Open Computing
Unix Unbound

About the Author

Harley Hahn is an internationally recognized writer, analyst and consultant. He is the author of thirteen books, including the best-selling *The Internet Complete Reference* and *The Internet Yellow Pages*, and the highly regarded *Assembler Inside & Out*. His Unix books include *A Student's Guide to Unix*, *Peter Norton's Guide to Unix* and *Mastering Xenix on the IBM PC AT*.

Hahn has a degree in Mathematics and Computer Science from the University of Waterloo, Canada; and a graduate degree in Computer Science from the University of California at San Diego. Before becoming a professional writer, he studied medicine at the University of Toronto Medical School.

Hahn enjoys writing computer books, because "I get to sleep in, and I like telling people what to do."

Hahn does not live in a converted farmhouse in Connecticut with his wife, three children, and a Labrador Retriever named Rolf. Nor does he commute frequently to New York.

His favorite pajamas are green.

Open Computing
Unix Unbound

Harley Hahn

Osborne **McGraw-Hill**

Berkeley New York St. Louis San Francisco
Auckland Bogotá Hamburg London Madrid
Mexico City Milan Montreal New Delhi Panama City
Paris São Paulo Singapore Sydney Tokyo Toronto

Osborne **McGraw-Hill**
2600 Tenth Street
Berkeley, California 94710
U.S.A.

For information on software, translations, or book distributors outside of the U.S.A.,
please write to Osborne **McGraw-Hill** at the above address.

Open Computing Unix Unbound

1234567890 DOC 9987654

ISBN 0-07-882050-2

Publisher Lawrence Levitsky	**Proofreader** Audrey Johnson
Acquisitions Editor Scott Rogers	**Illustrator** Marla Shelasky
Project Editor Kelly Barr	**Series Design** Jani Beckwith
Computer Designer Lance Ravella	**Quality Control Specialist** Joe Scuderi
Copy Editor Lunaea Hougland	**Cover Design** emdesign

List of Chapters

Contents

List of Figures

Introduction

This is the most important computer book you have ever seen.

Do you believe me?

I wouldn't if I were you. After all, this is just a Unix book. How could it possibly be the most important computer book you have ever seen?

Could it be because a lot of people use Unix? Well, Unix is used throughout the world so, in that sense, Unix is important. But it's not *that* important.

Anyway, a lot of people use Unix for years without buying a book and many of them get along just fine. It's nice to have a Unix book, but it is certainly not necessary to support life.

And even if you do want a Unix book, there are hundreds from which you can choose. What makes this one so important? Why should you buy this book?

Here's why.

When you first start using Unix, you will immerse yourself in learning the commands and the basic rules. There are many technical details to master and, at first, there is not much time for pondering.

But after a while, you will begin to realize that Unix is not like other computer systems. There is a feeling of elegance and charm that hides behind every esoteric command and within every technical rule. From time to time you will notice an odd perception — an impression, a pattern, a combination of ideas — an undeniable something that appears unexpectedly and then vanishes like the tail of a cat as he runs to hide under the bed.

Eventually these momentary sensations will coalesce into a startling idea: that there is something unexpectedly wonderful about Unix that transcends your computer system and the commands that you are using. You may hear people refer to this something as "the Unix philosophy", but there is a lot more to it.

I believe that all human cultures have a creative spirit that runs like a thread through the tapestry of history and forms an inseparable and inspiring counterpoint to human achievement. In each age, we find a handful of men and women who embody this spirit with their inventions and their ideas.

The basic development and refinement of Unix was the work of a small number of people and took only a few years. And yet, within this short time, these computer programmers managed to light a spark that would be fanned into many different flames of varying shades and intensity.

In retrospect, we can see that the ideas within Unix served as the basis of modern operating system design. Still, I suspect that the original Unix programmers did not fully understand the significance of what they had invented; for Unix is nothing less than a way of thinking: a modern implementation of the nucleus of human creativity. As I see it, when you use Unix, you are connecting with something that is as old as history and as deep as the ocean of our unconscious.

Okay, I realize that this may sound a bit strange (well, a lot strange). After all, philosophy aside, what you are holding in your hand is a computer book and an esoteric one at that. And yet... this is my fourth Unix book, and I am starting to see that Unix is more important than I ever imagined.

You see, unlike any other computer system that is popular today, Unix has much more to offer than a way to do your work by typing commands on a keyboard. Live with Unix long enough and you will change. You will become more creative, and you will come to understand the spirit of creation in others.

There will be times when you will puzzle over some elusive technical point that seems to make no sense whatsoever, and then... you will *get* it. And you will say to yourself, "So *that's* why they did it that way."

More than any other computer system today, Unix will repay every moment that you spend learning and experimenting. You will find that, as you teach yourself, you will come to follow the thought processes of those who have walked before you. This happens just as surely as you re-create mental images when you read poetry, or listen to music, or admire the logical reasoning within a mathematical proof.

In this sense, Unix is elegant, but it is an elegance that rides on the shoulders of utility. I am sure that no one ever decides to learn Unix just to experience beauty. We choose to use Unix for practical reasons: to do our work (or to play the games). But the wonderful thing is that the beauty comes by itself. As you work, you develop an appreciation that grows over months and years. And you don't have to do anything special: all *you* need to do is use Unix and it all happens automatically.

And that is where this book comes in.

I don't want to go on and on about elegance and beauty because, after all, this is a computer book and there is a good chance that you are standing in a bookstore trying to decide whether or not to buy the thing. (And if you have already bought this book, you are probably anxious to get on with your work.)

Fair enough. What I want you to remember is that if you use Unix long enough, it will become important to you. You may not care about this now, but I do, and I know what is going to change in you as you work with Unix. I understand this, and I care about it, and I have designed this book to help you and teach you for a long time to come. And that is why this book is so important: because Unix is so important.

I wrote this book to be your Unix companion and, I promise you, it will be a good one. Take a few moments and skim through the pages. This is not your ordinary Unix book, not by a long shot. There is a long journey ahead of you, and I will be with you every step of the way.

Buy this book, I am on *your* side.

— Harley Hahn

Acknowledgments

After I finish a book, the last thing I do is write the acknowledgments. Right now, the rest of the book has been written. Each chapter and appendix has been edited and typeset. Every figure and example has been checked and re-checked. I'm sitting at my desk, listening to The Who and to Liszt, and enjoying the Southern California ocean breeze as it moves gently through the peaceful summer night. My cat is swanking around like he owns the place, and the fragrance of cedar finds its way out of my shiny new incense holder and mingles with the quiet smells and sounds of the night.

It's late... very late. I just got off the phone with my editor, Scott Rogers, who reminds me that my next book is due in five weeks and when will I be sending him the first chapter? And where is the introduction for the Unix book, he asks. Will I get it tonight?

It's finished, I answer. All I have left are the acknowledgments.

What's so hard about writing acknowledgments, he says.

What's so hard about being an editor, I reply.

Well, if you really want to know, it's not at all easy being an editor. Personally, I wouldn't take the job for all the bagels in Los Angeles. Still, somebody has to do the job and I consider myself fortunate to have Scott. I had to run through a lot of editors to find him (some of whom are still living, after a fashion), and even the thought of having to write a book without him makes me feel like Mary setting off for school without her lamb.

There are many people within a publishing house that have the name "editor" somewhere in their job description. However, to each writer there is only one Editor: the guy who calls you late at night and asks you when the book will be finished. These people go by various appellations and, at Osborne McGraw-Hill, they are known as Acquisitions Editors. The idea is that it is their job to "acquire" books and build a list of successful titles.

Superficially, it would seem that that is a fairly easy job. You have lunch with authors, you send out a contract once in a while, and you spend most of your time on the phone chatting about this or that.

Actually, the life of an Acquisitions Editor ranks somewhere between a galley slave and the guy who works at the train station shining shoes. You see, the responsibilities of an Acquisitions Editor are supposed to end after the book has been acquired and the manuscript has been submitted. The reality of it is that these people never stop working. It seems that every job that no one else knows how to do is somehow foisted upon these gentle men and women. For example, suppose you are a writer reading the final page proofs and you decide that the typeface is not good enough. Who do you call?

Right. Your editor. After all, your mother certainly doesn't want to hear your theory about why they shouldn't have used a sans serif font with a ragged right margin.

Of course, such a life takes its toll and that, no doubt, is why Acquisitions Editors look the way they do. (Actually, I did want to include a picture of Scott here but, well... this *is* a family book and there is no point scaring the kids.)

So the next time you drive past a poor wretch in tattered clothes, with lines on his face and unkempt gray hair, standing in front of a bookstore and holding a sign that says "Will Read Manuscripts For Food", have pity. No doubt he was once one of Nature's noblemen who sacrificed himself for the good of mankind. "There," you must remind yourself, "but for the grace of God, go I."

But if you think that the lot of an Acquisitions Editor is tough, that's only because you have never met a Project Editor. My Project Editor is Kelly Barr and he has the gray hair to prove it. Kelly lives in a netherworld that is euphemistically referred to as "Editorial" — a way station between the place where a manuscript enters the office and the actual typesetters who render the thing into print. This means that Kelly must act as a liaison between authors who feel that their figures and listings are not being typeset properly and the production people who are rumored to live on the fifth floor.

I say "rumored", because as an author I never get to actually talk to them; everything must go through Kelly. In theory, this means that there is one central person to coordinate the project. In practice, this shortens Kelly's lifespan considerably.

So, where Acquisitions Editors can be forced to work around the clock for days at a time with only a short pizza break and a bowl of water, Project Editors must be treated gingerly, like fine china. Thus, in the course of producing this book, when it became necessary to send Kelly off to Switzerland under an assumed name for a short period of recuperation, we had to bring in a ringer: Wendy Rinaldi. Wendy, who served as the ersatz Project Editor in the closing days of production, demonstrated a level of sweetness, flexibility, and competence that would be difficult to overpraise.

Moving sideways on the food chain, we come to Jeff Pepper, the Osborne McGraw-Hill Editor-in-Chief and also an Acquisitions Editor (although he generally covers up the tattoo so you can't tell). Jeff was instrumental in planning this project from the beginning and was intimately involved with coordinating the details with McGraw-Hill's College Division. (You see, parts of this book are based on a textbook — A Student's Guide to Unix — that I wrote for the College Division.) Jeff spent a lot of time working within McGraw-Hill to move the necessary paper from one place to another. The financial details, were handled by Katherine "Money-is-no-object" Johnson, the Osborne McGraw-Hill Controller, whose tireless efforts were finally able to reconcile the cultural differences between the Osborne Division in Berkeley and the front office in New York.

Next, we come to several production people whose eclectic activities must not go unnoticed. Peter Hancik typeset and laid out the pages (even to the point to working all weekend on the final chapter). He was helped by Roberta Steele and Jani Beckwith while Marcela Hancik supervised. If it wasn't for these people, you would be holding several hundred sheets of blank paper along with thousands of mixed up letters and numbers that would fall onto the floor when you opened the book.

Kelly Vogel and Rachel Howes, both Editorial Assistants, fulfilled numerous jobs too appalling to mention, but without which the entire project would have floundered like a politician whose teleprompter is on the fritz.

Moving on, we have Lisa Kissinger, Manager of Publicity, and Claudia Ramirez, Grand Poobah of International Rights. If you are reading this book in the United States, you can thank Lisa. If you are reading this book outside the United States, you can thank Claudia.

And finally, as we carefully advance through the seventh floor hallway, avoiding the candy bar wrappers and piles of historically valuable manuscripts, we come to a corner office. It is here, in the only room that has a view of both the San Francisco Bay and an industrial waste facility, that we find the guiding force of the entire enterprise: the big man himself, Larry "L-Squared" Levitsky, the Osborne McGraw-Hill Publisher. However, we can stop but a moment. Larry is a busy man and we must leave him to his job. So with a quick wave and a short thank you for running such a smooth ship and making us so much money, we leave Osborne McGraw-Hill behind us and pass out into the night.

Any book like this one has thousands and thousands of things that can go wrong. For instance, an example might be incorrect; or a comma might be in the wrong place; or an index entry might point off to the middle of nowhere.

The reason that this book is of such high quality is that I have had superb help from three talented people. First, there is Eric Johannsen, my technical reviewer. Eric is from California but currently lives in Germany. Each chapter and appendix was sent to Eric over the Internet, and he read and critiqued every word quickly and competently. There may be something within Unix that Eric doesn't understand but I have yet to find it.

Next, we have Lunaea Hougland, my copy editor. However, to call her a mere "copy editor" is like calling the Grand Canyon a hole in the ground. Lunaea is the Queen of Copy Editors. Just between us, she is the only person in the world that I will let make changes in what I write. Actually, except for one thing, Lunaea would be perfect: she doesn't have a modem. Still, maybe it's all for the best. If she did get a modem she would be perfect, and it is not easy to work with a perfect person (just ask any of my editors).

And third, we have Wendy Murdock, the quintessential researcher, who stopped working on *The Internet Yellow Pages* long enough to prepare the index for this book. (See if you can find the secret entry she included that slipped by the editors.)

There are many people who helped me with *A Student's Guide to Unix*, which is the spiritual ancestor to this book. Within that book, you will see a long list of names. To that list I now thank the following people:

Timothy Tyndall and Marcy Montgomery at RAIN (Regional Alliance for Information Networking) in Santa Barbara, for access to the wonderful community-based Internet/Unix facility.

Rick Stout, for important technical advice and research. (Rick, by the way, is the person who actually wrote the textbook *Peter Norton's Introduction to Computers*. So, if you have that book, take a crayon and write Rick's name on the title page.)

Ronald van Loon, in the Netherlands, for contributing many valuable suggestions and ideas.

Ken Bracht, at IBM, for providing me with excellent PC hardware, software, and expertise.

Michael Tucker, the Executive Editor of *SunExpert Magazine*, for helping me work with Sun Microsystems to get a computer for testing purposes.

Laura Lilyquist, the Manager of Strategic Marketing at Sun, for helping me procure an excellent Sun workstation and for acting as an efficacious liaison between Sun and the outside world.

Mark Schildhauer, Joan Murdoch and Kevin Schmidt, of the Social Sciences Computing Facility at the University of California at Santa Barbara, for answering numerous questions about Suns and Macs. Special thanks goes to Mark who spent a lot of time with me working on the X Window screen shots that you see in Chapter 5.

Judy Howard at GTE World Headquarters in Irving, Texas, for helping me get the telephone sevices that I needed to connect to the Internet; Rhonda Bushno at GTE West in Thousand Oaks, California, for arranging and coordinating these services; and Sandee Ross of GTE West in Oxnard, California, for making sure that everything was installed and working.

Heidi Stettner, for furnishing me with the picture of her and Biff the Dog (Chapter 15). The picture, by the way, was taken by Carolyn Carr.

Alan Watson, of the Department of Astronomy, University of Wisconsin at Madison, for answering questions about the rc shell (see Chapter 10).

And finally, Kimberlyn Hahn, for helping me understand the basic philosophical underpinnings of Western culture.

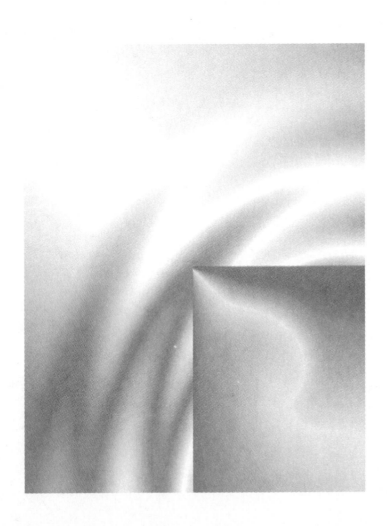

CHAPTER 1

Introduction to Unix

This book is about using Unix: a computer system that is used throughout the world and runs on virtually all types of computers.

The first Unix system was developed in 1969 by a programmer so he could run a program called Space Travel*. Unix today is nothing less than a worldwide culture, comprising many tools, ideas and customs.

The full details of Unix—which long ago ceased to be a single computer system—are well beyond human understanding. In other words, there is no single person who knows everything about Unix. In fact, there is no single person who knows even most of Unix.

*Space Travel simulated the movements of the sun and planets, as well as a spaceship that you could land in various locations. The programmer in question was Ken Thompson, who, with various other people at AT&T's Bell Labs, went on to develop the full-fledged Unix operating system (presumably, after they got tired of Space Travel).

The Unix culture—which you are about to enter—contains an enormous number of tools for you to use. You can create and manipulate information in more ways than you can imagine; you can send messages and talk with people almost anywhere in the world; you can play games, create documents, and write your own computer programs; and you can participate in ongoing discussions on hundreds of different subjects with people all over the world.

To use Unix, all you need is access to a Unix computer, preferably one that is connected to the Internet (the worldwide system of computer networks). Once you have such access, the facilities of Unix—the tools, the electronic mail system, the games, the discussion groups—are all waiting for you. All you need to do is learn how to use the system and how to participate in the culture.

This book will teach you what you need to know to get started and a lot more.

Although Unix (and the Internet) may be inexpensive to you, you should realize that someone, somewhere, is paying a lot of money and devoting a lot of time to maintain the system. Part of learning Unix is understanding what it means to be a responsible, honest and polite user—after all, we are sharing limited resources. In this book, we will discuss not only how to use Unix, but what it means to be a member of the Unix community.

The Unix Language

Around the world, the first language of Unix is American English. Nevertheless, Unix systems and documentation have been translated into many other languages, and it is not necessary to know English, as long as your system works in your language. However, as you explore the worldwide Unix-based network, you will probably find that much of the information and many of the discussion groups are in English.

In addition, the Unix community has introduced many new words of its own. In this book, we will pay particular attention to these terms. Each new word is explained and defined as it is introduced. For easy reference, all the definitions are collected into a glossary at the end of the book.

When we come to a name with a particularly colorful history, we will give a special explanation inside a box like the following:

What's in a Name?　Unix

In the 1960s, a number of researchers at Bell Labs (a part of AT&T) worked at MIT on a project called Multics, an early time-sharing operating system. Multics was a collaborative effort involving programmers from MIT, GE and Bell Labs. The name "Multics" was an acronym for "Multiplexed Information and Computing Service". ("Multiplex" refers to combining multiple electronic signals into a single signal.)

By the late 1960s, the management at Bell Labs decided not to pursue Multics and moved their researchers back into the lab. In 1969, one of these researchers, Ken Thompson, developed a simple, small operating system for a PDP-7 minicomputer. In searching for a name, Thompson compared his new system to Multics.

The goal of Multics was to offer many features to multiple users at the same time. Multics was large and unwieldy and had many problems.

Thompson's system was smaller, less ambitious and (at least at the beginning) was used by one person at a time. Moreover, each part of the system was designed to do only one thing and to do it well. Thompson decided to name his system Unics (the "Uni" meaning "one", as in unicycle), which was soon changed to Unix.

In other words, the name Unix is a pun on the name Multics.

Throughout the book, we print certain names in boldface, usually the names of commands. This allows you to see immediately that a word is a special Unix term. Here is an example:

"To copy a file, you use the Unix **cp** command. To remove (erase) a file, you use the **rm** command."

Hints for Learning Unix

As you read, you will notice many hints for learning Unix. These are ideas and shortcuts we have found to be important for newcomers and experienced users alike. To emphasize these hints, we present them in a special format that looks like this:

HINT
Unix is fun.

Getting the Most from This Book

We have designed this book to make it easy for you to find what you need quickly. Before you start, take a moment to examine the various parts of the book.

First, look at the Quick Index to Unix Commands on the inside back cover. This is a list of every command covered in this book and where to look for the discussion and examples.

Second, take a glance at the Quick Indexes for **vi** and **emacs** (the principal Unix text editing programs). Once you learn how to use **vi** or **emacs**, you will find these indexes especially helpful.

Of course, there is also the standard general index. Spend a few minutes now to skim through it (always a good idea with a new book). This will give a rough idea of the new ideas you will be meeting and what we will be emphasizing.

Aside from the glossary and the indexes, there are two summaries of Unix commands, also at the back of the book. These summaries contain one-line descriptions of each Unix command we cover in the book.

One summary lists the commands in alphabetical order; the other summary groups the commands by category. These summaries are a good place to check if you want to do something and are not sure what command to use. Once you have found your command, check with the Quick Index to see what page to read.

If you want to find the discussion of a particular topic, you can, of course, use the general index. Alternately, you can look up the appropriate term in the glossary. Along with each definition, you will find a reference to the chapter in which that term is explained. Once you know the chapter you want, a quick look at the table of contents will show you what section to read.

What We Assume in This Book

In this book, we make two important assumptions as to what type of Unix system you are using.

First, as you will see in Chapter 2, there are many versions of Unix, based on two principal variations: Berkeley Unix and System V Unix. Modern Unix systems combine the most important elements from both of these types. Thus, for the most part, it doesn't matter what type of Unix you are using.

We have oriented this book toward the needs of people who use Unix, not toward a particular type of Unix. For some aspects of your work, there will be a choice between the Berkeley or System V functionality. In such cases, we will lean toward the Berkeley conventions as these are the more popular.

Second, as you will see in Chapter 4, the program that reads and interprets the commands you type is called the "shell". In Chapter 10, we will explain that there are various shells you might choose to use. Almost all the time, it doesn't really matter what shell you use. However, in those few places where it does matter, we will use the C-Shell or the Korn shell. If you want to use another shell, that is fine. A few details may be different, but you won't have any real problems.

What We Do Not Assume in This Book

If you are an experienced computer user who wants to learn about Unix, this book will get you started and provide you with a firm background in all the important areas.

However, we do not assume that you have any prior experience. It's okay if you have never really used a computer. You do not need to know anything about Unix. You do not need to be a programmer, nor do you need to know anything about electronics or mathematics.

We will explain everything you need to know. Work at your own speed and enjoy yourself.

How to Use This Book

Before we start, it is important to realize that the world of Unix is bursting with information. As we mentioned earlier, it is impossible to learn everything about Unix, so don't even try. Concentrate on what you need and what you think you will enjoy. To get started, you should probably read the first six chapters. They will introduce you to Unix and teach you the basic skills.

HINT
It is impossible to learn everything about Unix. Concentrate on what you need and what you think you will enjoy.

After you are oriented to Unix, and you know how to start and stop a work session, enter commands and use the keyboard, you can read the rest of the book in any order you want.

Although every effort has been made to make each chapter as independent as possible, you should realize that each topic is dependent on other topics. There is no perfect place to start learning Unix and no perfect order in which to study the various topics.

For example, say that the main reason you want to learn Unix is to send and receive electronic mail. Naturally, it makes sense to read the chapter that explains how the Unix mail system is organized (Chapter 14). If you are using the mail program that comes with Unix, you will then want to read Chapter 15.

However, in order to compose messages, it is handy to already know how to use a text editing program (Chapters 20 or 21). And since you may want to save your messages, you should know how to store data in files. This means that you should already understand the file system (Chapter 22), the commands to display your files (Chapter 18), as well as the commands to manipulate your files (Chapters 23 and 24). And, of course, before you can type in messages, you need to understand how to start a work session (Chapters 4 and 5) and how to use the Unix keyboard (Chapter 6).

Obviously, this sort of approach leads nowhere fast, but it does underscore the most important principle that you need to understand at the outset: Unix was not designed to be learned; Unix was designed to be used. In other words, it can be confusing and time-consuming to learn Unix. However, once you have mastered the skills you need, for whatever work you want to do, working with Unix is fast and easy.

If you think back to when you learned how to drive a car, you will remember that it was anything but easy. Once you had some experience, though, your actions became smooth and automatic. By now, you can probably drive all day with one hand on the wheel as you listen to the radio and engage in conversation.

Let us embody this idea as the following hint:

HINT
Unix is easy to use, but difficult to learn.

Remember, once you have read the first few chapters of this book, you can teach yourself any topic in any order. If you come across an idea or skill you do not yet understand, you can either pause for a quick look at another chapter, or skip the part that confuses you and learn it later. This is how people learn Unix in real life: a bit at a time, depending on what they need at the moment.

Don't worry about memorizing every detail. In some chapters, we treat topics in depth. Learn what seems interesting and useful to you and just skim the rest. If you know the basics and you have an idea as to what is available, you can always return to the details when you need them.

HINT
Start by learning the basics. Then learn whatever you want, in whatever order you want.

CHAPTER 2

What Is Unix?

In this chapter, we will orient ourselves to the world of Unix: what it does, where we find it, the variations, and the culture that has grown up around it. To lay the groundwork, we start with a discussion of the fundamental component of any computer system: the operating system.

What Is an Operating System?

Computers perform tasks automatically by following instructions. A list of instructions is called a PROGRAM. As the computer follows the instructions, we say that it RUNS or EXECUTES the program. In general, programs are referred to as SOFTWARE, while the physical components of the computer are referred to as

HARDWARE. The hardware includes the keyboard, mouse, display screen, printers, disk drives and so on.

An OPERATING SYSTEM (which is software) is a complex master control program whose principal function is to make efficient use of the hardware. To do so, the operating system acts as the primary interface to the hardware. The operating system helps you (to do your work) and helps programs (as they execute).

For example, when you type a command to display the names of your data files, the operating system does the actual work of finding the names and displaying them on your screen. When you run a program that needs to open a new data file, the operating system sets aside storage space for the data and takes care of all the details.

As you work, the operating system is always there, waiting to serve you and to manage the resources of your computer. The most important jobs are: controlling how the computer's memory is used, maintaining a file storage system, scheduling work to be done, and providing accounting and security services.

Most operating systems come with a variety of programs for you to use. For example, there will be a program to display the names of your data files. A Unix operating system comes with literally hundreds of such programs, each of which is a tool to perform one specific job.

"Unix" Can Refer to One Specific Operating System

In Chapter 1, we described how the first Unix system—in fact, a primitive operating system—was developed in 1969 by a single programmer. The work was done at Bell Labs, the research arm of AT&T. Since then, a large number of people have developed Unix into a modern family of operating systems.

For many years, Bell Labs remained one of the centers of Unix development. In 1990, AT&T formed a new organization, called Unix Systems Laboratory or USL, to take over the work. In June 1993, AT&T sold USL to Novell Corporation. In October 1993, Novell transferred rights to the name "Unix" to X/Open, an international standards organization. At one time, the name "UNIX" referred to the product from AT&T. Now, we use the more generic "Unix" to describe any operating system that meets certain standards.

The most modern direct descendant of the original AT&T UNIX is System V version 4, often referred to as System V.4. The "V" is the Roman numeral 5, and the name is usually pronounced as "System five-dot-four". You may also see SVR4, which means System V Release 4. SVR4 is pronounced "System five-R-four".

"Unix" Can Refer to a Family of Operating Systems

Since the 1970s, many other Unix operating systems have been developed. As a family, Unix operating systems all share two important characteristics: they are multitasking and multiuser timesharing systems. MULTITASKING means that a Unix system can run more than one program at a time. MULTIUSER means that Unix can support more than one user at a time.

When people talk about Unix as an operating system, they mean any operating system that is Unix-like. In this sense, the word "Unix" refers to any member of the family of Unix-like operating systems. For example, somebody might say, "I am thinking of buying my own personal computer. What types of Unix will run on it?"

One of the most important Unixes comes from the University of California at Berkeley. At first, Berkeley Unix was based on AT&T UNIX. However, the newest version was designed to be as free as possible of AT&T System V UNIX programming.

The official name of Berkeley Unix is BSD, an acronym standing for Berkeley Software Distribution. Thus, although it seems strange, "BSD", like "Unix", is the name of an operating system. The most recent version of this operating system is BSD 4.4. The name is usually pronounced as "B-S-D four-point-four".

Although there are many types of Unix, virtually all of them are based on either BSD, System V, or both. In the academic and research communities, most people use a Unix that is based on both, with an emphasis on Berkeley Unix.

Figure 2-1 shows the names of Unix and Unix-like systems that you may encounter. The most common is Solaris or SunOS (the old name), running on a computer from Sun Microsystems. All of these Unixes are derived—at least in part—from Berkeley Unix and System V. This, of course, is not a complete listing.

What's in a Name?   BSD

Berkeley Unix did not start off with a typical name. The original release—a variation of AT&T UNIX—came to be known as "the first Berkeley software distribution", which was abbreviated to 1BSD. The next major release was known as 2BSD and so on.

Today, Berkeley Unix has taken on a life of its own and, as an operating system, is known as BSD. Thus, a purist might say that the newest version of Berkeley Unix should really be called 4.4BSD, not BSD 4.4.

There are many variations of Unix. For now, don't worry about all the different types. Generally speaking, Unix is Unix, and what you will learn in this book will be relevant no matter what type of Unix you are using.

NAME OF UNIX	COMPANY OR ORGANIZATION
386BSD	free on the Internet
AIX	IBM
A/UX	Apple
BSD	University of California at Berkeley
BSD-Lite	University of California at Berkeley
BSD/386	Berkeley Software Design (BSDI)
Coherent	Mark Williams Company
Dynix	Sequent
FreeBSD	free on the Internet
HP-UX	Hewlett-Packard (HP)
Hurd (GNU)	Free Software Foundation
Interactive Unix	Sun Microsystems
Irix	Silicon Graphics
Linux	free on the Internet
Mach	Carnegie-Mellon University
Minix	included with book by Andy Tanenbaum
MKS Toolkit	Mortice Kern Systems
NetBSD	free on the Internet
Nextstep	Next
OSF/1	Digital Equipment Corporation (DEC)
SCO Unix	Santa Cruz Operation
Solaris	Sun Microsystems
SunOS	Sun Microsystems
System V UNIX	various versions for personal computers
Ultrix	Digital Equipment Corporation (DEC)
Unicos	Cray Research
Unixware	Novell

FIGURE 2-1. *Types of Unix and the organizations that develop them*

People often ask, "How do you tell if a particular operating system is Unix?" Although there is no universal agreement, the best answer is: if an operating system looks like Unix to you as you work, and if it looks like Unix to your programs as they execute, then it's Unix. There are more technical answers to this question, but, realistically, Unix is whatever people call Unix.

"Unix" Is the Name of a Culture

Unix means much more than a family of operating systems. Unix means computer networks, electronic mail, a great many programs (including games) and a very real culture based on these tools. The third and most important way to use the word "Unix" is as a name for the global community we described in Chapter 1, the community that encompasses the Unix culture.

Some thoughtful people go further and consider Unix to be an abstract idea: an actual applied philosophy that dictates a particular approach to problem solving. This will make more sense to you as you learn more. In using Unix, you will learn to approach and solve problems by combining simple programs, like building blocks, into elegant structures. (You will learn about this in detail in Chapters 16 and 17.)

Perhaps the best definition of Unix—and the one we would like you to remember as you read this book—is the following:

Unix is a set of tools for smart people.

HINT

Unix is a set of tools for smart people.

What Is It Like to Use Unix?

Using Unix means interacting with a computer by using a keyboard, a display, and possibly a mouse. As you type (or move and click the mouse), you watch the screen on your display. From time to time, you may want to print something on paper.

To start a work session, you "log in". When you are finished working, you "log out". We will explain how all of this works in Chapter 4. Basically, you log in by typing your name and your password. After Unix verifies that you are allowed to use that particular computer system, you can start work. When you log out, it tells Unix you are finished working and you are ready to stop.

CHAPTER 3

The Unix Connection

T he reason why Unix is so important is that any Unix computer can connect with any other Unix computer. As a result, we have countless computer networks and a worldwide Unix community. In this chapter, we will take a look at the connections that make this all possible. We start with the most basic connection of all: the one between you and the computer.

Hosts and Terminals

As we explained in Chapter 2, Unix is a multiuser timesharing system. That means that Unix computers can support more than one user at the same time. The main computer — the piece of hardware that actually does most of the work — is called the HOST. One of the jobs of the operating system is to make sure that the resources of the host are shared among all the users.

To work with Unix you use a TERMINAL. A basic Unix terminal consists of a display screen, a keyboard and not much more. (However, as we will see later, some terminals are more complex. In particular, X terminals, which we will discuss in Chapter 5, allow you to use a mouse to manipulate graphical images.) Alternatively, a terminal might be a PC or a Macintosh. In such cases, the computer will run a program that makes it act like a terminal.

Your terminal is connected to the host. As you type, or as you move the mouse, signals are sent to the host. A program running on the host interprets these signals and reacts appropriately.

When a host program needs to display output, it sends signals to your terminal, which then displays the appropriate information on your screen. Figure 3-1 shows the relationship between the host and the terminals. All Unix systems use this host-terminal relationship.

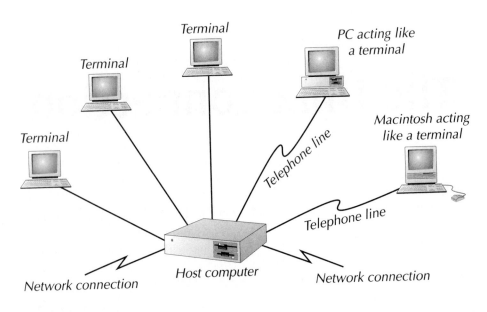

FIGURE 3-1. *The host-terminal relationship*

What Happens When You Press a Key?

Each time you press a key, a signal is sent to the host. The host responds by sending its own signal back to your terminal telling it to display the appropriate character on the screen. For example, as you type the **date** command (to display the current time and date), your display shows the letters "date". However, your terminal does not display each letter until the host tells it to do so.

At first, this may seem strange. When you press the D key, it does not cause the symbol "d" to be displayed on your screen. Rather, the "d" signal is sent to the host, which then sends a signal to your terminal, which then displays the letter "d". We say that the host ECHOES the character to your display. In most cases, it happens so fast that it looks as if your keyboard is connected directly to your screen.

When you learn more about Unix, you will see that it is possible to use a host computer that is many miles away. In such cases, there may be times when the characters you type will not be echoed for a second. In other words, you will press keys, but you will not see the letters appear on the screen immediately. This can happen if the host computer is far away and the communication line you are using happens to be slow.

HINT

You might ask, why was Unix set up so that the host echoes each character? Why not have the host silently accept whatever it receives and have the terminal do the echoing (which would be faster)?

The answer is that when the host does the echoing, you can see that what you are typing is being received successfully, and that the connection between the host and the terminal is intact. Moreover, as we will discuss in Chapter 6, you can press certain keys (such as BACKSPACE or DELETE) to make corrections as you type. Unix was designed to work with a wide variety of terminals, and it made much more sense for the operating system itself to handle the processing of these keypresses than to expect each different type of terminal to be able to do the job.

As you type, your position on the screen is marked by the CURSOR. On most terminals, the cursor is an underscore character (_), or a small box, that blinks. The cursor shows you where the next character you type will be displayed. As you type, the cursor advances, one position at a time.

How Multiuser Systems Are Connected

Many Unix hosts are connected directly to terminals. All you have to do is turn on the terminal and you are ready to work. Some places (like schools) have rooms full of such terminals or computers that act as terminals. If you look at the back of each machine, you will see a wire that leads, ultimately, to the host computer. You may never see the actual host, which might be locked away in an office somewhere.

This system works fine when all the terminals are used with only a single host computer. However, many computing facilities offer a variety of hosts. In such cases, your terminal may be connected to a special computer, called a TERMINAL SERVER, that acts as a switch.

After you turn on your terminal, you may need to type a command to the terminal server, telling it which host you want to use. For example, you might type:

```
connect compsci
```

to connect to a host named **compsci**. The terminal server then makes the connection for you. The advantage of using such a system is that any terminal can work with any of the host computers.

This configuration is illustrated in Figure 3-2.

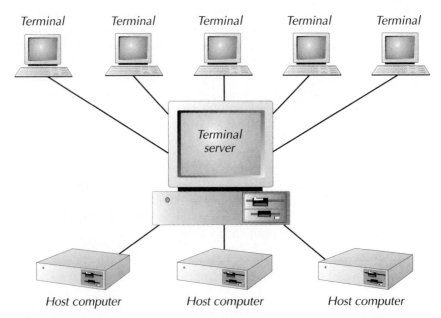

FIGURE 3-2. *Connections made by a terminal server*

The Console

Almost all host computers have a keyboard and display that are a part of the computer itself. As far as Unix is concerned, this keyboard and display are just another terminal. However, they are given a special name, the CONSOLE. In some sense, the console is built into the computer; all other terminals are separate and have to be connected.

A typical Unix system might use a host computer that sits in the office of the system manager. This computer could be connected to a room full of terminals or computers down the hall or on another floor. The system manager uses the console — the built in keyboard and display — to do his or her work, because it is more convenient. Everyone else uses a regular terminal.

However, as far as Unix is concerned, there is really nothing special about the console. The system manager could just as easily use any terminal to do whatever he or she needs to do.

You might ask, is it necessary for a Unix system to have a console? Not at all. Some computers do not come with a keyboard and display. The system manager uses a regular terminal, just like everybody else. The host computer, which is just a box, can be locked in a closet somewhere.

Workstations

In principle, all Unix systems can support multiple users. However, some Unix computers are used by only one person at a time. Such computers are called WORKSTATIONS.

When we refer to a computer as a workstation we mean that there is only one terminal, the console. When you use a workstation, you have the entire computer to yourself. This will be the case, say, if you have your own personal computer at home running Unix.

If someone were to give you a choice, would it be better to have a workstation or a terminal? You might think that it is always better to have your own computer. That way, you don't have to share, and the system won't slow down when a lot of people use it at the same time. If you are a knowledgeable user who demands a lot of resources — for example, if you are writing a lot of programs — having your own workstation is a good idea.

However, there are three important advantages to using a terminal. First, if you are paying for the equipment yourself, a terminal (which might be a PC or a Macintosh) is a lot less expensive. Second, a host computer that is shared by many users may offer more facilities than an isolated workstation. The host may be more powerful, have more data storage space, and offer a larger variety of programs.

Finally, if you use a terminal to access a host, it is likely that someone else is maintaining the system for you. If you have a workstation, you (or somebody) will have to install and maintain an entire Unix system. You will find, quite quickly, that administering a Unix system is not for the faint of heart or for those pressed for time. In the world of Unix, system administration is euphemistically referred to as a "non-trivial task". In other words, running your own Unix system is a great deal of work.

Moreover, when a system is administered by an experienced manager, it means that backups (extra copies of your data files, usually stored on tape) will be made regularly. If you have to administer your own computer, you may have to do your own backups.

Realistically, you will never have the time or inclination to organize and maintain a proper backup system. This puts you at risk of losing all your data when your disk fails (as it surely will one day).

As we will see in a moment, many workstations are connected to a network. Some network administrators make sure that all the workstations are backed up automatically over the network. For example, every night at 2 AM, a computer on the network may check each workstation for new files and copy those files to a tape.

Such a system may solve your backup problems, but someone will still have to manage your Unix system.

Network Connections

A NETWORK refers to two or more computers connected together. We connect computers into networks in order to share resources. For example, it is often convenient to allow all the users on a particular network to share a pool of printers.

Moreover, network users can share data files, send electronic mail, and even use one another's computers remotely. For example, say that you are using a workstation that is connected to another workstation over a network. You can run a program that allows your keyboard and display to act as a terminal for the other computer. As you work, signals are passed back and forth, over the network, between your keyboard/display and the remote host.

When computers are connected directly (using some type of cable), we call it a LOCAL AREA NETWORK or LAN. A typical LAN is contained within a single building, often on a single floor.

Connectivity, however, doesn't have to stop with a local network. Many LANs are connected to other networks, forming what is called a WIDE AREA NETWORK.

In many organizations, computers are connected together by local area networks. These LANs are sometimes connected with a high speed link (called a BACKBONE) that ties together the smaller LANs into one large wide area network. Large organizations with many departments may have more than one backbone.

This means, for example, that it is possible to send electronic mail from any computer in the organization to any other computer (as long as they are connected by the network). In fact, it can be as easy to send a message across the country as it is to send a message across the hall.

One mistake that beginners often make is thinking that they have to be near the computer they want to work with. If your organization is well connected, you can use a terminal in one building to work with a host computer in another building. For example, at a university, you might be in the psychology department using a PC (that is acting like a terminal) to access a host computer in the math department. This is especially important if you are using the X Window system, which we will explain in Chapter 5. Figure 3-3 shows the variety of connections that you might find in a large organization, such as a university.

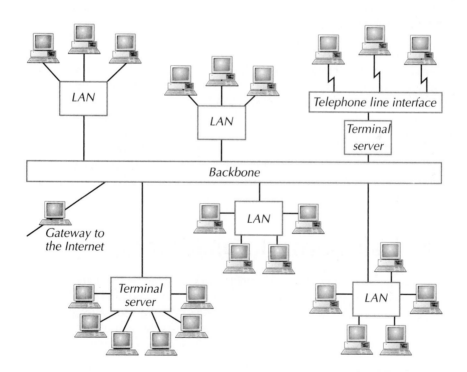

FIGURE 3-3.   *Network backbone connections*

The Client-Server Relationship

One of the principal reasons to create a network is to share resources. For instance, one computer may have a large amount of disk space to store files. This space can be shared throughout the network. It may well be that you will store your personal files not on the computer you are using, but on another computer. When your programs need to access a file, the data is sent to your computer over the network.

Such a system is common in large organizations. If all the data files are kept in one or two locations, it is easy for the system manager to make backup copies of the data.

In network terminology, any program that offers a resource is called a SERVER. A program that uses a resource is called a CLIENT. This terminology, of course, is taken from the business world. If you go to see a lawyer or an accountant, you are the client while they serve you.

If a program provides access to files over the network, it is called a FILE SERVER; a program that coordinates the printing of data using various printers is called a PRINT SERVER, and so on.

Sometimes the name "server" is used to refer to the actual computer, rather than a program. For example, you might hear someone say, "Our main file server sits in a closet in the system manager's office."

Here are two other common examples. On many networks, one computer on the network transmits electronic mail between the local computers and the outside world. This computer is called the MAIL SERVER.

Another computer (or perhaps the same computer) will provide users with access to the worldwide Usenet discussion group facility. This machine is called the NEWS SERVER (because Usenet groups are often referred to us as "newsgroups").

Unix system programmers will often talk about the connection between a client program and a server as the CLIENT-SERVER RELATIONSHIP. (Indeed, for many programmers, this is the most enduring relationship they have ever had.)

Large Scale Network Connections

Many organizational networks are connected to very large regional and national networks. Within such systems, designated computers, called GATEWAYS, will act as the links between the network and the outside world. For example, all electronic mail that is sent in and out of the organization will pass through one specific gateway computer. This computer will look at the address and route the message to the appropriate network.

Around the world (and especially in the United States), the major wide area networks are connected to a system known as the INTERNET. Any computer on the Internet — including the computers at most universities — can connect to any other computer on the Internet.

For example, from your computer, you can log into and use a computer across the continent. Even better, if you are working with someone in a remote location, you can use a simple command (called **talk**) to connect your two computers (as long as they are both on the Internet).

What is amazing is that the computers you connect to do not have to be the same type as your computer. As long as the remote computer communicates in the standard way, everything will work just fine.

When you are using a program that seems to react instantly, we say that the program is working in REAL TIME. Using an Internet connection, it is possible to use the **talk** command to type messages back and forth in real time. That is, as you type a message, it echoes not only on your screen, but on your friend's screen, which may be hundreds or even thousands of miles away.

As an example, while working on this book in California, we used **talk** to have long distance conversations with Unix experts in Ireland (Michael Peirce), Austria (Michael Schuster), and the Netherlands (Peter ten Kley), all of whom can now consider themselves famous.

Most other countries have large national networks that, through gateways, are connected to the Internet. Effectively, this connects many hundreds of thousands of computers into an enormous, worldwide network. This means that you can, with little trouble, send electronic mail and data files all over the world. There are even gateways to commercial computer networks. For example, you can exchange messages with people who use America Online, CompuServe, MCI Mail, Delphi, Prodigy, AT&T Mail, and so on.

Connecting Over a Phone Line

The network connections we have discussed so far are all set up and administered by experts. These connections usually use cables or leased telephone lines. The very large scale connections may use satellite links.

However, what if you have your own computer at home and you want to connect to a campus network or to the Internet? You can use a regular phone line and have your computer call the host computer and make the connection. To do so, you will need a special device to convert computer signals back and forth to phone signals.

Technically speaking, converting computer signals to telephone signals is called MODULATION. The reverse process is called DEMODULATION. Thus, the device that you need is called a MODEM (modulator/demodulator). You connect the phone line to your modem and the modem to your computer.

To run the whole show, you need to use a communication program. This program will dial the remote computer and establish the connection.

Now, remember that we said the only way to work with a Unix host computer is by using a terminal. Since your home computer is not a terminal, your communication program must make your computer act like a terminal. We say that your program is EMULATING a terminal. In a sense, this forces your full-fledged computer to act like a much less powerful device. (After all, a terminal is not much more than a keyboard and display.) The whole scheme is shown in Figure 3-4.

Unix systems can work with many different brands and types of terminals. However, there is one specific terminal that, by custom, is the one that is emulated when you need to work over a telephone line. This is the VT 100 terminal.

In other words, when you are using your home computer to work with a remote Unix system, the remote system thinks it is working with a VT 100 terminal. The job of your communication program is to make sure that your computer acts like a VT 100. (Ironically, the VT 100, which was made by the Digital Equipment Corporation, is quite old and has not been sold for years.)

A detailed discussion of communication programs is beyond the scope of this book. However, we will mention that most such programs offer a multitude of features, aside from the basic modem dialing and terminal emulation. Two of the most useful features are maintaining a directory of frequently dialed numbers and being able to transfer data files from one computer to another.

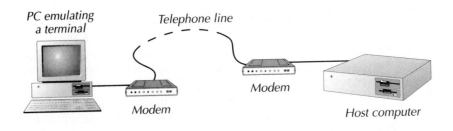

FIGURE 3-4. *Using a personal computer to access a Unix host*

Character Terminals and Graphics Terminals

As we explained earlier, you use a terminal to work with Unix. The terminal has a keyboard and a display screen. You type on the keyboard and read the characters on the display.

There are two classes of terminals that you can use with Unix. How you use Unix will vary somewhat depending on which type of terminal you are using.

The basic terminal furnishes not much more than a keyboard and a screen. This type of terminal, called a CHARACTER TERMINAL, displays only characters — such as letters, numerals, punctuation — but not pictures. Character terminals are inexpensive and are usually monochrome (for example, green characters on a black background). When you watch people access the computer in a bank or at an airport counter, you are usually looking at a character terminal.

If you use a PC or a Macintosh to emulate a terminal (especially over a phone line), you will most likely be using a character terminal.

The other type of terminal is called a GRAPHICS TERMINAL. It can display not only characters, but just about anything that can be drawn on a screen using small dots: pictures, geometric shapes, shading, and so on. Graphics terminals are more expensive than character terminals. Typically, a graphics terminal will have a large screen and will offer full color.

Most graphics terminals have a mouse and are designed to be used with a so-called graphical user interface. The most popular interfaces are based on a system called X Window. Terminals that are designed for X Window are known as X terminals.

Most of the time, using X Window calls for the same Unix skills as using a regular character terminal. However, there are a few special considerations. In this chapter, we discussed what everyone needs to know to start using Unix. In Chapter 5, we will go over the extra details that apply only to X Window users.

One last point: If you use a personal computer as a terminal (say, over a telephone line), you use a communication program that emulates a terminal. Such programs always emulate character terminals. Graphics terminals need a high-speed link between the terminal and the host because communicating in pictures requires a lot more data transmission than communicating in characters. The speed of a phone line is not fast enough to support graphics unless you are using a high speed modem.

Thus, an X terminal must be connected to the host either by a direct cable link or over a high-speed network. (Although, with very fast modems, it is possible to make X Window work over a telephone line if you fuss with it enough.)

CHAPTER 4

Starting to Use Unix

In this chapter, we'll take a look at what you need to know to start using Unix. You will learn how to start and how to stop a work session. To begin, let's talk about how Unix keeps track of who is allowed to use the system.

Userids and Passwords

All Unix systems require administration and maintenance. The person who performs these duties is called the SYSTEM MANAGER or SYSTEM ADMINISTRATOR. (Most people use the terms interchangeably.)

If you have your own Unix computer and you are the only one who uses it, you will have to act as the system manager. In a university or business, the system manager is usually a paid employee. With a large Unix computer, system administration is a full-time job that calls for a great deal of specialized knowledge; some system managers have a staff of assistants.

When you register to use a Unix system, the system manager will give you a name that identifies you to the system. This name is the USERID (pronounced "user-eye-dee"). Along with the userid, you will get a PASSWORD. The password is a secret code you must type in each time you use the system.

Once you have permission to use a system, we say that you have a Unix ACCOUNT on that computer. Even if you don't pay real money for your account, your Unix system may keep track of how much you use the computer. (Unix comes with a lot of built-in accounting, which your system manager can use to keep records of who is doing what.) In addition, your account will probably come with certain predefined limits, such as how much disk storage space you are allowed for your files.

One limit you are likely to encounter is an expiration date. For instance, if you are a student, your account may terminate automatically at the end of the semester.

What will your userid be? Usually, your system administrator will choose a userid for you. One common method is to base the userid on the person's real name. For example, for the name Harley Q. Hahn, the userid might be **harley**, **hahn**, **hhahn**, **harleyh** or **hqh**. Alternatively, your userid may reflect some completely objective criteria. For example, if you are a student and you are the 25th person in the Computer Science 110 class to ask for a Unix account, you might be assigned the userid **cs110-25**.

Each time you start a Unix session, you must enter your userid. This name is used by Unix to identify you. For example, any data files you create will be "owned" by your userid.

It is important to realize that userids are not secret. In fact, as you will see in Chapter 14, your userid is part of the address people use when they send you electronic mail and messages. However, to make sure that access to Unix is controlled, you will also be assigned a password that *is* secret.

Your password will probably be a meaningless group of characters, such as **H!lg%12**, which is difficult for someone else to guess. Later in the chapter, we will explain how to change your password if you don't like it.

Logging In (Starting Work with Unix)

When you sit down in front of your terminal, the process you go through to start work is called LOGGING IN. When we express this idea as a noun or an adjective, we use a single word, LOGIN. For example, "In order to log in, you need to learn the login procedure". Logging in consists of typing your userid and your password. Here is how it works:

When your Unix terminal is ready to use, it will display the following:

login:

This is an invitation to log in. Type your userid and press the RETURN key.

(We will talk about the Unix keyboard in Chapter 6. For now, all you need to know is that after you type a line you need to press the RETURN key. On some terminals, this key will be called ENTER. If you are using an IBM-compatible personal computer to emulate a terminal, you will press ENTER; if you are using a Macintosh to emulate a terminal, you will press RETURN.)

If you make an error while you are typing, some systems allow you to press the BACKSPACE or DELETE key, to erase one character at a time and correct your mistake. (You can experiment with your system, to see which key works.) Other systems require that you press RETURN, wait for the message that tells you the login was incorrect, and try again.

Once you have entered your userid, Unix will display:

Password:

Type your password and press RETURN. As you type, Unix will not echo your password—that is, the letters will not appear on your screen. This helps keep your password secret.

Once your userid and password are accepted, Unix will start a work session for you. If either your userid or password was incorrect, Unix will display:

Login incorrect

and let you try again. If you are connecting over a phone line or a network, some systems will disconnect you if you log in incorrectly too many times. This makes it difficult for someone who is trying to break into the system to keep guessing passwords indefinitely.

Whenever you type a userid, Unix always asks for a password, even if that particular userid was invalid. For example, if someone enters the userid **harley**, he or she will be asked for a password even if there is no such userid registered with the system. This makes it more difficult for evil-minded people to guess userids.

What Happens After You Log In?

After you log in successfully, Unix will display an informative message describing the system. Here is an example:

```
Last login: Tue May 17 00:00:11 from perseus.org
SunOS Release 4.1.3 (BEOWULF) #1: Sat Jul 10 20:29:29 PDT 1993
```

The first line tells you the last time you logged in. Take a minute to check this line. If the time is more recent than you remember, someone else may be using your account without your permission. If so, change your password immediately. (This is explained later in the chapter.) At the end of the first line, we see the name of the terminal server from which the last login occurred.

The second line shows that we are using the SunOS operating system on a computer named BEOWULF. We are using version 4.1.3 of the operating system, which was installed on July 10, 1993.

What happens next depends on how your system was set up by your system manager. As part of the login process, Unix executes a list of predefined commands that are kept in a special file.

Each person has their own file of login commands. The first time you log in, your file will contain whatever your system manager put in it. As you become more experienced, you can modify this file to suit your preferences. For example, you might have Unix execute a certain program automatically each time you log in.

One thing you may notice is the MESSAGE OF THE DAY. This is a message the system manager will update from time to time, showing important information. Some systems also have their own news facilities. News items are entered by the system manager and you can display them as you wish, usually by using a command named **news**. You may see the newest items displayed automatically each time you log in.

Another message you may see is one that looks like this (where *terminal-name* is the name of the terminal:

TERM = (*terminal-name* **)**

at which point everything will stop.

What is happening is that one of the startup commands (named **tset**) is asking you what type of terminal you are using. The name inside the parentheses is a guess. For example, if **tset** thinks you might be using a VT-100 terminal, you will see:

TERM = (vt100)

We will discuss terminal types in detail in Chapter 6. For now, all you need to do is type the name of your terminal and press the RETURN key. If the name that is displayed is correct, or if you are not sure what to do, just press RETURN.

Getting Down to Work: The Shell Prompt

Once your startup commands have finished executing, you are ready to start work. For the most part, your work will consist of entering one command after another until you are finished working. You then log out to end the session.

The program that reads and interprets your commands is called a "shell". When the shell is ready for you to type the next command, it will display a "prompt". We will talk more about the shell in Chapter 10.

For now, we will say that there are various choices of shells. In Chapter 11, we will discuss the C-Shell; in Chapter 12, we will discuss the Korn shell. Each shell allows you to interact with Unix in a somewhat different way. When you first log in, the shell you use will be chosen by your system manager. Once you become more knowledgeable, you can opt to use a different shell. Your prompt will vary depending on what shell you are using.

When you use the C-Shell, your prompt will be a **%** (percent sign). That is, when Unix is ready for you to enter a command, you will see:

%

If your system manager has customized your environment, the prompt may be somewhat different. For instance, it may show the name of the machine you are logged into. For example:

nipper%

In this case, the prompt shows us that we are logged into the machine called **nipper**. The important thing is that the **%** means the shell is telling you that you can type in a command.

With the Korn shell, your prompt will be a **$** (dollar sign):

$

You may also see a prompt that is customized, for example:

nipper$

The point is that **%** means you are using the C-Shell, and **$** means you are using the Korn shell.

Note: On some systems, a **$** prompt may mean that you are using the Bourne shell (see Chapter 10), the ancient ancestor of the Korn shell. But unless you are an advanced user, it's no big deal, so don't worry about it.

Whatever your shell, once you see the prompt, you can type any command you want and press the RETURN key. If you are logging in for the first time and you want to practice, try the **date** command (to display the time and date) or the **who** command (to display the userids of all the people who are currently logged in).

Logging Out (Stopping Work with Unix): `logout, exit, login`

When you are finished working with Unix, you must end your session by LOGGING OUT. (When we refer to this idea as a noun or adjective, we use a single word, LOGOUT.)

You log out to tell Unix that you are finished working under the current userid. Unix will stop your work session.

It is important to make sure that you log out when you are finished. If you were to just pick up and leave with your terminal logged in, anyone could come by and use it under the auspices of your userid.

At the very least, you run the risk of someone fooling around under your userid. At the other extreme, some mischievous person might erase files (including yours) and cause all types of trouble. If this happens, you will bear some responsibility: leaving a terminal logged in is like leaving your car unlocked with the keys in the ignition.

There are several ways to log out. The first way is to wait until you see the shell prompt and then press CTRL-D. This means you hold down the CTRL key and press the D key at the same time. (We will discuss the Unix keyboard in detail in Chapter 6.)

When you press CTRL-D, it sends a signal called "end of file". Essentially, this tells the shell (the program that interprets your commands) that there is no more data coming. The shell terminates, and Unix logs you out.

However, as you will find out, the end-of-file signal has other uses. It is altogether possible that you might press CTRL-D once too often and inadvertently log yourself out.

Thus, as a safeguard, most shells have a way for you to specify that you do not want to log out by pressing CTRL-D. Rather, you must enter a special command; in this way, it is impossible to log out accidentally.

It may be that your system manager has set up your system so that, by default, you cannot log out by pressing CTRL-D. If this is the case, you must use one of the logout commands. They are **logout** and **exit**.

To find out how to log out with your system, first try pressing CTRL-D. If it works, fine. If not, you may see a message like this:

Use "logout" to logout.

In this case, use the **logout** command. (Type "logout" and press the RETURN key.) If, instead, you see a message like this:

Use 'exit' to logout

you will need to use the **exit** command.

One final way to log out is to use the **login** command. This tells Unix to log you out and then get ready for a new person to log in. After you are logged out, Unix will display the:

login:

message, asking for a new userid. This command is handy if you want to leave your terminal ready for someone else to use.

HINT

On some systems, the **login** command will not disengage you completely. Instead, **login** will change the userid temporarily, but, officially, you will still be logged in under your original name. When the new person logs out, he will find himself back in your original session. If this is the case on your system, you should not use **login** because it could allow someone else to end up logged in under your userid.

You can find out how your version of **login** works by testing it: enter the **login** command, log in and log out, and then see if you are back in your original session. If so, it is not safe to use **login** for logging out. Use **logout** or **exit** instead.

How do you know for sure you have logged out successfully? The shell prompt will stop and, if you press RETURN, you may see the next **login:** prompt. On some systems, you may also see a message like "Session disconnected" or "Connection closed".

To summarize: to log out, press CTRL-D. If that doesn't work, use the **logout** or **exit** command. Alternatively, you can use the **login** command to allow someone else to log in right away.

SECURITY HINT

Do not, under any circumstances, walk away from your terminal and leave it logged in. Also, do not simply turn off your terminal and walk away. Someone else may come along, turn on the terminal, and take over your session (under the auspices of your userid).

Upper- and Lowercase

As you might have noticed, Unix distinguishes between small letters and capital letters. For example, when we discussed possible userids, we used the examples **harley** and **hahn**, both of which start with a small "h". At the same time, we suggested a possible password, **H!1g%12**, that contains two small letters and one capital letter.

Some computer systems are designed to ignore the differences between small and capital letters, a notable example being a personal computer using DOS. Unix, however, was written to be more specific.

For convenience, we refer to small letters as LOWERCASE and capital letters as UPPERCASE. The names come from typewriter terminology. When you use an old-fashioned typewriter, pressing the SHIFT key moves the "upper" case into position to print capital letters.

The idea of upper- and lowercase applies only to the letters of the alphabet, not to punctuation, numbers or any special characters.

When you type names or commands, you must be sure to be exact. For example, if your userid is **harley**, you must type all lowercase letters when you log in. If you type **Harley**, Unix considers it to be an entirely different userid. Similarly, when you log out, you must type **logout**, not **Logout**. When a program or system distinguishes between upper- and lowercase, we say that it is CASE SENSITIVE.

HINT

Unlike some other computer systems (such as DOS), Unix is case sensitive.

Since Unix considers uppercase letters to be different from lowercase letters, it is possible for a system manager to assign two different userids, such as **harley** and **Harley**. However, in practice, you would never see this because it would be too confusing; lowercase userids are used exclusively.

To maintain scrupulous accuracy in this book, we will not capitalize command names, even when they come at the beginning of a sentence—for instance: "**logout**, **exit** and **login** are three commands that you can use to log out."

Please appreciate that the distinction between upper- and lowercase applies only when you are logging in and entering Unix commands. When you use a program that works with regular textual data—for example, when you use a word processor to create a document—you type in the regular manner.

A Sample Session with Unix

Figure 4-1 shows a short work session with Unix. This session was taken from a computer that serves the social sciences departments at the University of California at Santa Barbara.

The session starts by logging in, using userid **harley**. Notice that Unix does not echo the password.

```
login: harley
Password:

Last login: Tue May 17 00:00:11 from perseus.org
SunOS Release 4.1.3 (BEOWULF) #1: Sat Jul 10 20:29:29 PDT 1993

***********************************************************
5/11/94
Welcome to the Social Sciences Computing Facility.
In the event of system problems, please send mail
to the system administrator using the command
"mail root".  System information is available
using the command "news".
***********************************************************

% date
Tue May 17 10:22:27 PDT 1994

% who
schild    console May 17 09:02
gwen      ttyp0   May 17 09:33   (colin.sscf.ucsb)
joan      ttyp1   May 17 07:48   (roc:0.0)
harley    ttyp2   May 17 10:19   (perseus.org)
schmidt   ttyp3   May 17 09:23   (sam.sscf.ucsb)
schild    ttyp4   May 17 09:03   (joyce:0.0)

% logout
Connection with BEOWULF closed.
```

FIGURE 4-1.   *Sample work session #1*

After the userid and password are accepted, the Unix system tells us when we last logged in and then identifies itself. We see that we are using the SunOS 4.1.3 operating system.

Next, we see the message of the day. We are welcomed to the system and told how to send messages to the system manager. We are also told that we can use the **news** command to look at other information (presumably local news).

Finally, the preliminaries are over, and we are presented with the **%** character. This is a prompt telling us that the shell (command interpreter) is ready for us to type in a command. In this case, we typed the **date** command. The system responded by displaying the current time and date.

Once the **date** command finished, the shell displayed another prompt. This time we type the **who** command. This command shows us what userids are currently logged in.

After the **who** command finishes, we see another shell prompt. We type the **logout** command, ending the session.

Notice that userid **schild** is logged in twice at different terminals. Unix allows you to log in as many times as you want without logging out. However, you would normally use only one terminal at a time. In our example, **schild** is the system manager, who has more than one terminal in his office.

If you ever enter the **who** command and see yourself logged in to more than one terminal, you should find out what is happening. You may have inadvertently finished a previous work session without logging out. Alternately, someone may be using your userid without your permission.

Figure 4-2 shows a second sample session. In this case, we used the **login** command to log out. Notice that the connection is not dropped. Instead, Unix (after logging us out) displays the **login:** prompt, asking for the userid of the next user.

Changing Your Password: **passwd**, **yppasswd**, **kpasswd**

When your Unix account is set up, the system manager will assign you a userid and a password. System managers usually have their own ways of organizing things, and you may not be able to get the userid you want.

```
login: harley
Password:

Last login: Tue May 17 10:21:27 from perseus.org
SunOS Release 4.1.3 (BEOWULF) #1: Sat Jul 10 20:29:29 PDT 1993


************************************************************
5/11/94
Welcome to the Social Sciences Computing Facility.
In the event of system problems, please send mail
to the system administrator using the command
"mail root".  System information is available
using the command "news".
************************************************************


% date
Tue May 17 10:43:56 PDT 1994


% login
login:
```

FIGURE 4-2. *Sample work session #2*

For example, you may want to use your first name as a userid, but the system manager may tell you that he or she has decided that all userids should be last names. Don't fight with your system manager. He or she has a great deal of responsibility—Unix systems are hard to manage—and is probably massively overworked.

You can, however, change your password whenever you want. Indeed, some Unix systems require you to change your password regularly for security reasons. As you change your password, the characters you type will not be echoed. This prevents anyone from reading your new password over your shoulder.

To change your password, use the **passwd** command. Unix will first ask you to enter your old password. This proves you are authorized to make the change. Otherwise, anyone who walks by a terminal that was left logged in could change that person's password.

Next, **passwd** will ask you to type in the new password. Some systems require all passwords to meet certain specifications. For example, your password may need to be at least eight characters. If your new password does not meet the local criteria, you will be so informed and asked to enter a new choice.

Finally, **passwd** will ask you to retype the new password. Remember, the characters are not echoed as you type. Entering your new password a second time ensures that you did not make a mistake.

Aside from **passwd**, there are two other password programs—named **yppasswd** and **kpasswd**—that you may encounter. These programs are used on computers that are part of a local area network (see Chapter 3). On such systems, passwords are sometimes kept in a network-wide database. If your computer is part of such a network, you may have to use either **yppasswd** or **kpasswd** instead of **passwd**.

What's in a Name? `passwd, yppasswd, kpasswd`

The standard Unix program to change passwords is named **passwd**. (Unix people don't like to type more letters than are really necessary.) The names **yppasswd** and **kpasswd** are variations.

Many Sun computers are connected into local area networks that use a facility called Networking Information System (NIS) to share information. The old name for NIS used to be "Sun Yellow Pages"; thus, the name **yppasswd** is used for the program that maintains the network-wide password database.

Other Unix networks use a security system called Kerberos. With Kerberos, the passwords are maintained in an "Authentication Database". On such systems, the name of the program to change passwords is **kpasswd**.

Choosing a Password

The reason we use passwords is to make sure that only authorized people use Unix accounts. This security is not mean-spirited. Many people depend on the computer to store their data and to run their programs. Moreover, computer resources, such as disk storage space, are limited and must be allotted deliberately.

As you might imagine, there are always a number of bright people who take pleasure in trying to break into a system. Such people are called CRACKERS. Some crackers want only to match wits against the Unix security system to see if they can log in on the sly. Other crackers enjoy causing real damage.

Thus, it behooves you to (1) never tell your password to anyone, and (2) choose a password that is not easy to guess. Remember: if you give your password to someone who damages the computer system, you are responsible.

What's in a Name?   Hacker, Cracker

There are two types of people who spend a lot of time programming: hackers and crackers. A HACKER is someone who spends his or her time working on useful (or at least benign) programming projects.

The word HACK is often used as a verb to indicate a larger-than-life devotion to programming. For example, "Gwen spent all weekend hacking at her MUD program". (A MUD is a computer-mediated role-playing game; MUDs can be extremely complex and, for some people, can become a way of life, like religion or **emacs**.)

Thus, the term "hacker" is often used in a positive sense, to describe someone who is capable of massive amounts of nerd-like effort. Hackers are socially useful people, though rarely cool. The most financially successful hacker in the world is Microsoft's Bill Gates.

A CRACKER is a bad guy: someone who enjoys breaking into computer systems and doing things that people in authority do not want him to do. (Notice we say "him". For some reason—perhaps a genetic deficiency—virtually all crackers are male.)

A cracker is someone you would not want your sister to marry. A hacker in the family would be okay: it's just that everyone would receive their wedding invitations by electronic mail. (And, at the reception, the wedding cake would have computerized sensors connected to the Internet, so that friends from all over the world could use the **finger** command—see Chapter 13—to determine how much cake remains at any given time.)

When you get your Unix account, the system manager will choose a password for you. Whenever you want, you can use the **passwd** command to change your password. (Remember, as we explained in the previous section, if your computer is on a local area network, you may have to use **yppasswd** or **kpasswd** instead of **passwd**.)

The rules for choosing a password are actually guidelines for what not to choose:

- Do not choose your userid. (This is like hiding the key to your house under the mat.)

- Do not choose your first or last name, or any combination of names.

- Do not choose the name of a loved one or friend.

- Do not choose a word that is in the dictionary.

- Do not choose a number that is meaningful to you, such as a phone number, important date (such as a birthday), social security number and so on.

- Do not choose a password that is even remotely related to *Star Trek* or *Monty Python.*

In addition, there are several routine precautions you should practice:

- Never write down your password on a piece of paper. (Someone is bound to find it after you lose it.)

- Change your password regularly.

Within the cracker community, there are programs that exist to guess passwords. Such programs not only make intelligent guesses (such as your first name, last name, and so on), but they use large lists of probable passwords to see if any of them will work. For example, there are lists of dictionary words, first and last names, movie actors, movie titles, Internet addresses, U.S. ZIP codes, nicknames of U.S. Congressmen, and much, much more, including of words from foreign languages.

So if you think of something well-known and amusing, chances are that the crackers have been there ahead of you. This is especially true for passwords that relate to popular TV shows. For example, if you're a student, both *Star Trek* and *Monty Python* were cool long before you were born, and there is probably no name or term you could use that is not in the standard cracker's list.

Password cracking programs are far more successful than you would imagine, so protect yourself (and your files) by choosing wisely. The best idea is to make up a pattern of meaningless characters. For good measure, mix in uppercase, lowercase, numbers and punctuation. (Some systems will force you to choose such characters.) As an example, consider the password **H!1g%12** which we used earlier in the chapter. Such a password would be hard to guess.

If you suspect that someone knows your password, change it right away. If you should forget your password, all you need to do is tell your system manager. He or she can assign you a new password without knowing the old one.

HINT

An ideal password is one that you can remember without writing down, but that no one will ever guess, and that will never appear on a cracker's word list. One good idea is to start with a phrase or sentence that makes sense to you and create an abbreviation. Here are some examples:

dontBL8	("Don't be late")
DhaCMan	(for Bart Simpson fans: "Don't have a cow Man")
2b||~2b	(for C programmers: "To be or not to be")
?8kin42NAW	(random meaningless phrase)

You get the idea. Just be sure that, in the excitement of creating a totally rad password, you resist the temptation to tell someone just to show off how smart you are.

Checking if Someone Has Been Using Your Unix Account: `last`

Whenever you log in, look carefully at the initial message: most systems will tell you the time and date you last logged in. If you don't remember logging in at this time, somebody might be using your account.

To check further, you can use the **last** command. Simply enter **last** followed by your userid. For example, if you are logged in as **harley**, enter:

```
last harley
```

You will see some information telling you the last time, or last several times, you logged in. (Note: This is a Berkeley Unix command so, if you are using an older System V system, **last** may not be available. See Chapter 2 for a discussion of the various types of Unix.)

If you accidentally enter the command without a userid:

```
last
```

you will see information about all the userids on the system. This may go on for some time so, if you want to terminate the command, press CTRL-C. (Hold down the CTRL key and press C at the same time.)

You might think, wouldn't it be fun to enter the **last** command without a userid and spy on all the other people by seeing when they logged in? Well, you can if you want, but it gets boring real fast. If you have nothing to do, you will probably have more fun playing one of the games we describe in Chapter 7.

Userids and Users

A USER is a person who utilizes a Unix system in some way. However, Unix itself does not know about users: Unix only knows about userids.

The distinction is an important one. If someone logs in using your userid, Unix has no way of knowing whether or not it is really you. That is why you need to protect your password.

Later in the book, we will describe how you can create files to hold your data. Such files are said to be "owned" by your userid. Thus, anyone who knows your password can log in with your userid and read (or even destroy) your files.

In the world of Unix, only userids have a real identity. It is userids, not users, who own files, send electronic mail, and log in and out.

Earlier in this chapter, we saw a sample session in which we used the **who** command to find out who was logged in. Here is the result of that command:

```
% who
schild     console May 17 09:02
gwen       ttyp0   May 17 09:33   (colin.sscf.ucsb)
joan       ttyp1   May 17 07:48   (roc:0.0)
harley     ttyp2   May 17 10:19   (perseus.org)
schmidt    ttyp3   May 17 09:23   (sam.sscf.ucsb)
schild     ttyp4   May 17 09:03   (joyce:0.0)
```

Notice that you see only userids, not people's names.

In Chapter 13, we will explain how you can use the **finger** command to display information about the person to whom a particular userid is registered. This is handy, for example, when you receive a message from, say, userid **wrm**, and you would like to know the name of the person behind the userid.

The Superuser Userid: `root`

Within Unix, all userids are considered equal, with one notable exception.

From time to time, it becomes necessary for the system manager to have special privileges. For example, he or she may need to add a new user to the system or change somebody's password.

Toward this end, Unix supports a special userid, called **root**, that has extraordinary privileges. A person who has logged in using the **root** userid can do anything he or she wants. (Obviously, the **root** password is a closely guarded secret.) When someone logs in as **root**, we refer to him or her as the SUPERUSER.

At first, the name **root** may not make any sense. However, in Chapter 22, we will see that the basis of the entire Unix file system is called the "root directory". Thus, the name **root** refers to a very important part of Unix.

Most of the time, a good system administrator will use his or her regular userid. He or she will change to superuser only to do work that requires special privileges. Once the work is done, the system administrator will change back to a regular userid. This prevents the power of the superuser from causing inadvertent damage.

For example, if you make a mistake entering the **rm** (remove) command, it is possible to erase data files accidentally. If you are logged in under your own userid, the worst that you can do is erase your own files. If you are logged in under **root**, you might erase everybody's files.

If you ever get a message from userid **root**, make sure you are polite. You are talking to someone who can wipe you out of the system with a single command.

Having Fun While Practicing Safe Computing

From its early days, Unix was designed for people working together who needed to share programs and documents. The basic design of the system assumes that everybody is honest and of good will. Even modern Unix, with its passwords and security measures, is not bulletproof, nor is it meant to be. People who use Unix are supposed to respect the other users and to share.

Since Unix is so complex, there are always a few crackers who get a kick out of trying to beat the system. In some environments, young programmers who figure out how to break into a system and perform clandestine acts are tolerated, perhaps even admired for their ingenuity.

Not so in the Unix community (which, as we described in Chapter 1, extends all over the world). Crackers and troublemakers are tracked down and punished. For example, we mentioned earlier that there exist programs that guess people's passwords. In some universities just being caught running such a program is grounds for immediate expulsion.

However, the wonderful thing about Unix is that there are so many challenging and pleasant diversions. For example, you may have acces to the worldwide Usenet network, which consists of hundreds of different discussion groups.

It is unlikely that you will ever become bored enough to get into mischief. Nevertheless, if you are ever so tempted, please remember that system managers are always overworked, and they have little patience with willful people who create unnecessary trouble.

If you find that you like Unix, you can get a great deal of pleasure out of helping other people. Two of the most important Unix traditions are to share and to help others.

CHAPTER 5

Starting with X Window

In Chapter 4, we discussed how to get started working with Unix. In particular, we explained how to log in and log out.

If you have a regular (character) terminal, the process is pretty much as we have described it, regardless of what type of terminal you are using. However, if you are using a graphics terminal with X Window, the procedures vary. Moreover, where users of regular terminals need only know how to use the keyboard, X Window users need some extra skills.

In this chapter, we'll examine X Window: a graphical system that lets you work within windows and run programs on any computer in your network. We will discuss the X Window system itself, what you can do with it, and how you log in and log out. If you do not use X Window, you can skip this chapter.

Before we can talk about X Window, though, we need to lay a foundation. Let's start with the idea of a graphical user interface.

GUI: Graphical User Interface

If you have ever used a Macintosh, or a PC with Microsoft Windows or OS/2, you know what a GRAPHICAL USER INTERFACE is. It is a system in which you use not only the keyboard, but also a mouse. Your screen contains not only characters, but boxes (windows) and pictures as well. You work by manipulating the boxes and pictures as objects. Sometimes a graphical user interface is called a GUI (pronounced "gooey").

There are several basic ideas you need to understand to work with a GUI. First, you need to learn to use two input devices: the keyboard and a POINTING DEVICE. As the name implies, you use the pointing device, from time to time, to point to a part of the screen. The most common pointing device is a mouse, but you may also see trackballs, touchpads, and so on. In this chapter, we will assume that you are using a mouse, but the differences are minor.

Typically, you will move the mouse around on your desktop. As you do, a pointer on the screen follows the motion. This pointer is a small picture, often an arrow. To point to a particular picture, you would move the mouse until the pointer on the screen rests within that picture. With some GUIs, you may find that the pointer changes as you move from one region of the screen to another.

Pointing devices usually have buttons that you can press. The X Window system uses three buttons, although it is possible to use fewer. By convention, these buttons are numbered from left to right. Button number 1 is on the left, number 2 is in the middle, and number 3 is on the right. When you use a GUI, you will find that you will use button 1, the left-most button, most often. (If you are left-handed, it is possible to change the order of the buttons.)

The next important idea about GUIs is that they divide the screen into a number of bounded regions called WINDOWS. As with real windows, the boundary is usually, but not always, a rectangle. The windows can overlap like pieces of paper on a desk. Moreover, you can change the size and position of the windows as you see fit.

Within each window, you can have a different activity. For example, you might use a number of different windows, each of which contains a different program. As you work, it is easy to switch from one window to another. This allows you to use each program whenever you want. On a regular character terminal, you can see only one program at a time (unless you have special software). In fact, one of the prime motivations behind the development of X Window—and of windowing systems in general—has been to allow a user to work with multiple programs.

There are other important ideas and skills that you need to understand in order to work with a GUI, but before we get to them, let's talk about X Window.

What Is X Window?

X Window is a system designed to support graphical user interfaces. For convenience, we usually refer to X Window as "X". Thus, you might ask a friend, "Does your computer run X?"

What's in a Name?   X Window

The roots of X lie in a particular operating system that was developed at Stanford University. This system was called V (the single letter "V"). When a windowing interface was developed for V, it was called W. Some time later, the W program was given to someone at MIT who used it as a basis for a new windowing system he called X.

Since then, the name has stuck, perhaps for two reasons. First, names of Unix systems often end in "x" or "ix" and X Window is used mostly with Unix. Second, if they kept changing the name, they would reach the end of the alphabet in just two more letters.

The idea behind X is to provide standard services to programs that display graphical data. You can, for example, run programs on one computer whose output is displayed on a screen attached to another computer. X stays behind the scenes, orchestrating all the details, providing the supporting structure.

X was developed at MIT as part of Project Athena. Currently, X is maintained by an independent organization called the X Consortium. In 1987, MIT released X version 11, referred to as X11. Various versions of X11 are known as X11.4, X11.5 and so on. Notice, by the way, that the proper name is "X Window", not "X Windows".

The Window Manager: `mwm`, `olwm`, `twm`

The actual graphical user interface is provided not by X itself, but by a program called the WINDOW MANAGER. The window manager controls the appearance and characteristics of the windows and the pictures.

There are several window managers that work with X. On your system there may be just one, or you may have a choice. As you work, you don't really interact with X, you interact with the window manager. Thus, the look and feel of your system depends on which window manager you use.

The three most common window managers are **mwm** (the Motif window manager), **olwm** (the Open Look window manager) and **twm** (the Tab window manager), although there are others. Motif is a product of the Open Software Foundation and is found on a variety of systems. Figure 5-1 shows what Open Look looks like. Open Look was developed by AT&T and Sun, and is found on many Sun systems. The Tab window manager comes with the basic X system. If you have a choice, you will probably opt for Motif or Open Look, which are easier to use and look nicer than Tab.

Using a graphical user interface is like using a car; if you know how to use one, it is easy to use another. We might carry the analogy one step further and say that

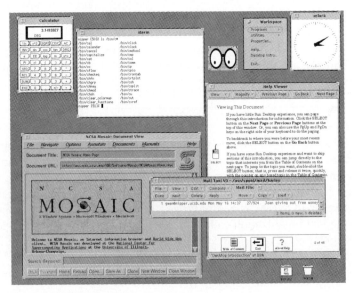

FIGURE 5-1. *The Open Look window manager*

twm is like a car with a manual transmission, while **mwm** and **olwm** are easier to use, like cars with automatic transmissions.

If you have ever used a Macintosh, or a PC with Microsoft Windows or OS/2, you have used a graphical user interface. You will have no trouble learning how to use one of the X-based GUIs. Indeed, if you have used OS/2 and are familiar with the Presentation Manager GUI, you will find **mwm** especially easy. Motif was designed to look and work like Presentation Manager.

X Servers and X Clients

Imagine yourself writing a computer program that offers a graphical user interface. You would find that it is a lot of work to attend to all the details of drawing windows, moving pictures around, keeping track of the mouse, and so on. Moreover, your program would have to know the exact hardware specifications of the screen, the keyboard and the mouse.

What would happen if your program became popular? People would want to use it on various types of computers. You would have to modify the program to work with all kinds of different screens, keyboards and mice. It wouldn't be long before most of the program was taken up with the details of maintaining the graphical user interface!

The X Window system was designed to make it easy to create and use graphical programs. To do this, X offers a standard service: a program called a DISPLAY SERVER. The display server takes care of all the details of interfacing with a graphical user interface.

Let's take a moment to review the terminology. As we explained in Chapter 3, a program or a computer that offers a resource over a network is called a server. A program that uses such a resource is called a client.

For example, say that you run a program that uses a file stored on another computer. Your program is the client. The file is sent over the network to your program by a file server. Similarly, you might send a file to another computer to be printed. The other computer acts as a print server.

In the world of X, the word "display" refers to more than just your screen display. DISPLAY is a technical term that refers to your screen, keyboard and mouse. That is, your display consists of all the equipment you use to interact with your programs.

The display server is a program that manages the screen, keyboard and mouse for other programs. When you write an X program, you do not need to worry about the input/output details. Your program can call on the display server to do the job.

For instance, if an X program needs to draw a window on the screen, it just tells the display server to draw a window of a certain size at a certain location. The display server takes care of the details. In particular, the X program does not need to know what type of screen is being used.

This means that X programs are highly portable. They can interact with any graphical user interface on any computer, using any screen, keyboard and mouse, as long as there is an X-based display server to perform the actual input and output.

Borrowing from the terminology of networks, the display server is usually referred to as an X SERVER. Similarly, any program that uses the display server is called an X CLIENT. In other words, an X client is a program that runs under X, using the resources of the X server to handle the input and output.

The X system comes with over 50 utility programs that run under X. For example, there is a program that displays a picture of a clock to tell you what time it is. In X terminology, we would say that the system comes with over 50 X clients.

When you use X, your computer executes a single X server program. This X server interfaces for all the X clients you want to use.

For instance, you may decide to run five X programs (X clients) at the same time, switching back and forth from one to another as you see fit. On your screen, each program is displayed within its own window. The input and output from all of these X clients are handled by a single X server program, which executes on your computer. The relationship between X clients and an X server is shown in Figure 5-2.

(As we explained in Chapter 2, Unix is a multitasking operating system that can run more than one program at the same time.)

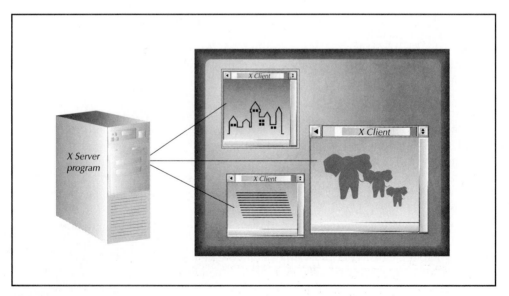

FIGURE 5-2.   *X clients and an X server*

Using X to Run Programs Remotely

You might ask, all these details are nice (and even mildly interesting), but do I really need to understand them just to use a graphical user interface? After all, there is no need to get so involved to learn how to use a Macintosh, Microsoft Windows or OS/2.

The reason that you must understand the X client-server relationship is that it provides a wonderful service. Since the display (screen + keyboard + mouse) is handled by a single X server for all X clients, we have effectively separated the input/output from the processing. Thus, the X server program that runs on your computer can service any X client no matter where it is executing.

Of course, your X server program serves X clients that execute on your computer. However, your X server can also interface for X clients that run on another computer—as long as there is a network connection between the two machines.

This is the beauty of the X system: using a graphical user interface, you can work with several windows at the same time, each of which contains a separate program. Although the X server runs on your computer, the programs in the window can be running on any computer on the network.

For instance, you might be running three programs on your own computer, one program on a friend's computer down the hall, and one program on the supercomputer in another building. Each program will run its own window. You control the whole thing by using a graphical user interface.

Thus, from a single computer, you can use any X-based graphical user interface to run any X client programs you want on any computers in the network. This idea is shown in Figure 5-3.

One last point: since X can work with various window managers, your screen may look somewhat different depending on what graphical user interface you are using.

For example, say that you and a friend are working, side by side, on two identical graphics terminals. You decide to use the **mwm** (Motif) window manager, while she is using the **olwm** (Open Look) window manager. You are both running the same set of five programs we just described. However, since you are using different GUIs, your screen display and interactions are different.

The Most Important X Client: `xterm`

As we explained in the last section, an X client is a program that runs under the X Window system. X, being a graphical system, is designed to support only graphics displays. However, much of the time you will want to enter Unix commands, one after the other, at the shell prompt (see Chapter 4). For such work, you need a plain vanilla character terminal.

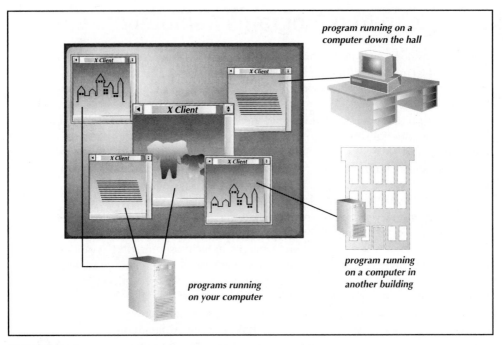

FIGURE 5-3. *X Window connections over a network*

Since this is a fundamental requirement, the X Window system comes with an X client whose sole purpose is to run within a window and emulate a terminal. This program is called **xterm**. When you start **xterm**, it sets up a window that acts like a small version of a terminal.

Thus, if you have four different **xterm** clients, each running in its own window, it's like having four different terminals, all logged in. You can move from one to the other whenever you want (see Figure 5-4).

xterm is capable of emulating two types of terminals: the ubiquitous VT-100 (see Chapter 3), to act as a character terminal, and the Tektronix 4014, for graphics work. Most of the time you will use **xterm** as a VT-100 (which is the default).

We mentioned earlier that X does not offer a full-featured graphical user interface. This is provided by whatever window manager you decide to use. The window manager, though, is itself an X client; that is, it is a program that runs under X. As we will see in a moment, the window manager may need to be started from within an **xterm** window.

In other words, out of all the X clients that come with the system, **xterm** is indispensable. You need it not only to act as a terminal, so you can enter Unix commands; you may also need it to start the window manager that creates your graphical user interface.

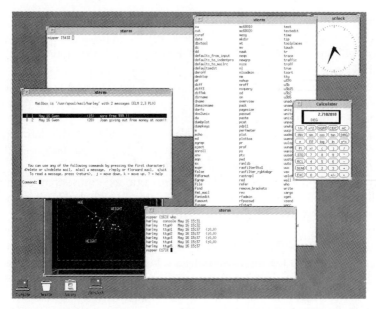

FIGURE 5-4. *Multiple `xterm` windows*

Starting Work with X Window: `xinit`, `xterm`, `twm`, `mwm`, `olwm`

In Chapter 4, we explained how you start work at a regular terminal. Essentially, all you need to do is wait for the login prompt and enter your userid and password. You will then see the shell prompt. You can now enter one Unix command after another. When you are finished, you log out, either by entering the **logout** or **exit** command, or by pressing **^D**.

If you are using X, getting started is more complex. How much work you have to do depends on whether or not your system manager has set up your system to start X and a window manager automatically. If not, you will have to enter the appropriate commands yourself.

There are three basic possibilities. Let's start with the most automated and work our way down. Before we start, realize that you can only use X if your terminal supports it. That is, you need to be using a workstation with a graphics display screen, or a special purpose terminal, called an X TERMINAL, designed just for running X. Moreover, the X Window software must already be installed and accessible on whatever host computer you are using.

To make starting X easy, some systems use a program called a DISPLAY MANAGER. The display manager moderates your login procedure. When you start work, you will see a message, such as "Welcome to the X Window System", as well as a login window in which you can enter your userid and password.

Once you log in, the display manager will start everything automatically. This involves starting X itself and then starting the window manager. Thus, if your system has a display manager, there is really nothing more for you to do than log in.

Without a display manager, Unix will present you with the standard login prompt that we discussed in Chapter 4. Log in by entering your userid and password. At this point, one of two things will happen.

First, your system manager may have set up your account so that, once you log in, X will start and the window manager will begin. As with the display manager, you are ready to start work without much trouble.

If, however, you are working at a terminal capable of using X, but nothing has been automated, you will have to start the system manually. You can tell this is the case because, after you log in, X will not start. Instead, you will find yourself at the regular shell prompt (see Chapter 4). You will have to enter two commands: one to start X Window, the other to start the window manager.

At the shell prompt, enter the command:

xinit

and wait for a few moments. **xinit** will start the X Window system and create the first **xterm**, which will be in a window. (On some systems, there may be another command that works better than **xinit**.)

Once X has started and you see the **xterm** window, you must indicate that you want to work with that particular window. Simply move the mouse so that the mouse pointer lies within the window.

Now that you are within the **xterm** window, enter the command to start your window manager. The command you use is the name of the window manager program followed by an **&** (ampersand) character. You will have to ask around to see what window managers are available on your system.

You can always use **twm** (Tab), the window manager that comes with X. However, if your system has either **mwm** (Motif) or **olwm** (Open Look), you are better off using those.

So, for example, if you are using Motif, enter the following command within the **xterm** window:

mwm &

After a few moments, your window manager will start. You are now ready to work.

To summarize: from the shell prompt, enter the **xinit** command. Once X has started, move to the **xterm** window and enter the name of your window manager, followed by an ampersand, for example, **mwm &**.

Why do we append the **&** character to the end of the command? The **&** tells Unix that the program we are starting should run by itself, in the "background". In other words, the window manager should have a life of its own.

If you forget the **&**, Unix will start the window manager, but will not release the keyboard and screen. If this happens, terminate the program by pressing the **intr** key (usually **^C** or DELETE). You can then reenter the command properly. (Note: Terminating programs using the **intr** key is discussed in Chapter 6.)

One last point: as you work with X, you will create and delete windows as you see fit. When you delete a window, any program that is running in the window will be terminated. Thus, if you were to delete the original **xterm** window, the program that is running in it—the window manager—will terminate and your graphical user interface will vanish!

To avoid this, it is a good idea to leave the original **xterm** window alone. If you want to enter Unix commands, you can create another **xterm**. In fact, you can create as many as you want. Some people like to minimize the original **xterm** window and move it out of the way. We will discuss how to perform such manipulations later in the chapter.

HINT
If you started your window manager manually from the original **xterm** window, iconize this window and move it out of the way. ("Iconize" means to turn a window into a small picture so as to take up less space on the screen. We discuss this later in the chapter.)

Learning to Use a Graphical User Interface

Learning to use a graphical user interface is easy; but the way to learn is by practicing and experimenting on your system, not by reading.

Because GUIs are mostly visual, the best way to learn is to have someone show you in person. Although it is possible to read about how to use a GUI, words do not convey the visual ideas well. You will find yourself reading and rereading instructions when what you really need is someone to take a few seconds and show you what to do. Using a GUI is so simple that once you see someone perform the basic operations, you will have no problems.

Although the various window managers offer GUIs that have a lot in common, there are small but important differences. It is difficult to write down a single set of instructions that will work for all the different interfaces. In addition, virtually every part of X Window can be customized. Your system manager may have set up your particular system to look and act in a certain way. Once you become a veteran X user, you can customize your system according to your own needs and preferences.

In the following sections, we will discuss the basic ideas that you must understand to use a GUI. However, make sure that after reading this chapter you take some time to practice with your particular window manager.

We have already covered the first few important ideas. A graphical user interface allows you to work with windows. A window is a bounded area of the screen, usually a rectangle. Windows can overlap. As the need arises, you can change the size of a window, or move it from one part of the screen to another.

Of Mice and Menus

On your screen will be a pointer. You use a pointing device, usually a mouse, to move the pointer around the screen. The shape of the pointer may change, depending on what you are doing and where you are on the screen.

You can indicate an action by moving the mouse to a particular position and pressing a button. Your mouse may have either one, two or three buttons. X Window is designed to use a three-button pointer, but a two-button device will also work.

There are only two things that you can do with a mouse button. First, you can press it and let go. When you do so, we say that you CLICK the button. If you press the button twice in rapid succession, we say that you DOUBLE-CLICK. On some occasions, you may also have to TRIPLE-CLICK: that is, press a button three times quickly.

The other thing you can do with a button is press it and hold it down.

Much of the time, you will make choices by selecting them from a list called a MENU. There are two types of menus. POP-UP menus appear out of nowhere after some action has occurred. For example, if you move the pointer to an empty area of the screen and hold down a button, a menu will pop up.

The other type of menu is a PULL-DOWN menu. With some X programs, there will be a horizontal list of words near the top of the window. If you move the pointer to one of these words and hold down the left button, a menu of related items will appear below the word.

One of the most common actions within a graphical user interface is to move the pointer to an object and click a mouse button. We call this POINT AND CLICK. For example, to change the size of a window, you may need to point and click on a particular part of that window.

Another common action is to move the pointer to an object, hold down the mouse button, move the pointer some more, and then let go of the mouse button.

For example, to move a window, you move the pointer to the title bar of the window (the place where the name is displayed near the top of the window). Hold down the left button and move the pointer to wherever you want the window to be. When you release the button, the window manager will redraw the window at the new location.

When we move something in this way, we say that we DRAG it. So we can say that to move a window, you drag the title bar to the new location.

Icons

It is possible to change the size of windows. We won't go into the details here, as they vary depending on your graphical user interface. It may be that you move the pointer to one of the borders of the window, hold down a button, and drag the border to a new location. Or you may click or hold down a button to bring up a menu and select a "size" option from that menu.

However, there will be times when you want to make a window as small as possible. For instance, you may have a window that contains a word processing program you are not using currently. It is nice to be able to shrink the window and move it out of the way. Later, when you want to return to the word processor, you can enlarge the window.

All GUIs have a facility for transforming a window into a small picture, called an ICON. How you do this depends on your GUI. You may click or double-click on a particular part of the window, or you may select an item from a menu. However you do it, we say that you ICONIZE or MINIMIZE the window.

Later, when you expand the window, either by clicking or by menu selection, we say that you MAXIMIZE the window.

It is often convenient to iconize a number of windows and drag them out of the way to a remote corner of the screen. Some GUIs have a special window to hold all your icons.

Controlling Your Focus

With a graphical user interface, you can have multiple windows, each of which contains its own program. However, when you type on the keyboard, the input will go to one specific window.

To choose a window to work with, you use the mouse to move the pointer to that window and then press the left mouse button. When you select a window in this way, we say that you are changing the keyboard FOCUS. (With some GUIs, you do not have to press a mouse button to change the focus; merely moving the pointer into the window is enough.)

Once you focus on a window, everything you type goes to the program that is running in that window. That is, to start working with a window, you need only move to it and click. The keyboard is now connected to that window.

When you focus on a window, it will be highlighted in some way to show that it is now the active window. In addition, if the window is partially obscured by another window, the window with the focus will be redrawn to be on top and will become completely visible.

Starting a Program: `xcalc`, `xclock`

There are two ways to start a program. First, when you move the pointer to a blank area of the screen and press a mouse button, you will pop up the MAIN MENU, sometimes called the ROOT MENU. (Which button you press, left or right, will depend on your window manager.) This menu may have a selection to allow you to start or "open" a new program. When you make such a selection, the program will start in its own window.

As we mentioned earlier, nearly every part of X can be customized. In particular, the items on your main menu can be modified. If the person who set up your system is an ambitious enthusiast, there may be all kinds of wonderful items on this menu, including a long list of programs.

The second way to start a program is to change your focus to an **xterm** window and type in a command at the shell prompt. Of course, you can type in any regular Unix command or program name.

If you are starting an X program that needs to reside in its own window—that is, an X client—you must type an **&** (ampersand) character at the end of the command. This tells Unix to let the program execute in the "background". In other words, this program has a life of its own; you do not want to wait for it to finish before you can enter the next command. We saw this earlier when we talked about starting the window manager from within an **xterm** window.

Here is an example. If you want to display the time and date, change your focus to an **xterm** window. At the shell prompt, enter:

```
date
```

Since **date** is a regular program, it will execute, display its output and end. Once the **date** program finishes, the shell prompt will be redisplayed.

On the other hand, let's say you want to start another **xterm** window. At the shell prompt, enter the command:

```
xterm &
```

A new **xterm** will start in its own window. Once it starts, the shell prompt will be redisplayed in the original window.

If you want to experiment with these ideas, try starting **xclock** and **xcalc**, two X clients that come with the X Window system. **xclock** displays a picture of a clock that shows the current time. **xcalc** provides a scientific calculator.

Starting a Program on a Remote System: xhost

As we described earlier, one of the most powerful features of X is that it allows you to work with an X client that is executing on a remote computer. Just make sure that there is a network connection between the remote computer and your computer, and that you have authorization to log in to the remote computer.

To run a program on a remote computer, you must tell your system what computer you plan to use, log in to that system, tell the remote system to work with the X server on your computer, then start the program. Follow these five steps:

1. Move the focus to an **xterm** window.

2. Use the **xhost** command to tell your X server that the remote computer is allowed to access your machine. After the command name, type the name of the remote computer. For example, if you will be accessing a supercomputer named **super**, enter the command:

```
xhost super
```

If the remote computer is not on your local network, you will have to specify its full address. For example:

```
xhost super.tsi.com
```

3. Log in to the remote computer. Normally you will use the **telnet** command. For example, to log in to the computer named **super**, you might enter:

```
telnet super
```

Again, if the remote computer is not on your local network, use the full address. For example:

```
telnet super.tsi.com
```

Enter your userid and password in the regular manner. You are now working on the remote system from within the **xterm** window on your screen.

4. Tell the remote system that any X clients you start should interact with the X server on your computer. To do this, use the **setenv** command to define a global variable named **DISPLAY** to point to your system. (We won't explain the details here.) Type **setenv**, followed by the word **DISPLAY**, followed by the name of your system, a colon, and the number **0**.

For example, if your system is named **nipper**, enter the command:

```
setenv DISPLAY nipper:0
```

This tells any X client you run on the remote computer to use the X server on computer **nipper**. The **0** refers to display number 0, the standard display. If you have a second display, it would be called **1**. Normally, you will only have a single display, so don't worry about the **0**, just put it in.

Note: The command we just described assumes that you are using a C-Shell on the remote system (see Chapter 4). If you are using a Bourne or Korn shell, you will need to use the following two commands:

```
set DISPLAY nipper:0
export DISPLAY
```

These commands can be combined onto a single line by separating them with a semi-colon:

```
set DISPLAY nipper:0; export DISPLAY
```

5. Start the X client. Remember to end the command with an **&** (ampersand) character so that the program will run in the background in its own window. For example, if you want to run a program named **statistics**, enter:

```
statistics &
```

To summarize, let's say that you want to run an X client named **statistics** on a remote system called **super** from your computer named **nipper**. From within an **xterm** window, enter the commands:

```
xhost super
telnet super
```

After logging in, enter:

```
setenv DISPLAY nipper:0
statistics &
```

When you are finished, terminate the program and log off the remote system in the usual manner.

HINT
It may happen that you find yourself repeatedly using X clients on the same remote computers. If so, X Window allows you to specify a list of such computers. Once a remote host is on this list, you do not need to use an **xhost** command each time you want to make a connection.

The list is kept in a file named **/etc/X0.hosts**. The **0** indicates that this list pertains to display number 0, the standard display; if you have a second display, you would use a file named **/etc/X1.hosts**; and so on.

(The name **/etc/X0.hosts** will make sense after we discuss the Unix file system in Chapter 22. Essentially, it refers to a file named **X0.hosts** that resides in a directory named **/etc**.)

For security reasons, you should not set up such a file unless you are the only person using your computer.

Stopping Your Work with X Window

When you work with a regular character terminal, logging out is simple. At the shell prompt, you enter either the **logout** or **exit** command, or press **^D**, whichever is appropriate for your shell. (This is all explained in Chapter 4.)

If you are using X, you must go through a few more steps. The details that we discuss in this section may seem a trifle involved and may not all be necessary for your computer. Ask around and find out what works best on your system. What you read in this section are general guidelines.

Before you log out, it is a good idea to terminate all your programs. Go to each window in turn and stop the program. If a window is an **xterm** in which you are logged into a remote system, you should log out of that system.

Once all your programs are stopped, close each window. You usually do this by selecting an item from a pop-up or pull-down menu associated with the window. You may also be able to double-click on part of the title bar. The details will depend on your window manager. With an **xterm** window, there is usually a menu with a "quit" selection.

Note: Closing a window terminates it. Do not confuse this with minimizing or iconizing a window. Minimizing a window simply shrinks it into a small icon. When you log out, you want to actually get rid of the window.

Finally, stop your window manager. With most window managers, all you need to do is pop up the main menu and select some type of "quit" operation.

With some systems, stopping the window manager will terminate X and log you out automatically. With other systems, you will be left at a shell prompt. If so, you can log out in the regular manner (using **logout**, **exit**, or **^D**, as appropriate).

If you had to start X and your window manager manually (by using the **xinit** command and so on, as we explained above), you may have to close the original **xterm** window in order to stop X.

HINT

To learn more about X on your system, check the Unix online manual (explained in Chapter 8). Try looking under **X** and **xterm**. Your system may or may not have such manual pages.

CHAPTER 6

Using the Keyboard with Unix

As we explained in Chapter 4, Unix works with many different types of terminals and computers. Of course, what you are probably most interested in is: how does Unix work with your particular system?

In this chapter, we will discuss how Unix uses the keyboard, and we will show you how to find out which keys have special meanings for you. Remember, as we explained in Chapter 3, Unix always assumes that you are using some type of terminal. (If you are using a computer—such as a PC or a Macintosh—to connect to a Unix host, the computer will be acting like a terminal.) So, to start, let's consider the problem of how Unix is able to work with any type of terminal.

TTYs: The First Terminals

When Unix was first developed, the programmers used Teletype ASR33 terminals, electromechanical devices that printed output on paper. The terminals had the letters of the alphabet, numbers, punctuation, a RETURN key, and a special "Control" key. (In fact, to this day, it is possible to use Unix using only these keys.) Many of the conventions used with modern terminals are based on these terminals.

For instance, the name "Teletype" was abbreviated as TTY. This quickly became a way to refer to any terminal. For example, the command to display the name of your terminal is **tty**, and one of the commands to set up your terminal is called **stty**.

What's in a Name?   *TTY*
In Unix, TTY means a terminal. The name comes from the abbreviation for the old Teletype terminals.

Another convention derived from Teletypes is how we use the word PRINT. As we mentioned, Teletypes printed output on paper. Now, of course, the same information would be displayed on a screen. However, the custom is still to refer to such operations as "printing".

For example, the **tty** command displays the name of the terminal you are currently using. However, the official description of the purpose of this command is "print current terminal name".

Similarly, the command to display the name of your working directory (see Chapter 23) is **pwd**, or "print working directory".

You might ask, if "print" means "display", what term do we use when we really mean print? Sometimes we can use the word "print" and it is clear by context that we mean real printing. Other times, we use the term "line printer" (an anachronism itself) to refer to a real printer. For example, the command to print a file is **lpr** with Berkeley Unix or **lp** with System V Unix. (We discuss the different types of Unix in Chapter 2.)

Since the time of the Teletypes, many different types of terminals have been developed. Most terminals do more than display a series of characters. They can also recognize and carry out certain commands.

For example, there is a command to clear the screen. The problem is that each type of terminal has its own characteristics and uses its own set of commands.

What would you do if you were writing a program that, at a certain point, needed to clear the screen of the terminal? The signal your program must send depends on what type of terminal is being used.

Every program would need to know about every different type of terminal—an enormous burden to place upon software developers. Moreover, what happens when a new terminal is introduced? If it uses different commands, it would not work properly with existing programs.

The solution used is to collect descriptions of all the different types of terminals into a database. With Berkeley Unix, this collection of information is called the TERMCAP ("terminal capabilities") database, and is stored in the file **/etc/termcap**. (The name will make sense after we discuss the Unix file system.) With System V Unix, the information is stored in a different format called TERMINFO ("terminal information"). Although you may want to remember the names termcap and terminfo, you do not need to worry about the details.

When you write a program that needs to send commands to the terminal, you use a standard programming interface called **curses**. (The name comes from the idea of controlling the cursor.) A program will tell **curses** what it wants to display on the screen. **curses** checks what type of terminal is being used and, referring to the termcap or terminfo database, sends the appropriate commands. This allows programs to be compatible with a wide variety of terminals.

The question is, how does Unix know what terminal you are using?

How Does Unix Know What Terminal You Are Using?

The part of the host computer to which a terminal is connected is called a PORT. Data moves in and out of the computer through the port. (Think of planes flying in and out of an airport.)

When the system manager sets up a system, he or she tells Unix what type of terminal will be attached to each port. This works well for terminals that are connected directly because, for such ports, the terminal type will always be the same. If the system manager changes the terminal, he or she changes the setup.

However, a port might not always connect to the same type of terminal. It may be attached to a terminal server or a network that services different types of terminals. Or the port may be attached to a modem that supports a dial-in connection.

When you log in, Unix looks at the port you are using and guesses what type of terminal you have, based on how the system manager set up that port. However, if you log in using a network, terminal server or modem, guessing is not enough. You must make sure that Unix knows exactly which terminal you are using.

As you use Unix, there are a number of quantities called GLOBAL VARIABLES that are always available to the shell and to any programs you may run. A global variable has a name and a value. At any time, a program can ask what is the value of the global variable with such-and-such name.

In particular, there is a global variable named **TERM** whose value is the type of terminal you are using. (You may remember that, in Chapter 4, we mentioned that the names of global variables are one of the few instances in Unix where we use uppercase letters.) You can display the value of any global variable by using the command **echo** **$**_name_. For example, if you enter:

```
echo $TERM
```

Unix will show you the value of the **TERM** variable.

Note: In Chapter 10, we explain that there are different shells you can use. If you use the C-Shell, the custom is to refer to global variables as "environment variables"; with the Korn shell, we call them "shell variables". We discuss such topics in detail in Chapter 11 (C-Shell) and Chapter 12 (Korn shell).

How Is the TERM Variable Set?

It is up to you to make sure the **TERM** variable is set properly. In other words, it is up to you to make sure that Unix knows what type of terminal you are using.

Usually, this is done automatically in one of two ways. First, if your terminal is directly connected to the port, the system manager will have set it up so that Unix knows what terminal you are using.

Second, every time you log in, your shell executes a list of predefined startup commands. One of these commands will set the **TERM** variable appropriately. As we mentioned in Chapter 4, one of your startup commands (**tset**) may guess at the terminal type you are using and ask you for confirmation.

For example, say that you are connecting via a phone line. The system manager knows that many communication programs will emulate a VT-100 terminal. He or she will set up the port to expect such a terminal. The specific **tset** command in your startup file will display the message:

```
TERM = (vt100)
```

whenever you log in using that port. You can either specify an alternate terminal type or simply press the RETURN key to continue.

What Happens If the TERM Variable Is Set Incorrectly?

If **TERM** is set incorrectly, you may not notice it when you use simple commands that display one line of output at a time. However, when you run programs that use the entire screen, such as the **vi** text editor which we will meet in Chapter 20, your terminal may not work properly.

To check that your setup is okay, enter the command:

```
echo $TERM
```

If Unix displays the correct terminal name, everything is okay. Otherwise, you will need to change your startup commands. Unfortunately, this requires advanced skills. Until you are more experienced, you will need to find someone to help you.

For specific information about how to set the **TERM** variable, see Chapter 11 for the C-Shell and Chapter 12 for the Korn shell. The idea is to place the appropriate command in your initialization file so that each time you log in, your terminal type will be set automatically. For the C-Shell, read about the **.login** initialization file; for the Korn shell, read about the **.profile** initialization file.

Understanding Your Keyboard: The CTRL Key

There are two aspects to using your terminal well. One is making sure that Unix knows what type of terminal you have, by making sure the **TERM** variable is set properly. We discussed this topic in the last three sections. The other aspect of using your terminal is learning about the various keys on your keyboard and how they are used.

Since Unix must work with any terminal, there is no such thing as a standard keyboard. Instead, Unix defines standard codes that are mapped onto different keyboards. Before we discuss the various codes, let's take a quick look at the keyboard.

Note: When we refer to an actual key, we will put the name in SMALL CAPITAL LETTERS. For example, the "Return" key is RETURN; the "Enter" key is ENTER.

The first thing you will notice is that most of your keyboard looks like the standard typewriter layout. There are keys for the letters of the alphabet, the numbers 0 through 9, and punctuation, as well as a SHIFT key for typing uppercase letters.

You will also see a number of miscellaneous keys, including ESC, BACKSPACE, DELETE and CTRL. The first three have special uses we will discuss later. However, let's spend a moment talking about CTRL.

The CTRL key (the name stands for "Control") was a feature on the early Teletype terminals we mentioned at the beginning of the chapter. The use of this key was adopted by the Unix developers and integrated into the system in several important ways.

To use the CTRL key, you hold it down (like the SHIFT key) while you press one of the other keys, usually a letter. For example, you might hold down CTRL and press the A key.

There are 26 such combinations based on the alphabet—CTRL-A through CTRL-Z—as well as a couple of others you might run into. Because it is awkward to write "Ctrl" over and over again, the Unix community uses a shorthand notation: the character ^ means "hold down the CTRL key". For example, **^A** means hold down CTRL and press the A key. (You might also see the notation CTRL-A or **c-a**, which mean the same thing.)

By convention, we always write a CTRL combination using a capital letter. For instance, we write **^A**, never **^a**. Using capital letters makes such combinations easier to read (compare **^L** to **^l**).

To get used to this notation, take a look at the following example. This is part of the output from an **stty** command we will meet later in the chapter.

```
erase kill werase rprnt flush lnext susp   intr quit stop   eof
^H    ^U   ^W     ^R    ^O    ^V    ^Z/^Y  ^C   ^\   ^S/^Q  ^D
```

This output tells us what keys to press to send certain codes. The details aren't important for now. What we want you to notice is the notation. In this example, we see that to send the **erase** code, you use **^H**. That is, you hold down CTRL and press H. For the **kill** code you use **^U**, for **werase** you use **^W**, and so on.

The Unix Keyboard Codes

In order to be able to work with any terminal, Unix defines a number of keyboard codes for standard operations. These codes are then mapped onto the keys of each particular keyboard.

For example, there is a code, called **intr** (interrupt), that tells Unix to abort the program that is currently running. Thus, to stop a program instantly, you can press the key that sends the **intr** code.

The idea of the **intr** code is standard: it is built into the definition of how Unix processes its input. What is not standard is the actual key you need to press to send this code. This varies from terminal to terminal.

Because the input codes are not mapped to a standard set of keys, there is flexibility in the definition of what each key does. For instance, on some terminals you press **^C** (CTRL-C) to send the **intr** code. However, if you want, you can change this so that you can press a different key, although there is usually no reason to do so.

With some keyboards, the **intr** code is mapped to the DELETE key instead of **^C**. If **^C** doesn't seem to work on your system, try DELETE. One of them should do the job.

In the next few sections we will describe the important keyboard codes and how you use them. We will then show you how to find out exactly what keys are used on your terminal and how you can change them if you want.

Special Keys to Use While Typing: `erase, werase, kill`

There are three keyboard codes that you can use to help you while you are typing. They are **erase**, **werase** and **kill**. **erase** deletes the last character you typed; **werase** deletes the last word you typed; **kill** deletes the entire line.

Each of these codes is mapped onto a particular key. The **erase** code is mapped onto either a BACKSPACE key or a DELETE key, depending on the configuration of your keyboard.

Take a look at the large key in the top right-hand corner of the main part of your keyboard. This will be your **erase** key. You can erase the last character you typed by pressing this key.

On most terminals—and on IBM-compatible PCs—you will have a BACKSPACE key. On a Macintosh, you will have a DELETE key. On a Sun computer, you will have both keys: BACKSPACE and DELETE; use the DELETE key (the one on top).

In other words, use whichever key works on your particular keyboard. You may remember we mentioned that some keyboards have a RETURN key, and some have an ENTER key. It's the same idea. As long as you press the right key, Unix doesn't care what it is named.

Here is an example. Say that you want to enter the **date** command (to display the time and date), but you spell it wrong, **datx**. Before you press the RETURN key, press BACKSPACE (or DELETE) to erase the last letter and make your correction:

datx\<Backspace\>**e**

On your screen, the **x** will disappear when you press BACKSPACE. If you want to delete more than one character, you can press BACKSPACE as many times as you want.

Throughout this book, when we refer to the BACKSPACE key, we mean either BACKSPACE or DELETE, whichever is used on your system. (Similarly, when we refer to the RETURN key, we mean either RETURN or ENTER.)

The next code, **werase**, tells Unix to erase the last word you typed. The **werase** key is usually **^W**. This key is useful when you want to correct one or more words you have just typed. Of course, you can always press BACKSPACE repeatedly, but **^W** is faster when you want to erase whole words.

Here is an example. You type the command to send mail to three friends whose userids are **curly**, **larry** and **moe**. The command to use is **mail curly larry moe**.

However, after you type the command (and before you press the RETURN key), you decide that you really only want to send mail to **curly**. Press **^W** twice to erase the last two words:

mail curly larry moe^W^W

On your screen, first the word **moe** and then the word **larry** will disappear.

The third code to use while typing is **kill**. The **kill** key is usually **^X** or **^U** (depending on how your system is set up). This code tells Unix to erase the whole line.

For example, let's say that you are just about to send mail to your three friends. You type the command, but, before you press RETURN, someone runs in the room and tells you they are giving away free money at the bank. Thinking quickly, you press **^X** (or **^U**):

mail curly larry moe^X

to cancel the command. On your screen, the entire line will disappear. Now you can log out. (Of course, you would never leave your terminal logged in, even to rush out to get free money.)

Note: The **kill** code does not stop programs. It only erases the line you are typing. To stop a program, use the **intr** code (which will be either **^C** or DELETE).

For reference, Figure 6-1 summarizes the keyboard codes to use when typing.

CODE	KEY	PURPOSE
erase	BACKSPACE, DELETE	erase the last character typed
werase	**^W**	erase the last word typed
kill	**^X, ^U**	erase the entire line

FIGURE 6-1. *Keyboard codes to use while typing*

What Happens When You Press BACKSPACE or DELETE

As we mentioned earlier, Unix was designed to use the basic keys that were available on the early terminals: the letters of the alphabet, numbers, punctuation, a RETURN key, and the CTRL key. The people who designed Unix did so very carefully, so that these keys were the only ones necessary to use Unix. Their goal was to be able to run Unix on different types of terminals. To this day, you can still use Unix with only these basic keys.

Modern keyboards have other keys — such as BACKSPACE, DELETE, the function keys, the cursor control keys, and so on — and your version of Unix will be able to use at least some of them. However, you only need the basic keys to perform all the fundamental keyboard operations.

In particular, you do not really need the BACKSPACE key to delete a single character. On most systems (except Sun computers — see below), the **erase** code is actually mapped to **^H** (CTRL-H). Pressing BACKSPACE simply sends a **^H** character.

Here is how to test this idea for yourself. Type a command and then, before pressing RETURN, make a correction using BACKSPACE. Now type some more, and make another correction using **^H**. You will see that these two keys, BACKSPACE and **^H**, are equivalent.

Technically speaking, **^ H** is the real **erase** key; the BACKSPACE key is only there as a convenience, because it is a lot easier to press BACKSPACE than **^H** each time you want to delete a character.

On some keyboards (such as Macintoshes), this same key is labeled DELETE instead of BACKSPACE, but it works the same way. When you press it, it sends a **^H**, the **erase** code.

It would be nice to say that this is a general rule, but life—at least, life with Unix—is not always so simple, and there is one notable exception to this rule: Unix systems running on Sun computers do not use **^H**.

Most Sun systems are set up so that a different character, called **del**, is used as the **erase** key. The **del** character is the last character of the ASCII code, and it does not really correspond to a particular CTRL key. The old name for the **del** character was "Rubout", and you may still see this name used from time to time.

(If you don't understand about the ASCII code, we discuss it in Chapter 17. Briefly, the ASCII code is a description of the 128 different characters that are used by Unix. If you want to take a quick look, check out Appendix E.)

So, as we were saying, Sun chose **del** rather than **^H** as the **erase** character. If you are using a Sun, you will have both a DELETE key and a BACKSPACE key. When you press DELETE, you get a **del** character; when you press BACKSPACE, you get a **^H** character. Sun systems almost always use the **del** character for **erase**, so when you want to delete a character, use DELETE.

To summarize: You can delete the last character you typed by pressing the key in the top right-hand corner of the main part of the keyboard. This key will be either BACKSPACE or DELETE. When you press this key, it will send whichever character is mapped to the **erase** code and Unix will make the correction. On non-Sun systems, pressing the key will send the **^H** character. On Sun systems, pressing this key (DELETE) will send the **del** character.

Regardless of how your system is set up, you can assign any character you want to the **erase** code by using the **stty** command (discussed later in this chapter). For example, if you are using a Sun computer, you can change the mapping so that **^H** deletes a character. You can then use the BACKSPACE key instead of DELETE.

HINT

Some people use a PC or a Macintosh to connect to a Sun computer over a telephone line. In such cases, you will use a communications program to dial the phone, maintain the connection, and emulate a VT-100 terminal (see Chapter 3).

If you do this regularly, you will find it inconvenient that your BACKSPACE key (or your DELETE key if you use a Mac) sends a **^H** and not the **del** character that the Sun expects. There are two ways to solve this problem.

First, you can use an **stty** command to tell the Sun computer that your **erase** key should be **^H**. (We discuss this command later in the chapter.) The exact command you want is:

```
stty erase ^h
```

Place this in your initialization file on the Sun so that, whenever you log in, the **stty** command will be executed automatically. If you use the C-Shell, put the command in your **.login** file (see Chapter 11). If you use the Korn shell, put the command in your **.profile** file (see Chapter 12).

The second solution is to leave the Sun alone and to change the character that is sent when you press the BACKSPACE or DELETE key. Your communications program should have a setting that controls what happens when you press this key. You can change this setting to have the program send a **del** instead of a **^H**. That way, the Sun will get the character it expects and you will not have to set the **erase** code to **^H**.

Note: As we mentioned, the old name for the **del** code was "Rubout", and you may see this name when you examine the settings for your communications program. All that it means is that the program was designed by an old person.

Connecting to a Sun Computer: The Case of the Mysterious ^H

Here is a common situation you should understand.

You are using a non-Sun system. You decide to connect to a remote computer on the Internet using the **telnet** or **ftp** commands. When you make the connection, the remote system asks you to enter a userid by displaying:

`login:`

You do so, but as you are typing the userid, you make a mistake. And when you try to make a correction by pressing BACKSPACE (or DELETE), it doesn't work.

For example, say that you want to enter **harley**, but you accidentally typed **harlqey**. On your screen, you see:

`login: harlqey`

So you press BACKSPACE three times to delete the last three characters. However, what you see is:

`login: harlqey^H^H^H`

What is happening?

Clearly, your keyboard is sending a **^H** character when you press BACKSPACE. However, the remote computer happens to be a Sun, and it expects a **del** character. The **^H** is not having the desired effect. What should you do?

You have several choices. The easiest thing to do it press **^W** to erase the entire word, and retype it.

The next choice is to press RETURN twice to bypass the login and password prompts, wait until you see a message telling you that the login failed:

`Login incorrect`

and then try again, typing more carefully.

The third choice is to give the Sun computer what it wants by pressing a key that will actually send a **del** character. This will allow you to delete one character at a time, which is really what you want to do.

The question is, what key do you press?

Here you will have to experiment. If your keyboard has both a BACKSPACE and a DELETE key, try pressing DELETE. If you are using a PC that is emulating a VT-100 terminal (see Chapter 3), try pressing CTRL-BACKSPACE. If you are using a Macintosh, try pressing OPTION-BACKSPACE. If any of these key combinations work, the Sun will detect a **del** and the previous character will vanish. If not, just press RETURN a couple of times and try again.

(For information on the **telnet** and **ftp** commands and connecting to remote computers, see the book, *The Internet Complete Reference* by Harley Hahn and Rick Stout, published by Osborne McGraw-Hill. (The ISBN is: 0-07-881980-6.)

Stopping a Program: `intr`

There are several keyboard codes that you can use to stop or pause a program. These codes are **intr**, **quit**, **stop** and **susp**. When you press a key that generates one of these codes, we say that you send a SIGNAL to the program. Either the program or Unix itself will notice the signal and take appropriate action.

On most systems, the **intr** key is **^C**. On some systems, you use the DELETE key instead. (You can try both and see which one works for you.)

The **intr** (interrupt) code actually has two uses. First, you can use it to stop a program dead in its tracks. For example, say that you enter a command to log in to a remote system. Nothing happens, and you decide to stop waiting. Just press **^C**. The remote login program will abort, and you will be back at the shell prompt.

Some programs are programmed to ignore the **intr** signal. In such cases, there will always be a well-defined way to end the program. By ignoring the **intr** signal, the program keeps you from accidentally causing damage by pressing **^C** inadvertently. We say that the program TRAPS the **intr** signal.

For example, consider what happens if you are using, say, a word processor, and you press **^C**. The word processor traps the **intr** signal and does not stop. In order to terminate the program you need to use the word processor's own quit command (whatever that is). If the word processor had not trapped the **intr** signal, pressing **^C** would abort the program and you would lose all the data that is not yet saved.

Note: You may sometimes see the **intr** key referred to as the "break" key. If you use an IBM-compatible PC, you may know that **^C** acts as a break key under DOS and OS/2. As you can see, this idea (along with many others) was taken from Unix.

The second use for the **intr** code arises when you are typing a Unix command at the shell prompt. If you are typing a command and you change your mind, you can press **^C** instead of RETURN to cancel the command completely.

Be sure that you do not confuse the **intr** key (**^C** or DELETE) with the **kill** key (**^U** or **^X**). When you are typing a command, **intr** cancels the command, while **kill** erases all the characters on the line. Effectively, this has the same result: whatever you were typing is discarded, and you can enter a new command.

However, only **intr** will stop a program. In spite of its name, **kill** will not "kill" a program.

Another Way to Stop a Program: `quit`

Aside from **intr** (**^C**), there is another keyboard code, **quit**, that will stop a program. The **quit** key is usually **^** (CTRL-BACKSLASH).

What is the difference between **intr** (**^C**) and **quit**? **quit** is designed for advanced programmers who may need to abort a test program. When you press **^**, it not only sends a **quit** signal (to stop the program), it tells Unix to make a copy of the contents of memory at that instant.

On some Unix systems, this information is stored automatically in a file named **core** (the old name for computer memory). A programmer can use special tools to analyze a **core** file.

The reason we mention this is that if a file named **core** mysteriously appears in one of your directories, it means that you have probably pressed **^**. Unless you really want the file, you can erase it. In fact, you should erase it because **core** files are rather large and there is no reason to waste the space.

Pausing the Display: `stop`, `start`

When a program writes a line of output to the bottom of your screen, all the other lines move up one position. We say that they are SCROLLED upward. If a program produces output too fast, data will scroll off the top of the screen before you can read it.

In such cases, you have three choices. First, if the lost data is not important, you can ignore it. Second, you can restart the program that generates the data and have it send the output to one of the so-called paging programs that will display the data nicely, one screenful at a time. (The names of the paging programs are **more**, **pg** and **less**. We will discuss them in Chapter 18.)

Finally, you can press a key to send the **stop** code. This tells Unix to pause the screen display temporarily. The **stop** key is usually **^S**. Once the display is paused, you can restart it by sending the **start** code. The **start** key is usually **^Q**.

Thus, when data is scrolling by too fast, press **^S** to pause, **^Q** to continue. (Think of "S" for Stop and "Q" for Qontinue.)

Using **^S** and **^Q** can be quite useful. However, you should understand that **^S** only tells Unix to stop displaying output. It does not pause the program that is executing. The program will keep going and will not stop generating output. However, Unix will store the output so that none will be lost. As soon as you press **^Q**, Unix will display what output remains. If a great many lines of new data were generated while the screen display was paused, they will probably whiz by rapidly once you press **^Q**.

Although it is handy to be able to pause and restart using **^S** and **^Q**, you may find that it is just too difficult to press the keys fast enough. If this is the case, you should use one of the paging programs (**more**, **pg** or **less**) to control the output.

HINT

If your terminal ever locks up mysteriously, try pressing **^Q**. You may have pressed **^S** inadvertently and paused the display. When everything seems to have stopped, you will never cause any harm by pressing **^Q**.

The End of File Code: eof

From time to time, you will work with programs that expect you to enter data from the keyboard. When you get to the point where there is no more data, you indicate this by pressing **^D** which sends the **eof** (end of file) code.

Here is an example. In Chapter 15, we will discuss the **mail** program that you can use to send electronic mail. As you compose your message, you type one line after another. When you are finished, you press **^D**. This indicates that there is no more data. **mail** knows the message is complete and sends it to the recipient.

Here is another example: The **bc** program provides the services of a built-in calculator. After you start **bc**, you enter one calculation after another. After each calculation, **bc** displays the answer. When you are finished, you press **^D** to tell **bc** that there is no more data. The program terminates.

The Shell and the eof Code

In Chapter 4, we explained that the shell is the program that reads your Unix commands and interprets them. When the shell is ready to read a command, it displays a prompt. You type a command and press RETURN. The shell processes the command and then displays a new prompt. Thus, your session with Unix consists of entering one command after another.

Although the shell may seem mysterious, it is really just a program. And, from the point of view of the shell, the commands that you type are just data that needs to be processed. So, you can stop the shell by indicating that there is no more data. Just press **^D**, the **eof** key.

But what does stopping the shell really mean? It means that you have finished your work. Thus, when the shell stops, Unix logs you out automatically. This is why you can log out by pressing **^D**. You are really telling the shell (and Unix) that there is no more work to be done.

Of course, there is a potential problem. What if you press **^D** by accident? You will be logged out immediately. The solution is to tell the shell to trap the **eof** code. With the C-Shell, you do this by entering the command:

```
set ignoreeof
```

With the Korn shell, you enter:

```
set -o ignoreeof
```

(We discuss the C-Shell in Chapter 11 and the Korn shell in Chapter 12.)

Once you set **ignoreeof**, it tells the shell to trap and ignore the **eof** signal. If you use the C-Shell and you press **^D**, the shell displays:

```
Use "logout" to logout.
```

If you use the Korn shell, you will see:

```
Use 'exit' to logout
```

You must deliberately enter a **logout** or **exit** command. In either case, it is impossible for you to log out inadvertently by pressing **^D**.

It is difficult to remember to set **ignoreeof** every time you start work with Unix. For this reason, most people put the appropriate command in their initialization file so that **ignoreeof** will be set automatically each time they log in. With the C-Shell, the initialization file is named **.login**; with the Korn shell, the file is named **.profile**. (Yes, the "." is part of the name.) For more details, see Chapters 11 and 12.

It is likely that, when the system manager set up your account, he or she gave you an initialization file that already contains this command. That is why, in Chapter 4, we said that you should try logging out by pressing **^D**, and if that doesn't work, use the **logout** or **exit** commands.

Note: What we have described here works for the C-Shell, the Korn shell, and other modern shells. If you are using the older Bourne shell, however, there is no way to prevent **^D** from logging you out. You will just have to be careful.

Checking the Special Keys for Your Terminal: stty

So far, we have mentioned a number of keyboard codes, each of which corresponds to some key on your keyboard. These are shown in Figure 6-2; the key assignments are the most common ones, but they are changeable.

To check how your Unix system uses your particular terminal, you can use the **stty** (set terminal) command. Enter the command:

stty -a

(The **-a** stands for "show me *all* the settings".) If this doesn't work on your system, try the command:

stty all

The **-a** form is for System V Unix; the **all** form is for Berkeley Unix. On many Unix systems, both commands will work. (We discussed the different types of Unix in Chapter 2.)

The **stty** command will display several lines of information about your terminal. The only lines we are interested in are the ones that show the keyboard codes and the keys to which they are mapped. Here is an example:

```
erase kill werase rprnt flush lnext susp  intr quit stop   eof
^H     ^X   ^W     ^R    ^O    ^V    ^Z/^Y ^C   ^\   ^S/^Q  ^D
```

CODE	KEY	PURPOSE
intr	^C	stop a program that is running
erase	BACKSPACE, DELETE	erase the last character typed
werase	^W	erase the last word typed
kill	^X, ^U	erase the entire line
quit	^\	stop a program and save **core** file
stop	^S	pause the screen display
start	^Q	restart the screen display
eof	^D	indicate there is no more data

FIGURE 6-2. *Summary of keyboard codes*

Notice that there are several codes we did not cover (**rprnt**, **flush**, **lnext**, **susp**). These are not as important, and you can ignore them for now.

If you would like to change a key assignment, the **stty** command will do that for you. Just type **stty**, followed by the name of the code, followed by the new key assignment. For example, to change the **kill** key to ^U, enter:

```
stty kill ^U
```

Type **^U** as two separate characters: the ^ character, followed by the **U** character.

Normally, the abbreviation **^U** stands for the single character CTRL-U. However, when you type the name of a CTRL key for the **stty** command (and only for this command), you literally type two characters: the **stty** command will know what you mean.

When you use **stty** with the name of a CTRL character, it is not necessary to type a capital letter. For instance, in the example above we could have used a small "u":

```
stty kill ^u
```

Remember to type two separate characters (in this case, ^ and **u**

Strictly speaking, we can assign a code to any key we want. For example, we could set the **kill** code to the letter "k":

```
stty kill k
```

Of course, such a command will only lead to problems. Every time we press the K key, Unix will erase the line we are typing!

Normally, we use only CTRL keys and, actually, it is best to stay with the standard assignments.

Here is another example. You are using a Sun computer which, by default, expects the **erase** key to be **del**. However, you are connecting from a computer that uses a BACKSPACE key which sends a **^H**. To make life more convenient, you wish to map the **erase** code to **^H**. Use one of the commands:

```
stty erase ^h
stty erase ^H
```

This will allow you to press BACKSPACE to delete a character.

Here is the opposite example. You are using a computer on which the **erase** code is set to **^H** by default, and you wish to change it to **del**. There is no actual key for **del**, so the convention is to refer to it as **^?**; that is, two separate characters, ^ followed by **?**. Use the command:

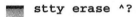

```
stty erase ^?
```

Note: The notation **^?** does not refer to an actual key combination CTRL-?. There is no such thing. **^?** is merely a two-letter abbreviation that we use with **stty** to stand for **del**.

If you want to verify the keyboard settings, enter the **stty -a** or **stty all** command as described above. Alternatively, you enter the **stty** command by itself:

```
stty
```

This will display an abbreviated report, showing only those keyboard settings that are nonstandard.

Teletype Control Signals

Note: The material covered in the rest of this chapter is not essential. It is included only for your interest. If you are getting bored, feel free to start skimming. However, if you still have patience, by all means push on. The following sections really are interesting (to certain strange types of people, anyway). In any event, be sure not to skip the fable at the end of the chapter.

There are a number of control characters that Unix uses in a special way. To understand how they are used, it is necessary to revisit the early Unix developers.

As we mentioned earlier in the chapter, the developers of Unix used Teletype ASR33 machines for terminals. A Teletype is an electromechanical device that was developed to send messages from place to place. A message would be typed on one Teletype and sent over a connection to another Teletype, where it would print on paper. The operator at the destination could rip off the paper and deliver the message.

The Teletype keyboard had the standard alphabet, some punctuation, and a CTRL key. Holding down CTRL while pressing one of the letters of the alphabet allowed for 26 auxiliary signals. These signals were used to control the operation of the Teletype.

A few of the CTRL signals affected the printing of the message. CTRL-H, or Backspace, caused the print carriage to back up a single space before printing the next character.

For example, if you wanted to underline a word, you could type the word, followed by a number of CTRL-Hs (which would move the print carriage backward), followed by some underscore characters.

CTRL-M, or Carriage Return, caused the print carriage to return to the beginning of the line. CTRL-J, or Linefeed, moved the paper vertically, up one position, so as to be ready to print on the next line. Thus, when a line had completed printing, the sequence CTRL-M, CTRL-J—Carriage Return, Linefeed—would position the carriage and the paper at the beginning of the next line.

Another signal, CTRL-I, made use of tab settings. These were predefined positions along the width of the print line. If you had a message that needed to print in columns—say, at positions 10, 15 and 30—you could physically set the tabs at those positions. When CTRL-I was encountered during printing, the carriage would move horizontally to the right to the next tab setting.

Finally, CTRL-G was called the Bell signal. The Bell signal literally rang a bell on the destination Teletype. This sound could be used to signal the operator. For example, you might send the following message:

NEXT REPORT REQUIRES YOU TO SET TABS AT 10 15 AND 30
Carriage Return
Linefeed
Bell
Bell

This message prints some instructions, moves the print carriage to the beginning of the next line, and rings the bell twice.

How Teletype Control Signals Are Used by Unix: ^H, ^I, ^G

Since the early Unix developers used Teletype machines for terminals, it was only natural that they should make use of some of the Control signals when they began to use display terminals.

CTRL-H, or **^H** as we write it now, is used to send the **erase** code. Thus, when you are typing a command, you can make corrections by using **^H** to erase the most recently typed character.

As a convenience, when you press the BACKSPACE key, Unix interprets the signal as being a **^H**. Thus, you can correct mistakes using BACKSPACE or **^H**, whichever is more convenient.

CTRL-I, or **^I**, is used as a horizontal tab code. It is possible to set your Unix terminal to specific tab positions. However, this is a lot of trouble, and it is rare that anyone bothers. Left to its own, Unix assumes that tabs are set every 8 positions, starting with position 1. In other words, Unix assumes that tabs are set at positions 1, 9, 17, 25 and so on.

For convenience, when you press the TAB key, Unix interprets it as a **^I**. Thus, if you need to use tabs, you can press either TAB or **^I**.

As an experiment, press TAB or **^I** as you type. Notice how the cursor moves to the right. Realize, though, that no matter how many positions the cursor moves, **^I** is still considered a single character. For instance, if you type three letters, press TAB, and type another letter,

ABC<Tab>**D**

Unix counts it as 5 characters.

As you remember, CTRL-G, or **^G**, rang the bell on a Teletype. Of course, modern terminals do not have a bell, but they can beep or make another sound. A Unix terminal will make a sound instead of displaying a **^G** character. For instance, say that you are using a program and you press the wrong key by mistake. The program may beep at you. It does this by "displaying" a **^G** character.

If you would like to try this for yourself, type the following **echo** command. (**echo** simply displays whatever you type after the name of the command.) Type **echo**, then a space, then press **^G** three times, then press RETURN:

echo ^G^G^G

You will hear three beeps.

So, as you can see, three of the Unix control characters, **^H**, **^I** and **^G**, owe their existence to the early Teletype machines. The manner in which Unix has adopted the last two control characters, CTRL-M and CTRL-J, is more complex, and will be discussed in the next section.

What Unix Does at the End of a Line: newline, return

As we explained earlier, the old Teletype terminals used the **^M** (Carriage Return) character to move the print carriage to the beginning of the line, and the **^J** (Linefeed) character to move the paper vertically up one line.

Unix borrows the Linefeed character as follows. Within a data file, it is usually convenient to divide the data into lines. To do this, Unix will use a **^J** character to mark the end of each line. When it is used in this way, **^J** is called **newline** rather than Linefeed.

When a program reads a data file, it knows it has reached the end of a line when it encounters a **newline**.

Unix borrows the Carriage Return character as well. When you are typing, you send the Carriage Return code (**^M**) to signal that you have reached the end of a line. To make life simple, Unix lets you press either the RETURN key or **^M**. Of course, we use the RETURN key most of the time because it is more convenient, but **^M** will work just as well. When used in this way, **^M** is called **return** rather than Carriage Return.

Now, one of the most elegant features of Unix is that data typed at the keyboard is treated the same as data read from a file. For example, say that you have a program that reads a series of names, one per line, and prints them. The program can read the names either from a disk file or from the keyboard.

The program does not need to be written in any special way to achieve this flexibility; this feature is called "standard input" and is built into Unix. (We will discuss standard input in Chapter 16.)

In order for standard input to work properly, each line must end with a **newline** (**^J**). But when you enter a line at the terminal, you are actually sending a **return** (by pressing RETURN or **^M**).

To make things more confusing, Unix must make sure that when it displays data each line ends with a **^M^J** sequence—the old Carriage Return, Linefeed characters (which we now call **return** and **newline**). This tells the terminal to move the cursor to the beginning of the next line.

How is this all reconciled?

As you type, every time you press RETURN, Unix changes the **return** code (**^M**) into a **newline** (**^J**). When you display data, each **newline** code (**^J**), is changed by Unix into a **return newline** (**^M^J**) combination.

At first, this may seem hopelessly confusing. Eventually, you will come to see that it all makes perfect sense, at which time you will know that you have finally started to think in Unix.

HINT

If you use DOS or OS/2 with a PC, your files will be stored with a Carriage Return + Linefeed (**^M^J**) at the end of each line. Unix uses only a solitary Linefeed (**^J**). Thus, when you copy files from DOS to Unix, each **^M^J** must be converted into **^J**. Conversely, when you copy files from Unix to DOS, each **^J** must be replaced by **^M^J**.

On PCs that run both Unix and DOS, there are special Unix commands that will do the conversion automatically. (See your documentation for details.) Similarly, if you are using a PC communication program to access a Unix host, computer, there is usually a way to specify that the DOS-Unix conversion should be performed whenever data is transferred between the two systems.

An Important Use for ^J: stty sane

As you might imagine, it is not really necessary to understand all the technical details regarding **return** and **newline** just to work with Unix (unless you want to be a programmer). Just remember to press RETURN at the end of each line and let Unix do the work.

However, there is one case where understanding these ideas is helpful. On rare occasions, the settings for your terminal may become so screwed up that the terminal does not work properly. There is a command you can use, **stty sane**, that will reset your terminal settings to reasonable values.

However, it may be that when you try to enter the command by pressing RETURN, the **return** to **newline** conversion does not work and Unix will not accept the command. Pressing **^M** instead of RETURN is no help because it is essentially the same key.

The solution is to press **^J**, the **newline**, which is all Unix wants anyway. Thus,

stty sane^J

may rejuvenate your terminal when all else fails.

You might ask, if that is the case, can you press **^J** instead of RETURN to enter a command at any time? Of course—try it.

The Fable of the Programmer and the Princess

A long time ago, there lived a young, handsome, charming programmer (you can tell this is a fable) who won the love of a beautiful princess. However, the night before their wedding, the princess was kidnapped.

The programmer followed the trail to a remote corner of the lawless Silicon Valley, where he discovered that his love was being held captive in an abandoned tech support center by an evil Vice President of Marketing.

Thinking quickly, the programmer took a powerful magnet and entered the building. He tracked down the princess and broke into the room where the VP of Marketing stood gloating over the terrified girl.

"Release that girl immediately," roared the programmer, "or I will use this magnet and scramble all your disks."

The VP pressed a secret button, and in the blinking of an eye, four more ugly, hulking vice presidents entered the room.

"On the other hand," said the programmer, "perhaps we can make a deal."

"What did you have in mind?" said the VP.

"You set me any Unix task you want," answered the programmer. "If I do it, the princess and I will go free. If I fail, I will leave and never return."

"Agreed," said the VP, his eyes gleaming like two toady red nuggets encased in suet. "Sit down at this terminal. Your task will have two parts. First, using a single command, display the time and date."

"Child's play," said the programmer, as he typed **date** and pressed the RETURN key.

"Now," said the VP, "do it again." However, as the programmer once again typed **date**, the VP added, "—but this time you are not allowed to use either the RETURN key or **^M**."

"RTFM, you ignorant buffoon!" cried the programmer, whereupon he pressed **^J**, grabbed the princess and led her to his waiting Ferrari and a life of freedom.

CHAPTER 7

Programs to Use
Right Away
(Including Games)

When you enter a command, you are telling Unix to run the program by that name. For example, when you enter the **date** command, Unix runs the **date** program.

Unix has literally hundreds of different programs, which means there are hundreds of different commands you can enter. Many of these commands require that you understand some theory. For instance, before you can use the file system commands you need to learn about the file system.

On the other hand, there are commands that you can use right away which require no special knowledge. In this chapter, we'll take a look at some of these commands. You will see they can be useful, interesting and even fun.

Your system may not have all the programs we discuss in this chapter (or in this book). The fundamental programs—such as the **date** command we will meet in the next section—are on every Unix system. However, some of the more esoteric programs (especially the games) may not be available.

If you enter a non-existent command, don't worry, it won't cause any problems. Unix will just tell you that it could not find that command.

Displaying the Time and Date: `date`

The **date** command is one of the most useful. Simply enter:

```
date
```

and Unix will display the current time and date. Here is some sample output:

```
Thu Aug  4 21:18:42 PDT 1994
```

If you live in a place that uses daylight savings time, Unix knows how to spring forward and fall back at the appropriate times. The example here shows Pacific Daylight Time.

Notice that **date** gives both the time and date. There is a Unix **time** command, but it does not display the time of day; **time** measures how long it takes to run a program.

Internally, Unix does not really run on local time. All Unix systems use Greenwich Mean Time (GMT). Unix silently converts between GMT and your local time zone as necessary. (The details about your local time are specified by the system manager when he or she installs Unix.)

Sometimes it is handy to see what time it is in GMT. To display the time in GMT (universal time), enter:

```
date -u
```

You will see a time and date like this:

```
Fri Aug  5 04:18:42 GMT 1994
```

This time, by the way, is the GMT equivalent of the time in the previous example.

Displaying a Calendar: `cal`

One of the nice things about Unix is that it was not designed by committee. When the programmers decided that they wanted a new tool, they just added it to the system. A good example of this is the `cal` command, which displays a calendar.

To display the calendar for the current year, enter:

```
cal
```

To display a calendar for a particular year, just specify the year. For example:

```
cal 1952
```

When you specify a year, be sure to type all four numbers. If you enter **cal 52**, you will get the calendar for 52 A.D. You can use any year between 1 and 9999.

HINT

When you display the calendar for a full year, the output is long enough so that it may not fit entirely on your screen. If the top part of the calendar scrolls out of sight before you get a chance to read it, there are two things you can do:

1. Press **^S** to pause the screen display; then press **^Q** to continue (Chapter 6).

2. Send the output to a paging program such as **more** (Chapter 18).

To display a calendar for only one month, specify that month as a number between 1 and 12 (1=January), as well as the year. For example, to display the calendar for December 1952, enter:

```
cal 12 1952
```

You will see:

```
December 1952
 S  M  T  W  T  F  S
    1  2  3  4  5  6
 7  8  9 10 11 12 13
14 15 16 17 18 19 20
21 22 23 24 25 26 27
28 29 30 31
```

If you want a specific month, you must always specify both the month and the year. For instance, if it is currently August of 1994, and you want a calendar for that month, you must enter:

```
cal 8 1994
```

If you enter:

```
cal 8
```

you will get the whole year for 8 A.D..

For Calendar Nerds

Our modern calendar—with regular years of 365 days and leap years of 366 days—is derived from the Julian calendar. This calendar was introduced by Julius Caesar in 46 B.C. (Actually, the calendar was developed by a grad student, but Caesar put his name on the paper.)

However, assuming that a year is exactly 365.25 days is too long by a matter of 11 minutes, 10 seconds. By the sixteenth century, this small error had accumulated into about 10 days, which meant that the calendar everyone was using did not match the sun and the stars.

To solve this problem, Pope Gregory XIII decreed in 1582 that the world should modify its calendar so that not all centenary years (1600, 1700, and so on) should be leap years. Only the centenary years that are divisible by 400 (such as 2000) would be leap years. This scheme is called the Gregorian or New Style calendar.

To calibrate the current calendar, Gregory further decreed that 10 days should vanish mysteriously.

The Gregorian calendar was not adopted in Great Britain until 1752, by which time the error had increased to 11 days. Thus, if you enter the command:

```
cal 9 1752
```

you will see that between September 2 and September 14, 1752, there is a gap of 11 days. This gap is necessary for the sun and stars to work properly (at least in Great Britain).

The Unix Reminder Service: `calendar`

The **cal** program we just discussed displays a calendar. Unix does have a command named **calendar**, but it is completely different. The **calendar** program offers a reminder service based on a file of important days and messages that you create yourself.

All you need to do is make a file named **calendar** in your home directory (see Chapter 22). Within this file, you put lines of text in which each line starts with a date (such as "January 23"). For example:

January 23   Gwen's birthday.

Whenever you enter the command:

calendar

the program will check this file and display all the lines that have today's and tomorrow's date. (Of course, before you can create such a file, you must know how to use a text editor program. We discuss the most popular Unix text editors later in the book: **vi** in Chapter 20 and **emacs** in Chapter 21.)

Many Unix systems are set up so that each day the **calendar** program is run automatically early in the morning. If you happen to have a **calendar** file in your home directory, the program will find it, check for lines with today's and tomorrow's dates, and send the output to you by electronic mail. In this way, Unix furnishes a built-in reminder service for anyone on the system who wishes to set up a **calendar** file.

For more information, see the documentation for the **calendar** command on your system. You can read the entry for **calendar** in the online Unix manual (see Chapter 8) by using the command **man calendar**.

How Long Has the System Been Up?
uptime, ruptime

If you want to check how long your particular computer has been up (running continuously), enter:

```
uptime
```

You will see something like this:

```
8:44pm up 4 days, 7:56, 3 users, load average: 0.13, 0.05, 0.00
```

In this case, the system has been up for 4 days, 7 hours and 56 minutes, and there are 3 userids currently logged in. The last three numbers show the number of programs that have been waiting to execute, averaged over the last 1, 5 and 15 minutes respectively. These numbers give you an idea of the load on the system. The higher the load, the more the system is doing.

If you want to see similar information about all the machines on your local network, enter the "remote" version of this command:

```
ruptime
```

Here is some typical output:

```
ccse      up      4:27,  0 users,  load 0.42, 0.08, 0.02
engrhub   up   4+07:56,  2 users,  load 0.16, 0.07, 0.00
hub       up  33+06:25,  0 users,  load 2.64, 3.97, 3.90
mondas    up      3:31,  0 users,  load 0.00, 0.00, 0.00
nowhere   up  37+05:58,  0 users,  load 0.41, 0.26, 0.00
topgun    up   2+04:42,  0 users,  load 0.45, 0.48, 0.01
```

This example was generated at night (when the best computer book authors tend to work). Notice that the only computer that has anyone logged in is **engrhub**. You will also notice that the computer with the highest loads is **hub**. It happens that, in this network, **hub** is the computer that provides the link to the Internet (see Chapter 14) and to the Usenet discussion group system.

Which computer has been up the longest? The prize goes to **nowhere**, which has been up for 37 days, 5 hours and 58 minutes. **mondas**, which has been up only 3 hours and 31 minutes, gets the James Dean live-fast-die-young-and-leave-a-good-looking-corpse award.

Finding Out What's New in Your Neighborhood: `news`, `msgs`

Many Unix systems provide some type of news service to keep users abreast of the local current events, such as new services becoming available, special meetings, scheduled downtime for the computer, and so on.

If your system has a local news service, it will probably be accessed by either the **news** command or the **msgs** (messages) command. Just type in the command name; the program will do the rest. If you are not sure which command to use, try both.

The **news** program displays messages that are created by the system administrator. If you have a **news** command on your system, it will display news items, from newest to oldest, one after the other. Each item will be displayed in full, one screenful at a time.

At the bottom of each screen, you will see something like:

```
--More--[Press space to continue, 'q' to quit.]
```

There are a number of responses, only two of which are really important. If you want to continue, press the SPACE bar. If you want to quit, type **q**. If you feel ambitious and you want to see all possible responses to this message, press **h** (for help).

If you keep pressing SPACE, **news** will display screen after screen of news items. Some versions of the **news** program do not remember what you have already read; they always start with the newest item and work their way backwards. If you have the patience, **news** will be glad to take you back through months or even years of local announcements. Most people press SPACE until they see stuff that looks familiar, and then type **q**.

The **msgs** program differs from **news** in that anyone—not just the system administrator—can post a message to the local user community. To post a message, you simply mail it to userid **msgs**. (We will discuss sending mail in Chapter 15. In the meantime, you can read the messages mailed in by other users.)

When you start **msgs**, it describes the oldest message you have not yet seen. For instance:

```
Message 4356:
From harley@nipper.ucsb.edu Sun Apr 24 23:03:35 1994
Subject:Free money
22 lines) More? [ynq]
```

In this example, we see a message from a userid named **harley**. The subject looks interesting, and the message is 22 lines long.

If you would like to see the entire message, enter **y** (for yes) or press the RETURN key. If you do not want to see the message, enter **n** (for no). Once you have disposed of this message, one way or the other, **msgs** will display information about the next message. Aside from **y** and **n**, you can enter – (the minus sign) to display the previous message.

When you are ready to quit, enter **q**. **msgs** will make a note of where you were; the next time you run the program, it will continue from where you left off.

If you see a particularly interesting message, you can enter **s** to save it to a file named **Messages**. Entering **s–** will save the previous message. If you want to specify an alternate file name, you can do so. Just make sure to leave a space after the **s** or **s–**. For example, you can enter **s money** to save the current message to a file named **money**.

Note: Your system may have access to the worldwide Usenet news network. This has nothing to do with the local news we just described. Although Usenet is often referred to as "the news", it is actually a collection of global discussion groups.

Information about You and Your System: `hostname, whoami, quota`

Here are a few quick commands to display information about you and your system.

The **hostname** command will display the name of the system you are using. This can come in handy if you are in the habit of logging in to more than one computer. If you forget what system you are using, all you need to do is enter **hostname**.

The **whoami** command displays the name of your userid. This command is handy when you come upon a terminal that someone has left logged in. Enter **whoami** to see the current userid. (This command is also useful if you are suddenly struck by amnesia and forget your name. Looking at your userid may give you a clue.) If your system doesn't have a **whoami** command, try entering the following (as three separate words):

`who am i`

(We will discuss the **who** command in Chapter 13.)

On many computers, the system manager will impose a limit as to how much disk storage space each user is allowed to use. If you want to check your limit, enter the **quota** command. Note: Unix measures disk space in KB or kilobytes; 1 KB = 1024 bytes (characters).

Locking Your Terminal: `lock`

As we mentioned in Chapter 4, it is a bad idea to leave your terminal logged in. Someone can come along and, under the auspices of your userid, cause a lot of trouble. For example, they may delete all your files, send rude messages to the system manager in your name, and so on. However, if you do need to step away from your terminal for a moment, it is irritating to have to log out and in again.

Instead, you can use the **lock** command. This tells Unix that you want to lock your terminal temporarily. The terminal will remain locked until you enter a special password.

To use this command, just enter:

```
lock
```

Unix will display:

```
Key:
```

Enter the password that you want to use to unlock the terminal. This password can be anything you want; it has nothing to do with your login password. Unix will not echo the password as you type, just in case someone else is looking at your screen.

After you enter the password, Unix will display:

```
Again:
```

This is asking you to retype the password, to ensure that you did not make a mistake.

As soon as you have entered and re-entered the special password, Unix will freeze your terminal. Nothing will happen, no matter what anyone types on the terminal, until you enter the password. (Don't forget to press the RETURN key.) As soon as you enter the password, Unix will reactivate your terminal and you can return to your work.

If you are working in a place where you must share terminals and there are people waiting, it is considered bad form to lock your terminal and leave for a long time—say, to eat dinner. Since Unix was developed in such an environment, the **lock** command has a built-in limitation: the terminal will unlock automatically after 15 minutes.

If you want to override this 15-minute default, some versions of **lock** will let you specify an alternate time limit when you enter the command. After the name of the command, leave a space, and then type **–** (a minus sign), followed by a number. For example, to lock your terminal for 5 minutes, enter:

```
lock -5
```

You might ask, what happens if someone locks a terminal and then leaves for good? Eventually, the command will time out and unlock. If the terminal needs to be reactivated right away, the system manager can enter the **root** (superuser) password. **lock** will always accept the **root** password (sort of like a master key).

Remember though, if you lock your terminal and don't come back, someone will come along eventually and find your terminal reactivated and logged in under your userid. Whatever trouble they cause under your userid will be your responsibility.

Asking Unix to Remind You When to Leave: `leave`

As you know, working on a computer can be engrossing, and it is easy to lose track of the time. To help you fulfill your worldly obligations, Unix has a command that reminds you when it is time to leave.

The name of the command is **leave**. When you enter this command, Unix will ask you:

```
When do you have to leave?
```

Enter the time that you want to leave in the form *hhmm*. For example, if you want to leave at 10:33, enter **1033**.

You can enter times using either a 12-hour or 24-hour system. For instance, **1344** means 1:44 PM. If you enter a number of hours that is 12 or less, Unix assumes that it is within the next 12 hours. For instance, if it is 8:00 PM and you enter **855**, Unix assumes you mean 8:55 PM, not 8:55 AM.

If you need to leave after a certain time interval, type a **+** (plus sign) followed by the number of minutes. For example, if you need to leave after 5 minutes, type **+5**. (Be sure not to leave a space after the **+** character.)

An alternate way to start the program is to enter the time right on the command line. After the name of the command, leave a space and type the time. For example, to leave at 10:30, enter:

```
leave 1030
```

To leave in 15 minutes, enter:

```
leave +15
```

HINT

When you log out, Unix discards a pending **leave** command. Thus, if you use **leave**, but then log out and in again, you will have to enter a new command.

Once you have entered the **leave** command, Unix checks periodically to see how much time is left. When it is five minutes before the time you specified, Unix will display:

`You have to leave in 5 minutes`

When there is one minute left, you will see:

`Just one more minute!`

When the time is up, Unix displays:

`Time to leave!`

From that point on, Unix will keep nagging you with reminders, once a minute:

`You're going to be late!`

until you log off. Finally, after ten such reminders, you will see:

`You're going to be late!`
`That was the last time I'll tell you. Bye.`

Perhaps this program should have been named **mother**.

A Built-in Calculator: bc

One of the most useful (and least appreciated) Unix programs is **bc**, which implements a full-fledged, programmable scientific calculator. Many people do not bother learning how to use **bc**. "I spit on **bc**," they sneer, "nobody uses it." Don't be misled. Once you learn how to use **bc**, you will find it invaluable for quick calculations.

If you use X Window (see Chapter 5), there is a program named **xcalc** that you can use. **xcalc** looks nice—it actually draws a picture of a calculator on your screen—but, for minute-to-minute work or for extensive calculation, **bc** is better. Moreover, **bc** does not require X Window and will work with any terminal.

To explain **bc**, we will start with a short technical summary. If you don't understand all the mathematical and computer terms, don't worry. In the next few sections, we will explain how to use **bc** for basic calculations (which is easy) along with a few examples.

A technical summary of **bc**: **bc** is a fully programmable mathematical interpreter. **bc** offers extended precision; each number is stored automatically with as many digits as necessary. In addition, you can specify a scale of up to 100 digits to the right of the decimal point. Numeric values can be manipulated in any base from 2 to 16. It is easy to convert from one base to another.

You can use **bc** either by entering calculations from the keyboard, which are interpreted immediately, or by running programs stored in files.

The programming syntax of **bc** is similar to the C programming language. You can define functions and use recursion. There are arrays, and local and global variables. You can write your own functions, store them in a file, and have **bc** load and interpret them automatically. **bc** comes with a library that contains the following functions: sin, cos, arctan, ln, exponential and Bessel function. (Everybody who knows what a Bessel function is, raise your hand...)

For more information, see the online manual description of the **bc** command. You can use the command **man bc**. (We will explain the online Unix manual in Chapter 8.)

Using bc for Calculations

Most of the time, you will use **bc** for routine calculations, which is simple. To start the program, enter:

```
bc
```

If you want to use the built-in library of mathematical functions (see below), start the program using the –l (library) option:

```
bc -l
```

Once you start **bc** there is no specific prompt; just enter one calculation after another. Each time you press RETURN, **bc** evaluates what you have typed and displays the answer. For example, if you enter:

```
122152 + 70867 + 122190
```

bc will display:

```
315209
```

You can now enter a new calculation. If you want to enter more than one calculation on the same line, separate them with semicolons (just like Unix commands). **bc** will display each result on a separate line. For example, if you enter:

```
10+10; 20+20
```

you will see:

```
20
40
```

When you are finished working with **bc**, stop the program by telling it there is no more data. To do this, press **^D**, the **eof** key (see Chapter 6). Alternatively, you can enter **quit**.

Within a calculation, you can use the following operations:

addition:	**+**
subtraction:	**–**
multiplication:	*****
division:	**/**
modulo:	**%**
exponentiation:	**^**
square root:	**sqrt(x)**

Modulo finds the remainder after a division. For example, **53%10** is 3. Exponentiation refers to taking a number to a power. For example, **3^2** means "3 to the power of 2", which is 9. The power must be a whole number, but can be negative. If you use a negative power, enclose it in parentheses; for example, **3^(-1)**.

bc follows the general rules of algebra: multiplication, division and modulo have precedence over addition and subtraction; exponentiation has precedence over everything. Just like algebra, you can change the order of evaluation by using parentheses. So, **1+2*3** is 7, where **(1+2)*3** is 9.

Aside from the standard operations, there are a number of useful functions in a special library. These functions are:

sin:	**s(x)**
cos:	**c(x)**
arctan:	**a(x)**
ln:	**l(x)**
exponential:	**e(x)**
Bessel function:	**j(n, x)**

If you want to use the functions in this library, you need to start **bc** using the command:

```
bc -l
```

When you use this command, **bc** automatically sets the scale factor to 20 (see below).

As we mentioned earlier, **bc** can compute to arbitrary precision. That is, it will use as many digits as necessary to perform a calculation. For instance, you can ask it to add two 100-digit numbers. (We tested this.)

However, by default, **bc** will assume you are working with whole numbers. That is, **bc** will not keep any digits to the right of the decimal point. If you want to use fractional values, you need to set a scale factor to tell **bc** how many digits you want to keep to the right of the decimal point. To do this, set the value of **scale** to the scale factor you want.

For example, to ask for three digits to the right of the decimal point, enter:

```
scale=3
```

From now on, all work will be done to three decimal places. Any extra digits will be truncated.

If at any point you want to check what the scale factor is, simply enter:

```
scale
```

bc will display the current value.

When you start **bc**, **scale** is set automatically to 0. One of the most common mistakes is to start calculations without setting a scale factor. For instance, let's say that you have just started **bc**. You enter:

```
150/60
```

bc displays:

```
2
```

You now enter:

```
35/60
```

bc displays:

```
0
```

Finally, you figure out what the problem is and set an appropriate scale factor:

```
scale=3
```

Now **bc** will display what you want to see. (Try it.)

Remember, when you use the mathematical library, **bc** automatically starts with a scale factor of 20.

Using Variables with bc

Like all programming languages, **bc** allows you to set and use variables.

A variable is a quantity with a name and a value. Variable names consist of a single lowercase letter; that is, there are 26 variables, from **a** to **z**. (Make sure that you do not use uppercase letters; these are used when working with bases—see below.)

You set the value of a variable by using an **=** (equals sign) character. For example, to set the value of the variable **x** to 100, enter:

```
x=100
```

To display the value of a variable, just enter its name. For example:

```
x
```

bc will respond with the current value. By definition, all variables are assumed to be zero unless you set them otherwise.

You will find that using variables is straightforward and adds a lot of power to your work with **bc**. Here is an example that illustrates the basic principles:

The Maharaja of Gaipajama has been impressed with your facility in Unix. As a token of his esteem, he offers you twice your weight in rubies, worth $1000 a pound, and one third of your weight in diamonds, worth $2000 a pound. (The Maharaja of Gaipajama buys his gems wholesale.)

You weigh 160 pounds. How much is the Maharaja's gift worth?

To solve this problem, start **bc** and enter:

```
w=160
r=(w*2)*1000
d=(w/3)*2000
r+d
```

The following answer is displayed:

```
426000
```

Thus, your gift is worth $426,000.

But wait: once the Maharaja realizes how much his promise will cost him, he says, "Did I say I would give you gems based on your weight in pounds? I should have said kilograms."

Since 1 kilogram is 2.2 pounds, you quickly convert the **w** variable to kilograms:

```
w=w/2.2
```

Now you re-enter the calculations for the value of rubies and diamonds:

```
r=(w*2)*1000
d=(w/3)*2000
r+d
```

The new answer is displayed:

```
192000
```

Thus, by adhering to the metric system, the Maharaja has saved $234,000 (and has allowed you to demonstrate how to set a new value for a variable, based on its old value; in this case, **w=w/2.2**).

Using bc with Different Bases

As you would assume, **bc** normally uses base 10 arithmetic. (If you don't know what a base is, you can skip this section with impunity and get on to the games.) However, there will be times when you may want to calculate using another base. For example, in computer science, it is sometimes necessary to use base 16 (hexadecimal), base 8 (octal) or base 2 (binary).

bc allows you to specify different bases for input and for output. To do so, there are two special variables that you can set: **ibase** is the base that will be used for input; **obase** is the base that will be used for output.

For example, if you want to display answers in base 16, enter:

```
obase=16
```

If you want to enter numbers in base 8, use:

```
ibase=8
```

In the last section, we said that, by default, variables have a value of 0 until you set them. **ibase** and **obase** are exceptions: they are automatically initialized to 10 so you can work in base 10. If you want to work in another base, you can set either of the variables to any value from 2 to 16.

You should appreciate that the values of **ibase** and **obase** do not affect how **bc** manipulates numbers internally. Their only effect is to specify how numbers should be translated during input or output.

To work with bases larger than 10, **bc** represents the values of 10, 11, 12, 13, 14 and 15 as the uppercase letters A, B, C, D, E and F, respectively. Always remember to use uppercase; if you use lowercase, **bc** will think you are referring to variables, and the result will be wrong.

For convenience, you can use these uppercase letters regardless of what input base you have set. For instance, even if you are working in base 10, the expression **A+1** will have the value 11.

As with all variables, you can find out the current values of **ibase** and **obase** by entering the names by themselves:

```
ibase
obase
```

However, you must be careful. Once you set **obase**, all output will be displayed in that base, and you may have trouble interpreting what you see. For instance, if you enter:

```
obase=16
obase
```

you will see:

```
10
```

This is because all output is to be displayed in base 16, and—in base 16—the value of "16" is expressed as 10.

Similarly, once you change **ibase**, you must be careful what you type as input. For example, say that you set:

```
ibase=16
```

You now want to set **obase** to base 10, so you enter:

```
obase=10
```

However, you have forgotten that input is now in base 16, and 10 in base 16 is really "16". Thus, you have set **obase**, as well, to base 16.

To avoid such errors, use the letters A though F, which retain the same value regardless of the **ibase** value. Thus, if things become confused, you can always reset the bases by entering:

```
obase=A
ibase=A
```

Here are two examples of changing bases. In the first, you want to add two hexadecimal (base 16) numbers, F03E and 3BAC. Enter:

```
obase=16
ibase=16
F03E + 3BAC
```

bc displays the answer:

```
12BEA
```

In the second example, you want to convert the hexadecimal number FFC1 to binary (base 2). Reset the bases:

```
obase=A
ibase=A
```

then enter:

```
obase=2
ibase=16
FFC1
```

bc displays the answer:

```
1111111111000001
```

Using the Unix Games

Almost since its inception, Unix has come with a number of games and curiosities. Unfortunately, a few commercial Unix vendors have removed some or all of the games from their versions of Unix, no doubt because they feel better knowing that their customers are not having too much fun. Other vendors, however, have kept the games and even added new ones. Even if there are no games on your system, once you have access to the Internet, you will find hundreds of free games in the public archives. In this section, we will look at what we might call the "standard Unix games"—the ones that have traditionally been available for years.

Virtually all of the standard games are old; indeed, some of them date way back to ancient versions of Unix that were developed at Bell Labs. However, as Shakespeare once put it (while playing Hunt the Wumpus), "Age cannot wither her, nor custom stale her infinite variety."

Your system may have a variety of new games. If you use X Window (see Chapter 5), there may be X games. There may also be games specially written for your computer. For instance, Next computers come with their own games.

Before we get into a description of the games, there are two points you should understand.

We said earlier that when you enter a command, Unix looks for a program by that name to execute. Where does Unix look? We won't go into the details here, but programs are stored in files, and files are collected into directories. Unix has a list, called the "search path", that describes which directories should be searched for programs. If you want to see the search path, enter:

```
echo $PATH
```

Whenever you enter a command, Unix looks in each directory in the search path, one after another, until it finds the program you want. If Unix can't find the program, it will tell you so. (This may happen if you misspell the name of the command.)

To start a game, you enter the name of the appropriate command. For example, to start Hunt the Wumpus, you enter:

```
wump
```

Now, the name of the directory in which all the games are kept is **/usr/games**. (This name will make sense after we discuss directories in Chapter 23.) When you enter the **wump** command, Unix must look in this directory to find a program named **wump**.

But, on some systems, the "games" directory is not in the search path. Unix will not be able to find the program and you will see:

```
wump: Command not found.
```

If this is the case on your system, you must tell Unix explicitly which directory to search. You do this by specifying the directory name, followed by a **/** (slash), before the name of the command:

/usr/games/wump

Now Unix will be able to find the program you want (as long as the game exists on your system), and the game will start.

In the following sections, we will give you the names of all the Unix games. You may find that, on your system, you will have to preface each name with **/usr/games/** when you enter the command. (Try it and find out.) For instance, to start the **fortune** program, you may have to enter:

/usr/games/fortune

When you enter such a command, be sure you do not put any spaces before or after the slashes. Also, make sure you do not spell **usr** with an "e".

The second point we want you to realize is that, although the games can provide pleasant diversions, they are not the main reason someone is spending a lot of money to provide you with a Unix system.

The games, of course, are Unix programs, just like many of the tools you will use. You will find that in learning how to start, stop and use a few games, you are also learning a great deal about how to use Unix programs in general. In other words, using the Unix games is, arguably, an educational experience.

Still, it behooves you to respect the wishes of your system manager. Do not tie up a terminal or workstation playing games when other people need to get more serious (and boring) work done.

Some system managers restrict game playing to certain off hours. Other system managers remove the games completely. (You may find, though, that even if all the other games are gone, the **fortune** program will be retained, simply because it is so amusing.)

How Do You Stop a Game (and Unix Programs in General)?

It is always a good idea to know how to stop a program. The hints that we give in this section apply to all Unix programs, not just to games.

Some programs are complex enough to have a whole list of commands you can use. For example, the **adventure** game allows you to enter commands as you explore a large cave. With such programs, there will be some type of prompt to let you know when you can enter a command.

If you need help, wait for the prompt and enter **help**. If that doesn't work, try **h** or **?** (a question mark).

When you are working with a program that reads commands, entering **quit** will often stop the program. If that doesn't work, try **q**, **Q** or **bye**. If none of these work, read the instructions.

Once you enter the quit command—whatever it is for that game—you may be asked if you really want to quit. This prevents you from accidentally losing hours of work (!) by typing the wrong word.

Since most games read input from your terminal, you can often end them by indicating that there is no more data. To do this, press **^D**, the **eof** key (see Chapter 6).

If all else fails, you may be able to stop a program by pressing the **intr** key, which will be either **^C** or DELETE (again, see Chapter 6).

Learning How to Play a Game

In the next section, we will give brief descriptions of each Unix game. Most of the complicated games are able to provide you with instructions as you play. However, for extra help, you can look in the online Unix manual.

We will discuss the online manual in detail in Chapter 8. For now, we will mention that to learn about a command—any command, not just a game—you use the **man** command. Enter **man** followed by the name of the program you want to learn about.

For example, to learn about the **fortune** program, enter:

```
man fortune
```

(To learn about the **man** command itself, enter **man man**.)

man will display information about the command you specify, one screenful at a time. At the bottom of the screen, you will see:

```
--More--
```

This tells you that there is more information. To display the next screen, press the SPACE bar. To quit, press the **q** key.

Before you start playing a new game, always check the description in the online manual. This will tell you how to start the game and, generally, how it works.

When you use a game for the first time, answer **y** (for yes) if it asks if you want instructions. Even if you think you know how to play—for example, the backgammon game—it will be different when you play it on a computer.

A Description of the Unix Games

When we refer to the Unix "games", we are really talking about two types of programs, all of which traditionally reside in the **/usr/games** directory.

First, there are a good many real games: blackjack, Monopoly, Hunt the Wumpus and so on. Second, there are diversions and curiosities (such as weird math programs and fortune telling programs) that are also part of Unix. In this section, we will describe the actual games. In the next section, we will discuss the other programs.

We can divide the standard Unix games into several categories. First, there are the games that you will find familiar. Several programs are based on well-known board games: **chess**, **mille** (Mille Bournes) and **monop** (Monopoly). There are also programs based on cards and gambling: **backgammon**, **btlgammon** (another backgammon), **bj** (blackjack), **canfield** (a form of solitaire), **craps**, **cribbage**, and the old standby, **fish**. In addition, there is a quiz program, **quiz**, as well as a guessing game called **moo**. Finally, there are two word games, **boggle** and **hangman**.

Next, there are games that will take you into some type of strange new world. All the information is textual; the program describes what you are looking at, what you are carrying with you, and so on. These games are habit-forming and are perfectly capable of occupying all your time for the foreseeable future.

The granddaddy of such games is **adventure**. In this game, you explore a large, labyrinth-like cave. Part of the charm of the game is that you have to figure out not only how everything works, but what it is exactly that you are supposed to do (just like real life). Indeed, before you can even start your explorations, you have to discover how to get into the cave. If you decide to play **adventure**, we have a hint for you: draw yourself a map (on paper) as you go. Another, more modern game in this genre—with a completely different scenario—is **battlestar**.

The third category consists of visual games that draw pictures on your terminal. First, there is **snake**, in which you try to make as much money as possible without getting eaten by the snake (another allegory for real life). Second, there is **worm**, in which you see how long you can keep a growing worm alive.

There are also visual games in which you shoot at something: **robots** (where you shoot at tiny robots), **trek** (based on Star Trek-like concepts) and **wump** (where you go after the cave-dwelling Wumpus with your bow and arrow).

The last two shooting games are **hunt** and **sail**. Both are multi-user, designed to be played by more than one person on the same network. Unlike **wump**, where you are restricted to the isolated pleasure of hunting an imaginary animal, **hunt** and **sail** afford the much more satisfying experience of tracking down and destroying your friends.

The final fantasy game is **rogue**, a popular visually oriented Dungeons and Dragons game, in which you evade the attacks of various monsters as you search for the Amulet of Yendor. If your system does not have **rogue**, it may have **hack**, a replacement for **rogue**. **hack** offers twice as many monster types (but requires three times the memory).

Diversions and Curiosities

Along with the games that we described in the previous section, Unix also contains a number of miscellaneous programs under the "games" heading.

For the mathematically inclined, there are **factor** (which decomposes any number into its prime factors) and **primes** (which generates all the prime numbers larger than a specified value). Note: The **primes** program will go on indefinitely until you stop it by pressing the **intr** key (which will be either **^C** or DELETE, depending on your system).

For the non-mathematically inclined, we have **arithmetic** (to practice simple computation) and **number** (which reads any integer and converts it to English words).

To create signs and notices, you can use **banner**, which takes any series of characters and displays them enlarged.

There are two versions of the **banner** program. The first displays letters that are just the right size for your screen. For example:

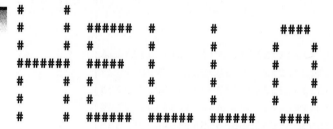

```
#     #
#     #  ######  #        #         ####
#     #  #       #        #        #    #
#######  #####   #        #        #    #
#     #  #       #        #        #    #
#     #  #       #        #        #    #
#     #  ######  ######   ######    ####
```

The other version of **banner** displays extremely large characters suitable for printing. These characters come out sideways and, when printed on continuous paper, make a nice sign. You will have to experiment to see which type of **banner** program is on your computer. In Chapter 19, we give an example of the commands you can use to print a sign using **banner**.

If you are a real old-timer, you may remember paper tape and punch cards. Well, Unix does, too. The **ppt** program reads a string of characters and shows how it would look encoded on paper tape. For example, the words "Harley Hahn" look like the following:

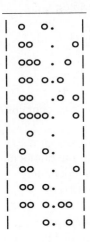

```
|  o  o.    |
|  oo   .  o|
|  ooo  . o |
|  oo o.o   |
|  oo  .o o |
|  oooo. o  |
|   o   .   |
|   o  o.   |
|  oo   . o |
|  oo o.    |
|  oo o.oo  |
|     o. o  |
```

The **bcd** program makes a similar translation to a punch card:

```
/HARLEY HAHN                                          |
|]]   ]   ]]]                                         |
|   ]]        ]                                       |
|      ]                                              |
|1]111111]111111111111111111111111111111111111111111  |
|222222222222222222222222222222222222222222222222     |
|333]333333333333333333333333333333333333333333       |
|444444444444444444444444444444444444444444444444     |
|5555]55555]55555555555555555555555555555555555       |
|66666666666666666666666666666666666666666666666      |
|7777777777777777777777777777777777777777777777       |
|]8]88]8]8]888888888888888888888888888888888888       |
|99999999999999999999999999999999999999999999999      |
|_____|
```

(If you are not sure what "bcd" stands for, ask an old person.)

If you have very little imagination and nothing to do, you might try **rain** or **worms**, which display moving shapes on the screen of your terminal. (Do not confuse **worms** with **worm**, the game we mentioned in the previous section.)

If you have a moderate imagination and nothing to do, you will love **fortune**. This program draws on a large database of pithy, humorous and offensive items. Every time you run **fortune**, it randomly selects and displays an item from the database.

To run **fortune**, simply enter its name:

```
fortune
```

Here is some sample output:

```
Any small object that is accidentally dropped
will hide under a larger object.
```

The idea is to simulate the type of fortune you might find inside a bizarre type of fortune cookie. Left to its own, **fortune** selects an item from the entire database, including the obscene entries. If you want to request an obscene fortune specifically, enter:

```
fortune -o
```

Here is one of the few examples that we can print in a family-oriented book like this one:

```
There was a young lady from Maine
Who claimed she had men on her brain.
But you knew from the view,
As her abdomen grew,
It was not on her brain that he'd lain.
```

Be aware that some Unix companies remove the obscene fortunes from the database. When you ask for such a fortune, you may see a message like this:

```
Sorry, no obscene fortunes. Don't want to offend anyone.
(Now that's obscene!)
```

As you will see in Chapters 11 and 12, there is a way to specify commands for Unix to run each time you log out. Some people add **fortune** to this list. Indeed, your system manager may have already set up your account in this way. If so, you will have noticed a different fortune every time you log out. Now you know where it comes from.

Finally, if you are one of those unusual people with enormous imaginations and nothing to do, try **ching**. This program draws on the I Ching, a Chinese book that has been a source of wisdom and advice for centuries. (Many calculus teachers use it to set final exams.) Enter the following:

```
ching
```

Now type a question, as many lines as you want. (If you are not sure what to ask, try "Is it time for me to get back to work?") When you are finished, press **^D**, the **eof** key (see Chapter 6).

ching will display the same type of cryptic analysis as the real I Ching. You now have many happy hours ahead of you, interpreting the results and deciding how they apply to your life. Perhaps, with a little practice, you may even be able to start your own religion. If so, be sure to mention Unix.

CHAPTER 8

The Online Unix Manual

When it comes to learning, there are two important parts of the Unix tradition that you should understand: first, you are expected to teach yourself; second, if you have tried your best and you still have a problem, a more advanced user will be glad to help you. (The converse of this, of course, is that once you are experienced you are expected to help anyone who knows less than you.)

Unix comes with a large, built-in manual that is accessible at any time from your terminal. Before you ask for help, it is expected that you will have looked in the manual. After all, it is available to everybody at all times.

In this chapter, we will discuss the Unix online manual: What is it? How do you use it? And what are the best strategies for finding information?

What Is the Online Manual? man

The ONLINE MANUAL is a collection of files, stored on disk, each of which contains the documentation about one Unix command or topic. You can access the online manual at any time by using the **man** command. Type the word **man**, followed by the name of the command you want to know about. Unix will display the documentation for that command.

For example, to display the documentation about the **cp** command, enter:

```
man cp
```

To learn about the **man** command itself, enter:

```
man man
```

HINT
The **man** command is the single most important Unix command because you can use it to learn about any command you want.

If you want, you can specify more than one command name. For example:

```
man cp mv ln
```

Unix will display the documentation for each command in turn.

What's in a Name?   The Manual

The online Unix manual has always been important. Indeed, at one time, when Unix was primarily a product of AT&T's Bell Labs, versions of Unix were named after the current edition of the manual: Unix Sixth Edition, Unix Seventh Edition, and so on.

Although there are many Unix books and references, there is only one online manual. When someone says, look it up in "the manual", he or she means to use the **man** command and check with the online manual. There is never any doubt as to which manual is The Manual.

Displaying the Online Manual on Your Terminal

Virtually all the entries in the online manual are longer than the number of lines on your screen. If an entry were displayed all at once, most of it would scroll off the screen so fast that you would not be able to read the text.

This is a common situation for which Unix has a good solution: send the output to a program that will display the output more carefully, one screenful at a time. There are three such programs, called paging programs, that are commonly used on Unix systems. Their names are **more**, **pg** and **less**.

In Chapter 18, we will talk about each of the paging programs. For now, we will give you a brief overview so that you will know enough to be able to read the online manual.

As we said, a paging program displays data one screenful at a time. After each screenful, the program pauses and displays a prompt at the bottom left-hand corner of the screen. The prompt differs depending on what paging program is being used.

The **more** program displays a prompt that contains the word "More". For example, you might see:

```
--More--(25%)
```

This means that there is more to come and you have read 25 percent of the data. (You can see where the name of the program comes from.) The **pg** program displays a prompt that is a simple colon:

```
:
```

The **less** program also displays a colon, possibly followed by some other information.

Once you have read what is on the screen, you can display more data by pressing the SPACE bar (for **more** and **less**) or the RETURN key (for **pg**). If you are not sure which paging program you are using, just experiment. Nothing bad will happen.

The idea is that by pressing SPACE (or possibly RETURN) repeatedly, you can page through the entire manual entry, one screen at a time. At any time, you can enter **q** to quit. (With **pg**, you will have to press RETURN after the **q**.)

When all the data has been displayed, the paging program will either stop by itself (**more**), stop when you press RETURN (**pg**), or stop when you enter the **q** command (**less**).

As you are reading, there are many commands that you can enter when the program is paused at a prompt. We will mention two of those commands here.

First, if you are looking for a specific pattern, press the **/** (slash), type the pattern, and then press RETURN. For example:

```
/output
```

In this case, the paging program will skip to the next line that contains the word "output".

Second, for instant assistance, you can enter the **h** (help) command at any time. (With **pg**, you will have to press RETURN after the **h**.) This command will display a summary of commands.

In Chapter 18, we will discuss the three paging programs in detail. If you want some extra information, look at the manual entries for these programs. You can use the commands:

```
man more
man pg
man less
```

Note: Not all systems have the **less** program.

HINT

If you are using X Window, there is an X client named **xman** that provides a graphical version of the **man** command. If you prefer to use the regular **man** command, you will need to execute it from within an **xterm** window.

How Is the Online Manual Organized?

The best way to think about the online manual is to imagine a gargantuan reference book that lives somewhere inside your Unix system. The book is like an encyclopedia in that it contains many entries, in alphabetical order, each of which covers a single topic.

You can't turn the pages of this book; hence, there are no page numbers and no formal table of contents or index. However, there are several layers of organization that are appropriate to an electronic book.

Section	Topic (Berkeley Unix)	Topic (System V)
(1)	Commands	Commands
(2)	System Calls	System Calls
(3)	Library Functions	Library Functions
(4)	Special Files	Administrative Files
(5)	File Formats	Miscellaneous Information
(6)	Games	Games
(7)	Miscellaneous Information	I/O and Special Files
(8)	Maintenance Commands	Maintenance Commands

FIGURE 8-1. *The eight main sections of the online Unix manual*

Traditionally, the entire manual is divided into eight main sections. These classic divisions are shown in Figure 8-1. Notice the minor differences between Berkeley Unix and System V.

As you might imagine from looking at the names, the most important sections are 1 and 6.

Section 1 contains descriptions of the bulk of the Unix commands. Most people can get by just fine with only this section of the manual.

HINT

The most important section of the online Unix manual is Section 1, which contains descriptions of most of the commands. It may be the only section you will ever need.

Section 6 contains descriptions of the Unix games (see Chapter 7). If the system manager has not installed the games on your system, you will probably find that Section 6 of the manual will also be missing. Otherwise, the system manager risks having complaints from users who can read about the games, but can't use them (sort of like Moses standing on Mount Pisgah and gazing down wistfully at the Promised Land).

The Miscellaneous Information section contains a grab bag of information, much of which pertains to using the Unix typesetting facilities.

If you are a programmer, Sections 2 and 3 will be important. Section 2 describes the system calls — ways in which your programs may call on Unix to perform certain tasks. Section 3 explains the built-in libraries of functions and subroutines you can use in your programs. In addition, the Special Files section describes the interfaces to various hardware devices, while the File Formats section shows the formats of the important files that are used by the system. Section 8 contains descriptions of the special commands that system managers use to carry out their work.

HINT

Except for Sections 1 (Commands) and 6 (Games), the bulk of the Unix manual is of interest only to programmers and system administrators.

Before we move on, we would like to mention that the eight-section organization, derived from the earliest Unix implementations, has pretty much remained intact. The modern Unix online manual, however, covers much more material than its venerable ancestor. Thus, you may see different, more comprehensive section names. For example, on one Unix system, Section 4, Special Files, is called "Devices and Network Interfaces", while Section 7, Miscellaneous Information, is called "Environments, Tables and Troff Macros". (**troff** is the name of the Unix typesetting program.)

You may also see sections broken down into subsections. For instance, Section 1 is always the main command reference. However, with System V, you may see Section 1m for system maintenance commands. You may also see Section 1c (for communication commands), Section 1g (graphics commands), Section 1X (X Window commands), and so on. Within a section, a single piece of documentation is called a PAGE or an ENTRY.

What's in a Name?   Page

In the beginning, Unix users had slow terminals, many of which printed on paper (because they did not have a display screen). Thus, it was convenient to print out pages of the manual, rather than access them on a terminal. At the time, most of the manual entries fit on a single page. To this day, each entry is still referred to as a "page", even though it may be hundreds of lines.

For example, you might overhear two Unix experts talking. One says, "I can't decide what to get my girlfriend for her birthday." The other replies, "Why not print her a copy of the manual page for the C-Shell?" The word "page" is used in this manner even though, in this case, the actual entry might take up many printed pages. In informal conversation or writing, the word "manual" is often abbreviated to "man". For example, "Last Mother's Day, I gave my mother a copy of the Korn shell man page."

Specifying the Section Number When Using the man Command

So far, we have seen how to use **man** by typing the name of the command you want to learn about. For example, to learn about the **kill** command (which can stop a runaway program), you can enter:

```
man kill
```

You will see the description of **kill** that resides in Section 1 of the manual.

However, it happens that there is also an entry for **kill** in Section 2 (System Calls). If this is what you are really interested in, you can specify the section number before the name of the command:

```
man 2 kill
```

This tells Unix that you are only interested in a particular section of the manual. If the section you are referencing is divided into subsections, you can be as specific as you want.

For example, there is an entry for **kill** in Section 3f, the part of the manual that documents Fortran subroutines. To display this description, enter:

```
man 3f kill
```

As we mentioned earlier, you can ask for more than one part of the manual at a time. For instance, if you want to see all three entries for **kill**, you can enter:

```
man 1 kill 2 kill 3f kill
```

When you do not specify a section number, Unix starts at the beginning of the manual (Section 1) and works its way through until it finds the first match. Thus, the following two commands will have the same result:

```
man kill
man 1 kill
```

Most of the time, you will be interested in the basic commands (Section 1), so it will not be necessary to specify a section number.

To orient you to the various parts of the manual, each section and subsection contains a page called **intro** that acts as a brief introduction. A good way to become familiar with the contents of a section is to display its **intro** page.

Here are some examples of commands that display such pages:

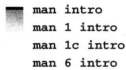
```
man intro
man 1 intro
man 1c intro
man 6 intro
```

As you know, **man** will assume Section 1 by default; thus, the first two examples are equivalent.

> **HINT**
> To learn more about using the online manual, use the following two commands:
>
> ```
> man man
> man intro
> ```

How Manual Pages Are Referenced

When you read about Unix, you will frequently see a name followed by a number in parentheses. This number tells you what section of the manual to look in for information about this item.

For example, here is part of a sentence taken from the Berkeley version of the man page for the **chmod** command (which we will meet in Chapter 24). For now, don't worry about what the sentence means, just look at the reference:

```
"...but the setting of the file creation mask,
    see umask(2), is taken into account..."
```

This reference tells us that we can enter the command:

```
man 2 umask
```

for more information. However, since we know that Section 2 describes system calls, we can guess that we would only care about this reference if we were writing a program.

At the end of the **chmod** man page are the following two lines:

```
SEE ALSO
    ls(1), chmod(2), stat(2), umask(2), chown(8)
```

These references tell us that there are five other man pages related to this one. As you can see, three of the references are in Section 2 and are for programmers. The last reference is in Section 8 (Maintenance Commands) and is for system administrators.

On the other hand, the first reference suggests that we look at the man page for **ls** in Section 1 of the manual. Since Section 1 describes general commands, there is a good chance that this reference will be of interest.

HINT

If you see a reference to a command that is in Section 1 of the online manual —for example, **ls(1)** —it is usually worth looking at. References to other sections can be ignored unless the Section 1 information is not adequate.

The Format of a Manual Page

Each man page explains a single topic. Some pages are short, while others are quite long. (For example, **csh(1)** — the man page that describes the C-Shell — is a reference manual in its own right.)

For convenience, each man page is organized according to a standard format using the headings shown in Figure 8-2. Not all man pages will have each of these headings. Moreover, some Unix systems use different headings. However, if you understand the standard headings, you should be able to figure out whatever your system uses.

Let's take a quick look at each of these headings. To show you how it all works, Figure 8-3 contains a typical man page. As you read Figure 8-3, remember that, in Unix, the word "print" usually refers to displaying text on your terminal, not actual printing (see Chapter 6).

```
       NAME: the name and purpose of the command
   SYNOPSIS: the syntax of the command
DESCRIPTION: a full description (may be long)
      FILES: list of files important to this command
   SEE ALSO: where to look for related information
DIAGNOSTICS: possible errors and warnings
       BUGS: mistakes, shortcomings and warnings
```

FIGURE 8-2. *The standard headings used in the online Unix manual*

```
MAN(1)                     USER COMMANDS                      MAN(1)
NAME
     man - display reference manual pages; find reference pages
     by keyword
SYNOPSIS
     man [-] [section] title ...
     man -k keyword ...
     man -f filename ...
DESCRIPTION
     Man is a program which gives information from the programmers manual.
     It can be asked for one-line descriptions of commands specified by
     name, or for all commands whose description contains any of a set of
     keywords. It can also provide on-line access to the sections of the
     printed manual.
     When given the option -k and a set of keywords, man prints out a one
     line synopsis of each manual section whose listing in the table of
     contents contains one of those keywords.
     When given the option -f and a list of names, man attempts to locate
     manual sections related to those files, printing out the table of
     contents lines for those sections.
     When neither -k or -f is specified, man formats a specified set of
     manual pages. If a section specifier is given man looks in that
     section of the manual for the given titles. Section is either an
     Arabic section number (3 for instance), or one of the words "new",
     "local", "old" or "public". A section number may be followed by a
     single letter classifier (for instance, 1g, indicating a graphics
     program in section 1). If section is omitted, man searches all
     sections of the manual, giving preference to commands over
     subroutines in system libraries, and printing the first section it
     finds, if any.
     If the standard output is a teletype, or if the flag - is given, man
     pipes its output through more(1) with the option -s to crush out
     useless blank lines and to stop after each page on the screen. Hit a
     space to continue, a control-D to scroll 11 more lines when the
     output stops.
FILES
     /usr/man          standard manual area
     /usr/man/man?/*    directories containing source for manuals
     /usr/man/cat?/*    directories containing preformatted pages
     /usr/man/whatis    keyword database
SEE ALSO
     apropos(1), more(1), whatis(1), whereis (1) catman(8)
BUGS
     The manual is supposed to be reproducible either on a
     photo-typesetter or on an ASCII terminal. However, on a terminal
```

FIGURE 8-3. *A sample manual page (the output of the command* **man man***)*

Name   In one line, this is what the command is all about. Be aware that some of the descriptions are vague.

Synopsis   This section shows the syntax of the command. This is the official explanation of how to enter the command. We describe command syntax in detail in Chapter 9.

Description   This section is the largest and usually takes up the bulk of the man page. On some systems, the full explanation is divided into two separate sections: Description and Options. Options allow you to control just how a command will execute. We discuss options in detail in Chapter 9.

Remember that this is a reference manual. Be prepared to find that many descriptions are not understandable until you know what you are doing. If you have trouble, keep reading until you run out of patience — some of what you read will stick — and when you learn more, you can try again.

There are some descriptions (like **csh(1)**) that you will probably never understand completely. If you become frustrated, remind yourself that the people who do understand everything are less attractive and less socially proficient than you.

Files   This section shows the names of the files that are used by this command. (File names are explained in Chapter 22.) If the information in this section makes no sense to you, you can ignore it.

See Also   This is an important section. It shows you other places to look in the manual for more information. In particular, you will see commands that are related in some way to the command under discussion. Following up these references is a good way to learn. Concentrate on the references to Section 1 man pages.

Diagnostics   This section can contain two types of information. First, there may be an explanation of possible error messages. Second, there may be a list of error codes that a command can return upon completion.

Error codes are important for programmers, who can use a command in a program or shell script and then test if the command completed successfully. (A shell script is a file containing a list of commands to be executed automatically.) If the command was successful, the error code will have a value of zero. Otherwise, the error code will be non-zero.

When a command returns an error code, its value is stored in the variable named **status**. You can display its value by entering:

```
echo $status
```

(This is if you are using the C-Shell or the Tcsh. If you are using the Bourne shell, the Korn shell, Bash or the Zsh, use **echo $?**. The various shells are described in Chapter 10.)

Bugs All programs have two kinds of bugs: the ones you know about and the ones you don't know about. The original developers of Unix recognized that no program is perfect and users deserve to know about the imperfections. Unfortunately, some vendors have decided that a section named Bugs gives the paying customers the wrong idea. Thus, you may see this section renamed to be less conspicuous (for example, Limitations).

A Quick Way to Find Out What a Command Does: `whatis`

When you enter the basic **man** command, Unix will display the full manual page. However, sometimes you are interested in just a quick description.

As we explained above, the Name section of each man page contains a one-line description. If all you want to see is this single line, use the **man** command as follows: type **man**, followed by **-f**, followed by the names of one or more commands. For example:

```
man -f time date
```

In this form of the **man** command, the **-f** is called an option. (We will discuss options in Chapter 9.) The letter "f" was chosen to stand for the word "files". Each man page is stored in a separate file; when you use the **-f** option, you are telling **man** which files to look at.

As a convenience, you can type the single word **whatis**, instead of **man -f**. For instance, if you want to display the time, but you are not sure whether to use the **time** or **date** command, enter:

```
whatis time date
```

You will see something like this:

```
date (1)          - print date and time
time (1)          - time a command
time (7)          - time a command
time, ftime (3)   - get date and time
```

You can ignore the last two lines as they do not refer to Section 1 of the manual. Looking at the first two lines, you see that the command you want is **date**. The **time** command actually measures how long it takes for a program or command to execute.

When you enter the regular **man** command, you can specify a particular section number (such as **man 1 date**). With **man -f** or **whatis**, you cannot be so specific. Unix will always search the entire manual.

Thus, a good way to find out what your manual contains is to enter:

whatis intro

You will see quick summaries of each **intro** page.

Note: For the **whatis** command to work properly, the man pages must be preprocessed in a certain way. All the one-line descriptions are collected and stored in certain files. It is these files that the **whatis** command searches, not the actual manual (that would be far too slow). Unless the preprocessing has been carried out, the **whatis** command will not be able to return useful information. If this is the case on your system, talk to your system manager.

Searching for a Command: `apropos`

When you want to learn about a command, you can use **man** to display the appropriate manual page. But what if you know what you want to do, but you are not sure which command to use?

The solution is to use **man** with the **-k** option to search for commands whose descriptions contain specified keywords. For example, say that you want to find all the entries in the online manual that have something to do with the manual itself. Enter:

man -k manual

As a convenience, you can use the single word **apropos** instead of **man -k**:

apropos manual

("Apropos of" is an elegant expression meaning "concerning" or "with reference to".)

When you use the **apropos** command, Unix searches through all the one-line command descriptions, looking for those that contain the same string of characters you specified. To make the command more powerful, Unix does not distinguish between upper- and lowercase.

Here is some sample output from the previous example.

```
catman (8)   - create the cat files for the manual
man (1)      - displays manual pages online
man (5)      - macros for formatting entries in REFERENCE manual
man (7)      - macros to typeset manual
route (8c)   - manually manipulate the routing tables
whereis (1)  - locate source, binary, and or manual for program
```

Notice there are only two commands of interest, **man** and **whereis** (the ones in Section 1). Notice also that the **route** command was cited because the characters "manual" happen to appear in its description.

You might ask, why don't **apropos** and **whatis** appear in this list? After all, they are important commands to help you access the online manual. To answer this question, enter:

```
whatis apropos whatis
```

You will see:

```
apropos (1) - locate commands by keyword lookup
whatis (1)  - display command description
```

The word "manual" does not appear in these descriptions.

The **apropos** command is not magic — all it can do is search for character strings. So if you can't find what you want, try asking in a different way.

HINT

Most commands are actually programs. For example, the **man** command is really a program named "man". However, some of the most basic commands are carried out by the shell (the command processor) itself. These commands will be documented within the man page for the shell. They will not have their own separate entries in the manual.

If you are looking for a command that you know exists, but you cannot find it under its own name, check the man page for the shell you are using. If you are using the C-Shell, check the man page for **csh**; for the Korn shell, check under **ksh**.

CHAPTER **9**

Command Syntax

Much of your work with Unix will be entering commands, one after another. As long as you work with Unix, you will never stop learning new commands — there are literally hundreds of them.

As you know, a command must be used just so, according to well-defined rules. Putting a comma in the wrong place, or spelling a word incorrectly, will invalidate the entire command. In the worst case, a mis-typed command may execute incorrectly and cause problems.

The formal description of how a command must be entered is called the COMMAND SYNTAX. In this chapter, we will explain this system and how you use it. Once you finish this chapter, you will be able to understand how to use any command just by reading its syntax in the online manual (see Chapter 8).

The Unix Command Line

When you enter a command, the entire line you type is called the COMMAND LINE. Usually, you will type one command at a time. However, the command line can contain multiple commands. Simply separate them with semicolons. For example:

```
date; cd; ls -l -F file1
```

You do not need a semicolon at the end of the command line.

When you enter a command, you type the name of the command, possibly followed by other information. The items that follow the name are called ARGUMENTS. For example, consider the following **ls** command. (**ls** lists information about files.)

```
ls -l -F file1
```

This particular command has three arguments, **-l**, **-F** and **file1**.

In order to process a command, Unix searches for, and then executes, a program with the name of the command. If you were to enter the previous **ls** command, Unix would find and start the **ls** program.

When Unix starts a program, it passes along the arguments. It is up to the program to figure out what to do with them.

Options and Parameters

There are two types of arguments, OPTIONS and PARAMETERS. Options come right after the command name and consist of a **-** (minus sign character) followed by a letter. Parameters come after the options. The example:

```
ls -l -F file1 file2 file3
```

has two options, **-l** and **-F**, and three parameters, **file1**, **file2** and **file3**. Occasionally, you will see an option that is a number, such as:

```
ls -1 file1 file2 file3
```

You will have to be careful not to confuse **-l** (the letter "l") with **-1** (the numeral "1").

You use options to tell the command exactly how you want it to work. In our example, the **-l** option tells the **ls** command to display the "long" listing. Normally, the **ls** command lists the names of files. When you use the **-l** option, **ls** lists extra information about each file, along with the names.

You use parameters to pass information to the program. In this case, we want **ls** to display information about three files named "file1", "file2" and "file3".

When we talk about a command, the tradition is to pronounce the **-** character as "minus", even though the **-** has nothing to do with arithmetic and acts more like a hyphen than anything else. For instance, if someone asks you how to make the **ls** command display a long file listing, you would say out loud, "Use the minus L option."

When a command has more than one option, you can combine them using a single **-** character. Moreover, you can specify options in any order. Thus, all of the following commands are equivalent:

```
ls -l -F file1
ls -F -l file1
ls -lF file1
ls -Fl file1
```

As with all Unix commands, you must make sure that you use the exact upper- or lowercase. For example, the **ls** command has both **-F** and **-f** options, and they are different. As a general rule, most commands have only lowercase options. (As we explained in Chapter 4, almost everything in Unix is lowercase.)

Whitespace

When you enter a command, you must make sure to separate each option and parameter. The rule is: between each word you must use one or more spaces or tabs. For example, here are several ways of entering the same command (we have indicated where we pressed the SPACE bar and TAB key):

```
ls<Space>-l<Space>-F<Space>file1
ls<Tab>-l<Tab>-F<Tab>file1
ls<Space><Tab>-l<Space>-F<Tab><Tab><Tab>file1
```

Normally, of course, you would just put a single space between each part of the command. However, the idea of using spaces and tabs as separators is important enough to have its own name: WHITESPACE. Whitespace means one or more consecutive spaces or tabs.

Thus, we can summarize the format of a Unix command as follows:

```
COMMAND-NAME   OPTIONS   PARAMETERS
```

the various options and parameters being separated by whitespace.

What's in a Name? Whitespace

The term "whitespace" refers to consecutive spaces and tabs that are used to separate two items. The name derives from the earliest Unix terminals that printed on paper. As you typed a command, there was real white space between each word.

The Unix command processor was designed to be flexible; it didn't care how much space there was, as long as the words were separated. Thus, "whitespace" came to mean any amount of spaces and tabs.

One or More; Zero or More

In the next section, we will discuss the formal method for describing commands. Before we do, however, we need to define two important expressions: "one or more" and "zero or more".

When you see the expression ONE OR MORE, it means that you must use at least one of something. Here is an example:

In Chapter 8, we discussed how you can use **whatis** to display a short description of a command, based on its entry in the online manual. When you use **whatis**, you must specify one or more command names as parameters. For instance:

```
whatis man cp
whatis man cp rm mv
```

The first example has two parameters; the second example has four parameters. Because the specifications of this command call for "one or more" names, we must include at least one — it is not optional.

The expression ZERO OR MORE, on the other hand, means that you can use one or more of something, but it is also okay to leave it out.

For instance, we said earlier that the **ls** command, along with the **-l** option, lists information about the files you specify. The exact format of the command requires you to specify zero or more file names. Here are three examples:

```
ls -l
ls -l file1
ls -l file1 file2 data1 data2
```

Whenever you see a specification that requires zero or more of something, you should ask, "What happens if I don't use any?" Frequently, there is a DEFAULT — an assumed value — that will be used.

With **ls**, the default is the set of files in your working directory (explained in Chapter 23). Thus, if you do not specify any file names — as in the first example — **ls** lists information on all the files in your working directory.

HINT

Whenever you can specify zero or more of something, ask: "What is the default?"

The Formal Description of a Command: Syntax

A good approach to learning a new command is to answer the following three questions:

- What does the command do?

- How do I use the options?

- How do I use the parameters?

You can learn what a command does by using the **man** command to look up the command in the online manual (see Chapter 8).

When you check the man page, you will see the exact, formal specification for using the command. This specification is called the command syntax. Informally, we can say that the syntax for a command is its "official" description.

The syntax that is used to describe Unix commands follows five simple rules:

1. Items in square brackets are optional.

2. Items not in square brackets are obligatory and must be entered as part of the command.

3. Anything in boldface must be typed exactly as written.

4. Anything in italics must be replaced by an appropriate value.

5. Any parameter that is followed by an ellipsis (...) may be repeated any number of times.

Here is an example to show how it all works.

The following is the syntax for the **ls** command on one particular Unix system:

ls [-aAcCdfFgilLqrRstu1] [*filename...*]

From looking at the syntax, what can we say about this command?

- The command has 18 different options. You can use **-a**, **-A**, **-c**, **-C** and so on. Since the options are optional, they are enclosed in square brackets.

- There is one parameter, *filename*. This parameter is optional, so it too is enclosed in square brackets.

- The name of the command and the options are printed in boldface. This means that they must be typed exactly as they appear.

- The parameter is in italics. This means that you must replace it with an appropriate value (in this case, the name of a file or a directory of files).

- The parameter is followed by "..."; this means that you can use more than one parameter (to specify the name of more than one file). Since the parameter is itself optional, we can be precise and say that you specify zero or more file names.

Based on this syntax, here are some valid **ls** commands. Remember, options can be typed separately or grouped together with a single – (minus) character.

```
ls
ls -l
ls file1
ls file1 file2 file3 file4 file5
ls -Fl file1 file2
ls -F -l file1 file2
```

Here are some invalid **ls** commands:

ls -lz file1 file2 (There is no **-z** option.)
ls file1 -l file2   (All options must precede the parameters.)

This last example is tricky and shows why you must follow the syntax exactly.

Unix expects the options first. Since the first argument (**file1**) does not begin with a – character, Unix assumes that this argument, and all the other arguments, are parameters. Thus, the **ls** program thinks you are specifying the names of three files: **file1**, **-1** and **file2**. Of course, there is no file named **-1**, so the results of this command will not be what you wanted.

Learning Command Syntax from the Unix Manual

When you read a printed manual, you will see boldface and italics as we described. However, when you use **man** to display the online manual on your terminal, you will not see any special typefaces. On some systems, the boldface and italics may be highlighted in some way. On other systems, you will have to be careful and deduce, from the context, which of the arguments are parameters. Usually, this is not difficult.

All man pages explain each option and parameter. However, some manuals use a simplified form of syntax in which all the options are represented by the word "options". Here is an example. Earlier we showed the syntax for the **ls** command:

ls [**-aAcCdfFgilLqrRstu1**] [*filename...*]

Using the simplified system, the syntax would be:

ls [**options**] [*filename...*]

In either case, each option would be explained separately as part of the description of the command.

How Can You Learn So Many Options?

You will have noticed that the example we have been using, the **ls** command, has 18 different options. How can you ever learn so many options? The answer is, you don't.

Nobody remembers all the options for every command they use. The best idea is to memorize only the most important options. When you need to use other options, look them up — that is what the online manual is for.

One of the characteristics of Unix programmers is that they tend to write programs with many options, most of which you can safely ignore. Moreover, it is not uncommon to find that different versions of Unix have different options for the same command.

The **ls** command we have been using is from one particular type of Unix. Other systems will have **ls** commands that have a different number of options. However, the most important options — the ones you will use most of the time — do not vary much from system to system.

In this book, we explain many Unix commands. We will make a point to describe only the most important options and parameters. When you feel a need to learn more about a command, check with the manual on your system. You will see the exact syntax and description that pertain to you.

As an example, here is the syntax for the **man** command we described in Chapter 8:

```
man [section] title...
man -f command-name...
man -k keyword...
```

Since this command can be used in three different ways, it is easiest to show three different syntax descriptions.

The first way to use **man** is with an optional *section* name and one or more *title* values. The second way uses the **-f** option and one or more *command-name* values. The third way uses the **-k** option and one or more *keyword* values.

These are not the only options that **man** uses, just the most important ones. On some systems, **man** has a large number of options. However, for most day-to-day work, **-f** and **-k** are the only ones you will need.

To conclude this chapter, here are two final examples. As we explained in Chapter 8, you can use the **whatis** command instead of **man -f**, and the **apropos** command instead of **man -k**. The syntax for these two commands is:

```
whatis command-name...
apropos keyword...
```

The syntax shows us that, to use either of these commands, you enter the command name followed by one or more parameters.

CHAPTER 10

The Shell

The program that reads and interprets your commands is called the "shell". From the beginning, Unix was designed so that the shell is an actual program separate from the main part of the operating system. Today, there are a number of shells in use. If your system has more than one shell, you can use the one you want.

In this chapter, we will answer the questions: What is a shell, and why is it important? What shells are there and which shell should you use? In the following two chapters we will discuss the two most popular shells: the C-Shell and the Korn shell. So read this chapter first, and then read either Chapter 11 (the C-Shell) or Chapter 12 (the Korn shell), whichever one pertains to you.

What Is a Shell?

Once you start using Unix, you will hear a lot of talk about the SHELL. Just what is this "shell" thing, anyway?

There are several answers.

The simplest answer is that the shell is a COMMAND PROCESSOR — a program that reads and interprets the commands you enter. Every time you type a Unix command, it is the shell that figures out what to do. Some shells offer facilities to make your minute-to-minute work more convenient. For instance, a shell may let you recall, edit, and re-enter previous commands. You may also be able to execute and control more than one program at a time.

Aside from being a command interpreter, the shell is also a programming language. You can write programs, called "scripts", for the shell to interpret. These scripts can contain regular Unix commands, as well as special shell programming commands. Each shell has its own programming language and rules.

However, neither of these explanations really captures the aura of *je ne sais quoi* — that certain something — that surrounds the idea of the shell. You see, the shell is your main interface into Unix. Using the facilities that are built into your shell, you can create a highly customized environment for yourself (although most people have no need to do so).

Moreover, since there are several shells, you may have a choice as to which interface you want to use. As you can imagine, there are all kinds of arguments among the cognoscenti as to which shells are best and which shells should be avoided at all costs.

HINT

Until you are an experienced Unix user, it does not really matter what shell you use.

Once you get used to Unix, you will understand the mysterious feeling people have for the shell. You can't see it or touch it, but it always there, ready to serve you by interpreting your commands and running your programs and scripts. (If you are a pantheist, all of this will make perfect sense.)

What's in a Name?   The Shell

There are three ways to think of the name "shell". First, the shell provides a well-defined interface to protect the internals of the operating system. In this sense, a Unix shell acts like the shell of an oyster, shielding its vulnerable parts from the harsh realities of the outside world.

Second, you can imagine the cross section of one of those sea shells that wind around and around in a spiral. With the Unix shell, you can pause what you are doing and start another shell or another program. Thus, you can put as many programs as you want on hold, each one "inside" its predecessor, just like the layers of the spiral.

However, the best way to think of the name "shell" is as a brand new word. Let the meaning come solely from your experience with Unix. The analogies to sea shells are somewhat far-fetched and can only lead to disillusionment and disappointment.

The Bourne Shell Family: `sh, ksh, bash, zsh, rc`

The earliest Unix shell that is still in use is the BOURNE SHELL. This shell is named after its primary developer, Steven Bourne of AT&T Bell Labs. A modern version of the Bourne shell — the original dates from the late 1970s — is available on every Unix system in the world. The Bourne shell is a command interpreter with its own programming language.

As we mentioned, shells are themselves programs. The name of the Bourne shell program is **sh**.

In the mid-1980s, another Bell Labs scientist, David Korn, created a replacement for the Bourne shell, called the Korn shell. The name of the Korn shell program is **ksh**.

The Korn shell is an upwards compatible extension to the Bourne shell. That is, anything that works with the Bourne shell will work with the Korn shell. In addition, the Korn shell provides four important features: a history file, command editing, aliasing, and job control. (We discuss the Korn shell in Chapter 12.)

The next member of the Bourne shell family is BASH, which stands for "the Bourne Again Shell". This shell was first released in 1989 and is the product of the Free Software Foundation. The primary authors were Brian Fox and Chet Ramey.

The Free Software Foundation is an organization dedicated to the proposition that all software should be freely available (at least to individuals). They have developed many widely used tools. Their project to develop an entire Unix system is called GNU. (GNU is a recursive acronym that stands for "GNU's Not Unix". GNU is pronounced, "guh-new", to rhyme with "canoe".)

Bash extends the capabilities of the basic Bourne shell in a manner similar to the Korn shell. The name of the Bash program is **bash**.

Another member of the Bourne shell family is the Zsh (pronounced "zee-shell"). This shell offers all of the important features of the other Unix shells, as well as new capabilities which are not widely available. For example, you can tell the Zsh to notify you when a particular userid has logged in.

The Zsh was developed by Paul Falstad in 1990. His philosophy was to "take everything interesting that I could get my hands on from every other shell". As he explains, "I wanted a shell that can do anything you want."

Within a short time of being released, the Zsh developed a cult following around the world and became popular among programmers and advanced Unix users. The name of the Zsh program is **zsh**.

Falstad created the shell when he was an undergraduate at Princeton University. Today, the Zsh program is maintained by various members of the worldwide Unix community.

The final member of the Bourne shell family is **rc**. This shell was developed by Tom Duff of Bell Labs to replace the Bourne shell as part of a project called Plan 9 (an experimental operating/networking system). Another programmer, Byron Rakitzis, wrote a more portable version of rc that has been implemented on many different systems (the original rc runs only on two versions of Unix). As you would imagine, the name of the rc program is **rc**.

The idea behind rc was to create a small, elegant shell that eliminated all the technical shortcomings of the Bourne shell. Conceptually, rc is much more manageable than any of the other shells: it is actuallly possible for a knowledgeable person to understand thoroughly the entire shell and its programming language (which is based on the C language).

Since rc is small, it does not have some of the advanced features that you find in other shells, such as job control and command line editing (although the latter can be implemented as an add-on). However, if you are a purist with a computer science background, you will love rc.

The C-Shell Family: `csh`, `tcsh`

There are two members of the C-Shell family. The first is the C-Shell itself, written by Bill Joy (who was a student at the University of California at Berkeley). The C-Shell was designed to be the Berkeley Unix alternative to the Bourne shell which, at the time, was the standard shell. The name of the C-Shell program is `csh`.

Like all shells, the C-Shell is a command interpreter that offers a programming language. In addition, the C-Shell offers many advantages over the Bourne shell, including a history mechanism, aliasing, and job control. (We discuss the C-Shell in Chapter 11.) The C-Shell is very popular among experienced Unix users, especially at universities and research organizations, where it is often the default shell.

The other member of the C-Shell family is the Tcsh (pronounced "Tee See Shell"). The development of the Tcsh was started in the late 1970s by Ken Greer at Carnegie-Mellon University and carried on in the 1980s by Paul Placeway at Ohio State. Since then, many people have contributed to the shell, which is distributed over the worldwide Internet network. The Tcsh is maintained primarily by a group at Cornell University.

This shell is an enhanced C-Shell that offers a constellation of advanced features. We won't describe all the details here, but if you are an experienced user, you may want to check out the Tcsh manual page. The name of the Tcsh program is `tcsh`.

What's in a Name?   *C-Shell, Tcsh*

The developer of the C-Shell designed its programming facilities to work like the C programming language. Thus, the name C-Shell (which is also a pun on "seashell").

The "T" in the name Tcsh stands for Tenex, an operating system used on the old PDP-10 computers. The original work that led to the Tcsh was done on a Tenex system.

For reference, the table in Figure 10-1 shows each shell along with the name of its program. To display the reference manual for a shell, use the **man** command with the name of the appropriate program. For example, **man csh**.

SHELL	NAME OF THE PROGRAM
Bash	`bash`
Bourne Shell	`sh`
C-Shell	`csh`
Korn Shell	`ksh`
rc	`rc`
Tcsh	`tcsh`
Zsh	`zsh`

FIGURE 10-1.   *The Unix shells*

What Shell Should You Use?

We have described seven different shells, all of which are in widespread use: the Bourne shell, the Korn shell, Bash, the Zsh, the C-Shell and the Tcsh.

Worldwide, the most widely used shells are the Bourne shell and its replacement, the Korn shell. However, in the academic, research and programming communities, the C-Shell is the most popular shell. (Although there are significant numbers of people who use Bash, the Zsh, rc, and the Tcsh).

The Tcsh is designed to be upwards compatible with the C-Shell. This means that if you ignore the extra features, everything works just the same as the C-Shell.

Similarly, both the Korn shell and Bash are upwards compatible with the Bourne shell. On many systems, the Korn shell is the default and veteran Bourne shell users don't even notice a difference.

Remember, though, a shell has two main purposes: to act as a command processor and to provide a programming language for shell scripts. As a command processor, the C-Shell family provides a good all-around working environment. However, the programming language used by the Bourne shell family is easier and more pleasant to use than the C-Shell language.

Thus, many people use the C-Shell as a command processor, for minute-to-minute work, but write their shell scripts for the Bourne shell. So, here is our advice: Use the C-Shell or Korn shell as your principal shell, but use the Bourne shell to execute your scripts. (On many systems, these choices are the default.) Once you become an experienced Unix user, look at the documentation for Bash, the Zsh, rc, and the Tcsh, and see if the extra features appeal to you.

What's in a Name? C

Both the C-Shell and the Tcsh are named after the C programming language. But how did such an odd name arise for a language?

In 1963, a language called CPL was developed in England during a project involving researchers from Cambridge and the University of London. CPL stood for "Combined Programming Language" and was based on Algol 60, one of the first well-designed modern programming languages.

Four years later, in 1967, a programmer at Cambridge named Martin Richards created BCPL, "Basic CPL". BCPL itself gave rise to yet another language, known by the single letter, B.

The B language was taken to Bell Labs, where Ken Thompson and Dennis Ritchie made modifications and renamed it NB. In the early 1970s, Thompson (the original Unix developer) used NB to rewrite the basic part of Unix for its second edition. Up to then, all of Unix had been written in assembly language. Not long afterwards, the NB language was extended and renamed C. C soon became the language of choice for writing new utilities, applications and even the operating system itself.

You might ask, where did the name C come from? Was it the next letter after B in the alphabet, or was it the second letter of BCPL? This has philological implications of cosmic importance: would the successor to C be named D or P?

The question proved to be moot when, in the early 1980s, Bjarne Stroustrup (also of Bell Labs) designed the most popular extension of C, which he called C++ (pronounced C-plus-plus).

In the C language, "++" is an operator that adds 1 to a variable. For instance, to add 1 to the variable "total" you can use the command "total++". Thus, C++ is one of those wonderful programming puns that make people scratch their heads and wonder if Man is really Nature's last word.

HINT
Use the C-Shell or Korn shell as your principal shell, but use the Bourne shell to execute your scripts.

How complex are each of the shells? A complicated program will have extra features and capabilities, but it will also demand more of your time to master. Moreover, like a lot of Unix programs, the shells have many esoteric features and options that you will never really need. These extra facilities are often a distraction.

One crude way to measure the complexity of a program is by looking at the length of the documentation. The table in Figure 10-2 shows the number of bytes (characters) in the manual pages for each of the shells. For comparison, we have also normalized the numbers, assigning the smallest a value of 1.0. (Of course, these numbers change from time to time as new versions of the documentation are released.)

From these numbers, it is easy to see why the C-Shell provides a nice middle ground between the older, less capable Bourne shell and the other, more complex shells. (The rc shell is relatively small and simple, but it is not distributed as a standard shell.)

Of course, someone may argue that the more complicated shells are all upwards compatible, either with the Bourne shell or the C-Shell. If you don't want the added features, you can ignore them and they won't bother you.

However, you must remember that documentation is important. The manual pages for the more complex shells take a long time to read and are much more difficult to understand. Even the manual page for the Bourne shell is too large to peruse comfortably.

Changing Your Shell Temporarily

By default, you will be assigned a shell to start automatically whenever you log in. If you want to change your shell, you can do so in two ways.

NAME OF SHELL	SIZE OF MAN PAGE (BYTES)	RELATIVE COMPLEXITY
rc	37,885	1.00
Bourne Shell	44,500	1.17
C-Shell	76,816	2.03
Bash	127,361	3.36
Zsh	133,565	3.53
Korn Shell	141,391	3.73
Tcsh	199,834	5.27

Note: All the manual pages are self-contained except for the Tcsh. This page is actually a large addendum, describing only those extra features that are not part of the C-Shell. In this table, the number for the Tcsh includes the C-Shell documentation. The Tcsh manual page on its own is 123,018 bytes.

FIGURE 10-2.   *The relative complexity of the different shells*

When you log in, the shell that Unix starts automatically is called your LOGIN SHELL. From the shell prompt, you can start a new shell any time you want simply by entering the name of that shell (see Figure 10-1). For example, say that you are using the C-Shell and you want to try out the Korn shell. Enter:

ksh

(Of course, the new shell must be available on your system.)

The original login shell will put itself on hold and execute the Korn shell. This is exactly the same as when you enter a command to run a program. After all, a shell is just a program.

When you are finished with the new shell, you can stop it. Either enter the **exit** command or press **^D**, the **eof** key (see Chapter 6). When the new shell is finished, the old shell will restart and wait for a new command.

One point to remember is that you can only log out from the original shell. If you have started one or more new shells, you must back out to the login shell before you can end your work session.

Changing Your Default Shell: **chsh**

Unix maintains a password file of userids to keep track of who is allowed to log in to the system. Each userid has one entry in the password file. Within this entry, Unix keeps the name of the shell to start when that userid logs in.

If you want to change your default shell, use the **chsh** command. The syntax is:

chsh *userid name-of-shell*

When you specify the shell, you are really telling Unix what program to run. As part of this specification, you must include the name of the directory that contains the shell program. (We will discuss directories in Chapter 23.) This is called the "pathname" of the program.

On most systems, the shells are contained in the **/bin** directory. For reference, the table in Figure 10-3 shows the pathname of each shell program, assuming that they are in this directory. On your system, though, one or more of the shells may be in a different directory, and you will have to modify the specification accordingly.

On many systems, the list of all the available shells is kept in a file called **/etc/shells**. You can display this file by using the command:

more /etc/shells

(The **more** command is explained in Chapter 18.)

SHELL	FULL NAME
Bash	**/bin/bash**
Bourne Shell	**/bin/sh**
C-Shell	**/bin/csh**
Korn Shell	**/bin/ksh**
rc	**/bin/rc**
Tcsh	**/bin/tcsh**
Zsh	**/bin/zsh**

FIGURE 10-3.   *The full pathname of each shell*

Here is a quick example. You want to change your default shell to the Korn shell, which, on your system, is in the **/bin** directory. Your userid is **harley**. Enter the following command:

chsh harley /bin/ksh

On some systems, you can enter the command name by itself:

chsh

and Unix will prompt you to enter the name of the new shell. You may also be shown a list of all the available shells. Try it and see how it works on your system.

When you use **chsh**, you are making a change to your password file. Thus, the change will not take effect until the next time you log in (just like when you change your password).

NOTE
On some systems, the **chsh** command will not be enabled and you may have to ask your system manager to help you.

CHAPTER 11

Using the C-Shell

This chapter describes the most important features of the C-Shell. If you are using a different shell, the principles will be more or less the same although the exact particulars may differ. If you are using the Korn shell, read Chapter 12 instead of this chapter.

Many people do not take enough time to learn how to use the shell well. This is a mistake. To be sure, the shell has many features you really do not need to understand. However, there are a handful of fundamental ideas that are of great practical value.

The time you spend reading this chapter will repay you well. You will find that the skills you learn here will save you a lot of time in your day-to-day work. There are many topics in this chapter, and you don't need to understand them all immediately. Just read the chapter once so you know what is available. As you become more experienced, you can reread parts of the chapter as you need them.

If, after reading this chapter, you decide that you want to know more details, check the C-Shell manual page (**man csh**). This is the ultimate reference as to how the shell works on your particular system.

Shell Variables That Act as Switches: set, unset

One of the ways the shell lets you customize your working environment is by using SHELL VARIABLES. A shell variable is an item, known by a name, that represents a value of some type. As the term "variable" implies, the value of a shell variable can be changed.

There are two types of shell variables. First, there are variables that act as off/on switches. Second, there are variables that store a particular value as a string of characters.

You can create your own shell variables, but, unless you write programs, you will usually make do with the ones that are built in. Figure 11-1 shows the predefined shell variables that act as switches. (Your list of variables may vary slightly, depending on the version of your C-Shell.) Don't worry if you don't understand what all these variables do; this list is for reference. By the time you learn enough to care about using a variable, you will understand its purpose.

VARIABLE NAME	PURPOSE
echo	display each command before execution
filec	enable file name completion
ignoreeof	must log out with **logout** rather than **eof** key (**^D**)
nobeep	no beep, command completion has ambiguous file name
noclobber	do not allow redirected output to replace a file
noglob	inhibit expansion of file names
nonomatch	no error if file name expansion matches nothing
notify	notify about job completions at any time
verbose	display full command after history substitution

Note: The name **nonomatch** is spelled correctly.

FIGURE 11-1. *Built-in shell variables: switches*

To turn on switch variables, use the **set** command. The syntax is:

set [*variable-name*]

For example, to turn on the **ignoreeof** switch, enter:

set ignoreeof

To turn off a switch, use **unset**. For example:

unset ignoreeof

To display all the shell variables and their current settings, enter the command with no arguments:

set

If a variable is set, its name will appear in the list. If a variable is unset, its name will not appear.

Shell Variables That Store Values: `set`

Aside from shell variables that act as off/on switches, there are variables that store values. Some of these values can be set by you to modify the shell's behavior. Other values are set by the shell to pass information to you.

Figure 11-2 shows the predefined shell variables that store values, along with their uses; don't worry if you don't understand them all. (Your list of variables may vary slightly, depending on the version of your C-Shell.) Whenever you log in, the shell automatically initializes the **argv**, **cwd**, **home**, **path**, **prompt**, **shell** and **status** variables.

To set a variable of this type, use the **set** command with the following syntax:

set [*variable-name* **=** *value*]

For example, to set the **history** variable to the value "50", use:

set history = 50

To display all the variables and their values, use:

set

VARIABLE NAME	PURPOSE
argv	list of arguments for current command
cdpath	directories to search to find a subdirectory
cwd	pathname of current working directory
fignore	suffixes to ignore during file name completion
hardpath	no symbolic link pathnames in directory stack
histchars	the two characters used for history substitution
history	size of the history list
home	pathname of your home directory
mail	pathnames where shell should check for mail
path	list of directories to search for programs
prompt	string of characters to use for command prompt
savehist	number of history lines to save upon logout
shell	pathname of the shell program
status	return status of last command
term	type of terminal you are using
time	threshold value for reporting of command timing
user	name of the userid currently logged in

FIGURE 11-2. *Built-in shell variables that store values*

On occasion, you may want to give a variable a value that contains spaces, punctuation or other special characters. In that case, you must put single quotes around the value. For example:

```
set prompt = 'nipper% '
```

Another alternative is to assign a value of a variable that is a list of words, by enclosing the list in parentheses. The most important example of this occurs when you are setting the **path** variable (discussed in detail later in the chapter).

As an example, here is a **set** command that defines the value of the **path** variable to be a list of four words: **/usr/local/bin**, **/bin**, **/usr/bin** and **/bin**.

```
set path = ( /usr/local/bin /bin /usr/bin ~/bin )
```

Displaying the Value of a Variable: `echo`

We mentioned that you can use the **set** command to display the names and values of all your shell variables. If you only want to display the values of one or more variables, you can use the **echo** command. This command simply displays the value of anything you give it. For example, if you enter:

`echo I think that Unix is a lot of fun`

You will see:

`I think that Unix is a lot of fun`

(which is true...)

To display the value of a variable, use its name preceded by a dollar sign (**$**) character. For example, to display the value of the **term** variable, enter:

`echo $term`

If the value of this variable is, say, "vt100", you will see:

`vt100`

Of course, you can combine this with anything you want. For instance, you can display a more informative message:

`echo The terminal type is $term`

If the value of **term** is as shown above, you will see:

`The terminal type is vt100`

If you want to display punctuation characters, you must place them within double quotes. For example:

`echo "Working directory is $cwd; home directory is $home."`

Although the **echo** command can be useful to check on one or more variables, it is usually easier to simply use the **set** command and ignore the variables you don't want. The real use for the **echo** command is to display informative messages within shell scripts. (Shell scripts, discussed later in the chapter, are programs written in the shell's own programming language.)

Even if you are not a programmer, you might want to use some **echo** commands in your **.login** initialization file (which we also discuss later in the chapter). For example, you might place the following command in your **.login** file:

```
echo "Hi. Welcome to Unix."
```

This way, you will see a nice message each time you log in.

Environment Variables: `setenv`, `printenv`

The shell variables we have just described are used only within the shell to control preferences and settings. However, there is a whole other set of variables that the shell maintains for passing values between programs. These are called ENVIRONMENT VARIABLES or GLOBAL VARIABLES.

By convention, environment variables have uppercase names. Figure 11-3 shows the most common environment variables; don't worry if you don't understand them all. (The variables on your system may differ slightly.)

VARIABLE NAME	PURPOSE
EDITOR	pathname of your text editor
HOME	pathname of your home directory
LOGNAME	name of the userid currently logged in
MAIL	pathname of your mail program
MANPATH	list of directories to search for manual pages
PAGER	name of paging program you prefer (Chapter 18)
PATH	list of directories to search for programs
SHELL	pathname of the shell program
TERM	type of terminal you are using
USER	name of the userid currently logged in

Note: Some versions of the C-Shell use only **USER** and not **LOGNAME**.

FIGURE 11-3. *Common environment variables*

The value of a global variable is available to any program or shell. For example, many programs look at the **TERM** variable to see what type of terminal you are using. If this variable is not set correctly, the output may not be displayed properly.

> **HINT**
> Some programs cannot display their output properly unless they know exactly what type of terminal you are using. If a program that uses the full screen for output—such as the **vi** editor or **more**—displays its output in a strange manner, make sure that your **TERM** variable is set correctly.

To set the value of an environment variable, use the **setenv** command. The syntax is:

setenv [*variable-name value*]

Notice that, unlike the **set** command, you do not use an equals sign. For example, to set the name of your terminal to **vt100**, use:

setenv TERM vt100

To display the value of one or more environment variables, use the **printenv** command. The syntax is:

printenv [*variable-name*]

If you enter the command with no parameters:

printenv

it will display all the environment variables. To display the value of a single variable, there are two choices. You can use **printenv** with the name of the variable, such as:

printenv TERM

or you can use **echo** with the syntax:

echo $*variable-name*

such as:

■ `echo $TERM`

Another way to display all the environment variables is to use **setenv** with no parameters:

■ `setenv`

However, do not try to display a single variable with **setenv**. If you were to enter, say:

■ `setenv TERM`

it would not display the value of **TERM**. Rather, it would set **TERM** to a null value.

How Environment and Shell Variables Are Connected

There are six common shell variables that have the same names as environment variables (except that environment variables have uppercase names). The shell variables are **home**, **mail**, **path**, **shell**, **term** and **user**. We can divide these variables into three groups.

First, **home** and **shell** contain information that is stored as part of your userid profile. **home** contains the pathname of your home directory; **shell** contains the pathname of the shell program you use.

(A pathname is an exact description of the location of a file or directory. The home directory is where you store your personal files. We will discuss these ideas in detail in Chapter 23.)

Whenever you log in, Unix automatically sets the values of **home** and **shell** (and **HOME** and **SHELL**). Your programs will examine these variables from time to time, but you will probably never need to change them yourself.

The next group of shell variables—**term**, **path** and **user**—also have global variable analogs. The difference is that these local variables are tied to the corresponding global variables. Whenever you change the shell variable, the shell will automatically update the global variable.

Later in the chapter, we will explain how you specify initialization commands in two special files, named **.cshrc** and **.login**. Within these files you will set the values of **term** and **path**. You will not have to set **TERM** and **PATH**, because they are updated automatically.

Try this. Display the value of **term** and **TERM** by entering:

```
echo $term; echo $TERM
```

Now change the value of **term**:

```
set term=hello
```

Redisplay both variables:

```
echo $term; echo $TERM
```

Notice that the value of **TERM** has been updated automatically. (When you are finished, don't forget to set **term** back to its original value.)

Note: The bond between **HOME**, **TERM** and **USER**, and **home**, **term** and **user** only works in one direction. Changing the environment variable does *not* change the shell variable. So changing **TERM** does not change **term**.

The final shell variable we'll mention is **mail**. There is a global variable named **MAIL**, but it has a different meaning, so **mail** and **MAIL** are not connected. (See Figures 11-2 and 11-3).

Commands That Are Built into the Shell

When you enter a command, the shell breaks the command line into parts that it analyzes. We say that the shell PARSES the command. The first part of each command is the name, the other parts are options or parameters (see Chapter 9).

After parsing the command, the shell decides what to do with it. There are two possibilities. Some commands are internal to the shell; this means that the shell can interpret the command directly. The table in Figure 11-4 shows the various shells and the number of commands that are built in.

If you want to see a full list of all the built-in commands, check the C-Shell manual page (use the command **man csh**). This is the place to look for help with such commands. All the other commands will be separate programs with their own manual pages.

HINT

If you are looking for help for a particular command and you can't find it in the manual, check with the documentation for your shell: the command may be internal.

NAME OF SHELL	INTERNAL COMMANDS
rc	15
Bourne shell	32
Korn shell	43
Bash	50
C-Shell	52
Tcsh	56
Zsh	73

FIGURE 11-4. *The number of internal commands in each shell*

The Search Path

If a command is not built into the shell—and most commands are not—the shell must find the appropriate program to execute.

For example, when you enter the **date** command, the shell must find the **date** program. The shell then starts the program and puts itself on hold. When the program finishes, the shell regains control. It is now ready for you to enter another command.

The **path** variable tells the shell where to look for programs. The value of **path** is a series of directory names called the SEARCH PATH. (We will discuss directories in Chapter 23. Basically, a directory holds a collection of files.)

When the shell is looking for a program to execute, it checks each directory in the search path in the order they are specified. As soon as the shell finds the program, it stops the search and executes the program. Thus, you should specify the directory names in the order you want them to be searched.

Here is a typical **set** command to define a search path:

```
set path = ( /usr/local/bin /usr/ucb /bin /usr/bin ~/bin )
```

This command sets the **path** shell variable's value to be a list of five directories. Each of these directories is a place where programs are kept.

The names will make more sense after we cover directories in Chapter 23. For now, all we will say is that **bin** is often used to indicate a directory that holds programs, and the tilde (~) character is an abbreviation for the name of your home directory. In other words, **~/bin** indicates a directory that holds programs that lie within your home directory. The **/usr/ucb** directory holds programs specific to Berkeley Unix. (**ucb** stands for University of California at Berkeley.)

If you are a programmer, you may find it convenient to have the shell also check your working directory when it looks for a program. (The term "working directory" refers to the directory in which you are currently working.) To do this, add the dot (`.`) character to the search path:

```
set path = ( . /usr/local/bin /usr/ucb /bin /usr/bin ~/bin )
```

Remember, you can place the entries in any order you want. In this case, Unix will search your working directory before it searches any other directories.

For example, say that you create a program and name it **date**. You are working in the directory that holds this program, and you enter:

```
date
```

What happens?

First the shell checks to see if this an internal command. The answer is no, so the shell starts searching for a program named **date**. Since the search path tells the shell to check your working directory first, it finds and executes your program named **date**, not the Unix **date** command (which is in the **/bin** directory).

Now, suppose you had defined the search path with your working directory after **/bin**:

```
set path = ( /usr/local/bin /usr/ucb /bin /usr/bin . ~/bin )
```

In this case, the shell will find the Unix **date** command first (in **/bin**).

A detailed discussion of search paths is beyond the scope of this book (and not all that necessary). Normally, you can accept the search path that is set up for you by default. The only thing you must remember is that if you modify the search path, order is important.

One final note: as we mentioned earlier, the shell automatically copies the value of **path** to the environment variable **PATH**. This allows any program to look at your search path. (Remember, programs can only examine environment variables, not shell variables.) However, if you display the value of **PATH**, you will see that its format is slightly different from **path**. This is to maintain compatibility with the older Bourne shell.

The value of **PATH** is not a word list; rather, it is one long string of characters in which the various directory names are separated by colons. The working directory is specified by an empty directory name, not by a dot (`.`).

For example, if you wanted to explicitly set **PATH** to have the value of **path** in our last example, you would use:

```
setenv PATH /usr/local/bin:/usr/ucb:/bin:/usr/bin::~/bin
```

The empty directory name (the working directory) is specified by the two colons in a row. If the working directory were at the end of the list, the character string would end in a colon:

```
setenv PATH /usr/local/bin:/usr/ucb:/bin:/usr/bin:~/bin:
```

The Shell Prompt

As we explained in Chapter 4, the shell displays a prompt whenever it is ready for you to enter a command. By default, the C-Shell displays a percent character:

```
%
```

while the Korn shell and Bourne shell display a dollar sign:

```
$
```

As we will see in a moment, most people set up their prompt to include other information. However, it is customary to always include either the **%** or **$** character to remind you which type of shell you are using.

The C-Shell uses the value of the shell variable **prompt** as its command prompt. Thus, you can change your prompt to whatever you want by setting the value of this variable. (This is also true for the other shells.)

Here is an example. You are in the habit of logging in remotely to various computers on your network, and you want to use a different, unique prompt with each system to remind you where you are.

Say that one of the systems is named **nipper**. On that system, you can set your prompt as follows:

```
set prompt = 'nipper% '
```

(Remember, if you assign a value that contains spaces or punctuation, you must enclose it in single quotes.) For a system named **princess**, you can use:

```
set prompt = 'princess% '
```

Later in the chapter, we will discuss history substitution. When we do, you will see that it is useful to have a value called the "event number" as part of the prompt. (The event number is a value that is increased by 1 every time you enter a new command. This value is used to identify specific commands that you have already entered.)

To display the event number within a prompt, use an exclamation point (**!**). Whenever the shell displays the prompt, it will replace the **!** with the current event number.

When you use an **!** in a **set** command, there is one point you need to remember. As you will see later, the **!** has a special meaning on the command line. When you set the prompt, you must take precautions to make sure the **!** is interpreted correctly.

Let's say that you want your prompt to be the name **nipper**, followed by a space, followed by the event number in square brackets, followed by a percent sign, followed by a space. If you were to enter the command:

```
set prompt = 'nipper [!]% '
```

the **!** would retain its special meaning and the command would fail. You need to precede the **!** with a backslash (****). A backslash tells the shell, "Interpret the next character literally", the backslash itself is ignored. So the correct command would be:

```
set prompt = 'nipper [\!]% '
```

If, for example, the value of the event number happens to be 21, the prompt will be:

```
nipper [21]%
```

When you enter a new command, the event number changes to 22 and the prompt will be:

```
nipper [22]%
```

Setting Up History Substitution: `history`

After you use Unix for awhile, you will know the frustration of having to type a command over and over because of spelling mistakes. There are two mechanisms that the C-Shell provides to make it easier to enter commands: history substitution and aliasing. These features are one reason why many people prefer to use the C-Shell over the Bourne shell. We will discuss each feature briefly. For more information, see the C-Shell manual page (use the command **man csh**).

HISTORY SUBSTITUTION is a feature that lets you change and re-enter a previous command without having to retype it. History substitution in the C-Shell has many esoteric rules and features. If you know them all, that's great; you will have enormous facility in recycling your commands. However, most people just memorize and use a few of the simpler features: the ones we will describe in this section.

At all times, the shell saves your commands in a list called the HISTORY LIST. Each command is given an identification number, starting at 1. Whenever you enter a command, the identification number increases by 1. Thus, you can refer to command number 6, or command number 46, and so on.

You determine how long the history list should be—that is, how many commands the shell should save—by setting the shell variable named **history**. For example, to tell the shell to save the last 50 commands, enter:

```
set history = 50
```

If the **history** variable is not set, the shell, by default, will save only the last command. For many people, this may be enough.

To display the history list, use the **history** command. The syntax is:

```
history [-r] [number]
```

If you enter the command with no arguments:

```
history
```

the shell will display the entire history list. Here is some sample output:

```
21   ls
22   datq
23   datw
24   date
25   history
```

If you specify a number, the shell will display only that many commands. For example:

```
history 3
```

might display:

```
24   date
25   history
26   history 3
```

If you use the **-r** option, the shell will display the commands in reverse order (most recent first). For example:

```
history -r
```

might display:

```
27   history -r
26   history 3
25   history
24   date
23   datw
```

Notice that every command you enter is added to the history list, including commands with mistakes, as well as the **history** commands themselves.

Displaying the history list is important for two reasons. First, as we will describe in a moment, you can edit and recall previous commands. Second, you can check back and see what commands you have already entered. ("Did I really delete all those files?") If you think that you may want to keep a long record of your work, you should set the **history** variable to a large number, say, 100.

In the world of the C-Shell, past commands are referred to as EVENTS. (That should make you feel important every time you enter a command.) The number that identifies each command is called an EVENT NUMBER. If you decide to use history substitution, you will find it handy to display the current event number as part of your prompt. We explained how to do this in the section on the shell prompt. Here is an example:

```
set prompt = 'nipper [\!]% '
```

This prompt displays a reminder that you are using a system named **nipper**, followed by the current event number (in square brackets) and a percent sign. A sample prompt might be:

```
nipper [24]%
```

Using History Substitution

The C-Shell supports a large variety of complex substitutions. In this section, we will discuss the simplest, most useful substitutions. For more details, see the C-Shell manual page (**man csh**).

The two most useful substitutions use **! !** and **^ ^**. To reuse the previous command, exactly as you typed it, enter:

```
!!
```

The shell will redisplay and then execute this command.

To replace a string of characters in the previous command, type **^**, followed by the characters you want to replace, followed by another **^**, followed by the new characters. Here is an example. You want to use the **date** command to display the time and date, but you accidentally enter:

```
datxq
```

You can correct the command by entering:

```
^xq^e
```

HINT
If you remember nothing else about history substitution, make sure to memorize how to use **! !** and **^^**.

To reuse an older command, use an **!** followed by the event number for that command. For example, say that the history list is:

```
21   ls
22   datq
23   datw
24   date
25   history
```

If you enter:

```
!24
```

the shell will re-execute the **date** command.

It is also possible to add characters to the end of a command. For example, event number 21 is the **ls** command, which lists the names of files. As we will see in Chapter 23, **ls** with no arguments displays the names of all the files in your current directory. However, if you want to display only those names that begin with the letters "temp", you can use **ls temp***. We can reuse event number 21 to create this new command by entering:

```
!21 temp*
```

To reuse a command that begins with a particular pattern, enter **!** followed by that pattern. For example, to reuse the last command that began with **ls**, enter:

```
!ls
```

If you need to use certain commands repeatedly, this facility can really come in handy. For example, say that you are working on a C program named **summary.c**. You use the **vi** text editor to modify the program. After each modification, you use the **cc** command to recompile the program. The two commands you will be using are:

```
vi summary.c
cc summary.c
```

Once you enter the commands for the first time, you can refer to them as **!v** and **!c**, respectively. This makes it easy to go back and forth from one command to the other.

You can also reference a command by specifying a pattern within question marks (**?**). The shell will execute the last command that contained this pattern. For example, you can reuse the command **ls temp*** by entering:

```
!?temp?
```

As you can see, most history substitutions begin with an **!** character. Whenever the shell sees such a character in a command line, it assumes you are referring to some type of event. If you want to use a command that contains a real **!**, you must put a backslash (****) in front of it. This tells the shell that the **!** is not part of a history substitution. (The shell will ignore the backslash itself.) We saw this earlier when we used the **set** command to redefine the command prompt:

```
set prompt = 'nipper [\!]% '
```

History Substitution Example: Avoid Deleting the Wrong Files

The final substitution we will explain uses an exclamation point followed by an asterisk (**!***). This combination stands for everything on the command line after the name of the command.

For example, say that you have just entered:

```
ls temp* extra?
```

You can enter a new command and use **!*** to stand for **temp* extra?**.

Most of the time, such substitutions are complicated and not worth the effort. However, there is one case in which using **!*** is invaluable.

As we will discuss in Chapter 24, the **rm** (remove) command will delete files. When you use **rm**, you can specify patterns to stand for lists of files. For example, the pattern **temp*** stands for any file name that begins with **temp** followed by zero or more characters; the pattern **extra?** refers to any file name that starts with **extra** followed by a single character.

The danger with **rm** is that once you delete a file it is gone for good. If you discover that you have made a mistake and erased the wrong file—even the instant after you press the RETURN key—there is no way to get the file back.

Now, let's say that you want to delete a set of files with the names **temp**, **temp_backup**, **extra1** and **extra2**. You are thinking about entering the command:

```
rm temp* extra?
```

However, you have forgotten that you also have an important file called **temp.important**. If you enter the preceding command, this file will also be deleted.

A better strategy is to first enter the **ls** command using the patterns that you propose to use with **rm**:

```
ls temp* extra?
```

This will list the names of all the files that match these patterns. If this list contains a file that you have forgotten, such as **temp.important**, you will not enter the **rm** command as planned. If, however, the list of files is what you expected, you can go ahead and remove the files by entering:

```
rm !*
```

You may ask, why do I need to use **!*** ? Now that I have confirmed that the patterns match the files I want, couldn't I just type the **rm** command using those patterns?

The answer is, when you use **!*** you are guaranteed to get what you want. If you retype the patterns, you may make a typing mistake and, in spite of all your precautions, end up deleting the wrong files.

To make the whole process easier, you can use an alias, as you will see in the next section.

Command Aliasing: `alias, unalias`

An ALIAS is a name that you give to a command or list of commands. You can then type the name of the alias instead of the commands.

For example, say that you often find yourself entering the following command:

```
ls -l temp*
```

If you give the command an alias of **lt**, you can enter it more simply by typing:

```
lt
```

To create an alias, use the **alias** command. The syntax is:

```
alias [name [command]]
```

Here is an example in which we create the alias we just mentioned:

```
alias lt 'ls -l temp*'
```

As you can see, we enclosed the command in single quotes. Certain punctuation characters (such as *****) have special meanings to the shell. The single quotes tell the shell to treat the characters literally. This is a good idea when you specify an alias for any command that has punctuation. Here is an example that creates an alias for a list of two commands:

```
alias info 'date; who'
```

You can now enter **info** to find out the time and date, and then check who is logged in to the system. One of the most useful aliases is:

```
alias a alias
```

This allows you to use **a** instead of typing the whole word "alias". For example, once you define this alias, you can enter:

```
a info 'date; who'
```

Another useful alias, along the same lines, is to define **h** to stand for the **history** command:

```
alias h history
```

If you want to check the current value of an alias, enter the **alias** command with a name only. For example:

```
alias info
```

If you want to display all the aliases, enter the command name by itself, with no arguments:

```
alias
```

To remove an alias, use the **unalias** command. The syntax is:

```
unalias alias-name
```

For example, to remove the alias we just defined, use:

```
unalias info
```

Using Arguments with an Alias

When you use an alias, you can add arguments (options and parameters) to the end of the command line. (These terms are explained in Chapter 9.) Here is an example.
  The **ls** command lists the names of files. When you use the **-l** option, **ls** displays a "long" listing with extra information. Many people use the following alias to make it easy to use **ls -l** (which is easy to mis-type):

```
alias ll ls -l
```

By default, **ls** lists all the files in your working directory (explained in Chapter 23). Thus, you can display a long listing of all such files by entering:

```
ll
```

If you want information only on certain files, you specify their names as parameters. For example:

```
ls -l myfile yourfile
```

Using our alias, you can enter:

```
ll myfile yourfile
```

The shell replaces the **ll** alias and then tacks the parameters onto the end of the command.

If you want to insert arguments into the middle of an alias, you can refer to them as **!***, just as we did with history substitution. (In fact, many of the history substitutions work with aliases. See the C-Shell manual page for details.) However, you must remember to put a backslash (****) before the **!** so the shell does not interpret it as an event specification. This is true even if you use single quotes.

The following example shows how this works. The alias **lld** displays long listings for the files you specify, and then displays the time and date.

```
alias lld 'ls -l \!*; date'
```

So now, if you enter:

```
lld myfile yourfile
```

the shell replaces it with:

```
ls -l myfile yourfile; date
```

Alias Example: Keeping Track of Your Working Directory

Here is an example that uses the concepts from the previous section to produce a particularly useful alias.

In Chapter 23, we will explain the idea of a working directory. Briefly, directories contain files, and, at any time, the particular directory you are working within is called your "working directory". To change your working directory, you use the **cd** (change directory) command. (This is also discussed in Chapter 23.)

To use the **cd** command, you specify the name of the directory to which you want to change. For example, to change to a directory named **bin**, you would use:

```
cd bin
```

To display the name of your working directory, you use the **pwd** (print working directory) command. (Don't worry about the details right now.)

If you change directories a lot, you will find that it is easy to lose track of where you are. However, it is a bother to type **pwd** repeatedly. As an alternative, we will develop an alias to display an automatic reminder whenever you use **cd** to change your working directory.

If you refer to Figure 11-2, the table of built-in shell variables, you will see a variable named **cwd**. At all times, this variable contains the name of your current working directory. You can display the contents of **cwd** by using:

```
echo $cwd
```

What we want to do is issue this **echo** command every time we change directories. To do so, we will alias the **cd** command to two separate commands: a **cd** command followed by the **echo** command:

```
alias cd 'cd \!*; echo $cwd'
```

Now, whenever we change directories, we will know exactly where we are.

Alias Example: Avoid Deleting the Wrong Files

In this section, we will show you how to combine an alias with a history substitution to produce an exceptionally handy tool.

Earlier in the chapter, we showed how to use the **ls** command to check which file names would be matched by a particular set of patterns. We performed this check before using those same patterns with the **rm** (remove) command to delete files. This allowed us to make sure that the files we removed were the ones we meant to remove. This is important because once Unix deletes a file it is gone forever.

The example we used deleted the files that match the patterns **temp*** and **extra?**. First, we checked what files these patterns match by entering:

```
ls temp* extra?
```

If the results were what we expected, we entered:

```
rm !*
```

to delete using the exact same pattern.

It would be nice to define an alias for this command. Unfortunately, for technical reasons, we cannot. (In an alias, the `!*` would refer to the current command, not to the previous command. For details, see the C-Shell manual page.)

However, it is possible to define an alias that does the job:

```
alias del 'rm \!ls:*'
```

(Again, we won't go into the details here. Basically, we are extracting the arguments from the last command that contained the characters "`ls`".)

Once this alias is defined, you can use the following procedure to delete files that match a particular pattern:

First, enter an `ls` command with the pattern that describes the files you wish to delete. For example:

```
ls temp* extra?
```

If the pattern displays the names you expect, enter:

```
del
```

If not, re-enter the `ls` command with a different pattern until you get what you want, then use **del**. In this way, it is impossible to delete the wrong files by accident because of a mismatched pattern.

If you make a habit of using `ls` with a **del** alias in this way, we promise you that, one day, you will save yourself from a catastrophe. (In fact, we have mathematical proof—using Bessel functions—that this one trick alone is worth the price of this book.)

Initialization and Termination Files: `.cshrc`, `.login`, `.logout`

So far, we have met several types of commands that are useful for setting up your working environment. In addition, we have discussed variables that must be set before you can start work. How can you be sure everything is prepared properly? You certainly don't want to have to enter a long sequence of commands each time you log in. In addition, there may be certain commands you want to run each time you log out.

The shell provides a way for you to specify such commands once and have them executed at the appropriate time. Here is how it works.

The C-Shell recognizes three special files, named **.cshrc**, **.login** and **.logout**, in which you can store commands to be run automatically.

Every time a new shell is started, the commands in the **.cshrc** file are executed. This happens, of course, whenever you log in and your initial shell is started. It also happens whenever you run a shell script—we discuss shell scripts later in the chapter—or pause a program to start a temporary shell. The commands in the **.login** file are executed only once: when you log in, right after the **.cshrc** file is processed. As you might imagine, the **.logout** commands are also executed only once, just after you log out.

(Files whose names start with a period are called "dotfiles". We discuss dotfiles in Chapter 23.)

What's in a Name?   The **.cshrc** File

Although few people know it, the "**rc**" stands for "run commands"—that is, initialization commands that are run automatically.

The name derives from the CTSS operating system (Compatible Time Sharing System), developed at MIT in 1963. CTSS had a facility called "runcom" that would execute a list of commands stored in a file.

Aside from the C-Shell itself, other programs automatically look for "**rc**" initialization files in your home directory. Three examples are **.exrc** for the **ex** and **vi** text editors, **.mailrc** for the **mail** program, and **.newsrc** for the Usenet news program.

There is an important reason why these file names start with a dot: when you use the **ls** command to list your files, the names that begin with a dot are normally not displayed. This means that you do not have to look at these names each time you list your files. On those rare occasions when you want to display the names of all your files, including the names that begin with a dot, you can use **ls** with the **-a** (list all) option (see Chapter 23).

Most system managers set up their systems so that all new C-Shell users have **.cshrc** and **.login** files in their home directories. (There may or may not be a **.logout** file.) In most cases, you will not have to make any changes to these files. Your shell and environment variables will be set up for you. You may also have some useful aliases. If you want to take a look at these files, use the **more** command. For example:

◼ `more .cshrc`

From time to time, you may decide to modify these files. For example, you might want the system to display the message:

◼ `HELLO, GOOD LOOKING!`

each time you log in. Or you may wish to start the mail program automatically if there are messages for you. To make such changes, you will have to know how to use a text editor, either **vi** or **emacs**, which are discussed later in the book.

HINT

Which commands should go in the `.cshrc` file and which should go in the `.login` file? Here's what works best:

Your `.cshrc` file should contain commands to:

    —set your shell variables
    —define your aliases

Your `.login` file should contain commands to:

    —set up your terminal
    —define environment variables
    —set the user mask for default file permissions (Chapter 24)
    —perform initialization tasks each time you log in

The `.logout` file is less essential than `.cshrc` and `.login` and may be omitted if you want. This file holds commands that are executed whenever you log out. A nice command to put in your `.logout` file is **fortune** (see Chapter 7). Every time you log out you will see a funny remark. Some system managers (the ones with a good sense of humor) put this command in everybody's `.logout` file.

Shell Scripts

As we explained in Chapter 10, the shell is more than a command processor. The shell also supports a full programming language. In addition to regular Unix commands, you can also use special shell programming commands.

A file of such commands is called a SHELL SCRIPT. As the shell processes a script, it reads one command at a time. (Think of an actor reading a script, one line at a time.) To describe the processing, we say that the shell INTERPRETS each command.

In general, any program that reads and processes SCRIPTS—lists of sequential commands—can be called an INTERPRETER. Unix has a number of interpreters. For example, some of the text editors can interpret predefined scripts.

The details of programming the shell are beyond the scope of this book. However, for your interest, we have included two sample scripts, one in the Bourne shell programming language (Figure 11-5) and one in the C-Shell programming language (Figure 11-6). Within the scripts, lines that begin with a number sign (**#**) are comments that are ignored by the shell.

```
#! /bin/sh
# SHOWINFO: Bourne shell script to display an information file

# If the information file exists, display its contents.
# Otherwise, if the file does not exist, but if an older
#   version exists, display the older version.
# If neither file exists, display an error message
   if [ -f info ]
   then
      echo "The information file has been found.";
      more info
   elif [ -f info.old ]
   then
      echo "Only the old information file was found.";
      more info.old
else
   echo "The information file was not found."
fi
```

FIGURE 11-5. *A sample Bourne shell script*

```
#! /bin/csh
# SHOWINFO: C-Shell script to display an information file

# If the information file exists, display its contents.
# Otherwise, if the file does not exist, but if an older
#   version exists, display the older version.
# If neither file exists, display an error message
   if (-f info ) then
       echo "The information file has been found.";
       more info
   else if (-f info.old) then
   echo "Only the old information file was found.";
       more info.old
else
  echo "The information file was not found."
endif
```

FIGURE 11-6. *A sample C-Shell script*

Many C-Shell users feel that the Bourne shell language is better for writing scripts than the C-Shell language. Thus, it is common to find people who use the C-Shell (or Tcsh) as a command interpreter, but write Bourne shell or Korn shell scripts. (As we discussed in Chapter 10, the Korn shell was designed to be an upward compatible replacement for the Bourne shell. The Korn shell can run all Bourne shell scripts while offering enhanced programming features.)

In the sample Bourne shell script, you will notice that the first line is:

```
#! /bin/sh
```

This tells Unix to run the script under a Bourne shell. On many systems, this is the default.

Some people feel that the design of any shell programming facility is necessarily compromised because the shell must do double duty: as a command interpreter and as a programming language. Such people prefer to use an alternate interpreter designed only for scripts.

The most popular such interpreter is Perl, the Practical Extraction and Report Language. Perl was designed by Larry Wall, one of the Unix folk heroes. Perl provides a much more powerful scripting facility than the shell and is widely used by system managers. However, Perl programming is more difficult than shell programming and is not for the faint of heart.

CHAPTER 12

Using the Korn Shell

This chapter describes the most important features of the Korn shell. If you are using a different shell, the principles will be more or less the same, although the exact particulars may differ. If you are using the C-Shell, read Chapter 11 instead of this chapter.

As we explained in Chapter 10, the Korn shell is an upwards compatible extension to the Bourne shell (the original Unix shell). This means that everything that works with the Bourne shell will work with the Korn shell; however, the Korn shell can do a lot more. From its inception, the Korn shell was designed to replace the older Bourne shell. Indeed, on some systems, when you ask for the Bourne shell, you get the Korn shell and, unless you know what to look for, you may never know the difference.

Many people do not take the time to learn how to use the shell well. This is a mistake. To be sure, the shell has many features that you do not really need to understand. However, there are a handful of fundamental ideas that are of great practical value.

The time you spend reading this chapter will repay you well. You will find that the skills you learn here will save you a lot of time in your day-to-day work. There are many topics in this chapter, and you don't need to understand them all immediately. Just read the chapter once so you know what is available. As you become more experienced, you can reread parts of the chapter as you need them.

If, after reading this chapter, you decide you want to know more details, check the Korn manual page (**man ksh**). This is the ultimate reference as to how the shell works on your particular system.

Shell Options: `set -o`, `set +o`

One of the ways the shell lets you customize your working environment is by using SHELL OPTIONS. A shell option is a setting that controls a particular aspect of the shell's behavior. Shell options act like on/off switches. When you SET an option (turn it on), it tells the shell to act in a certain way. When you UNSET an option (turn it off), it tells the shell to stop acting in that manner.

Figure 12-1 shows the shell options you can set and unset. (Your list of options may vary slightly, depending on the version of your Korn shell.) Don't worry if you don't understand what all these options do; this list is for reference. By the time you learn enough to care about using a option, you will understand its purpose. To set or display a shell option, you use the **set** command. The syntax to set an option is:

set -o *option*

(The **-o** stands for "option".)

Here is an example. Normally, you can terminate a shell by pressing **^D** (the **eof** key). However, if the shell happens to be your login shell, you will be logged out. (Your login shell is the top-level shell, the one that was started when you logged in.) You will find that it is all too easy to press **^D** by accident and log yourself out unexpectedly. To guard against this you can set the **ignoreeof** option. This tells the shell to not log you out when you press **^D** while in your login shell. Instead, you must enter **exit** to log out. To set this option, use the following command:

set -o ignoreeof

SETTING	PURPOSE
allexport	set export attribute for defined variables
bgnice	run background jobs at lower priority
emacs	use **emacs** built-in editor
errexit	execute **ERR** trap after a non-zero exit status
gmacs	use **gmacs** built-in editor
ignoreeof	must logout with **exit** rather than **eof** key (**^D**)
markdirs	pathname expansion: append **/** to directory names
monitor	enable job control
noclobber	do not allow redirected output to replace a file
noexec	read commands, check syntax, but do not execute
noglob	inhibit expansion of file names
nolog	do not store function definitions in history file
nounset	treat expanding an unset variable as an error
privileged	do not run user's initialization/environment files
protected	old version of **privileged** setting
trackall	aliases: substitute full pathnames for commands
verbose	display each command before running it
vi	use **vi** built-in editor

FIGURE 12-1.   *Korn shell options*

To unset an option, you use the syntax:

set +o *option*

For example, to unset the **ignoreeof** option, you would enter:

set +o ignoreeof

To display all the shell options and their current settings, enter the command with **-o** but with no option name:

set -o

The shell will show you a list of all its options and tell you whether they are on (set) or off (unset).

HINT

Unless you are an advanced user, the only options you need concern yourself with are **ignoreeof**, **monitor** and **noclobber**, and one of either **emacs** or **vi**. The **monitor** option enables job control, which we discuss in Chapter 25. The **noclobber** option prevents you from accidentally removing a file when you redirect the standard output (see Chapter 16). The **emacs** and **vi** options are used to specify which built-in editor you want to use to recall and edit previous commands. This is explained later in the chapter.

These options are best set from within your environment file. This is an initialization file that is executed automatically each time a new shell is started. We discuss this file later in the chapter.

Built-In Shell Variables: `set`

The shell options we have just discussed are used only within the shell to control preferences and settings. However, there is a whole other set of items, called SHELL VARIABLES, that the shell maintains for passing values between programs. A shell variable is an item, known by a name, that represents a value of some type. As the term "variable" implies, the value of a shell variable can be changed.

Here is an example. As we discussed in Chapter 6, Unix needs to know what type of terminal you are using in order to display characters (or graphics) properly on your screen. More precisely, it is not Unix itself, but the actual programs that need to know what type of terminal you are using. To meet this need, it is up to you to set that value of a particular variable (called **TERM**) to the name of your terminal. Once this is done, any program that must know your terminal type needs only to examine the value of **TERM**. The **TERM** variable—along with other important variables—should be set automatically from the Korn shell initialization file (named **.profile**) which we discuss later in the chapter.

HINT

Some programs cannot display their output properly unless they know exactly what type of terminal you are using. If a program that uses the full screen for output—such as the **vi** or **emacs** editor—displays its output in a strange manner, make sure that your **TERM** variable is set correctly.

You can create your own shell variables, but, unless you write programs, you will usually make do with the standard ones. There are two types of shell variables that you will encounter. First, there are a number of variables that are used by the shell itself. To display the shell variables on your system, along with their values, enter the **set** command by itself:

```
set
```

By convention, shell variables that are to be shared with other programs are always given uppercase names. In technical terms, we sometimes describe such items as GLOBAL VARIABLES or ENVIRONMENT VARIABLES, although this terminology is more commonly used with the C-Shell.

Figure 12-2 shows the most common variables that are used by the Korn shell. (Your list of variables may vary slightly, depending on the version of your Korn shell and how it has been set up.) Don't worry if you don't understand what all these variables do; this list is for reference. By the time you learn enough to care about using a variable, you will understand its purpose.

The second type of shell variable are those that are used by other programs. For example, many programs depend on a pager (see Chapter 18) to display output on your screen. If you set the shell variable called **PAGER** to the name of your favorite pager, these programs will use the designated pager instead of what would otherwise be the default.

To set the value of a shell variable, simply type the name of the variable (remember to use uppercase letters), followed by an equals sign, followed by the value you want to assign to the variable. The syntax is:

```
name=value
```

For example, to set the name of your terminal to **vt100**, use:

```
TERM=vt100
```

Note: Do not put a space on either side of the **=** character. For example, the command:

```
TERM = vt100
```

will not work. The shell will think you are trying to run a program named **TERM**.

If the value of a variable contains spaces or punctuation characters, you should enclose it within single quotes. For example:

```
PS1='nipper [!]$ '
```

(We will discuss the **PS1** variable and this particular example later in the chapter.)

VARIABLE NAME	PURPOSE
CDPATH	list of directories searched by the **cd** command
COLUMNS	width (in characters) of your screen or window
EDITOR	name of default editor
ENV	name of file executed when **ksh** is invoked
FCEDIT	name of editor for **fc** command to use
HISTFILE	name of the command history file
HISTSIZE	number of lines kept in the command history file
HOME	name of your home directory
MAIL	name of file to check for new mail
MAILCHECK	how often (in seconds) the shell checks for new mail
MAILPATH	list of files to check for new mail
OLDPWD	name of your previous working directory
PATH	list of directories to search for programs
PS1	primary shell prompt
PS2	secondary shell prompt
PS3	prompt used by **select** command
PS4	prompt used with trace option
PWD	name of your current working directory
RANDOM	a random number between 0 and 32,767
SECONDS	number of seconds since the shell was invoked
SHELL	pathname of the shell program
TERM	type of terminal you are using
TMOUT	seconds to wait before auto-logout if no command
VISUAL	name of default editor (overrides **EDITOR** variable)

FIGURE 12-2. *Korn shell variables*

Displaying the Value of a Variable: `print`

We mentioned that you can use the **set** command to display the names and values of all your shell variables. If you only want to display the values of one or more variables, you can use the **print** command. This command simply displays the value of anything you give it. For example, if you enter:

`print I love Unix`

You will see:

`I love Unix`

(which, by now, should be true).

To display the value of a variable, use its name preceded by a dollar sign (**$**). For example, to display the value of the **TERM** variable, enter:

`print $TERM`

If the value of this variable is, say, "vt100", you will see:

`vt100`

Of course, you can combine this with anything you want. For instance, you can display a more informative message:

`print The terminal type is $TERM`

If the value of **term** is as shown above, you will see:

`The terminal type is vt100`

If you want to display punctuation characters, you must place them within double quotes. For example:

`print "Working directory is $PWD; previous one was $OLDPWD."`

Although the **print** command can be useful to check on one or more variables, it is usually easier to simply use the **set** command and ignore the variables you don't want. The real use for the **print** command is to display informative messages within shell scripts. (Shell scripts, discussed later in the chapter, are programs written in the shell's own programming language.)

Even if you are not a programmer, you might want to use some **print** commands in your **.profile** initialization file (which we also discuss later in the chapter). For example, you might place the following command in your **.profile** file:

```
print 'Hi. Welcome to Unix.'
```

This way, you will see a nice message each time you log in.

HINT

With most shells (including the C-Shell), the command to display text and variables on the screen is named **echo**. For example, you might type:

```
echo The terminal type is $TERM
```

The **echo** command will work with the Korn shell. However, the inventor of the Korn shell (David Korn) purposely created the **print** command to replace **echo**. The main reason is that **echo** has different options on different systems, while **print** works the same everywhere. This is important when you are writing shell scripts that must run on all types of systems.

So unless you are writing shell scripts that will be widely distributed, it doesn't really matter if you use **print** or **echo** in your day-to-day life. Still, within the Korn shell community, **print** is the preferred command, and when you use it—especially if someone is watching you—you show yourself to be an official Korn shell person and not simply a C-Shell transplant who doesn't know any better.

Exporting Shell Variables: `export`

Some of the variables the shell maintains are considered to be part of the ENVIRONMENT: a collection of information that is passed along to a program when it is started by the shell.

For example, consider what happens when you enter the command to start the **vi** editor. Within the environment, there should be a variable named **TERM** that contains the type of terminal you are using (for example, **vt100**). When the shell starts the **vi** program, this variable is passed to **vi** as part of the environment. In this way, **vi** knows what type of terminal you are using. If this were not to happen, **vi** would not be able to display characters on your screen properly.

When variables are passed to a program as part of the environment, we say the shell EXPORTS those variables. Thus, we can say the shell exports the **TERM** variable to **vi**.

We have already discussed the most common shell variables and described how they are used (see Figure 12-2). Some of these variables are crucial to the working of your Unix session and are automatically defined for you when you log in. You can count on these variables being exported automatically. However, if you define your own variables (or redefine existing ones), you must tell the shell that they should be exported. To do so, you use the **export** command. The syntax is:

```
export [name[=value]]...
```

To tell the shell to export a variable, type **export** followed by the name of the variable.

Here is an example. Later in the chapter we will show how to set the **PS1** variable to customize your shell prompt. A typical choice is to set the prompt to be the name of your system followed a dollar sign and a space. Say that your system is named **nipper**. The following command will set the prompt accordingly (don't worry about the details for now):

```
PS1='nipper$ '
```

Thus, when the shell is ready to read a new command, it will display:

```
nipper$
```

instead of the default:

```
$
```

If you typically use more than one Unix system, such a prompt is handy as it reminds you which system you are using.

Now, to ensure that this new prompt is placed in the environment, you would use the **export** command. Together, the two commands look like:

```
PS1='nipper$ '
export PS1
```

If you would like to combine these into a single command, you can do so by defining the variable within the **export** command itself:

```
export PS1='nipper$ '
```

Most of the time, you will want to set up these commands so that they are executed automatically each time you log in. You can do so by putting them into your **.profile** initialization file (which we will discuss later in the chapter). For example, this is the place to define and export the **TERM** variable to ensure that all the programs that you invoke know what type of terminal you are using.

If you want to check which of your shell variables will be exported, you can enter the **export** command by itself:

```
export
```

The shell will display a list of each variable that is part of the environment, along with its current value. If you compare this list with the output of the **set** command (which shows you all the shell variables), you will be able to see which ones will be exported and which ones will not.

HINT

If you have ever used the C-Shell, you may know that it has a command named **setenv** that defines and exports a variable in one step. Thus, with the C-Shell, you can use:

```
setenv TERM vt100
```

rather than:

```
TERM=vt100
export TERM
```

You might wonder, why does the Korn shell require you to explicitly export a variable to make it part of the environment?

There are three reasons. First, the Korn shell was written to be upwards compatible with the Bourne shell, and the Bourne shell requires you to export variables explicitly. Second, the Korn shell does allow you to define and export in one step, using the alternative form of the **export** command that we described above. For instance:

```
export TERM=vt100
```

Finally, there may be times when you want to define a variable but not have it be part of the environment. With the Korn shell, all you have to do is not export the variable. The C-Shell works differently. It recognizes two types of variables: those that are exported automatically (environment variables) and those that are not (shell variables). Thus, C-Shell users must learn how to work with the two types of variables (see Chapter 11 for the details). This can be a major source of confusion for beginners (at least, for those beginners who do not have this book).

Commands that Are Built into the Shell: type

When you enter a command, the shell breaks the command line into parts that it analyzes. We say that the shell PARSES the command. The first part of each command is the name; the other parts are options or parameters (see Chapter 9).

After parsing the command, the shell decides what to do with it. There are two possibilities. Some commands are internal to the shell; this means that the shell can interpret the command directly. The table in Figure 12-3 shows the various shells and the number of commands that are built in.

If you want to see if a command is built into the shell, you can use the **type** command. The syntax is:

type *command-name*

All you have to do is specify the name of a command and the shell will tell you what type of command it is. For example, say that you want to know whether or not the **print** command is built into the shell. Enter:

type print

You will see:

print is a shell builtin

This shows you that **print** is an internal command. Now, say that you enter:

type date

NAME OF SHELL	INTERNAL COMMANDS
rc	15
Bourne shell	32
Korn shell	43
Bash	50
C-Shell	52
Tcsh	56
Zsh	73

FIGURE 12-3. *The number of internal commands in each shell*

You will see something like:

`date is a tracked alias for /bin/date`

At this point, it's not important to understand what is meant by a "tracked alias"; it is a technical distinction you can ignore. The important thing is that we see that **date** is not a built-in command.

If you want to see a full list of all the built-in commands, check the Korn shell manual page (use the command **man ksh**). All the other commands will be separate programs with their own manual pages.

HINT
If you are looking for help for a particular command and you can't find the manual page, check with the documentation for your shell: the command may be internal.

The Search Path

If a command is not built into the shell—and most commands are not—the shell must find the appropriate program to execute.

For example, when you enter the **date** command, the shell must find the **date** program. The shell then starts the program and puts itself on hold. When the program finishes, the shell regains control. It is now ready for you to enter another command.

The **PATH** variable tells the shell where to look for programs. The value of **PATH** is a series of directory names called the SEARCH PATH. (We will discuss directories in Chapter 23. Basically, a directory holds a collection of files.) Normally, you will set this variable from within the **.profile** initialization file (discussed later in the chapter). This ensures that **PATH** is set properly each time you log in.

When the shell is looking for a program to execute, it checks each directory in the search path in the order they are specified. As soon as the shell finds the program, it stops the search and executes the program. Thus, you should specify the directory names in the order you want them to be searched.

Here is a typical command to define a search path:

`PATH=/usr/local/bin:/usr/ucb:/bin:/usr/bin:$HOME/bin`

This command sets the **PATH** variable's value to be a list of five directories. Notice that the directory names must be separated by colons. Each of these directories is a place where programs are kept.

The names will make more sense after we cover directories in Chapter 23. For now, all we will say is that **bin** is often used to indicate a directory that holds programs, and the **HOME** variable contains the name of your home directory. In other words, **$HOME/bin** indicates a directory that holds programs that lies within your home directory. The **/usr/ucb** directory holds programs specific to Berkeley Unix. (**ucb** stands for University of California at Berkeley.)

If you are a programmer, you may find it convenient to have the shell also check your working directory when it looks for a program. (The term "working directory" refers to the directory in which you are currently working.) To do this, add the dot (**.**) character to the search path:

```
PATH=.:/usr/local/bin:/usr/ucb:/bin:/usr/bin:$HOME/bin
```

Remember, you can place the entries in any order you want. In this case, Unix will search your working directory before it searches any other directories.

For example, say that you create a program and name it **date**. You are working in the directory that holds this program, and you enter:

```
date
```

What happens?

First the shell checks to see if this an internal command. The answer is no, so the shell starts searching for a program named **date**. Since the search path tells the shell to check your working directory first, it finds and executes your program named **date**, not the Unix **date** command (which is in the **/bin** directory).

Now, suppose you had defined the search path with your working directory after **/bin**:

```
PATH=/usr/local/bin:/usr/ucb:/bin:/usr/bin:.:$HOME/bin
```

In this case, the shell will find the Unix **date** command first (in **/bin**).

A detailed discussion of search paths is beyond the scope of this book (and not all that necessary). Normally, you can accept the search path that is set up for you by default. The only thing you must remember is that if you modify the search path, order is important.

An alternate way to specify your working directory within a search path is to use an empty name. Thus, the following command is equivalent to the previous one:

```
PATH=/usr/local/bin:/usr/ucb:/bin:/usr/bin::$HOME/bin
```

Both commands place your working directory as the second to last in the list. The empty directory name (the working directory) is specified by the two colons in a row. If you want the current directory to be at the end of the list, put a colon at the end:

PATH=/usr/local/bin:/usr/ucb:/bin:/usr/bin:$HOME/bin:

This tells the shell to search your working directory last. Similarly, you can place your working directory at the beginning of the list:

 PATH=:/usr/local/bin:/usr/ucb:/bin:/usr/bin:$HOME/bin

This tells the shell to search your working directory first.

The Shell Prompt

As we explained in Chapter 4, the shell displays a prompt whenever it is ready for you to enter a command. By default, the Korn and Bourne shells display a dollar sign character:

 $

while the C-Shell displays a percent sign:

 %

As we will see in a moment, most people set up their prompt to include other information. However, it is customary to always include either the **$** or **%** character to remind you which type of shell you are using.

The Korn shell uses the value of the shell variable **PS1** as its command prompt. Thus, you can change your prompt to whatever you want by setting the value of this variable. (This is also true for the other shells.)

Here is an example. You are in the habit of logging in remotely to various computers on your network, and you want to use a different, unique prompt with each system to remind you where you are.

Say that one of the systems is named **nipper**. On that system, you can set your prompt as follows:

 PS1='nipper$ '

(Remember, if you assign a value that contains spaces or punctuation, you must enclose it in single quotes. Remember, also, that you must not put spaces on either side of the **=** character.) For a system named **princess**, you can use:

 PS1='princess$ '

Later in the chapter, we will discuss the history file (which stores the commands that you enter) and how you can reuse a command without having to type it in again. When we do, you will see that it is useful to have a value called the "command number" as part of the prompt. (The command number is a value that is increased by 1 every time you enter a new command. This value is used to identify specific commands you have already entered.)

To display the command number within a prompt, use an exclamation point (**!**). Whenever the shell displays the prompt, it will replace the **!** with the current command number.

Let's say that you want your prompt to be the name **nipper**, followed by a space, followed by the command number in square brackets, followed by a dollar sign, followed by a space. Enter the command:

```
PS1='nipper [!]$ '
```

If, for example, the value of the command number happens to be 29, the prompt will be:

```
nipper [29]$
```

When you enter a new command, the command number changes to 30, and the prompt will be:

```
nipper [30]$
```

Another useful way to define your prompt is to have it display the name of your working directory. (We discuss the idea of a current directory in Chapter 23. Briefly, your keep your files in "directories". As you work, you can move from one directory to another. The directory in which you are working at a particular time is called your working directory.)

At all times, the shell maintains the name of your working directory in the **PWD** variable. When you change directories, the shell changes the value of **PWD**. (The name **PWD** comes from the **pwd** command—"print working directory"—which you can use to display the name of your working directory.)

Here is an example. You decide to have your prompt display the name of your working directory in square brackets, followed by a dollar sign and a space. Set the **PS1** variable as follows:

```
PS1='[$PWD]$ '
```

If your working directory happens to be, say, **/usr/harley/books**, your prompt would be:

```
[/usr/harley/books]$
```

If you change to the directory **/usr/harley/reviews**, the prompt will become:

```
[/usr/harley/reviews]$
```

As a final example, here is a command that sets your prompt to display both the name of your working directory and the command number:

```
PS1='[$PWD] [!]$ '
```

If your working directory is **/usr/harley/books**, and the command number is 21, the prompt would be:

```
[/usr/harley/books] [21]$
```

Remember, of course, the square brackets are optional. You can put whatever you want in your prompt.

The History File: `history`

After you use Unix for awhile, you will know the frustration of having to type a command over and over because of spelling mistakes. There are three mechanisms that the Korn shell provides to make it easier to enter commands: reusing commands, built-in editing, and aliasing. These features are one reason why many people prefer to use the Korn shell over the Bourne shell or C-Shell. (The C-Shell does have similar capabilities, but they are not as powerful.) We will discuss each feature in turn briefly. For more information, see the Korn shell manual page (use the command **man ksh**).

The Korn shell lets you change and re-enter a previous command without having to retype it. This facility has a number of esoteric rules and features. If you know them all, that's great; you will have enormous facility in recycling your commands. However, most people just memorize and use a few of the simpler features: the ones we will describe in this section. For more powerful means of editing and reusing commands, you can use the built-in editors we describe later in the chapter.

At all times, the shell saves your commands in a list called the HISTORY FILE. Each command is given an identification number, starting at 1. Whenever you enter a command, the identification number increases by 1. Thus, you can refer to command number 6, or command number 46, and so on.

By default, the shell will save the most recent 128 commands. If you want to change this number, you can do so by setting the value of the **HISTSIZE** variable. For example, to tell the shell to save only the most recent 25 commands, enter:

HISTSIZE=25

To display the history list, use the **history** command. The syntax is:

history [**-r**] [*first* [*last*]]

If you enter the command with no arguments:

history

the shell will display the previous 16 commands along with their numbers. (The numbers, of course, are not part of the commands.) Here is some partial output of a sample **history** command:

```
20   cp tempfile backup
21   ls
22   who
23   datx
24   datq
25   date
26   mail
27   w
28   history
```

You can display a range of commands by specifying a starting and ending number. For example:

history 25 27

might display:

```
25   date
26   mail
27   w
```

If you display only a single number, the shell will display from that number all the way up to the current command. For example:

```
history 25
```

This displays from command number 25 up to the current command.

Finally, if you use the **-r** option, the shell will display the commands in reverse order (most recent first). For example:

```
history -r 25 27
```

might display:

```
27   w
26   mail
25   date
```

To display the previous 16 commands in reverse order, enter:

```
history -r
```

Notice that every command you enter is added to the history list, including commands with mistakes, as well as the **history** commands themselves.

Displaying the history list is important for two reasons. First, as we will describe in a moment, you can recall, edit and then execute previous commands. Second, you can check back and see what commands you have already entered. ("Did I really delete all those files?") If you think that you may want to keep a long record of your work, you can set the **HISTSIZE** variable to a large number, although the default (128) should be adequate for most people.

If you decide to use the history file (and you should), you will find it handy to display the current command number as part of your prompt. We explained how to do this in the section on the shell prompt. Here is an example:

```
PS1='nipper [!]$ '
```

This prompt displays a reminder that you are using a system named **nipper**, followed by the current command number (in square brackets) and a dollar sign. A sample prompt might be:

nipper [29]$

Reusing Commands from the History File: r

To reuse a command from the history file, you can use the **r** command. The syntax is:

r [*old=new*] [*command*]

If you enter the command name by itself, the shell will re-execute the previous command. For example, say that you want to display the time and date. You enter:

date

After waiting awhile (without typing another command), you enter:

r

The shell will re-execute the **date** command and you will see the new time.
    If you want to recall a particular command, you can do so in several ways. First, you can specify a command number. For example, to re-execute command number 24, enter:

r 24

If you specify a negative number, the shell will subtract it from the current command number. For example, let's say that the current command number is 29. You enter:

r -3

The shell will re-execute command number 26.
    The final way to indicate which command you want is to specify one or more characters. The shell will re-execute the most recent command that starts with

those characters. For example, say that the current command is number 29, and the history file contains the following lines:

```
20   cp tempfile backup
21   ls
22   who
23   datx
24   datq
25   date
26   mail
27   w
28   history
```

You enter:

```
r w
```

The shell will re-execute the most recent command that begins with "w" (command number 27). Now you enter:

```
r wh
```

The shell will re-execute the most recent command that begins with "wh" (command number 22).

One of the most useful features of the **r** command is that it allows you to make a replacement before you re-execute the command. All you have to do is specify the old pattern, followed by an equal sign, followed by the replacement pattern. For example, say that you want to display the time and date, but you accidentally enter:

```
datx
```

All you need to do is tell the shell to replace the "x" with an "e", and then re-execute the command:

```
r x=e
```

The shell will execute the command:

```
date
```

Here is another example. You have just entered the command:

```
ls -l backup
```

You want to change "backup" to "book/chapters" and repeat the command. Enter:

```
r backup=book/chapters
```

The shell will execute:

```
ls -l book/chapters
```

When the shell makes such a substitution, it does so only for the first occurrence of the old pattern, so be careful. For example, say that you enter the command:

```
ls -l book/chapters/1.new book/chapters/2.new
```

You want to change both occurrences of "new" to "old" and re-execute the command, so you enter:

```
r new=old
```

However, the shell will only make one substitution and you will get:

```
ls -l book/chapters/1.old book/chapters/2.new
```

In this case, the easiest way to make the change is to use one of the built-in editors (described later in the chapter).

When you use the **r** command, you can recall a command from the history file and change it at the same time. For example, let's say that command number 20 was:

```
cp tempfile backup
```

You want to change "backup" to "extra" and re-execute this command. Simply enter:

```
r backup=extra 20
```

This shell will execute the command:

```
cp tempfile extra
```

With a little practice, such substitutions can save you a lot of time and effort.

HINT FOR NERDS

Both the **history** and **r** commands are actually aliases, not "real" commands. (We will discuss aliases later in the chapter. Basically, an alias is an alternate name for a command. For example, you could make an alias named **d** to stand for the **date** command. That way, every time you want to display the time and date, you need only type **d**.)

The command that actually does the work of recalling items from the history file is called **fc**. The name stands for "fix command", as in "I entered the command incorrectly so now I can use **fc** to fix it and run it again."

The **fc** command is a powerful one: it can recall one or more commands from the history file, make substitutions, even allow you to edit a previous command with your favorite editor program, and then submit the whole thing to the shell to be re-executed. Unfortunately, the syntax of **fc** was designed poorly and the details of the command itself are awkward to remember and to use. Thus, it is better to use the aliases **history** and **r**. In case you are interested, the alias **history** stands for:

```
fc -l
```

The **-l** option tells **fc** to list part of the history file. The alias **r** stands for:

```
fc -e -
```

(Don't even ask.)

If you want more information about the **fc** command and its various options, see the Korn shell manual page (use the command **man ksh**).

History List Example: Avoid Deleting the Wrong Files

As we will discuss in Chapter 24, the **rm** (remove) command will delete files. When you use **rm**, you can specify patterns to stand for lists of files. For example, the pattern **temp*** stands for any file name that begins with **temp** followed by zero or more characters; the pattern **extra?** refers to any file name that starts with **extra** followed by a single character.

The danger with **rm** is that once you delete a file it is gone for good. If you discover that you have made a mistake and erased the wrong file—even the instant after you press the RETURN key—there is no way to get the file back.

Now, let's say that you want to delete a set of files with the names **temp**, **temp_backup**, **extra1** and **extra2**. You are thinking about entering the command:

```
rm temp* extra?
```

However, you have forgotten that you also have an important file called **temp.important**. If you enter the preceding command, this file will also be deleted.

A better strategy is to first enter the **ls** command using the patterns that you propose to use with **rm**:

```
ls temp* extra?
```

This will list the names of all the files that match these patterns. If this list contains a file you have forgotten, such as **temp.important**, you will not enter the **rm** command as planned. If, however, the list of files is what you expected, you can go ahead and remove the files by entering:

```
r ls=rm
```

You may ask, why do I need to use **r** to reuse the previous command? Now that I have confirmed that the patterns match the files I want, couldn't I just type the **rm** command using those same patterns?

The answer is, when you reuse the command you are guaranteed to get what you want. If you retype the patterns, you may make a typing mistake and, in spite of all your precautions, end up deleting the wrong files. Also—in this case anyway—it is faster to type a simple **r** command than to type a long **rm** command.

To make the whole process easier, you can use an alias, as you will see later in the chapter.

Command Aliasing: `alias`, `unalias`, `whence`

An ALIAS is a name that you give to a command or list of commands. You can then type the name of the alias instead of the commands.

For example, say that you often find yourself entering the following command:

```
ls -l temp*
```

If you give it an alias of **lt**, you can enter the command more simply by typing:

```
lt
```

To create an alias, use the **alias** command. The syntax is:

```
alias [name=command]
```

(There are some options, but you don't need to bother with them.) Notice that—just like when you define a variable—you must not put a space before or after the **=** character.

Here is an example in which we create the alias that we just mentioned:

```
alias lt='ls -l temp*'
```

As you can see, we enclosed the command in single quotes. This is necessary when the alias contains spaces. In addition, certain punctuation characters (such as *****) have special meanings to the shell. The single quotes tell the shell to treat the characters literally. This is a good idea when you specify an alias for any command that has punctuation.

Here is an example that creates an alias for a list of two commands:

```
alias info='date; who'
```

You can now enter **info** to find out the time and date, and then check who is logged in to the system. One of the most useful aliases is:

```
alias a=alias
```

This allows you to use **a** instead of typing the whole word "alias". For example, once you define this alias, you can enter:

```
a info='date; who'
```

If you want to check the current value of an alias, enter the **alias** command with a name only. For example:

```
alias info
```

If you want to display all the aliases, enter the command name by itself, with no arguments:

```
alias
```

To remove an alias, use the **unalias** command. The syntax is:

```
unalias name
```

For example, to remove the alias that we just defined, use:

```
unalias info
```

You may remember the **type** command we discussed earlier in this chapter. (You specify the name of a command, and **type** will tell you what type of command it is.) The reason we mention it here is that **type** will let you know if a particular command is an alias. For example, say that you define the **info** alias as shown, and then enter:

```
type info
```

You will see:

```
info is an alias for date; who
```

Interestingly enough, **type** itself is an alias. It is one of several aliases that are built into the shell. (Two others are **history** and **r**.) Try entering:

```
type type
```

You will see a message like the following:

```
type is an exported alias for whence -v
```

Thus, whenever you enter **type**, you are really using the command **whence   -v**. We won't go into the **whence** command in detail. Suffice it to say that, without the **-v** option, **whence** displays the pathname of the specified command. (We discuss pathnames in Chapter 23.) With the **-v** (verbose) option, **whence** tells you what type of command you specified.

As you might imagine, you are likely to develop a whole set of aliases that you use all the time, and it is bothersome to have to retype the alias definitions each time you log in. Instead, you can place them in your "environment file", so that they will be defined automatically for you. We will discuss this file and how to initialize your working environment later in the chapter.

Alias Example: Avoid Deleting the Wrong Files

In this section, we will show you how to combine an alias with a command recalled from the history file to produce an exceptionally handy tool.

Earlier in the chapter, we showed how to use the **ls** command to check which file names would be matched by a particular set of patterns. We performed this check before, using those same patterns with the **rm** (remove) command to delete files. This allowed us to make sure that the files we removed were the ones we meant to remove. This is important because once Unix deletes a file it is gone forever.

The example we used deleted the files that matched the patterns **temp*** and **extra?**. First, we checked what files these patterns matched by entering:

```
ls temp* extra?
```

If the results were what we expected, we entered:

```
r ls=rm
```

to delete using the exact same pattern.

In order to make this command easy to use, we can define an alias for it named **del**. The obvious way to do this would be to use the definition:

```
alias del='r ls=rm'
```

The idea is that, when you enter **del**, the characters "ls" in the previous command are replaced by "rm" and the command is then re-executed. This means that you can reuse the same pattern of file names without having to retype it.

However, such an alias definition will not work properly. Here is why. We explained earlier that the **r** command is itself an alias, one that is built into the shell. The actual command that **r** represents is:

```
fc -e -
```

For example, the following two commands will have the same effect:

```
r oldname=newname
fc -e - oldname=newname
```

Both commands will recall the previous command from the history file, change the first occurrence of "oldname" to "newname", and then re-execute the command.

In other words, the **r** alias stands for **fc** (fix command) followed by the **-e** and **-** options. We won't go into the details here. It is enough to say that they are complex and that this is why the **r** alias is built into the shell

The problem with our **del** alias is that we tried to define it in terms of the **r** alias, and you cannot use an alias within another alias. This is because when you enter a command, the shell only expands an alias once. If you define the alias described above, you will find that when you go to use it, the shell will not replace the "r" properly.

However, in this case, we know that the **r** command represents a form of the **fc** command (which you can verify by entering the command **type r**), so we can simply use the **fc** command directly. Thus, we can define our **del** alias as follows:

```
alias del='fc -e - ls=rm'
```

Once this alias is defined, you can use the following procedure to delete files that match a particular pattern:

First, enter an **ls** command with the pattern that describes the files you wish to delete. For example:

```
ls temp* extra?
```

If the pattern displays the names you expect, enter:

```
del
```

If not, re-enter the **ls** command with a different pattern until you get what you want, then use **del**. In this way, it is impossible to delete the wrong files by accident because of a mismatched pattern.

If you make a habit of using **ls** with a **del** alias in this way, we promise you that, one day, you will save yourself from a catastrophe. (In fact, we have mathematical proof—using mathematical induction and hypergeometric functions—that this one trick alone is worth the price of this book.)

The Built-In Editors

One of the most important features of the Korn shell are the two BUILT-IN EDITORS. These are facilities that let you recall, edit, and re-execute commands from the history file. You can also edit the command you are currently typing. What makes the built-in editors so powerful is that you can use virtually all of the commands from either **vi** or **emacs** (your choice), the two most popular Unix editors. Thus, if you already know how to use either of these editors, you know almost everything you need to edit shell commands. Here is how it works.

As we explained earlier, the shell saves your commands in the history file (which you can look at by using the **history** command). At any time, you can use **vi**- or **emacs**-like instructions to recall and edit a command. Once the command is modified to suit your needs, you can execute it by pressing RETURN.

Before you can use this facility, you must set an option to tell the shell which built-in editor you want to use. You do this by issuing one of the following commands:

```
set -o vi
set -o emacs
```

Typically, you will place one of these commands in your environment file (discussed later in the chapter), so that your preference will be set automatically.

It is important to understand that once you make your choice, you are not using the real editor program. Rather, you are using a facility that is built right into the Korn shell. In the following sections, we will show how each of these built-in editors works with the shell. Before we do, let's take a moment to discuss how you might choose which one to use.

First, if you do not know how to use either **vi** or **emacs**, there is nothing you can do, and you are more to be pitied than censured. The easy way to remedy the situation is to teach yourself one of these editors. Unfortunately, neither editor is easy to learn, but—and this is an important "but"—once you learn either editor, you will find it easy to use. Listen: no matter what anyone tells you, you really do need to know how to use one of the two Unix editors, so don't put it off. We discuss **vi** in Chapter 20, and **emacs** in Chapter 21.

If you already know how to use **vi** or **emacs**, you are all set. However, just because you know one editor doesn't mean you shouldn't learn the other, or at least enough of the other to edit shell commands. Each editor has its good and bad points, and you may want to use one for general text editing and the other for command editing. For example, we like to use **vi** to edit files and **emacs** for editing commands.

Why? As you may know, **vi** has two modes: input mode and command mode. When you are typing a shell command, you are automatically in input mode. To make changes, or to recall a previous command from the history list, you must press ESC to change into command mode. **emacs**, though, only has one mode. At any time, even while you are typing, you can issue an **emacs** command. Thus, it is faster to use **emacs**.

However—and this is a big "however"—in order for **emacs** to have only one mode, it can only use commands that do not look anything like the characters you might want to type as input. In practice, this means that you must memorize a lot of CTRL and ESC key combinations.

For instance, with **vi** you can delete from the cursor to the end of the line by typing **D** (in command mode). With **emacs**, you use **^K**. With **vi**, you move back one word by typing **b**. With **emacs**, you use ESC-B. **You get the idea.**

Thus, before you make up your mind which built-in editor you want to use to edit shell commands, you might want to read both of the following sections and experiment. Remember, you can switch from one built-in editor to another simply by entering one of the commands:

```
set -o vi
set -o emacs
```

Once you decide which one you want to use permanently, you can put the appropriate command in your environment file.

Using the **vi** Built-In Editor

To use the **vi** built-in editor, you must first set the appropriate option:

```
set -o vi
```

Normally, you would do this from within your environment file. Once this option is set, you can use any of the **vi** commands whenever you want. If you do not already know how to use **vi**, you should learn to do so before you read this section. We explain the **vi** editor in Chapter 20. In addition, there is a **vi** command summary in Appendix C.

Whenever you begin to type a shell command, you can consider yourself to be in input mode. To use a **vi** command, press ESC to enter command mode. You can now use any **vi** command you want. Once you have modified the line to be just the way you want it, you can execute it by pressing RETURN.

Note: You do not need to be at the end of the line to press RETURN; nor do you have to be in command mode. Whenever the line looks correct, just press RETURN to execute the command.

A quick example will make it all clear. You have just typed the following command but you have not as yet pressed RETURN:

```
who | gred melissa
```

What you want to do is use the **who** command to generate a list of all the people using the system, and then send the output to the **grep** program to extract all the lines that contain the characters "melissa". Don't worry if you don't understand the example. What is important is that you accidentally typed "gred" instead of "grep".

At this point, the cursor is at the end of the line. (Remember, you have not as yet pressed RETURN.) You decide to edit the command before executing it, so you press ESC to change to command mode. Now, type **2b** to move backward two words. (Alternatively, you could have pressed **b** two times.) The cursor is now under the "g". Type **cw** to change one word. Type **grep**. The line now reads:

```
who | grep melissa
```

The cursor is under the "p". If you do not want to make any further changes, press RETURN. The shell will now execute the new command.

The best way to think about using the built-in **vi** editor is to imagine that you are editing the history file (including the current line). However, you can only see one command at a time. To move up and down within the history file, you use the same **vi** commands that move up and down within an editing buffer: **k** (or **-**) moves up, **j** (or **+**) moves down. Each time you move up one line, the shell moves back within the history list and displays the command in that position.

Here is an example that you can try for yourself. Enter the following commands, one at a time:

```
who | grep melissa
date
ls -l
print Unix is fun
```

After pressing RETURN to enter the **print** command, you decide to re-enter the **who** command with the name "gwen" instead of "melissa". Here is what to do:

Start by pressing ESC to change to command mode. Then press **k** to move up one line within the history file. The shell will redisplay the **print** command. Press **k** again. You will see the **ls** command. Press **k** again. Now you see the **date** command. Press **k** one last time and you will see the **who** command.

The cursor will be at the beginning of the line. To change the name "melissa", type **3w** to move 3 words to the right. Then press **C** to change the rest of the line. Type **gwen** and press RETURN.

As a **vi** user, you know that there are many ways of doing the same thing. Indeed, the art of using **vi** well is in knowing how to do whatever you want with as few keystrokes as possible. In this case, we could have jumped up four lines at once by pressing ESC to enter command mode and then typing **4k**. The shell would have displayed:

```
who | grep melissa
```

We could have then have moved right to the "m" character by typing **fm** (find "m").

As you can see, the built-in **vi** editor works a lot like the real **vi** editor. There is, however, one important exception. When you use the **/** (search) command, it searches backward (up) within the history file. With the regular editor, the **/** command searches forward (down). Similarly, the **?** command searches forward (down), and the **G** command jumps directly to the oldest line in the history file. If you think about it, this is what you want these commands to do. Otherwise you would have to use **?** to search for a previous command and **1G** to jump to the oldest command.

As you might expect, using **/** by itself repeats the search. For example, to search for the last command that contained the characters "who", press ESC to enter command mode and then enter:

```
/who
```

If this is not the command you want, enter:

```
/
```

and the shell will find the next command that contains "who". You can repeat this as often as you need, in order to find the exact line you want.

Except for these few exceptions, the **vi** commands for the built-in editor work just like the regular **vi** commands: you can insert by using **i**, **a**, **I** or **A**; you can jump to the beginning of the line by pressing **0** and to the end of the line by pressing **$**; and so on. Thus, we will not go into all the commands in detail. For more information, see Chapter 20 where we discuss **vi** in depth. For a summary of **vi** commands, see Appendix C. If you want to read the definitive description of how the **vi** built-in editor works on your system, see the Korn shell manual page (use the command **man ksh**).

HINT
Editing shell commands is cool. Take a few minutes and experiment. Once you get started, you will wonder how you ever lived without it.

Using the emacs Built-In Editor

To use the **emacs** built-in editor, you must first set the appropriate option:

```
set -o emacs
```

Normally, you would do this from within your **.profile** initialization file. Once this option is set, you can use any of the **emacs** commands whenever you want. If you do not already know how to use **emacs**, you should learn to do so before you read this section. We explain the **emacs** editor in Chapter 21. In addition, there is an **emacs** command summary in Appendix D.

You can use **emacs** commands at any time. (Unlike **vi**, you do not have to enter a special command mode.) This means that you can mix **emacs** commands with regular characters as you type. Once you have modified a line to be just the way you want it, you can execute it by pressing RETURN. Note: You do not need to be at the end of the line to press RETURN.

A quick example will make it all clear. You have just typed the following command, but you have not as yet pressed RETURN:

```
who | gred melissa
```

What you want to do is use the **who** command to generate a list of all the people using the system, and then send the output to the **grep** program to extract all the lines that contain the characters "melissa". Don't worry if you don't understand the example. What is important is that you accidentally typed "gred" instead of "grep".

At this point, the cursor is at the end of the line. (Remember, you have not as yet pressed RETURN.) You decide to edit the command before executing it. Press ESC-B twice to move back two words. The cursor is now pointing to "gred". Press ESC-D to delete one word. Type **grep**. The line now reads:

```
who | grep melissa
```

If you do not want to make any further changes, press RETURN. The shell will now execute the new command.

The best way to think about the built-in **emacs** editor is to imagine that you are using a simplified version of **emacs** to edit the history file (including the current line) from within a single, one-line window. Thus, you can only see one command at a time. To move up and down within the history file, you use the same **emacs** commands that move up and down within a regular buffer: **^P** moves up, **^N** moves down, and so on. Each time you move up one line, the shell moves back within the history list and displays the command in that position.

Here is an example you can try for yourself. Enter the following commands, one at a time:

```
who | grep melissa
date
ls -l
print Unix is fun
```

After pressing RETURN to enter the **print** command, you decide to re-enter the **who** command with the name "gwen" instead of "melissa". Here is what to do:

Press **^P** to move up one line within the history file. The shell will redisplay the **print** command. Press **^P** again. You will see the **ls** command. Press **^P** again. Now you see the **date** command. Press **^P** one last time and you will see the **who** command.

The cursor will be at the end of the line. To change the name "melissa", press ESC-H (or ESC-DELETE) to delete one word backward. Type **gwen** and press RETURN.

As you can see, the built-in **emacs** editor works a lot like the real **emacs** editor. Of course, it doesn't have all the advanced functionality (like a built-in programming language or the games), but all the basic commands are there. There is, however, one difference you should know about. The **^Y** command will restore the last thing that you deleted. With the real **emacs** editor, **^Y** will not restore a single character; the built-in version of **emacs** will.

In general, the **emacs** commands for the built-in editor work just like the regular **emacs** commands: **^B** moves backward one character, **^F** moves forward one character, ESC-B moves backward one word, ESC-F **moves forward one word,** **^A** moves to the beginning of the line, **^E** moves to the end of the line; and so on. Thus, we will not go into all the commands here. For more information, see Chapter 21 where we discuss **emacs** in depth. For a summary of **emacs** commands, see Appendix D. If you want to read the definitive description of how the **emacs** built-in editor works on your system, see the Korn shell manual page (use the command **man ksh**).

HINT

Editing shell commands is cool. Take a few minutes and experiment. Once you get started, you will wonder how you ever lived without it.

HINT

There is a special command hidden within the Korn shell **emacs** editor. Once you have set the **emacs** option (with **set -o emacs**), you can press **^V** at any time to display information about which version of the Korn shell you are using. Here is a typical response:

Version 11/16/88e

This means that you are using the November 16, 1988, version of the Korn shell (modification "e").

Initialization and Termination Files: `.profile`, `.kshrc`, `.logout`

So far, we have met several types of commands that are useful for setting up your working environment. We have also discussed options and variables that must be set before you can start work. How can you be sure that everything is prepared properly? You certainly don't want to have to enter a long sequence of commands each time you log in. In addition, there may be certain commands you want to run each time you log out.

The shell provides a way for you to specify such commands once and have them executed at the appropriate time. Here is how it works.

The Korn shell recognizes a special file, named **`.profile`**, in which you can store commands to be run automatically. Each time you log in, the shell looks for a file by this name in your home directory. If the file is there, the shell reads it and executes the commands it finds. Having a **`.profile`** file is important and, if you do not already have one, you should create one.

(Files whose names start with a period are called "dotfiles". We discuss dotfiles in Chapter 23.)

What types of commands should be in your **`.profile`** file? Well, you can put in just about anything you want (like a welcoming message) but, at the very least, you must set up your shell variables, such as **TERM** (to show what type of terminal you are using), **PATH** (the set the search path), and so on. (See the discussion on shell variables earlier in this chapter.)

Most system managers set up their systems so that all new Korn shell users have a **`.profile`** file in their home directories. In most cases, you will find that your shell variables will be set up for you, although, as you become experienced, you may wish to make changes.

HINT

Whenever you put a variable definition in your **`.profile`** file, don't forget to export the variable as well. This ensures that all the programs you use will have access to that variable. (See our discussion earlier in the chapter.)

If you want to take a look at your **.profile** file, use the **more** command:

```
more .profile
```

From time to time, you may decide to modify your **.profile** file. For example, you might want the system to display the message:

```
HELLO, GOOD LOOKING!
```

each time you log in. Or you may wish to start the mail program automatically if there are messages for you. To make such changes, you will have to know how to use a text editor: either **vi** or **emacs**, which are discussed later in the book.

As we mentioned, the shell executes the commands in your **.profile** file each time you log in. However, there are certain commands that you will want to execute each time a new shell is started. For example, the options that you set with the **set -o** command are not exported. If you want to preserve them, you must redefine them every time a new shell starts. Similarly, you may decide to define functions (which we do not discuss in this book), and they too must be redefined for each invocation of a shell.

Why is this important? Well, say that you are editing a file and, from time to time, you pause the editor to go to a shell to issue some commands. When you are finished, you end the shell and return to the editor. You want to make sure that this new temporary shell has the same options as your login shell.

Here is how you can do this. Each time a new shell is started, the first thing it does is look for an ENVIRONMENT FILE. If this file exists, the new shell reads it and executes the commands it finds. To check for an environment file, the shell looks for a variable named **ENV** that contains the pathname of the environment file. (We explain pathnames in Chapter 23.) Thus, to use an environment file—and you should definitely have one—all you need to do is use an editor to create the file, and then put a line in your **.profile** file defining and exporting the **ENV** variable.

You can give your environment file any name you want, but we suggest that you use the name **.kshrc** and place it in your home directory. The following command, in your **.profile** file, will do the job:

```
export ENV=$HOME/.kshrc
```

What's in a Name?   The `.kshrc` File

Although few people know it, the "rc" stands for "run commands"—that is, initialization commands that are run automatically.

The name derives from the CTSS operating system (Compatible Time Sharing System), developed at MIT in 1963. CTSS had a facility called "runcom" that would execute a list of commands stored in a file.

Many Unix programs automatically look for "rc" initialization files in your home directory. For example, the C-Shell looks for a `.cshrc` file, the **ex** and **vi** text editors look for a `.exrc` file, the **mail** program looks for a `.mailrc` file, and so on.

With the Korn shell, you can choose any name you want for your environment file, so using `.kshrc` is appropriate.

There is an important reason why these names start with a dot: when you use the **ls** command to list your files, the names that begin with a dot are normally not displayed. This means that you do not have to look at these names each time you list your files. On those rare occasions when you want to display the names of all your files, including the names that begin with a dot, you can use **ls** with the **-a** (list all) option (see Chapter 23).

Every time a new shell is started, the commands in your environment file are executed. This happens, of course, whenever you log in and your initial shell is started. It also happens whenever you run a shell script—we discuss shell scripts later in the chapter—or pause a program to start a temporary shell. The commands in the `.profile` file are executed only once: when you log in, just before the environment file is processed.

HINT

If you are a C-Shell user, you may know that when you log in, your environment file (`.cshrc`) is processed *before* your login initialization file (`.login`). With the Korn shell, the `.profile` file is processed first. If this were not the case, the shell would not know where to find the environment file, as the **ENV** variable would not yet be defined.

Or, if you are inclined to be teleological, you might say that the Korn shell processes your `.profile` file first to allow you the flexibility of choosing your own name for the environment file, rather than being forced to use the standard name.

The last file we want to discuss is one that can hold commands that will be executed whenever you log out. For example, you can display a nice message each time you finish your work with Unix. Or, more likely, you might enjoy running the **fortune** program (see Chapter 7) so that every time you log out you will see a funny remark.

The C-Shell has a built-in facility to find such a termination file. If you have a file named **.logout** in your home directory, the C-Shell will read it and execute the commands it finds each time you log out.

The Korn shell does not do this automatically. However, you can tell it to do so by placing the following command in your **.profile** file:

```
trap '$HOME/.logout' EXIT
```

We won't go into the technical details here. Essentially, you are telling the shell to "trap" the signal named **EXIT**, which is sent whenever you log out. When this signal is detected, the shell will process the file you specify: in this case, a file named **.logout** in your home directory. Like the environment file, you can specify any file you want, but we suggest using the name **.logout** and keeping it in your home directory.

HINT

Which commands should go in your **.profile** file and which should go in your environment file? Here's what works best.

Your **.profile** file should contain commands to:

—set up your terminal
—define shell variables
—set the user mask for default file permissions (Chapter 24)
—perform initialization tasks each time you log in

Your environment (**.kshrc**) file should contain commands to:

—define aliases
—define functions

Shell Scripts

As we explained in Chapter 10, the shell is more than a command processor. The shell also supports a full programming language. In addition to regular Unix commands, you can also use special shell programming commands.

A file of such commands is called a SHELL SCRIPT. As the shell processes a script, it reads one command at a time. (Think of an actor reading a script, one line at a time.) To describe the processing, we say that the shell INTERPRETS each command.

In general, any program that reads and processes SCRIPTS—lists of sequential commands—can be called an INTERPRETER. Unix has a number of interpreters. For example, some of the text editors can interpret predefined scripts.

The details of programming the shell are beyond the scope of this book. However, for your interest, we have included a sample script in the Korn shell programming language (see Figure 12-4). Within the script, lines that begin with a number sign (**#**) are comments that are ignored by the shell. (If you want to see a sample script in the C-Shell language, look at the end of Chapter 11.)

In the sample script, you will notice that the first line is:

```
#! /bin/ksh
```

This tells Unix to run the script under a Korn shell.

```
#! /bin/ksh
# SHOWINFO: Korn shell script to display an information
file

# If the information file exists, display its contents.
# Otherwise, if the file does not exist, but if an older
#   version exists, display the older version.
# If neither file exists, display an error message
   if [ -f info ]
   then
      echo "The information file has been found.";
      more info
   elif [ -f info.old ]
   then
      echo "Only the old information file was found.";
      more info.old
   else
      echo "The information file was not found."
   fi
```

FIGURE 12-4. *A sample Korn shell script*

Some people feel that the design of any shell programming facility is necessarily compromised because the shell must do double duty: as a command interpreter and as a programming language. Such people prefer to use an alternate interpreter designed only for scripts.

The most popular such interpreter is Perl, the Practical Extraction and Report Language. Perl was designed by Larry Wall, one of the Unix folk heroes. Perl provides a much more powerful scripting facility than the shell and is widely used by system managers. However, Perl programming is more difficult than shell programming and is not for the faint of heart.

CHAPTER 13

Communicating with Other People

One of the wonderful things about Unix is that every time you log in you become a member of a global electronic community, especially if your computer is connected to the Internet. In this chapter, we will show you how you can find out about members of this community. You will learn how to see who is doing what on your computer and how to display the public information Unix keeps about each userid.

We will then show you how to hold a "conversation" with anyone: on your own computer or anywhere in the world. With a simple command, you can connect your computer to another and type messages back and forth in real time.

To start, let's take a look around your own local system.

Displaying Userids Who Are Logged In: `users`

Unix is not a world of secrets. For example, to find out who is currently logged in to your system, simply enter the command:

```
users
```

Unix will display the name of each userid that is logged in. If a userid is logged in more than once, it will be displayed more than once. For example, say that in response to a **users** command you see:

```
gwen gwen harley tln kim
```

This means that there are five userids currently logged in. One of them, **gwen**, is logged in twice. Usually this means either 1) the same person is logged in at two different terminals or 2) the person is using X Window and is logged in within two different windows.

Information About Logged-In Userids: `who`

The **users** command only shows the names of the userids that are currently logged in to your system. For more information, use the **who** command. Here are some examples. You enter:

```
who
```

and you see:

```
gwen      console Jul  8 10:30
gwen      ttyp0   Jul 12 16:45
harley    ttyp1   Jul 12 17:46
tln       ttyp4   Jul 12 21:22    (cat)
kim       ttyp3   Jul 12 17:41    (tintin.ucsb.edu)
```

The first column shows the userids (the same information as the **users** command) that are logged in to your computer. The next column shows the name of the terminal at which each userid is logged in. Most terminal names start with "tty" (which, as we pointed out in Chapter 6, is often used as an abbreviation for "terminal").

Following the terminal name is the date and time at which the userid logged in. In this example, you can see that userid **gwen** has been logged in to terminal **console** for a long time. This userid may represent a system manager who has a terminal in her office permanently logged in.

Finally, if a userid has logged in from another computer, the name of this computer will be shown following the time. In our example, **gwen** and **harley** have logged in to the host directly from a terminal. **tln** and **kim**, on the other hand, have logged in via network connections. In other words, they have first logged in to their own computers and, from there, logged in remotely to our computer.

When a userid has logged in remotely from a computer on the local network, you will see only a simple name. For example, **tln** has logged in from the computer named **cat** which is on our local network.

When a userid has logged in remotely from a computer on a different network, you will see the full network address. For example, **kim** has logged in from the computer **tintin.ucsb.edu** which is on a totally different network. (We will discuss addresses in Chapter 14.)

Information About Local Network Logged-In Userids: `rwho`

The **users** and **who** commands display information about your computer. However, there may be times when you want to see who is logged in to the computers on the same local network as your computer. The **rwho** (remote **who**) command will display this information. The syntax is:

`rwho [-a]`

Here is some typical output:

```
gwen      nipper:ttyp0    Jul 12 16:45
harley    nipper:ttyp1    Jul 12 17:46
kim       nipper:ttyp3    Jul 12 17:41 :10
melissa   princess:ttyp1  Jul 12 20:01
randy     law:ttyp3       Jul 12 20:35
```

We see some of the userids from the **who** example above, all of which are logged in to our system (**nipper**). We also see two other userids: **melissa**, who is logged in to **princess**, and **randy**, who is logged in to **law**.

Like the **who** command, **rwho** also shows the date and time at which the userid logged in. To the right of this information, **rwho** displays information about users who have been idle—have not pressed a key—for at least a minute. In this example, we see the user logged in as **kim** has not pressed a key for 10 minutes.

Notice, however, that two userids seems to be missing. When we entered the **who** command above, we saw that userid **gwen** was logged in twice. What happened to the second session? Furthermore, userid **tln** has disappeared completely.

The answer is that **rwho**, unlike **users** or **who**, does not display the names of userids that have been idle for more than an hour. If you want **rwho** to list all the userids, use the **-a** option:

```
rwho -a
```

Here is some sample output:

```
gwen       nipper:console Jul  8 10:30 99:59
gwen       nipper:ttyp0   Jul 12 16:45
harley     nipper:ttyp1   Jul 12 17:46
tln        nipper:ttyp4   Jul 12 21:22   1:40
kim        nipper:ttyp3   Jul 12 17:41    :10
melissa    princess:ttyp1 Jul 12 20:01
murray     princess:ttyp3 Jul 12 10:11   3:09
randy      law:ttyp3      Jul 12 20:35
```

Now we see userid **tln** as well as the other session for **gwen**. We also see another userid named **murray** who is logged in to **princess** and is idle.

To the right of the login time and date, we see the idle time in hours and minutes. In our example, **tln** has been idle for 1 hour, 40 minutes, **kim** has been idle for 10 minutes, and **murray** has been idle for 3 hours, 9 minutes. The maximum time that **rwho -a** will display is 99 hours and 59 minutes (about 4 days, 4 hours). Thus, we know that **gwen** has been idle at the console for at least that long.

HINT
To find out who is logged in to your computer, use **users** or **who**. To find out who is logged in to any computer on your local network, use **rwho** or **rwho -a**.

Finding Out What Someone Is Doing: w

The commands we have discussed so far merely tell you who is logged in to your computer or to a computer on your network. If you want to find out what somebody is doing, use the **w** command. The syntax is:

```
w [-hsu] [userid]
```

Think of the name **w** as meaning "Who is doing what?"

Note: The **w** command, like the **who** command, displays information only about users on your computer, not about all the users within the network.

The output of **w** consists of two parts: First, there is a one-line summary showing overall system statistics. This summary is the same as the output of the **uptime** command that we discussed in Chapter 7. Next, there is information describing the activities of each userid that is logged in.

You can control what output you get by using the options. With no options, you get all the output. For example, if you enter:

```
w
```

you will see output like this:

```
8:44pm up 9 days, 7:02, 5 users, load average: 0.11, 0.02, 0.00
User       tty       login@  idle  JCPU   PCPU  what
gwen       console  Wed10am 4days 42:41  37:56  -csh
gwen       ttyp0     4:45pm         1:40   0:36  vi existential
harley     ttyp1     5:47pm        15:11         w
tln        ttyp4     9:22pm  1:40    20      1   -rn rec.pets.cats
kim        ttyp3     5:41pm    10  2:16     13   -csh
```

The first line shows the system statistics, which we explained in Chapter 7. In this case, the system has been up for 9 days, 7 hours and 2 minutes, and there are 5 userids currently logged in. The last three numbers show the number of programs that have been waiting to execute, averaged over the last 1, 5 and 15 minutes, respectively. These numbers give you an idea of the load on the system.

The next line shows the headings for the information that is to follow. For each userid, we see the following:

User:	userid
tty:	terminal name
login@:	time of login
idle:	time since the user last pressed a key (idle time)
JCPU:	processor time used by all processes (jobs) since login
PCPU:	processor time used by the current process
what:	the command (and its arguments) that is currently running

Note the term IDLE TIME. This refers to the elapsed time since the user has typed anything. Thus, if you are waiting for a time-consuming job to finish and you are not typing while you are waiting, the **w** will show you being "idle".

What's in a Name?   CPU

In the days of mainframes, the "brain" of the computer—what we would now call the processor—was a large box. This box was referred to as the central processing unit or CPU (and still is for large computers). In Unix, we sometimes use the term "CPU" to mean "processor".

Thus, we use the term "CPU time" to refer to processor time. You may hear someone say, "Ron's program slows down the system because it takes up too much CPU time." This means that Ron's program is so demanding that, when it runs, it makes all the other programs wait.

In our example above, we can see that userid **gwen** is logged in to more than one terminal. First, **gwen** is logged in to the console, although there has been no activity for about 4 days. A C-Shell (**csh**) is running, probably waiting for input. At another terminal, **ttyp0**, userid **gwen** is active, editing a file named **existential** with the **vi** editor (which we will meet in Chapter 20).

Userid **harley** is logged-in to the terminal **ttyp1** and is running the **w** program. The processing time used by this program is so small (less than 1/100th of a second) that it is not even displayed.

(Note: Whenever you run the **w** command, you will see yourself running the **w** command. However, you won't really see yourself, you will see your userid, just like **harley** in our example. This situation is fraught with important philosophical implications.)

Finally, you can see that userids **tln** and **kim** are both idle. **tln** is reading the Usenet discussion group about cats and has not pressed a key for

1 minute and 40 seconds. **kim** is running a C-Shell that is probably waiting for a command and has not pressed a key for 10 seconds.

By default, the **w** command will display all of this information. You can use the options to specify that you want less information.

If you specify a userid, **w** will display information about that userid only. Using the previous example, if you enter:

w gwen

you would see:

```
8:44pm up 9 days, 7:02, 5 users, load average: 0.11, 0.02, 0.00
User       tty          login@  idle   JCPU    PCPU   what
gwen       console   Wed10am 4days   42:41   37:56  -csh
gwen       ttyp0        4:45pm            1:40    0:36   vi existential
```

The **-s** option displays a short report. For example, if you enter **w -s** the report looks like this:

```
8:44pm up 9 days, 7:02, 5 users, load average: 0.11, 0.02, 0.00
User       tty       idle    what
gwen       co       4days   csh
gwen       p0                vi
harley     p1                w
tln        p4        1:40    rn
kim        p3         10     csh
```

This report is a lot simpler. The name of the terminal has been abbreviated. The processing times have been omitted. Finally, only the name of the current command is displayed; the arguments are omitted. If you use **w -h**, you will get the long report, but without the headings:

```
gwen       console   Wed10am 4days   42:41   37:56   -csh
gwen       ttyp0        4:45pm            1:40    0:36   vi existential
harley     ttyp1        5:47pm          15:11             w
tln        ttyp4        9:22pm  1:40      20       1   -rn rec.pets.cats
kim        ttyp3        5:41pm    10     2:16      13   -csh
```

This is handy if you are going to send the output of **w** to another program for further processing, since each line represents a single userid. (Sending the output of one program to another program is called "piping" and is explained in Chapter 16.)

Perhaps the most useful form of this command is to combine these two options: **w -sh**. The output looks like the following:

```
gwen      co      4days   csh
gwen      p0              vi
harley    p1              w
tln       p4      1:40    rn
kim       p3        10    csh
```

This is an easy way to have a quick look at what is happening in the system. You might even want to create an alias for this. (See Chapters 11 if you use the C-Shell or Chapter 12 if you use the Korn shell.) For the C-Shell, put the following alias in your **.cshrc** initialization file:

alias snoop w -sh

If you use the Korn shell, here is the equivalent command for your environment file:

alias snoop='w -sh'

You can now check out the system whenever you want by entering:

snoop

Finally, if you use **w -u**, the command will display only the first line of the heading. For example:

8:44pm up 9 days, 7:02, 5 users, load average: 0.11, 0.02, 0.00

This is the same as the **uptime** command (see Chapter 7).

Note: The **w** command will not display system information about other computers in your network. You will have to use **ruptime** (also Chapter 7).

Public Information About a Userid: The Password File

Unix maintains information about userids that is available to anyone. This information is kept in your computer's PASSWORD FILE. On many systems, this file is named **/etc/passwd** and you can display it by entering the command:

more /etc/passwd

(We will discuss the **more** command in detail in Chapter 18. For now, we will say that you can use this command to display the contents a file, one screenful at a time. While the file is being displayed, press the SPACE bar to display the next screenful, and press **q** to quit.)

The name **/etc/passwd** refers to a file named **passwd** that lies in the **/etc** directory. We will discuss directories and file names in Chapters 23 and 24.

The standard password file holds the information the system needs to identify you and to help you log in: your userid, your real name, what shell you use, your home directory (discussed in Chapter 23) and other information. Actually, the name of this file is a misnomer. It might better be called the "userid information file".

Note: In some networks, all the userid/password information is gathered into one or more central network files. This may allow you to use any computer on the network. In such cases, the **/etc/passwd** file will contain only a few basic entries; the bulk of the userid information will be elsewhere. You may have to ask around to find out where this information is kept on your system.

Knowing that all sorts of information, including userids, is kept in the password file, it is natural to ask: what about passwords? Are they kept in the password file? The answer is, maybe.

On some systems the passwords are kept right in the password file. On other systems the passwords are kept, along with special password data, in what is called a SHADOW FILE. In either case, the actual password is encoded.

Thus, it is safe to let anyone read the password file, which allows the basic information about each userid to be public. This method of organization is a long-standing Unix tradition.

Understanding What's in the Password File

One way to find out all the public information about a particular userid is to display the line of the password file that pertains to that userid. For example, the following command searches the password file for a line that contains "harley":

```
grep harley /etc/passwd
```

(We won't explain the details here; see Chapter 17. Briefly, **grep** displays all the lines in a file that contain a specified pattern.) Here is some typical output: the entry for userid **harley** within a password file.

```
harley:62VvAhkOJI:101:90:&Hahn,,,2024561414:/usr/harley:/bin/csh
```

The standard Unix password file (which may be modified on your system) contains seven fields, separated by colons.

■ The first field is the userid, in this case, **harley**.

■ The second field is the password (encoded, of course).
   By the way, it is impossible to figure out the actual password from the encoded pattern. It is also impossible to guess the encoding algorithm by using **passwd** to feed Unix different passwords and seeing what patterns are created. Don't waste your time trying to beat the system. Even the system manager, who can log in as superuser, has no way to find out your password.

■ The next two fields contain the numeric value for the userid and the groupid.
   As you know, all users have a login name, or userid. As we will discuss later, each userid belongs to a group, and each group has its own name, called a groupid.
   For example, if someone gives you a complimentary account on their computer, just for fun, your userid might be put into a group named **guests**. Groups and groupids are important when you use file permissions, which we will discuss in Chapter 24.
   Internally, Unix assigns each userid and groupid a unique number. In this example, the userid is number **101** and the groupid is number **90**. We know that the userid is **harley**, but we don't know the actual groupid (the name of the group). This information is stored in the file **/etc/group**, which you can display by using the command:

```
more /etc/group
```

■ The fifth part of a password file entry is called the GECOS FIELD. (We will explain why in a minute.) Traditionally, this entry has four components, separated by commas:

   — your full name
   — the room number of your office
   — the phone number of your office
   — your home phone number

Some systems maintain this structure; others have modified it somewhat. However, at the very least, the GECOS field should contain your real name. In the example above, the GECOS field contains:

```
&Hahn,,,2024561414
```

The **&** character means that the first name is the same as the userid (which, in this case, is **harley**). Although there is no room number or phone number, there is a home phone number: (202) 456-1414.

- The sixth field shows the userid's home directory: the place where that user keeps his or her files. (We will discuss home directories in Chapter 23.)

- The last field contains the name of the shell that is started automatically for the userid upon login. In this case, the userid will be using the C-Shell (**/bin/csh**).

What's in a Name?   The GECOS Field

The fifth field within each entry in the Unix password file is called the GECOS field. Typically, this field contains the user's real name and, perhaps, other information such as a phone number.

Where does the name come from?

Around 1970, programmers at General Electric (then in the computer business) developed a clone of IBM's System/360 low-end DOS operating system. The GE system was called GECOS: General Electric Comprehensive Operating System.

Some years later, Honeywell bought out GE's computer division and changed the name of the system to GCOS: General Comprehensive Operating System. It happened that some early Bell Labs Unix systems used GCOS machines for printing and other services. (Bell Labs is where Unix was first developed.) For this reason, someone at Bell Labs added a field to the password file to hold the GCOS identification information.

It has been a long time, of course, since this field has actually held real GCOS information; the space is now used to hold personal data. However, for the sake of historical obscurity, the entry is still known as the GECOS field (or, occasionally, the GCOS field).

Displaying Public Information About a Userid: `finger`

In the last section, we explained how you can look at your system's password file to display public information about a particular userid.

However, the information that is displayed in this manner is not all that easy to read. In addition, some networked systems keep the password information in central files that are not directly accessible to most users.

In this section, we will show you how to use the **finger** command to get at all this information easily. Moreover, as we will see later, **finger** has a reach that goes far beyond your local computer. The syntax for the **finger** command is:

finger [**-ls**] [*name...*]

The most common way to use this command is to specify the name of a particular userid, such as:

finger harley

The command will display the public information about this userid. For example:

```
Login name: harley                In real life: Harley Hahn
Phone: 202-456-1414
Directory: /usr/harley                Shell: /bin/csh
On since Aug  9 21:01:56 on ttyp3 from nipper.ucsb.edu
```

Aside from the information that can be found in the password file, **finger** will let you know if the userid happens to be logged in at the time. In this case, userid **harley** was logged in from the remote computer **nipper.ucsb.edu** using terminal **ttyp3**.

If you are not sure of someone's userid, try using his or her name. For example:

finger Hahn

On some systems, **finger** will check in the GECOS fields of the password file, looking for names. Other systems are less sophisticated and you can use only userids. If you specify more than one userid, for example:

finger harley gwen tln

finger will display information about each one in turn. Alternatively, you can use **finger** without any names at all:

finger

You will get a short report that contains one line for each userid that is currently logged in. For example:

```
Login       Name           TTY  Idle    When
harley      Harley Hahn    p1    1:    Wed 17:45
kenn        Kenn Nesbitt   p0          Wed 17:46
ron         Ron Dragushan  p6          Mon 09:17
rick        Rick Stout     p4   10:    Mon 09:17
```

Some systems may show you extra information, such as the computer from which the userid has logged in or the information in the userid's GECOS field.

To control the output, you can use the **-s** and **-l** options to force **finger** to display a short or long report. For example, to display a short report on several specific userids, you can use:

```
finger -s harley gwen tln
```

To display a long report on all the userids who are logged in, use:

```
finger -l
```

Your system may have other options. Check the **man** page (use **man finger**).

Note: We sometimes use the word FINGER as a verb, meaning to use the **finger** program to check out someone. For example, you might say to someone that you meet at a dance, "If you forget my home phone number, just finger me." (Yes, Unix people really do talk like this.)

Changing Your Publicly Accessible Information: chfn

As we explained earlier in the chapter, your entry in the password file contains public information about your userid. Some of this can be changed only by your system manager: for example, your userid and your home directory.

However, you can change some of the information. First, as we explained in Chapter 10, you can use the **chsh** command to change your default shell. Second, you can use the **chfn** (change finger information) command to modify whatever is in the GECOS field. Just enter:

```
chfn
```

and follow the instructions.

The GECOS field contains information about you: your name, and possibly your office number, office phone number and home phone number. The **chfn** allows you to modify or remove this information whenever you want by making the appropriate changes to the system password file.

In fact, the **chfn** command is really just the **passwd** command with a **-f** option. This makes sense because what you are doing is changing the system password file, just like when you use the **passwd** command to change your password.

Note: Some systems will not allow you to use **chfn**. On such systems, all changes must be performed by the system manager.

The **finger** Command and the **.plan** and **.project** Files

Aside from the public information in the password file, **finger** will display information from two other files you can control directly. Their names are **.plan** and **.project**. If one or both of these files exists in your home directory, **finger** will read them.

(Why do these file names begin with a period? You list the names of your files by using the **ls** command. The **ls** command will not list file names that begin with a period unless you use the **-a** [all] option. Many system files have names that begin with a period so you don't have to look at the names each time you list your files. This is discussed in Chapter 23.)

(What is your home directory? It is the directory that has been created for you to store your own personal files. We will discuss the home directory in Chapter 23.)

It is up to you to create the **.plan** and **.project** files; they are purely optional. To create these files, you will need to know how to use a text editor like **vi** (Chapter 20) or **emacs** (Chapter 21). Make sure the files have the appropriate permissions for other people to read them. (File permissions are explained in Chapter 24.)

Here is how the **.plan** and **.project** files are used. If you have a **.plan** file, **finger** will display its contents. If you have a **.project** file, **finger** will display the first line.

Remember, Unix was designed in academic and research environments where just about everybody had a project to work on (and a few people even had plans). You would describe your project in your **.project** file, and everyone who fingered you would know what you were doing.

The **.plan** file was intended to be a description of your current location and upcoming plans. The idea was that you could change your **.plan** file whenever necessary to let people know where you were.

Nowadays, people use these files to hold all types of information. For example, if you are giving a party, you can put the directions for getting to your house in your **.plan** file. You can then mail people invitations, telling them to finger you if they need directions. In a university setting, one common use of the **.plan** file is for professors and teaching assistants to list their office hours.

If you finger a variety of people, you will see a variety of **.plan** files: jokes, poems, drawings, quips, and, very occasionally, an actual plan.

Here is one example so you can see what it looks like. You enter:

```
finger harley
```

and you see:

```
Login name: harley              In real life: Harley Hahn
    Phone: 202-456-1414
Directory: /usr/harley              Shell: /bin/csh
On since Aug  9 21:01:56 on ttyp3 from nipper.ucsb.edu
Project: writing a Unix book
Plan:
    To live forever, or die in the attempt.
```

If you finger someone who does not have a **.project** file, **finger** will silently omit it. However, if the person does not have a **.plan** file, you will see:

```
No Plan.
```

(which is usually appropriate).

Displaying Mail Status with `finger`

Some versions of **finger** will display information about a userid's mailbox. (We will discuss mail in Chapter 15.)

If the user has read and disposed of all the mail in his or her mailbox, **finger** will display the message:

```
No unread mail
```

along with the regular information. If the user has read all the mail, but has not disposed of it, you will see a message like this:

```
Mail last read Wed May 18 17:06:10 1994
```

Finally, if there is mail waiting to be read, the message will look like this:

```
New mail received Wed May 18 17:22:26 1992;
  unread since Wed May 18 17:06:10 1992
```

Some systems may also show the amount of unread mail in kilobytes (1 kilobyte = 1K = 1,024 characters).

You might think this will come in handy when you need to know if someone has read the mail you sent. However, looks are deceiving. **finger** actually has no way to know if someone has read his or her mail. All it can find out is the last time that the mail file was accessed.

Isn't this the same thing as knowing if someone has read his or her mail? Not at all.

In Chapter 15, we will learn that you can use the **from** command to display a summary of mail that is waiting for you. When you use **from**, you do not actually read the mail, you just see a summary.

Many people put the **from** command in their initialization file so they can see a summary of their mail each time they log in. Since the **from** command accesses the mail file, it fools **finger** into thinking the mail has already been read by a person.

Here is a common scenario. You have sent someone an urgent mail message and you want to know if he has read it yet. You use a **finger** command, which reports that the mail was last read on such and such a date.

Since your message was urgent, you are annoyed that, after having read your message, the recipient did not even bother to reply. (We won't say you are disgruntled, but you are certainly far from gruntled.)

So you send him a nasty note in which you tell him exactly what you think of people who do not respond to important messages in a timely fashion.

Meanwhile, unbeknownst to you, the recipient has never actually read your message. All that happened is a **from** command in his initialization file has looked at the mail file once.

When the recipient gets your second note, he gets so mad that he sends over two plug-uglies to break both your legs.

Imagine your embarrassment!

Fingering the World

If **finger** could only display information about the userids on your own computer, that would be useful enough. But **finger** can do a lot more: it can tell you about any userid on any computer that is connected to yours (as long as it supports this facility).

We are referring to more computers than the ones in your local network. If your computer is connected to the Internet—the global collection of networks—you can finger anyone on any other Internet computer, anywhere in the world. All you need is his or her electronic address.

In Chapter 14, we will discuss addresses. For now, we will explain briefly that standard Internet addresses are of the form:

```
userid@domain
```

where *domain* is the official name of the person's computer. Here is an example:

```
harley@nipper.ucsb.edu
```

So you could enter the command:

```
finger harley@nipper.ucsb.edu
```

Your computer will send a request to the remote computer. Its **finger** program will service the request and send the response back to your computer.

If you leave out the userid, **finger** will ask for information regarding which userids are currently logged in to the computer whose name you specify. For example, to see a short report about all the userids who are logged in to the computer named **nipper.ucsb.edu**, enter:

```
finger @nipper.ucsb.edu
```

Be sure not to leave out the **@** character, or **finger** will think you are specifying a userid, not a computer name.

On your own network, you can usually refer to a computer using only the first part of its full name. For example, if there is a computer in your network named **misty**, you can display a short report about all the userids currently logged in by entering:

```
finger @misty
```

Systems that support remote fingering have a finger daemon (see below) that receives and processes finger requests. Some system managers do not like the idea of their userids and computers being fingered from anywhere in the world. They will specify that their finger daemon should not service remote requests. If you ask **finger** to connect to such a system, you will get a message like:

```
connect: Connection refused
```

Note: A DAEMON (yes, that is how you spell it) is a program that executes in the background and provides a useful service. We will discuss such programs in Chapter 19 when we meet the daemon that handles the Unix printing services.

Checking to See if a Computer Is Alive and Well: `ping`

If your computer has trouble contacting another computer you think is on the Internet, you may see a message like:

    unknown host: nipper.ucsb.edu

This can mean one of three things. First, you may have entered a bad name (check your spelling). Second, one of the links between your computer and the remote computer may be down temporarily. The third possibility is that the destination computer may exist, but it may not be connected to the Internet. This can be confusing because there are many computers that have names that look like official Internet addresses, but that are not really connected to the Internet.

If you want to check if a computer is actually connected, you can use the **ping** command. The syntax is:

    ping computer-name

For example, you might enter:

    ping nipper.ucsb.edu

You will get one of three responses. If the computer is on the Internet and is responding, you will see a message like this:

    nipper.ucsb.edu is alive

If the computer is on the Internet, but is not responding, you will see a message (after a while) like this:

    no answer from nipper.ucsb.edu

Finally, if the computer is not connected to the Internet, you will see a message like this:

    ping: unknown host nipper.ucsb.edu

The **ping** command is useful if you are trying to connect to someone using the **talk** command (explained later in this chapter) and you are having trouble making the connection.

Note: There are various versions of the **ping** command. The one on your system may work differently, but the main idea will be the same.

What's in a Name? Ping

On a ship, a single sonar pulse that is sent out to reflect off another ship is called a "ping". You can see the analogy to a computer command which sends out an electronic query to check the status of another system. Thus, we have the **ping** command. Officially, the name stands for "Packet Internet Groper". (On the Internet, data is sent in packets.)

In conversation, the word "ping" is used as a verb: "I couldn't connect to the other computer, so I pinged it to see if it was alive." If you ever call someone who answers the phone by saying "ping", you know you have reached a Unix expert (or a sonar operator).

Communicating with Someone Directly: talk

If you need to send a message to someone, you can always use the Unix mail system (see Chapter 15). However, there will be times when you really want to talk with someone directly, back and forth, like a telephone call.

If that person is logged in to a computer that is connected to yours, you can use the **talk** command. The syntax is:

```
talk user-name [terminal-name]
```

If the person you want to talk to is logged in to your computer, all you need to do is specify their userid. For example:

```
talk harley
```

If the person is logged into another computer, specify the full address (as we described for the **finger** command). For example:

talk harley@nipper.ucsb.edu

(How do you tell if a particular userid is logged in? For your own computer, use the **users** or **who** commands; for remote computers, use the **rwho** or **finger** commands. To see what computers are connected to your local network, use **ruptime**.)

When you use **who** or **rwho**, you may see that the userid you want to talk to is logged in to more than one terminal. If so, you will want to connect to the terminal that is active. The output of **who** and **rwho** shows you what is happening on each terminal. Pick the one that looks the best. You can then specify that terminal name as part of the **talk** command.

For example, say that you want to talk to a userid named **gwen**. The **who** command shows you:

```
User      tty        login@  idle   JCPU   PCPU  what
gwen      console    Wed10am 4days  42:41  37:56 -csh
gwen      ttyp0      4:45pm         1:40   0:36  vi existential
```

In this case, it is best to talk to the **ttyp0** terminal. Enter:

talk gwen ttyp0

Once you enter the **talk** command, you will see the message:

[Waiting for your party to respond]

At the other end, the **talk** daemon is displaying a message for the recipient:

Message from Talk_Daemon@nipper at 13:19 ...
talk: connection requested by harley@nipper.
talk: respond with: talk harley@nipper

The message means that someone with the userid of **harley**, on a computer named **nipper**, is trying to talk with you. To establish the connection, you must enter your own **talk** command, in this case:

talk harley@nipper

You will then see a message telling you the connection has been established.

If you enter a **talk** command and the other userid is not logged in, you will see:

[Your party is not logged on]

If the other person is logged in, but is not responding, **talk** will display:

[Ringing your party again]

If you see this last message repeatedly, you should probably give up. Abort the **talk** command by pressing the **intr** key (usually **^C**, see Chapter 6).

Once you make a connection, **talk** will take control of your screen and divide it into two parts. From now on, everything you or the other person types will be echoed on both screens. The top half of the screen shows what you type. The bottom half of the screen shows what the other person types.

If the data is not being displayed properly—for example, if the characters are dribbling down the left-hand side of the screen—make sure you have set the global **TERM** variable correctly (see Chapters 4, 11 and 12).

The nice thing about **talk** is that both people can type at the same time, just like talking over the telephone. However, to keep from getting confused there are two conventions you should follow.

First, when you are finished typing something, press RETURN twice to put in a blank line. This tells the person, who may have been waiting patiently, that you are finished for the moment. Second, it is polite to say good-bye ("bye") before terminating a conversation.

As you are typing, you can use any of the regular correction keys we discussed in Chapter 6. These keys are shown in Figure 13-1. In addition, if the screen becomes garbled, you can tell **talk** to redisplay it by pressing **^L**.

To quit talking, you can either press **^D** (the **eof** key) to tell **talk** there is no more data, or you can press **^C** (or whatever your **intr** key is) to abort the command. Either person can sever the connection by pressing one of these two keys.

Replacements for the `talk` Program: `ntalk`, `ytalk`

If your system has a program called **ytalk**, you should use it instead of **talk**. **ytalk** is a replacement for **talk** that works better and has more features. For example, **ytalk** will let you talk with more than one person at the same time, and if each person has **ytalk**, you can all talk together.

KEY	PURPOSE
BACKSPACE, DELETE	erase the last character typed (**erase**)
^W	erase the last word typed (**werase**)
^X, ^U	erase the entire line (**kill**)
^L	redisplay the entire screen

FIGURE 13-1.   *Special keys to use with* **talk**

In addition, the **talk** program has a problem you may encounter when you try to talk to people over the Internet. The details have to do with how data is stored.

Sun computers and Macintoshes store data using a scheme called "big-endian", while VAX computers and PCs use a system called "little-endian". The **talk** program will not connect two computers unless they store data the same way. When you try to connect to a computer that is not compatible with yours, you will see the message:

[Checking for invitation on caller's machine]

Although this looks like a nice message, it is misleading. It really means your two computers cannot communicate using **talk** and nothing is going to happen.

A newer program, called **ntalk**, will connect computers that are not alike, but only if they are both using **ntalk**. The great thing about the **ytalk** program is that it will work with any other computer, whether it stores data using big-endian or little-endian, and whether the other person is using **talk**, **ntalk** or **ytalk**.

If your system does not have **ytalk**, you might ask your system manager to get it for you.

HINT FOR NERDS

Within a computer, bytes are stored within words. A BIG-ENDIAN computer (such as a Sun or Macintosh) stores the bytes with the most significant byte (the "big end") first. A LITTLE-ENDIAN computer (such as a VAX or PC) stores the least significant byte (the "little end") first.

Communicating with Someone Directly: `write`

Aside from **talk**, there is another, older program named **write** that you can use to talk with someone directly. The syntax is:

write *userid* [*terminal-name*]

Unlike **talk**, **write** does not divide the screen into two parts. Once you establish a connection, all **write** does is copy data from your terminal directly to the other person's terminal and vice versa. This has two immediate disadvantages:

- If you both type at the same time, the characters will be mixed together. You will have to take turns.

- You can only use **write** to connect to a terminal on your own computer. You cannot connect to someone who is using a different computer.

However, there are advantages to **write**:

- Some systems do not have a **talk** command, but **write** is almost always available. You will at least be able to communicate with people on your computer.

- When you are using **write**, it is possible to enter a regular Unix command without severing the connection. With **talk**, there is no easy way to do this.

To write to someone, specify their userid. For example:

write harley

If they are logged in to more than one terminal, you can specify the one to which you want to connect. (See the discussion for the **talk** command above.) For example:

write harley ttyp0

If you mistakenly enter an Internet-style remote address, such as:

`write harley@nipper.ucsb.edu`

write will try to interpret it as a userid and you will see a message telling you the userid is not logged in:

`harley@nipper.ucsb.edu not logged in`

This message is misleading, as it implies that **write** could connect to the remote computer if only the userid were logged in. (If you want to see who is logged in to your computer, use the **users** command.)

HINT
You can use the **talk** command to communicate with anyone who is logged in to any computer that is connected to yours (as long as their computer has a **talk** program).

You can use the **write** command only with people who are logged in to your own computer.

When you enter a write command, the other person will see a message. Here is an example:

`message from gwen@nipper on ttyp1 at 16:56 ...`

In this example, someone with the userid of **gwen** is trying to connect to you. To make the connection, you must enter your own **write** command. In this case:

`write gwen`

The connection will now be completed.

Note: When you enter a **write** command, you will not see anything until the other person responds. Thus, if you have entered a **write** command and nothing happens for a while, you should probably give up. Abort the **write** command by pressing the **intr** key (usually **^C**, see Chapter 6).

Once you have established a connection, each line that is typed by either person is echoed on both screens. Thus, you need to take turns. By convention, the person who initiated the connection goes first.

To keep things straight, there are two simple rules you should follow. First, don't type until the other person is finished. Second, when you are finished, let the other person know by typing a lowercase **o** in parentheses. For example:

```
blah blah blah blah blah
blah blah blah blah blah
(o)
```

This stands for "over". When the other person sees this signal, he will type as long as he wants, again finishing with **(o)**. It is now your turn. When you want to stop the conversation, you tell the other person by typing:

```
(oo)
```

which stands for "over and out".

At any time, you can enter a regular Unix command by starting the line with an **!** (exclamation mark) character. For example, say that you are talking with someone who asks if you have a particular file. Tell him to hold on for a moment and then type:

```
!ls
```

This will run the **ls** command to list the names of your files. After the output of the command is displayed, you will see a second **!** character. You can now continue your conversation.

As you are typing, you can use any of the regular correction keys that we discussed in Chapter 6. These keys are shown in Figure 13-2.

KEY	PURPOSE
BACKSPACE, DELETE	erase the last character typed (**erase**)
^W	erase the last word typed (**werase**)
^X, **^U**	erase the entire line (**kill**)

FIGURE 13-2. *Special keys to use with* `write`

To quit talking, you can either press **^D** (the **eof** key) to tell **write** there is no more data, or you can press **^C** (or whatever your **intr** key is) to abort the command. Either person can sever the connection by pressing one of these two keys.

Keeping Others from Sending You Messages: mesg

You can use the **mesg** command to keep other people from connecting to your terminal with **talk** or **write**. This is handy if you are using the full screen and unsolicited messages would mess up what you are doing. The syntax is:

mesg [**n**] [**y**]

To indicate that you do not want interruptions, enter:

mesg n

To indicate that you will accept messages, enter:

mesg y

To check the current status, enter the command with no parameters:

mesg

The response will be either **y** or **n**.

Some system managers put a **mesg n** command in everyone's initialization file. Check the **mesg** status next time you log in. If it is set to **n** and you want to talk with people, you will have to change your initialization file. If you use the C-Shell, this will be your **.login** file (see Chapter 11). If you use the Korn shell, it will be your **.profile** file (see Chapter 12).

Note: The **mesg** command does not affect the sending and receiving of mail.

HINT
You cannot use **talk** or **write** if **mesg** is set to **n**. If people are having trouble connecting to your terminal, check to see if your **.login** file contains a **mesg n** command.

Being Courteous and Conventional While Talking

When you talk in person or over the telephone, you use various verbal and visual cues.

For example, imagine you are a male college student talking (in person) to your roommate. He is wondering if he should ask out the woman he met who is working on her thesis about Political Commitment in Twentieth Century Literature.

You look at him, raise your eyebrows and, with a mocking lilt to your voice, say, "Do you really think she would go out with someone like you?" All in good fun, of course.

Now, imagine that, instead of talking in person, you are communicating over a computer connection using the **talk** program. You type:

```
Do you really think she would go out with someone like you?
```

This time, there is no look, no raised eyebrows and no actual voice. What would have been subtle irony has become gross sarcasm.

This phenomenon— the ease with which you can insult someone over a computer connection— was noticed years ago. The solution used in the Unix community is to tell people explicitly whenever there may be any doubt that you are making a joke. You do this by typing what is called a SMILEY. It looks like this:

```
:-)
```

(Turn your head to the left and look at it sideways.)

You should type a smiley face every time you write something that may be offensive. (Another way to look at it is you should type a smiley face every time you want to point out to someone that you are being subtly ironic.) For example:

```
Do you really think she would go out with someone like you? :-)
```

As you use the Internet, you will find there are many variations on the basic smiley. For example, here is someone winking at you:

```
;-)
```

Here is a sad face:

```
:-(
```

And here is a cool, California surfer-dude who writes Unix books:

`|-)`

All such pictograms are referred to as smileys, even though many of then are not really smiling.

Aside from the smiley, there is one alternative you might encounter when you mix with people who have used commercial networks where the proletariat gather (such as CompuServe). Such people often type **<g>** or **<grin>** instead of a smiley face:

Do you really think she would go out with someone like you? <g>

Get into the habit of using a real smiley. This will make you look like an experienced, worldly Internet person. When you use **<g>** or **<grin>**, it makes you look like an immature CompuServe person who doesn't know what he is doing. `:-)`

HINT

Communicating with **talk** or **write** is a lot slower than speaking, and it is easy to get bored if someone is typing too slowly.

Don't worry about simple mistakes in grammar or spelling. Instead of stopping to backspace and correct, plunge on with abandon. Your recipient will figure out what you mean.

The Importance of Universal Addressing

As we explained earlier, when you use **talk** or **finger** with a userid from a remote system, you must specify the full electronic address. On the Internet, this address takes the form:

userid@domain

for example:

harley@nipper.ucsb.edu

(We will explain more about addresses in Chapter 14.)

In the world of Unix, you use the same address for everything: mail, fingering, talking, and so on. In addition, you can also receive mail at this address from most of the public commercial mail systems, such as CompuServe, MCI Mail, America Online, and so on.

Compared to a postal address, your electronic address is much easier to understand and remember. Moreover, you will find computer communication to be more reliable and a lot faster. We happen to think this is an amazing achievement, and we would like you to take a moment to think about it.

HINT
A single electronic address allows you to receive any type of computer communication from anywhere in the world (as long as the connection is there).

CHAPTER 14

Networks and Addresses

Once you are a part of the Unix community, you can communicate with people and transfer data all over the world. All you need is an electronic address and a knowledge of how to use the networking programs.

In this chapter, we will explain the fundamental ideas. We start by giving you an overview of the Unix mail system. We then discuss the large Internet network and what it offers. Finally, we explain how electronic addressing works.

In the next chapter, you will learn how to send and receive mail. However, this chapter explains the basic principles, so read it first.

An Overview of the Unix Mail System

MAIL or EMAIL refers to the sending and receiving of messages or files. When Unix people use the word "mail", you can take it for granted they mean electronic mail, not regular post office mail. Similarly, when you see the word ADDRESS, it refers to an electronic mailing address, not a postal address.

Mail is an important part of Unix, and all Unix systems come with a built-in mail system. Even if your computer is not connected to other computers, you can still send mail to other people on your system and even to yourself. If your computer is connected to the Internet (which we will discuss later in the chapter), you can send mail to people all over the world.

You can exchange mail with anyone whose computer is connected to yours, as long as the systems are configured properly. The recipient's system does not necessarily have to run Unix. Mail system configuration is not easy, but it is a job for the system manager and there is no reason for you to care about the details. All you need to know is what capabilities are available and how to use them.

You will find that sending mail across the world is as easy as sending mail across the hall. Moreover, mail travels fast. If the network is not too busy, sending messages over long distances may take only seconds. Even on slow days, electronic mail on the Internet is always faster than the regular postal service.

What's in a Name?   Snail Mail

When Unix people talk about "mail", they always mean electronic mail. When they refer to regular post office mail, they will always make it clear by context.

One term that is often used to refer to post office mail is SNAIL MAIL. This name describes the relative pace of mailing through the post office compared to mailing via an electronic network.

Working with mail is easy. Here is a quick overview of how it works using the Unix **mail** program. In Chapter 15, we will describe everything in detail. To send mail you enter:

mail *address*

where *address* is the address of the person to whom you want to send a message. For example:

```
mail harley@nipper.ucsb.edu
```

If the recipient is on your own system, you only need to specify a userid:

```
mail harley
```

Note: It is not necessary for someone to be logged in to receive mail. The remote Unix system will receive and store the message. The next time the person logs in, Unix will display a message saying that mail is waiting.

After entering the **mail** command, you type the message, one line at a time. At the end of each line, you press RETURN. When you are finished, you press **^D** (the **eof**) key to tell the **mail** program there is no more data. The message will be sent automatically and you will see:

```
EOT
```

This stands for "end of transmission".

To read mail, just enter:

```
mail
```

The **mail** program will show you a list of all the messages that are waiting for you. Using simple commands, you can read one message at a time. When you have read it, you can save it, delete it, reply to it, or forward it to someone else. You can even have Unix tell you when mail arrives so you don't have to keep checking for yourself.

Of course, there are some particulars you need to learn (there always are with Unix programs). We will discuss the **mail** program in detail in Chapter 15.

Where can you send mail? It makes sense that you should be able to send mail to anyone on your own computer, your own network, and (if you are a student) even to any computer on your campus. However, if your host computer is connected to the Internet, you can send mail to computers in every part of the world. All you need to know is the address of the recipient.

However, before we get into addressing, we need to talk about the Internet, the mysterious network that holds together the worldwide electronic community. The best place to start is with TCP/IP, the glue that holds the Internet together.

TCP/IP: **traceroute**

The Internet is a collection of networks, all over the world, that contain many different types of systems. Something must hold it all together. That something is TCP/IP (plus a lot of volunteer labor).

The details of TCP/IP are highly technical and well beyond the interest of almost everybody. However, there will be many times when you see or hear the term "TCP/IP", so we might as well spend a few minutes talking about it.

TCP/IP is the common name for a collection of more than 100 different protocols. (A PROTOCOL is a set of rules that allow different machines and programs to coordinate with one another.) The TCP/IP protocols are used within the Internet (and other networks) to connect computers, communications equipment and programs. Not all computers on the Internet run Unix, but they all use TCP/IP.

What's in a Name?   TCP/IP

The name TCP/IP is derived from two of the basic protocols: TCP is an acronym for Transmission Control Protocol; IP is an acronym for Internet Protocol.

Within a TCP/IP system, data that is to be transmitted is divided into small packets. Each packet has the address of the recipient computer along with a sequence number. For example, the system may divide a mail message into 10 different packets; each of those packets will have its own sequence number.

The various packets are sent out over the network, and each packet is transported, on its own, to the destination. When the packets are all received, the destination system uses the sequence numbers to put them back together. If, for some reason, a packet has arrived in garbled condition, the destination system will transmit a message to the sender asking for that particular packet to be resent.

Breaking data into packets has several important benefits. First, communication lines can be shared among many users. All kinds of packets can be transmitted at the same time, and they will be sorted and recombined when they arrive at their respective destinations.

Compare this to how a telephone conversation is transmitted. Once you make a connection, the circuits are reserved for you and cannot be used for another call, even if you put the other person on hold for twenty minutes.

The second advantage of the TCP/IP system is that data does not have to be sent directly between two computers. Each packet is passed from computer to computer until it reaches its destination. This, of course, is the secret of how you can send messages and data between any two computers, even if they are not directly connected to one another.

What is amazing is that it may take only a few seconds to send a good size file from one machine to another, even when they are thousands of miles apart and the data must pass through multiple computers. One of the reasons for this speed is that, when something goes wrong, only a single packet may need to be retransmitted and not the whole message.

Another benefit of this system is that every packet does not need to follow the same path. This allows the network to route each packet from place to place, using the best connection available at that instant. Thus, your message packets do not necessarily all travel over the same route, nor do they necessarily all arrive at the same time.

Finally, the flexibility of the system makes for high reliability. If one particular link goes down, the system will use a different one.

When you send a message, it is TCP that breaks the data into packets, sequences the packets, adds some error control information and then sends packets out to be delivered. At the other end, TCP receives the packets, checks for errors, and combines all of the packets back into the original data. If there is an error somewhere, the destination TCP program will send a message asking for the required packets to be resent. (TCP would have done a lot better at putting Humpty Dumpty back together than did all the King's men.)

The job of IP is to get the raw data—the packets—from one place to another. The computers that direct data from one network to another—called ROUTERS—use IP to move the data.

In other words, IP moves the raw data packets, while TCP manages the flow and ensures that the data is correct.

Historical aside: During the Persian Gulf war of 1991, the Allies had trouble destroying the Iraqi command network even when some of the computers were damaged. Why? The Iraqis were using commercial IP routers that were able to find alternative routes quickly whenever a link went down.

HINT

Do not sell IP routers to hostile governments.

So, when someone asks you what TCP/IP is, you can give three different answers. First, you can say that TCP and IP are two protocols that manage and perform data transmission between networks. Second, you can say that the term TCP/IP is often used to refer to a collection of more than 100 different protocols that are used to organize computers and communication devices into a network.

Or you can simply wave your hands and say that TCP/IP is the glue that holds the Internet together.

HINT

If you are interested in seeing the route from your computer to another, you can use the **traceroute** command.

This command is not available on all systems. If your system does have **traceroute**, just enter the command name followed by the address of another computer on the Internet. (We will discuss addresses below.)

For example, to see the route from your computer to the computer whose address is **traceroute ds.internic.net**, enter:

```
traceroute ds.internic.net
```

The output will show you each step in the path between the two computers. From time to time, you may see a different path as conditions change in the network.

The **traceroute** command has many technical options and is really meant for people who maintain network connections. However, you may find it fun to check a connection path once in a while.

What Is the Internet?

There are two ways to think of the Internet.

First, we can define it in a technical sense. We can say the Internet is a worldwide collection of networks that transmit data using the IP protocol.

This is a good definition in the sense that it is accurate. However, it is not satisfying. What we really want to know is, what can we do with the Internet?

There are seven main services the Internet has to offer you. Here is a short description so you can orient yourself:

■ Mail: You can send and receive messages.

■ File transfer: You can copy files from one computer to another.

■ Remote login: You can log in to another computer and work with it, just as if your terminal were attached directly.

■ Discussion groups: You can read and post articles to the thousands of Usenet discussion groups.

■ Sharing software: You can get free copies of all kinds of software, and you can share your own programs with others.

■ Accessing information: You can search for and retrieve any kind of information. If you are not sure where to look, there are special programs to help you.

■ Talking with other people: You can have a conversation with other people using your keyboard and screen, either one person at a time or in a group.

Thus, here is a good, practical definition of the Internet: the Internet is a worldwide network that offers the services of mail, file transfer, remote login, discussion groups, sharing software, accessing information, and talking with other people. For more information about the Internet and how to use it see the book, *The Internet Complete Reference*, by Harley Hahn and Rick Stout, published by Osborne McGraw Hill. (ISBN 0-07-881980-6)

Are You Really Part of the Internet?

As we will see later in this chapter, there are other large networks that have mail connections to the Internet. However, just being able to exchange mail with the Internet does not mean that a computer is actually part of the Internet. For example, people using Compuserve or MCI Mail can send mail to Internet addresses. However, they do not have file transfer, remote login and all the rest.

Similarly, there are many people who use non-Internet systems to participate in the Usenet discussion group system. Most of these people can send mail to Internet addresses, but they do not have access to the resources that require a direct connection.

Some people are confused about all of this and think they are connected to the Internet when they are not. Usually, this means that they have some sort of mail or Usenet service, but not a full connection.

If you can log on to a remote Internet computer, you are probably on the Internet. If you are in a university, you will find that almost every computer will afford you access to the Internet, either directly or via another local system.

Some people ask: All I want to do is send mail; do I really need an Internet connection? The answer is: No, you don't *need* an Internet connection, as long as your computer has some way to route mail to the outside world.

However, if you send mail regularly to people on Internet computers, you will find that an Internet connection is a lot faster. It is not uncommon for Internet mail to be transmitted in seconds. This is because the Internet uses permanent, high-speed connections. When mail is sent from the outside, the transmission is slower and all the data must be routed through whatever computer provides the mail connection to the Internet.

Moreover, if you have a chance to use an Internet connection, there are many wonderful services available that go well beyond simple mail delivery.

Standard Internet Addresses

The key to using the Internet (and the mail system) is to understand the addresses. The amazing thing about the Internet addressing scheme is that each userid and each computer needs only a single address no matter what service is being used. For instance, when you send mail to someone, you use the same address as when you have a conversation via the **talk** command (see Chapter 13).

As you will come to appreciate, this system really is remarkable. Imagine being able to use the same address or identification number to mail someone a postcard, call them on the telephone, or send them a fax. Yet with a single Internet address, you can do much more.

An Internet address consists of a userid, followed by an **@** character (the "at" sign), followed by the name of a computer. The part of the address that contains the computer name is called the DOMAIN. Thus, the standard Internet address looks like this:

*userid***@***domain*

Here is an example:

harley@nipper.ucsb.edu

In this example, the userid is **harley**, and the domain—the name, or address, of the computer—is **nipper.ucsb.edu**. (Unix computers always have a name.) To use the Unix mail program to send a message to this userid, you would enter:

mail harley@nipper.ucsb.edu

The notation using the **@** character is appropriate. As you enter this command, you can say to yourself, "I am sending mail to Harley, who is at the computer named **nipper.ucsb.edu**."

The parts of the domain that are separated by periods are called SUBDOMAINS. The address above has three subdomains: **nipper**, **ucsb** and **edu**. The rightmost subdomain (in this case, **edu**) is referred to as the TOP-LEVEL DOMAIN.

To read an address, look at the subdomains from right to left. This will take you from the most general name to the most specific name. The leftmost subdomain will usually refer to a specific computer.

When you type an Internet address, you can mix upper- and lowercase letters. For example, the following addresses are equivalent:

```
mail harley@nipper.ucsb.edu
mail harley@NIPPER.UCSB.EDU
```

As a general rule, it is a good habit to stick with lowercase, especially for userids, although some people do mix upper- and lowercase. Here are two common variations:

```
mail harley@nipper.Ucsb.Edu
mail harley@nipper.ucsb.EDU
```

The first variation emphasizes the name of the main computer at the site; the second emphasizes the name of the top-level domain. In either case, the uppercase letters are optional.

HINT

If you are using an Internet address in which some of the letters are uppercase, it is safe to change the letters to lowercase.

Internet Addresses: The Old Format

There are two types of top-level domains: the old format and the newer, international format. The old format is used mainly in the United States and Canada, and has seven different top-level domains. These domain names are shown in Figure 14-1.

The address:

```
harley@nipper.ucsb.edu
```

has a top-level domain of **edu**, which shows it to be an educational institution (in this case, a university). Within the United States, most of the addresses that you will encounter will use either the **edu** or **com** domains. The **int** domain is used for international organizations, such as NATO.

After you look at the top-level domain, look at the other subdomains, from right to left. They will become progressively more specific. In our example, the

DOMAIN	MEANING
com	commercial organization
edu	educational institution
gov	government
int	international organization
mil	military
net	networking organization
org	non-profit organization

FIGURE 14-1.   *Old-style top-level domains*

domain refers to a computer named **nipper** at the University of California at Santa Barbara.

Variations on the Standard Internet Address

Sometimes you will see addresses that use extra subdomains to be more specific. A common subdomain is **cs**, referring to a computer science department. For example, the address:

samuel@emmenthaler.cs.wisc.edu

refers to userid **samuel** at a computer named **emmenthaler**, within the computer science department at the University of Wisconsin.

Once you see enough addresses, you will start to notice patterns among computer names. For example, at the University of Wisconsin—which is in a state that is well known for its dairy products—many computers are named after a type of cheese.

Sometimes you will see Internet addresses that are as simple as can be, having just the name of the organization and a top-level domain. For example:

melissa@ucsd.edu

This address refers to userid **melissa** at the University of California at San Diego.

Whenever you see such an address, it means that the organization uses one main computer to receive and distribute mail. In this case, the computer named `ucsd.edu` has a directory of many of the userids in the university. When you mail a message to one of these userids, for example, `melissa`, this computer knows which of the campus computers is used by `melissa`.

The nice thing about this system is that the addresses are simple. Of course, someone has to maintain the central mail service and keep the list of userids up to date.

A final variation that you may see is an address that uses a `%` (percent) character. This is used occasionally to specify a more complex recipient name. Here is an example:

`randy%anaconda@ucsd.edu`

The idea is that the computer that receives the message (in this case, `ucsd.edu`) will look at everything to the left of the `@` character (in this case, `randy%anaconda`) and make sense out of it.

Typically, the `%` separates a userid from a local computer name. In this case, it may be that mail for `randy` should go to the computer named `anaconda`. However, there may be several local paths to that computer, and the main computer (`ucsd.edu`) will figure out the best path at the time.

Don't worry too much about the details; just use whatever address your recipient gives you. A lot of people know what their address is, but they don't understand it. Many sites have more than one way to address mail, and the system managers will usually tell their users which address works best.

Standard Internet Addresses: The International Format

We said earlier that there are two types of top-level domain names. The old-style uses abbreviations that describe the type of organization: **edu**, **com** and so on. This type of address was developed for the old Arpanet network, an ancestor of the Internet, and was meant to be used only in the United States.

As the Internet expanded, it became clear that a better system was needed. The solution was to use top-level domains that represented countries. For most countries, the top-level domain is the two-letter international abbreviation. Figure 14-2 shows some of these abbreviations. For a full list, see Appendix F.

Here are two typical addresses that use an international top-level domain:

`sean@unix1.tcd.ie`
`hans@physik.tu-muenchen.de`

DOMAIN	MEANING
at	Austria
au	Australia
ca	Canada
ch	Switzerland ("Confoederatio Helvetica")
de	Germany ("Deutschland")
dk	Denmark
es	Spain ("España")
fr	France
gr	Greece
ie	Republic of Ireland
jp	Japan
nz	New Zealand
uk	United Kingdom (England, Scotland, Wales, Northern Ireland)
us	United States

FIGURE 14-2.   *Some of the international top-level domains*

The first address is for a computer named **unix1** at Trinity College in Dublin, Ireland. The second address is for a computer in the physics department (physik) at the Technical University in Munich (Muenchen) in Germany (Deutschland).

Some countries use a subdomain, just to the left of the top-level domain, to divide the top-level domain into categories. Thus, you may see **ac**, for academic sites, and **co**, for commercial sites. For example, the following address:

`otto@spam.tuwien.ac.at`

refers to a computer named **spam** at the Technical University in Vienna (Wien) Austria.

HINT

The British and New Zealanders may reverse the order of the subdomains in their addresses. For example, you may see an address like:

`victoria@uk.ac.cambridge.history`

If you need to use such an address (outside that country), be sure to reverse the order of the subdomains:

`victoria@history.cambridge.ac.uk`

so that they form a standard address.

Outside the United States, virtually all Internet sites use the newer international style of addressing, in which the top-level domain shows the country code. However, within the United States (and to some extent in Canada), most Internet computers still use the old-style addresses, the ones with top-level domains of **edu**, **com** and so on.

Of course, there are international-style addresses for the United States (using the country code **us**). It's just that most American sites have not yet moved away from the old system. Regardless of what type of address your location uses, you can communicate with any computer on the Internet.

Pseudo-Internet Addresses

There are many system managers who would like their computers to be on the Internet, but who do not have the time or money to maintain a permanent Internet connection. As an alternative, they arrange to connect regularly with an Internet site and then register their address as if it were an Internet address. (We won't go into the details here.)

For example, a small company named Sigma Star Research might have an address of **sigstar.com**. From time to time, their computer calls another computer (which is on the Internet) to exchange mail. From your point of view, you can send mail to **sigstar** in the usual way. For instance, to send mail to userid **ron** at this company, you would enter:

`mail ron@sigstar.com`

However, you do need to remember that mail to such an address will not be as fast as mail to a real Internet address.

When you see an Internet-like address, there is often no way to tell, just from the address, whether or not that computer is really on the Internet. If you

see an address like **small-company-name.com**, you might have your
suspicions. However, even some large, well-known companies do not have a full
Internet connection.

HINT

The best way to find out if a computer is on the Internet is to use the
ping command (Chapter 13). On the Internet, it is not enough just to
look like a duck and feel like a duck. You must also **ping** like a duck!

UUCP Addresses and Bang Paths

All Unix systems have a built-in networking system, called UUCP, that allows any
Unix machine to exchange messages with any other Unix machine. With UUCP,

---

What's in a Name?   UUCP

The UUCP system is implemented as a family of commands. The most well-known
command is **uucp**. It is this command that gives its name to the system as a whole.

The **uucp** command copies files from one computer to another. Thus, the
name, which stands for "Unix to Unix copy".

---

messages are passed from one computer to another until they reach their final
destination. However, unlike the Internet, the address you use must specify every
step along the way.

Using UUCP, it is possible to form a network in which the computers do not
have to be connected at all times. They can use modems to call one another over
the phone line. This makes for an inexpensive system in which messages can be
passed from computer to computer over vast distances.

Here is an example. You are working on a computer that, from time to time,
connects over the phone to another computer named **beta**. You have sent
messages to two different userids, one on your local system, the other on
computer **beta**.

After you send the messages, the mail daemon examines the addresses.
(Daemons are explained in Chapter 19.) Since the first message is going to a local
userid, the message is delivered immediately. However, the daemon recognizes the
second address as being a UUCP address. Thus, it puts the second message in a
queue of messages waiting for a UUCP connection.

Later, when your computer connects to computer **beta**, this message, along with any others that have been waiting, is sent on its way. Conversely, any messages that **beta** is holding for your machine are passed over to your computer at the same time.

The format of UUCP addresses is conceptually simple. All you need to do is specify exactly what path you want your mail to take. Separate each computer name with an **!** character (exclamation mark). At the end of the path, put a final **!** followed by the userid of the recipient.

For example, to send mail via UUCP to a userid named **arthur**, who uses computer **beta**, use:

```
mail beta!arthur
```

Here is another example. You want to send a message to a userid named **chance** who uses a computer named **evers**. This computer does not have a UUCP connection with your machine. However, your computer connects to a machine named **tinker** that does have a UUCP connection to **evers**. You can have UUCP pass the mail along for you by using:

```
mail tinker!evers!chance
```

A list of names, separated by **!** characters in this way, is called a BANG PATH (because one of the slang names for the **!** character is "bang").

Each time mail is passed from one computer to another, we call it a HOP. Thus, the address above contains two hops. The UUCP address:

```
alpha!beta!gamma!delta!epsilon!username
```

contains five hops. It is not at all unusual to encounter addresses that have more than ten hops.

When we refer to the UUCP NETWORK (or, sometimes, just plain "UUCP"), we mean the thousands of computers that are reachable using a UUCP-style bang path address. Some of these machines are on the Internet, but many are not.

Note: If you are using the C-Shell, you must make sure the **!** characters are not interpreted as event indicators (see Chapter 11). To do so, you must put a **** (backslash) in front of each **!** character. This tells the shell to take the **!** literally. For example:

```
mail beta\!arthur
mail tinker\!evers\!chance
alpha\!beta\!gamma\!delta\!epsilon\!username
```

If you forget the \ characters, you will see a message like:

```
Event not found.
```

Simplified UUCP Addressing

Using UUCP and bang path addresses, it is possible to send messages vast distances as long as 1) you know the exact path to use, and 2) the connections are made properly.

The nice thing about UUCP is that it is cheap and accessible to anyone who has a Unix system and a modem. All that is needed is a connection to one other computer in the UUCP network.

The disadvantage, however, is that to send messages via UUCP you must use exact path names for addresses (which can become quite long), and mail delivery is slow and, at times, unreliable.

Moreover, it can be difficult to give someone a correct UUCP address, because how mail should travel to a recipient depends very much on where the mail originates. For example, the route that someone in New York uses to send mail to a computer in Los Angeles may not be the same route used by someone in San Francisco to send mail to Los Angeles.

With Internet addresses, you specify only the name and location of the recipient. The routing software decides which is the best path to follow. Thus, Internet addresses are well-defined and relatively short.

To bring the same conveniences to UUCP, the UUCP MAPPING PROJECT was created. This group publishes regularly updated maps of data that are sent to many UUCP computers. The mail routing software on these computers can use this data to decide the best path to take between any two points. This allows you to send mail to a UUCP address simply by specifying its location. You do not need to use a complete bang path.

Some of the addresses you will encounter will look like Internet addresses, but really contain the names of computers that have UUCP connections. For example, if you see the address:

```
mail ron@sigstar.com
```

it may well be that the machine **sigstar** is actually on the Internet or connects to an Internet computer regularly. However, it may also be that **sigstar** is really a UUCP computer that is several hops away from an Internet machine. When you send mail to **sigstar**, the routing software will decide the best path to take. It will all be invisible to you.

In practice, such a message will probably be sent to a machine near **sigstar**, say, the closest Internet computer. Once this computer receives the message, its routing software will figure out the best way to pass the message to **sigstar**.

Occasionally, you will see addresses that use a top-level domain of **uucp**. For example:

```
rick@tsi.uucp
```

The name **uucp** is not an Internet subdomain. Rather, it is a signal to the mail routing software to look up the computer name in the UUCP mapping data and construct the best possible address.

Mailing to Other Networks

From the Internet, there are gateways (connections) to many other networks. If you know the right address, you can send mail through a gateway to anyone on these networks. What is nice is that, even if the recipient uses a commercial system that charges for mail, you, as an Internet user, can send and receive for free.

There are numerous networks that have gateways to the Internet. In this section, we will discuss the most popular ones.

First, there are the commercial mail systems: America Online, AT&T Mail, Compuserve, Delphi, MCI Mail, and Prodigy. To send mail to users on these systems, just use one of the following domains:

```
aol.com
attmail.com
compuserve.com
delphi.com
mcimail.com
prodigy.com
```

As a general rule, you can use the standard format: the user name or identification number, followed by an **@** character, followed by the domain. Note: Compuserve uses identification numbers that contain a comma, such as **12345,678**. When you use such as number in an Internet address, you must change the comma to a period.

Here are some examples:

```
nipper@aol.com
nipper@attmail.com
123456.789@compuserve.com
nipper@delphi.com
nipper@mcimail.com
nipper@prodigy.com
```

Aside from the commercial networks, you may encounter an address from FidoNet, a large network of personal computers that connect via dial-up telephone lines. (Conceptually, Fidonet is similar to UUCP.) There are several Fidonet sites that act as gateways to the Internet. You can reach these sites by sending mail to **fidonet.org**. (Be forewarned: because of the nature of the connections, Fidonet mail often moves slowly.)

Fidonet addresses consist of three parts: a zone number, a net number and a node number. Here is a typical Fidonet address: 1:123/456. To send mail to Fidonet, you encode the three-part address, in reverse order, as follows:

f*node*.**n***net*.**z***zone*.**fidonet.org**

Fidonet uses full names for recipients. Just separate each name by a period. Thus, to send a message to Ben Dover at address 1:123/456, use:

mail Ben.Dover@f456.n123.z1.fidonet.org

Finally, the last gateway we will mention is the one that goes to Bitnet, a collection of networks based in Europe, Canada, the United States and Mexico. To mail to a Bitnet user, simply use a top-level domain of **bitnet**. The subdomain to the left will be the name of the Bitnet host computer.

For example, to send mail to a friend of yours named Jack, whose Bitnet name is **jjones**, at the Bitnet host **cunyvm**, use:

mail jjones@cunyvm.bitnet

Note: Many Bitnet host names end in "vm" because they are IBM mainframes running the Virtual Machine operating system.

CHAPTER 15

Mail

Mail is one of the most important services provided by Unix. In this chapter, we will discuss the standard Unix mail program. You will learn everything you need to know to send and receive messages.

As you will see, the mail program offers many facilities and is quite complex. Although we will be explaining a lot of details, you really only need to memorize the few parts that are necessary for everyday work. What is important is that you develop an appreciation of what the mail program can do for you. You can always look up the technical points as you need them.

In Chapter 14, we discussed the mail system in general terms, as well as the Internet and electronic addressing. If you have not yet read Chapter 14, it would be a good idea to at least skim it before you read this chapter.

The Unix Mail Programs: `mail`, Pine, Elm, MH, Mush, Rmail

As we explained in Chapter 14, Unix comes with a built-in mail system. The most important part of this system is the user interface, the program that you use to send and read messages. The most common such program is named `mail`.

In this chapter, we will show you how to use `mail` effectively. Even if you decide to use a different program, it is a good idea to be familiar with `mail`. It is the basic Unix mail program, and you will find it, in one form or another, on all Unix systems. Moreover, the concepts you will learn in this chapter are basic to any mail program you may choose to use.

On many systems, you will have an alternative to the `mail` program. Although we won't be able to go into the details of such programs, you might find it useful to take a quick look at what else may be available on your computer.

What's in a Name? `mail`

Originally, there was a simple program called `mail`. This program was adequate, but limited.

Years ago, `mail` was replaced by more powerful programs. System V Unix had a program named `mailx` ("extended mail"), while Berkeley Unix had `Mail` (with an uppercase "M").

Both `mailx` and `Mail` are upwards compatible with `mail` and are actually quite similar to one another. When these programs first came out, users had to enter the `mailx` or `Mail` command. This, of course, was not as simple as using a command named "`mail`". Moreover, if someone forgot the new name and did type `mail`, he or she would end up with the clunky, old `mail` program.

These days, just about all systems are set up to execute automatically the newer program when you type `mail`. In other words, the name `mail` will point to either `mailx` or `Mail`, whichever is appropriate. If you really want the old `mail` program, there is usually a way to get at it, but it is rarely used.

The evolution of `mail` illustrates one of the Unix traditions: when a program is replaced by a new one, the old one is not thrown away. Even if the new program eventually usurps the old name, the old program is still kept around (possibly under a different name) for the sake of continuity.

This is one of the reasons why Unix grows ever larger.

Aside from the basic **mail** program, the most popular programs you may encounter are Pine, Elm, MH, Mush and Rmail. One thing all of these systems have in common is that they greatly extend the functionality of **mail** by offering extra features.

HINT

Many advanced mail programs depend on using the full screen. If you are accessing a Unix computer via a slow phone line, you may find it faster and easier to use the standard line-oriented **mail** program.

If one of these other programs is available on your system and you get serious about mail (or if you start to receive a lot of messages), it is certainly worth your time to learn how to use an advanced mail program. All of them are complete mail-handling systems with many capabilities. If you become a mail fanatic, some of these programs even allow you to create your own customized mail-handling system.

The two most popular Unix mail programs among Internet users are Elm and Pine. Elm is a menu-driven program that was developed as a replacement for the standard Unix **mail** program. Elm is both easy to use and powerful. If you have ever used a mail program before — especially the **mail** program — you will probably be able to start using Elm within minutes. Once you get used to Elm, you will find it to be fast and sophisticated. There are many opportunities for customization, including advanced features that let you build your own personalized mail-handling system.

Pine was designed to be easy to learn and is a favorite of casual users, especially those with no previous electronic mail experience. Pine is more forgiving of mistakes than Elm, and provides immediate feedback each time you issue a command. With only a short introduction, just about anyone can start using Pine immediately. Pine has an interesting feature in that it comes with its own simple text editor (called Pico) for creating messages, and its own paging program for reading messages. The down side is that Pine and Pico are not all that powerful and are not as well suited to experienced users.

Note: If both Elm and Pine are available on your system, be sure to read the next section of this chapter in which we discuss how to choose between them.

The MH system is actually a large set of commands. Rather than working within one main program, you enter separate commands for whatever you want to do. This means you can intersperse handling your mail with doing other work. If you receive a great deal of mail and you like memorizing new commands, you will love MH.

Mush (the "mail user's shell") is a program with two faces. It can be used with a line-oriented interface (like **mail**) or with a screen-oriented interface (like Elm or Pine).

Rmail is the name of the mail facility that is built into some versions of **emacs**. If you are an **emacs** user, you will find it useful to learn how to use Rmail.

Although you can use any mail program and specify **emacs** as your text editor, Rmail is more convenient as it is integrated into the **emacs** environment. (We discuss **emacs** in Chapter 21.)

Choosing Between Elm and Pine

Many Unix users have both Elm and Pine installed on their system. Which one is best to use?

If you don't read or send mail very often, you are probably better off with Pine. It is simple, easy to learn, and the built-in Pico editor is far more accessible than either **vi** or **emacs**.

However, we firmly believe that, in the long run, just about everyone is better off taking the time to learn a mail program like Elm and to learn a text editor like **vi** or **emacs**. The reason is that, as human beings, we do ourselves a disservice when we opt for tools that are easy to use on the first day, but prove stifling after the first month. It takes a little longer to learn to use Elm (and a lot longer to learn **vi** or **emacs**), but once you master these tools, they are faster and better.

The crucial idea is to not confuse "easy to learn" with "easy to use". It is easier to learn how to use Pine than to learn how to use Elm. But once you understand both programs, you will find Elm to be a lot faster and much more attuned to the workings of an intelligent mind.

With respect to Pico, the text editor, the situation is even more polarized. Pico is very easy to learn— even beginners can use it—and both **vi** and **emacs** are very difficult to learn. Only a sadist would put an inexperienced person in front of a computer and tell him that he cannot send mail until he learns how to use **vi** or **emacs**. (Indeed, in some jurisdictions such behavior is considered a felony and is punishable by law.)

Fortunately, if Pine is installed on your system, you can employ Pico as a separate program by using the **pico** command. For example, to edit a file named **message**, simply enter:

```
pico message
```

This means that, no matter what mail program you use, you can use Pico as your text editor.

Specifically, Elm lets you choose which text editor you want to use and, if you have not yet learned **vi** or **emacs**, you can select Pico. (Use the **o** command to bring up the "Options" screen and then press **e** to change the name of your editor.)

Still, even if you start with Pico (which is reasonable), you do need to learn either **vi** or **emacs**. Why? Because once you become an experienced Unix person, editing with Pico will drive you bananas faster than watching Monty Python with a laugh track.

(Note to Americans: The original Monty Python shows did not have a laugh track; it was added for the American market. No doubt, this decision was made by the sort of people who use Pico exclusively and are fond of expressing the idea that computers should be "intuitive" to use.)

HINT

There is one area in which Pine is definitely better than Elm: attaching files to messages.

Normally, mail messages consist of simple text. However, there are times when you will want to send someone a non-textual file, such as a picture, a spreadsheet, or a word processing document. On the Internet, a facility called MIME (Multipurpose Internet Mail Extensions) exists for attaching such files to a mail message. At the other end, the recipient uses a mail program to detach the file and recover the data in its original form.

We discuss MIME—along with alternatives for mailing non-textual files—in our book *The Internet Complete Reference*. The point here is that Pine is better than Elm at handling MIME attachments, so if you need to send non-textual files through the mail, Pine may be a better choice than Elm (at least in this limited area).

Orientation to the `mail` Program

Although your Unix system may have more than one mail program, you can count on it having the standard program **mail**. Even if you are going to use another program, there are two good reasons why you should at least become familiar with **mail**. First, it is the only mail program that you can count on seeing in every Unix system. Second, the ideas that you will learn with **mail** are basic to all mail programs.

HINT

Learn how to use the standard Unix **mail** program. Once you understand **mail**, other mail programs will be variations on a familiar theme.

Using **mail** is actually like using two different programs: one for sending mail and one for receiving mail. We will discuss each task in turn. Along the way, we will explain a number of ancillary topics that you will need to understand in order to work efficiently.

Before we start, here is a quick summary of how you send and receive messages. This summary leaves out the details and the power of **mail** (which we will get to presently).

To send mail, enter the **mail** command followed by the address of the recipient. For example:

```
mail harley@nipper.ucsb.edu
```

Type your message, one line at a time. When you are finished, press RETURN (to move to a new line) and then press **^D** (the **eof** key). The message will be sent automatically.

While you are composing a message, you can edit and review it. You can also include text from a file or from another message.

To read your mail, enter:

```
mail
```

You will see a summary of your messages. Using the various commands, you can now read and dispose of each message in turn. When you are finished, enter the **q** command to quit. The program terminates, leaving you back at the shell prompt.

Sending Mail

To send mail, use the **mail** command with the following syntax:

```
mail [-v] [-s subject] address...
```

The most common way to send mail is to specify only the address of the recipient. (Chapter 14 explains the various types of addresses.) If the recipient is on your system, you need only specify the userid. For example:

```
mail rick
```

If the recipient is on a different system, you must specify the full address. For example:

```
mail melissa@misty.acme.com
```

If the recipient is within your local network, you can often leave out part of the address. For example, say that your address is **myname@alpha.ucal.edu** and you are mailing to a friend who uses a different computer on the network. His address is **friend@beta.ucal.edu**. You are usually safe in leaving off the part of the address that you both have in common: that is, the part of the address that describes your local network. So, in this case, you could use:

```
mail friend@beta
```

The mail software should be able to figure out that this is a local address and deliver the message properly. If you have a problem, you may have to use the full address.

Every system should have a userid named **postmaster** to whom you can send queries. For example, say that you have trouble finding the address of someone who uses a computer named **misty.acme.com**. You can send a message asking for the person's mail address to:

```
postmaster@misty.acme.com
```

For more help with mail addresses, see *The Internet Complete Reference*, by Harley Hahn and Rick Stout, published by Osborne McGraw-Hill. (The ISBN is 0-07-881980-6.) That book contains an entire chapter devoted to finding someone on the Internet.

HINT

If you have a problem with mail not reaching its destination:

1. Check the spelling of the address.

2. Make sure you have specified the full address.

3. Ask an experienced person for help.

4. If all else fails, send a query to the **postmaster** userid.

When you want to send the same message to more than one person, simply specify more than one userid:

```
mail curly larry moe melissa@misty.acme.com
```

Each recipient will get a copy of the message. If you want to receive a copy yourself, put your userid in the list.

Once you enter the **mail** command, you will be able to compose your message. (We describe the details below.) However, there will be times when you have a message stored in a file, all ready to go, and there is no need to go through the process of typing and editing. If so, you can send your message directly by telling **mail** where to find the file.

At the end of the **mail** command, type a **<** (less than) character, followed by the name of the file. (The **<** character tells **mail** to redirect the "standard input" from the keyboard to a file. We will explain such techniques in Chapter 16.)

For example, to send a message contained in a file named **notice** to three userids named **curly**, **larry** and **moe**, enter:

```
mail curly larry moe < notice
```

mail will send the message and return you to the shell prompt immediately. Note: Be careful to use the **<** (less than) character, not the **>** (greater than) character.

In Chapter 14, we explained that some addresses use the **!** character. However, when you are using the C-Shell, the **!** is used for history substitution to specify an event (see Chapter 11). Thus, you must make sure that the **!** characters in an address are not interpreted by the shell.

To do so, you must put a **** (backslash) character in front of each **!** character. For example, to send mail to **alpha!beta!murray** you would enter:

```
mail alpha\!beta\!murray
```

A backslash tells the shell to take the next character literally.

If you forget to use the ****, the shell will try to interpret the **!** characters, and you will see a message like:

```
beta!murray: Event not found.
```

Re-enter the command and put in the **** characters.

HINT
If you are using the C-Shell, don't forget to put a backslash in front of each **!** character that appears in an address. For example:

```
mail alpha\!beta\!murray
```

Specifying the Subject of the Message

All messages have a few lines of information at the beginning of the message. One of these lines shows the subject of the message.

When you check your mail, the first thing you will see is a summary of all the messages that are waiting. This summary shows the userid who sent the message, the time it was received, the size of the message, and the subject.

Thus, it is always a good idea to specify the subject when you send a message. This allows the recipient to see the topic of the message without having to read it. If you are sending mail to a person who receives many messages a day (such as a system manager), he or she will scan the summaries before reading the messages. If you have left out the subject, the person may take a long time to get around to reading your message. (It is not unusual for busy people to get over a hundred messages a day.)

When you enter the **mail** command, you can specify the subject directly by using the **-s** option. For example:

```
mail -s Hello rick
```

In this case, the subject is "Hello".

If your subject has space characters or punctuation, you must enclose it in single quotes. Otherwise, the shell will interpret the spaces and punctuation in a way that will be incorrect. Using single quotes tells the shell to pass the character string to **mail** exactly as you typed it. For example:

```
mail -s 'Do you want free money?' rick
```

If we had left out the single quotes:

```
mail -s Do you want free money? rick
```

the command would have been interpreted as a message with subject "Do", that should be sent to five different userids (**you**, **want**, **free**, **money?** and **Rick**). Moreover, the shell would have interpreted the **?** character in a special way (which we will explain in Chapter 23).

HINT

When you send mail, keep the subject line short (less than 35 characters is a good rule of thumb). Excess characters may be truncated when the recipient looks at a summary of messages.

If you do not specify a subject, **mail** will prompt you to enter one by displaying:

```
Subject:
```

Since **mail** is now reading your input directly, you do not need to use single quotes.

HINT
If your **mail** program does not prompt you for a subject, you can force it to do so by including a **set ask** command in your **.mailrc** initialization file (explained later in the chapter).

Having entered the **mail** command along with the subject, you are now ready to enter your message.

Entering Your Message

Entering a message is simple. Type the message, one line at a time. At the end of each line, press the RETURN key. After you press RETURN for the last line, press **^D** (the **eof** key that we discussed in Chapter 6). This tells **mail** that there is no more data. Mail will display **EOT** (end of transmission) and send your message. You will then be returned to the shell prompt.

As you type, you can make corrections by using the special keys we discussed in Chapter 6. These are shown in Figure 15-1. (The **^C** key is discussed below.)

Here is a typical session with **mail**. The **%** characters indicate a shell prompt.

```
% mail -s 'Do you want free money?' rick harley
They will be giving free money away today at 3PM.
Do you want some?
Harley
EOT
%
```

In this example, we have entered the **mail** command with two recipient userids. The first indicates the person to whom we are sending the message (**rick**); the second is our own userid (**harley**), so that we will receive a copy of the message.

CODE	KEY	PURPOSE
erase	BACKSPACE, DELETE	erase the last character typed
werase	^W	erase the last word typed
kill	^X, ^U	erase the entire line
eof	^D	send the message
intr	^C	cancel the message

FIGURE 15-1. **mail:** *Special keys to use when composing messages*

The message consists of three lines. After typing the third line, we pressed RETURN, and then pressed **^D**. mail responded by displaying **EOT**, sending the message, and returning us to the shell.

If, while entering a message, you decide that the whole thing was a mistake, press the **intr** key (usually **^C**, see Chapter 6). **mail** will display:

```
(Interrupt -- one more to kill letter)
```

This means that **mail** has recognized that you pressed the **intr** key. However, it might have been by accident. **mail** is asking you to confirm that you really want to kill the message. If so, press the **intr** key once more. **mail** will save the message in a file named **dead.letter** and then return you to the shell prompt. If you really did press the **intr** key by accident, just keep typing.

HINT

Pressing **^C** to cancel a message only works while you are composing. Once you have actually sent a message, there is no way to get it back.

So if you are angry at someone, take a long, deep breath and count to 100 before you mail anything you might later regret. Better yet, use a text editor to create the letter as a separate file. You can always mail it later.

Watching Your Message Being Delivered: The **-v** Option

Sometimes, you may want to ensure that the message is actually delivered. One idea is to send yourself a copy, as we did in our previous example. If you receive your copy, you might infer that the other person received theirs.

Of course, such an inference is not always correct. For example, say that you enter a message correctly, but that you make a mistake in the other person's address. You will receive your copy, but the other person will not receive theirs.

If you want to watch your message being delivered, just use the **-v** (verbose) option when you enter the **mail** command:

```
mail -v -s 'New time for the meeting' melissa@misty.acme.com
```

This option tells **mail** to show you the details as the message is being delivered.

If your computer is on the Internet, and you are sending a message to another computer on the Internet, you will be able to see the connection being made. If the address is wrong, it should be obvious.

If the message is being sent to a non-Internet computer, you will not be able to see all the connections. If you have made a mistake in the address, it will not be immediately obvious.

In any event, if a message cannot be delivered, it will be mailed back to you. When you read it, there will be notes from the various computers that handled it along the way. You should be able to read these notes and figure out what went wrong.

For your interest, here is a sample session with **mail** using the **-v** option. We start by entering the command:

```
mail -v -s 'Mail Test' navarra@madsci.nwu.edu
```

Next, we enter a short, meaningless message. At the end of the message, we press **^D** (the **eof** key). **mail** displays "**EOT**" (end of transmission):

```
This is a test.
EOT
```

Now the mail delivery program (**sendmail**) sends the mail on its way. (**sendmail** is a type of program called a DAEMON. A daemon executes in the background and provides a service of general interest. See Chapter 19.)

As we watch, we see our computer (**nipper**) issue the appropriate commands (**HELO**, **VERB** and so on) to send the message. The actual message is being sent following the **DATA** command. Finally, we are told that the message has been sent.

```
navarra@madsci.nwu.edu... Connecting to hub.tcplocal...
220 hub.ucsb.edu Sendmail ready at Sat, May 21 94 12:22:32
>>> HELO nipper
250 hub.ucsb.edu Hello nipper.ucsb.edu, pleased to meet you
>>> VERB
200 Verbose mode
>>> ONEX
200 Only one transaction
>>> MAIL From:<harley@nipper>
250 <harley@nipper>... Sender ok
>>> RCPT To:<navarra@madsci.nwu.edu>
250 <navarra@madsci.nwu.edu>... Recipient ok
>>> DATA
354 Enter mail, end with "." on a line by itself
>>> .
```

```
250 Mail accepted
>>> QUIT
221 hub.ucsb.edu delivering mail
navarra@madsci.nwu.edu... Sent
```

Depending on how your system is configured, you may or may not see this much detail. Some systems are configured to display an interesting remark (like "pleased to meet you") as each command is processed; you may see some strange things.

Note: You may be able to check that someone has received his or her mail by using the **finger** command. See Chapter 13 for the details and the caveats.

The Tilde Escapes

As you type a message, there are various commands that you can send to the **mail** program. However, it is important that **mail** be able to distinguish between commands and text. Thus, the commands have a special format: they all start with a ~ (tilde) at the beginning of the line.

Here is an example. You are typing a message and, after pressing RETURN, you enter:

`~p`

This tells **mail** to display (print out) what you have typed so far.

When used in this way, the tilde is called an ESCAPE CHARACTER. An escape character tells a program that what follows is to be treated in a special way. That is, it tells the program to "escape" from its standard way of interpreting data. For this reason, these commands are called the TILDE ESCAPES.

Figure 15-2 contains a list of the tilde escapes. The most important is ~?. This is the command that will display a summary of all the tilde escapes. If you forget the commands, you can always enter the ~? command.

You might ask, what do you do if you really want to enter a line that begins with a tilde? Just use two tildes at the beginning of the line. For example:

`~~This line starts with a tilde.`

The first tilde tells **mail** that the second tilde is just a regular character. In your message, there will be only one tilde.

We will describe each tilde escape in turn. But first, we must talk about the two parts of a message: the header and the body.

The Parts of a Message: Header and Body

Each message has two parts. The HEADER consists of a number of lines of information at the beginning of the message. The BODY consists of the text of the message. Here is a typical message:

```
To: rick
Subject: 'Do you want free money?'
Cc: melissa randolph
Bcc: murray

They will be giving free money away today at 3 PM.
```

COMMAND	DESCRIPTION
~?	help: display summary of tilde escapes
~b *address...*	add addresses to "Blind Copy" line
~c *address...*	add addresses to "Copy" line
~d	read in contents of **dead.letter** file
~e	invoke text editor
~f *messages*	read in old messages
~h	edit header lines
~m *messages*	read in old messages, shift right one tab
~p	display (print) current message
~q	quit (same as pressing **intr** key twice)
~r *file*	read in contents of a file
~s *subject*	change "Subject" line
~t *address...*	add new addresses to the "To" line
~v	invoke alternative editor (usually same as ~ e)
~w *file*	write current message to a file
~! *command*	execute shell command, then return to message
~| *command*	pipe current message through a filter
~~	at beginning of line: a real tilde character

Note: Tilde escapes must start at the beginning of a line and must be the only thing on the line.

FIGURE 15-2. `mail:` *Summary of tilde escape commands*

```
Do you want some?
Harley
```

In this example, the header consists of the first four lines. The body consists of the last three lines.

There are four basic lines in the header. The first is the "To" line. This is the only header line that is required; the others are optional. The "To" line shows the recipients of the message. In this case, there is only one recipient, **rick**.

Next is the "Subject" line. We explained above how to specify the subject. If you want to change it as you are typing the message, use the **~s** tilde escape. For example, you can enter:

```
~s Do you want extra free money?
```

The next line of the header is the "Copy" line. This line begins with **Cc** and indicates who should receive a copy of the message.

There is no important difference between putting an address in the "To" line or the "Cc" line. However, for political reasons, you may find it better to list certain people as receiving a "copy" of a message. Moreover, when you send someone a copy, there is an assumption that the message is being sent only for that person's information and they should not feel obligated to reply.

To add one or more addresses to the "Copy" line, use the **~c** tilde escape. For example:

```
~c marilyn
```

If you want to replace the "Copy" line completely, use the **~h** tilde escape (described below).

The final part of the header is the "Blind Copy" line. This functions like the "Copy" line, but will not be sent as part of the message. In our original example, the message will contain the lines:

```
To: rick
Subject: 'Do you want free money?'
Cc: melissa randolph
```

However, the line:

```
Bcc: murray
```

will not be included. Thus, no one else knows that **murray** was sent a copy of the message.

To add one or more addresses to the "Blind Copy" line, use the **~b** tilde escape. For example:

```
~b mitch
```

HINT

The most convenient way to replace all four lines of the header is to use the **~h** tilde escape. This will prompt you for each line in turn. After you change the header, you may want to check the new header by using the **~p** tilde escape to display the message.

What's in a Name?   cc, bcc

A long time ago, before there were copy machines and computers, there was only one easy way to send a copy of a typewritten letter to someone: you had to use carbon paper to make an extra copy as you typed the letter. You would send the original copy to the principal recipient and the "carbon copy" to the second person. (In addition, most business people made at least one extra carbon copy for their files.)

When a carbon copy was sent to somebody (say Ben Dover), a notation would be made in the bottom left-hand corner of the first page:

```
cc: Ben Dover
```

This would tell the person reading the letter that Ben Dover also received a copy.

It has been a long time since carbon paper has been used regularly to make copies. Still, the custom in Unix is to use **cc:** in the header to refer to a copy of a message. When the idea of blind copies was invented, the notation was extended to **bcc:**.

Using a Text Editor to Compose Messages

You enter a message one line at a time. While you are typing, you can use the special keyboard codes (**erase**, **werase** and **kill**) to make corrections. However, if you are composing a long message it is usually more convenient to use a text editor. You can do this by using either the **~e** or **~v** tilde escape.

Why are there two tilde escapes to start the same program? Originally, **~e** invoked a standard text editor that was provided by **mail**, while **~v** started the **vi** ("visual") screen-oriented editor. (We will discuss **vi** in Chapter 20.) These days, only **vi** is used, so both commands are essentially the same.

When you enter a ~e or ~v tilde escape, **mail** starts **vi** with a copy of your message in the editing buffer. When you finish editing, quit **vi** in the usual way. You will be back in **mail**. As always, press ^D (the **eof** key) to send your message.

After you learn how to use **vi**, you should make a point of memorizing one of these two tilde escapes. Using a text editor makes typing messages a lot easier.

Reading Data into Your Current Message

There will be times when you want to copy existing text into the body of your message. There are several ways to do this.

First, you can use the ~d tilde escape to copy the contents of the **dead.letter** file. (As we explained earlier, this is the file into which a message is placed when you abort the **mail** command.) Using ~d is a convenient way to recall the old, unsent message.

Similarly, you can copy the contents of any file into your message by using the ~r (read) tilde escape. For example, to read in a file named **announcement**, use:

```
~r announcement
```

If you are responding to a message you have just read, you can use the ~f and ~m tilde escapes to place a copy of that message into the current message. (We will explain how this works later in the chapter.)

Finally, you can save the message you are composing to a file by using the ~w (write) tilde escape. For example, the command:

```
~w safekeeping
```

will save the message you are typing to a file named **safekeeping**.

Executing Shell Commands While Composing a Message: fmt

There are two ways to execute regular shell commands as you type a message. First, you can use the ~! tilde escape, followed by the name of the command you want to execute. For example, if you want to find out the time and date, you can enter:

```
~! date
```

When the command is finished, you will be returned to **mail** automatically.

If you want to enter more than one command, you can start a brand new shell. Just enter the name of your shell as a command. For instance, to start a C-Shell, enter:

```
~! csh
```

To start a Korn shell, use:

```
~! ksh
```

You can now enter as many commands as you want. When you are finished, end the shell by pressing **^D** (the **eof** key). You will be returned to **mail**.

The second way you can use a regular shell command is as a filter through which you can pipe the contents of the current message.

(Briefly, a filter is a program that reads data, modifies it in some way, and outputs the result. When we send data to such a program, we say that we "pipe" the data through the filter. For example, if you need to sort some data, you can pipe it through the **sort** filter. We will discuss pipes in Chapter 16 and filters in Chapter 17.)

To pipe the current message through a filter, use the ~| tilde escape (a |, vertical bar character, is used in Unix as the "pipe" symbol). The data that comprises the message will be replaced by the output of the filter. For example, if for some reason you wanted to sort the contents of the current message, you could enter:

```
~ | sort
```

HINT

After you have used the ~| command to pipe the contents of the current message, you may want to use **~p** to see what the new, filtered message looks like.

If the filter command fails, **mail** will make sure that the original message is not changed. This protects you against, say, misspelling the name of the command.

The most useful filter for processing a message is the **fmt** command. This command was designed specifically to format messages prior to mailing (although it is also useful for other simple tasks).

What **fmt** does is read the input and, using the same text, generate lines that are as close as possible to 72 characters long. **fmt** will preserve spaces at the beginning of lines, spaces between words and blank lines. In other words, **fmt** will make your message look nice without changing the paragraph breaks.

For example, say that you are in the middle of entering a message, line by line. To check what it looks like, you enter the **~p** command and you see:

```
Ron,
    Be sure to visit me when you come to the
university next Thursday.
    I will be glad to
show you around and introduce
you to all the people in the Computer Science department.
We can see the movie you wanted to see,
as it is playing at the campus theater.
    —Harley
```

Now you format the message by piping it through the **fmt** filter:

```
~| fmt
```

To check the output, you use **~p** to display the formatted message:

```
Ron,
    Be sure to visit me when you come to the university next Thursday.
    I will be glad to show you around and introduce you to all the
people in the Computer Science department.  We can see the movie
you wanted to see, as it is playing at the campus theater.
    —Harley
```

If the message now meets with your approval, you can press **^D** to send it on its way.

> **HINT**
> To make your messages easy for people to read, use:
>
> ```
> ~| fmt
> ```
>
> to format them before they are mailed.

Sending Mail to a File or to a Program

Most people do not know it, but you can send messages to files (for storage) or to programs (for special processing).

To send a message to a file, specify an address that is the name of the file. If the file already exists, **mail** will add the message to the end of the file.

How does **mail** know if a recipient is a file name? It will assume this to be the case if the address contains a **/** (slash) character. If you want to specify the name of a file in your current directory, use **./**, for example, **./message**. (File names and directories are explained in Chapter 23.)

Here is an example. You regularly send notes to three userids named **curly**, **larry** and **moe**. However, you would like to keep a copy of all these notes. Use the command:

```
mail curly larry moe ./stooges
```

This will send a copy of the message to a file named **stooges** in your current directory.

As strange as it sounds, you can send messages not only to a userid or to a file, but to a program as well. The program will receive the message and do whatever it does with input. For instance, you might have a program named **broadcast** that sends a copy of its input to a large number of people. Thus, you could send a message in this manner by mailing it to **broadcast**.

To mail to a program, use an address that consists of a | (vertical bar), followed by the name of the program. Because the | character has a special meaning to the shell, you must enclose the whole thing within single quotes. For example, to mail a message to a program named **broadcast**, use:

```
mail '|broadcast'
```

(The | is called a "pipe" symbol. It tells Unix to take the output of one program and use it as the input for another program. We discuss pipes in Chapter 16.)

Here is an easy way for you to test this facility. In Chapter 17, we will see that the **wc** program counts the number of lines, words and characters in its input. Try sending a message to **wc**:

```
mail '|wc'
```

Note: **mail** is picky about how you specify the program name: it can be only a single argument. Thus, you must be careful not to put any spaces within the quotes.

You will run into trouble if you try to mail to a command that consists of more than one argument. For example, with Berkeley Unix, the command **lpr -p** will format and print a file. However, you can't send mail directly to **'|lpr -p'**. The solution is to use a mail alias in your **.mailrc** file (described later in the chapter). This allows you to use a single word to refer to a complex name. For example, you might define the mail alias:

```
alias lprp '|lpr -p'
```

You can now specify the "address" **lprp** whenever you want to print a copy of a message. For example, the command:

```
mail harley lprp
```

will send a message to userid **harley** and to the printing command **lpr -p**.

Hints for Practicing Safe Mail

If you are new to electronic mail, it may take you a while to appreciate the subtleties. Here are some hints to save you trouble.

First, assume that there is no privacy. Do not send messages that, within the bounds of reason, you would not want everyone to see. It is a good idea to avoid intimate love letters, temperamental tirades, mean-spirited insults, and so on.

HINT

All mail programs make it easy to forward a message to another person. Some people love to forward mail, just as some people like to gossip. Don't assume that just because you send a message to only one person the message is private.

Moreover, don't assume that when you delete a message it cannot be restored. More than likely, your system manager does regular backups of the file system. If you delete a sensitive message on Tuesday, chances are it was preserved as part of the regular Monday night backup. Unix does not have a paper shredder.

Second, develop an appreciation for the fact that electronic messages do not carry the body language or voice inflection of regular conversation. It is all too easy to be insulting when you mean to be funny.

Thus, whenever you write something that has a chance of being misinterpreted, use the smiley face. (We talked about this in detail in Chapter 13, at the end of the discussion on the **talk** command.)

The smiley face looks like this:

`:-)`

(Turn your head sideways to the left and you will see the smile.)

Use the smiley face to indicate irony that is so subtle your correspondent might miss it. For example:

`Are you always such a jerk? :-)`

The next hint is: be careful what you promise. It is the nature of electronic mail that people tend to take messages they receive more seriously than messages they send. Moreover, it is easy to save messages — as we will see later in the chapter—and some people keep their mail forever.

Don't let yourself get in the position where someone can say to you: "What do you mean you are too busy to help me paint my house? I have a message right here from four years ago in which you told me that if I ever needed any help I should just ask."

Finally, make it a point to be polite and keep your temper. If someone sends you a message that really bothers you, wait a day before you respond. This is especially true with people you have not met in person and whose motivations may not be clear.

HINT

When you send mail on the Internet to another country, remember that many people speak English as a second language. When you write metaphonically or use slang, it is easy for someone from another culture to misinterpret what you are saying. In particular, sarcasm and irony do not travel well across national boundaries.

How Do You Know Mail Has Arrived? `from`, `biff`, `xbiiff`

How do you know when mail has arrived? To read mail, you enter the **mail** command with no arguments:

```
mail
```

If there are no messages, you will be told that there is no mail for your userid. For instance, if your userid is **harley**, you will see:

```
No mail for harley
```

If you do have mail, you will see a summary of the messages. For example:

```
Mail version SMI 4.0 Sat 10/13/90   Type ? for help.
"/usr/spool/mail/harley": 2 messages 2 new
>N  1 rick   Sun Aug 28 12:12   15/385   I would like some free
 N  2 melissa@misty.acme.com  Sun Aug 28 12:12   15/367   No th
```

However, there are three ways for you to know that you have mail waiting without having to actually start the **mail** program. First, whenever you log in, Unix will check to see if there is mail for you. If so, you will see:

```
You have new mail.
```

Second, from the shell prompt, you can use the **from** command:

```
from
```

This will display a quick summary of all the mail you have waiting. For example:

```
From rick Sun Aug 28 12:12 1992
From melissa@misty.acme.com Sun Aug 28 12:12 1992
```

The **from** command is handy when new mail arrives. Using **from**, you can quickly scan your mailbox without having to start the **mail** program.

   Many people put a **from** command in their initialization file, so they will automatically see what mail is waiting each time they log in. If you use the C-Shell, you would put the command in your **.login** file (see Chapter 11). If you use the Korn shell, you would put the command in your **.profile** file (see Chapter 12).

   The third way to check for mail is to use the **biff** command. This tells Unix whether or not you want a special announcement whenever a new message arrives. If you want such an announcement, enter:

```
biff y
```

(The **y** stands for "yes".) Whenever a new message arrives, you will see a notice, followed by a summary of the message. For example:

```
New mail for harley@nipper has arrived:
----
Date: Sun, 28 Aug 92 14:41:54 -0500
From: rick
To: harley
Subject: Re:  I would like some free money.
Harley,
I would like some free money.
...more...
```

The last line, **...more...**, shows us that there is more to the message than we see. If you do not want to be bothered with such announcements, use:

```
biff n
```

(The **n** stands for "no".) If you want to see the current **biff** setting, enter the command with no arguments:

```
biff
```

Many people execute **biff y** in their **.login** or **.profile** file to make sure that Unix always tells them when mail arrives.

If you are an X Window user (see Chapter 5), there is an X client named **xbiff** that you can use. Typically, **xbiff** displays a small picture of a mailbox. When mail arrives, **xbiff** will make a sound and raise the flag on the mailbox.

What's in a Name? `biff`

You might think the name "biff" stands for something like "Be notified if mail arrives and show who it is from". Actually, **biff** is named after a dog.

Biff the dog belonged to Heidi Stettner, who, in the summer of 1980, was about to become a Computer Science graduate student at the University of California at Berkeley (see Figure 15-3). She spent that summer working for a professor in Evans Hall, where the latest version of Berkeley Unix was being developed. (This was the version that introduced virtual memory to Unix.)

There is an apocryphal story that the **biff** command—which tells you when new mail has arrived—was named after Biff the dog because he always barked when the mailman came.

Here is the real story: Biff the dog was a universal favorite at Evans Hall. He was one of the first dogs who regularly visited the Computer Science department, and he had a sociable, friendly disposition. People liked to come to Heidi's office to visit Biff and play with him by throwing a ball down the long hallway. Biff even had his photo on the bulletin board that showed pictures of all the Computer Science graduate students. (Biff was described as studying for his Ph.Dog degree.)

Heidi remembers: "Biff used to come to classes with me. In one instance, a compiler class, he even got a grade. The teacher gave Biff a B, which was higher than some of the students."

One day, John K. Foderero, one of the grad students who was working on Berkeley Unix, decided to create a command named after Biff. He came up with the idea of writing a program to check for mail. In Heidi's words: "I had no idea that the **biff** command was in the works until after it was done. The hardest thing was for someone to think of what the name could mean. Bill Joy and John were the ones who racked their brains to come up with a long name that biff could stand for."

[Note: John Foderero wrote the compiler for Berkeley's version of Lisp (a programming language) which was called Franz Lisp. Bill Joy wrote much of Berkeley Unix, including the C-Shell and the **vi** editor. He later went on to found Sun Microsystems.]

Today, Heidi Stettner is an accomplished Unix programmer. Biff, alas, passed away in August of 1993 at the age of fifteen, after a long and happy life with Heidi and her family (John Raskin, her husband, and Sam and Max, her sons).

FIGURE 15-3.   *Heidi Stettner and Biff, circa 1980*

How Mail Is Stored

Before we talk about the details of reading your mail, let's take a moment to discuss how mail is stored.

All mail is kept by the system in a set of files, one for each userid. Typically, mail is kept in a directory named **/usr/spool/mail**, although this may vary from system to system. Thus, if your userid is **harley**, your mail will be kept in a file named **/usr/spool/mail/harley**. (We will discuss directories and file names in Chapter 23.) This file is called your SYSTEM MAILBOX.

When you enter the **mail** command with no arguments:

```
mail
```

the **mail** program checks your system mailbox, looking for messages.

All your messages are stored together, as one long file. **mail** can tell where one message ends and another begins by looking for the distinctive lines that lie within the header of each message.

To read your mail, you examine each message. After reading a message, you can save it to a file of your own. If the file already exists, **mail** will append the new message to the end of the file.

After you are finished with a message, you delete it, which removes it from your system mailbox. If you do not delete a message, it will be saved for you automatically in a file called **mbox** in your home directory. (We discuss the home directory in Chapter 23.)

It is a good idea to read and dispose of your messages in a timely fashion so they do not accumulate in the system mailbox. On some systems, you will receive automatic warnings (by mail) when your mailbox becomes too large. If your mailbox grows past a certain point, it may be moved to your **mbox** file (where, presumably, the disk space is charged to your personal account).

The nice thing about saving messages is that they are stored in the same format as incoming mail. Thus, you can use the **mail** program itself to examine and manipulate old messages. If you want to examine such a file, start **mail** using the **-f** option, followed by the name of the file. For instance, if you enter the command:

```
mail -f personal
```

mail will look in the file named **personal**, rather than in your system mailbox. By default, **mail** will read from a file named **mbox** when you use the **-f** option without a file name. Thus, the following two commands are equivalent:

```
mail -f mbox
mail -f
```

Either one will read the messages that have been stored in your **mbox** file.

Starting to Read Your Mail

Once you start the **mail** program (with or without the **-f** option), you will see a summary of all the messages that are waiting for you. Here is a typical summary.

```
Mail version SMI 4.0 Sat 10/13/90  Type ? for help.
"/usr/spool/mail/harley": 2 messages 2 new
>N  1 rick  Sun Aug 30 12:12  15/385  I would like some free
 N  2 melissa@misty.acme.com  Sun Aug 30 12:12  15/367  No th
```

The first line shows the version of the **mail** program (the date refers to the **mail** program itself) followed by the suggestion that we can use the **?** command to display help.

The next line shows us what file we are reading. In this case, it is our system mailbox. We have two messages, both of which are new.

The last two lines show a summary of these messages. Each one-line summary shows the userid who sent the message, the time and date it was received, the size of the message (lines/characters), and as much of the subject as will fit on the rest of the line.

We can see that the first message is 15 lines long and has a subject that starts with "I would like some free".

Once the summary is displayed, **mail** will display an **&** (ampersand) character. This is a prompt, to tell you that you can now enter a command.

At this point, you have 60-75 different commands you can use to read and process your messages. (The total number of commands depends on what version of **mail** you are using.)

Fortunately, there are only a few crucial commands you need to remember. These commands are summarized in Figures 15-4 and 15-5. You can use either the full name or the abbreviation. Most people use abbreviations exclusively.

At any time, you can display a summary of the most important commands by entering **?** (a question mark). You can also display a list of all the commands—without a description—by entering the **1** (list) command.

Displaying Header Information

When you start **mail**, the first thing you will see is a summary of your messages. This summary is taken from the information in the message headers. At any time, you can redisplay the summary by entering the **h** (header) command. This is a convenient way to remind yourself what messages remain to be read.

If you have a lot of messages, the summary will not list them all at once. To see the next group, enter **z**. If you have many messages, you can move through the list by entering one **z** command after another.

To display the summary for the previous group of messages (that is, to move backwards) enter **z-**.

ABBREVIATION	FULL NAME	DESCRIPTION
?	—	display summary of important commands
!	—	execute a single shell command
+	—	display the next message
-	—	display the previous message
RETURN	—	display the next message
number	—	display message *number*
d	**delete**	delete messages
dp	—	delete current msg, display next msg
e	**edit**	use text editor on messages
h	**headers**	display header summaries
l	**list**	list names of all available commands
m	**mail**	send new message to specified userid
n	**next**	display the next message
p	**print**	display (print) messages
pre	**preserve**	keep messages in system mailbox
q	**quit**	quit **mail**
r	**reply**	reply to sender and all other recipients
R	**Reply**	reply to sender only
s	**save**	save messages to specified file
sh	**shell**	pause **mail**, start a new shell
to	**top**	display top few lines of messages
u	**undelete**	undelete previously deleted messages
w	**write**	same as **s**, only do not save header
x	**exit**	quit **mail**, neglect any changes
z	—	show next set of header summaries
z-	—	show previous set of header summaries

Note: On some systems, the sense of **r** and **R** is reversed.

FIGURE 15-4. `mail:` *Important commands in alphabetical order*

ABBREVIATION	FULL NAME	DESCRIPTION
Stopping `mail`		
q	`quit`	quit `mail`
x	`exit`	quit `mail`, neglect any changes
Help		
?	—	display summary of important commands
l	`list`	list names of all available commands
Headers		
h	`headers`	display header summaries
z	—	show next set of header summaries
z-	—	show previous set of header summaries
Displaying Messages		
+	—	display the next message
-	—	display the previous message
RETURN	—	display the next message
number	—	display message *number*
n	`next`	display the next message
p	`print`	display (print) messages
to	`top`	display top few lines of messages
Replying and Mailing		
m	`mail`	send new message to specified userid
r	`reply`	reply to sender and all other recipients
R	`Reply`	reply to sender only
Processing a Message		
d	`delete`	delete messages
dp	—	delete current msg, display next msg
e	`edit`	use text editor on messages
pre	`preserve`	keep messages in system mailbox
s	`save`	save messages to specified file
u	`undelete`	undelete previously deleted messages
w	`write`	same as **s**, only do not save header
Shell Commands		
!	—	execute a single shell command
sh	`shell`	pause `mail`, start a new shell

Note: On some systems, the sense of **r** and **R** is reversed.

FIGURE 15-5. `mail:` *Important commands grouped by function*

Displaying a Message

At all times, **mail** recognizes one of your messages as being the CURRENT MESSAGE. By default, **mail** commands are interpreted relative to the current message. When you display the message summary, the current message is marked with a **>** character. In the following example, the current message is #1.

```
Mail version SMI 4.0 Sat 10/13/90  Type ? for help.
"/usr/spool/mail/harley": 2 messages 2 new
>N  1 rick   Sun Aug 28 12:12   15/385   I would like some free
 N  2 melissa@misty.acme.com  Sun Aug 28 12:12   15/367   No th
```

You can display the current message by entering the **p** (print) command. To display the next message, simply press RETURN (with no command). Thus, you can display all your messages, one at a time, by pressing RETURN repeatedly. (**mail** knows to start with message #1.)

As an alternative, you can also display the next message by entering either the **n** (next) or **+** (plus) command.

To display the previous message, enter the **-** (minus) command.

To display a specific message, simply enter its number. For example, if you have 20 messages and you only want to see message #15, enter:

```
15
```

Finally, if you only want a preview of a message, enter the **to** (top) command. This will display the first few lines of a message.

HINT

In Chapter 18, we will explain how to use the paging programs: **more**, **pg** and **less**. These programs can be used to display a long message one screenful at a time so that the data does not scroll off the top of your screen.

Once you learn how to use one of the paging programs, set the **PAGER** environment variable. This will tell **mail** which program you want to use. (All of this is explained in Chapter 18.)

Saving a Message

After you display a message, you have to decide what to do with it. There are several choices.

First, you can write the body of a message to a file by using the **w** (write) command. Enter the command, followed by the name of the file. For example, to write a message to a file named **personal**, enter:

    w personal

As an alternative, the **s** (save) command will write the entire message, including the header. For example:

    s personal

If you save messages to a file using this command, you can later read the file using **mail** with the **-f** option.

Another way to process a message is to edit it. If you enter the **e** (edit) command, **mail** will start the text editor using the message as data. (The editor will probably be **vi**, which we will discuss in Chapter 20.) Within the editor, you can make any changes you want and save your work using the editor's commands. When you quit the editor, you will be returned to **mail**.

Replying to a Message

You can reply to a message by using the **R** command. After entering this command, you type your message in the regular manner, one line at a time, just as we described earlier in the chapter. When you are finished, press **^D** (the **eof** key). Your reply will be sent automatically to the userid who sent you the original message.

While you are typing the message, you can use all the regular tilde escape commands. In particular, you can use **~p** to display (print) the new message and **~e** (edit) to start the text editor. Remember that you can change all or part of the header by using the **~s**, **~t**, **~c**, **~b** or **~h** tilde escapes. (Don't forget that tilde escapes must start at the beginning of a line and must be the only thing on the line.)

If you are replying to a message that was sent to more than one recipient, you can send your reply to all the recipients, not just the sender of the message, by using the **r** (lowercase "r") command.

HINT

Before you reply to a message, check to see if there were other recipients. If so, make sure to use the **R** command (not **r**) unless you really want everybody to see your reply.

On some systems, the sense of **r** and **R** is reversed. You will have to test these commands for yourself. If you don't like the default, you can change it by setting the **Replyall** option, discussed later in the chapter.

When you are replying to a message, there are several other tilde escapes that are particularly useful. You can copy the old message into the new message by using the **~f** tilde escape. This is handy if you want to incorporate all or part of the old message into your reply.

A similar tilde escape is **~m**. This also copies the old message into the new one. However, each line of the old message is indented by a single tab.

Finally, you can include text from a file into the new message by using the **~r** (read) tilde escape. For example, to include the text from a file named **info**, enter:

```
~r info
```

A common technique is to use **~m**, followed by **~e**, to set yourself up to reply to a message. The **~m** copies the old message; the **~e** starts the editor.

Within the editor, it is a simple task to delete the lines you don't want. You can then reply to various portions of the original message by placing your replies directly under the appropriate lines. For example, if someone sends you a message that contains several questions, you can frame a reply in which you type each answer directly under the original question.

HINT

When you are using the **vi** editor to reply to a message that you have copied by using the **~m** tilde escape, change the tab at the beginning of each line to **>>**. To do this, enter the command:

```
:%s/<Tab>/>> /
```

(The "<Tab>" after the first **/** means press the TAB key.)

This will preface each line of the original message with **>>**, which looks nicer than a plain indentation.

Originating a New Message

There may be times when, as you read your mail, you decide to send a brand new message. Of course, you could quit reading and enter a new **mail** command, but this is a lot of bother.

Instead, you can use the **m** (mail) command. Enter the command followed by the recipient addresses. For example, say that you are reading your mail and you suddenly decide to send a new message to a person whose userid is **harley**. At the **&** prompt, enter the command:

```
m harley
```

You can now compose a message in the usual manner.

When you are finished, press **^D** (the **eof** key) to send the message. You will be returned to the **&** prompt.

You can now continue reading your mail.

Deleting a Message

Once you have displayed and (possibly) saved or replied to a message, you should delete it by using the **d** command. If you display a message, but do not delete or save it before you quit, **mail** will automatically save it to a file named **mbox**. If you make a mistake, you can undelete a message by using the **u** command.

As a convenience, you can enter the **dp** (delete/print) command. This will delete the current message and display the next one.

Finally, if you have read a message and you are not ready to delete or save it, you can use the **pre** (preserve) command. This tells **mail** to retain this message when you quit. The message will be preserved as if it were new; it will not be saved to the **mbox** file.

Note: When you preserve a message, Unix may incorrectly tell you that you have just received new mail.

Message Lists

By default, almost all commands will act upon the current message. However, wherever it makes sense, you can specify a MESSAGE LIST to specify one or more messages. The command will act on all the messages.

For example, to delete messages 3 through 5, you can enter:

```
d 3-5
```

To display all the messages from userid **root**, use:

```
p root
```

Figure 15-6 contains a summary of the different ways to specify a message list. Figure 15-7 shows examples, using the **p** (print) command.

Note: In general, **mail** assumes you do not want to refer to deleted messages unless it makes sense to do so. Thus, where **d *** will delete all messages that have not yet been deleted, **u *** will undelete all messages that have already been deleted.

SPECIFICATION	MEANING
. [a period]	the current message
n	message number *n*
n-m	all messages from *n* to *m* inclusive
^ [a circumflex]	the first message
$ [a dollar sign]	the last message
* [an asterisk]	all messages
userid	all messages from specified *userid*
/pattern	all messages containing *pattern* in subject
:n	all new messages
:o	all old messages
:r	all messages that have been read
:u	all messages that are still unread

FIGURE 15-6. `mail:` *Ways to specify a message list*

COMMAND	MEANING
p .	display the current message
p 3	display message 3
p 3-5	display messages 3 through 5 inclusive
p ^	display the first message
p $	display the last message
p *	display all messages
p harley	display all the messages from userid **harley**
p /hello	display all the messages with "hello" in subject
p :n	display all the new messages
p :o	display all the old messages
p :r	display all the messages that have been read
p :u	display all the messages that are still unread

FIGURE 15-7. `mail:` *Examples of specifying a message list*

Stopping the `mail` Program

When you are finished reading your messages, you stop the **mail** program by entering the **q** (quit) command.

When you quit, **mail** will remove all the messages you have saved or deleted. If there were any messages you read but did not save or delete, **mail** will save them in a file named **mbox**. Later, you can read these messages by using the command:

```
mail -f mbox
```

If you have previously used the **pre** command to preserve a message, it will be treated as a new message. When you quit, it will not be saved to **mbox**.

If you quit by using the **x** (exit) command instead of the **q** command, **mail** will leave your mailbox completely unchanged. This is handy when you make a mess of your mailbox by deleting the wrong messages. Using **x** puts everything back the way it was.

Hints for Managing Your Mail

Once you build up a correspondence, it doesn't take long before you have more messages than you have time to deal with. Many people routinely ignore (or preserve) messages, with the result that their mailboxes become clogged past the point of no return.

As we mentioned at the beginning of this chapter, there are other mail programs, besides **mail**, that have more sophisticated features. Some of these features are designed to make it easy to handle large amounts of mail.

However, the secret of maintaining control over your mailbox is not really what program you use. The secret is your approach to managing your mail. All you need to do is use the following guidelines:

- Look at each message only once.
- Reply or save immediately.
- Before you move on to the next message, delete the one you have just read.

Finally, the most important rule of all:

- When in doubt, throw it out.

Thus, a typical session of reading mail should look like this:

1. To start, enter the **mail** command.

2. Press RETURN to read the first message.

3. Save or reply to the message as you wish.

4. Enter **dp** to delete the message and display the next one.

5. Repeat steps 3 and 4 until all your messages have been read.

6. Enter **q** to quit.

Customizing **mail**: The **.mailrc** File

Each time **mail** starts, it looks for a file named **.mailrc** in your home directory. (The home directory is discussed in Chapter 23.) If **mail** finds such a file, it reads it and executes all the commands that it finds.

Thus, you can initialize **mail** to your liking by creating a **.mailrc** file to hold certain commands. To create such a file, you will have to use a text editor like **vi** (which is discussed in Chapter 20).

There are four commands that are especially useful within **.mailrc** files.

First, any lines that begin with a **#** (pound sign) are assumed to be comments and are ignored. Blank lines are also ignored.

Second, you can use the **alias** command to define an abbreviation for one or more addresses. The syntax is:

```
alias name address...
```

Here are two examples:

```
alias melissa melissa@misty.acme.com
alias workgroup melissa randolph peter karin pixie
```

Once an alias is defined, you can use the name as an address and **mail** will make the substitution for you automatically.

Using the first alias, we can mail to **melissa** instead of trying to remember the full address each time. Using the second alias, we can send a message to five different userids simply by using the address **workgroup**. Notice that once we define an alias (for example, **melissa**), we can use it in subsequent alias definitions.

Aliases are also useful for defining a name that stands for a command. For example, the Berkeley Unix command **lpr -p** will format and print data. Say that you define the alias:

```
alias lprp '|lpr -p'
```

You can now format and print a message by mailing it to **lprp**. (This technique was explained earlier in the chapter.)

The last two commands that are useful within a **.mailrc** file are **set** and **unset**. These commands allow you to modify a number of built-in options.

Most of the options are esoteric and can be ignored. However, there are a few you might want to use. These are shown in Figure 15-8. If you want to see all the available options and the defaults for your system, look at the manual page for the **mail** command (**man mail**).

The **ask** and **askcc** options tell **mail** to ask you to specify the "Subject" line and "Copy" line every time you create a new message.

The **autoprint** option tells **mail** that each time you delete a message, you want to automatically display the next message. In other words, the **d** command should act like the **dp** command.

The **verbose** option tells **mail** to show you the details each time a message is delivered. This is the same as invoking **mail** with the **-v** option that we explained earlier in the chapter.

The **Replyall** option reverses the meaning of the **r** and **R** commands. One of these commands sends a reply to everyone who received a copy of a message; the other command replies only to the person who sent the message. Not all systems are the same. You will have to experiment on your system to see which command does what. If you don't like the default, set the **Replyall** option.

The **set** and **unset** commands turn an option on or off respectively. Thus, to have **mail** prompt you for a "Subject" line, but not for a "Copy" line, use:

```
set ask
unset askcc
```

Figure 15-9 contains a sample **.mailrc** file.

OPTION	MEANING
`ask`	prompt for the "Subject" line of each message
`askcc`	prompt for the "Copy" line of each message
`autoprint`	after deleting, display the next message
`verbose`	show details of mail delivery (same as **-v** option)
`Replyall`	reverse the sense of the **r** and **R** commands

FIGURE 15-8. `mail:` *Useful options for the* `.mailrc` *file*

```
# .mailrc file for Harley Hahn

# OPTIONS -----------------------
set ask
unset askcc
set autoprint
unset verbose


# ALIASES -----------------------
# Melissa the Expert
alias melissa melissa@misty.acme.com
# The Anaconda Research Society
alias workgroup peter karin pixie randolph melissa
# format and print a message
alias lprp '|lpr -p'
```

FIGURE 15-9. `mail:` *A sample* .mailre *file*

CHAPTER 16

Redirection and Pipes

From the beginning, Unix has always had a certain something that makes it different from other operating systems. That "something" is the Unix toolbox: the large variety of programs that are a part of every Unix system, and the simple, elegant ways in which we can use them.

In this chapter, we will explain the philosophy behind the Unix toolbox. We will then show you how to combine basic building blocks into powerful tools of your own. In Chapter 17, we will survey the most important of these programs, so that you will have a good feel for what resources are available for your day-to-day work.

The Unix Philosophy

In Chapter 1, we explained how the original developers of Unix had worked previously on an operating system called Multics. One of the problems with Multics was that it was too unwieldy. The Multics design team had tried to make their product do too many things to please too many people.

When Unix was designed — at first, by only two people — the developers felt strongly that it was important to avoid the complexity of Multics and other such operating systems.

Thus, they developed a Spartan attitude in which economy of expression was paramount. Each program, they reasoned, should be a single tool with, perhaps, a few basic options. A program should do only one thing, but should do it well. When you need to perform a complex task, you should do so by combining existing tools, not by writing a new program.

Here is a common example. Virtually all programs generate some type of output. When you display a large amount of output, the data may come so fast that all but the last part will scroll off the screen before you can read it.

One solution is for each program to be able to control its output. Whenever output is to be displayed on the screen, the program can present it one screenful at a time. This is just the type of solution that the original Unix developers wanted to avoid. Why should each program need to incorporate the same functionality?

Moreover, why should each program need to know where its output is going? Sometimes you may want to look at data on the screen; other times you may want to send it to a file. You may even want to send output to another program for more processing.

So the Unix designers built a single tool whose job was to display data, one screenful at a time. Whenever you used a program that generated a lot of output, you could specify that the output was to be sent to the screen display tool. Thus, no matter how many different programs you used, you needed only one tool to display output on the screen.

This approach has three important advantages. First, when you design a new program, you can keep it simple. You do not have to give it every possible capability. For example, you do not have to endow your new program with the ability to display data one screenful at a time: there is already a tool to do that.

The second advantage is that, since each tool only does one thing, you can concentrate your effort. When you are designing, say, a screen display program, you can make it the best possible screen display program; when you are designing a sorting program, you can make it the best possible sorting program, and so on.

The third advantage is ease of use. As a user, once you learn the commands to control the standard screen display program, you know how to control the output for *any* program.

Thus, in two sentences, we can summarize the Unix philosophy:

■ Each program or command should be a tool that does only one thing and does it well.

■ When you need a new tool, it is better to combine existing tools than to write new ones.

Some people describe this philosophy as: "Small is beautiful."

Since Unix is well into its second decade as an operating system, it makes sense to ask if the Unix philosophy has been successful. The answer is, yes and no.

To some extent, the original philosophy is still intact. As you will see in Chapter 17, there are a great many single-purpose tools, and Unix makes it easy to combine them as the need arises.

However, the original philosophy has proved inadequate in two important ways. First, too many people could not resist creating alternative versions of the basic tools. This means that you must sometimes learn how to use more than one tool in a single category.

For example, there are three screen display programs in common use: **more**, **pg** and **less**. Although you may decide to use **more**, for example, you should probably also have some familiarity with **pg**. One day you will log in to a system that employs **pg** to display screenfuls of output and, if you only know **more**, you will be confused.

On the other hand, many systems do use **more** as a default and you cannot get by knowing only **pg**. Finally, many people have a personal preference for **less** (which is not available on all systems). Such people need to make sure they have at least a passing acquaintance with **more** and **pg**.

Second, the idea that small is beautiful has a lot of appeal. But as users grew more sophisticated and their needs grew more demanding, it became clear that simple tools were often not enough.

For instance, the original mail program had only a few commands. It was simple to use and could be learned in a short time. However, as electronic mail systems grew in size and importance, the original mail program became seriously inadequate.

The result is that, as we described in Chapter 15, a wide variety of mail programs have been developed. Moreover, the original Unix mail program has been replaced with an enhanced program that has many, many commands. (Although you may think that Chapter 15 — the mail chapter — is long, we covered fewer than half the available commands and settings.)

What this means is that you must approach the learning of Unix carefully. In 1980, the original design of Unix was still intact, and you could learn just about everything about all the common commands. Today, there is so much more to learn that you can't possibly know it all. This means that you should be selective about which programs you want to learn, and, within each program, you should be selective about which options and commands you want to remember.

As you read this chapter, make an effort to understand the basic ideas. By all means, work in front of your terminal as you read and enter commands to test them out as you learn. However, don't try to memorize the details of each program. Just remember what is available and where to look for help when you need it.

HINT

When you learn how to use a new program, do not try to memorize every detail. Learn:

1. What the program can do for you

2. The basic details

3. Where to look for help when you need it

Standard Input and Standard Output

If there is one single idea that is central to using Unix effectively, it is the concept of standard input and output. Understand this one idea, and you are a long way toward becoming an effective Unix user.

The basic idea is a simple one: every program should be able to accept input from any source and write output to any target.

For instance, say that you have a program that sorts lines of data. You should have your choice of typing the data at the keyboard, using data from an existing file, or even accepting data that is the output from another program. Similarly, the sorting program should be able to display its data on your screen, write it to an output file, or send it to another program for more processing.

Such a system has two wonderful advantages. First, as a user, you have enormous flexibility. You can define the input and output for a program as you see fit. Moreover, you need to learn how to use only one program for each task. The same program that displays sorted data on your screen will also send its output to a disk file.

The second advantage is that designing and writing programs becomes a lot easier. When you write a program, you don't need to worry about all the variations of input and output. You can concentrate on the details of your program and depend on Unix to handle the standard resources for you.

The crucial idea is that the source of input and the target of output are not specified by the programmer. Rather, he or she writes the program to read and write in a general way. Later, *at the time you run the program*, the shell will connect the appropriate source to the input and the appropriate target to the output.

To implement this idea, the developers of Unix designed a general way to read data called STANDARD INPUT and a general way to write data called STANDARD

OUTPUT. We refer to these ideas together as STANDARD I/O (pronounced "standard eye-oh").

In practice, we often speak of these terms informally as if they were actual objects. Thus, we might say, "To save the output of a program, send the standard output to a file." What we really mean is, "To save the output of a program, tell the shell to set the output target to be a file." It is a good idea to remember that standard input and output are really ideas, not actual repositories of data.

Redirecting Standard Output

When you log in, the shell automatically sets standard input to be your keyboard and standard output to be your screen. This means that, by default, most programs will read from your keyboard and write to your screen.

However — and here's where the power of Unix comes in — every time you enter a command, you can tell the shell to reset the standard input or output, just for the duration of that command.

Thus, you might tell the shell: "I want to run the **sort** command and save the output to a file named **names**. Thus, for this command only, I want you to send the standard output to that file. After the command is over, I want you to reset the standard output back to my screen."

Here is how it works. If you want the output of a command to go to your screen, you don't have to do anything. This is automatic.

If you want the output of a command to go to a file, type a **>** (greater-than sign) followed by the name of the file, at the end of the command. For example, the command:

```
sort > names
```

will send its output to a file named **names**. The **>** character is nice because it looks like an arrow showing the path of the output.

If the file does not exist, Unix will create it. If the file already exists, its contents will be replaced. (So be careful.)

If you use two **>>** characters in a row, Unix will append data to the end of an existing file. Thus, consider the command:

```
sort >> names
```

If the file **names** does not exist, Unix will create it. If it does exist, the new data will be appended to the end of the file.

When we send the standard output to a file, we say that we REDIRECT it. Thus, both of these **sort** commands redirect their output to the **names** file.

When you redirect output, it is up to you to decide whether to use **>** (and replace data) or **>>** (and append data). When the file does not yet exist, there is no difference.

Protecting Files from Being Replaced by Redirection

In the previous section, we explained that when you use the **>** character to redirect standard output to a file, any data that already exists in the file will be replaced. We also explained that when you use **>>** to append output to a file, the file will be created if it does not already exist.

There may be times when you do not want Unix to make such assumptions on your behalf. For example, say that you have a file called **names** that contains 5,000 lines of data. You want to append the output of a **sort** command to the end of this file. In other words, you want to enter the command:

```
sort >> names
```

However, you make a mistake and accidentally enter:

```
sort > names
```

What happens? All of your original data is wiped out.

To prevent such catastrophes, you can tell the shell to not replace an existing file when you use **>** to redirect output, and to not create a new file when you use **>>** to append data. This ensures that no files can be replaced or created by accident.

If you use the C-Shell (see Chapter 11), you set a variable named **noclobber**. If you use the Korn shell (see Chapter 12), you set the option named **noclobber**. Once you set **noclobber**, the shell does exactly what you ask, but no more.

To set this variable using the C-Shell, use:

```
set noclobber
```

To unset this variable, use:

```
unset noclobber
```

(Note: There is no built-in C-Shell variable named **clobber**. Thus, entering **set clobber** will not do anything. You must set and unset **noclobber**.)

To set the option using the Korn shell, use:

```
set -o noclobber
```

To unset this option, use:

```
set +o noclobber
```

Once **noclobber** is set, you have built-in protection. For example, if the file **names** already exists and you enter:

```
sort > names
```

you will see:

```
names: File exists.
```

If you really want to replace the file, type an **!** (exclamation mark) after the character:

```
sort >! names
```

This will override the automatic check. (Be sure not to put a space between the **>** and **!** characters.) Similarly, if you try to append data to a file that does not exist, for example:

```
sort >> notfile
```

You will see a message like:

```
notfile: No such file or directory
```

If you really want to create a file, type an **!** after the **>>** characters:

```
sort >>! notfile
```

This will override the automatic check.

When you use an **!** character in this way, you can think of it as meaning "Do what I tell you!"

HINT

There are four common uses for the **!** (exclamation mark) character in Unix. Do not be confused.

1. The **!** is used to indicate event information when you use the C-Shell history mechanism. (See Chapter 11.) For example, when you enter **! !** the C-Shell will re-execute your previous command.

Note: When you use **!** as part of a command and you do not want it to be interpreted as an event indicator, you must preface it with a **** (backslash) character. This tells the C-Shell to take the **!** literally.

2. The **!** is used to delimit the parts of a UUCP bang path address. (See Chapter 14.) For example:

```
mail tinker\!evers\!chance
```

3. The **!** is used within some interactive programs to execute a single shell command.

For example, when you are using **mail** to read your mail, you can display the time and date by entering:

```
!date
```

When the **date** command is finished, you will be returned to the original program.

When the **!** is used in this way, it is sometimes called the SHELL ESCAPE CHARACTER.

4. The **!** character is sometimes used to override an automatic check.

For instance, if you set the **noclobber** variable (or option), the shell will not replace an existing file when you use **>** to redirect the standard output. To override this automatic check, you can use **>!**. For example:

```
sort >! notfile
```

Pipelines

If you want the output of a command to go to another program for further processing, type a | (vertical bar) followed by the name of the program. For example, to send the output of the **sort** program to the **lpr** command (which will print the data), use:

```
sort | lpr
```

When we send the standard output to another program, we say that we PIPE the output. Thus, the **sort** program pipes its output to the **lpr** program.

Once you know how to pipe output, you can build a command in which output is passed from one program to another in sequence. For example, the following command sends the output of the **cat** program to **grep**, the output of **grep** to **sort**, and finally, the output of **sort** to **lpr**:

```
cat newnames oldnames | grep Harley | sort | lpr
```

You don't need to worry about the details for now.

(Okay, we can worry about a few of the details. The **cat** program combines files; **grep** extracts all the lines of data that contain a specified string of characters, in this case, the letters "Harley"; **sort** sorts the data; and **lpr** prints the data. Thus, we end up with a printed, sorted list of all the lines in the files **newnames** and **oldnames** that contain the characters "Harley".)

When we combine commands in this manner, we call it a PIPELINE. The image of a pipeline, in which data is sent in at one end and emerges at the other end, is a clear one. However, you would be better off thinking of it as an assembly line in which each program performs a different function on the data. The raw data goes in one end of the assembly line and comes out the other end in finished form.

HINT

The art of using Unix well is in knowing when and how to solve a problem by combining programs into a pipeline.

Redirecting Standard Input

By default, the standard input is set to your keyboard. This means that when you enter a command that needs to read data, Unix expects you to enter the data by typing it, one line at a time. When you are finished entering data, you press **^D** (the **eof** key that we discussed in Chapter 6). Pressing this key indicates that there is no more data.

Here is an example that you can try for yourself. Enter:

```
sort
```

The **sort** command is now waiting for you to enter data from the standard input (the keyboard). Type as many lines as you want. For example, you might enter:

```
Harley
Addie
Melissa
Randolph
```

After you have pressed RETURN on the last line, press **^D** to indicate that there is no more data. The **sort** program will now sort all the data alphabetically and write it to the standard output (which, by default, is the screen).

With the data in our example, you would see the output:

```
Addie
Harley
Melissa
Randolph
```

There will be many times when you want to redirect the standard input to a file. In other words, you will want the shell to tell a program to read its data from a file, not from the keyboard. Simply type a **<** (less-than sign), followed by the name of the file, at the end of the command.

For example, to sort the data contained in a file named **temp**, use the command:

```
sort < temp
```

As you can see, the **<** character is a good choice as it looks like an arrow showing the path of the input.

Here is an example you can try for yourself. As we mentioned in Chapter 13, the system information about each userid is usually contained in the file **/etc/passwd**. You can display a sorted version of this file by entering the command:

```
sort < /etc/passwd
```

Here is a common use for redirecting standard input. When you have prepared a message that you want to mail, you can tell the mail program to read its input from a file. (The Unix mail program is discussed in Chapter 15.)

For example, say that you have a file named **notice** which contains a message you want to mail to three userids, **curly**, **larry** and **moe**. You can use the command:

```
mail curly larry moe < notice
```

As you might imagine, it is possible to redirect both the standard input and the standard output at the same time. For example, the command:

```
sort < rawdata > names
```

reads data from a file named **rawdata**, sorts it, and writes the output to a file called **names**.

HINT

When you enter a command that redirects or pipes standard I/O, it is not necessary to put spaces around the **<**, **>** or **|** characters. However, it is a good idea to use such spaces.

For example, instead of:

```
cat newnames oldnames|grep Harley|sort|lpr
sort <rawdata >names
```

it is better to use:

```
cat newnames oldnames | grep Harley | sort | lpr
sort < rawdata > names
```

This makes your commands easier for you to understand and minimizes the chances of a typing error. Remember, do not put a space between the characters **>!** or **>>!** when you are overriding a **noclobber** setting (explained earlier in the chapter). For example:

```
sort >! names
sort >>! notfile
```

Splitting a Pipeline with Tees: `tee`

There may be times when you want the output of a program to go to two places at the same time. For example, you may want to save the output to a file, but you may also want to send the output to another program for more processing.

Take a look at this example:

```
cat newnames oldnames | grep Harley | sort | lpr
```

This command uses **cat** to combine the two files **newnames** and **oldnames**. It then sends the output to **grep**, which extracts all the lines of data that contain the characters "Harley". Next, the output of **grep** is sent to **sort** to be sorted.

Now, let us say you want to save the sorted output to a file named **save**. However, you also want to send the sorted data to **lpr** (to be printed). The solution is to use what is called a TEE. This is a mechanism that sends a copy of its input to a file as well as to the standard output. (The name comes from the world of plumbing in which a "tee" joins two pipes while providing an extra right-angled connection.)

To create a tee, use the **tee** command. The syntax is:

```
tee [-a] file...
```

Normally, you use the command with a single file name. For example:

```
cat newnames oldnames | grep Harley | sort | tee save | lpr
```

In this case, the output of the **sort** program will be saved in the file **save**. At the same time, the output will also be sent to the **lpr** program for further processing.

The syntax of the **tee** command allows you to create duplicate copies of the output by specifying more than one file name. For example, the **tee** command in the following pipeline copies the output to two files, **c1** and **c2**.

```
cat newnames oldnames | grep Harley | sort | tee c1 c2 | lpr
```

If a file you name in a **tee** command does not exist, **tee** will create it for you. However, if a file already exists, **tee** will overwrite it and the original contents will be lost. If you want to have **tee** add data to the end of an existing file instead of replacing it, use the **-a** (append option). For example:

```
cat newnames oldnames | grep Harley | sort | tee -a save | lpr
```

This command will save the output of the **sort** command in a file named **save**. If this file already exists, the output will be appended to the end of the file.

CHAPTER 17

Filters

I n Chapter 16, we explained how the Unix philosophy led to the development of many programs, each of which can be used as a tool to perform a single function. We showed how to use redirection to control the source and target of input/output, and we showed how to build pipes to create assembly lines where data is passed from one program to the next.

In this chapter, we will discuss a number of the most useful Unix tools. Using these programs, and the techniques from Chapter 16, you will be able to build flexible, customized tools to solve a wide variety of problems.

At the end of this chapter, we will explain two important Unix facilities: command substitution and regular expressions.

Filters

In Chapter 16, we saw how a series of programs could be joined using a pipeline. For example, the following command passes data through four programs in sequence: **cat**, **grep**, **sort** and **lpr**.

```
cat newnames oldnames | grep Harley | sort | lpr
```

By now, you should be able to appreciate how useful a program can be if it is designed to be part of a pipeline. Such a program will read data, perform some operation on the data, and then write out the results.

We call such programs FILTERS. Strictly speaking, a filter is any program that reads from standard input and writes to standard output. Informally, we also expect that a filter will do only one task and will do it well.

> ### HINT
> If you use filters to develop a pipeline that you use a lot, define it as an alias and place it in your **.cshrc** file (C-Shell) or your environment file (Korn shell). This will allow you to use the pipeline without having to type the whole thing every time.
>
> We discuss aliases in Chapter 11 (for the C-Shell) and Chapter 12 (for the Korn shell).

If you are a programmer, it is not hard to create your own filters. You can use a programming language (like C) or the built-in language that comes with the shell. All you need to do is make sure that your program reads and writes using the standard I/O, and your program will be a filter. In other words, if your program or shell script reads from standard input and writes to standard output, it can be part of a pipeline.

Interestingly enough, the first and last programs in a pipeline do not have to act like filters. In our last example, for instance, the **lpr** program is used to print the output of the **sort** program. Clearly, the output of **lpr** is not going to the standard output, it is going to the printer. (More precisely, the output is going to a system file where it will wait to be printed.)

Similarly, the first command in the pipeline, **cat** (which combines files), does not read from the standard input. In this case, it reads from two files, **newnames** and **oldnames**.

The Simplest Possible Filter: cat

A filter reads from standard input, does something, and then writes the results to standard output.

What would be the simplest possible filter? The one that does nothing at all. Its name is **cat** (we will see why in a moment). All **cat** does is copy data from standard input to standard output.

Here is a simple example you can perform for yourself. Enter the command:

```
cat
```

The system is now waiting for data from the standard input. That is, **cat** is waiting for you to type something. (Remember, by default, the standard input is the keyboard.)

When you press the RETURN key at the end of each line, the line will be sent to **cat**, which will copy it to the standard output (the screen). The result is that each line you type is displayed twice. For example:

```
this is line 1
this is line 1
this is line 2
this is line 2
```

When you are finished, press **^D** (the **eof** key). This tells Unix that there is no more input. The **cat** command will end, and you will be returned to a shell prompt.

You might ask, what use is a filter that does nothing? Of course, there is no need to use **cat** within a pipeline. However, you can take advantage of the mechanics of standard I/O to use **cat** as a quick way to create short files. Consider the following command:

```
cat > data
```

In this command, the standard input is still the keyboard, but the standard output has been redirected to a file named **data**. Each line that you type is copied to this file. If the file does not already exist, Unix will create it for you. If the file does exist, its contents will be replaced.

You can type as many lines as you want and end by pressing **^D**. Thus, using **cat** with redirected output is an easy way to create a file that contains a small amount of data. (Unfortunately, if you notice a mistake after you have pressed RETURN at the end of a line, you have to re-enter the command and start typing all over again.)

If you want to append data to the end of an existing file, use **>>** to redirect the standard output:

```
cat >> data
```

(As we explained in Chapter 16, when you redirect output with **>>**, the shell will append the output, rather than replace an existing file.)

You can also use **cat** to display a short file. Simply redirect the standard input to the file you want to display. For example:

```
cat < data
```

By default, the standard output will go to your screen.

Finally, you can use **cat** to make a copy of a file by redirecting both the standard input and output. For example, to copy the file **data** to another file named **newdata**, enter:

```
cat < data > newdata
```

Now, for day-to-day work, there are better ways to perform these functions. Normally, you would use a paging program (like **more** or **pg**) to display a file, a text editor (like **vi** or **emacs**) to create a file, and the copy command (**cp**) to copy a file.

However, it is important that you read and understand these examples. They will help you appreciate the power of standard I/O and filters. Look how much we can do with a filter that does nothing!

Putting **cat** through its paces provides us with a good example of the elegance of Unix. What seems like a simple concept—that data should flow from standard input to standard output—turns out to bear fruit in so many unexpected ways.

HINT

Part of the charm of Unix is, all of a sudden, having a great insight and saying to yourself, "So *that's* why they did it that way."

Increasing the Power of Filters

By making one significant change to a filter, it is possible to increase its usefulness enormously. That enhancement is to allow you to specify the names of input files.

As you know, the strict definition of a filter requires it to read its data from the standard input. If you want to read data from a file, you must redirect the standard input to that file.

However, what if we also had the option of reading from a file whose name we would specify as a parameter. For example, instead of having to enter:

```
cat < data
```

we could enter:

```
cat data
```

At first, such a small change seems insignificant. True, we make the command line slightly simpler, but at a price. The **cat** program itself must be more complex. It not only has to be able to read from the standard input, it also has to be able to read from any file. Moreover, by extending the power of **cat**, we have lost a little of the beauty and simplicity of a pure filter.

However, many filters are extended in just this way. The reason is not because it makes it easier to read from one file, but because it makes it possible to read from multiple files.

Here is an abbreviated version of the syntax for the **cat** command:

```
cat file...
```

where *file* is the name of a file from which **cat** will read.

Notice the three dots after the *file* parameter. This means that we can specify more than one file name. (Command syntax is explained in Chapter 9.)

Thus—and this point is important—in extending the power of **cat** to read from a file, we have also allowed it to read from more than one file. This means we can specify multiple files, and **cat** will read from each of them in turn and then write all the data (in the order it was read) to the standard output.

In other words, we can use **cat** to combine the data from multiple files. Take a look at the following examples:

```
cat name address phone
cat name address phone > info
cat name address phone | sort
```

The first example combines the data from three files (**name**, **address** and **phone**) and writes it to the screen. The second example combines the data from three files and writes it to a fourth file (**info**). The third example combines the data from three files and pipes it to another program (**sort**).

We have already mentioned that other filters, not just **cat**, can read input from multiple files. Technically, this is not necessary. If we want to operate on data from more than one file, we can collect the data with **cat** and then pipe it to whatever filter we want. For example:

```
cat name address phone | sort
```

This is appealing in one sense. By extending **cat** to read from files, not just the standard input, we have lost some of the elegance of the overall design. However, by using **cat** to feed other filters, we can at least retain the purity of the other filters.

However, as in many aspects of life, utility has won out over beauty and purity. It is just too much trouble to combine files with **cat** every time we want to send such data to a filter. Thus, most filters allow us to specify multiple file names as parameters.

For example, the following commands will sort the data in more than one file:

```
sort name address phone
sort name address phone > info
sort name address phone | grep Harley
```

The first command displays the output on the screen. The second command saves the output to a file. The third command pipes the output to another command for further processing.

To summarize, let us ask the following esoteric techno-nerd question. Strictly speaking, a filter reads its data from the standard input. Does this mean that a program is not really a filter if it reads its input from a file?

There are two answers. First, we can decide that when a program like **cat** or **sort** reads from standard input, it is a filter, but when it reads from a file, it is not a filter. Or we can broaden the definition of a filter to allow it to read from either the standard input or from one or more files.

Talk about controversy!

A List of Useful Filters

Having explained the basics of using filters, we will spend the rest of the chapter discussing the most important of these programs. Figure 17-1 shows a list of useful filters. We will discuss all of these in this chapter except for **fmt** (Chapter 15), **head**, **less**, **more**, **pg** and **tail** (Chapter 18), and **nl** and **pr** (Chapter 19).

FILTER	PURPOSE
`cat`	combine files; copy standard input to standard output
`colrm`	remove specified columns from each line of data
`crypt`	encode or decode data using a specified key
`cut`	extract selected portions (columns) of each line
`fmt`	format text to fit a 72-character line
`grep`	extract lines that contain a specified pattern
`head`	display the first few lines of data
`less`	display data, one screenful at a time
`look`	extract lines beginning with a specified pattern
`more`	display data, one screenful at a time
`nl`	create line numbers
`paste`	combine columns of data
`pg`	display data, one screenful at a time
`pr`	format data, suitable for printing
`rev`	reverse order of characters in each line of data
`sort`	sort or merge data
`spell`	check data for spelling errors
`tail`	display the last few lines of data
`tr`	translate or delete selected characters
`uniq`	look for repeated lines
`wc`	count number of lines, words or characters

FIGURE 17-1. *A list of useful filters*

As we discuss each filter, bear in mind that we will cover only the most important material. If you want to learn all the details, including the more esoteric options, use the **man** command to check the online manual. (The online manual is explained in Chapter 8.)

In addition, you may find that not all of these programs are available on your system. If you have any doubts, check the online manual or use the **whatis** command (Chapter 8).

Note: If you decide to skim through the rest of this chapter, be sure to read the last two sections on command substitution and regular expressions.

Combining Files: cat

The **cat** program copies data, unchanged, to the standard output. The data can come from the standard input or from one or more files. The syntax is:

```
cat [-bns] file...
```

where *file* is the name of a file.

You can use **cat** to combine files, for example:

```
cat name address phone
cat name address phone > info
cat name address phone | sort
```

You can also use **cat** to display one or more files:

```
cat name
cat name address phone
```

to create a file:

```
cat > newfile
```

to append data to an existing file:

```
cat >> oldfile
```

and to copy a file:

```
cat < data > newdata
```

There is one common mistake you must be sure to avoid: do not redirect output to one of the input files. For example, say that you want to append the contents of **address** and **phone** to the file **name**. You cannot use:

```
cat name address phone > name
```

This is because Unix sets up the output file before starting the **cat** program. Thus, the file **name** is already cleared out *before* **cat** reads and combines its input. By the time **cat** looks in **name**, it is already empty.

If you enter a command like the one above, you will see a message like:

```
cat: input name is output
```

However, it is too late. The original contents of **name** have been lost.

The safe way to append the contents of **address** and **phone** to the file **name** is to use:

```
cat address phone >> name
```

Notice you do not use **name** as an input file; rather, you append the contents of the other two files to **name**.

The options for **cat** are as follows. The **-n** (number) option will place a line number in front of each line. The **-b** (blank) option is used with **-n** and tells **cat** not to number blank lines. The **-s** (squeeze) option changes more than one consecutive blank line to a single blank line.

HINT

Although you can display a file with **cat**, it is best to get in the habit of using a paging program, such as **more** (see Chapter 18), which will display data one screenful at a time.

People like to use **cat** because it is cute and is easy to type. However, unless the file is short, most of the data will scroll off the top of the screen before you can read it.

What's in a Name?   cat

Many people believe that the name **cat** stands for "concatenate". Not really.

The name **cat** actually comes from the archaic word "catenate" which means "to join in a chain". (And, as all classically educated computer programmers know, "catena" is the Latin word for "chain".)

Removing Columns of Data: `colrm`

The **`colrm`** command reads from the standard input, removes specified columns of data, and then writes the remaining data to the standard output. The syntax of the **`colrm`** command is:

`colrm` [*startcol* [*endcol*]]

where *startcol* and *endcol* specify the starting and ending range of the columns to be removed. Numbering starts with column 1.

Here is an example: You are a tenured professor at a university in California and you have to print a list of grades for all the students in your PE 201 class ("Intermediate Surfing"). This list should not show the students' names.

You have a master data file, named **students**, that contains one line of information about each student. Each line has a student number, a name, the final exam grade and the course grade:

```
012-34-5678   Ambercrombie, Al   95%   A
123-45-6789   Barton, Barbara    65%   C
234-56-7890   Canby, Charles     77%   B
345-67-8901   Danfield, Deann    82%   B
```

To construct the list of grades, you need to remove the names, which are in columns 14 through 28, inclusive. Use the command:

```
colrm 14 28 < students
```

The output is:

```
012-34-5678       95%   A
123-45-6789       65%   C
234-56-7890       77%   B
345-67-8901       82%   B
```

To print this list, all you need to do is pipe the output to the **`lpr`** program:

```
colrm 14 28 < students | lpr
```

(Using **`lpr`** to print files is explained in Chapter 19.)

If you specify only a starting column, **colrm** will remove all the columns from that point to the end of the line. For example:

```
colrm 14 < students
```

displays:

```
012-34-5678
123-45-6789
234-56-7890
345-67-8901
```

If you specify neither a starting nor ending column, **colrm** will delete nothing.

Extract Selected Columns of Each Line: cut

The **cut** command extracts columns of data. This command has a great deal of flexibility. You can extract either specific columns or delimited portions of each line (called fields). If you are a database expert, you can consider **cut** as implementing the projection of a relation. (If you are not a database expert, don't worry. Nobody really understands that stuff anyway.)

In this section, we will concentrate on the basic features of **cut**; we will not deal with fields. If you want more details, check the online manual (described in Chapter 8) by using the **man cut** command.

The syntax of the **cut** command is:

```
cut -clist [file...]
```

where *list* is a list of columns to extract, and *file* is the name of an input file.

You use the list to tell **cut** which columns of data you want to extract. Specify one or more column numbers, separated by commas. Do not put any spaces within the list. For example, to extract column 10 only, use **10**. To extract columns 1, 8 and 10, use **1,8,10**.

You can also specify a range of column numbers by joining the beginning and end of the range with a hyphen. For example, to extract columns 10 through 15, use **10-15**. To extract columns 1, 8, and 10 through 15, use **1,8,10-15**.

Here is an example of how to use **cut**. Say that you have a file named **info** that contains information about a group of people. Each line contains data pertaining to one person. In particular, columns 14-30 contain a name and columns 42-49 contain a phone number. Here is some sample data:

```
012-34-5678   Ambercrombie, Al   01/01/72   555-1111
123-45-6789   Barton, Barbara    02/02/73   555-2222
234-56-7890   Canby, Charles     03/03/74   555-3333
345-67-8901   Danfield, Deann    04/04/75   555-4444
```

To display the names only, use:

```
cut -c14-30 info
```

You will see:

```
Ambercrombie, Al
Barton, Barbara
Canby, Charles
Danfield, Deann
```

To display the names and phone numbers, use:

```
cut -c14-30,42-49 info
```

You will see:

```
Ambercrombie, Al 555-1111
Barton, Barbara  555-2222
Canby, Charles   555-3333
Danfield, Deann  555-4444
```

To save this information, you can redirect the standard output to a file. For example:

```
cut -c14-30,42-49 info > phonelist
```

If you want to rearrange the columns of a table, you can use **cut** with the **paste** command (explained later in this chapter).

The **cut** command is handy to use in a pipeline. Here is an example. You want to make a list of the userids that are currently logged in to the system. Since some userids may be logged in more than once, you want to show how many times each userid is logged in.

Start with the **who** command we described in Chapter 13. This command will generate a report with one line for each userid that is logged in. Here is a sample:

```
addie      console Jul  8 10:30
harley     ttyp1   Jul 12 17:46
tln        ttyp4   Jul 12 21:22    (feline)
addie      ttyp0   Jul 12 16:45
kim        ttyp3   Jul 12 17:41    (tintin.ucsb.edu)
```

As you can see, the userid is displayed in columns 1 through 8. Thus, we can extract the userids by using:

```
cut -c1-8
```

Next, we sort the list of userids using **sort**, and count the number of duplications using **uniq -c**. (Both the **sort** and **uniq** commands are explained later in the chapter.)

Putting the whole thing together, we have:

```
who | cut -c1-8 | sort | uniq -c
```

(As you can see, there is no problem using options within a pipeline.)

If the output of the **who** command was the same as our example above, the result of this pipeline would be:

```
2 addie
1 harley
1 kim
1 tln
```

An interesting variation is to solve the following problem: How can you display the names of all userids who are logged in twice? The solution is to search the output of **uniq** for all the lines that begin with "2". You can do so using the **grep** command (explained later in the chapter):

```
who | cut -c1-8 | sort | uniq -c | grep 2
```

The output is:

```
2 addie
```

Encoding and Decoding Data: `crypt`

The **crypt** command encodes data. To use **crypt**, you specify a password called a KEY. **crypt** uses the key to create an encoded version of the data. The encoded data itself looks like nonsense. However, if you know the key, you can use **crypt** to decode the data and recover the original message.

The **crypt** command is useful to protect sensitive data such as payroll data, love letters or student grades. Although Unix does provide for specific file permissions (see Chapter 24), it is possible that someone might find a way to read your files. Thus, if you have top secret data lying around, you may wish to encode it.

For cryptography buffs: the **crypt** command implements a one-rotor machine similar to the German Enigma used during World War II. The main difference is that **crypt** uses a 256-element rotor.

Note: This command is not available on all systems. In particular, for reasons of national security, this command is not supposed to be available on systems that are shipped outside of the United States. (This may seem silly, but we in America do sleep more soundly at night.)

The syntax of the **crypt** command is:

crypt [*key*]

where *key* is the password to be used to encode the data.

To use **crypt**, enter the name of the command, with or without a key. If you do not specify a key, **crypt** will ask you for one. **crypt** will read from the standard input, encode what it reads, and write the result to the standard output.

Here is an example. You want to create a quick message in code and save it in a file named **message**. Enter:

crypt > message

You will be asked for a key:

Enter key:

Enter whatever key you want and press RETURN. For secrecy, the key will not be echoed as you type, just like when you type your login password.

You can now type your message, as many lines as you want. After you have pressed RETURN for the last line, press **^D** (the **eof** key) to tell **crypt** that there is no more data from the standard input. **crypt** will encode your message and write it to the file you specified.

To view the coded message, enter:

```
crypt < message
```

Once again, **crypt** will ask you for the key. After you enter it, **crypt** will decode the message and display the output on your screen (the default standard output).

Here is another example: You have a file named **bigsecrets** that you want to protect from prying eyes. You decide to encode it, using the key **duckface**, and save the encoded data in a file named **notimportant**. Enter the command:

```
crypt duckface < bigsecrets > notimportant
```

Now you can remove the original file by using the **rm** command (explained in Chapter 24):

```
rm bigsecrets
```

When you want to recover the original data, you can display it on your screen by using:

```
crypt duckface < notimportant
```

You can restore it to a file (in this case, **bigsecrets**) by using:

```
crypt duckface < notimportant > bigsecrets
```

Hint for Paranoids

To be extra careful, do not enter the key as part of your command. The person who is spying on you can use the **w** or **ps** commands to see your entire command line and read your key.

If you encrypt files, make sure to keep your keys secret. Anyone who can access the files will be able to read them if they know your key. Without a key, even the system manager cannot read an encrypted file.

However, make sure you do not forget the key. If you do, there is no way to recover the original data.

Extracting Lines That Contain a Specified Pattern: grep

(Note: After you read about **grep**, be sure to look at the section on regular expressions, at the end of this chapter. Regular expressions allow you to specify search patterns that can be used with **grep**.)

The **grep** command will search for all the lines in a collection of data that contain a specified pattern and write these lines to the standard output. For example, you can search a file for all the lines that contain the word **Harley**.

The **grep** command is actually part of a family. The other members are **fgrep** and **egrep**. At the time that **grep** was first developed, computer speed and memory were limited. Three separate programs were developed, each with trade-offs.

grep was designed to be the general purpose program. It can search for patterns that are exact characters (such as "Harley"), or for patterns that match a more general specification. For example, the specification **H[a-z]*y** will match the letter "H", followed by any number of lowercase letters, followed by the letter "y". (We will explain what the name **grep** means at the end of the chapter.)

fgrep was designed to be a faster searching program. However, it can only search for exact characters, not for general specifications. The name **fgrep** stands for "fixed character **grep**" (not "fast **grep**").

egrep was designed to be the most powerful **grep** program. It can search for more complex patterns than **grep**, and it is usually the fastest of the three programs. However, the method that **egrep** uses sometimes requires more memory than **grep** or **fgrep**. The name **egrep** stands for "extended **grep**".

These days, computers are faster and memory is more plentiful. There is rarely any need to use **fgrep**. In fact, some people say the best idea is to use **egrep** almost all the time.

However, most people still use **grep** for two reasons. First, **grep** is well-known among Unix people, who, like all of us, do preserve a certain amount of tradition. Second, the name **grep** is cuter and easier to type than the name **egrep**.

Thus, we suggest that, as a rule, you use **grep** unless you need the extended features of **egrep**. You can forget about **fgrep**.

The **grep** family provides a wide range of text searching capabilities. In this section, we will discuss only the most useful features of the basic **grep** program. If you want more details, or if you want to learn about **egrep**, check the online manual (described in Chapter 8) by using the **man grep** command.

The syntax of the **grep** command is:

grep [**-cilnvw**] *pattern* [*file...*]

where *pattern* is the pattern to search for, and *file* is the name of an input file.

grep reads all the input data and selects those lines that contain the specified pattern. Here is an example.

In Chapter 13, we explained that most Unix systems keep general login information in the file named **/etc/passwd**. Each userid has one line of information in this file. You can display the information about your userid by using **grep** to search the file for that pattern. For example, if your userid is **harley**, use the command:

grep harley /etc/passwd

If **grep** does not find any lines that match the specified pattern, there will be no output or warning message. Like most Unix commands, **grep** is terse. When there is nothing to say, **grep** says nothing.

When you specify a pattern that contains punctuation or special characters, you should place them in single quotes so the shell will interpret the command properly. For example, to search a file named **info** for all the lines that contain a colon followed by a space, use the command:

grep ': ' info

Much of the flexibility of **grep** comes from the fact that you can specify not only exact characters, but a more general search pattern. To do this, you use what are called "regular expressions".

Regular expressions are extremely important in Unix, so we will describe them in a separate section at the end of the chapter. In that section, we will give examples using **grep**.

As useful as **grep** is for searching files, it really comes into its own in a pipeline. What makes **grep** so handy is that it can reduce a large amount of raw data to a small amount of useful information. Here are some examples.

The **w** command (discussed in Chapter 13) displays information about all the users and what they are doing. Here is some sample output:

```
8:44pm  up 9 days,  7:02,  5   users,  load average: 0.11, 0.02, 0.00
User    tty          login@   idle   JCPU     PCPU   what
addie   console      Wed10am  4days  42:41    37:56  -csh
addie   ttyp0        4:45pm          1:40     :36    vi existential
harley  typ1         5:47pm          5:11            w
tln     ttyp4        9:22am   1:40   20       1      -rn rec.pets.cats
kim     ttyp3        5:41pm   10     2:16     13     -csh
```

Say that you want to display all the users who logged in during the afternoon or evening. You can search for lines of output that contain the pattern "pm". Use the pipeline:

```
w -h | grep pm
```

(Notice that we use **w** with the **-h** option to suppress the header information, the first two lines.) Using the above data, the output of the previous command would be:

```
addie     ttyp0     4:45pm          1:40      0:36   vi existential
harley    ttyp1     5:47pm          15:11            w
kim       ttyp3     5:41pm    10    2:16      13     -csh
```

Suppose we just want to display the userids and not all the other information. We can pipe the output of **grep** to the **cut** command and extract the first 8 columns of data:

```
w -h | grep pm | cut -c1-8
```

The output is:

```
addie
harley
kim
```

The **grep** command has several options that you can use. The **-c** (count) option will display the number of lines that have been extracted, rather than the lines themselves. For example, to count the number of users who logged in during the afternoon or evening, use:

```
w -h | grep -c pm
```

The **-i** option ignores the difference between upper- and lowercase letters when making a comparison. (Note that, with the **look** and **sort** commands, discussed later in the chapter, the same option is named **-f**.)

The **-n** option writes a relative line number in front of each line of output. Your data does not have to actually contain line numbers; **grep** will count lines as it processes the input. The **-n** option is useful when you are searching a large file. If you need to, say, use a text editor to change the lines that **grep** finds for you, the line numbers will help you locate the data quickly.

The **-l** (list file names) option is useful when you want to search a number of files for a particular pattern. This option will output not the lines that contain the pattern, but the names of files in which such lines were found.

For example, say that you have three files, **names**, **oldnames** and **newnames**. You want to see which files, if any, contain the pattern "Harley". Use:

```
grep -l Harley names oldnames newnames
```

The **-w** option specifies that you want to search only for complete words. For example, say that you have a file named **memo** that contains the following lines:

```
We must, of course, make sure that all the
data is now correct before we publish it.
I thought you would know this.
```

You want to display all the lines that contain the word "now". If you enter:

```
grep now memo
```

you will see:

```
data is now correct before we publish it.
I thought you would know this.
```

grep did not distinguish between "now" and "know" because they both contain the specified pattern. However, if you enter:

```
grep -w now memo
```

you will see only the output you want:

```
data is now correct before we publish it.
```

Finally, the **-v** (reverse) option will select all the lines that do *not* contain the specified pattern. For example, let's say you are a student and you have a file, named **homework**, to keep track of your assignments. This file contains one line for each assignment. Once you have finished an assignment, you mark it "DONE". For example:

```
Math: problems 12:10-33, due Monday
Basket Weaving: make a 6-inch basket, DONE
Psychology: essay on Animal Existentialism, due end of term
Surfing: catch at least 10 waves, DONE
```

To list all the assignments that are not yet finished, enter:

```
grep -v DONE homework
```

If you want to see the number of assignments that are not finished, you can use:

```
grep -cv DONE homework
```

Extracting Lines Beginning with a Specified Pattern: look

The **look** command will search data that is in alphabetical order and will find all the lines that begin with a specified pattern. The syntax of the **look** command is:

```
look [-df] pattern [file]
```

where *pattern* is the pattern to search for, and *file* is the name of a file.

There are two ways to use **look**. First, you can use sorted data from one or more files. For example, say that the file **evaluations** contains data regarding student evaluations of professors. The data consists of a ranking (A, B, C, D or F) followed by the name of the professor. For example:

```
A    William Wisenheimer
C    Peter Pedant
F    Norman Knowitall
```

You want to display the names of all the professors who received an "A" rating. Use **look** to search for all the lines of the file that begin with "A":

```
look A evaluations
```

If you want to prepare data to use with **look**, you should be aware that it cannot read from the standard input. (Thus, **look** is not really a filter and cannot be used within a pipeline.) This is because **look** uses a search method—called a "binary search"—that needs to access all the data at once. With standard input, a program can read only one line at a time.

However, all you need to do is prepare your data and save it in a file, then use the **look** command. For example, say that the four files **frosh**, **soph**, **junior** and **senior** all contain evaluations. To search all of them for professors who received an "A", use the **sort** command to sort and combine the files. Then use **look** to find the information you want:

```
sort -dfu frosh soph junior senior > evaluations
look A evaluations
```

(The **sort** command is explained later in the chapter.)

When you use **look** to select lines, there are two options that will control the comparisons. The **-d** (dictionary) option tells **look** to consider only upper- and lowercase letters, numerals, tabs and spaces.

The **-f** (fold) option tells **look** to treat uppercase the same as lowercase.

The second way to use **look** is to specify only a search pattern, but not a source of input. In this case, **look** will examine the file **/usr/dict/words**, using both the **-d** and **-f** options.

The name **/usr/dict/words** refers to the file **words**, which lies within the **/usr/dict** directory. (Such names are explained in Chapter 23.) **/usr/dict/words** is a master file of correctly spelled words and is used by the **spell** command (which is discussed later in the chapter).

Since the master word file is sorted, **look** can search it successfully. You can display all the words that start with a particular pattern by using:

```
look -df pattern /usr/dict/words
```

However, as we mentioned, the **-d** and **-f** options and the file name **/usr/dict/words** are defaults. Thus, you can simplify the command to:

```
look pattern
```

Using **look** in this way is handy when you are not sure how to spell a word. For example, say that you want to use the word "simultaneous", but you are not sure how to spell it. Enter:

```
look simu
```

You will see the list:

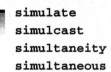

simulate
simulcast
simultaneity
simultaneous

You can now pick the correct word.

HINT
If you are working with the **vi** text editor (see Chapter 20), you can display words by using **:r!** to issue a quick **look** command. For example:

:r !look simu

will insert all the words that begin with "simu" into your editing buffer. You can now delete all but the word that you wanted.

Combining Columns of Data: `paste`

The **paste** command combines columns of data. This command has a great deal of flexibility. You can combine several files, each of which has a single column of data, into one large table. You can also combine consecutive lines of data to build multiple columns.

In this section, we will concentrate on the basic feature of **paste**: combining separate files. If you want more details, check the online manual (described in Chapter 8) by using the **man paste** command.

The syntax of the **paste** command is:

paste [**-d** *char*] *file*...

where *char* is a character to be used as a separator, and *file* is the name of an input file.

You use **paste** to combine columns of data into one large table. For example, say that you have four files named **idnumber**, **name**, **birthday** and **phone**. These files contain the following data:

idnumber

```
012-34-5678
123-45-6789
234-56-7890
345-67-8901
```

name

```
Ambercrombie, Al
Barton, Barbara
Canby, Charles
Danfield, Deann
```

birthday

```
01/01/72
02/02/73
03/03/74
04/04/75
```

phone

```
555-1111
555-2222
555-3333
555-4444
```

You want to build one large file named **info** that combines all this data into a single table. Use:

paste idnumber name birthday phone > info

If you display the data in **info**, it will look like this:

```
012-34-5678    Ambercrombie, Al    01/01/72    555-1111
123-45-6789    Barton, Barbara     02/02/73    555-2222
234-56-7890    Canby, Charles      03/03/74    555-3333
345-67-8901    Danfield, Deann     04/04/75    555-4444
```

HINT
Think of **cat** as combining data vertically and **paste** as combining data horizontally.

The reason for the spacing of the output in our last example is that, by default, **paste** puts a tab character between each column entry. As we explained in Chapter 6, Unix assumes that tabs are set every 8 positions, starting with position 1. In other words, Unix assumes that tabs are set at positions 1, 9, 17, 25 and so on.

If you would like **paste** to use a different character between columns, use the **-d** (delimiter) option followed by an alternative character in single quotes. For example, to create the same table with a space between columns, use:

```
paste -d' ' idnumber name birthday phone > info
```

Now your output looks like this:

```
012-34-5678 Ambercrombie, Al 01/01/72 555-1111
123-45-6789 Barton, Barbara  02/02/73 555-2222
234-56-7890 Canby, Charles   03/03/74 555-3333
345-67-8901 Danfield, Deann  04/04/75 555-4444
```

Note: **paste** will allow you to specify more complex delimiters than what we have shown here. For more details, check the online manual (**man paste**).

Using **cut** and **paste** in sequence, you can change the order of columns in a table. For example, say that you have a file named **pizza** with the following columns of data:

```
mushrooms regular sausage
olives    thin    pepperoni
onions    thick   meatball
tomato    pan     liver
```

You want to change the order of the first and second columns. First, save each column to a separate file:

```
cut -c1-9 pizza > vegetables
cut -c11-17 pizza > crust
cut -c19-27 pizza > meat
```

Now combine the three columns into a single table, specifying the order that you want:

```
paste -d' ' crust vegetables meat > pizza
```

To display this file, use the **more** command (see Chapter 18):

```
more pizza
```

The data now looks like this:

```
regular mushrooms sausage
thin    olives    pepperoni
thick   onions    meatball
pan     tomato    liver
```

Finally, use the **rm** command (see Chapter 24) to remove the three temporary files:

```
rm crust vegetables meat
```

Reversing the Order of Characters: rev

The **rev** command reverses the order of characters in each line of input. The data may come from the standard input or from one or more files. The syntax of the **rev** command is:

```
rev [file...]
```

where *file* is the name of a file.

The output of **rev** is written to the standard output. **rev** does not change the original file.

Here is an example. You have a file named **data** that contains:

```
12345
abcde
AxAxA
```

You enter:

```
rev data
```

The output is:

```
54321
edcba
AxAxA
```

Later in the chapter, we will show you an example of how using **rev** (with command substitution) might save your life.

Sorting and Merging Data: `sort`, the ASCII Code

The **sort** command performs two main tasks. First, as you would expect, it sorts data. You will find that **sort** is highly useful for sorting files of data and for sorting data within a pipeline. Second, **sort** will read files that contain previously sorted data and merge them into one large, sorted file.

sort has a great deal of flexibility. You can compare entire lines or selected portions of each line (called fields). In this section, we will concentrate on the basic features of **sort**; we will not deal with fields. If you want more details, check the online manual (described in Chapter 8) by using the **man sort** command.

The syntax for using **sort** to sort data is:

```
sort [-dfnru] [-o outfile] [infile...]
```

where *outfile* is the name of a file to hold the output, and *infile* is the name of a file that contains input.

The syntax for using **sort** to merge data is:

```
sort -m [-o outfile] sortedfile...
```

where *outfile* is the name of a file to hold the output, and *sortedfile* is the name of a file that contains sorted data.

The simplest way to use **sort** is to sort a single file and display the results on your screen. Say that you have a file called **names** that contains:

```
Barbara
Al
Deann
Charles
```

To sort this data and display the results, enter:

`sort names`

You will see:

`Al`
`Barbara`
`Charles`
`Deann`

To save the sorted data to a file named **masterfile**, you can redirect the standard output:

`sort names > masterfile`

This last example saves the sorted data in a new file. There will be times when you want to save the data in the same file. That is, you will want to replace a file with the same data in sorted order.

Unfortunately, you cannot use a command that redirects the output to the input file:

`sort names > names`

As we explained earlier (in the discussion about the **cat** command), when you redirect the standard output, Unix sets up the output file before starting the command. This means that by the time **sort** is ready to read from **names**, it will be empty. Thus, the result of your entering this command would be to wipe out all your data.

sort provides a special option just for this situation. You can use **-o** (output) followed by the name of the file you want to use for output. If the output file is the same as one of your input files, **sort** will be sure to protect your data.

Thus, to sort a file and save the output in the same file, use a command like:

`sort -o names names`

In this case, the original data in **names** will be replaced by the sorted data.

If you need to sort the combined data from more than one file, just specify more than one file name. For example, to sort the data from the files **names**, **oldnames** and **extranames**, and save the output in the file **masterfile**, use:

`sort names oldnames extranames > masterfile`

To sort the same files but save the output in **names** (one of the input files), use:

`sort -o names names oldnames extranames`

The **sort** command is often used as part of a pipeline to process data that has been produced by another program. The following example combines two files, extracts only those lines that contain the characters "Harley", sorts those lines, and then sends the results to be printed.

```
cat newnames oldnames | grep Harley | sort | lpr
```

By default, data is sorted in ascending order according to a specification called the ASCII CODE. The ASCII code is a description of the entire set of 128 different characters that was adopted by Unix. This set includes lowercase letters, uppercase letters, numerals, punctuation and miscellaneous symbols. It also contains the space, the tab, and the control characters (which, as we described in Chapter 6, are used for special purposes). For reference, we have included a copy of the ASCII code in Appendix E.

What is important here is that the ASCII code is like our regular alphabet in that the characters are in a certain order, and it is this order that **sort** uses for comparisons.

The order of characters in the ASCII code is as follows:

— control characters (including the tab)
— the space character
— (symbols) ! " # $ % & ' ( ) * + , - . /
— (numerals) 0 1 2 3 4 5 6 7 8 9
— (more symbols) : ; < = > ? @
— (uppercase letters) A B C ... Z
— (more symbols) [\ ] ^ _ `
— (lowercase letters) a b c ... z
— (more symbols) { | }~
— the del (null) character

HINT
As a rule of thumb, all you need to remember about the ASCII code is: space, numerals, uppercase letters, lowercase letters, in that order. Think of "SNUL".

Thus, if you use **sort** to sort the following data (in which the third line starts with a space):

```
hello
Hello
 hello
1hello
:hello
```

The output will be:

```
 hello
1hello
:hello
Hello
hello
```

The **sort** command has several options that you can use to affect the sorting order:

The **-d** (dictionary) option considers only letters, numerals and spaces, and ignores other characters.

The **-f** (fold) option treats uppercase letters as if they were lowercase.

The **-n** (numeric) option will recognize numbers at the beginning of a line and sort them numerically. Such numbers may include leading spaces, negative signs and decimal points.

The **-r** (reverse) option sorts the data in reverse order.

Finally, the **-u** (unique) option will look for identical lines and suppress all but one. For example, if you use the command:

```
sort -u
```

to sort the following data:

```
Barbara
Al
Barbara
Barbara
Deann
```

the output will be:

```
Al
Barbara
Deann
```

Aside from sorting data, **sort** will also merge multiple files that contain sorted data. To use **sort** in this way, specify the **-m** (merge) option.

For example, say that you have three files, **names**, **oldnames** and **extranames**, that contain the following data:

names	oldnames	extranames
Al	Barbara	Deann
Barbara	Charles	Fred
Edward	Edward	

The following command will merge all the data into a single file named **masterfile**:

```
sort -m names oldnames extranames  masterfile
```

If you want to merge the three files, and save the output to **names** (replacing the original data), use the **-o** (output) option:

```
sort -m -o names names oldnames extranames
```

Check Data for Spelling Errors: spell

The **spell** command will read data and generate a list of all the words that look as if they are misspelled. This command has a number of esoteric options and capabilities. In this section, we will cover only the basic functions. For more details, check the online manual (see Chapter 8) by using the **man spell** command.

The syntax of the **spell** command is:

```
spell [-b] [file...]
```

where *file* is the name of an input file.

Using **spell** is straightforward. For example, say that you have a file named **document**. To display a list of misspelled words, one word per line, use:

```
spell document
```

Each word is listed only once, even if it appears in several places.

To count the number of different misspelled words, pipe the data to the **wc** filter (discussed later in the chapter) using the **-1** (line count) option:

```
spell document | wc -1
```

Aside from specifying an input file, you can pipe data to **spell**. For example, to look for spelling mistakes in the **spell** manual page, enter:

```
man spell | spell
```

By default, **spell** uses American spelling. If you would like **spell** to use British/Canadian spelling, use the **-b** option. For example, the word "colour" will be used instead of "color".

The **spell** command is actually one of a family of programs that uses a master file of sorted words to provide a spell-checking service. This file is **/usr/dict/words**. You can look at all the words by entering:

```
more /usr/dict/words
```

(The **more** program displays one screenful of data at a time [see Chapter 18]. When you use **more**, press the SPACE bar to display the next screenful; press the **q** key to quit.)

Since the master word file is sorted, you can search it with the **look** command. (See the description of **look** for more details.)

Translate or Delete Selected Characters: **tr**

The **tr** (translate) command will read data and replace specified characters with other characters. It will also delete specified characters. For example, you might change all uppercase letters to lowercase. Or you might delete all the left and right parentheses.

The syntax of the **tr** command is:

```
tr [-cds] [set1 [set2]]
```

where *set1* and *set2* are sets of characters.

The idea is that **tr** reads data from the standard input and looks for any characters from *set1*. Whenever **tr** finds such a character, it replaces the character with the corresponding character from *set2*.

For example, say that you have stored information in a file named **olddata**. You want to replace all the **a** characters with **A** and store the translated output in a file named **newdata**. Use the command:

```
tr a A < olddata > newdata
```

By defining longer sets of characters, you can replace more than one different character. The following command looks for and makes three different replacements: **a** is replaced by **A**, **b** is replaced by **B**, and **c** is replaced by **C**:

```
tr abc ABC < olddata > newdata
```

If the second set of characters is shorter than the first, the last character in the second set is duplicated. Thus, the following two commands are equivalent:

```
tr abcde Az < olddata > newdata
trabcde Azzzz < olddata > newdata
```

They both replace **a** with **A**, and the other four characters with **z**.

If you want to specify characters that have a special meaning to the shell, you must place these characters within single quotes. This tells the shell to treat these characters literally. For example, say that you want to change all the colons, semicolons and question marks to periods. Use:

```
tr ':;?' '.' < olddata > newdata
```

When you specify a set of characters, you can define a range by using a hyphen. For example, you can use **a-z** to stand for all the lowercase letters, from "a" to "z". Thus, the following command will change all uppercase letters to lowercase:

```
tr A-Z a-z < olddata > newdata
```

If you want to use a character that cannot be typed easily, you can look it up in the ASCII code and use its three-digit numeric value. (We discussed the ASCII code in the section describing the **sort** command.)

Each character within the ASCII code corresponds to a three-digit number. This number is actually the position within the code, expressed as an octal value (base 8). If this doesn't mean anything to you, just use the number and forget about it. Base 8 is not all that important.

To use such a value, simply type a \ backslash, followed by the three digits. Place the entire expression within single quotes. Here are those values that you are likely to need:

NAME	OCTAL VALUE
backspace	010
tab	011
newline	012

(The **newline** character marks the end of each line. See Chapter 6 for details.) Thus, to translate all the tabs in a file to spaces, use:

```
tr '\011' ' ' < olddata > newdata
```

The **tr** command has three options that let you affect the processing of data. The **-d** option deletes all the characters that you specify. When you use **-d**, you only define one set of characters. For example, to delete all the left and right parentheses, use:

```
tr -d '()' < olddata > newdata
```

The **-s** (squeeze) option changes all repeated characters that match the specified set into a single character from the replacement set. For example, the following command replaces any occurrence of more than one consecutive space by a single space:

```
tr -s ' ' ' ' < olddata > newdata
```

What we are doing is replacing one space by another space, while squeezing out repeated characters.

Finally, the **-c** option tells **tr** to match all the characters that are *not* in the first set. For example, to replace all the characters that are not upper- or lowercase letters with a period, use:

```
tr -c A-Za-z '.' < olddata > newdata
```

The **-c** stands for "complement". In mathematics, the complement of a set is all the elements that are not part of the set. (Notice that you do not put a comma or a space between **A-Z** and **a-z**, as they define one single set of characters.)

Here is an interesting example that combines two options and shows the power of **tr**. You have two files named **document** and **essay**. You want to know how many different words are used in the files.

The best plan is to use a pipeline. First, use **cat** to combine the two files.

Next, use **tr** to place each word on a separate line by replacing each non-alphabetic character with a **newline**. Use the **-c** option to define all characters that are not upper- or lowercase letters, and the **-s** option to squeeze out all such repeated characters. Finally, use numeric code **012** to stand for **newline**. The **tr** command is:

```
tr -cs A-Za-z '\012'
```

Now, after isolating each word on its own line, use the **sort** filter with the **-u** (unique) option to sort the data and eliminate the repeated lines.

Finally, use the **wc** filter with the **-l** (line count) option to count the number of lines. (The **wc** command is explained later in the chapter.)

The completed pipeline looks like this:

```
cat document essay | tr -cs A-Za-z '\012' | sort -u | wc -l
```

Thus, you have a single Unix command line that will tell you how many different words are contained in a collection of input files.

Look for Repeated Lines: uniq

The **uniq** command will examine data, line by line, looking for consecutive, duplicate lines. **uniq** can perform four different tasks: retain only duplicate lines, retain only unique lines, eliminate duplicate lines, or count how many times lines are duplicated.

In making its comparisons, **uniq** can work with parts of each line rather than the entire line. However, in this section we deal with whole line comparisons only. If you want more details, check the online manual (described in Chapter 8) by using the **man uniq** command.

The syntax of the **uniq** command is:

```
uniq [-cdu] [infile [outfile]]
```

where *infile* is the name of and input file, and *outfile* is the name of an output file.

The **-d** option will retain one copy of all lines that are duplicated. Remember, though, the duplicate lines must be consecutive. For example, say that the file **data** contains:

```
Barbara
Al
Al
Charles
Barbara
```

The command:

```
uniq -d data
```

produces:

```
Al
```

The **-u** (unique) option retains only those lines that are not duplicated. For example, the command:

```
uniq -u data
```

produces:

```
Barbara
Charles
Barbara
```

With no options, **uniq** behaves as if both **-d** and **-u** are specified. This effectively eliminates all duplicate lines. Thus, the command:

```
uniq data
```

produces:

```
Barbara
Al
Charles
Barbara
```

Finally, the **-c** option counts how many times each line is found. The command:

```
uniq -c data
```

produces:

```
1 Barbara
2 Al
1 Charles
1 Barbara
```

So far, we have used simple examples. The real power of **uniq** is when you use it with sorted data in a pipeline. When data is sorted, it guarantees that all duplicate lines will be consecutive.

For example, say that you are a professor and you have two files that contain the names of students enrolled in two different courses, **math100** and **math150**. To show which students are taking both courses, use:

```
sort math100 math150 | uniq -d
```

To show which students are taking one course only, use:

```
sort math100 math150 | uniq -u
```

To show all the students, with no duplications, use:

```
sort math100 math150 | uniq
```

(You could also use **sort -u math100 math150**.) Finally, to list each student, showing how many courses he or she is taking, use:

```
sort math100 math150 | uniq -c
```

Counting Lines, Words and Characters: wc

The **wc** (word count) command counts lines, words and characters. The data may come from the standard input or from one or more files. The syntax of the **wc** command is:

```
wc [-lwc] [file...]
```

where *file* is the name of a file.

This command is straightforward. Its output is three numbers: the number of lines, words and characters in the data. If you specify the name of a file, **wc** will write the name after the three numbers. If you specify more than one file, **wc** will also give you total statistics.

Note: **wc** considers a "word" to be an unbroken sequence of characters, delimited by spaces, tabs or **newline** characters. (The **newline** character marks the end of a line; see Chapter 6.)

Here is an example. You have a file named **poem** that contains the following:

```
There was a young man from Nantucket,
Whose girlfriend had told him to
```

The command:

```
wc poem
```

displays the following output:

```
2       13        71 poem
```

In this case, your file has 2 lines, 13 words and 71 characters. If you forget which number is which, just remember that there will usually be more words than lines, and more characters than words.

When **wc** counts characters, it also includes characters that are usually hidden from you, such as the **newline** at the end of each line. (The **newline** character is explained in Chapter 6.)

If you specify more than one file at a time, you will also see total statistics. For example:

```
wc poem message story
```

might write output like this:

```
 2       13        71 poem
 1        4        17 message
31      178      1200 story
34      195      1288 total
```

If you do not want all three numbers, you can use the options: **-l** counts lines, **-w** counts words, and **-c** counts characters. For example, to see how many lines are in the file named **story**, use:

```
wc -l story
```

To see how many words and characters are in the file named **message**, use:

```
wc -wc message
```

There are two important uses for **wc**. First, there are times when you need a quick measure of the size of a file. For example, say that you send a file to someone over a network. The file is important, and you want to double-check that it arrived intact. Run the **wc** command on the original file. Then tell the recipient to run **wc** on the other file. If the two sets of results do not match, you know that some data was lost (or that some spurious data was included).

The second use for **wc** is far more important. You can pipe the output of another command to **wc** and check how many lines were generated. Many commands will generate one item of information per line. By counting the lines, you know how much information was generated. Here are two examples.

The **ls** command (see Chapter 23) lists the names of files in a directory. If you enter:

```
ls /etc
```

you will see the names of all the files in the **/etc** directory. (Directories are explained in Chapter 23.)

The **ls** command has many options. However, there is no option for counting the number of files. To do so, simply pipe the output of **ls** to **wc**. Thus, to count the number of files in the **/etc** directory, enter:

```
ls /etc | wc -l
```

This example demonstrates an important principle. When you learn about **ls**, you will see that it normally displays its output in columns, with more than one name per line. However, when **ls** knows that its output is going to a file or pipeline, it will write only one name per line.

In other words, when **ls** thinks that you might want to process the data further, it will be cooperative and write its data in a form that is easy to process.

HINT

Many Unix commands (especially filters) generate output in which each piece of information is on a separate line. This makes it possible to pipe the data to another program.

Here is one final example. In Chapter 13, we showed how to use the **who** command to find out which userids are logged in to your system. We can use the pipeline:

```
who | wc -l
```

to count the number of userids that are currently logged in.

Command Substitution: `tset`

Command substitution allows you to use the output of one command as part of another command.

In order to show an example, we would first like to remind you about the **echo** command (see Chapter 11). This command simply displays the values of its parameters. For example, if you enter:

echo Hello there

you will see:

Hello there

The **echo** command is usually used within a shell script (a program written in the shell's programming language).

Now, to use command substitution, you place part of a command within ` (backquote) characters. The shell will evaluate the part within backquotes as a command on its own. Then the shell will substitute the output of this command into the larger command.

Here is an example. If you enter:

echo The time is date.

you see:

The time is date.

If you enter:

echo The time is `date`.

you will see something like this:

The time is Fri May 20 16:31:56 PDT 1994.

The shell has executed the **date** command, substituted its output into the **echo** command, and then executed the newly constituted **echo** command.

If you are a Korn shell user, the preceding example will work, but there is a more up-to-date syntax you should use. Instead of enclosing the command in backquotes, you use a dollar sign character (**$**), followed by the command in parentheses. For example, here is the Korn shell equivalent of the last command:

```
print The time is $(date).
```

(Remember, as we explained in Chapter 12, the Korn shell has a **print** command that replaces **echo**. You can use **echo**, but **print** is better.)

In Chapter 23, we will explain how the **pwd** command displays the name of your working directory. Try the following example (the second one is for the Korn shell):

```
echo My working directory is `pwd`.
print My working directory is $(pwd).
```

Be sure not to confuse the backquote with the single quote.

There is one common situation in which you might use command substitution. As we explained in Chapter 11 (C-Shell) and in Chapter 12 (Korn shell), your initialization file contains commands that are to be executed each time you log in. With the C-Shell, you have a **.login** file; with the Korn shell, you have a **.profile** file. One of these commands should set the variable **TERM** to the type of terminal you are using.

Let's say that you are using a VT100 terminal. With the C-Shell, you would use the command:

```
setenv TERM vt100
```

With the Korn shell, you would use:

```
TERM=vt100
```

You can use command substitution to help you set this variable correctly.

With Berkeley Unix, there is a command named **tset** (terminal setup) that can be used to help choose the type of terminal you are using and to initialize the terminal. Using **tset** is complicated and the details are beyond the scope of this book. However, the following is a typical example.

Say that, most of the time, you use a terminal at school or work that is connected directly to the Unix host computer. However, you sometimes use your personal computer at home to emulate a VT100 terminal and connect over the telephone line. (These concepts are explained in Chapter 3.)

The following **tset** command writes the name of the appropriate terminal to the standard output:

```
tset - -m 'dialup:vt100'
```

You can use one of the following commands to set the **TERM** variable to the output of the **tset** command. With the C-Shell, put this command in your **.login** file:

```
setenv TERM `tset - -m 'dialup:vt100'`
```

With the Korn shell, use the following command in your **.profile** file:

```
TERM=$(tset - -m 'dialup:vt100')
```

In this way, **TERM** will be set correctly no matter which terminal you happen to use to log in.

Note: There are other ways to use **tset** that we do not explain here. For more information, see the online Unix manual (use the command **man tset**).

A Real-Life Example of Command Substitution

Here is an example of how using the **rev** filter with command substitution might save your life.

You are an international spy and you need to send a secret message. You want to use **crypt** to encode the message and save it as a file. You can leave the file for your partner to decode and read.

Unfortunately, the system manager for your computer is a spy for a rival country. You know that he can easily access the file with the encoded message. However, unless he knows the key you used with **crypt**, he will not be able to decode the message. So he arranges that one of his flunkies should accidentally walk by your terminal just as you are typing the key.

For good luck, you decide to use a key of "harley". Normally, you would enter the command:

```
crypt > message
```

and let **crypt** prompt you for the key. After you enter **harley**, you would enter your message. Once you press **^D** (the **eof** key), **crypt** would encode the message and save it in a file named **message**.

However, without letting anyone see, you actually enter the command:

```
crypt 'rev' > message
```

At this point, the flunky (who knows you are about to enter the key) watches your fingers as you type. You enter:

```
harley
```

The flunky hurries away to report to the system manager. What he doesn't know is that **rev** has effectively reversed the key to **yelrah**.

Meanwhile, you press **^D** (to end the **rev** command) and enter your message:

```
Secret meeting tonight. Midnight, at abandoned warehouse.
The system manager is a spy.  Take care.
```

Again, you press **^D**, this time to end the message.

You now have an encoded file named **message** which you can leave for your partner. He enters the command:

```
crypt < message
```

and, using the key **yelrah**, decodes your message.

The system manager, on the other hand, sneaks a copy of your file, but works in vain for hours, trying to decode it with a key of **harley**.

Regular Expressions

A REGULAR EXPRESSION is a compact way of specifying a general pattern of characters. There are many places in Unix where you can use a regular expression instead of an exact pattern. For example, you might want to use **grep** to search for all the lines in a file that contain the letter "H", followed by any number of lowercase letters, followed by the letter "y".

You can use regular expressions with many commands, including the text editors (such as **vi**, Chapter 20) and the paging programs (such as **more**, Chapter 18).

Unfortunately, the details of what regular expressions are acceptable may vary slightly from program to program. For example, the **egrep** (extended **grep**) program will recognize more complex regular expressions than will **grep**.

However, regular expressions are an integral part of Unix and you *must* learn how to use them. In this section, we will discuss the regular expressions that you can use with **grep**. The rules you learn in this section are typical of regular expressions in general. Remember these rules, and you will need to learn only a few variations as the need arises.

The name "regular expression" comes from computer science and refers to a set of rules for specifying patterns. Within a regular expression, certain symbols have special meanings. These symbols are summarized in Figure 17-2.

Here are some examples that will show you how this all works. Each of these examples uses the **grep** command to search a file named **data**.

First, within a regular expression, any character that does not have a special meaning stands for itself. For example, to search for lines that contain "Harley", use:

```
grep Harley data
```

(This is nothing new.)

To indicate that you want to match only patterns at the beginning of a line, use ^ (the circumflex). For example, to search for lines that start with "Harley", use:

```
grep '^Harley' data
```

Notice that we placed the pattern within single quotes. Be sure to do this whenever you use special characters. Otherwise, some of them may be interpreted incorrectly by the shell. Using the single quotes tells the shell to leave these characters alone and pass them on to the program (in this case, **grep**).

SYMBOL	MEANING
.	match any single character except newline
*	match zero or more of the preceding characters
^	match the beginning of a line
$	match the end of a line
\<	match the beginning of a word
\>	match the end of a word
[ ]	match one of the enclosed characters
[^]	match any character that is not enclosed
\	take the following symbol literally

FIGURE 17-2. *Summary of symbols used in regular expressions*

The **$** (dollar sign) indicates that you want to match patterns at the end of a line. For example, to search for lines that end with "Harley", use:

```
grep 'Harley$' data
```

You can combine **^** and **$** in the same regular expression as long as what you are doing makes sense. For example, to search for all the lines that contain only "Harley", use:

```
grep '^Harley$' data
```

Another way of thinking about this is that you are telling **grep** to search for all lines that consist entirely of "Harley".

You can also specify that a pattern must occur at the beginning or at the end of a word. You indicate the beginning of a word by using **\<**. For example, to find the pattern "kn", but only if it occurs at the beginning of a word, use:

```
grep '\<kn' data
```

To find the pattern "ow", but only at the end of a word, use:

```
grep 'ow\>' data
```

To search for complete words, use both **\<** and **\>**. For example, to search for "know", but only as a complete word, use:

```
grep '\<know\>' data
```

This would find the line:

```
I know who you are, and I saw what you did.
```

but not the line:

```
Who knows what evil lurks in the minds of men?
```

Using **grep** with **\<** and **\>** gives the same results as the **-w** (word) option. (See the section on **grep**.)

The **.** (period) symbol will match any single character except **newline**. (As we explained in Chapter 6, the **newline** character marks the end of a line.) For example, to search for all lines that contain the letters "Har" followed by any two characters, followed by the letter "y", use:

```
grep 'Har..y' data
```

This command will find lines that contain patterns like:

```
Harley      Harxxy      Harlly
```

To match a character from a set, you can enclose the set in square brackets. For example, to search for all lines that contain the letter "H", followed by either of the letters "a" or "A", use:

```
grep 'H[aA]' data
```

If you want to specify a range of characters, use a hyphen to separate the beginning and end of the range. For example, to search for all the lines that contain the letter "H", followed by any single lowercase letter (from "a" through "z"), use:

```
grep 'H[a-z]' data
```

When you specify a range, the order must be the same as in the ASCII code (discussed earlier in this chapter).

You can use more than one range of characters in the same pattern. For example, to search for all the lines that contain the letter "H", followed by any single lowercase or uppercase letter, use:

```
grep 'H[A-Za-z]' data
```

Remember, a range stands for only one character. Thus, the previous regular expression stands for two characters.

You can use the ***** (asterisk) to match multiple characters. The ***** symbol stands for zero or more occurrences of the preceding character. (We discussed the idea of "zero or more" in Chapter 9.) For example, to search for all the lines that contain the letter "H", followed by zero or more lowercase letters, use:

```
grep 'H[a-z]*' data
```

This command will find patterns like:

```
H     Harley     Halloween     Hint     Hundred
```

Sometimes, you may want to search for one or more occurrences of a character. Simply specify the character, followed by zero or more occurrences of that character. For example, to search for all the lines that contain the letter "H", followed by one or more lowercase characters, use:

```
grep 'H[a-z][a-z]*' data
```

Literally, you are asking for the letter "H", followed by a single lowercase character, followed by zero or more lowercase characters.

It is often convenient to combine the **.** (period) with the ***** (asterisk). For example, to search for all the lines that contain a colon, followed by zero or more occurrences of any other characters, followed by another colon, use:

```
grep ':.*:' data
```

The final rule you need to remember is that if you want to include one of the special symbols as part of a regular expression, precede it by a backslash. This indicates that the following symbol is to be taken literally. For example, to search for all the lines that contain a dollar sign, use:

```
grep '\$' data
```

If you want to search for a backslash character itself, use two of them. For example, to find all the lines that contain the characters *****, followed by any characters, followed by **$**, use:

```
grep '\\\*.*\$' data
```

We can break this down as follows:

****	a single backslash
*	a single asterisk
.*	any number of other characters
\$	a single dollar sign

Next, here are two examples that search the file **/usr/dict/words**. This file contains the master word list used by the **spell** program (discussed earlier in the chapter).

The first example finds all words that begin with "qu" and end with "y":

```
grep '^qu[a-z]*y$' /usr/dict/words
```

The second example solves an old riddle: Can you name an English word that contains the letters "a, e, i, o, u", in that order? The letters do not have to be adjacent, but they must be in order.

To solve this problem, we must search for the letter "a", followed by zero or more other letters, followed by "e", followed by zero or more other letters, and so on. The full command is:

```
grep 'a[a-z]*e[a-z]*i[a-z]*o[a-z]*u' /usr/dict/words
```

To end the suspense, we will tell you that this command found three such words:

```
adventitious
facetious
sacrilegious
```

Finally, here is a command to search the Unix system itself for historical artifacts. In the olden days, many Unix commands were two letters long. The text editor was **ed**, the copy program was **cp**, and so on. Let us find all such commands.

The older Unix programs are contained in the **/bin** directory. To list all the files in this directory, we can use the command:

```
ls /bin
```

(The **ls** command is discussed in Chapter 23.)

To analyze the output of **ls**, we can pipe it to the **grep** filter. **ls** will automatically place each name on a separate line because the output is going to a filter. With **grep**, we can search for lines that consist of only two lowercase letters. The full pipeline is:

```
ls /bin | grep '^[a-z][a-z]$'
```

This will display all the basic Unix commands whose names consist of only two characters. If you want to see how many such commands there are, use **grep** with the **-c** (count) option:

```
ls /bin | grep -c '^[a-z][a-z]$'
```

What's in a Name?   `grep`

The name **grep** is a strange one. It is actually an acronym for the expression "global regular expression print".

- ■ "global" reminds us that **grep** searches all of the input data
- ■ "print" is traditionally used in Unix to mean "display"

Thus, the name tells us that this command will search all of its input for a regular expression, and then display the results.

Within the old **ed** text editor, the command to perform such a search was **g/**, followed by the regular expression, followed by **/p**. In other words, the **ed** command was:

> **g/**re**/p**

where re stands for a regular expression. It is this serendipitous abbreviation that first suggested the name **grep**.

It is the custom among Unix people to use the word "grep" as a verb. Thus, you might say to someone, "If you want to find all the words that end with a particular pattern, you can grep the **/usr/dict/words** file."

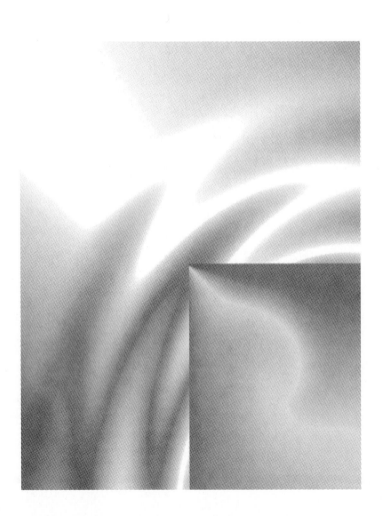

CHAPTER 18

Displaying Files

With all the time we spend using the computer, it is interesting to remind ourselves that the main product of all our effort is some type of output, either displayed on our screen or printed on paper. Unix has a number of important commands you can use to control the displaying and printing of data.

In this chapter, we will discuss the commands that provide the service of displaying data in a manageable fashion. We will start by showing you how to display the beginning or end of a file. Next, we discuss the commands that let you page though an entire file, one screenful at a time.

In Chapter 19, we will complement what we cover in this chapter by showing you how to print files.

Note: When we refer to "files", we assume the intuitive idea that a file has a name and contains information. For example, you might have a file named **memo** that contains the text of a memorandum. In Chapter 22, we will discuss the Unix file system in detail, at which time we will give the strict definition of a file.

Displaying the Beginning of a File: head

To display the beginning of a file, use the **head** command. The syntax is:

head [-*count*] [*file...*]

where *count* is the number of lines you want to display, and *file* is the name of a file. By default, **head** will display the first 10 lines of a file. This is useful when you want to get a quick look at a file to check its contents. For example, to display the first 10 lines of a file named **memo**, use:

head memo

If you want to display a different number of lines, specify that number as an option. For example, to display the first 20 lines of the same file, use:

head -20 memo

The **head** command is useful at the end of a pipeline. Here is an example that combines three operations. The **cat** command combines the two specified files. The **grep** command extracts all the lines that contain the specified pattern. The **sort** command sorts the result.

cat newnames oldnames | grep Harley | sort

If you enter this command line, you will see the entire output of the **sort** command. If you only want to see the first five lines, pipe the output to the **head** command:

cat newnames oldnames | grep Harley | sort | head -5

(Pipelines are discussed in Chapter 16. The **cat**, **grep** and **sort** commands are discussed in Chapter 17.)

Displaying the End of a File: tail

To display the end of a file, use the **tail** command. There are two forms of this command:

tail [+*start***fr**] [*file*]
tail [-*start***fr**] [*file*]

where *start* is the line number at which you want to start, and *file* is the name of a file. By default, **tail** will display the last 10 lines of a file. For example, to display the last 10 lines of a file named **memo**, use:

tail memo

To start displaying at a particular line, you can use either **+** or **-**, followed by a number. If you use **+**, **tail** counts from the beginning of the file. If you use **-**, **tail** counts from the end of the file. For example, to display the last 20 lines of the file, use:

tail -20 memo

To display from line **35** to the end of the file, use:

tail +35 memo.

(As you can see, **tail** is one of the few Unix commands that has an option that does not start with a **-** character.)

Like the **head** command, **tail** is useful at the end of a pipeline. For example:

cat newnames oldnames | grep Harley | sort | tail -5

This **tail** command displays the last 5 lines of output from **sort**.

The **-r** option displays the output in reverse order. By default, **-r** displays all the lines in the file, not just 10 lines. For example, to display the entire file named **memo** in reverse order, use:

tail -r memo

To display the last 10 lines of the file, in reverse order, use:

tail -10r memo

To display from line 35 to the end of the file, in reverse order, use:

tail +35r memo

HINT
To reverse the order of all the lines in a file, use **tail -r**.

The final option, **-f**, is useful when you are waiting for data to be written to a file. This option tells **tail** not to quit when it reaches the end of the file. Rather, **tail** will wait and display more output as the file grows.

For example, say that over the next few minutes, a particular program will be adding output to the end of a file named **results**. You want to follow the progress of this program. Enter:

```
tail -f results
```

tail will start by displaying the last 10 lines of the file. As new lines are added, **tail** will display them as well. When you get tired of watching, you stop the command by pressing **^C** (the **intr** key; see Chapter 6). The command will not stop by itself.

The Paging Programs

In the next few sections, we will discuss three programs you can use to display a file. They are named **more**, **pg** and **less**.

The distinguishing feature of these programs is that they display an entire file, one screenful at a time. These programs are sometimes called PAGING PROGRAMS, or PAGERS, because you can page through a file at your own speed. As you read, there are a multitude of commands to use. For example, you can enter a command to search for a particular pattern.

What's in a Name?   **pg, more, less**

The three paging programs have strange names. Here is how they originated:

pg   An abbreviation for "pager".

more   After displaying a screenful of data, this program displays the prompt **--More--** to show there is more to come. The program is named after this prompt.

less   This program was developed as a replacement for **more** and **pg**. The name **less** was chosen as a sardonic comment that insiders with a sense of irony would understand. Although the name is **less**, the program actually offers a lot more than **more**.

All three of the paging programs have a variety of options and many internal commands you can use as you are displaying a file. It may take a while to learn all the nuances.

Generally speaking, you only need to learn the details of one paging program for your personal use. However, you do need at least a passing acquaintance with all three programs, as you will be called upon to use them at various times.

This is especially true when you use the Internet. There will be times when you will connect to a remote computer and display information. When you do so, you will have to be able use whichever paging program was chosen by the person who set up that particular system. You will find that the three pagers — **more**, **pg** and **less**—are used all over the world and you never know which one you will encounter. Thus, you need to understand the basic operation of all three.

The basics, however, are not much. You just need to understand how to move from one screenful to the next, how to search for a pattern, and how to stop the program. Ten minutes of practice should do it.

HINT

Pick one of the paging programs — **more**, **pg** or **less** — and learn it well.

The **less** program has an important advantage in that it allows you to move backward and forward through a file easily. With the other programs, it is more awkward to move backward.

If you are not sure which pager to choose, use **more** because it is the easiest, most commonly-used paging program.

Whichever pager you choose, you should learn the basics of all three.

Should You Use `cat` to Display Files?

Aside from the paging programs, the **cat** command will also display a file. Why? The job of **cat** is to combine files and write the result to standard output. By default, the standard output is the screen of your terminal. Thus, a command like:

```
cat memo
```

will write the contents of **memo** to your screen. (Standard output is explained in Chapter 16. **cat** is explained in Chapter 17.)

The problem is that, much of the time, the files you display will be longer than the size of your screen. With **cat**, all the output is written without interruption. Unless the file is a short one, most of the output will scroll by so fast that you won't be able to read it.

The best idea is to pick one pager — either **more**, **pg** or **less**—as your favorite. Get in the habit of using that program when you need to display a file. Even when the file is short enough to fit completely on the screen, there is no real advantage to using **cat**.

HINT
Using the **cat** program to display files is a bad habit. Instead, pick either **more**, **pg** or **less** to use exclusively. For example, instead of using:

```
cat memo
```

you should use one of the following:

```
more memo
pg memo
less memo
```

Displaying a File Using more

The **more** program is a pager you can use to display data one screenful at a time. The syntax is:

```
more [-cs] [+startline] [+/pattern] [file...]
```

where

startline:	number of the line at which you want to start
pattern:	an initial pattern to search for
file:	the name of a file

In this section, we will describe the basic options and features of the **more** program. For more information, look at the manual page by using **man more**. (The online Unix manual is described in Chapter 8.)

The **more** program displays the contents of the files you specify. The data is displayed one screenful at a time. After each screen is written, you will see a prompt at the bottom left corner of the screen. The prompt looks like this:

```
--More--(40%)
```

(You can see where the name **more** comes from.)

At the end of the prompt is a number in parentheses. This shows you how much of the data has been displayed. In our example, the prompt shows that you are 40 percent of the way through the file.

The simplest way to use **more** is to specify a single file name. For example:

```
more memo
```

If the data fits on a single screen, it will be displayed all at once. Otherwise, the data will be displayed, one screenful at a time, with the prompt at the bottom.

Once you see the prompt, you can enter a command. The most common command is simply to press the SPACE bar. This will page to the next screen. You can press SPACE repeatedly to page through the entire file. After displaying the last screenful of data, **more** will stop automatically.

One of the most common uses of **more** is to display the output of a pipeline, one screenful at a time. Here are two examples:

```
cat newnames oldnames | grep Harley | sort | more
ls -l | more
```

(Pipelines are explained in Chapter 16. Filters, the programs that are used within a pipeline, are explained in Chapter 17.)

When you use **more** in a pipeline, the prompt will not show the percentage:

```
--More--
```

This is because **more** displays the data as it arrives and has no idea how much there will be.

When **more** pauses, there are many commands you can use. For most commands, you do not have to press RETURN; just type the name. The most important command is **h** (help). This will display a summary of all the possible commands.

Figure 18-1 contains a summary of the most useful **more** commands. The best way to learn about **more** is to type the **h** command, see what is available, and experiment.

When you use the **/** command to search for a pattern, you can use the same type of regular expression we described at the end of Chapter 17. When **more** finds the pattern you want, it will display two lines before that location so you can see the line in context.

There are a number of options you can use when you start **more**. The two most useful are **-s** and **-c**. The **-s** (squeeze) option replaces multiple blank lines with a single blank line. This is useful for condensing output in which multiple blank lines are not meaningful. Of course, this does not affect the original file.

BASIC COMMANDS

h	display help information
SPACE	display the next screenful
q	quit the program

MORE ADVANCED COMMANDS

RETURN	go forward one line
n RETURN	go forward *n* lines
d	go forward (down) a half screenful
*n***f**	go forward *n* screenfuls
b	go backward one screenful
*n***b**	go backward *n* screenfuls
v	start the **vi** editor using file you are displaying
/pattern	search forward for the specified pattern
n	repeat the previous search command
! *command*	execute the specified shell command
=	display the current line number
.	repeat the previous command

Do not press RETURN after any command except with **/** and **!**.

FIGURE 18-1. *Summary of the most useful **more** commands*

The **-c** (clear) option tells **more** to display each new screenful of data from the top down. Each line is cleared before it is replaced. Without **-c**, new lines scroll up from the bottom line of the screen. Some people find that long files are easier to read with **-c**. You will have to try it for yourself.

Two other options allow you to control the line at which **more** starts to display data. You can use a **+** (plus sign) followed by a number to tell **more** to start at that line number. For example, to display the contents of the file **memo** starting at line 37, use:

```
more +37 memo
```

Second, you can use **+/** (plus, slash) followed by a pattern, and **more** will search for that pattern before it starts displaying data. For example, to display the same file, starting with a search for the word **Harley**, use:

```
more +/Harley memo
```

Note: You cannot use both the **+** and **+/** options at the same time.

HINT

If you are used to using **pg**, there are two basic differences. With **more**:

■ You press SPACE, not RETURN, to display the next screenful of data.

■ You do not press RETURN after each command.

Displaying a File Using **pg**

The **pg** program is a pager you can use to display data one screenful at a time. The syntax is:

pg [**-cn**] [**+**startline] [**+/**pattern] [file...]

where:

startline:	number of the line at which you want to start
pattern:	an initial pattern to search for
file:	is the name of a file

In this section, we will describe the basic options and features of the **pg** program. For more information, look at the manual page by using **man pg**. (The online Unix manual is described in Chapter 8.)

The **pg** program displays the contents of the files you specify. The data is displayed one screenful at a time. After each screen is written, you will see a prompt at the bottom left corner of the screen. The prompt will be a colon:

```
:
```

The simplest way to use **pg** is to specify a single file name. For example:

```
pg memo
```

The data will be displayed one screenful at a time, with the prompt at the bottom.

Once you see the prompt, you can enter a command. The most common command is simply to press RETURN. This will page to the next screen. You can press RETURN repeatedly to page through the entire file.

After displaying the last screenful of data, **pg** will not stop automatically. You will see the following prompt (which stands for "End of File"):

```
(EOF):
```

To quit, press RETURN.

One of the most common uses of **pg** is to display the output of a pipeline, one screenful at a time. Here are two examples:

```
cat newnames oldnames | grep Harley | sort | pg
ls -l | pg
```

(Pipelines are explained in Chapter 16. Filters, the programs that are used within a pipeline, are explained in Chapter 17.)

When **pg** pauses, there are many commands you can use. After each command, you must press RETURN (unless you use the **-n** option which we will discuss below). The most important command is **h** (help). This will display a summary of all the possible commands.

Figure 18-2 contains a summary of the most useful **pg** commands. The best way to learn about **pg** is to enter the **h** command, see what is available, and experiment.

When you use the **/** or **?** commands to search for a pattern, you can use the same type of regular expressions we described at the end of Chapter 17.

There are a number of options you can use when you start **pg**. The two most useful are **-n** and **-c**. The **-n** (newline) option tells **pg** to execute the single letter commands without your having to press RETURN (just like the **more** program).

The **-c** (clear) option tells **more** to display each new screenful of data from the top down. Before new data is written, the entire screen is cleared. Without **-c**, new lines scroll up from the bottom line of the screen. Some people find that long files are easier to read with **-c**. You will have to try it for yourself. If your system has a very fast connection, you may not notice much difference.

HINT

When you use the **-c** option, **pg** clears the entire screen at once before displaying new data. When you use **-c** with **more**, it clears one line at a time. Compare the two programs and see which one you like better.

BASIC COMMANDS

h	display help information
RETURN	display the next screenful
q	quit the program

MORE ADVANCED COMMANDS

*n***l**	go to line *n*
l	go to the next line
+*n***l**	go forward *n* lines
*n***l**	go backward *n* lines
d	go forward (down) a half screenful
-d	go backward (up) a half screenful
l	go to the first line of the data
$	go to the last line of the data
/*pattern*	search forward for the specified pattern
?*pattern*	search backward for the specified pattern
! *command*	execute the specified shell command

You must press RETURN to enter a command unless you start **pg** with the
-n option.

FIGURE 18-2.   *Summary of the most useful* **pg** *commands*

Two other options allow you to control the line at which **pg** starts to display
data. You can use a **+** (plus sign) followed by a number to tell **pg** to start at that line
number. For example, to display the contents of the file **memo** starting at line 37,
use:

```
pg +37 memo
```

Second, you can use **+/** (plus, slash) followed by a pattern, and **pg** will search for
that pattern before it starts displaying data. For example, to display the same file,
starting with a search for the word **Harley**, use:

```
pg +/Harley memo
```

Note: You cannot use both the **+** and **+/** options at the same time.

HINT

If you are used to using **more**, there are two basic differences.
With **pg**:

■ You press RETURN, not SPACE, to display the next screenful of data.

■ You must press RETURN after each command.

Displaying a File Using less

The **less** program is a pager you can use to display data one screenful at a time.
The syntax is:

less [**-cmsCM**] [**-x**tab] [+command] [file...]

where:

> command: is a command to be executed automatically
>   file: is the name of a file
>   tab: is the tab spacing you want to use

Like **more** and **pg**, **less** is a paging program. It is designed as a replacement
for both of these programs. However, it is not a standard part of Unix and may not
be on your system.

For basic work, **less** acts much like the other two programs. However, for
advanced users, **less** is a lot more sophisticated. It has many commands and
allows a great deal of customization. One of the major advantages of **less** is that
it is easy to move backward and forward through a file.

The commands in **less** are based on those found in **more** and in the **vi** editor
(Chapter 20). They make it particularly easy to move around in the file. If you are a
serious Unix user, it is worth your while to master **less**.

In this section, we will describe the basic options and features of the **less**
program. For more information, look at the manual page by using **man less**. (The
online Unix manual is described in Chapter 8.)

The **less** program displays the contents of the files you specify. The data is
displayed one screenful at a time. After each screen is written, you will see a
prompt at the bottom left corner of the screen. The first prompt will show you the
name of your file. Each subsequent prompt will be a colon:

:

If you use the **-m** option, **less** will display a prompt that is similar to that of the **more** command by showing you how far you are through the file. For example:

40%

In this example, the prompt shows that you are 40 percent of the way through the file.

HINT

For ambitious fanatics with a lot of time, **less** offers more flexibility for customizing your prompt than any paging program in the history of the world.

The simplest way to use **less** is to specify a single file name. For example:

```
less memo
```

The data will be displayed, one screenful at a time, with the prompt at the bottom.

Once you see the prompt, you can enter a command. The most common command is simply to press the SPACE bar. This will page to the next screen. You can press SPACE repeatedly to page through the entire file.

After displaying the last screenful of data, **less** will not stop automatically. You will see the following prompt:

```
(END)
```

To quit, press **q**.

One of the most common uses of **less** is to display the output of a pipeline, one screenful at a time. Here are two examples:

```
cat newnames oldnames | grep Harley | sort | less
ls -l | less
```

(Pipelines are explained in Chapter 16. Filters, the programs that are used within a pipeline, are explained in Chapter 17.)

When **less** pauses, there are many commands you can use. For most commands, you do not have to press RETURN; just type the name. The most important command is **h** (help). This will display a summary of all the possible commands.

Figure 18-3 contains a summary of the most useful **less** commands. The best way to learn about **less** is to type the **h** command, see what is available, and experiment. There are many **less** commands. In particular, **less** uses many of the same screen control commands as the **vi** editor (Chapter 20).

Some of the commands have more than one name. In Figure 18-3, we show the simplest name. For more information, use the **h** (help) command. If you don't like the command names, you can make your own by using the **lesskey** command. (Enter **man lesskey** for the details.)

BASIC COMMANDS

h	display help information
SPACE	go forward one screenful
q	quit the program

MORE ADVANCED COMMANDS

RETURN	go forward one line
n RETURN	go forward *n* lines
b	go backward one screenful
y	go backward one line
*n***y**	go backward *n* lines
d	go forward (down) a half screenful
u	go backward (up) a half screenful
g	go to the first line
*n***g**	go to line *n*
G	go to the last line
*n***p**	go to the line that is *n* percent through the file
v	start the **vi** editor using file you are displaying
/*pattern*	search forward for the specified *pattern*
?*pattern*	search backward for the specified *pattern*
n	repeat the previous search command
!*command*	execute the specified shell *command*
=	display the current line number and name of file
-*option*	change specified *option*
_*option*	display the current value of *option*

Do not press RETURN after any command except **/**, **?** and **!**.

FIGURE 18-3. *Summary of the most useful **less** commands*

When you use the **/** command to search for a pattern, you can use the same type of regular expressions we described at the end of Chapter 17.

There are a large number of options you can use when you start **less**. The two most useful are **-s** and **-c**. The **-s** (squeeze) option replaces multiple blank lines with a single blank line. This is useful for condensing output in which multiple blank lines are not meaningful. Of course, this does not affect the original file.

The **-c** (clear) option tells **less** to display each new screenful of data from the top down. Without **-c**, new lines scroll up from the bottom line of the screen. Some people find that long files are easier to read with **-c**. The **-C** (uppercase "C") option is like **-c** except that the entire screen is cleared before new data is written. You will have to try these options for yourself and see what you prefer.

The **-m** option, which we mentioned earlier, makes the prompt look like the **more** prompt by showing the percentage of the file that has been displayed. The **-M** (uppercase "M") option makes the prompt show even more information: the name of the file, the line number, and the percentage that has been displayed. For example, say that you start **less** to view a file named **memo** by using:

```
less -M memo
```

A typical prompt would look like this:

```
memo line 48/75 93%
```

Note: The line number refers to the top line on the screen while the percentage includes all the lines on the screen. In our example, line 48 (of 75) is at the top of the screen. However, once you have read all the lines on the screen, you are 93 percent of the way through the file.

The **+** (plus sign) option allows you to control the line at which **less** starts to display data. Whatever appears after the **+** will be executed as an initial command. For example, to display the file **memo**, with the initial position at the end of the file, use:

```
less +G memo
```

To display the same file, starting with a search for the word **Harley**, use:

```
less +/Harley memo
```

As a special case, a number after the **+** tells **less** to start at that line. For example, to start at line 37, use:

```
less +37 memo
```

This is really an abbreviation for:

```
less +37g memo
```

Finally, the **-x** option followed by a number tells **less** to set the tabs at the specified regular interval. This controls the spacing for data that contains tab characters. For example, to set the tabs to every 5 spaces, use:

```
less -x5 memo
```

The default value is to set the tabs to every 8 spaces. (This is the case for most Unix programs.)

If you want to change an option while you are viewing a file, use the – (hyphen) command at the prompt. Type – followed by the new option. For example, to change the prompt to the **-M** version, type:

```
-M
```

To display the current value of an option, use an _ (underscore) followed by the option. For example, to check how the prompt is set, use:

```
_m
```

HINT

To learn **less**, use the – (change option) and _ (display option) commands to experiment with the various options. This is especially useful if you want to use the **-P** option (which we did not discuss) to change the prompt.

Using Environment Variables to Customize Your Paging Program

As we explained in Chapter 16, the Unix philosophy is that each program should do only one thing and should do it well. The paging programs are examples of this philosophy: they are designed specifically to display data.

The paging programs are available to any other program that wants to display data. For example, the **man** command will automatically call upon a paging program to display data from the online Unix manual. Other programs, such as your mail program, will also use a paging program when necessary.

Once you decide what paging program you like best, you can make sure that other programs use it by setting the **PAGER** global variable to the name of the pager you want to use. When other programs need to display data, they will look at this variable and use the paging program you specify.

With the C-Shell, global variables are called "environment variables"; with the Korn shell, they are called "shell variables". We discuss these variables and how to use them in Chapter 11 (C-Shell) and Chapter 12 (Korn shell).

For the C-Shell, you use the **setenv** command to set an environment variable. Normally, you place such a command in your **.login** initialization file, so the command will be executed each time you log in.

For the Korn shell, you set the variable to the value you want by using an **=** character and then export the variable by using the **export** command (see the examples below). Such commands normally go in your **.profile** initialization file.

Once you place the commands to set **PAGER** in your initialization file (either **.login** or **.profile**), the value of this variable will be set automatically each time you log in and will be available to every program that you use.

The following C-Shell command specifies that you want to use the **more** program for your pager:

```
setenv PAGER more
```

Similarly, you might choose to use one of the other paging programs:

```
setenv PAGER pg
setenv PAGER less
```

Here are the equivalent commands for the Korn shell:

```
PAGER=more; export PAGER
PAGER=pg; export PAGER
PAGER=less; export PAGER
```

Note: Be sure not to put a space on either side of the **=** character.

The **more** and **less** programs offer an added degree of customization. You can define an environment variable named **MORE** (or **LESS**) that contains the options you want to use each time you start the program. For example, say that you always use **more** with the **-c** and **-s** options. With the C-Shell, you can define:

```
setenv MORE '-cs'
```

With the Korn shell, use:

```
MORE='-cs'; export MORE
```

From now on, whenever you start **more**, it will automatically use these options without your having to specify them. If you always use **less** with the **-s**, **-C** and **-M** options, you can use one of the following commands to set the **LESS** variable:

```
setenv LESS '-sCM'
LESS='-sCM'; export LESS
```

Unfortunately, the **pg** program does not support this type of customization.

CHAPTER 19

Printing Files

In Chapter 18, we explained how to display data at your terminal. In this chapter, we finish the discussion of processing output by showing you how to print data.

We start by explaining how Unix offers the service of printing and what happens when you start a print job. From there, we will move on to the commands. First, we will explain how to format a file before you print it. Next, you will see how to print a file, how to check which files are waiting to be printed, and how to cancel a print job. Finally, we will show you how to print pages from the online Unix manual, which we discussed in Chapter 8, and how to print large signs.

Orientation to Printing

When we refer to "files", we are using the intuitive idea that a file has a name and contains information. For example, you might have a file named **memo** that contains the text of a memorandum. In Chapter 22, we will discuss the Unix file system in detail, at which time we will give the strict definition for a file.

In principle, printing a file is similar to displaying a file. They both involve copying data to an output device. However, there are some important differences. Printing has its own special considerations, its own commands, and its own terminology.

Perhaps the biggest difference between printing and displaying is that printing is slow. If every file you printed was finished within a few seconds, you wouldn't mind waiting for it. Of course, this is rarely the case. Even with modern printers, it can take awhile for your output to be ready. Moreover, you may not have a printer of your own. Your file may have to wait its turn if someone else is using the community printer.

The Unix system was designed to assume that all printing requests may have to wait. When you enter the command to print a file, Unix generates a PRINT JOB. Most systems will display an identification number called the JOB NUMBER that you can use to keep track of the job.

To print a file and to control the print job, you use certain commands. Unfortunately, Berkeley Unix has different commands from System V Unix. (See Chapter 2 for a discussion of the different types of Unix.) In this chapter, we will explain both the Berkeley and System V commands. Many Unixes, including the modern version of System V, contain both sets of commands, so you may be able to use whichever ones you want. If you want more information than we provide in this chapter, you can use the **man** command to look up a specific command in the online Unix manual (see Chapter 8).

For reference, Figure 19-1 compares the commands for each system. For the most part, they perform the same functions, although they do have different options.

BERKELEY UNIX	SYSTEM V	DESCRIPTION
lpr	lp	send a file to be printed
lpq	lpstat	show what print jobs are waiting
lprm	cancel	cancel a print job

FIGURE 19-1.   *Printing commands: Berkeley Unix and System V*

What's In A Name? 1p

You will notice that all but one of the print commands start with the letters **1p**. What does this mean?

As we described in Chapter 6, the earliest Unix terminals printed output on paper. For this reason, it became traditional to refer to the output of a terminal as being "printed". For example, the command to display the name of your working directory (Chapter 23) is **pwd**: print working directory.

To refer to the actual printer, Unix uses the term "line printer". (This describes the type of printer that was used by the first developers of Unix.) Thus, whenever you see a command or system name that begins with **1p**, it refers to real printing.

What Happens When You Print a File: Spooling

At all times, Unix maintains a list of all the print jobs that are waiting to be processed. This list is called the PRINT QUEUE. When you use the **1pr** or **1p** command to print a file, Unix makes a temporary copy of the file and saves it in a special directory. It then adds your job to the print queue and displays the job number.

As soon as the printer becomes available, Unix starts printing the next job in the queue. At any time, you can use the **1pq** or **1pstat** command to check what is in the print queue, and the **1prm** or **cancel** command to remove a job from the queue.

When your print job finishes, Unix removes the temporary file and goes on to the next job. By using the **-m** option with **1pr** or **1p**, you can have Unix mail you a message to tell you when a print job is completed.

The most important idea about this entire process is that Unix does not print a file the moment you enter the **1pr** or **1p** command. Rather, Unix keeps track of the file and prints it at an appropriate time (for example, when the printer is available). This arrangement is called SPOOLING. The word "spool" is a flexible one. It can be used:

- as an adjective: "The temporary file is called a SPOOL FILE."

- as a noun: "The program that handles all the details is called the PRINT SPOOLER or, sometimes, just the SPOOLER."

- even as a verb: "The system SPOOLED my job six hours ago and it still hasn't printed."

HINT
"Spool" is a cool word.

What's in a Name? *Spool*

The term "spool" dates from the olden days of mainframes (the early 1960s). In those days, the main processor was expensive and, by our standards, slow. When output needed to be sent to a peripheral device, such as a printer, the processing time involved in sending the data was considerable.

On the larger computers, a system was used where the output was kept in a temporary storage area. Another processor, perhaps a smaller, cheaper computer, would take over the job of sending the output to the peripheral device. This freed the main processor for more important tasks, thus making the whole system more efficient.

This type of organization was called spooling, which stood for "simultaneous peripheral operations offline". (In case you haven't guessed, this term was invented at IBM.)

Daemons and Dragons

The print spooler is an example of a DAEMON, a program that executes in the background and provides a service of general interest. Unix has a number of such programs. Some daemons are started automatically when the system is initialized and are always available. Other daemons sleep most of the time, waking up at predefined intervals or in response to some event.

Daemons perform all kinds of functions to keep the system running smoothly: managing memory, overseeing print jobs, sending and receiving mail, executing commands at specific times, responding to remote finger requests (see Chapter 13), and so on.

The print spooling daemon is called **lpd** (line printer daemon). The finger daemon is called **fingerd**. The most common mail daemon is **sendmail**. The most well-known daemon is **cron**, whose purpose is to execute jobs at predefined times.

What's in a Name?   Daemons, Dragons

Although the name is pronounced "dee-mon", it is correctly spelled "daemon". Nobody knows if the name used to be an acronym or why we use a British variation of the spelling. (In Celtic mythology, a daemon is usually good or neutral, merely a spirit or inspiration. A demon, however, is always an evil entity.)

You may occasionally read that the name stands for "Disk and Executing Monitor", a term from the old DEC 10 and 20 computers. However, this explanation was made up after the fact.

The name "daemon" was first used by MIT programmers who worked on CTSS (the Compatible Time-sharing System), developed in 1963. They coined the name to refer to what were called DRAGONS by other programmers who worked on ITS (the Incompatible Time-sharing System).

CTSS and ITS were both ancestors to Unix. ITS was an important, though strange, operating system that developed a cult following at MIT. To this day, ITS is still revered among aging East Coast hackers.

Strictly speaking, a dragon is a daemon that is not invoked explicitly but is always there, waiting in the background to perform some task. The **cron** daemon, for example, might be called a dragon. Although many Unix users have heard of daemons, very few people know about dragons. (But now you do.)

Formatting a File for Printing: `pr, nl`

Before we get down to the business of printing a file, let's take a moment and discuss two filters that are used to format data before you print it: **pr** and **nl**.

(Filters are discussed in Chapter 17. Basically, they are programs that read from the standard input and write to the standard output. As such, filters can be combined with other programs into a pipeline in which each program reads data, does something to it, and passes it on the next program. Pipelines are discussed in Chapter 16.)

The **pr** command reads from the standard input or from a text file and produces output which is paginated and labeled. **pr** can also arrange text into columns. The intention is that you will use **pr** to prepare data before you print it. The **pr** command does not change the original file. Like all filters, **pr** writes to the standard output. Thus, if you do not redirect the output, it will be displayed on your terminal. The syntax for the **pr** command is:

pr [**-h** *title*] [**-l***pagelength*] [*file...*]

where:

> *title*: is what you want to print in the header
> *pagelength*: is the number of lines per page
> *file*: is the name of a file

Unless you specify otherwise, **pr** will format and paginate according to certain defaults. It assumes that the length of a page is 66 lines (the number of lines that normally print on an 11-inch piece of paper). Of these lines, the first 5 are used as a header, the last 5 are used as a trailer. Thus, **pr** will use 56 lines per page for your output.

The header consists of 2 blank lines, 1 line of text, and another 2 blank lines. The line of text will show the date, the name of the file, and the page number. The trailer is just 5 blank lines.

Normally, you pipe the output of **pr** to the **lpr** or **lp** program (discussed later in the chapter) which will print the file. For example, to format and print a file named **memo**, you can use:

pr memo | lpr

A common way to use **pr** is to send its output from a pipeline. For example, the following command uses **cat** (Chapter 17) to combine three files, and then formats and prints the result.

cat names extra.names old.names | pr | lpr

The next command formats and prints a long directory listing of the **/bin** and **/usr/bin** directories:

ls -l /bin /usr/bin | pr | lpr

(We discuss pipelines in Chapter 16, and directories and the **ls** command in Chapter 23.)

There are several options you can use to change the default formatting values. We will explain only the most important ones. For more information, including a description of how to format text into columns, look at the manual page for **pr** by using the command **man pr**. (The online Unix manual is discussed in Chapter 8.)

The **-l** (length) option changes the number of lines on a page. Use **-l** followed by the number, but do not put a space after the **-l**. For example, to format and print the **memo** file using 50 lines per page, use:

```
pr -150 memo | lpr
```

The length you specify includes both the header and the trailer.

> ### HINT
> You normally print the output of **pr** by piping it to the **lpr** or **lp** program. If you are testing various options, first send the output to a paging program (such as **more**; see Chapter 18), so you can preview it at your terminal. For example:
>
> ```
> pr -150 memo | more
> ```
>
> Once you are happy with what you see, you can send the same output to **lpr** or **lp**:
>
> ```
> pr -150 memo | lpr
> ```

The **-h** (header) option allows you to specify a title for the header instead of the name of the file. Use **-h** followed by whatever you want to print. If you want to use more than a single word or if you want to use special characters, enclose your specification in single quotes.

For example, to print "Important Memo" within the header of each page, use:

```
pr -h 'Important Memo' memo | lpr
```

Note: The **-h** option replaces only the file name. You will still get the date and the page number.

> ### HINT
> When you format data from a pipeline, there will be no file name for the header. In such cases, it is a good idea to use **-h** to specify a title for the printout. For example:
>
> ```
> ls -l /bin /usr/bin | pr -h 'Directory List' | lpr
> ```

The second filter you can use to format data before printing is **nl**, a program to create line numbers. The input can be from the standard input or from a file. (Note: Not all Unix systems have this program.)

There are many options that give you exquisite control over how the line numbers are generated and formatted. However, most of the time you will ignore the options and use the defaults, so we will not discuss the details. If you want more information, see the manual page for **nl**. (Use the command **man nl.**) Ignoring the options, the syntax for **nl** is simple:

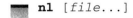

nl [*file...*]

Here are several examples. Say that you want to number each non-blank line of the file **memo**, starting from line number 1 (these are the defaults). You want to format and then print the output. Use:

nl memo | pr | lpr

The next example combines three files, numbers each non-blank line, formats the output and then prints the result:

cat names extra.names old.names | nl | pr | lpr

A second use for **nl** is to create a file with actual line numbers. For example, say that you have a file named **raw.data** that you want to have line numbers. You want the numbered text to be stored in a file named **master.data**. Use:

nl raw.data > master.data

(We explain how to use **>** to redirect output to a file in Chapter 16.)

■ Printing a File: lpr (Berkeley Unix)

With Berkeley Unix, you print a file by using the **lpr** (line printer) command. The syntax is:

lpr [**-mprh**] [**-#***num*] [**-J** *name*] [**-P** *printer*] [**-T** *title*] [*file...*]

where:

num:	is the number of copies you want
name:	is the name of the job
printer:	is the name of a printer
title:	is the title that you want to print in the header
file:	is the name of a file

The **lpr** command has many options. In this section, we will discuss only the most important ones. If you want to find out more about **lpr**, look at the manual page by using the command **man lpr**. (The online Unix manual is covered in Chapter 8.) In particular, there are special options you can use if you are printing output from a text formatter such as **troff**, **ditroff** or TeX.

The basic way to use **lpr** is to specify the names of one or more files to be printed. For example, to print a file named **memo**, use:

```
lpr memo
```

You can also use **lpr** at the end of a pipeline to print the output. For example, the following command line uses **cat** to combine three files. The output of **cat** is sent to **nl** to be numbered and then to **pr** to be formatted. The result is piped to **lpr** to be printed:

```
cat names extra.names old.names | nl | pr | lpr
```

When you use **lpr**, most systems will display a job number that identifies your print request. You can use this job number with the **lpq** command to check on the progress of the job and with the **lprm** command to remove the job from the print queue. If your system does not display a job number automatically, you can use the **lpq** command to display the number.

As a convenience, **lpr** can send you mail to tell you the job has finished printing. Just use the **-m** option:

```
lpr -m memo
```

To print more than one copy, use **-#** followed by the number of copies. Do not put a space before the number. For example, to print 5 copies of the file **memo**, use:

```
lpr -#5 memo
```

If you have created a file only to hold data for printing, you may want to remove it once the print job has finished. The **-r** (remove) option will do this for you. For example, to print and then remove a file named **raw.data**, use:

```
lpr -r raw.data
```

(The idea of removing a file is discussed in detail in Chapter 24.)

Many systems have more than one printer. If this is the case with your system, each printer will have a name. To send your output to a specific printer, use the **-P** (uppercase "P") option followed by the name of the printer. For example, to print the file **memo** on the printer named **laser2**, use:

```
lpr -P laser2 memo
```

If you do not use the **-P** option, **lpr** will use whatever printer is the default for your system. If you want to specify your own default printer, you can set the **PRINTER** global variable. This is similar to the **PAGER** variable that we discussed in Chapter 18.

For example, say that you want **lpr** to consider the printer named **laser1** to be the default printer. For the C-Shell, use the following command in your **.login** file:

```
setenv PRINTER laser1
```

For the Korn shell, use the following commands in your **.profile** file:

```
PRINTER=laser1; export PRINTER
```

(With the C-Shell, global variables are called "environment variables". With the Korn shell, they are called "shell variables". For more information on setting such variables, see Chapter 11 for the C-Shell and Chapter 12 for the Korn shell.)

HINT

Ask around and find out what printers are available on your system and which is the default printer. Otherwise, you may find yourself waiting for output at the wrong printer.

At the beginning of each printout, **lpr** will print an extra page that contains identification information, including a job name and a job classification. The page is called a BURST PAGE.

What's in a Name?   *Burst Page*

When you print on continuous fan-fold paper, the burst page indicates where to separate one printout from the next. The word "burst" refers to the act of tearing apart the pages of a printout.

Normally, the job name on the burst page is the name of the first file you are printing. You can change this name by using the **-J** option followed by a different name. If the name is more than one word or if it contains special characters, enclose it in single quotes. For example, to print the file **memo** with a job name of "Privileged Information", use:

```
lpr -J 'Privileged Information' memo
```

If you are printing a document on your own printer, you will probably want to dispense with the burst page entirely. You can do so by using the **-h** (omit header) option. For example:

```
lpr -h memo
```

In the previous section, we explained how you can use the **pr** filter to format data before printing. For example, the following command line formats and prints a file named **memo**:

```
pr memo | lpr
```

An alternative to using a pipeline is to use the **-p** option. This tells **lpr** to use **pr** to format the data before printing it. For example, the following command is equivalent to the previous one:

```
lpr -p memo
```

If you invoke **pr** in this way, you can use the **-T** (uppercase "T") option to tell **pr** what title to use in the page headers. Use **-T** followed by the title. For example, the following two commands are equivalent:

```
pr -h 'Important Memo' memo | lpr
lpr -p -T 'Important Memo' memo
```

If you want to use other formatting options, you will have to invoke **pr** directly and pipe the output to **lpr**.

Checking the Status of Print Jobs: lpq (Berkeley Unix)

With Berkeley Unix, you check on the status of a print job by using the **lpq** (line printer queue) command. The syntax is:

```
lpq [-l] [job...] [-P printer]
```

where:

> *job*: is a job number
> *printer*: is the name of a printer

The **lpq** command has other, less important options which we do not cover here. For more information, display the manual page by using the command **man lpq**. (The online Unix manual is discussed in Chapter 8.)

If you enter the command with no options, it will show you information about all the jobs in the print queue for the default printer. (If you have set the **PRINTER** variable, **lpq** will use that as the default.) Here is some sample output:

```
lp is ready and printing
Rank    Owner       Job  Files      Total Size
active harley       773  memo       25646 bytes
```

Of course, with a busy system, the print queue will often be long and you may have to wait a while for your printout.

Normally, **lpq** will display only a small amount of information to ensure that the description of each print job fits on a single line. If you want to see more information, you can use the **-l** (long listing) option:

```
lpq -l
```

To display information about the print queue of a particular printer, use the **-P** (uppercase "P") option followed by the name of the printer. For example, to look at the print queue for a printer named **laser2**, use:

lpq -P laser2

Finally, if you specify one or more job numbers, **lpq** will display information about those jobs only. For example:

lpq 773

HINT
Some systems operate the print queues on a first-come, first-served basis. Other systems look at the file to be printed and give priority to small jobs.

Canceling a Print Job: `lprm` (Berkeley Unix)

To cancel a print job, use the **lprm** (line printer remove) command. This command will remove an entry from the print queue. The syntax is:

lprm [-] [*job...*] [**-P** *printer*]

where:

> *job*:   is a job number
> *printer*:   is the name of a printer

If you use the command with no options:

lprm

it will cancel the job that is currently active (as long as it is one of your jobs). To cancel a specific job, specify the job number. For example:

lprm 773

To cancel all your print jobs, use the - option:

lprm -

HINT
The **lprm** command will remove only jobs that were sent by your userid. Don't waste your time trying to remove other people's jobs to make yours print faster.

Normally, **lprm** will cancel jobs for the default printer. (If you have set the **PRINTER** environment variable, **lpq** will use that as the default.) If you want to cancel jobs from a particular printer, use the **-P** (uppercase "P") option followed by the name of the printer. For example, to cancel all your jobs for a printer named **laser2**, use:

```
lprm - -P laser2
```

When **lprm** cancels a print job, you will see some type of message. Here is a typical example:

```
dfA773nipper dequeued
cfA773nipper dequeued
```

This message indicates that two files have been removed from the print spool directory. The first file, **dfA773nipper**, contains the data to be printed. The other file, **cfA773nipper**, contains the control information. The spool files were named using a suffix of **nipper** because that is the name of the computer.
If **lprm** does not cancel anything, there will be no message.

Printing a File: lp (System V Unix)

With System V Unix, you print a file using the **lp** (line printer) command. The syntax is:

```
lp [-mw] [-dprinter] [-nnum] [-ttitle] [file...]
```

where:

printer:	is the name of a printer (destination)
num:	is the number of copies you want
title:	is the title that you want to print in the header
file:	is the name of a file

The **lp** command has other options. In this section, we will discuss only the most important ones. If you want to find out more about **lp**, look at the manual page by using the command **man lp**. (The online Unix manual is covered in Chapter 8.)

The basic way to use **lp** is to specify the names of one or more files to be printed. For example, to print a file named **memo**, use:

```
lp memo
```

To print two files named **names** and **addresses**, use:

```
lp names addresses
```

You can also use **lp** at the end of a pipeline to print the output. For example, the following command line uses **cat** to combine three files. The output of **cat** is sent to **nl** to be numbered and then to **pr** to be formatted. The result is piped to **lp** to be printed:

```
cat names extra.names old.names | nl | pr | lp
```

When you use **lp**, the system will display a job number, called a REQUEST ID, that identifies your print request. You can use the request id with the **lpstat** command to check on the progress of the job and with the **cancel** command to remove the job from the print queue. If you specify more than one file to be printed, **lp** considers the whole thing to be a single job and issues only one request id.

As a convenience, **lp** can send you mail to tell you the job has finished printing. Just use the **-m** (mail) option:

```
lp -m memo
```

If you would like to get a message at your terminal instead, use the **-w** (write) option. For example:

```
lp -w memo
```

When the job has printed, the system will check if you are logged in locally. If so, it will send a message to your terminal. If you are logged in via a remote connection (or not logged in at all), the message will be mailed to you instead. The idea is that if you are working near the printer, it makes sense for you to know right away that your job is ready. Otherwise, a mail message is all you need.

To print more than one copy, use **-n** followed by the number of copies. Do not put a space before the number. For example, to print 5 copies of the file **memo**, use:

```
lp -n5 memo
```

Many systems have more than one printer. If this is the case with your system, each printer will have a name. There may also be names for a particular class of printer (for example, "postscript"). To send your output to a specific printer or printer class, use the **-d** (destination) option followed by the name of the printer or class. For example, to print the file **memo** on a specific printer named **laser2**, use:

```
lp -d laser2 memo
```

To print the same file on the first available printer in the class named **postscript**, use:

```
lp -d postscript memo
```

If you do not use the **-d** option, **lp** will use whatever printer is the default for your system.

You can control which printer will be the default (for you) by setting a global variable named **PRINTER**. This is similar to the **PAGER** variable we discussed in Chapter 18. For example, say that you want **lp** to consider the printer named **laser1** to be the default printer. For the C-Shell, use the following command in your **.login** file:

```
setenv PRINTER laser1
```

For the Korn shell, use the following commands in your **.profile** file:

```
PRINTER=laser1; export PRINTER
```

(With the C-Shell, global variables are called "environment variables". With the Korn shell, they are called "shell variables". For more information on setting such variables, see Chapter 11 for the C-Shell and Chapter 12 for the Korn shell.)

Technical note: When you print a file without using the **-d** option, **lp** first checks for a global variable named **LPDEST** for the name of a default printer. If this variable exists, it takes priority over the **PRINTER** variable.

HINT

Ask around and find out what printers are available on your system and which is the default printer. Otherwise, you may find yourself waiting for output at the wrong printer.

At the beginning of each printout, some systems will print an extra page, called a BANNER PAGE, that contains identification information. Normally, the job name on the banner page is the name of the file you are printing. You can change this name by using the **-t** option followed by a different name. If the name is more than one word or if it contains special characters, enclose it in single quotes.

For example, to print the file **memo** with a job name of "Privileged Information", use:

```
lp -t 'Privileged Information' memo
```

Checking the Status of Print Jobs: `lpstat` (System V Unix)

With System V Unix, you check on the status of a print job by using the **`lpstat`** (line printer status) command. The syntax is:

`lpstat [-o [id-list]] [-p [printer-list]]`

where:

> *id-list*: is a list of one or more request id numbers
> *printer-list*: is a list of one or more printers

The **`lpstat`** command has other, less important options which we do not cover here. For more information, display the manual page by using the command **man `lpstat`**. (The online Unix manual is discussed in Chapter 8.)

If you enter the command with no options, **`lpstat`** will show you information about all your jobs that are printing or waiting in the print queue:

`lpstat`

To see information about specific jobs, you can use the **-o** (output) option followed by the request id of that job:

`lpstat -o 773`

You can specify more than one request id if you want. If so, enclose them in double quotes:

`lpstat -o "773 776 779"`

If you use **-o** by itself, you will see information about all jobs in the print queue:

`lpstat -o`

To display information about a specific printer, use the **-p** option followed by the name of that printer:

`lpstat -p laser2`

To display information about all the printers, use **-p** by itself:

```
lpstat -p
```

Note: When you enter a **lpstat** without a **-p** option, the command uses the value of the **PRINTER** global variable as the default. (And, as we explained in the discussion of the **lp** command, if the **LPDEST** variable is set, it takes precedence over **PRINTER**.)

HINT
Some systems operate the print queues on a first-come, first-served basis. Other systems look at the file to be printed and give priority to small jobs.

Canceling a Print Job: `cancel` (System V Unix)

To cancel a print job, use the **cancel** command. This command will remove an entry from the print queue. There are several forms of this command:

```
cancel id...
cancel printer...
cancel -u userid
```

where:

> *id*: is the request id number
> *printer*: is the name of a printer
> *userid*: is your userid

To cancel one or more jobs, specify their id request numbers. For example:

```
cancel 773
cancel 773 776
```

To cancel all of your jobs on one or more printers, specify the names of those printers. For example:

```
cancel laser2
cancel laser2 laser5
```

HINT

If you forget the id request number or printer name for a particular job, you can find out by using the **lpstat** command.

To cancel all your print jobs on all printers, use the **-u** option followed by your userid. For example, if your userid is **harley** and you want to cancel all your print jobs, enter:

```
cancel -u harley
```

HINT

The **cancel** command will remove only jobs that were sent by your userid. Don't waste your time trying to remove other people's jobs to make yours print faster.

Interesting Things to Print: Manual Pages and Signs

There are two interesting things you might like to print. First, it can be handy to print selected pages from the online Unix manual (see Chapter 8). When you use the **man** command, it automatically formats the output for printing. Thus, all you need to do is pipe the output of **man** to the **lpr** or **lp** command.

For example, to print a copy of the manual page for the **who** command on the default printer, use:

```
man who | lpr
```

If for some reason your **man** command does not format the data, you can always pipe it through **pr**. Either of the following commands will do the job:

```
man who | pr | lpr
man who | lpr -p
```

The second interesting thing to print is a sign made up of large letters. You can generate such a sign by using the **banner** command we described in Chapter 7. To print a sign, all you have to do is pipe the output of **banner** to **lpr** or **lp**. For example:

```
banner 'This sign is silly.' | lpr
```

Note: The **banner** program is in the **/usr/games** directory. If this directory is not in your search path, you will see an error message when you try to run the program because Unix will not be able to find the program:

```
banner: Command not found.
```

If so, you will have to preface the command with the name of the directory that contains the **banner** program. Use:

```
/usr/games/banner 'This sign is silly.' | lpr
```

This consideration is explained in Chapter 7. Directories are explained in Chapter 23.

HINT

When you use **banner** to generate a sign, print the output on continuous paper. If you use separate sheets of paper, you will have to tape them together.

CHAPTER **20**

The **vi** Editor

An EDITOR, or TEXT EDITOR, is a program you use to create and modify files of data. Editors are used to modify TEXT, data that consists of letters, numbers, punctuation and so on.

This chapter covers one of the most important topics in Unix: the **vi** editor. It is important to learn **vi** or, at least, some editor program such as **emacs** (Chapter 21). Even if you don't want to create documents or programs, there are many times when you will need to use an editor.

For example, if you want to mail someone a message, you can type it directly, line by line. (This is all explained in Chapter 15.) But without an editor, there is no way to make changes in the message. Moreover, you cannot prepare a message in advance.

Similarly, if you participate in Usenet (the world-wide system of discussion groups), you may want to post an article of your own. Unless you can use an editor, you will have no way to create the article. In fact, any time you need to manipulate textual data directly, you need an editor.

A number of Unix programs have built-in commands to start an editor should you need one. Most often, this editor will be **vi** and you must know how to use it.

In this chapter, we will explain the basics of using **vi**. Although we will not be able to explain everything—that would take at least several chapters—we will show you most of what you need to know.

HINT

If you use a non-Unix computer to access Unix—say, a Macintosh or a PC—it is possible to create a file on that computer and send it to Unix. However, in many cases, you are better off doing the work on the Unix computer.

Thus, no matter how you access Unix, you do need to learn to use a Unix editor. If you know how to use **vi**, you can edit files on any Unix system you may encounter.

Which Editor Should You Use?

As a Unix user, you must to learn how to use an editor. (This is mandatory.) The three main choices are **vi**, **emacs** and **pico**. Both **vi** and **emacs** are powerful, full-featured programs that will take you some time to learn. **pico** is a simple, much less powerful program that is easy to learn quickly. **pico** comes with the **pine** mail program (see Chapter 15). Even if you do not use **pine** to read and send mail, you can still use **pico** as your editor for regular work.

Which editor should you use? Our advice is to use either **vi** or **emacs** (the choice is up to you), and leave **pico** to rot slowly in benign neglect.

Strong words? Yes, they are, but this *is* a no-holds-barred, industrial-strength Unix book and we do speak our mind. The thing is, **pico** was designed to be simple—so much so that you can use it immediately with little training or assistance. Unfortunately, because it is so simple, **pico** is about as brain-dead as a congressman, and using **pico** for your day-to-day work will be frustrating to the point of dementia. Just believe us, there will be many times you want to do something reasonable with your text, and **pico** will just not be able to do it.

You see, the spirit of Unix is to use powerful, logically designed tools: tools that encourage you to think, innovate, and to do your work with elegance and a minimum of fuss. Both **vi** and **emacs** are such programs; **pico**, on the other hand, will cause permanent, degenerative changes in your brain tissue.

This is not to say that no one anywhere should use **pico** (and other such tools, such as the **pine** mail program). Not at all. It's just that if you are the type of person who is smart enough to learn Unix, you are better off with **vi** or **emacs**.

There are many ordinary people using **pico** who still manage to live useful, productive lives.

HINT

When you walk by a computer and see someone using **pico**, be kind. Pause for a second, and remind yourself that: "There, but for the grace of God, go I."

If you were to ask experienced Unix people what editor they use—and all experienced Unix people use *some* editor—you would find their loyalties divided between **vi** and **emacs**.

In this chapter, we will show you how to use **vi**. This is because **vi** is available on every Unix system and will do just fine. Moreover, **vi** is a standard tool. It has not changed in years, nor will it change in the future. **emacs** will also suffice, but it is not always available. It is our opinion that, unless you have a good reason to do otherwise, you should learn **vi** first. You can always learn **emacs** later.

However, if you do decide to learn **emacs**, this is a good time to skip directly to Chapter 21.

HINT

If you are learning **vi** and you become temporarily discouraged, take a break and try a little **emacs**. **emacs** will seem so complex and impossible that you will feel a lot better about using **vi**.

What Is **vi**?

In Chapter 6, we explained that the early Unix developers used teletype-like terminals that printed on paper. Later, they used rudimentary display terminals that were, by today's standards, slow and awkward.

The first Unix editor, called **ed**, was a LINE-ORIENTED EDITOR or LINE EDITOR. This means the lines of text were numbered and you would enter commands based on these numbers. For example, you might enter a command to print lines 10 though 20, or delete line 17. Such an approach was necessary because of the slowness of the terminals. (It is from these early terminals, by the way, that the Unix tradition developed of using the word "print" to mean "to display data".)

Later, at U.C. Berkeley, Bill Joy developed a more powerful line editor that he named **ex** (extended editor). **ex** was far more comprehensive and powerful than **ed**. (Bill Joy also wrote a great deal of early Berkeley Unix, including the C-Shell. He later founded Sun Microsystems.)

Line editors display data, line by line, at the bottom of the screen. As each new line is displayed, the others scroll up. With the availability of fast, flexible terminals, there arose a need for SCREEN EDITORS that would take advantage of the increased functionality. Such editors allow you to enter and display data anywhere on the screen, much like a modern word processing program.

Joy wrote a screen-oriented interface for **ex** which he called **vi** (visual editor). **vi** supports all of the **ex** commands, but it has its own special commands and conventions that make use of the full screen. **vi** became the standard Unix editor and, as we mentioned earlier, is included with all Unix systems.

Interestingly enough, **vi** and **ex** are really the same program. If you start the program with the **ex** command, it uses a line-oriented interface. If you start the program with the **vi** command, it uses the screen-oriented "visual" interface. Consequently, as you are using **vi**, all the **ex** commands are still available. Indeed, as you will see, it is often more effective to use an **ex** command than a **vi** command.

What's in a Name? ed, ex, vi

In the early days of Unix, many commands were given short, two-letter names. The convention is to pronounce these names as two separate letters. For example, "ee-dee" (**ed**), "ee-ex" (**ex**) and "vee-eye" (**vi**). It is incorrect to pronounce **vi** as a single syllable "vie".

There were two practical reasons why so many commands were given such small names. First, smart people tend to prefer short, easy-to-use abbreviations. Second, the old terminals were agonizingly slow, and it was convenient to use short command names that were easy to type correctly.

This same limitation also gave rise to one of Unix's distinguishing characteristics: its terseness. When a program has nothing to say, it says nothing. For example, if you enter a command to search for data and it finds none, it does not display a message. It simply returns you to the shell prompt. Similarly, Unix error messages are short and to the point.

Like the two-letter command names, the tradition of brevity was the product of smart, quick people who were forced to work with slow equipment. Today, the esthetic of "small is beautiful" is still an important (though vanishing) part of the Unix culture.

If you are interested in seeing what two-letter command names are still in use, look in Chapter 17 at the end of the section on regular expressions. In that section, we show how to use the **grep** command to find these names on your own system. If you have a few moments, you might look up these commands in the online manual. You will find some forgotten gems.

How to Start `vi`

To start **vi**, you enter the **vi** command. The basic syntax is:

`vi [file...]`

where `file` is the name of a file you want to edit. (There are also two useful options which we will cover later.)

In Chapter 22, we will discuss the concept of a file in detail. For now, it is enough to assume the intuitive idea that a file is a repository of data, usually stored on a disk, that you can access by using a name.

Thus, if you want to edit a file named **memo**, you can enter:

`vi memo`

If the file does not already exist, **vi** will create it for you.

It is okay to start **vi** without a file name. **vi** will let you specify a name when it comes time to save the data.

Command Mode and Input Mode

When you work with **vi**, all the data is kept in what is called the EDITING BUFFER. This means that when you use **vi** to edit an existing file, you are not working with the actual file. **vi** copies the contents of the file to the editing buffer. It is not until you tell **vi** to save your data that the contents of the editing buffer are stored in the file. Thus, if you accidentally mess up the data in the editing buffer, you can simply opt to discard the editing buffer and preserve your original file.

vi operates in two distinct ways, called INPUT MODE and COMMAND MODE. When **vi** is in input mode, everything you type is inserted into the editing buffer. When **vi** is in command mode, the characters you type are interpreted as commands. There are many different commands you can issue: delete certain lines, move from place to place in the file, search for a pattern, make changes, and so on.

If you have ever used a word processor program, you know that it allows you to move to any place in the file and start typing. With a personal computer, you would move around the file by using special keys like PAGEUP, PAGEDOWN, HOME and END, as well as the cursor control (arrow) keys. You might also use a mouse. When **vi** was developed, terminals did not have these special keys or a mouse. There were only the regular keyboard and the CTRL key.

For this reason, **vi** uses two different modes. The effect of what you type depends on what mode **vi** is in at the time. For example, if **vi** is in command mode and you press D, it acts as a delete command. If **vi** is in input mode, pressing D will actually insert the character "D" into the editing buffer, and the "D" will appear on your screen. In this way, you do not need any special keys and **vi** will work on any type of terminal.

Here is what it's like to work with **vi**: Say that you want to add some data to the middle of a file. When you start **vi**, you are automatically in command mode. The cursor shows your current position in the editing buffer. Using appropriate commands, you move the cursor to the place where you want to add the data. You type a command to change to input mode and start typing. At this point, everything you type is inserted into the editing buffer. When you are finished, you change back to command mode.

Although it is **vi** that changes from one mode to another, we usually talk as if you, the user, are making the change. For example, we might say "There are many commands you can use when you are in command mode." Or we might say, "To add text to the editing buffer, you must first change to insert mode."

As you work with **vi**, you frequently change back and forth between command mode and insert mode. In command mode, there are a number of different commands you can use to change to input mode. Each of these commands is a single letter. For example, the **I** command allows you to start inserting text at the beginning of the current line. The **A** (append) command allows you to start inserting text at the end of the current line. We will explain all these commands in due time.

When you are in insert mode (typing characters), there is only one way to change to command mode: you press the ESC key. (If you are already in command mode and you press the ESC key, **vi** will beep at you.) At first, it will seem strange to have to change to a special mode just to start typing data. Don't worry, it will not take you long to get used to it.

If you are not sure what mode you are in, you can always press ESC twice. This is guaranteed to leave you in command mode and to beep. Why? If you are in insert mode, the first ESC will change to command mode, and the second ESC will beep. If you are already in command mode, both ESCs will beep.

HINT

When using **vi**, if you are not sure what mode you are in, press ESC twice. You will be in command mode, and you will hear at least one beep.

You might ask, why doesn't **vi** do something to show you what mode you are in? There are two answers to this question. First, some versions of **vi** have an option named **showmode** that you can set. To do so, enter the command:

```
:set showmode
```

Once you set this option, **vi** will remind you that you are in insert mode by displaying a short message at the bottom right-hand corner of the screen.

(If you decide you always want to set this option, you can place the command in your **.exrc** file—discussed at the end of this chapter—so the option will be set automatically each time you start **vi**.)

Second, once you get used to **vi** and you have some experience with switching from command mode to insert mode and back again, you will always just know what mode you are in: it's really not that much of a problem. Most experienced **vi** users do not bother to set the **showmode** option even if it is available. They don't really need it and—after a little practice—neither will you.

vi was designed extremely well. At first, many things may seem awkward. However, once you become experienced, everything will make sense, and **vi** will seem natural and easy to use. This suggests the following hint which, in Chapter 1, we applied to Unix in general:

HINT

vi is easy to use, but difficult to learn.

If you are a touch typist, you will find that **vi** is particularly easy to use once you have memorized the basic commands. You will be able to do anything you want without taking your hands off the keyboard. The only special keys you ever need are CTRL and ESC. As you may know, this is not the case with word processors that use keys like PAGEUP or PAGEDOWN, or that use a mouse.

Starting **vi** as a Read-Only Editor: The **-R** Option, **view**

There may be times when you want to use **vi** to look at an important file that should not be changed. There are two ways to do so. First, you can start **vi** with the **-R** (read-only) option. This tells **vi** that you do not want to save data back into the original file. Second, you can start the editor by using the **view** command.

There is really no difference between **vi -R** and **view**. You can use whichever is easier to remember. Thus, the following two commands are equivalent:

```
vi -R importantfile
view importantfile
```

They both start **vi**, using a file named **importantfile** for reading only. Using **vi** in this way protects you from accidentally replacing important data.

Recovering Data After a System Failure: The **-r** Option

From time to time, it may happen that the system will go down while you are working with **vi**. If this occurs, **vi** will usually make it possible for you to recover all or most of your data. Remember, when you use **vi** to edit a file, you are not editing the actual file; you are working with an editing buffer. This buffer is usually preserved, even when the system goes down unexpectedly.

Once the system is restarted, a daemon (see Chapter 19) will mail you a message similar to this one:

```
You were editing the file "memo"
at <Wed May 11 16:24> on the machine ``nipper''
when the editor was killed.

You can retrieve most of your changes to this file
using the "recover" command of the editor.
An easy way to do this is to give the command "vi -r memo".
This method also works using "ex" and "edit".
```

As the message implies, you can recover your data by starting **vi** with the **-r** (recover) option. First, enter:

```
vi -r
```

and **vi** will show you all the files you may recover. If the file you want is available, enter the same command, but this time specify the name of the file. For example:

```
vi -r memo
```

This will start **vi** and, hopefully, leave you where you were when the system went down.

Note: Be careful not to confuse the **-r** (recover) option with the **-R** (read-only) option.

How to Stop `vi`

There are two situations in which you may find yourself when you are ready to stop **vi**. Usually, you will want to save the contents of the editing buffer to a file and then stop. Occasionally, you may decide to quit without saving your work.

In either case, you must be in command mode to enter the command to quit. If you are in input mode, press ESC to change to command mode.

To save your work and then stop, the command is:

ZZ

That is, hold down the SHIFT key and press Z twice. You do not need to press RETURN.

What's in a Name?   **ZZ**

This command, used to stop **vi**, certainly has a strange name, but there is a reason. The name **ZZ** was chosen because it is difficult to type by accident. If you are in command mode, but for some reason, you think you are in input mode, it is unlikely that you would type **ZZ** as input. If **vi** used a simple command like **s** (for "stop"), it would be easy to type it accidentally.

To quit without saving your work, the command is:

:q!

After you type this command, you do need to press the RETURN key. Later in the chapter, we will explain why the command starts with a colon and why you need to press RETURN. Rest assured, it all makes sense.

Be careful: When you use **ZZ** to stop **vi**, it will check to see if you have saved your data. If not, **vi** will save it for you. However, when you use the **:q!** command, **vi** will not save your data.

In Unix, the **!** character is often used to indicate that you want to override some type of automatic check. In the case of **:q!**, the **!** tells **vi** not to check if you have saved your data. (For a summary of how the **!** character is used in Unix, see Chapter 16.)

How **vi** Uses the Screen

As we explained in Chapter 6, many Unix programs look at the global variable **TERM** to see what type of terminal you are using. Whenever you start **vi**, it uses the **TERM** variable to make sure it sends the correct commands to control your terminal. In particular, **vi** will try to use as many lines as your terminal can display.

HINT

If you ever find that **vi** is displaying data strangely, make sure that your **TERM** variable is set correctly.

We explain how to set this variable in Chapter 11 (for the C-Shell) and Chapter 12 (for the Korn shell); in Chapter 17 we show how the **tset** command can help with this initialization.

The bottom line of your screen is called the COMMAND LINE. As we will see in a moment, **vi** uses this line to display certain commands as you type them. All the other lines are used to display data. **vi** will show as much of the editing buffer as will fit onto your screen at one time.

When you have a small amount of data, there may not be enough lines to fill up the screen. For example, say that your terminal has 25 lines. The bottom line is the command line, leaving 24 lines to display data. Now, say that the editing buffer contains only 10 lines. It would be confusing if **vi** displayed the empty 14 lines as being blank. After all, you might actually have blank lines as part of your data.

Instead, **vi** marks the beginning of each empty line with a ~ (tilde) character. As you add new lines, they will take up more and more of the screen, and the tildes will disappear.

If at any time your screen becomes garbled—for instance, if someone sends you a message—you can tell **vi** to redisplay everything by pressing **^L**. Some people set **mesg** to **n** before they use an editor so their work won't be interrupted by a message. (The **mesg** command is explained in Chapter 13.)

Most of the time, your data will consist of regular characters, letters, numbers, punctuation and so on. However, if the need arises, you can enter control characters (see Chapter 6) into your editing buffer. To do so, press **^V** followed by the control character you want to enter. For example, if you want to type an actual **^C** character, press **^V^C**. If, for some strange reason, you actually want to type **^V**, enter **^V^V**.

When **vi** displays control characters, you will see the **^** character followed by a letter, for example, **^C**. Remember that this is really only a single character, even though it takes up two spaces on your screen.

As we explained in Chapter 6, the tab character is **^I**. **vi**, like Unix in general, assumes that tabs are set for every 8 positions. (You can change the positioning, but most people don't bother.) When you enter a tab in the editing buffer, **vi** does not display **^I**. Rather, **vi** displays as many spaces as necessary to make it look as if your data is aligned according to the tab. This is just for your convenience. Remember that these extra spaces do not really exist. The editing buffer contains only a single tab character.

Using vi and ex Commands

We explained earlier that **vi** and **ex** are really different faces of the same program. This means that when you use **vi**, you have access to both **vi** and **ex** commands.

Most **vi** commands are one or two letters. For example, to move the cursor forward one word, you use the **w** command. (Just type **w**.) To delete the current line, you use the **dd** command. (Just type **dd**.) Since **vi** commands are so short, they are not echoed as you type.

For most **vi** commands, you do not press RETURN. For example, as soon as you type **w**, the cursor moves forward one word. As soon as you type **dd**, the current line disappears.

If you make a mistake and type a bad **vi** command, you will hear a beep. There will not be an error message.

ex commands are longer and more complex than **vi** commands. For this reason, they are echoed on the command line as you type. All **ex** commands start with **:** (colon). For example, the command:

```
:1,5d
```

deletes lines 1 through 5. The command:

```
:%s/harley/Harley/g
```

changes all occurrences of "harley" to "Harley".

As soon as you type the first colon, **vi** will move the cursor down to the command line (the bottom line of your screen). As you type the command, each character will be echoed. When you are finished typing the command, you must press RETURN.

If you make a mistake before you press RETURN, you have two choices. First, you can press ESC. This will cancel the command completely. Second, you can correct the command using the special keys we discussed in Chapter 6. These are shown in Figure 20-1. You can use these same keys when you are in input mode to make corrections as you type.

CODE	KEY	PURPOSE
erase	BACKSPACE, DELETE	erase the last character typed
werase	^W	erase the last word typed
kill	^X, ^U	erase the entire line

FIGURE 20-1. vi: *Special keys to use while typing*

When you make a correction, the cursor will move backward. However—and this is important—**vi** will not erase the characters from the screen. Logically, they will be gone, but physically, they will still be on the screen.

For example, say that you enter:

```
:1,5del
```

Before you press RETURN, you realize that you did not need to type **el** at the end of the command. So you press BACKSPACE twice and the cursor will move back two positions. However, the "e" and "l"—even though they are not really there any longer—will not be erased from the screen. Just ignore them. You can now press RETURN.

A Strategy for Learning **vi** Commands

As you know, the cursor shows your position on the screen. When you want to add data into the editing buffer, you must follow these steps:

1. Move the cursor to the place at which you want to add data.

2. Type a command to change to input mode.

3. Enter the data.

4. Press ESC to change back to command mode.

Once your editing buffer has data, there are various commands you can use to make changes. So, there are three main types of commands you need to learn:

■ commands to move the cursor

■ commands to enter input mode

■ commands to make changes

We will describe each family of commands in turn.

One thing that may surprise you is the large number of commands in **vi**. For example, there are 12 different commands you can use to enter input mode. And there are 40 different commands just to move the cursor. (These are just the *simple* cursor commands.)

As you might guess, you don't really need to know 40 different ways to move the cursor. However, it is useful to know as many commands as possible. What makes **vi** so easy to use—once you are experienced—is that there are so many ways to do the same task.

For example, say that you want to move from the top left of the screen to a word halfway down and to the right. You could move the cursor one position at a time, which would be slow and awkward. But if you knew all 40 cursor movement commands, you could quickly choose the best ones to use and, by typing three or four keys, quickly jump to where you want to be.

HINT

The art of using **vi** well is in being familiar with so many of the commands that, in any situation, you know the best way to do what you want quickly.

In this chapter, we will be able to cover only the basic commands. For reference, Appendix C contains a thorough summary of **vi**. Every now and then, take a moment and teach yourself a new command. They are all useful.

As you read the rest of the chapter, work in front of your terminal and follow along. As you learn about each new command, try it out. If you need a file of data to practice with, use either of the following commands:

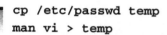

```
cp /etc/passwd temp
man vi > temp
```

The first command copies the system password file to a file named **temp**. The second command copies the manual page for **vi** to a file named **temp**. (The **cp** command is explained in Chapter 24; the password file in Chapter 13; the online manual in Chapter 8; and the redirection of standard output using **>** in Chapter 16.)

Either of these commands will leave you with a file named **temp** that you can use for practice. Once you have such a file, you can edit it by entering the command:

```
vi temp
```

When you are finished, you can remove the file by using:

```
rm temp
```

(The **rm** command is explained in Chapter 24.)

Moving the Cursor

A good strategy for using **vi** is to teach yourself a variety of ways to move the cursor. Each time you want to jump to a different part of the editing buffer, take a moment and think about which sequence of commands will work best. After a while, choosing the right commands will become second nature.

In some cases, there are several ways to make the exact same cursor movement. For example, as you will see in a moment, there are three different commands that will move the cursor one position to the left. There is no need to learn all of them. Pick the commands you like the best and practice those.

To move the cursor a single position, you have a lot of choices. The best commands to use are **h**, **j**, **k** and **l**. They work as follows:

h	move cursor one position left
j	move cursor one position down
k	move cursor one position up
l	move cursor one position right

Why such an odd choice of keys? When you type using the proper finger positions, these four keys are easy to press with your right hand. (Take a look at your keyboard.)

If you are not a touch typist, there are alternatives that are easier to remember. If your terminal has cursor control keys (arrow keys), you can use those. (We will call them LEFT, DOWN, UP and RIGHT.) You can also use BACKSPACE to move left and the SPACE bar to move right.

LEFT	move cursor one position left
DOWN	move cursor one position down
UP	move cursor one position up
RIGHT	move cursor one position right
BACKSPACE	move cursor one position left
SPACE	move cursor one position right

Another way to move up and down is to use the **–** and **+** commands. Pressing **–** moves to the beginning of the previous line; pressing **+** moves to the beginning of the next line. As an alternative, pressing RETURN also moves to the beginning of the next line.

–	move cursor to beginning of previous line
+	move cursor to beginning of next line
RETURN	move cursor to beginning of next line

These keys are handy if you have a PC-type keyboard with a numeric keypad. The rightmost keys will be **-**, **+** and ENTER. (ENTER is the same as RETURN.)

Within the current line, the **0** (number zero) command moves to the beginning of the line. The **$** (dollar sign) command moves to the end of the line. If the current line is indented, you can use the **^** (circumflex) to move to the first character in the line that is not a space or tab.

0	move cursor to beginning of current line
$	move cursor to end of current line
^	move cursor to first non-space/tab in current line

Aside from moving by character or line, there are several commands you can use to move from word to word. To move forward, use the **w** or **e** commands. **w** moves to the first character of the next word; **e** moves to the last character (end) of the next word. By using either **w** or **e**, you can move exactly where you want and save keystrokes.

To move backward, use **b** to move to the first character in the previous word.

w	move cursor forward to first character of next word
e	move cursor forward to last character of next word
b	move cursor backward to first character of previous word

One thing about the **w**, **e** and **b** commands is that they stop at each punctuation character. This is okay if your data does not contain many such characters. However, if your data does contain much punctuation, **w**, **e** and **b** can be rather slow. Instead, use the **W**, **E** and **B** commands. These work the same way except they recognize only spaces and **newline** characters as ending a word.

W	same as **w**; ignore punctuation
E	same as **e**; ignore punctuation
B	same as **b**; ignore punctuation

For example, say that the cursor is at the beginning of the following line:

```
this is an (important) test; okay
```

If you press **w** several times, you will stop at each parenthesis and at the semicolon, as well as at the beginning of each word. That is, you will have to press **w** eight times to reach the last word of the line. If you use **W**, you will stop only after each space. You will have to press **W** only five times to reach the last word of the line. Try it for yourself.

If you are editing a document, you can use the parentheses commands to jump from sentence to sentence, and the brace bracket commands to jump from paragraph to paragraph.

)	move forward to next sentence beginning
(	move backward to previous sentence beginning
}	move forward to next paragraph beginning
{	move backward to previous paragraph beginning

Again, these are commands you should try for yourself to make sure you understand exactly how they work.

Within **vi**, the official definition of a SENTENCE is a string of characters, ending in a period, comma, question mark or exclamation mark, and followed by at least *two* spaces or a **newline** character. (The **newline** character marks the end of a line; see Chapter 6.)

In other words, for **vi** to recognize a sentence, it must either be followed by two spaces or the end of the line. The reason for this requirement is that putting in two spaces allows **vi** to distinguish sentences from words (which are separated by single spaces). Consider the following text, which consists of two sentences separated by a period and two spaces:

```
Meet me at 6 p.m. at the Shell Tower.   Is this o.k. with you?
```

Similarly, a PARAGRAPH is defined as a section of text that starts and ends in a blank line. Thus, putting a tab at the beginning of a line is not enough.

HINT

When you use **vi**, remember to put two spaces between sentences and a blank line between paragraphs. This will do three things:

First, it will allow you to use **(** and **)** to move from one sentence to another, as well as **{** and **}** to move between paragraphs.

Second, it will make your writing easier to read.

Third, if you send text to someone who will later edit it, that person will find your text a lot easier to manipulate. For example, say that you mail a message to someone who is polite enough to edit your text when he replies. It is a lot easier for him to delete whole sentences if the original message was formatted nicely. This may seem like a minor point, but it really isn't.

Prediction: After you get comfortable with **vi**, you will find yourself annoyed at people who use only a single space between sentences.

Note for nerds: If you use **nroff** or **troff** for text formatting, **vi** will also recognize paragraph macros (such as **.P**) as starting a new paragraph. If this idea makes no sense to you, ignore it.

There will be times when you want to make a large move from one part of your screen to another. To start such a move, you can use the **H**, **M** or **L** commands. They jump to the top, middle or bottom of the lines that are currently on your screen.

H	move cursor to top line
M	move cursor to middle line
L	move cursor to last line

(Think of "high", "middle" and "low".)

The art of moving the cursor is to get where you want to be in as few keystrokes as possible. Here is an example. Say that the cursor is on the top line of the screen. The last line of data on the screen contains:

today if you can.   Otherwise give me a call.

You want to move to the "c" in call so you can insert the word "phone".

You could press DOWN many times to move to the line you want, and then press RIGHT many times to move to the word you want. However, you can do the whole thing in three keystrokes:

L$b

This means: **L** (last line), **$** (end of line), **b** (back up one word).

Wherever it makes sense, you can have **vi** automatically repeat a cursor movement command by typing a number—called a "repeat count"— before the command. For example, to move forward 10 words, type:

10w

Notice that you do not put a space after the number.

Here are two more examples. To move down 50 lines, type any of the following commands:

50j
50<Down>
50+
50<Return>

To move back three paragraphs, type:

3{

As a general rule, you can repeat any **vi** command—not just cursor commands—by typing a number in front of it, as long as doing so makes sense.

HINT
Whenever you need to move from one place to another, challenge yourself to do it in as few keystrokes as possible.

(If you are a student, this may help you work your way through college. You can go into bars and bet that you can move the **vi** cursor faster than anyone. At first, use a lot of short movement commands like UP and DOWN. After you have lost a few bets and the odds increase, you can use **H**, **M** and **L**, followed by repeated sentence and word commands, and clean up.)

Moving Through the Editing Buffer

vi will display as much of the editing buffer as will fit on your screen. To display different parts of the editing buffer, there are several commands you can use.

First, you can use the **^F** (forward) command to move down one screenful. (Remember, **^F** refers to CTRL-F.) The opposite command is **^B** (backward), which moves up one screenful. There are also two variations: **^D** moves down a half screenful, and **^U** moves up a half screenful.

^F	move down (forward) one screenful
^B	move up (back) one screenful
^D	move down a half screenful
^U	move up a half screenful

If you type a number in front of **^F** or **^B**, it acts, as you would expect, as a repeat factor. For example, to move down 6 screenfuls, type:

6^F

Since you can use **^F** and **^B** to jump over many lines in this manner, you do not need to be able to repeat **^D** and **^U** commands. Thus, when you type a number in front of **^D** or **^U**, it is used for something different: it sets the number of lines that either of these commands should jump. For example, if you type:

```
10^D
```

(or **10^U**), it not only jumps 10 lines, it tells **vi** that all subsequent **^D** and **^U** commands should also jump 10 lines (until you reset it). You can also set the number of lines to a larger amount. For example, if you would like to be able to jump 100 lines at a time, use **100^D** (or **100^U**). Until you change this number, all **^D** and **^U** commands will jump 100 lines.

Searching for a Pattern

Another way to move around the editing buffer is to jump to a line that contains a particular pattern. To do so, use the **/** and **?** commands.

When you type **/**, **vi** will display a **/** on the command line (at the bottom of the screen). Now type any pattern you want and press RETURN. **vi** will search for the next occurrence of that pattern. If you want to search again for the same pattern, just type **/** again and press RETURN.

Here is an example. You are editing a list of people to whom you want to send money, and you wish to find the next occurrence of the pattern "Harley". Type:

```
/Harley
```

and press RETURN. **vi** will jump to the next line that contains the pattern. To repeat the search and jump once more, type:

```
/
```

and press RETURN. Since you did not specify a new pattern, **vi** will assume that you want the same one as the previous **/** command.

When **vi** looks for a pattern, it starts from the cursor position and searches forward. When it gets to the end of the editing buffer, **vi** wraps around to the beginning. Thus, **vi** will search the entire editing buffer.

If you want to search backward, use the **?** command. For example:

```
?Harley
```

This works the same as **/** except that **vi** searches in the opposite direction. Once you use **?** to specify a pattern, you can search backward for the same pattern by using **?** by itself:

?

When **vi** gets to the beginning of the editing buffer, it will wrap around to the end and continue to search backward.

Once you have specified a pattern with a **/** or **?** command, there are two convenient commands to continue searching for the same pattern. The **n** (lowercase "n") command searches in the same direction as the original command. (Think of **n** as standing for "next".) The **N** (uppercase "N") command searches in the opposite direction. For example, say that you have already entered the command:

/Harley

You now want to find the next occurrence of the same pattern. All you have to do is press **n**. (Do not press RETURN.) This is the same as if you had entered the **/** command with no pattern. To search repeatedly for the same pattern, press **n** as many times as you want. If you press **N**, **vi** will make the same search backward.

Now, say that you have entered the command:

?Harley

Pressing **n** will search backward (the same direction) for the next occurrence. Pressing **N** will search forwards (the opposite direction).

For flexibility, you can use a regular expression to specify a pattern. (A regular expression is a compact way of specifying a general pattern of characters.) We discussed regular expressions in detail at the end of Chapter 17; you can look there for a lot of examples. **vi** uses the same type of regular expressions, so everything from Chapter 17 will work here.

For reference, Figure 20-2 shows the various symbols that have special meanings within a regular expression. Here are a few examples. To search for the next occurrence of an "H", followed by any two characters, use:

/H..

To search for an "H" followed by any two lowercase characters, use:

/H[a-z][a-z]

SYMBOL	MEANING
.	match any single character except **newline**
*	match zero or more of the preceding characters
^	match the beginning of a line
$	match the end of a line
\\<	match the beginning of a word
\\>	match the end of a word
[ ]	match one of the enclosed characters
[^]	match any character that is not enclosed
\\	take the following symbol literally

FIGURE 20-2. `vi:` *Symbols used in regular expressions*

To search for an "H", followed by zero or more lowercase characters, followed by "y", use:

`/H[a-z]*y`

To search for the next line that begins with "Harley", use:

`/^Harley`

As you can see, regular expressions are particularly useful. For more examples and a longer discussion, see Chapter 17. To summarize:

/*rexp*	search forward for specified regular expression
/	repeat forward search for previous regular expression
?*rexp*	search backward for specified regular expression
?	repeat backward search for previous regular expression
n	repeat last **/** or **?** command, same direction
N	repeat last **/** or **?** command, opposite direction

Using Line Numbers

Internally, **vi** keeps track of each line in the editing buffer by assigning it a line number. If you would like to see these numbers, enter the command:

```
:set number
```

For example, say that you are a graduate student using **vi** to write your Applied Philosophy dissertation. The editing buffer contains:

```
I have a little shadow that goes
in and out with me,
And what can be the use of him
is more than I can see.
```

If you enter the **:set number** command, you will see:

```
1    I have a little shadow that goes
2    in and out with me,
3    And what can be the use of him
4    is more than I can see.
```

It is important to realize that the numbers are not really part of your data. They are only there for your convenience. If you want to get rid of the numbers, enter:

```
:set nonumber
```

There are two important uses for line numbers. First, as we will see later, you can use them with many of the **ex** commands. Second, you can use the **G** (go to) command to jump to a specific line. Simply type the number of the line, followed by **G**. Do not type a space or press RETURN. For example, to jump to line 100, type:

```
100G
```

To jump to the beginning of the editing buffer, type:

```
1G
```

If you want to jump to the end of the editing buffer, type **G** by itself:

```
G
```

To summarize:

*n***G**	jump to line number **n**
1G	jump to first line in editing buffer
G	jump to last line in editing buffer

Most of the time, you will use only **G** and **1G**.

Inserting Data into the Editing Buffer

With a word processor, you move the cursor to where you want to insert data and start typing. With **vi**, you must type a command to change to input mode before you can enter your data. When you are finished entering data, you must press ESC to leave input mode and return to command mode.

(When you press ESC in command mode, **vi** will beep. If you are not sure what mode you are in, press ESC twice. When you hear the beep, you will know you are in command mode.)

There are twelve commands to change to insert mode. Half of these commands are for entering new data; the other half are for replacing existing data.

Of course, you will ask, why do I need so many different commands just to change to input mode? The answer is that each command opens the editing buffer in a different place. Here are the commands for entering new data:

i	change to insert mode: insert before cursor position
a	change to insert mode: insert after cursor position
I	change to insert mode: insert at start of current line
A	change to insert mode: insert at end of current line
o	change to insert mode: open below current line
O	change to insert mode: open above current line

To see how this all works, let's say you are a student editing a term paper for your Advanced Classical Music class. The current line is:

For a dime you can see Kankakee or Paree

The cursor is under the letter "K" and you are in command mode.

If you type **i**, you will change to command mode. As you type, the data will be inserted before the "K". The letters to the right will be moved over to make room. For example, say that you type:

iAAA<Esc>

(The ESC returns you to command mode.) The current line would look like:

For a dime you can see AAAKankakee or Paree

Now, instead, suppose you type **a** to change to insert mode. As you type, the data will be inserted after the "K". If you start with the original line and type:

aBBB<Esc>

the current line would look like:

For a dime you can see KBBBankakee or Paree

HINT
To remember the difference between the **i** and **a** commands, think of **i**=insert, **a**=append.

By using the **I** (uppercase "I") and **A** (uppercase "A") commands, you can insert data at the beginning or end of the current line, respectively. For example, if you start with the original line and type:

ICCC<Esc>

the current line would look like:

CCCFor a dime you can see Kankakee or Paree

If the current line is indented using spaces or tabs, **vi** will do the intelligent thing and start inserting after the indentation. If you start with the original line and type:

ADDD<Esc>

the data you type is appended to the end of the line. The current line would now look like:

For a dime you can see Kankakee or PareeDDD

Finally, to insert below the current line, use the **o** (lowercase letter "o") command. To insert above the current line, use the **O** (uppercase "O") command. In either case, **vi** will open a brand new line for you.

HINT

To remember the difference between the **o** and **O** commands, think of the command name as being a balloon filled with helium. The larger balloon, **O**, floats higher, above the current line. The small balloon, **o**, floats lower, below the current line.

As we explained earlier, there are many commands to move the cursor. In particular, the **^** (circumflex) command moves to the beginning of the current line (after any indentation); the **$** (dollar sign) command moves to the end of the current line.

Thus, if you want to insert data at the beginning of the current line, you can type **^** followed by **i**, instead of **I**. Similarly, you can insert at the end of the line by using **$a** instead of **A**.

Here then is a wonderful illustration of the beauty of **vi**. By learning a couple of extra commands, you can often type one character (**I** or **A**) instead of two (**^i** or **$a**). If you are a beginner, this may not seem like much. But after just a few days with **vi**, you will see that anything that saves keystrokes for common operations is a real convenience. Of course, you do have to learn the extra commands. This is why we say that **vi** is easy to use, but difficult to learn.

If you are used to using a mouse with your editor, do not scoff at **vi**'s older, command-oriented design. Take some time to learn all the important **vi** commands. Once you do, you will be pleased with how easy it is to edit data without having to take your hands away from the keyboard to move a mouse or to press special keys. Moreover, you will find that using **vi**'s powerful cursor movement commands is a lot easier and a lot faster than using a mouse to click on a scroll bar.

HINT

Tools that are simple enough to use the first day are often a real pain after the first month.

As you work in input mode, remember:

- You can use the keys listed in Figure 20-1 to correct mistakes. For example, if you mistype a word, you can erase it by pressing **^W** without having to leave insert mode.

- You can enter a control character by prefacing it with **^V**; for example, to enter a backspace, type **^V^H**. On the screen it will look like the two characters **^H**, even though it is really a single character.

Making Changes to the Editing Buffer

In the last section, we looked at the commands that change to input mode so you can insert new data into the editing buffer. In this section, we will examine how to change data that is already in the editing buffer.

First, we will discuss seven **vi** commands. All but one of these replace data by changing to insert mode. Let's start with the one command that does not change to insert mode.

To replace a single character with another character, type **r** followed by the new character. For example, let's say you are a student writing one of your professors a letter explaining why you were not able to finish your term paper. You are in command mode, and the current line is as follows:

```
would mean missing The Simpsons. I gm sure you
```

You notice that the word "gm" is wrong. Move the cursor to the "g" and type:

```
ra
```

The current line now looks like:

```
would mean missing The Simpsons. I am sure you
```

Since you changed only one character, there was no need to enter insert mode.

Suppose you want to replace more than one character by overwriting. Move to where you want to start the replacement and type **R** (uppercase "R"). Now each character you type will replace one character on the current line. When you are finished, press ESC to return to command mode. Here is an example. The current line is as you left it above. You move the cursor to the **T** character in the word "The" and type:

```
RMa's funeral<Esc>
```

The current line is now:

```
would mean missing Ma's funeral. I am sure you
```

Sometimes, you will want to replace one or more characters with data that is not exactly the same size. There are a number of commands you can use. The **s** (substitute) command allows you to replace a single character with many characters. In our example, move the cursor to the **a** in "Ma" and type:

```
s
```

vi will change the **a** to a **$** and put you in insert mode. You will see:

would mean missing M$'s funeral. I am sure you

The **$** shows you which character is being replaced. Type as much as you want and press ESC when you are done. Say that you type:

other<Esc>

The current line would be:

would mean missing Mother's funeral. I am sure you

The **C** (uppercase "C") command is a variation of this type of change. It allows you to replace all the characters from the cursor to the end of the line. In our example, say that you move to the **I** and type:

C

vi will put you in insert mode and mark the last character to be replaced with a **$**. You will see:

would mean missing Mother's funeral. I am sure yo$

Now type whatever you want and press ESC. If you type:

We all hoped that<Esc>

The current line is now:

would mean missing Mother's funeral. We all hoped that

Sometimes the easiest thing to do is replace an entire line. There are two commands that will do the job: **S** or **cc**. Just move to the line you want to replace and type either of these commands. You will be in insert mode. When you press ESC, whatever you typed will replace the entire line.

Why are there two identical commands whose names look so different? If you were to look at all the **vi** commands, you would see that the names follow a pattern (most of the time). There are names with one lowercase letter, two lowercase letters, or one uppercase letter. According to this pattern, both **S** and **cc** should be the command to replace an entire line. Thus, you can use whichever one makes more sense. (If you can't see the pattern right now, don't worry about it. Wait until you learn some more commands.)

The final **vi** command to replace data is extremely useful. This command is **c** followed by one of the **vi** commands that move the cursor. Once again, you will be put into insert mode. This time, whatever you type will replace everything from the cursor up to the position indicated by the move command.

This can be a tad confusing, so here are a few examples. Say that the current line is:

would mean missing Mother's funeral. We all hoped that

The cursor is at the **M**. You want to replace the entire word "Mother" with "my dog". Type:

cw

vi will put you in insert mode and mark the last character to be replaced with a **$**. You will see:

would mean missing Mothe$'s funeral. We all hoped that

Now you type:

my dog<Esc>

The current line is now:

would mean missing my dog's funeral. We all hoped that

In other words, **cw** allows you to change one word.

You can use **c** with any of the cursor movement commands that are single characters, possibly with a repeat count. For example, if you use **c4b**, it will replace from the current position back 4 words. If you use **c(**, it replaces back to the beginning of the sentence. If you use **c}**, it replaces to the end of the paragraph. To replace 6 paragraphs, move the beginning of the first paragraph and type **c6}**.

The following summary shows the **vi** replacement commands:

r	replace exactly 1 character (does not enter input mode)
R	replace by typing over
s	replace 1 character by insertion
C	replace from cursor to end of line by insertion
cc	replace entire current line by insertion
S	replace entire current line by insertion
c*move*	replace from cursor to *move* by insertion

Replacing a Pattern

If you want to replace a particular pattern with something else, you can use the **ex** command named **:s** (substitute). To make a substitution on the current line, use:

:s/_pattern_**/**_replace_**/**

where _pattern_ is the pattern you want to replace, and _replace_ is the replacement text. For example, to replace "UNIX" with "Unix" on the current line, use:

:s/UNIX/Unix/

Using **:s** by itself will replace the first occurrence of the pattern. If you want to replace all occurrences, put **g** (global) at the end of the command. For instance, to change all occurrences of "UNIX" to "Unix" on the current line, use:

:s/UNIX/Unix/g

If you want **vi** to ask your permission before making the change, you can add **c** (confirm) to the end of the command:

:s/UNIX/Unix/c

At the bottom of the screen, **vi** will display the line that contains the pattern, point out the location of the pattern and wait for your decision. If you want to make the replacement, type **y** (for yes). Otherwise, type **n** (for no). Of course, you can combine both **c** and **g**:

:s/UNIX/Unix/cg

If you want to remove a pattern, just replace it with nothing. For example, to remove all the occurrences of "UNIX" on the current line, use:

:s/UNIX//g

For convenience, if you do not use a **c** or a **g** at the end of the command, you can omit the final **/** character. As an example, the following two commands are equivalent:

```
:s/UNIX/Unix/
:s/UNIX/Unix
```

There are two important variations of the **:s** command. First, you can specify a particular line number after the colon. **vi** will make the substitution on that line. For example, to change the first occurrence of "Unix" to "UNIX" on line 57, use:

```
:57s/UNIX/Unix/
```

Remember, as we explained earlier, you can tell **vi** to display line numbers by entering the command:

```
:set number
```

You can tell **vi** to stop displaying line numbers by entering:

```
:set nonumber
```

Instead of a single line number, you can indicate a range by separating two line numbers with a comma. For example, to make the same replacement on lines 57 through 60, use:

```
:57,60s/UNIX/Unix/
```

Most of the time, you won't use specific line numbers. However, there are two special symbols that really make this command useful: a **.** (period) stands for the current line, and a **$** (dollar sign) stands for the last line in the editing buffer. The following command replaces all occurrences of "UNIX" with "Unix", from the current line to the end of the editing buffer:

```
:.,$s/UNIX/Unix/g
```

To make the same change from the beginning of the editing buffer (line 1) to the current line, use:

```
:1,.s/UNIX/Unix/g
```

Another useful abbreviation is **%** (percent sign), which stands for all the lines in the editing buffer. Thus, to change every occurrence of "UNIX" to "Unix" on every line in the editing buffer, use:

```
:%s/UNIX/Unix/g
```

This is the same as making the substitution from line 1 to line **$** (the end of the editing buffer):

:1,$/UNIX/Unix/g

Obviously, using **%** is a lot more convenient. If you want to make such a change and have **vi** ask for confirmation before each substitution, use:

:%s/UNIX/Unix/gc

If you use such a command, and you want to stop it part way through, press **^C** (the **intr** key). The aborts the entire command, not just the current substitution.

Here is a summary of the **:s** command. To replace the first occurrence of a pattern on each line:

:s/*pattern*/*replace*/	substitute, current line
:*line***s**/*pattern*/*replace*/	substitute, specified line
:*line,line***s**/*pattern*/*replace*/	substitute, specified range
:%s/*pattern*/*replace*/	substitute, all lines

At the end of the command, you can use **c** to tell **vi** to ask for confirmation, and **g** (global) to replace all occurrences on each line. For line numbers, you can use an actual number or **.** (period) for the current line, and **$** for the last line in the editing buffer.

To finish this section, here is a particularly useful substitution. Say you want to save a copy of the manual page of a particular command. (The online manual is explained in Chapter 8.) You enter:

man vi > vipage

This command saves a copy of the **vi** manual page in the file named **vipage**. Now take a look at the file using **vi**:

vi vipage

You will probably see a lot of instances of:

_^H

For example:

_^Hv_^Hi is a display-oriented text editor based on _^He_^Hx.

Although **^H** takes up two spaces on your screen, it is really a single character. In fact—as we explained in Chapter 6—**^H** is the backspace character. So, _**^H** is just an underscore followed by a backspace. This means that when this line is printed (and the online manual is formatted for printing), each character following a _**^H** will be underlined.

This is fine for paper, but on your screen the _**^H** characters just get in the way. The best thing to do is to get rid of them all by replacing them with nothing. Here is the command:

:%s/_^H//g

Since **^H** is a control character, you can't enter it directly. You must first press **^V** and then **^H**. Of course, you do not type four separate characters: **^ V ^ H**. You type the two characters CTRL-V and CTRL-H:

:%s/_<Ctrl-V><Ctrl-H>//g

You type **^V** only to tell **vi** to take the next character literally; only the **^H** will be displayed. If you were to enter this command, our example above would become:

vi is a display-oriented text editor based on ex.

After entering this command, there may still be some **^H** characters left in the editing buffer. If so, you can get rid of them all by using:

:%s/^H//g

The reason you couldn't just use this command straight off is that it would not remove the underscores that precede **^H** characters.

Undoing or Repeating a Change

Once you start making substitutions, it becomes important to be able to undo such changes. For instance, say you wanted to change all the occurrences of the word "advertisement" to "ad". So you decide to enter:

:%s/advertisement/ad/g

However, you make a typing mistake and accidentally leave out the second "d":

:%s/advertisement/a/g

You have replaced all occurrences of "advertisement" with the letter "a". You can't just change "a" to "ad" because the letter "a" occurs all over the place. You could use the **:q!** and quit without saving your work—if you were working with an existing file—but then you would lose all your changes for that editing session.

vi has two commands for just such emergencies. They are:

u   undo last command that modified the editing buffer

U   restore current line

The **u** (lowercase "u") command will undo the last command that changed the editing buffer: an insertion, a substitution, a change or a deletion. In our example above, all you would have to do is type **u** and your substitution would be nullified.

If, after pressing **u**, you decide that you really did want the change, simply press **u** again. The **u** command can undo itself.

The **U** (uppercase "U") command will undo all the changes you made to the current line since you last moved to it. For example, let's say you move to a line and start doing a lot of editing. You make a big mess of it. Finally, you decide that all you want is for the line to be just as it was when you last moved to it. Simply type **U**. If you type the **U** command, but you don't like the results, you can undo them with a **u** command.

The **U** command will undo as many changes as necessary. Remember, though, **U** will only work as long as you stay on the line with the changes. As soon as you move to a new line, the **U** command will apply to that line.

Aside from **u**, there is another important command that involves the previous change to the editing buffer. It is the **.** (period) command:

.   repeat last command that modified the editing buffer

The **.** command will repeat the last insertion, substitution, change or deletion. Here is an example of how you might use it.

Say that you want to insert the name "Mxyzptlk" at several different places in the editing buffer. This is a difficult name to spell, and it is a bother to have to type it more than once.

Here's what to do. Move to the place where you want to make the first insertion and type:

```
iMxyzptlk<Esc>
```

Now move to the place where you want to make the next insertion and type:

```
.
```

The insertion will be repeated for you.

You can use the . command as many times as you want. Be careful, though: as soon as you make another change, even a tiny one-character deletion, the effect of the . command will change as well.

Changing the Case of Letters

It may happen that you will need to change letters from lowercase to uppercase, or from uppercase to lowercase. To do so, you can use the ~ (tilde) command:

~   change the case of a letter

Simply move to the letter you want to change and press:

~

vi will change the case of the letter and advance the cursor one position. For example, say that the current line contains:

```
"By Jove," he said, "that's a CAPITAL idea."
```

The cursor is at the "C". You press:

~

The current line will look like:

```
"By Jove," he said, "that's a cAPITAL idea."
```

The cursor is now at the "A".

Since ~ moves the cursor one position to the right, you can type ~ repeatedly to change a sequence of letters. In our example, you can change the rest of the word to lowercase by typing:

~~~~~~

(6 tildes).

If you type ~ when the cursor is at a character that is not a letter, such as a punctuation symbol, vi will advance the cursor, but will not make a change. Thus, it is safe to "tilde" your way across a vast distance. **vi** will simply skip over the non-alphabetic characters.

It would be useful if you could put a repeat count in front of this command. For example, to change the case of a 7-letter word, it would be nice to be able to type **7~**. Some versions of **vi** will allow this, but many will not. You will have to check your system to see if it works.

Controlling the Length of Lines

When you type a document, you will have to break the text into lines. One way to do this is to press RETURN at the end of each line. Pressing RETURN will insert a **newline** character and—as we explained in Chapter 6—a **newline** marks the end of a line.

Of course, as you edit, there will be times when you need to break long lines into two. For example, say that you have the following line:

This line is much too long and must be broken into two.

You want to break it after the word "and". The easiest way is to move the cursor to the space following "and" and type:

r<Return>

Using the **r** command replaces a single character with another character. In this case, the **r** command replaces the space with a **newline**, effectively breaking the line. If you need to join two lines, you can use the **J** command:

J   join lines

All you need to do is move to the first line and type **J**. **vi** will join that line and the next line into one large line.

When **vi** joins lines, it automatically inserts spaces in appropriate places. For example, **vi** will put a single space between words. If the end of the first line was the end of a sentence, **vi** will insert two spaces.

If you want to join more than one line, you can put a repeat count before the **J** command. Here is an example. Your editing buffer contains the following lines:

This sentence
is short.
This sentence is also short.

You move the cursor to the first line and type:

2J

The result is:

This sentence is short. This sentence is also short.

The **r** and **J** commands are handy when it comes to small adjustments. But when you are typing large amounts of text, it is a lot easier to let **vi** break your lines for you. To do this, use the **:set wm** command:

:set wm=n auto line break within n positions of right margin

This command affects only input mode. The command tells **vi** to break a line into two when it gets within n characters of the right margin. For example, to have **vi** break your lines automatically when they get within 6 characters of the right margin, use:

:set wm=6

The name **wm** is an abbreviation for "wrap margin". If you wish, you can spell it out (with no space):

:set wrapmargin=6

Use whatever you find easier to remember. If you want the longest possible lines, you can use:

:set wm=1

However, it is usually a good idea to leave room for small changes.

> **HINT**
> When setting the automatic margin control, leave enough room for small changes by setting **wm** to between 6 and 10.

To turn off the automatic margin control, set **wm** to **0**:

:set wm=0

If you make changes to existing text and you want to reformat it, you can use the **fmt** command as described later in this chapter.

Deleting Data from the Editing Buffer

There are several ways to delete data from the editing buffer. There are five **vi** commands:

x	delete character at cursor
X	delete character to left of cursor
D	delete from cursor to end of line
d_move_	delete from cursor to _move_
dd	delete the entire current line

and two variations of an **ex** command:

:_line_**d**	delete specified line
:_line_**,**_line_**d**	delete specified range

No matter what command you use, you can undo any deletion by using the **u** command.

The simplest delete command is **x** (lowercase "x"). It deletes the character at the current cursor position. For example, say you are a college freshman writing a letter to your parents telling them all about life at school. The current line of the editing buffer contains:

`I always go to heiQnous paWrties and avoid the library as a rule`

You notice that there is a mistake in the fifth word. You move the cursor to the "Q" and type:

`x`

The current line is now:

`I always go to heinous paWrties and avoid the library as a rule`

The **X** (uppercase "X") command also deletes a single character. The difference is that **X** deletes the character to the left of the cursor. For example, you notice that there is another mistake in the sixth word. You move to the "r" and press:

`X`

The current line is now:

I always go to heinous parties and avoid the library as a rule

The **D** (uppercase "D") command deletes from the cursor to the end of the line. For example, say that you move to the space following the word "library" and type:

D

The current line becomes:

I always go to heinous parties and avoid the library

The next **vi** deletion command is **d** (lowercase "d") followed by a cursor movement command. **vi** will delete from the cursor up to the position indicated by the move command. This is similar to the **c** (change) command we discussed earlier. Here are some examples:

dw	delete 1 word
d10w	delete 10 words
d10W	delete 10 words (ignore punctuation)
db	delete backward, 1 word
d2)	delete 2 sentences
d5}	delete 5 paragraphs

HINT
Two of the most useful **d** commands are:

dG	delete from current line to end of editing buffer
d1G	delete from current line to beginning of editing buffer

To continue our example, say that you move to the beginning of the word "heinous" and type:

d4w

The current line becomes:

I always go to the library

The final **vi** deletion command is **dd**. This deletes the entire current line. If you want to delete more than one line, you can put a repeat count in front of the command. For example, to delete 10 lines, use:

```
10dd
```

There will be times when it is more convenient to delete using line numbers. At such times, you can use the **ex** command **:d**. Remember, as we explained earlier, you can tell **vi** to display line numbers by entering the command:

```
:set number
```

You can tell **vi** to stop displaying line numbers by entering:

```
:set nonumber
```

To use the **:d** command, you can specify either a single line number or a range (two numbers separated by a comma). For example, to delete line 50, use:

```
:50d
```

To delete lines 50 through 60, use:

```
:50,60d
```

As with the other **ex** commands, the symbol **.** (period) stands for the current line and **$** (dollar sign) stands for the last line in the editing buffer. For example, to delete from the beginning of the editing buffer to the current line, use:

```
:1,.d
```

To delete from the current line to the end of the editing buffer, use:

```
:.,$d
```

To delete the entire editing buffer, use either of the following commands:

```
:1,$d
:%d
```

(Remember, as we explained earlier, **%** stands for all the lines in the editing buffer.)

Copying the Last Deletion

At all times, **vi** keeps a copy of the last thing you deleted. You can copy this deletion to any place in the editing buffer by using the **p** and **P** (put) commands.

The **p** (lowercase "p") command inserts the last deletion after the current position of the cursor. For example, say that the current line contains:

`This good is a sentence.`

You move to the "g" and delete one word by typing:

`dw`

The current line now looks like:

`This is a sentence.`

Now you move to the space between "a" and "sentence", and type:

`p` *(the lowercase "p")*

The deleted word is inserted to the right of the cursor. The current line is now:

`This is a good sentence.`

Here is an example that uses the **P** command. Say that the current line contains:

`This is right now.`

You move to the space before the word "right" and type:

`de`

This erases up to the end of the word and leaves you with:

`This is now.`

Now move to the period and type the uppercase **P**:

`P`

The deletion is inserted to the left of the cursor. The current line becomes:

This is now right.

Consider now the combination **xp**. The **x** command deletes the character at the current cursor position. The **p** command inserts the deletion to the right of the cursor. The net result is to transpose two characters. For example, say that the current line is:

I ma never mixed up.

You move to the first "m" and type:

xp

The current line is now:

I am never mixed up.

Another important combination is **deep**. Here is an example. Say that the current line contains:

I am mixed never up.

Move to the space before the word "mixed". (Take care to move to the space before the word, not to the first letter of the word.) Now type:

deep

The **de** deletes the space and the following word, after which the current line looks like:

I am never up.

The **e** moves forward to the end of the next word. The **p** inserts the deletion after the cursor. The net result is:

I am never mixed up.

Thus, the effect of **deep** is to transpose two words.

When you delete whole lines, **p** and **P** will insert whole lines. **p** will insert below the current line; **P** will insert above the current line.

Consider, then, what happens when you type **ddp**. The **dd** command deletes the current line. The next line becomes the new current line. The **p** inserts the deletion below the new current line. The net result is to transpose two lines.

HINT

Remember the following **vi** command combinations:

xp	transpose two characters
deep	transpose two words (start cursor to left of first word)
ddp	transpose two lines

To summarize:

p	copy last deletion; insert after/below cursor
P	copy last deletion; insert before/above cursor

As we explained earlier, using a repeat count in front of the **dd** command will delete multiple lines. One way to move lines is to use **dd** to delete them, and then use **p** or **P** to insert the lines in their new location. For instance, say that you want to move 10 lines. Position the cursor on the first line and type:

`10dd`

This deletes the 10 lines. Now position the cursor at the line below which you want to make the insertion. Type:

`p`

The 10 deleted lines will be inserted. You can even move to another part of the editing buffer and use the **p** command to insert the same lines once again.

Copying and Moving Lines

There will be times when it is convenient to copy or move lines while referring to them by number. For these operations, you can use the **ex** commands **:co** (copy) and **:m** (move).

Remember, as we explained earlier, you can tell **vi** to display line numbers by entering the command:

`:set number`

You can tell **vi** to stop displaying line numbers by entering:

`:set nonumber`

The **:co** and **:m** commands use the same format. The only difference is that **:m** deletes the original lines while **:co** makes a copy.

    To use these commands, you specify a single line number, or a range of line numbers, before the command name. After the command name, you specify the target line number. The new lines will be inserted below the target line. Here are some examples:

`:5co10`	copy line 5, insert below line 10
`:4,8co20`	copy lines 4 through 8, insert below line 20
`:5m10`	move line 5, insert below line 10
`:4,8m20`	move lines 4 through 8, insert below line 20

As with other **ex** commands, you can use a **.** (period) to refer to the current line and a **$** (dollar sign) to refer to the last line in the editing buffer. For example:

`:1,.m$`	move lines 1 through current line, to bottom

You can also use line 0 (zero) to refer to the beginning of the editing buffer:

`:.,$m0`	move current line through last line, to top

These last two commands are interesting. They both swap the top and bottom parts of the editing buffer. However, there is a subtle difference. With the first command, the current line ends up at the bottom of the editing buffer. With the second command, the current line ends up on top.

    To summarize, the **ex** copy and move commands are:

`:line co`*target*	copy specified line; insert below target
`:line,line co`*target*	copy specified range; insert below target
`:line m`*target*	move specified line; insert below target
`:line,line m`*target*	move specified range; insert below target

Entering Shell Commands

There are several ways to enter regular shell commands from within **vi**. First, you can issue a command by typing **:!** followed by the command. **vi** will send the command to the shell to be executed. For example, to display the time and date, enter:

:!date

After the command is finished, **vi** will display:

[Hit return to continue]

Press RETURN and you will be back in **vi**.

To repeat the most recent shell command—regardless of long it has been since you entered it—use:

:!!

For example, if the last shell command you entered was **date**, you can display the time and date once again by using **:!!**.

If you would like to enter a number of shell commands, you can start a new shell. There are two ways to do this. First, you can use the **:sh** command:

:sh

This will pause **vi** and start a new copy of whatever shell you use. You can now enter as many commands as you want. When you are finished with the shell, stop it—by pressing **^D** or by entering the **exit** command—and you will be returned to **vi**.

If, for some reason, this doesn't work on your system, you can run a new copy of the shell as an actual command. For example, to start a new C-Shell, run the **csh** program:

:!csh

To start a new Korn shell, use:

:!ksh

(The names of the various shells are discussed in Chapter 10.) When you end the shell, you will be returned to **vi**.

HINT

When you start a shell by using the **:!** command, you can specify any shell you want. For example, if you normally use a C-Shell, the **:sh** command will start a C-Shell. If, for some reason, you would like a Korn shell just this once, you can start one by using the **:!ksh** command.

Here is a summary:

:!command	pause **vi**, execute specified shell command
:!!	pause **vi**, execute previous shell command
:sh	pause **vi**, start a shell
:!csh	pause **vi**, start a new C-Shell
:!ksh	pause **vi**, start a new Korn shell

If you want to insert the output of a shell command directly into the editing buffer, you can use the **:r !** command, described in the next section.

Reading Data into the Editing Buffer

To read data from an existing file into the editing buffer, use the **:r** command. Here is an example:

```
:10r info
```

Before the command name, you specify the line number where you want to insert the new data. **vi** will insert the data *after* the specified line. After the command name, leave a space and specify the name of the input file. Our example inserts the contents of the file **info** into the editing buffer after line 10.

If you want to refer to the beginning of the editing buffer, use line 0 (zero). For example, to insert the contents of **info** at the beginning of the editing buffer, use:

```
:0r info
```

To refer to the end of the editing buffer, use **$**:

```
:$r info
```

If you omit the line number, **vi** will insert after the current line. This is probably the most useful form of the **:r** command. For example, to insert the contents of the file **info** into the editing buffer, move to where you want the data and enter:

```
:r info
```

There is a variation of the **:r** command that is especially useful. If, instead of a file name, you type an **!** (exclamation mark) followed by a regular shell command, **vi** will execute that command and insert its output into the editing buffer. Here is an example. In Chapter 23, you will learn how the **ls** command displays a list of your files. If you are editing and you want to insert such a list after the current line, enter:

```
:r !ls
```

If you want to insert the time and date at the end of the editing buffer, use:

```
:$r !date
```

Here is a wonderful time-saving idea. In Chapter 17, we showed you how to use the **look** command to help you find out how to spell a word. For example, say that you want to use the word "simultaneous", but you are not sure how to spell it. You can use the command:

```
look simu
```

In this case, the output is:

```
simulate
simulcast
simultaneity
simultaneous
```

When you are using **vi**, you can use **:r** to insert the output of such a command directly into the editing buffer. Press ESC to change to command mode and enter:

```
:r !look simu
```

The output of the **look** command will be inserted after the current line (the line you were last typing). Now delete all but the word you want. (If you don't want any of the words, use the **u** command to undo the change.) Once you have deleted all but the correct word, move up to the last line you typed and type:

```
J
```

This will join the new word onto the end of the line. Finally, to return to insert mode at the end of the line, type:

A

(Remember, the **A** command allows you to append data to the end of the current line.) This sequence of commands may seem a bit complex, but it is actually quite simple. Try it. It's way cool.

Here is a summary of the **:r** command:

:_line_**r** _file_	insert contents of _file_ after specified _line_
:r _file_	insert contents of _file_ after current line
:_line_**r** **!**_command_	insert output of _command_ after specified _line_
:r **!**_command_	insert output of _command_ after current line

HINT

If you don't like the result of a **:r** or **:r !** command, you can reverse it with the **u** (undo) command.

Using a Shell Command to Process Data

Using the **!** and **!!** (exclamation mark) commands, you can send lines from the editing buffer to a regular shell command. The output of the command will replace the original lines. For example, you can replace some lines with the same data in sorted order.

To do this, move to the line where you want to start. Type the number of lines you want to process, followed by **!!**, followed by the shell command, followed by RETURN.

For example, say you have five lines that contain the following data:

```
entertain
balloon
anaconda
dairy
coin
```

Move to the first line and enter:

```
5!!sort
```

(The **sort** command is discussed in Chapter 17.)

Once you type the second !, **vi** will move the cursor to the command line and display an !. You can now type your shell command directly on the command line. If necessary, you can back up and make corrections before you press RETURN. In our example, the original 5 lines will be replaced by:

```
anaconda
balloon
coin
dairy
entertain
```

HINT

If you use ! or !! to process data in the editing buffer with a shell command and you don't like the results, you can undo the change by using the **u** command.

Here is another example that is especially useful. In Chapter 15, we described the **fmt** (format) command. This command reads its input and, using the same text, generates lines that are as close as possible to 72 characters long. **fmt** will preserve spaces at the beginning of lines, spaces between words and blank lines. In other words, **fmt** will make your message look nice without changing the paragraph breaks.

fmt is useful for formatting all or part of your editing buffer when you are creating documents. If you use **fmt**, you don't have to worry so much about line breaks as you are entering and editing your data. The following command will format 10 lines, starting from the current line:

```
10!!fmt
```

The ! command works much the same as the !! command, except that you have more flexibility in specifying the range of input lines. Type ! followed by a command that moves the cursor, followed by the shell command. For example:

```
!}fmt
```

This command sends all the data from the current line, up to and including the line specified by the cursor move, to be processed by the **fmt** command. In this example, we will process all the lines to the end of the paragraph (because the } command moves to the end of the paragraph).

Once you type the !, **vi** will move to the command line and display !, just as with the !! command.

Here is an easy way to format the entire editing buffer. Move to the first line of the editing buffer by typing:

1G

Then enter:

!Gfmt

(Remember, the **G** command moves to the end of the editing buffer.) Similarly, you could sort the entire editing buffer by using:

!Gsort

To summarize:

n!!*command*	execute *command* on *n* lines
!*move command*	execute *command* from cursor to *move*

Writing Data to a File

When you stop **vi** using the **ZZ** command, it automatically saves your data. However, there are several commands you can use to write data to a file whenever you want.

:w	write data to original file
:w *file*	write data to specified *file*
:w>> *file*	append data to specified *file*

The **:w** command will write the contents of the editing buffer back to the original file. For example, say that you started **vi** by entering the command:

vi memo

The contents of the file **memo** are copied to the editing buffer. No matter how many changes you make to the editing buffer, the original file, **memo**, is not changed. This arrangement is important as it allows you to quit without changing your file (by using the **:q!** command). However, at any time, you can enter:

:w

This will copy the editing buffer back to the file. Normally, you don't need to do this unless you are going to use the **:e** command to start editing a new file (see below). However, if you have made a lot of changes, you might want to take a moment and save them back to the original file. This will protect you against losing your work if something goes wrong.

If you specify the name of a file after the **:w** command, **vi** will write the data to that file. For example, to save the contents of the editing buffer to a file named **extra**, enter:

:w extra

If the file does not already exist, **vi** will create it. If the file does exist, **vi** will replace its contents.

Remember this: If you use **:w** to write to a file that exists, the old contents will be lost. If you want to append the new data to the end of an existing file, type **>>** (two greater-than signs) after the command name. For example:

:w>> memo

Using **>>** will preserve the old data. (Note: The **>>** notation is also used to redirect the standard output of a command to an existing file. See Chapter 16.)

If you want to write only certain lines of the editing buffer, you can specify them in the usual manner. For example, to write line 10 to a file named **save**, enter:

:10w save

To append lines 10 through 20 to a file named **save**, use:

:10,20w>> save

Changing the File You Are Editing

When you start **vi**, you usually specify the name of the file you want to edit. For example, to edit a file named **memo**, you enter:

vi memo

If you are within **vi** and you decide you want to edit a different file, you do not have to quit and restart the program. Instead, you can use the **:e** and **:e!** commands:

:e *file*	edit the specified *file*
:e! *file*	edit the specified *file*, omit automatic check

To change to a new file, use the **:e** command, followed by the name of the file. For example, to begin editing a file named **document**, enter:

:e document

When you start editing a new file, the old contents of the editing buffer are lost. Thus, make sure to use the **:w** command first and save your data. When you use the **:e** command, **vi** will check to see if you have saved your data. If there is unsaved data, **vi** will not let you change to a new file. If you would like to override this protection, use the **:e!** command. For example, say that you start **vi** using the command:

vi memo

The contents of **memo** are copied to the editing buffer. As it happens, you make so many mistakes that you would rather just start over. The last thing you want to do is save the contents of the editing buffer back to the original file. Enter:

:e! memo

You are now editing a copy of the original file. The previous changes have been thrown away.

Using Abbreviations

By using the **:ab** command, you can create abbreviations for frequently used words or expressions. For example, say you are working on a résumé for a summer job. You would find it tiresome to type "exceptionally gifted" over and over. Instead, you can establish an abbreviation of, say, "eg".

Type **:ab**, followed by the short form, followed by the long form. For example,

:ab eg exceptionally gifted

From now on, whenever you type **eg** as a separate word (in input mode), **vi** will automatically replace it with **exceptionally gifted**. **vi** is smart enough not to replace **eg** within a word, such as "eggplant".

If you want to see a list of all the current abbreviations, enter the command name by itself:

:ab

If you want to remove an abbreviation, use the **:una** (un-abbreviate) command. Type **:una** followed by the name of the short form you wish to remove. For example:

:una eg

To summarize:

:ab *short long*	set *short* as an abbreviation for *long*
:ab	display current abbreviations
:una *short*	cancel abbreviation *short*

■ Using the **.exrc** File to Initialize **vi**

When **vi** starts, it looks for a file named **.exrc** in your home directory. If such a file exists, **vi** will read and execute any **ex** commands that it finds. This allows you to initialize your working environment automatically. The name **.exrc** stands for "**ex** run commands".

(We discuss the home directory in Chapter 23. We discuss the idea of initialization files in Chapter 11 for the C-Shell, and Chapter 12 for the Korn Shell.)

A **.exrc** file is a great place to put **:set** and **:ab** commands that you use all the time. You can also put in regular shell commands by using the **:!** command.

Before we continue, we want to take a moment to describe one more **ex** command — **:map** — that is especially useful within a **.exrc** file.

You use the **:map** command to define what is called a MACRO: a one-character abbreviation for a command. Macros are not used all that often, and we won't go into the details. However, there is one particular macro that is handy and should always be defined. It lets you use the letter **g** as a synonym for **1G**. The command to create this macro is:

:map g 1G

Once you define this macro, you can move to the beginning of the editing buffer by typing **g** (lowercase "g"), and to the end of the editing buffer by typing **G** (uppercase "G"). (Of course, you must be in command mode.)

Now, to continue, **vi** will ignore any lines within the **.exrc** file that begin with **"** (a double quote). You can use such lines to hold descriptive comments. In addition, **vi** will ignore space and tab characters at the beginning of a command.

This allows you to indent commands to make them easier to read. Finally, within an `.exrc` file, you do not need to start any of the commands with a colon.

Here is a sample `.exrc` file:

```
" set the options
    set showmode
    set wrapmargin=6
" set abbreviations
    ab eg exceptionally gifted
" define the g macro
    map g 1G
" display the time and date and pause for 2 seconds
    !date; sleep 2
```

(Note: The **sleep** command tells Unix to pause for the specified number of seconds.)

If your `.exrc` file contains a bad command, **vi** will quit executing the file at that command. Although **vi** will start properly, the rest of the commands in the `.exrc` file will not be processed. **vi** will usually display some type of error message, but it will probably go by so fast that you will have trouble reading it. Make sure you test each command carefully before you place it in your `.exrc` file.

CHAPTER 21

The emacs Editor

An EDITOR, or TEXT EDITOR, is a program you use to create and modify files of data. TEXT is data that consists of letters, numbers, punctuation and so on.

Unix has two main editors: **vi** and **emacs**. The **vi** editor is a standard part of every Unix system. However, **emacs** is a popular alternative you will find on many systems. As a Unix user, it is important that you learn how to use *some* editor, even if you don't want to create documents or programs.

For example, if you want to mail someone a message, you can type it directly, line by line. (This is all explained in Chapter 15.) But without an editor, there is no way to make changes in the message. Moreover, you cannot prepare a message in advance.

Similarly, if you participate in Usenet (the worldwide system of discussion groups), you may want to post an article of your own. Unless you can use an editor, you will have no way to create the article. In fact, any time you need to manipulate textual data directly, you need an editor.

In this chapter, we will explain the basics of using **emacs**. Although we will not be able to explain everything—that would take several books—we will show you most of what you need to know for straightforward day-to-day work.

HINT

If you use a non-Unix computer to access Unix—say, a Macintosh or a PC—you might think you don't need to learn how to use a Unix editor because you can do all your editing on your own computer. For example, say that you want to mail a message to a friend. You could use your own computer to create the message, copy it to the Unix computer, and then mail it to your friend.

Although this is possible, it is a lot more trouble than it is worth. Just believe us, no matter how you access a Unix computer, it is much easier to use **vi** or **emacs** and work directly with Unix. Depending on your Mac or PC for all your editing is like depending on your mother to do your laundry for you. It will work—after a fashion—but it is unlikely to impress anyone over the age of sixteen.

What Is emacs?

We have introduced **emacs** as a text editor, but it is a lot more: **emacs** is nothing less than a total environment in which you can spend all your time in the Unix universe. From within **emacs**, you can not only create and modify text files, you can play games, send and receive mail, participate in Usenet discussion groups, manipulate files and directories, and develop computer programs. In other words, you can spend your whole life within **emacs** doing just about everything modern man needs to be happy (including sending out for pizza over the Internet).

Moreover, all **emacs** systems come with full source code—that is, the actual programs that make up **emacs** itself—and if you are willing to learn how to use the computer language in which **emacs** is written (called Lisp), you can customize your **emacs** environment up the wazoo.

HINT

For many people, **emacs** is a way of life, like religion or football.

In this chapter, we will discuss **emacs** as you would use it under Unix. However, **emacs** has been implemented on a number of computing platforms and, even within the Unix world, there are variations. In particular, we will describe the most popular version of **emacs**—GNU **emacs**—that is distributed by the Free

Software Foundation. Still, what we will be covering here are basic principles and, as such, will be applicable with just about any type of **emacs** you may encounter.

Our goal is to show you how to use **emacs** as a text editor. If you want to learn how to use **emacs** for more esoteric purposes, you can start by reading the official documentation. You may also want to get yourself one or more **emacs** books. As we said, there is a lot to learn.

> ### HINT
>
> If you want to master **emacs**, it helps to believe in reincarnation, because there is no way you are going to learn it all in a single lifetime.

Where Did emacs Come From?

Many people believe that **emacs** is of divine origin, but that is only partially correct.

The first **emacs** was developed by Richard Stallman at MIT in 1975. At the time, Stallman was working in the MIT Artificial Intelligence Lab on a system called ITS (the Incompatible Time-sharing System) using a PDP-10 computer. One of the programs in wide use at the time was a text editor named TECO. TECO was used by many people, but was complex and difficult to use, driving even experienced programmers to the point of dementia.

Stallman developed a set of macros whose purpose was to make TECO easier to use. (In this sense, a macro is a tool that lets you specify something complex by using a relatively simple abbreviation.) The macros Stallman developed were, collectively, referred to as Emacs (the name is explained below).

Since then, **emacs** has been rewritten as separate program—multiple times—and greatly improved. It is available in a number of versions, the most popular being GNU **emacs**, a product of the Free Software Foundation (FSF). This is the version of **emacs** you are most likely to encounter on a Unix system.

HISTORICAL NOTE: The Elder Days
The Golden Age of Hackerdom—the pre-1980 era of the PDP-10, TECO, Lisp and ITS—is sometimes referred to as the ELDER DAYS, a term taken from J.R.R. Tolkien's *Lord of the Rings*. The elder days also saw the development of the Arpanet—the ancestor of the Internet—as well as Unix itself, although, strictly speaking, neither Unix nor the Arpanet were hacks.

The foci of Lisp hacking in the elder days were the MIT AI Lab; the Stanford AI Lab (SAIL); Bolt, Beranek and Newman (BBN); Carnegie-Mellon University (CMU); and Worcester Polytechnic Institute (WPI).

What's in a Name?   *TECO*, `emacs`

As we mentioned, the original **emacs** was a set of editing macros written to run under the TECO editor. Originally, the name TECO stood for "Tape Editor and Corrector". Later, the name was changed to "Text Editor and Corrector".

The name **emacs** is a simple abbreviation for "editing macros".

What's in a Name?   *GNU, Lisp*

GNU is the name Richard Stallman chose to describe the Free Software Foundation's project to develop Unix-like tools and programs. The name itself is an acronym meaning "GNU's Not Unix" and is pronounced "ga-new".

Notice that, within the expression "GNU's Not Unix", the word GNU can be expanded indefinitely:

```
GNU
(GNU's Not Unix)
((GNU's Not Unix) Not Unix)
(((GNU's Not Unix) Not Unix) Not Unix)
((((GNU's Not Unix) Not Unix) Not Unix) Not Unix)
```

and so on. Thus, GNU is actually a recursive acronym.

When you expand the word GNU in this way, you create the type of structure you would use if you were programming with Lisp, a computer language popular among artificial intelligence people. Stallman used Lisp when he worked in the MIT AI Lab, and, in fact, **emacs** itself is written in Lisp and comes with an entire Lisp programming environment.

The name Lisp stands for "List Processing language".

The Free Software Foundation, or FSF, was founded by Stallman in 1985. The philosophy of the FSF is that high-quality software should be freely available without the usual commercial restrictions. Towards this end, Stallman wrote a manifesto in which he set forth his philosophy that software should be shared. Stallman's idea is not so much that software should always be completely free and unrestricted. Rather, he believes that programmers like to share their work and, when they do, everyone benefits.

Stallman's initial goal was an ambitious one: to create an entire Unix-like operating system—including all the programs and tools—that would be freely distributed along with the source code.

Excerpts from the GNU Manifesto

As we mentioned, Richard Stallman wrote a manifesto whose philosophy forms the foundation of the Free Software Foundation. His basic idea—that *all* software should be shared freely—is, at best, naive. However, with the rise of the Internet, the development and distribution of free software has become an important economic and social force in our world. There are literally tens of thousands of programs available for free, and their contribution to the world at large (and to the happiness of their programmers) is beyond measure.

The FSF has been one of the leaders in this area, not only with **emacs**, but with a C compiler (**gcc**), a C++ compiler (**g++**), a powerful debugger (**gdb**), a Unix shell (**bash**), and many, many other tools. All of this software—which is part of the GNU project—is used around the world and is considered to be of the highest quality.

Stallman's public declaration was not as sophisticated as other well-known manifestos, such as "95 Theses" (Martin Luther, 1517), or "The Playboy Philosophy" (Hugh Hefner, 1962-1966). Still, the work of the Free Software Foundation continues to make important contributions to our culture and, for this reason, you may be interested in reading a few excerpts from Stallman's 1985 essay. (If you want to read the entire essay, you can do so—within some versions of GNU **emacs**—by using the command CTRL-H CTRL-P.)

Here, then, are a few passages from the original GNU Manifesto. Note that when Stallman says software should be free, he does *not* mean that anyone—including for-profit corporations—should be able to use any program for no money. He means that no one should have to pay for *permission* to use a program, although there may be a charge for distribution or support.

Excerpts from the GNU Manifesto

"I consider that the Golden Rule requires that if I like a program I must share it with other people who like it. Software sellers want to divide the users and conquer them, making each user agree not to share with others. I refuse to break solidarity with other users in this way. I cannot in good conscience sign a nondisclosure agreement or a software license agreement. For years I worked within the Artificial Intelligence Lab to resist such tendencies and other inhospitalities, but eventually they had gone too far: I could not remain in an institution where such things are done for me against my will.

"So that I can continue to use computers without dishonor, I have decided to put together a sufficient body of free software so that I will be able to get along without any software that is not free. I have resigned from the AI lab to deny MIT any legal excuse to prevent me from giving GNU away...

"Many programmers are unhappy about the commercialization of system software. It may enable them to make more money, but it requires them to feel in conflict with other programmers in general rather than feel as comrades. The fundamental act of friendship among programmers is the sharing of programs; marketing arrangements now typically used essentially forbid programmers to treat others as friends. The purchaser of software must choose between friendship and obeying the law. Naturally, many decide that friendship is more important. But those who believe in law often do not feel at ease with either choice. They become cynical and think that programming is just a way of making money...

"Copying all or parts of a program is as natural to a programmer as breathing, and as productive. It ought to be as free...

"In the long run, making programs free is a step toward the post-scarcity world, where nobody will have to work very hard just to make a living. People will be free to devote themselves to activities that are fun, such as programming, after spending the necessary ten hours a week on required tasks such as legislation, family counseling, robot repair and asteroid prospecting. There will be no need to be able to make a living from programming..."

A Strategy for Learning emacs

With most text editors, the way to start is to learn some of the basic keystrokes — how to move the cursor, how to page up and down, how to search for a pattern, and so on—and practice, practice, practice.

With **emacs** you need a different strategy. **emacs** is wonderful in that it is a full-fledged working environment. However, it is this very same exhaustive complexity that makes **emacs** difficult to learn. So here then are some helpful guidelines. First, what *not* to do:

1. Do not jump in and start by learning the basic keystrokes. Keystrokes are easy to learn. To understand **emacs**, you must first have the proper background.

2. As you will see later, **emacs** comes with a built-in tutorial. Do not begin by starting **emacs** and firing up the tutorial. All that will happen is you will become confused and discouraged. (At least, that's what happened to us.)

So what should you do?

3. Read each section of this chapter in order. We will start by teaching you all the basic concepts (and there are a lot of them). At the proper time, we will show you how to use the fundamental keystrokes, and then you can practice, practice, practice. At the end of the chapter, we will show you how to run the **emacs** tutorial, and you can use it as a post-graduate course.

HINT

If you are learning **emacs** and you become temporarily discouraged, take a break and try a little **vi**. **vi** will seem so complex and impossible, you will feel a lot better about using **emacs**.

The **CTRL** Key

emacs has a lot of key combinations, far more than you will ever memorize. Later in the chapter, we will explain why there are so many combinations. First, though, you need to understand how **emacs** uses the keyboard.

Like all text editors, **emacs** uses all the regular keys (letters of the alphabet, numbers, punctuation, and so on). However, **emacs** also uses two special keys: CTRL and META.

The CTRL key is used in the usual way. You hold it down as you press another key. For example, the command CTRL-H starts the built-in help facility: hold down the CTRL key and press **h**. No surprise here.

What will be new to you is that many **emacs** commands consist of more than one CTRL combination in a row, or a CTRL combination followed by a single letter. Here are two examples:

■ To quit **emacs**, you use CTRL-X CTRL-C. That is, press CTRL-X and then press CTRL-C.

■ To start the built-in tutorial, you use CTRL-H **t**. That is, you press CTRL-H and then press the letter **t**.

In order to make the description of such key combinations readable, **emacs** uses its own notation. As you know, the Unix convention for describing CTRL keys is to use a **^** (circumflex) character to represent the CTRL key. For example, **^X** means CTRL-X. Part of the convention is that, when we describe a CTRL key, we write the letter of the alphabet in uppercase. For instance, we write **^X**, not **^x**. We do this because it is easier to read. (You don't actually press the SHIFT key when you type the **x**).

In **emacs**, the CTRL key is represented by the letter "C", and letters are written in lowercase. For example, instead of writing CTRL-X or **^X**, an **emacs** person would write **C-x**. Similarly, the combination CTRL-X CTRL-C is written as **C-x C-c**; and CTRL-H followed by the letter **t** is written as **C-h t**. It is important that you recognize this notation because that is what you will see when you read the **emacs** documentation. To help you get used to these conventions, we will use them consistently throughout this chapter.

The **META** Key

In addition to CTRL, **emacs** uses another special key, called the META key. You use it the same way you use the CTRL and SHIFT keys. That is, you hold it down while you press another key.

For example, to type a capital "A", you would hold down the SHIFT key and press the "A" key. To type CTRL-A, you would hold down the CTRL key and press the "A" key. And, to use META-A, you hold down the META key and press the "A" key.

The **emacs** notation used to indicate a META key combination is similar to what we use with CTRL keys, except that we use an "M" instead of a "C". For instance, to indicate the combination META-A, we would write **M-a**.

Here is an example. When you are editing a file, the command to move down one screenful is **C-v**, while the command to move up one screenful is **M-v**.

Thus, we have four possible ways to use each letter of the alphabet. The letter "a", for example, can be used as a lowercase letter (**a**), an uppercase letter (SHIFT-**a**), a CTRL combination (**C-a**) or a META combination (**M-a**).

By now, you are probably saying: What META key? Ain't no stinkin' META key on my keyboard. Indeed, most keyboards do *not* have such a key. The META key is a legacy from the elder days of hackerdom (described earlier in this chapter), when there actually were keyboards that had this key.

Your keyboard will have some key that acts as a META key and, before you start learning **emacs**, it is up to you to figure out which key it is. (Clearly, **emacs** is not for weenies.)

Here are a few hints. On many keyboards, there are small identical keys to the left and right of the SPACE bar. Try these keys first. If you are running **emacs** on a Sun computer, these will be the keys with the small diamond on them. If you are running **emacs** on an IBM-compatible PC, try the ALT keys. And if you are running **emacs** on a Macintosh, try the COMMAND keys (the ones with the cloverleaf design) or the OPTION keys.

On virtually all systems, you can use the ESCAPE (or ESC) key as a META key. However, when you use ESCAPE, you do not hold it down. You press it, let go, and then press the second key.

For example, say that you are running **emacs** on a Sun computer and you want to use the **M-f** (META-F) command. You can either (1) hold down the diamond key and press **f**, or (2) press ESCAPE, let it go, and then press **f**.

This may sound confusing when you read it, but in practice it is easy. Either find your META key (if there is one for your system) or use ESCAPE. If you want to practice, start **emacs** (we will tell you how in the next section) and type a sentence or two. You can now use **M-f** to move the cursor forward one word at a time, and **M-b** to move backward one word at a time.

HINT

If you are an X Window user, you can use the **xmodmap** utility to define the META key to be anything you want. A good choice is whichever key happens to be just next to your SPACE bar.

One final point: when you are looking for your META key, remember that the hints we gave apply to the computer on which the **emacs** program is running. This may not be the same as the computer whose keyboard you are using.

For instance, say that you are using a PC to connect to a remote Unix host over a telephone line. As we described in Chapter 3, your PC runs a communications program that emulates a terminal. When you use **emacs** under these conditions, it is running on the remote computer, not on your PC. In such a case, the ALT key on your PC will not serve as a META key. (This is because ALT key combinations are not recognized by the terminal emulator and are not sent to the remote computer.) Instead, you can use the ESCAPE key, which always works.

However, if you are running **emacs** on your own personal PC, you will be able to use the full keyboard, and chances are that the ALT key will work just fine.

HINT

If you have read any of the Don Juan books by Carlos Castaneda, you may remember Don Juan's instruction to his beginning student to "find your spot".

Well, as a beginning **emacs** student, it is incumbent upon you to find your META key. If you can't, you should not be using **emacs**. We mentioned earlier that **emacs** is not for weenies, but the reality of it is much more profound. Learning **emacs** will make permanent, irreversible changes to your brain cells. If the possibility of modifying your nervous system in this way bothers you, this is a good time to switch to Chapter 20 and learn **vi** instead.

HINT FOR NERDS

The plain vanilla ASCII code uses only 7 bits and, thus, defines characters from 0 to 127. The original purpose of the META key was to turn on the top (8th) bit to allow you to use characters 128 through 255.

The tradition of using a special key to modify the top bits of a character started with the keyboard developed for special-purpose Lisp computers at SAIL (the Stanford Artificial Intelligence Lab) in the 1980s. On these keyboards, there were two extra keys called CONTROL and META. A later keyboard, designed at MIT's AI (Artificial Intelligence) Lab, extended this idea. This device, known as the Knight keyboard, was used on the legendary MIT Lisp Machines and heavily influenced Richard Stallman when he designed **emacs**.

The Knight keyboard had seven extra keys. Three of these—SHIFT, TOP and FRONT—were like regular shift keys. The four other keys—CONTROL, META, HYPER and SUPER—modified the bits of the actual character. In all, you could use a Knight keyboard to type over 8,000 different characters. This phenomenon gave rise to the **emacs** (and general hacker) philosophy that it is worthwhile to memorize the meanings of a great many strange key combinations, if it will reduce typing time.

The extra bits modified by these special keys are known as "Bucky bits". They are named after Niklaus Worth (the inventor of the Pascal programming language) whose nickname is Bucky. When Worth was at Stanford, he suggested adding an extra key (called EDIT) to set the 8th bit of the otherwise 7-bit ASCII character set.

One last point: the Knight keyboard was named after Tom Knight, one of the Lisp Machine's principal designers. However, the name also has more metaphysical connotations in that it recalls a semi-mythical organization of Lisp hackers called the Knights of the Lambda Calculus. (The Lambda Calculus is the mathematical theory upon which Lisp is based.)

Special Key Names

Within **emacs**, there are a few names that are used for special keys. These are shown in Figure 21-1.

We have already met the CTRL and META keys. The only thing you need to remember is that **C-** stands for "hold down the CTRL key", and **M-** stands for "hold down the META key". If you can't find a META key on your keyboard, you can press ESCAPE instead. For example, **M-x** means hold down META and press **x**. Instead, you could press ESCAPE, let it go, and then press **x**.

You will occasionally see key combinations that use both CTRL and META. For example, one such command is META-CTRL-S.

You will see these double key combinations written in three different ways, but they all mean the same thing: hold down both the CTRL and META keys at the same time, and press a third key. For example, if you see any of the following:

```
C-M-s
M-C-s
ESC C-s
```

it means hold down CTRL and META, and press the **s** key.

If you use the ESCAPE key instead of a META key, simply press ESCAPE, let it go, and then press the CTRL combination. For example, ESCAPE CTRL-S.

The other keys are straightforward. If you have any questions, you should take a look at Chapter 6, where we discuss how the various keys are used with Unix and what variations you might expect to find on your keyboard.

Name	Actual Key
C-	CTRL
M-	META
DEL	DELETE
ESC	ESCAPE
LFD	LINEFEED (CTRL-J)
RET	RETURN
SPC	SPACE
TAB	TAB

FIGURE 21-1.   **emacs**: *Names for special keys*

However, there is one comment we would like to make right now. As an **emacs** user, the **DEL** key will be especially important to you because, as you type, you use **DEL** (not BACKSPACE) to correct a mistake. Thus, make sure you know which key this is on your particular keyboard.

If you have any problems, read the discussion about the DELETE key in Chapter 6. You need to find the key that sends the **del** code. On most keyboards, this key is labeled DELETE or DEL. The old name for this key was RUBOUT, so if you encounter that name, you will know it refers to **DEL**.

How to Start the **emacs** Editor:
emacs, gmacs, gnuemacs, gnumacs

To start **emacs**, you enter the **emacs** command. The basic syntax is:

emacs [*file...*]

where *file* is the name of a file you want to edit. (The **emacs** command does have some options, but you probably won't need them, so we won't mention them here.) The recommended way to start **emacs** is to simply enter the command by itself:

emacs

Once **emacs** starts, you can either create a brand new file or tell **emacs** to read in an existing file.

It is possible to specify the name of a file when you start the program. As **emacs** starts, it will automatically load the file you specified. For example, say that you want to edit an existing file named **document**. You can enter:

emacs document

Once **emacs** has started, you will be ready to edit the file. If you want, you can enter more than one file name. For example:

emacs document names addresses phone-numbers

emacs will read them all into separate work areas, and you can switch back and forth as necessary.

If your system uses GNU **emacs**, it is possible that the name of the actual program will be different. Some common names are **gmacs**, **gnuemacs**, and **gnumacs**. When you enter the **emacs** command you will see a message like:

```
emacs: Command not found.
```

If this is the case, try using one of the other names, such as **gmacs** instead of **emacs**. For example:

```
gmacs
gmacs document
gmacs document names addresses phone-numbers
```

If you still get an error, check with your system administrator to make sure that **emacs** is installed on your system.

HINT

Although it is possible to specify a file name (or multiple file names) when you start **emacs**, this is not the recommended procedure. Why? Because it runs counter to the **emacs** philosophy.

emacs was designed to provide a total working environment. Unlike other editors, **emacs** makes it easy to handle more than one file at the same time (as well as read your mail, work with directories, participate in Usenet discussion groups, write programs, issue shell commands, and so on).

The intention is that you should start **emacs** by entering the command without file names, and then initiate as many different tasks as you want, switching from one to another as the mood takes you. Once you get good at **emacs**, you can do just about anything you want from within it. Indeed, some people virtually live within emacs (leaving only to get something to eat).

So, you can specify a file name when you start **emacs**, but, in the long run, you are better off thinking of **emacs** as home away from home and not simply a text editor.

HINT FOR X WINDOW USERS

Modern versions of **emacs** have been written to work well under X Window. When you start **emacs** under X, **emacs** creates its own window to run in, and there are special X menus you can use.

It is a good idea to start **emacs** as a background process so that it frees up the original window. For example, if you are starting **emacs** from within an **xterm** window, you will probably not want to tie up the original **xterm** while **emacs** is running. All you need to do is put an **&** (ampersand) character at the end of the command. Here are some examples:

```
emacs &
emacs document &
emacs document names addresses phone-numbers &
```

When you start **emacs** within X, you can use the typical constellation of X-oriented options (to set the window border, the colors, the geometry, and so on). For more information, see the entry for **emacs** in the online manual by using the command **man emacs**. (The online Unix manual is explained in Chapter 8.)

Starting emacs as a Read-Only Editor

There may be times when you want to use **emacs** to look at an important file that should not be changed. To do this, start **emacs** using the following syntax:

```
emacs   -f toggle-read-only file...
```

For example, say that you need to look at a file named **secrets**. You want to use **emacs** to look at the file, but you want to be sure you don't accidentally make any changes to it. Enter the command:

```
emacs   -f toggle-read-only secrets
```

When **emacs** starts, the file will be marked as being read only. This means you can look at it, but not make any changes.

HINT FOR NERDS

When you start **emacs** by using the **-f** option, it tells **emacs** to execute the function that is specified after the option. In this case, you are telling **emacs** to execute a function named **toggle-read-only**. This function tells **emacs** to consider the file you are editing as being read-only.

Recovering Data After a System Failure

If your computer goes down (or if you lose your connection), you stand to lose all the data you typed since the last time you saved your work. For this reason, it is a good idea to pause and save your work regularly.

Still, accidents do happen, and **emacs** works behind the scenes to protect you from losing data in case of a system failure. Whenever you are editing a file, **emacs** automatically saves a copy of that file at regular intervals (by default, every 300 keystrokes). This backup file is called the AUTO-SAVE FILE.

emacs creates the auto-save file in the same directory as the file you are editing. (We explain directories in Chapter 22.) The name of the file will be the same as the file you are editing, except that there will be a **#** (number sign) character at the beginning and end of the name. For example, if you are editing a file named **document**, **emacs** will create an auto-save file named **#document#**. So if you are looking at a directory and you see a file with such a name, you will understand what it is and how it got there.

Whenever you save a file, **emacs** automatically removes the auto-save file. If you make more changes to the file, **emacs** creates a new auto-save file. Thus, under normal circumstances, you should never see an auto-save file. However, if your **emacs** session is terminated abnormally—before you have a chance to save your work—the auto-save file is preserved.

Each time you tell **emacs** to begin work with an existing file, **emacs** first checks to see if there exists a corresponding auto-save file. If so, it means that the last time you edited the file, you were unable to save your work properly. In such cases, **emacs** will display a message like the following:

```
Auto save file is newer; consider M-x recover-file
```

This means **emacs** thinks you need to recover your file. To do so, simply follow the instructions. Enter the command:

```
M-x recover-file
```

emacs will display the name of the original file. If this is correct, press RETURN. **emacs** will now ask your permission to restore the auto-save file. At the same time, **emacs** will create a new window on your screen (windows are explained later). Within this window, you will see the directory information for the original file. If you understand such information (which is explained in Chapter 23), it can help you decide whether or not to restore the file.

If you do decide to restore the file, type **yes**. **emacs** will replace the text you are editing with the contents of the auto-save file. If you do not want to restore the auto-save file, just type **no**.

To summarize, if your work is interrupted abnormally, **emacs** will probably have saved what you were doing in an auto-save file. If so, you will see a message suggesting that you recover the file the next time you start to edit it. To recover the file, enter:

M-x recover-file

When **emacs** displays the name of the file, press RETURN. Then, when **emacs** asks for permission to restore the file, enter **yes**.

Stopping **emacs**

To stop **emacs**, use the command **C-x C-c**. If there is no need to save any files, **emacs** may display a message like:

(No files need saving)

and quit. You will be returned to the shell prompt.

If you have been working with one or more files that have not yet been saved, **emacs** will give you a chance to do so before it quits. For each file that has not been saved, **emacs** will display the name of the file along with several choices.

Here is an example. You have been working with a file named **document** that has not as yet been saved. You press **C-x C-c** and you see the following:

Save file /usr/harley/document? (y, n, !, ., q, C-r or C-h)

emacs is asking if you want to save the file. Notice that **emacs** displays the full pathname of the file:

/usr/harley/document

This shows the file name and the directory in which it resides. (We explain pathnames in Chapter 22.)

At this point, you have a number of choices. Most likely, you will want to save the file and quit. To do so, press **y** (for yes). If you don't want to save the file, press **n** (for no), and **emacs** will quit without saving. Be careful: if you press **n**, any changes you have made to the file since the last time you saved it will be lost.

HINT

If you are editing an existing file and you happen to make a lot of mistakes, you may decide to abandon everything you have done. Simply press **C-x C-c**, and then press **n** to quit without saving.

When you are editing more than one file, **emacs** will display the name of each file that needs to be saved, one at a time, and ask you what to do. As before, you can press **y** to save and **n** to not save. However, you also have a few other choices.

To save all of the files at once and then quit, press **!** (exclamation mark). To quit immediately, without saving anything more, press **q**. To save the current file only, but quit without saving anything else, press **.** (period).

If you try to quit when there are still files that are not saved, **emacs** will ask you to confirm your intentions. You will see a message like:

 `Modified buffers exist; exit anyway? (yes or no)`

In this case, you must enter either **yes** or **no** (the full words).

Notice that the message refers to "buffers". We will explain what they are in a moment. For now, you can consider each buffer to be a separate working area.

HINT

When **emacs** wants to be especially sure you are making the right decision, it will ask you to answer **yes** or **no** (as opposed to **y** or **n**). In such cases, you must type the full word. This prevents you from making a serious mistake by accidentally pressing a single wrong key.

When you are working with only a single file, you can see the file on your screen when **emacs** asks if you want to save it. However, when you are editing more than one file, **emacs** will ask you about each file in turn, and you may have forgotten what was in one of the files. If so, when **emacs** asks what to do with that particular file, press **C-r**. **emacs** will show you the file, so you can make an informed decision. As you are looking at the file, you will be in VIEW MODE, which means you can read the file, but not make any changes. To quit viewing the file, press **q** (for quit).

Finally, if you forget what any of the choices mean, you can press **C-h** to display a quick help summary. To get rid of the help information, press **q**.

To summarize, you stop **emacs** by pressing **C-x C-c**. If there are files to be saved, you have the following choices:

y	save the specified file
n	do not save the specified file
!	save all the remaining files
q	quit immediately without saving
.	save the specified file and then quit
C-r	view the specified file
C-h	display help information

Commands and Key Bindings

emacs has hundreds of different commands. As with other programs, you issue a command by pressing a particular key. For example, while you are editing, you can move the cursor to the previous line by pressing **C-p**. To move the cursor to the next line, you press **C-n**.

There are many such key combinations and—in one sense—learning to use **emacs** means learning how to use the various commands (or at least, the most useful ones). Thus, in order to learn how to edit with **emacs**, you will need to memorize the various key combinations for moving the cursor, displaying text, loading and saving files, and so on.

Each particular **emacs** command has its own name. For example, the command that moves the cursor to the previous line is called **previous-line**. The command that moves the cursor to the next line is called **next-line**. Whenever you press a key, you are really telling **emacs** to execute the command that is associated with that key. For example, when you press **C-p**, you are telling **emacs** to execute the **previous-line** command. When you press **C-n**, you are telling **emacs** to execute the **next-line** command.

Here is another example. To move the cursor forward one character (that is, one position to the right), you press **C-f**. This invokes a command called **forward-char**. To move the cursor forward one word, you press **M-f**. This invokes a command called **forward-word**.

In **emacs** terminology, the connection between a key combination and the command it invokes is called a KEY BINDING. Thus, we say that **C-p** is BOUND to the **previous-line** command; **C-n** is bound to the **next-line** command; **C-f** is bound to the **forward-char** command; **M-f** is bound to the **forward-word** command; and so on.

Most of the time, you don't really need to know the official names of the commands you use; all you need to remember is which keys to press. However, there is a reason we are telling you all this. **emacs** has so many commands that there just aren't enough simple key combinations to go around. This means that many **emacs** commands are not bound to a particular key, and to execute such commands you need to specify the full name of the command.

What you do is press **M-x**, then type the name of the command, then press RETURN. **emacs** will then execute that command.

Here is an example. There happens to be a command called **spell-buffer** that helps you check the spelling of all the words in your buffer. (We will discuss buffers later; basically, a buffer is a work area.) The **spell-buffer** command is not bound to any particular key combination. Thus, you cannot run it by pressing a key. Instead, you must press **M-x**, then type **spell-buffer**, then press RETURN.

Here are several experiments you can try for yourself. First, you might be wondering, can I use **M-x** to execute any command by specifying its full name, rather than pressing its key? Of course.

For example, we mentioned that **C-p** moves the cursor to the previous line by executing the **previous-line** command. Try this. Start **emacs** and type a few lines of text. Now press **C-p**. Notice that the cursor moves up one line. Now press **M-x**, then type **previous-line** and press RETURN. Again, the cursor moves up one line.

Of course, you would never move the cursor by typing **M-x previous-line**; pressing the **C-p** key is a lot easier. However, this example does show how it all works.

Here is one last example. **emacs** comes with a number of games and diversions you can use by executing the appropriate programs. One such game is **doctor**: a program that acts like a psychiatrist. (This is actually a modern version of a program called Eliza that was written many years ago at MIT.)

We will discuss the **emacs** games later in the chapter. For now, though, you may want to try talking to the built-in **emacs** psychiatrist. Press **M-x**, type **doctor**, and then press RETURN. (Note: If **emacs** displays a message saying "no match", it means this program is not installed on your system.)

Once the **doctor** program starts, you can talk to it by typing whatever you want, one line at a time. If you make a typing mistake, correct it by pressing the DELETE key (not BACKSPACE). Each time you finish talking, press RETURN twice and the program will respond. When you are ready to quit, press **C-x k**, and then press RETURN. (The **C-x k** command kills the buffer in which the program is running.)

Buffers

One of the nice features of **emacs** is that it lets you do more than one thing at a time. For example, you can edit as many files as you want, jumping from one to another as the mood takes you.

In order to offer this flexibility, **emacs** keeps a separate storage area, called a BUFFER, for each particular task. For example, if you are editing three different files, **emacs** will maintain three separate buffers, one for each file.

Understanding buffers and how to use them is a crucial skill you must develop in order to become comfortable with **emacs**. So let's take a few moments to explore what these things are and just how they work.

There are two ways in which buffers are created. First, you can make a new buffer whenever you want. Second, **emacs** will automatically create a buffer when the need arises.

The thing to remember is that *everything* you see and everything you type within **emacs** is kept in one buffer or another. For example, **emacs** contains a built-in help facility that you can use whenever you want. When you press the key to ask for help (it happens to be **C-h**), **emacs** creates a new buffer to hold the help information.

Here is another example. Earlier, we mentioned that **emacs** comes with a program called **doctor** that acts like a psychiatrist. (You tell it your problems and it responds with meaningless platitudes.) When you enter the command to start it (**M-x doctor**), **emacs** creates a new buffer in which to run the program.

One last example. To keep track of your resources, you can use a command that tells **emacs** to display a list of all your buffers (the command is **C-x C-b**). When you use this command, **emacs** creates yet another buffer to hold the actual list as it is being displayed.

To keep track of all your buffers, **emacs** assigns each one of them a unique name. When you start editing a file, **emacs** creates a buffer with the same name as the file. Thus, if you tell **emacs** you want to edit a file named **document**, it will create a buffer named **document** to hold that file.

When **emacs** is called upon to create a buffer on its own, it will choose an appropriate name. For example, when you tell **emacs** to display help information, it creates a buffer named ***Help***. Or when you run the **doctor** program, **emacs** creates a buffer named **doctor**.

At all times, **emacs** makes sure that you have at least one buffer. When you start **emacs** by specifying a file to edit, **emacs** will create a buffer by that name. If the file already exists, **emacs** will read its contents into the buffer. If not, **emacs** will create a brand new file by that name, and the buffer will be empty. For example, if you enter the command:

```
emacs document
```

you will start working with a buffer named **document**.

When you start **emacs** without a file name:

```
emacs
```

you will find yourself with an empty buffer named ***scratch***. Since **emacs** does not know what file you want to use, it creates the ***scratch*** buffer, so you will have someplace to work.

One of the most important uses for a buffer is to act as a temporary work area when you need to make some quick notes. For example, say that your mother calls you on the phone as you are typing a letter. She tells you to write down the name of a wonderful book you should read (*The Internet Complete Reference*), but you don't want to take the time to look for a piece of paper and a pen. Instead, you quickly create a new buffer and type the information. Once your mother hangs up, you switch back to the buffer that contains the letter you are typing. The new buffer remains hidden from view, where you can deal with it at your leisure.

Later in the chapter, we will discuss the commands you can use to manipulate your buffers. For now, just remember the following five important ideas:

■ Everything you do with **emacs** is contained in a buffer.

■ Each buffer has a unique name.

■ You can create a new buffer whenever you want.

■ You can kill (delete) a buffer whenever you want.

■ Some buffers are created by you, some are created automatically by **emacs**.

As you become an experienced **emacs** person, you will find that being able to use buffers is an essential skill. Later in the chapter, we will discuss the commands that you can use to create and delete buffers, and to change from one buffer to another. At that time, we suggest that you take a few moments to experiment and become familiar with these commands.

HINT

Buffers are your friends.

Windows

As we have explained, everything you do with **emacs** takes place within a buffer. You can have as many buffers as you want and, much of the time, you will have several things going on at once.

But how do you see what is in your buffers? The answer is that **emacs** creates one or more WINDOWS on your screen and, within each window, you can view the contents of a single buffer. Some people prefer to use one large window and look at only one buffer at a time. Other people like to use multiple windows. For example, say that you are working with three different files. You might decide to have three windows, each of which displays a different file (in its own buffer).

As you become experienced with **emacs**, you will develop your own personal style. Most of the time, you will probably use one or two windows, creating and deleting extra ones as the need arises.

Just so you can see what it looks like, Figure 21-2 shows a typical **emacs** screen with a single window; Figure 21-3 shows a screen with two windows.

```
This is the first line in a file named "starting with emacs".
When you first start using emacs it can be a bit confusing.
The best way to learn emacs is to go slow.  Start with
the basic concepts and then practice.

emacs is designed to provide a total working environment
and to be exquisitely customizable.  That means that there
are a multitude of complicated features that, at the beginning,
may overwhelm you.

Don't worry.  Go slow and be content in the knowledge that
everyone who learned emacs felt disoriented at the beginning.




-----Emacs: starting-with-emacs        (Fundamental)--All-------

Wrote /usr/harley/starting with emacs
```

FIGURE 21-2. **emacs**: *A screen with one window*

One nice thing about **emacs** is that it lets you display a particular buffer in more than one window at a time. This comes in handy when the contents of the buffer are too large to fit into a single window. You can use two windows to look at different parts of the same file at the same time.

For example, say that you are editing a long document. You can display the beginning of the document in one window and the end of the document in another window. This makes it easy to copy or move text from one part of the buffer to another.

The best way to think of a window is as a fixed-size opening into a buffer. When you look into a window, you are looking into the part of the buffer that is currently being displayed. If you want to look at another part of the buffer, you can move the window up or down (or even sideways).

Here is something interesting. Let's say that you have two windows, each of which is displaying the same part of a particular buffer. What do you think will happen if you make a change to the text in one of the windows? Well, since each

```
This is the first line in a file named "typing-advice".
This file is displayed in the top window.

As you type, you can backspace and make a correction
by pressing the <Delete> key.

Do not press the <Backspace> key.  This will send
a Ctrl-H character which will start the Help facility.
If you do this by accident, press the q key to quit Help.



--**-Emacs: typing-advice           (Fundamental)--30%--------

This is the first line in a file named "window-advice".
This file is displayed in the bottom window.

To move the cursor from one window to another,
    press C-x o (the letter "o").

To expand the selected window to take up the whole screen,
    press C-x 1.

To kill (delete) the selected window,
    press C-x 0 (the number "0").



--%%-Emacs: window-advice            (Fundamental)--Top--------

C-x-
```

FIGURE 21-3. emacs: *A screen with two windows*

window is showing you the same buffer, changing the text in one window should affect the text in the other window and, indeed, that is what happens. As you type or edit the text in one window, you can see both windows change at the same time.

To see how this all works, try it for yourself. Start **emacs** by entering the command:

emacs

You now have a single large window containing an empty buffer named ***scratch***. (You may see some informative messages when **emacs** starts, but they will go away as soon as you begin to type.)

Now create a duplicate of the window by pressing **C-x 2** (the command is explained later). You should now have two windows, each of which shows the empty ***scratch*** file.

Start typing anything. Notice that everything you type shows up in both windows. Press **DEL** (the DELETE key) a few times to erase the most recently typed character. Notice that, as you erase a character, the change is updated in both windows.

When you are finished, press **C-x C-c** to stop **emacs**.

At any time, the cursor is in one particular window, which we call the SELECTED WINDOW or CURRENT WINDOW. As you type, the characters are inserted into the selected window at the position of the cursor. If you want to insert characters into a different window, you must first move the focus to that window. (We will explain how to do this later in the chapter.) When you do, the cursor will move to that window and it will become the selected window.

The Mode Line / Read-Only Viewing

At the bottom of each window is a special line called the MODE LINE. The mode line contains information about the buffer that is currently being displayed in that window. On most terminals, the mode line is displayed in reverse colors.

Take a look at the screen in Figure 21-2. This screen has a single window and, hence, one mode line at the bottom of that window. In this particular case, the mode line is:

```
-----Emacs: starting-with-emacs         (Fundamental)--All--------
```

Now take a look at Figure 21-3. This screen has two windows, so there are two mode lines. They are:

```
--**-Emacs: typing-advice                (Fundamental)--30%--------
```

```
--%%-Emacs: window-advice                (Fundamental)--Top--------
```

Each mode line starts with two hyphens (**--**). Following these hyphens are two characters that tell you about the status of the buffer. The meaning of these characters is shown in Figure 21-4. In our first example, the two characters are **--** (two hyphens). This indicates that the buffer has not yet been modified in any way. Thus, if you were to quit now, there would be nothing to save.

In the next example, the two characters are ****** (two asterisks). This means that the buffer has been modified in some way. This reminds you that you must save the contents of the buffer before you quit.

In the final example, the two characters are **%%** (two percent signs). This means that the buffer cannot be modified; that is, the buffer is in Read-only mode.

Characters	Meaning
`--`	the buffer has not yet been modified
`**`	the buffer has been modified
`%%`	the buffer cannot be modified (Read-only mode)

FIGURE 21-4.   `emacs`: *Status characters within the mode line*

As we explained earlier, when you start the **emacs** program with the name of a file, you can tell **emacs** you want to edit in Read-only mode by using the **-f** option to execute the **toggle-read-only** command. For example, to edit a file named **secrets** in Read-only mode, you can use the command:

```
emacs -f toggle-read-only secrets
```

When you start **emacs** in this way, you will see that the left side of the mode line contains the characters **%%**. This shows that the buffer is in Read-only mode.

At any time, you can change to and from Read-only mode by executing the **toggle-read-only** command directly. For example, if you are editing a file in Read-only mode and you decide that you want to be able to make changes, you can press **M-x**, then type **toggle-read-only**, then press RETURN. When you do, the status characters in the mode line will change from **%%** to **--**. This indicates that the buffer is no longer in Read-only mode.

Similarly, if the mode line shows **--**, you can change to Read-only mode by executing the **toggle-read-only** command. The status characters will change to **%%**, indicating that your buffer is protected from changes.

To continue: the next item of information on the status line is the word **Emacs**. This is to remind you what program you are using. Isn't that nice.

A little further to the right is the name of the buffer. In our examples, these names are **starting-with-emacs**, **typing-advice**, and **window-advice**. These are names we chose when we created the buffers. As we mentioned earlier, **emacs** sometimes creates buffers on its own. In particular, when you start **emacs** without specifying a file name, **emacs** will create an empty buffer named ***scratch***. Also, when you start the help facility, **emacs** creates a buffer named ***Help*** to hold the help information.

To the right of the buffer name, you will see one or more words in parentheses. These words show you the mode in which **emacs** is operating for that particular buffer. We will discuss modes later in the chapter. For now, we will just say that **emacs** can act in different ways to suit the type of work you are doing. For example, if you are editing English text, **emacs** will work a little differently than if you are writing a Lisp program. The mode shows what personality **emacs** is using at the moment. (This, by the way, is where we get the name "mode line".) In all three of our examples, **emacs** is in Fundamental mode (which we will explain later).

Finally, near the far right of the mode line is information that gives you a rough idea of the current position within the buffer. If the entire buffer is small enough to be contained within the window, you will see **All**. This is the case in our first example.

If the buffer is too large to fit into the window all at once, you will see three possible position descriptions. If the window is currently showing the beginning of the buffer, you will see **Top**. (This is the case in our third example.) If the window is showing the end of the buffer, you will see **Bot** (bottom). Otherwise, you will see a number. This number indicates what percentage of the buffer is above the top in the window. In our second example, 30 percent of the buffer is above what we see in the window.

The Echo Area / Typing `emacs` Commands

As you know, when you type a regular Unix command (at the shell prompt), Unix echos the command. This means that Unix displays each character as you type it. **emacs** is different: it only echos some commands. When it does, the characters are displayed on bottom line of your screen, which is called the ECHO AREA.

Here is how it works. **emacs** does not echo any commands that consist of only a single character combination. For example, the command **C-n** moves the cursor to the next line. When you press this key combination, you do not see the letters "**C-n**" in the echo area; all you see is that the cursor moves.

emacs echos only multi-character commands. However, it waits one second after you press a character before it echos it. If, within that time, you press a second character, **emacs** does not echo the first one.

For example, the command **C-x k** kills (deletes) the current buffer. When you type the first character (**C-x**), **emacs** waits for you to type another one. If you do not type another character within one second, **emacs** echos what you have already typed. That is, the letters "**C-x**" will appear on the bottom line of the screen. However, if you complete the command quickly, nothing will echo; **emacs** will simply carry out the command.

The reason that **emacs** echos in this way is to give quick typists a fast response, while providing slower, more hesitant typists with as much feedback as possible. In practice, this means that when you type the commands with which you are the most familiar, things move fast, but when you type commands that are still new to you, **emacs** prompts you as necessary. The overall feeling is that the system speeds up or slows down to match your comfort level.

The echo area is also used by **emacs** to display messages. These may be error messages, warnings, or simply informative comments. Whenever it displays an error message, **emacs** will make a sound to make sure to get your attention.

If you look at Figures 21-2 and 21-3, you will see examples of how **emacs** uses the echo area. At the bottom of the screen in Figure 21-2 is the following message:

```
Wrote /usr/harley/starting-with-emacs
```

This message tells us that **emacs** has successfully saved the contents of the buffer to a disk file. At the bottom of the screen in Figure 21-3, you can see:

```
C-x-
```

This means that we have pressed the **C-x** key and that **emacs** is waiting for us to type something else to complete the command.

As is usually the case with Unix, you can type ahead as much as you want: that is, you can press the keys as fast as you want, and **emacs** will remember what you type. However, when you make a mistake that generates an error message, **emacs** will throw away all the pending keystrokes. This prevents a mistake from causing unexpected problems.

If you are typing a command and you change your mind, you can press **C-g** to cancel the command. We will discuss this in the next section.

The Minibuffer

Many commands require you to enter further input once you press the initial key combinations. For example, the command **C-x f** tells **emacs** to read a disk file into the buffer. Once you press **C-x f**, **emacs** will ask you for the name of the file. If the file exists, **emacs** will copy it from the disk into the buffer. If the file doesn't exist, **emacs** will create it for you.

When **emacs** displays a message asking for information, it writes it to the bottom line of your screen. You are expected to type the information and then press RETURN. Whatever you type is echoed on the bottom line of the screen and, up until the time you press RETURN, you can make corrections.

Thus, the bottom line of your screen has two purposes: First, as we explained earlier, **emacs** uses this line to echo your regular keystrokes and to display messages. Second, **emacs** uses this same line to ask you for information and to echo such information as you type it.

For this reason, the bottom line of your screen has two different names. When **emacs** is echoing your commands, this line is called the echo area. And when **emacs** is asking you for information and reading your reply, this line is called the MINIBUFFER.

As you type information into the minibuffer, you can use **DEL** (the DELETE key) to correct mistakes. Each time you press **DEL**, it erases one character.

HINT

Remember to make corrections by pressing **DEL**, not the BACKSPACE key. The BACKSPACE key sends the **C-h** code which will start the Help facility. If you do start Help by accident, you can press **q** (for "quit") to kill it.

As an **emacs** user, you will often find yourself typing information into the minibuffer. To help you, **emacs** does two things that make your life easier. First, whenever possible, **emacs** will display a default value in parentheses when it prompts you for information. This default value is **emacs'** guess as to what you might want to type. If indeed this is what you want, all you need to do is press RETURN. Otherwise, you can type a different value.

Here is an example. You are working with three different buffers: **names**, **addresses** and **phone-numbers**. At the current time, you are editing the **names** file, and you decide to switch to **addresses**. The command to change to another buffer is **C-x b**. As soon as you type this, **emacs** displays the following in the minibuffer (the bottom line of your screen):

Switch to buffer: (default addresses)

emacs is asking you for the name of the buffer to which you want to switch. The message in parentheses is telling you that the default value is **addresses**.

Thus, if you want to switch to the **addresses** buffer, all you need to do is press RETURN. If you want to switch to another buffer (such as **phone-numbers**), you would have to type its name and then press RETURN.

The second way in which **emacs** makes it easy to enter information into the minibuffer is a facility called "completion". Completion is a process by which you can tell **emacs** to guess what you are going to type, so you don't have to actually type all the characters yourself. Completion is an important topic, and we will discuss it in more detail in the next section.

As you now understand, **emacs** uses the bottom line of your display for both the echo area and for the minibuffer. Occasionally, **emacs** will need to display something (such as an error message) while you are typing in the minibuffer. When this happens, **emacs** will display the message and the minibuffer will disappear temporarily. After a few seconds, **emacs** will erase the message and the minibuffer will reappear. In other words, the bottom line of your screen will be transmogrified from the minibuffer into the echo area and then, after a few seconds, back to the minibuffer.

Occasionally, you will be typing in the minibuffer when you realize that you are making a big mistake. **emacs** makes it easy to cancel the whole command: all you need to do is press **C-g** (before you press RETURN).

This is a key worth remembering: **C-g** within **emacs** acts a lot like the **^C** (**intr**) key within Unix (see Chapter 6). One day it may save your life.

HINT
If you get yourself into a situation within **emacs** where things are getting weird and you don't know what to do, try pressing **C-g** to cancel the current command. If it doesn't work, press **C-g** a second time.

Completion

One of the nice ways that **emacs** makes your minute-to-minute work easier is that, at various times, you can tell **emacs** to guess what you are going to type and complete it for you. This facility is called COMPLETION and here is how it works.

Whenever you are typing in the minibuffer—that is, providing information in response to a prompt from **emacs**—you can use one of the completion commands (explained below). This is a signal to **emacs** to try to complete what you are typing. **emacs** will display what it thinks you want to type. If **emacs** has guessed correctly, all you have to do is press RETURN. Otherwise, you can press **DEL** (the DELETE key) to make whatever correction is necessary and then press RETURN.

For example, let's say that you would like to switch to a different buffer. At the current time, you have three buffers, called **names**, **addresses** and **phone-numbers**. Right now, you happen to be editing the **names** buffer, but you want to switch to the **phone-numbers** buffer.

The command to switch to a different buffer is **C-x b**. When you type this command, **emacs** will display a prompt in the minibuffer. In this case, you might see:

```
Switch to buffer: (default addresses)
```

This means that **emacs** is asking you for the name of the buffer to which you want to switch. The default is **addresses**, so if this is the buffer you want, you need only press RETURN.

In this case, you want to switch to a different buffer, **phone-numbers**. So you could type the entire name and then press RETURN. The shortcut, though, would be to type only a **p** and then type a completion command. **emacs** will then guess what you want, and type the rest of the name for you. In this case, you would see:

```
Switch to buffer: (default addresses) phone-numbers
```

Now all you have to do is press RETURN.

The completion facility—like much of **emacs**—has a lot of complex details. However, all you really need to know are the four completion commands. They are all single keys: **TAB** (the TAB key), **SPC** (the SPACE bar), **RET** (the RETURN key), and **?** (question mark). Figure 21-5 summarizes how these keys work.

Most of the time, you will only need the **TAB** key. This key tells **emacs** to complete as much as possible and then wait for you to press RETURN. Here is how it would work in our example. **emacs** has just displayed the message:

Switch to buffer: (default addresses)

We want to switch to the **phone-numbers** buffer. So we type the single letter **p** and then press **TAB**. **emacs** looks through its list of buffers to see if any of them begin with **p**. In this case, it happens there is only one, the **phone-numbers** buffer. So **emacs** types the rest of the name for us. We can now press RETURN and complete the command.

The **SPC** command is similar to **TAB** except that **SPC** will only complete up to the end of the word. In this case, if we had pressed **SPC** instead of **TAB**, **emacs** would have completed only up to the hyphen after the word **phone**. We would have seen:

Switch to buffer: (default addresses) phone-

To complete the command, we would have to either type the rest of the name, or type an **n** and press **TAB** or **SPC**.

SPC is handy when you want to use part of a name and finish the rest for yourself. For example, say that we wanted to create a new buffer named **phone-messages**. We can press **C-x b**, then press **p** and **SPC** to get the response described above. Now we can type **messages** and then press RETURN. Since this buffer does not already exist, **emacs** will create it for us. Thus, we will have a brand new buffer named **phone-messages**.

Key	Action
TAB	complete text in minibuffer as much as possible
SPC	complete text in minibuffer up to end of word
RET	same as **TAB**, then enter the command
?	create new window, display list of possible completions

FIGURE 21-5. *emacs: Completion keys*

The third completion key is **RET**. This works like **TAB** with the added effect that, after the completion is finished, **emacs** will enter the command for you automatically. Thus, pressing **RET** is like pressing **TAB** followed by RETURN. In other words, if you are sure that there is only one way for **emacs** to complete what you are typing, you can press **RET** instead of **TAB** RETURN and save yourself a keystroke.

The last completion key is **?** (a question mark). If you press **?**, **emacs** will create a new window and, within it, display a list of all the possible completions it can find. This is handy when there are a number of completions, and you are not sure which one you want. Once you see the one you want, you can type it and press RETURN. If you don't see the one you want, you can press **C-g** and cancel the command.

Here is an example. There is a command named **auto-fill-mode** which is useful when you are typing English text. It tells **emacs** to break long lines for you automatically as you type, so you don't keep pressing RETURN. To execute this command, you would press **M-x**, then type **auto-fill-mode**, and then press RETURN.

So, you decide that you want to execute this command, but you forget the full name. You remember that it starts with the word **auto**. Press **M-x** and then type **auto**. The minibuffer now looks like this:

```
M-x auto
```

Now press the **?** key. **emacs** will create a new window with a buffer named ***Completions***. Within this window you will see all the possible completions. In this case, there are two:

```
auto-fill-mode
auto-save-mode
```

To finish the command, all you need to do is type **-f** and press **RET**. Since there is only one possible completion, **emacs** will type it for you and enter the command.

The power of the completion facility lies in the fact that you can use it just about any time you are called upon to type something into the minibuffer. You can use completion for file names, buffer names, **emacs** commands, and so on. Once you get used to the completion keys—and remember, most of the time, all you really need is **TAB**—you will come to appreciate the power of **emacs**.

Here is one last example. Earlier in the chapter, we described a command named **toggle-read-only**, that switches back and forth from Read-only mode. It would be a great bother to have to type the full name of this command each time you want to use it. But with completion, all you need to type is:

```
M-x tog RET
```

Thus, you can see why it is okay that so many **emacs** commands have long names. Most of the time, you never really have to type the full name.

HINT

When you use the **?** completion command, **emacs** creates a new buffer named ***Completions*** and, within it, displays a list of all the possible completions. If you want, you can make a choice by changing to the ***Completions*** window, moving to the selection you want, and pressing RETURN. (We explain how to change from one window to another later in the chapter.)

However, most of the time, it is easier to complete the command on your own by typing a few more keystrokes and then pressing either **TAB** or **RET**.

Practicing with emacs

In order to practice with **emacs**, you need to start the program and have some text to edit. Here is an easy way to do just that. Start the program by entering the **emacs** command by itself:

```
emacs
```

You may see some informative messages. Don't worry, they will go away as soon as you start to type.

You are now in **emacs** with an empty buffer named ***scratch***. Press **C-h**. This will start the Help facility. At the bottom of the screen, you will see a message like:

```
C-h (Type ? for further options)-
```

Press **b**. This tells **emacs** to display information about key bindings. (This is a list of all the **emacs** key combinations and what they do.)

In order to display this list, **emacs** will create a new buffer named ***Help***. **emacs** will then split your screen into two windows. The top window will contain the empty ***scratch*** buffer; the bottom window will contain the ***Help*** buffer. In the bottom window, you will see the beginning of the key bindings list.

At this point, your cursor will be in the top window. What you want to do is get rid of the top window and work exclusively with the bottom window. To do this, press **C-x 0** (the number zero). This tells **emacs** to kill the selected window.

You will now have one large window containing a long list of key bindings. This is a good place to practice using **emacs** (because, while you are practicing, you will be reading about all the different **emacs** keys and what they do).

When you are finished, press **C-x C-c** to stop **emacs**.

If anything weird happens, press **C-h b** to get back to the list of key bindings. If this doesn't solve the problem, just bail out by pressing **C-x C-c** and start all over again.

To summarize, here is what you can do each time you want to practice with **emacs**:

1. Start **emacs**.

2. Press **C-h b** to display the information about key bindings.

3. Press **C-x 0** to remove the ***scratch*** window.

4. Practice as much as you want.

5. When you are finished, press **C-x C-c** to quit.

Typing and Correcting

To create text, all you have to do is move the cursor to where you want the characters to be inserted and start typing. That's all there is to it. (Later in the chapter, we will show you how to move the cursor wherever you want.)

If you want to practice, start **emacs** as follows:

```
emacs
```

As we mentioned, you may see some informative messages when the program starts, but as soon as you type anything, these messages will go away. Once you start, you will have a single window called ***scratch***. Just start typing. When you are finished, you can stop by pressing **C-x C-c**.

As you type, there are two ways to make simple corrections. To erase the character you have just typed, press **DEL** (the DELETE key). If you do not have a DELETE key— or if it doesn't work properly— just press whatever key sends the **del** code. We discuss this idea in Chapter 6.

Notice that you do not press BACKSPACE to make corrections. If you press BACKSPACE, it will start the built-in Help facility. (Try it now.) This is because—as we explained in Chapter 6—the BACKSPACE key is really CTRL-H and, in **emacs**, **C-h** starts the Help facility. (We will discuss the Help facility later in the chapter.) If you do press BACKSPACE by accident, just press **q** to quit Help.

The second way to make a simple correction is to press **C-d**. This will erase the character that the cursor is under. In other words, **DEL** erases to the left; **C-d** erases to the right. These keys are described in Figure 21-6.

When you want to insert a new line, there are two ways to do it. First, you can move to where you want to put the line, type whatever you want, and press the

Key	Action
DEL	delete one character to the left of cursor
C-d	delete one character at the position of cursor
C-o	open a new line
C-_	undo the last change to the buffer
C-x u	same as **C-_**
C-q	insert the next character literally

Note: **C-_** is CTRL-underscore.

FIGURE 21-6. **emacs**: *Keys to use while typing*

RETURN key. Alternatively, you can move to where you want the new line and press **C-o**. This will create a new line for you. (You can think of the "o" as meaning "open".)

Here is how it works. If you are at the beginning of a line, **C-o** creates a new, empty line above the current line. If you are at the end of a line, **C-o** creates a new, empty line below the current line. And if you are within a line, **C-o** breaks it into two separate lines. Just experiment a little and it will all make sense.

As you read through this chapter, you will find many commands you can use to make changes in the buffer: to erase text, to replace text, to move text, and so on. You will sometimes find yourself in the situation of having made a change that you really don't want. For example, you may have deleted a large chunk of the buffer and realized immediately that you made a mistake.

In such cases, you can use the **C-_** command to undo the last change to the buffer. If you press **C-_** again, you will undo the change before that. If you want, you can press **C-_** repeatedly, to undo one change after another, moving backward in time. Most of the time, however, you will catch your mistake right away and you will need only to undo the very last change.

The notation **C-_** stands for CTRL-underscore. On many keyboards, the underscore character is on the same key as the **-** (minus) character. Thus, **C-_** is the same as **C--** (because you don't use the SHIFT key with CTRL). If, for some reason, this key does not work on your terminal, there is an alternative: you can use **C-x u**, which will work with all keyboards.

HINT
Take a moment to memorize the **C-_** (undo) key. It may save your life one day.

From time to time, you may want to enter a special character. For example, you may want to put an actual CTRL-C into your text. (Why, we can't imagine, but still, everyone has their own needs.) The trouble is that many of the CTRL keys have special meanings in **emacs**, as do ESCAPE, TAB, DELETE and so on. If you want to insert one of these characters into your text, you must first press **C-q**. This tells **emacs** that the next character is to be taken literally. Thus, to insert a CTRL-C character, type **C-q C-c**. To insert a CTRL-Q, type **C-q C-q**.

The only problem with this is that it won't work in Unix, because CTRL-Q sends the **start** signal. (This is the key you press to restart after you have paused the screen display by pressing CTRL-S. See Chapter 6 for the details.)

Near the end of the chapter, we will show you how to customize your work environment so that you can use a different key instead of **C-q**. In the meantime, just remember that **C-q** tells **emacs** that the next character is to be taken literally, and be patient: it will all make sense eventually, we promise.

Aside from this, there is really no trick to entering characters: just type and be happy.

Why emacs Commands Are So Weird

The **vi** editor (Chapter 20) has two distinct modes (ways of working). They are command mode and insert mode. Before you can type text, you must first change to insert mode. And before you can use a command, you must change back to command mode. Thus, in **vi**, you are always changing from one mode to another.

emacs is a "mode-less" editor. That means that you can type text whenever you want. (In **vi** terms, we might say that you are always in insert mode.) Thus, in one sense, **emacs** is simpler to use than **vi**, because you never have to change from one mode to another.

But this simplicity does not come for free. In **vi**, the names of the commands are simple, and easy to type and remember. (Well, relatively easy to remember.) For example, to delete from the cursor to the end of the line, you type **D**; to save (write) your text to a file, you type **:w**; and to search for a pattern using a regular expression (see Chapter 17), you press **/** (slash) and then type the expression.

In **emacs**, all the commands must use special keys like CTRL and META (ESCAPE) so they will not be confused with the letters, numbers and punctuation you might be typing. Thus, **emacs** commands tend to be strange and can take longer to memorize. For example, to delete from the cursor to the end of the line, you press **C-k**; to save your text to a file, you press **C-x C-s**; and to search for a pattern using a regular expression, you press **M-C-s** (META-CTRL-S) and then type the expression.

So is all this complexity worth it? We think so. All you need to do is memorize about 40 to 50 basic **emacs** commands (which is a lot easier than you might think) and you will be as comfortable as a brother-in-law living in the spare room. Since you won't always have to be switching back and forth from one mode to another, a part of your brain is freed up to think about other things (such as remembering all the key combinations).

Common Problems and What to Do

As you work with **emacs**, it is inevitable that strange things will happen. Here are a few of the more common problems and what you can do about them.

Problem #1: *You are in the middle of typing a command when you change your mind. You decide that you would just as soon forget the whole thing.*

Solution: Press **C-g** to cancel the command.

Problem #2: *You have started a command and it is not doing what you want.*

Solution: Press **C-g** to cancel the command. If that doesn't work, press **C-g** again.

Problem #3: *Something is happening that you want to stop.*

Solution: Press **C-g**. It not only cancels commands, it stops programs that are running within **emacs**.

Problem #4: *You press the* BACKSPACE *key to erase a character, and the Help facility appears out of nowhere.*

Solution: In **emacs**, you use the **DEL** (DELETE) key to erase a character. The BACKSPACE key is the same as **C-h**, which is the command to start the Help facility. To get rid of the Help junk on your screen, either press **q** (for "quit") or press **C-g**. To fix this problem permanently, you need to redefine the meaning of BACKSPACE within the **emacs** environment. We will show you how to do this later in the chapter.

Problem #5: *You press the **ESC** (ESCAPE) key twice, and strange messages appear about a "disabled command". **emacs** seems to be waiting for you to do something.*

Solution: Certain commands are disabled by **emacs**, because they can cause trouble for beginners. If you accidentally press the keys that start such a command, **emacs** will display a confusing message that asks if you really want to use the command. It happens that **ESC ESC** starts such a command. To get rid of the message, either press **n** (for "no") or press **C-g**. To fix the problem permanently, you need to tell **emacs** to ignore the **ESC ESC** sequence. We will show you how to do this later in the chapter.

Problem #6: *You are quietly minding your own business when you notice a message on the bottom line of the screen that says "**Garbage collecting**".*

Solution: **emacs** is written in a programming language called Lisp. Within the Lisp environment, storage areas that are no longer needed are discarded. From time to time, **emacs** runs a program that collects all of the discarded areas so they can be reused. This process, which is normal, is known as garbage collection. You can ignore the message.

Problem #7: *You press the **C-s** key and your terminal stops dead.*

Solution: Within Unix, the **C-s** and **C-q** characters are used for what is called "flow control". **C-s** pauses the screen display; **C-q** restarts it (see Chapter 6). Unfortunately, some **emacs** commands use these two characters and, whenever you press **C-s**, your screen display will stop. To bring **emacs** back to life, press **C-q**. To solve the problem permanently, you need to tell **emacs** to use two other keys instead of **C-s** and **C-q**. We will show you how to do this later in the chapter.

Problem #8: *You press the **C-q** key and nothing happens*

Solution: See the solution to the previous problem.

Problem #9: *Your screen has become filled with junk.*

Solution: A common cause of junk on the screen is a noisy phone line. Whatever the reason, press **C-l** (the lowercase letter "L"), and **emacs** will redraw the screen.

Commands to Control Windows

One of the tricks to being an **emacs** virtuoso (or, at least, looking like an **emacs** virtuoso) is to become a whiz at manipulating windows.

When you are editing a single buffer, **emacs** puts it in one large window. Thus, much of the time, you will be working with one buffer and only one window.

At various times, though, **emacs** will create another window. This will happen automatically whenever **emacs** has some information it needs to display. For example, when you start the Help facility (explained later in the chapter), **emacs** will create a new window and, within this window, display a buffer named ***Help***.

In addition, you can create a new window for yourself whenever you want. You can use the new window to display the same buffer as the old window or a completely different buffer. Remember, at any particular time, one window is designated as the selected window. This is the window that contains the cursor.

The commands to work with windows are shown in Figure 21-7. With a little practice, you will be zipping around from one window to another, creating and deleting like nobody's business.

Here is a good way to practice. Start **emacs** as follows:

    emacs

You will have one large window with a ***scratch*** buffer. Now start the Help facility and tell it to display a list of all the key bindings. Press **C-h b**. You now

Command	Description
C-x 0	delete the selected window
C-x 1	delete all windows except selected window
C-x 2	split selected window vertically
C-x 3	split selected window horizontally
C-x o	move cursor to the next (other) window
C-x }	make selected window wider
C-x {	make selected window narrower
C-x ^	make selected window larger
M-x shrink-window	make selected window smaller

Note: In older versions of **emacs**, the command to split a window horizontally was
    C-x 5, not **C-x 3**.

FIGURE 21-7. **emacs**: *Commands for controlling windows*

have two windows that you can use to practice the commands in Figure 21-7. When you are finished, you can stop **emacs** by pressing **C-x C-c**.

The best way to become comfortable controlling windows is to just spend some time experimenting with the commands. At first, you will feel a little awkward, but soon it will become second nature to move from one window to another, delete a window, create a new one, and so on.

Be sure you understand the difference between windows and buffers. As we explained earlier, a buffer is a work area, and you can have as many as you want. A window is simply what **emacs** uses to display the contents of a buffer. Thus, when you delete a window, you are *not* deleting the buffer that is displayed in that window. Any buffers that are not currently displayed are maintained invisibly in the background. Thus, you can have many buffers, only some of which are actually displayed in windows at the current time.

Before we leave this topic, there are a few points we would like to make about the commands in Figure 21-7. First, notice that there are two commands whose names might be a tad confusing. The "delete selected window" command is **C-x 0** (the number zero). The "move cursor to next window" command is **C-x o** (the lowercase letter "o"). It may help if you think of the letter "o" as standing for "other window".

Strictly speaking, **C-x o** moves to what is called the NEXT WINDOW. When you have more than one window on your screen, **emacs** moves from one to another in a specific order. If you have only two windows, the next window is simply the other window. If you have more than two windows, **emacs** cycles from one to another, going from left to right and from up to down.

If you want to check this out for yourself, try the following experiment. Start **emacs** as follows:

emacs

You now have one large window containing an empty buffer named ***scratch***. Now press **C-x 2** and split the window into two windows, one on top of the other. Press **C-x o** a few times and watch how the cursor moves from one window to another.

Now press **C-x 3** and split one of the windows into two side-by-side windows. Again, press **C-x o** a few times and see how **emacs** cycles through the three windows. Try using **C-x 2** and **C-x 3** to create some more windows and, each time, watch how **C-x o** moves the cursor. When you are finished, press **C-x C-c** to quit **emacs**.

To continue, look back at Figure 21-7. Notice that the command to make the selected window smaller (**shrink-window**) is not bound to a specific key combination. Thus, you must execute this command explicitly by using **M-x**. Normally, though, you won't need the **shrink-window** command because whenever you make a window larger (by using **C-x ^**), **emacs** automatically makes the other windows smaller. Thus, you can get by just fine simply by making a window larger as the need arises and letting **emacs** adjust the other windows as it sees fit. Indeed, this is what most people do most of the time, which is why the **shrink-window** command does not really need to be bound to a key.

HINT
You will notice that commands to delete and split windows are similar: **C-x** followed by a number (**0**, **1**, **2** or **3**). It looks as if there might be a pattern. There isn't, so don't bother trying to invent one. Just practice and, after a few days, you will find that each individual command will become familiar on its own.

Commands to Control Buffers

As we explained earlier, a buffer is a work area that is maintained for you by **emacs**. You can have as many buffers as you want at the same time, each with its own name. At all times, you will have at least one buffer. If you start **emacs** without specifying the name of a specific file, **emacs** will create a buffer for you named ***scratch***.

Not all of your buffers need to be displayed in a window. Indeed, it is common to have an assortment of buffers (to use as separate work areas), of which only one or two are actually displayed in a window. As the need arises, you can change which buffers are displayed.

Figure 21-8 shows the commands you can use to control your buffers. These commands work together with the window-oriented commands we described in the previous section (see Figure 21-7).

Command	Description
C-x C-b	display a list of all your buffers
C-x b	display a different buffer in selected window
C-x k	kill (delete) a buffer
C-x 4 b	display a different buffer in next window
C-x 4 C-o	same as **C-x 4 b**, but don't change selected window

FIGURE 21-8. **emacs**: *Commands for controlling buffers*

The most important of these commands is **C-x b**. You use this command to tell **emacs** that you want to work with another buffer. This new buffer will be displayed in the window in which you are currently working (the selected window). The buffer that is currently in the window will be replaced, but not lost.

When you press **C-x b**, **emacs** will wait for you to enter the name of the buffer with which you want to work. If this buffer already exists, **emacs** will just move it into the window. Otherwise, **emacs** will create a brand new empty buffer in the window. Thus, **C-x b** is the command to use when you want to create a new buffer.

If you have more than a few buffers, it is easy to forget their names. To remind yourself, you can press **C-x C-b** to display a list. When you do, you will notice that **emacs** has created a new buffer called ***Buffer List*** to hold the list itself.

We mentioned that when you change the contents of a window, the buffer that was replaced is not destroyed: it exists in the background and you can recall it whenever you want. However, from time to time, you may actually want to delete a buffer. To do so, use the **C-x k** (kill) command. When you do, **emacs** will wait for you to enter the name of the buffer you want to kill. The default will be whatever buffer is in the selected window. If this is the buffer you want to delete, just press RETURN. Otherwise, type the name of another buffer and then press RETURN. If you decide to cancel the command, press **C-g**, the **emacs** cancel key.

HINT

You will not be allowed to delete all of your buffers. At the very least, **emacs** will force you to have a single buffer named ***scratch***.

There will be many times when you are working with one buffer and you want to display another buffer in a different window. To do so, there are two commands you can use. The command **C-x 4 b** tells **emacs** to display whichever buffer you specify in a different window. This new window then becomes the selected window. Thus, the **C-x 4 b** command allows you to switch to another buffer while still being able to see the contents of the old buffer. As with **C-x b**, if the buffer does not already exist, the **C-x 4 b** command will create a new buffer for you.

Sometimes you will want to look at the contents of another buffer without changing the selected buffer. For example, say that you are typing a letter to someone and you need to display his or her address, which is in a different buffer. You will want to display the contents of this second buffer without moving away from the window in which you are typing.

In such cases, use the **C-x 4 C-o** command. This is similar to the **C-x 4 b** command, except that the selected window does not change. One restriction (which only makes sense) is that you must specify the name of a buffer that already exists. After all, there is no point in displaying an empty buffer in another window.

HINT

Most **emacs** commands act on the selected buffer. However, commands that begin with **C-x 4** act on another buffer. Learning how to use the **C-x 4** commands allows you to control your buffers smoothly and quickly.

There are also **C-x 4** commands that deal with files. These commands are explained in the next section.

Commands for Working with Files

The crucial thing to understand about files is how they relate to buffers. In Chapter 22, we discuss the Unix file system and give a strict definition of a file. For now, let's just assume that a file is a collection of information that is given a name and that is kept on some type of storage device (usually a disk).

As we explained earlier, you can specify the names of one or more files when you start **emacs**. If you do, **emacs** will read the contents of each file into its own buffer and set them all up for you when the program begins.

Most of the time, however, you start work with a file by using a command that tells **emacs** to read the contents of the file into a buffer. Remember, though, a buffer is just a work area—a temporary work area—and, as such, it disappears when you quit **emacs**. Thus, if you want to save the contents of a buffer, you must do so *before* you quit.

The commands to work with files are summarized in Figure 21-9. Most of the commands act on the selected window. However, the commands that begin with **C-x 4** act on the next window. This makes it easy to load a file into another window without moving from your current window. (We discussed the idea of the next window earlier in the chapter.)

The commands in Figure 21-9 look a bit confusing, so here is some quick advice: the only file commands you really need to memorize are **C-x C-f** to read a file, and **C-x C-w** to save a file.

Okay, here is what it all means. The **C-x C-f** command tells **emacs** to read the contents of a file into a buffer. **emacs** will use the name of the file as the name of the buffer. If the file does not already exist, **emacs** will create a new buffer by that name. When **emacs** copies the contents of a file into a buffer, we say that you VISIT the file.

The idea of visiting a file is important because it implies an association between a buffer and a file. When you visit a file, **emacs** remembers that your buffer is associated with that particular file. If you make changes to the buffer, **emacs** will not let you quit without giving you a chance to save the contents of the buffer back to the file. (The idea is to make it difficult to lose your work by accident.) However,

Command	Description
C-x C-f	switch to buffer containing specified file
C-x C-v	replace buffer contents with specified file
C-x C-s	save a buffer to file
C-x C-w	save a buffer to specified file
C-x i	insert contents of a file into buffer
C-x 4 C-f	read contents of file into next window
C-x 4 f	same as **C-x 4 C-f**
C-x 4 r	same as **C-x 4 C-f**, read-only

FIGURE 21-9. **emacs**: *Commands for working with files*

when you create a new buffer that is not tied to a particular file, **emacs** will be more than glad to let you quit without reminding you to save your work.

Here is an example. You have two windows. In the first window, you have used the **C-x C-f** command to read in a file named **griffin** that contains a letter to a friend in the South Seas. When you entered this command, **emacs** created a buffer named **griffin** in which to copy the file. It is this buffer that you are looking at in the window. In the second window, you have used the **C-x b** command to create a brand new buffer named **sabine**, into which you have typed a letter to a friend in England.

Now, both windows are similar in that they each contain a buffer that holds some text. However, in the first window, a file is being visited, while in the second window no file is being visited. Thus, if you were to quit **emacs**, you would be asked if you want to save the contents of the **griffin** buffer back to the file, but you would not be asked if you want to save the **sabine** buffer.

Now, let's say you want to start editing a new buffer. You have two ways to create the buffer. You can use **C-x b**, or you can use **C-x C-f**. (Remember, each of these commands will create a new buffer if the one you specify does not already exist.) The difference is that if you use **C-x b**, emacs will create a buffer that is not tied to any particular file. If you use **C-x C-f**, the new buffer will be associated with a file of the same name. (That is, you will be visiting that file.) Thus, when you quit, you will be asked if you want to save the contents of the buffer to a file.

HINT

When you want to create a new buffer for work that you do not want to save, use the **C-x b** command. When you want to create a new buffer for work that you want to save in a file, use the **C-x C-f** command.

The **C-x C-v** command copies the contents of a file into the current buffer, replacing the current contents of the buffer. Thus, you use **C-x C-v** when you want to switch to a new file and you don't mind losing what you are working on.

When you replace the contents of a buffer using **C-x C-v**, whatever was in the buffer will be deleted. So, for your own protection, **emacs** will ask for your confirmation before it replaces a buffer that has not been saved.

If you want to insert the contents of a file into the current buffer without losing what is already in the buffer, use the **C-x i** command. The contents of the file you specify will be copied into the buffer at the current cursor position. The original contents of the buffer will be moved to make room for the new data, but will not be deleted.

There are two commands you can use to save the contents of a buffer to a file. Use the **C-x C-s** command when you are visiting a file and you want to save the contents of the buffer back to that same file. For example, if you are editing a file named **griffin**, the **C-x C-s** command will copy the current contents of the **griffin** buffer to the file named **griffin**. Obviously, this is a command you should use frequently to save your work.

The only trouble is, this command will probably not work on your system. As we explained earlier, when you press the **C-s** key, Unix will pause your screen display. To continue, you must press **C-q**. That means when you press **C-x C-s**, all that will happen is that the screen display will stop (and you will think that your computer has hung). If you have the presence of mind, you will remember to press **C-q** to continue, but that still won't let you save your file.

There are two solutions to this problem. The simplest is to use the **C-x C-w** command to save your file. This command is similar to **C-x C-s** except it allows you to save the buffer contents to any file you want, not just the one you are visiting. When you type **C-x C-w**, **emacs** will prompt you for the name of the file to which you want to save. The default will be the file you are visiting, so if this is the file to which you want to save, you need only press RETURN. If you want to save to a different file, simply type the name and press RETURN.

The important thing is that pressing **C-x C-w** followed by RETURN is the same as pressing **C-x C-s**. Thus, you need not feel deprived that the **C-s** key is off limits.

The better solution, though, is to customize **emacs** so you can use another key instead of **C-s**. We explain how to do this later in the chapter.

Whenever you need to specify a file name, **emacs** will start you off by displaying the name of the current directory in the minibuffer. You can then type the name of the file you want. (Remember, if the beginning of the file name is unique, you can save keystrokes by using the completion facility we described earlier in the chapter.)

Here is an example. Your current directory is named **memos**. This directory lies within your home directory. (All these ideas are explained in Chapter 22.) When you press **C-x C-f**, emacs will display the following prompt in the minibuffer:

```
Find file: ~/memos/
```

The ~ character—also explained in Chapter 22—is an abbreviation for your home directory.

This particular prompt tells you that **emacs** is guessing that you want a file in this particular directory. Type the name of the file and press RETURN. If you want a file in a different directory, you can use the **DEL** key to erase the directory name and specify your own. At the end of this new directory name, type a **/** (slash), then the file name, and then press RETURN.

As we mentioned earlier, the commands that begin with **C-x 4** are used to manipulate the next window. The **C-x 4 C-f** command works like **C-x C-f** except that it acts on the next window. As a convenience, you can use **C-x 4 f** instead of **C-x 4 C-f**.

The **C-x 4 r** command is similar except that it sets the buffer to be read-only when it reads in the file. This allows you to examine an important file in another window without having to worry about changing the file by accident.

The Cursor and the Idea of Point

In **emacs**, there is a special name for the current position of the cursor. This location, within the buffer, is called POINT (not "the point", just "point"). The idea of point is important because it is at this location that whatever you type is inserted into the buffer. Moreover, when you read the **emacs** documentation and the descriptions in the built-in Help facility, you will see many references to point.

Although the cursor lies under a particular character, point is actually between two characters: the one at the cursor position and the character immediately to its left. For example, say that, in your buffer, you are reading the word **tergiversate** and the cursor is under the **g**. Point is considered to be between the **r** and the **g**.

What's in a Name?   Point
The original **emacs** was developed to be a set of editing macros for an obtuse text editing facility named TECO. Within TECO, you used the **.** (period) character as the command for accessing the current location within the text. Since the **.** character was really just a dot, the command that it represented was referred to as the "point" command. In **emacs**, the current location within the current buffer is marked by the cursor and is referred to as "point".

It is important to realize that each buffer has its own point which is carefully maintained by **emacs**. Of course, there is only one cursor, and it is used to show where point is in the buffer that is currently active. However, **emacs** remembers where point is in each buffer so that, as you switch from one buffer to another, **emacs** knows exactly where to place the cursor.

Moving the Cursor

Moving the cursor is straightforward. You can move it up and down, and backward and forward. The commands for moving the cursor are summarized in Figure 21-10.

Notice that there are two types of commands. First, there are the commands that move forward or backward by a particular amount. For example, you can move to the left or right by a single character by using **C-b** and **C-f**, respectively. There are similar commands to move by a single word, line, sentence or paragraph.

As a convenience, you can use the cursor control keys to move a single position at a time. Thus, pressing the LEFT key is the same as **C-b**, and pressing the UP key is the same as **C-p**.

Backward	Forward	
C-b	**C-f**	a single character
LEFT	RIGHT	a single character
M-b	**M-f**	a word
C-p	**C-n**	a line
UP	DOWN	a line
M-a	**M-e**	a sentence
M-{	**M-}**	a paragraph
Beginning	**End**	
C-a	C-e	the current line
M-<	M->	the entire buffer

FIGURE 21-10. **emacs**: *Commands for moving the cursor*

Second, there are commands that move to the beginning or end of something. (You will find these commands to be especially useful.) For example, to jump to the very beginning of the buffer, use **M-<** (META less-than sign). To jump to the end of the buffer, use **M->** (META greater-than sign).

Note: Within **emacs**, a "paragraph" of regular text is defined as a block of characters that begins with one or more space or tab characters, or that is preceded by a blank line. Thus, you can put blank lines between your paragraphs, or start them with a space or tab (or any combination).

If you look at the key combinations, you can see some patterns. For example, the letters **b** and **f** stand for **backward** and **forward**; the letters **p** and **n** stand for **previous** and **next**; and so on. Still, you don't really need to memorize **emacs** keys in this way. Just practice for a few days, and you will remember without even trying.

Repeating a Command: Prefix Arguments

To perform an **emacs** command a specified number of times, you type what is called a PREFIX ARGUMENT in front of the command. For example, you can type the prefix argument that means "repeat the following command 6 times" and then press **C-p**. This will move the cursor up 6 lines. Because the prefix argument specifies a number, it is also referred to as a NUMERIC ARGUMENT. (The term "argument" is a programming word that describes a value passed to a program when it is executed.)

To specify a prefix argument, hold down the META key and type a number. For example, to move the cursor up 6 lines, press **M-6 C-p**. An alternative (especially if your keyboard does not have a META key) is to use the ESCAPE key instead. Thus, to move 15 characters to the right, you can press **ESC 15 C-f**.

You can use a prefix argument with any command, and **emacs** will interpret the numeric value in the way that makes the most sense for that particular command. Where prefix arguments really come in handy is when you combine them with the cursor movement commands we discussed in the previous section.

HINT

Take a few moments and practice various combinations of prefix arguments with the cursor movement commands in Figure 21-10.

The number you specify can be either positive or negative. If you use a negative number with a cursor movement command, it will move in the opposite direction. For example, to move the cursor up 6 lines, use either **M-6 C-p** or **M--6 C-n**. (Perhaps this last command would be clearer if we wrote it as **ESC -6 C-n**.)

If your terminal has a META key, you will hold it down as you type a prefix argument. For example, when you use the **M-6 C-p** command, you will have to hold down the META key as you type the **6**. Some people find this inconvenient, so there are two alternatives. First, as we mentioned, you can press **ESC** instead of holding down META. Second, you can press **C-u** instead. (The name comes from the fact that this key executes a command called **universal-argument**.) Thus, to move the cursor down 6 lines you can use either **M-6 C-n** or **C-u 6 C-n**. Although this looks like an extra keystroke, it is actually easier, especially when you are using a multi-digit prefix argument. For example, to move the cursor down 120 lines, you can use **C-u 120 C-n**.

As a final shortcut, the **C-u** command has a special meaning when you use it before a command *without* specifying a number. In such cases, the **C-u** key tells **emacs** to repeat the next command 4 times. And you can use more than one **C-u** keypress in a row to multiply this effect.

This may seem a bit strange at first, but it is really useful, so take a moment to figure it out.

Here is a simple example. To move the cursor down 4 lines, you can use **M-4 C-n** or **C-u 4 C-n**. But, as a shortcut, you can use **C-u** by itself: **C-u C-n**. Similarly, to move the cursor 4 characters to the left, you can use **C-u C-b**.

The power of the **C-u** prefix comes when you use more than one in a row. Because each such prefix multiplies the next command by a factor of 4, using two in a row tells **emacs** to repeat a command 16 times. And using three in a row repeats a command 64 times.

For example, to move the cursor down 16 lines, you can use **C-u C-u C-n**. Or, to move the cursor 64 characters to the right, you can use **C-u C-u C-u C-f**. Although this may seem a bit awkward, it is actually quick and easy to type.

To summarize, the various prefix argument combinations are shown in Figure 21-11.

Prefix	Effect
M-*number*	repeat command specified number of times
ESC *number*	repeat command specified number of times
C-u *number*	repeat command specified number of times
C-u	repeat command 4 times
C-u C-u	repeat command 16 times
C-u C-u C-u	repeat command 64 times
C-u C-u C-u C-u	repeat command 256 times

FIGURE 21-11.   **emacs**: *Prefix argument combinations*

HINT

The **C-u C-u** prefix is especially useful when you are working with characters and lines. This is because 16 characters is about one fifth of a line and 16 lines is about one third of a standard-sized screen. It is worth a few moments of your time to practice putting together the **C-u C-u** prefix with your favorite character and line commands, just to fix them firmly in your mind. For example, try:

C-u C-u C-f	move 16 characters to the right
C-u C-u C-b	move 16 characters to the left
C-u C-u C-n	move 16 lines down
C-u C-u C-p	move 16 lines up

You may find it handy to hardwire these particular combinations directly into your motor cortex (the lump of gray matter in your prefrontal gyrus, just anterior to the central sulcus). The details for doing so, however, are beyond the scope of this book.

Moving Through the Buffer

There will be many times when you want to page through the buffer. Perhaps the most common example is wanting to read something from beginning to end. You start at the top of the buffer and read one screenful at a time.

When you tell **emacs** to display information that is just beyond the border of your window, we say that you are SCROLLING. For example, if you have read what is on the screen and you move down to the next screenful, we say that you scroll down. Similarly, you can scroll up (and display the previous screenful). If the buffer contains very long lines, they may not completely fit on the screen. In such a case, you might scroll right (to read the rightmost portion of the line) and scroll left (to move back to the left-hand margin).

Notice that we talk about scrolling as if *you* do it, rather than as if **emacs** is doing it. For example, someone might ask a friend, "What command do I use to scroll to the right?" This is a common way of speaking that reminds us that computers are actually extensions of our minds.

Figure 21-12 shows the **emacs** commands you can use to move throughout the buffer. The scrolling commands are completely straightforward, and there is not much that we want to say about them other than be sure to memorize **C-v** and **M-v** *this very minute.* These are two crucial commands that you will use every day of your life, so don't even leave this paragraph without committing them to memory. The right and left scrolling commands are less important: you need them only when you are dealing with unusually long lines.

One variation on the scrolling commands is **M-C-v**. This command scrolls down in the next window. (We discussed the idea of the next window earlier in the chapter.) Using **M-C-v**, you can scroll through the next window without having to leave the window in which you are working. Unfortunately, there is no easy way to scroll *up* in the next window.

For completeness, we have included the **M-<** (jump to the beginning of the buffer) and **M->** (jump to the end of the buffer) commands in Figure 21-12. We described these commands earlier in the chapter in the section on moving the cursor. However, they also belong here because they are handy for zipping around.

Finally, there is the **C-l** (lowercase letter "L") command. This command redisplays the screen so that the line on which the cursor lies is in the middle of the screen. This command is handy when the cursor is near the bottom of the screen and you want to pull it up somewhat to read the lines underneath. **C-l** is a useful command that is all too often neglected. Try it for yourself to see how useful it can be.

Command	Description
C-v	scroll down one screenful
M-v	scroll up one screenful
C-x >	scroll to the right
C-x <	scroll to the left
M-C-v	scroll down in the next window
M-<	jump to the beginning of buffer
M->	jump to the end of buffer
C-l	redisplay the screen, current line in middle

FIGURE 21-12.   **emacs**: *Commands to move throughout the buffer*

Using Line Numbers

Most of the time you will move around the buffer in small and large jumps or (as we will explain shortly) by searching for a particular pattern. However, there will be times when it is handy to be able to jump right to a specific line based on its position in the buffer. For example, you may want to jump to line 43.

There are two commands you can use in this regard. They are described in Figure 21-13.

First, you can use the **M-x line-number-mode** command to tell **emacs** to display the line number of the current line. Once you enter this command, **emacs** will display the current number on the mode line. Here is an example:

```
--**-Emacs: *Help*            (Fundamental)--L43--65%--------
```

In this case, we are looking at a buffer named ***Help***. The cursor is currently on line 43, and the top line of the screen is 65 percent of the way through the buffer. (The top line of the buffer is considered line 1.)

To jump to a particular line, use the **M-x goto-line** command. When you type this command, **emacs** will prompt you to enter a line number. Type the number you want and press RETURN. **emacs** will jump to the line that you want to specify.

Mark, Point, and the Region

Within **emacs** there are commands that operate on various character groupings. For example, you can work with single characters, words, lines, sentences and

Command	Description
M-x line-number-mode	display current line number
M-x goto-line	jump to line with specified number

FIGURE 21-13.   **emacs**: Commands to use line numbers

paragraphs. To provide flexibility, **emacs** also lets you define an area of the buffer—called a REGION—which can be as long or short as you want. Once you define a region, you can operate on it using any one of several commands. For example, you can define a region of, say, thirteen and a half lines, and then erase it. Or you can define a region of ten words, and then change them all to uppercase.

Here is how it works. A region is defined as all the characters between two locations: MARK and point. Point you already know; it is the location of the cursor. Mark is a location you can set for yourself.

There are several ways to define mark. The simplest is to move the cursor to wherever you want mark to be, and then press **C-SPC** (CTRL-SPACE). Mark is now at that location. You can then move the cursor to a new location (which becomes point). The region is now all the characters between mark and point.

Perhaps the best way to think of mark and point is as two locations in the buffer, both of which you can set. However, since there is only one cursor, **emacs** can only show you one of these locations (point); you will have to remember where mark is. Still, it's not all that hard once you get used to it. Most people set mark for a particular purpose, and then use it right away before they forget where it is.

A simple example will make it all clear. In order to understand the example, we will tell you that the command **C-x C-u** converts all the characters in the region to uppercase (capital letters).

Let's say that you have a line in the buffer that reads as follows:

If you are reading this in a bookstore, buy this book now!

You decide that the last four words ("buy this book now") should be in uppercase. The plan is to define the region to consist of these four words, then use **C-x C-u** to change all the characters in the region to uppercase.

To start, move the cursor to the **b** at the beginning of **buy**. Point is now at this location. Now press **C-SPC**. This sets mark to be at this location as well. Next, move the cursor to the **!** character after **now**. Now mark is at the **b** and point is at the **!**. Press **C-x C-u** to convert all the characters from **b** to **!** to uppercase. The line looks as follows:

If you are reading this in a bookstore, BUY THIS BOOK NOW!

Since these are important concepts, let's take a moment to be precise. As you may remember from our discussion earlier in the chapter, point is not exactly the same as the cursor. The cursor sits under a particular character. Point is really between two characters, the one at the cursor and one to its left. For example, consider the line:

abcdefghijklmnopqrstuvwxyz

If the cursor were under the **m**, point would be between the **l** and the **m**. When you set mark, it works the same way. Say that while the cursor is under the **m**, you press **C-SPC**. Mark (and point) are now both between the **l** and the **m**. Now, say that you move the cursor to be under the **g**. Mark is still between the **l** and the **m**, and point is now between the **f** and the **g**. Thus, the region consists of the letters **ghilkl**. If you were to press **C-x C-u**, the line would change to:

abcdefGHIJKLmnopqrstuvwxyz

This is why, in our previous example, we had to make sure that the rightmost boundary of the region was set to the character *after* the last one on which we wanted to operate. (You will remember that we had the word **now!** and that we moved the cursor to the **!** .)

Using Mark and Point to Define the Region

A region is defined as all the contiguous characters between mark and point. Point is always at the position of the cursor. Thus, to define a region, all you need to do is set mark.

Broadly speaking, there are two ways in which mark can be set. First, you can use a command that sets mark. Second, many commands that perform some function or other automatically set mark to a new value. (When this happens, you will see a message telling you that mark has been set.)

For example, when you use a command that inserts text into the buffer, **emacs** will finish the operation by setting mark at one end of the new text and point at the other end. Thus, the region will contain the newly inserted text.

Figure 21-14 shows the commands that explicitly set mark. Two of these commands set mark without changing point (**C-SPC** and **M-@**). Two other

Command	Description
C-SPC	set mark to current location of point
C-@	same as **C-SPC**
M-x set-mark-command	same as **C-SPC**
C-x C-x	interchange mark and point
M-@	set mark after next word (do not move point)
M-h	put region around paragraph
C-x h	put region around entire buffer

FIGURE 21-14.   **emacs**: *Commands to set mark and define a region*

commands set both mark and point (**M-h** and **C-x h**). A final command interchanges the location of mark and point (**C-x C-x**).

Strictly speaking, the command to set mark is **C-@**. However, it happens that with many terminals, pressing **C-SPC** will generate the same character as **C-@**. Thus, although **C-SPC** is not a real character, we say that you can use it to set mark. When you do so, you are really using **C-@**, but **C-SPC** is a more convenient key combination. If **C-SPC** does not work on your terminal—for example, if it generates a regular **SPC** character—you will have to use **C-@**.

(Note: On most keyboards, you use **C-@** by pressing **C-2**, because the **2** is the same key as **@**. You do not need to hold down the SHIFT key.)

If neither **C-SPC** nor **C-@** work on your system, you can execute the command directly by using **M-x set-mark-command**. Typing this command by hand is not as bad as it looks: with completion (explained earlier in the chapter) all you really need to type is **M-x set-m RET**.

Once you set mark, it stays where it is until you change it or until another command changes it. When you define a region, it does not matter whether mark comes before or after point. Nor does it matter which one you set first.

As we explained earlier, you can work with as many buffers as you want at one time. Within **emacs**, each buffer has its own point and its own mark. Thus, if you set mark in one buffer and then move to another buffer, the original mark will still be there when you return.

Because mark is invisible, you may forget where it is. Unlike point, which is marked by the cursor, there is no way to look at the screen and see mark. In such cases, you can use the **C-x C-x** command to exchange the location of mark and point. Thus, the new location of the cursor will be where point was. To move the cursor back to its original location, simply press **C-x C-x** again.

HINT

Normally, you will set and use mark within a short time, so you will not forget its location. However, if you do, you can visualize the region by pressing **C-x C-x** twice. The cursor will jump back and forth from one boundary to the other.

You can always set mark by moving to wherever you want it and pressing **C-SPC** (or whatever command works for you). However, there are three other commands that provide handy shortcuts.

The **M-@** command sets mark after the current word. For example, let's say that you are editing some text that contains the sentence:

`Okay boys, let's defenestrate him.`

The cursor is currently under the **d** in **defenestrate**. You press **M-@**. This sets mark to be at the space at the end of the word (after the **e**). Point will not change.

You can verify this by pressing **C-x C-x**. This is a good way to set the region to contain a particular word on which you want to perform an operation.

If you want to set mark to be more than one word away, you can use a prefix argument (explained earlier in the chapter). In our previous example, for instance, let's say that the cursor is once again under the **d** in **defenestrate**, and you want to set mark to be after the end of word **him** (2 words away). Use **ESC 2 M-@**. This leaves mark at the period. To set mark to be 10 words away, use **ESC 10 M-@**, and so on.

The next command, **M-h**, sets the region by moving both mark and point to contain an entire paragraph. (Within **emacs**, a "paragraph" starts with one or more space or tab characters, or is preceded by a blank line.) If the cursor is within a paragraph, **M-h** sets point to the beginning of the paragraph and mark to the end of the paragraph. Thus, when you press **M-h**, it not only sets the region, it also moves the cursor to the beginning of the paragraph. If you press **M-h** when the cursor is on a blank line, point and mark will be set to the beginning and end of the following paragraph.

The final command, **C-x h**, marks the entire buffer as being in the region. It does this by moving point to the beginning of the buffer and mark to the end of the buffer.

Operating on the Region

In the previous two sections, we explained how to set mark and point, and thereby define the region. The reason we do this is to make it easy to perform an operation on all the characters in the region. Figure 21-15 shows the **emacs** commands you can use.

Generally speaking, the most useful of these commands is **C-w**. This command kills (erases) the entire region. If you change your mind after the deletion, you can press **C-_** (CTRL-underscore) to undo the operation.

Command	Description
C-w	kill (erase) all the characters
C-x C-l	convert the characters to lowercase
C-x C-u	convert the characters to uppercase
M-=	count the lines and characters
M-|	run a shell command, use characters as data

FIGURE 21-15. **emacs**: *Commands that act upon the region*

The **C-x C-l** and **C-x C-u** commands convert all the characters in the region to upper- and lowercase, respectively. These commands work well with the mark-setting commands to change the case of a word or group of words.

For example, to change one word to uppercase, move the cursor to the beginning of the word, and press **M-@** (set mark at end of word) followed by **C-x C-u**. To change 5 words to lowercase, move to the beginning of the first word, and press **ESC 5 M-@** (set mark at end of fifth word) followed by **C-x C-l**.

Here is one last example. Your cursor is in the middle of a line, and you want to change the entire line to uppercase. Type **C-a** (move to beginning of line), **C-SPC** (set mark), **C-e** (move to end of line), and finally, **C-x C-u** (change region to uppercase).

The **M-=** (META equal-sign) command will count all the lines and characters in the region. This command is handy if you are a writer who has to keep measuring his output in order to convince his editor that he is making progress. (We are not mentioning any names here.) Combined with the region-defining commands, **M-=** works quickly and easily.

For example, say that you want to find out how many lines are in the buffer. The **C-x h** command will set the region to the entire buffer. Thus, to count all the lines in the buffer, all you need to type is **C-x h** and then **M-=**. Here is some typical output:

Region has 108 lines, 1724 characters

Try it: it's too cool for words.

Finally, the **M-|** (META vertical-bar) command will send the contents of the region to a shell command to be processed. To store the output, **emacs** will create a buffer named ***Shell Command Output***. If this buffer already exists, its contents will be replaced by the output of the new command.

This command is incredibly useful, so let's look at a few examples. First, let's say that you want to sort all the lines in the buffer. All you have to do is use the **C-x h** command to set the region to the entire buffer, and then use **M-|** to run the **sort** command. To test this out, let's create a customized list of all the **emacs** commands in alphabetical order.

To get the raw material, we can use the built-in Help facility (described later in the chapter). The command to use Help is **C-h**. If you type **C-h b**, **emacs** will create a new buffer, named ***Help***, that contains a full set of one-line descriptions for every key. (The **b** stands for **key bindings**.) Each line contains the name of the key, followed by the name of the function it invokes. Here are two examples:

```
C-h b              describe-bindings
ESC |              shell-command-on-region
```

(Notice that the META key is described as **ESC**.)

So all we have to do is generate a buffer full of key descriptions and sort them. When we do, we will use the **sort** command with the **-u** (unique) option. This option eliminates all duplicate lines. (See the discussion of **sort** in Chapter 17.) In this case, the **-u** option will effectively eliminate all but one of the blank lines.

So, here is how to create your own cool, personalized, alphabetical list of **emacs** commands:

1. **C-h b**: Create a buffer named ***Help*** that contains the key descriptions.

2. **C-x o**: Change to the ***Help*** buffer.

3. **C-x h**: Set the region to be the entire buffer.

4. **M-| sort -u**: Sort all the lines in the buffer.

5. **C-x o**: Change to the ***Shell Command Output*** buffer.

At this point, you may want to save the list to a file for future reference. If so, use the command:

6. **C-x C-w**: Save the buffer to a file.

Before we leave this topic, here is one more useful example. In Chapter 15, we described the **fmt** command you can use to format text. The **fmt** command makes your text look as uniform as possible, while preserving paragraphs and indentations. This is a nice command to smooth out ragged text that has been the victim of brutal modifications and editing. (In **emacs**, this is known as "filling" text.)

To format the entire buffer, use **C-x h** (set the region), followed by **M-| fmt** (process the region with the **fmt** command).

Note: **emacs** has a command, **M-x fill-region**, that has much the same effect. This main difference is that **M-x fill-region** changes the original region. Using **M-| fmt** creates a new buffer containing only the formatted text.

Kill and Delete: Two Ways to Erase Text

There are a variety of **emacs** commands you can use to erase text from the buffer. As a convenience, **emacs** will remember the erased text so you can insert it back into the buffer at a later time. For example, to move a paragraph from one place to another, you can erase it and then insert it somewhere else.

Once you start using these commands, it won't be long before you see there is no need to preserve everything. For example, when you erase a single character or an empty line, there is really no need to save it. However, when you erase a whole paragraph line or an entire region, it does make sense to keep a copy of the text.

For this reason, **emacs** is designed so that some commands save the erased text while others do not. In general, **emacs** saves the text from commands that erase more than a single character. Such commands are called KILL COMMANDS. **emacs** does not save the text from commands that erase only a single character or whitespace. These commands are called DELETE COMMANDS. ("Whitespace" refers to space, tab or **newline** characters. See Chapter 9 for details.)

The custom within **emacs** is to use these two terms—kill and delete—as verbs. When we talk about KILLING some text, we imply that the text is being removed and saved. When we DELETE some text, we imply that the text is removed and not saved.

In the next few sections, we will discuss first the delete commands and then the kill commands. Then we will explain how **emacs** saves erased text, and what commands you can use to insert such text back into the buffer. You will find that these commands are especially useful, as you can use them to copy or move text from one part of the buffer to another, or even between two different buffers.

Commands to Delete Text

As we explained, delete commands erase only a single character or whitespace. These commands are shown in Figure 21-16. Remember, unlike the kill commands, the erased text is not saved for later recall. Still, you can't lose more than one character at a time.

We have already covered the first two commands. **DEL** erases the character to the left of the cursor. This is the key to use when you are typing and you need to back up and fix a mistake. The **C-d** key erases the character that is at the cursor position. More precisely, **DEL** erases to the left of point and **C-d** erases to the right of point.

Command	Description
DEL	delete one character to the left of cursor
C-d	delete one character at the position of cursor
M-	delete spaces and tabs around point
M-SPC	delete spaces and tabs around point; leave one space
C-x C-o	delete blank lines around current line
M-^	join two lines (delete **newline** + surrounding spaces)

FIGURE 21-16. emacs: *Commands to delete text*

As with other **emacs** commands, you can use a prefix argument (explained earlier in the chapter) with these two commands to operate on more than one character at a time. For example, to erase 5 characters to the left, you can use **ESC 5 DEL**; to erase 18 characters to the right, you can use **ESC 18 C-d**.

When you use such commands, you are erasing more than one character and, as such, you are killing and not deleting. For this reason, **emacs** does save the erased text when you use **DEL** or **C-d** to erase more than one character.

SECRET HINT

Here is a way to make a bit of money for yourself.

Take this book and go to a bar where Unix people hang out. Look for some people who are learning **emacs** and practicing on a portable computer, and sit down next to them. Open the book so that Figure 21-17 (shown in the next section on page 61) is clearly visible and casually leave it where the people next to you can see it. This figure contains a summary of all the **emacs** kill commands. Pretend you are not looking at the book.

Next, strike up a casual conversation with the people next to you and carefully work the topic around to the **emacs** kill commands. Offer to bet them a small sum of money that they can't think of a way to kill text without pressing any upper- or lowercase letters.

When they sneak a look at the book, pretend you don't see. They will see that **M-DEL** is a kill command, and accept the bet. When they press **M-DEL**, pretend to be annoyed with yourself, and tell them you would like a chance to make back your money. Offer them a much larger bet that you can kill text without using **M-DEL** and without pressing any alphabetic keys.

Now, look the other way for a second, which will give them another chance to check out Figure 21-17. Aside from **M-DEL**, they will not see any other kill commands that do not use a letter of the alphabet.

As soon as they take your bet, press **ESC 5 DEL** and clean up.

To continue, the **M-** command erases any **space** or **tab** characters that happen to be on either side of point. This command provides a quick way to clean up a section of whitespace. For example, say that you have typed the following text and the cursor is under one of the spaces between **tea** and **ch**:

```
Everything we tea      ch you is true.
```

If you press **M-**, **emacs** will erase all the surrounding spaces. The line now looks like:

Everything we teach you is true.

The **M-SPC** (META-SPACE) command is similar, except that it leaves exactly one space. Here is an example. You have just typed the line:

The sentence above is   only partially correct.

You would like to erase the extra spaces. Move the cursor to one of the spaces between **is** and **only** and press **M-SPC**. The line is changed to the following:

The sentence above is only partially correct.

The **C-x C-o** command performs the analogous operation for blank lines. This command will erase all the blank lines surrounding the current line. For example, say that the buffer contains the following text:

Everything we teach you is true.

The sentence above is only partially correct.

Don't believe everything you read.

You would like only a single blank line between each line of text. Move to one of the blank lines following the first line, and press **C-x C-o**. The extra blank lines will be erased and you will be left with the following:

Everything we teach you is true.

The sentence above is only partially correct.

Don't believe everything you read.

Finally, the **M-^** command will join two lines into one long one. This command joins the current line to the one immediately above it, while leaving a single space between the two groups of text. Any extra spaces (at the end of the first line or at the beginning of second line) are removed. For example, say that you have the following lines of text:

This is the first sentence.
This is the second sentence.

You want to join these two lines. Move the cursor to the second line and press **M-^**. You will now have one long line:

This is the first sentence. This is the second sentence.

The cursor will be at the place where the lines were joined, in this case, under the space between the two sentences.

Commands to Kill Text

Most of the commands that erase text are kill commands. When you use a kill command, **emacs** saves the text that is erased in case you want to insert it back into the buffer. Figure 21-17 summarizes the various kill commands.

The **C-k** command erases all the characters from the cursor to the end of the line. More precisely, **C-k** erases from point to the end of the line. (Remember, point is between the cursor and character to its left.) If you are at the beginning of a line when you press **C-k**, it will erase all the characters on the line. If you are on a blank line, **C-k** will erase the line itself. Thus, you can erase a line completely by (1) moving to the beginning, (2) erasing all the characters, and then (3) erasing the line itself. The sequence to do this is **C-a C-k C-k**.

HINT

To erase an entire line: if you are at the beginning of the line, press **C-k C-k**. If you are not at the beginning of the line, press **C-a C-k C-k**.

There are two kill commands that erase a word. The **M-d** command erases from point to the end of the word. The **M-DEL** command erases from point to the

Command	Description
C-k	kill from cursor to end of line
M-d	kill a word
M-DEL	kill a word backward
M-k	kill from cursor to end of sentence
C-x DEL	kill backward to beginning of sentence
C-w	kill the region
M-z *char*	kill through next occurrence of *char*

FIGURE 21-17. **emacs**: *Commands to kill text*

beginning of the word. Remember that point lies between the cursor and the character to its left. Thus, **M-DEL** does not erase the character above the cursor.

Here are a few examples. Say that you have just typed the following text:

This book is not the best Unix book ever written.

You decide you want to erase the word **not**. There are two ways to do it. First, you can move the cursor to the space between **is** and **not** and press **M-d** to erase the next word. Or you can move to the **t** at the beginning of **the** and press **M-DEL** to erase the previous word.

Until you practice these commands, the exact positioning may seem a little odd. However, when you look carefully at the location of point, it all starts to make sense. Earlier in the chapter, we described how **M-f** moves the cursor forward by one word, and **M-b** moves the cursor backward by one word. When you use **M-f**, it leaves you on the space between two words. When you use **M-b**, it leaves you on the first character of a word. Take a few moments and experiment. You will see that **M-f** and **M-d** work well together when you are moving forward, and **M-b** and **M-DEL** work well together when you are moving backward.

The next two kill commands erase text within a sentence. The **M-k** command erases forward, from point to the end of the sentence. The **C-x DEL** command erases backward, from point to the beginning of the sentence. When you use these commands, it is helpful to remember the commands that move the cursor one sentence at a time. **M-e** moves forward by one sentence; **M-a** moves backward by one sentence. These relationships are summarized in Figure 21-18.

The next kill command, **C-w**, is one you will use frequently, as it allows you to kill the entire region. (As we described earlier in the chapter, the region consists of all the characters between mark and point.) **C-w** is particularly handy when you want to move a section of text. All you need to do is set mark and point to enclose the text, use **C-w** to kill the region, and then insert the text back into the buffer at a different location (or even into another buffer). We will discuss this idea—which is called "yanking"—later in the chapter.

The final kill command is **M-z**. When you type this command, **emacs** will prompt you to specify a single character. **emacs** will kill all the text from point

	WORDS		SENTENCES	
	Backward	*Forward*	*Backward*	*Forward*
Move:	M-b	M-f	M-a	**M-e**
Kill:	M-DEL	M-d	C-x DEL	**M-k**

FIGURE 21-18. **emacs**: *Commands to move and kill by word or sentence*

(your current position) to the next occurrence of that character. When you use this command, we say that you are "zapping" the characters; thus, the name **M-z**.

Here is an example. You are editing an important document that was typed by someone who is not as smart as you. You come across a line that reads:

```
I can't imagine how anyone could prefer emacs to vi.
```

Having read this, it is the work of a moment to move to the space following the **I** (at the beginning of the sentence) and type **M-z d**. This erases all the characters from the space up to (and including) the **d** in **could**. The line now reads:

```
I prefer emacs to vi.
```

The Kill Ring and Yanking; Moving and Copying

We have already explained that there are two types of commands that erase text. The delete commands erase single characters and whitespace. The kill commands erase more than one character. Whenever you use a kill command, **emacs** saves the text in what is called a KILL RING. (The name will make sense in a moment.) This allows you to move to a different location and insert the text should the need arise. **emacs** has a number of commands that let you work with the kill ring and its contents. These commands are summarized in Figure 21-19.

The kill ring is really a set of storage areas, each of which holds text that has been killed. Each storage block is called a KILL RING ENTRY. When you kill some text, it is stored as the most recent kill ring entry. To insert this text back into the

Command	Description
C-y	yank most recently killed text
C-u C-y	same as **C-y**, cursor at beginning of new text
M-y	replace yanked text with earlier killed text
M-w	copy region to kill ring, without erasing
M-C-w	append next kill to newest kill ring entry
C-h v kill-ring	display the actual values in the kill ring

FIGURE 21-19.   **emacs**: *Commands to yank text*

buffer, you move the cursor to where you want to insert the text, and press **C-y**. When you insert such text into a buffer, we say that you YANK the text. (Thus, the name **C-y**.)

What's in a Name?   Kill, Yank

In the **emacs** culture, "killing" means deleting text that is saved to the kill ring; "yanking" means copying this text back into the buffer. In most other systems, these operations would be referred to by the more civilized names of "cutting" and "pasting".

In other words, if you understand how to cut and paste, you understand how to kill and yank.

When you use the **C-y** command to yank some text into the buffer, **emacs** sets mark at the beginning of the text and point at the end of the text. This means that the text is now defined to be the region, in case you want to operate on it in some way. It also means that the cursor is at the end of the text.

If you use the **C-u C-y** command instead, **emacs** will yank the exact same text, but the locations of mark and point will be reversed. So, although the region will still enclose the newly inserted text, the cursor will be at the beginning. This is useful when you want to yank some text and then insert something in front of it.

HINT
Before you yank text, think about where you want the cursor. If you want it at the beginning of the text, use the **C-u C-y** command. If you want the cursor at the end of the text, use the **C-y** command.

Let's talk for a moment about what happens as you kill more than one section of text. The first time you kill text, **emacs** stores it in a kill ring entry. Later, when you kill more text, **emacs** stores it in a different entry. Since the kill ring has a number of entries, there is no need to throw away old text until you fill up each of the entries. And even then, you need discard only the very oldest material in order to make room for the new text.

By default, the kill ring has 30 entries. Thus, **emacs** can store the last 30 collections of killed text. (You can change this number if you want, but it is rarely necessary.) So what happens when all the kill ring entries are filled, and you kill some more text? **emacs** discards the oldest entry and uses it to hold the new text.

Some people like to visualize the kill ring as a number of entries organized into a circle. As **emacs** needs to store text, it works its way around the circle, using one entry after another. Thus, we have the idea of a ring.

This means it is possible to yank not only the most recent kill ring entry, but the entry before that, and the entry before that, and so on (up to 30 different entries). To do so, you use the **M-y** command.

Here is how it works. Just after you have used one of the **C-y** or **C-u C-y** commands, take a look and see if the newly inserted text was what you wanted. If what you wanted is stored in a previous kill ring entry, press **M-y**. **emacs** will erase the text and replace it with the previous entry. If this is what you wanted, fine. If not, press **M-y** again. You can continue pressing **M-y** until you run out of kill ring entries. In conceptual terms, you can think of the **M-y** command as working its way around the kill ring, showing you one entry after another.

HINT

If you are using **M-y** repeatedly to search for an old kill ring entry, and you can't find what you want, you can always use **C-x u** to undo the last insertion and forget the whole thing.

emacs maintains only one kill ring for all the buffers. This means that you can kill some text in one buffer, and yank it into another buffer. Indeed, this is exactly how you move text from one buffer to another: kill some text, move to another buffer, then yank the last kill ring entry.

This procedure works well, but it does have one drawback: You have to erase something before you can move it. What if you merely want to copy something without destroying the original?

The solution is to define the region (using mark and point) so as to contain the text, and then use the **M-w** command. This tells **emacs** to copy the text to the kill ring without erasing anything. You can then yank the text wherever you want.

Thus, to copy something from one buffer to another, you set mark and point to enclose the text, press **M-w**, change to the other buffer, move to where you want to insert the text, and then yank it with **C-y**. Of course, this will also work with two locations in the same buffer.

When you use more than one kill command in a row, **emacs** will automatically collect all the killed text into the same kill ring entry. This allows you to move from place to place, killing text and accumulating it into a single large block. You can then yank all of it with a single **C-y** or **C-u C-y** command.

As soon as you use a non-kill command, **emacs** stops the accumulation. The next time you kill something, it will be put into a different kill ring entry. However, there is a way to tell **emacs** to place killed text into the previous entry. All you need to do is press **M-C-w** before you kill the text. (If you don't have a META key, press ESCAPE and then **C-w**.)

For example, let's say that you have been moving around the buffer, using the **M-k** command to kill one sentence after another. As long as you do not interrupt these commands with a non-kill command, the sentences will be stored in the same kill ring entry. As it happens, you have to use a few non-kill commands for some reason, after which you would like to yank yet another sentence into the same kill ring entry. All you need to do is move to the beginning of that sentence, press **M-C-w** (to tell **emacs** not to start a new entry), and then press **M-k** (to yank the new sentence).

The final kill-oriented command is **C-h v kill-ring**. This tells **emacs** to display the actual contents of the kill ring. You will rarely have to do so, but it is interesting to look at the entire kill ring from time to time. This command makes use of the built-in Help facility (described later in the chapter). In technical terms, **emacs** stores the kill ring as a "variable" called **kill-ring**. (We can ignore the details.) The **C-h v** command simply tells **emacs** to display the value of this variable.

Correcting Common Typing Mistakes

emacs has a number of commands that have been specifically designed to make it easy to correct typing mistakes. These commands are shown in Figure 21-20. As you can see, there are three types of commands: erasing, case changing, and transposing. Notice that the erasing and case changing commands act upon characters you have just typed (that is, characters to the left of the cursor).

We have already discussed the delete and kill commands. **DEL** erases the character you have just typed; **M-DEL** erases the word you have just typed; and, **C-x DEL** erases to the beginning of the sentence.

Command	Description
DEL	delete one character to the left of cursor
M-DEL	kill the previous word
C-x DEL	kill to the beginning of sentence
M--M-l	change the previous word to lowercase
M-- M-u	change the previous word to uppercase
M--M-c	change previous word to lowercase, initial cap
C-t	transpose two adjacent characters
M-t	transpose two adjacent words
C-x C-t	transpose two consecutive lines

Note: **M--** is "META minus-sign".

FIGURE 21-20. `emacs:` *Commands for correcting common typing mistakes*

HINT

Your typing habits will influence which commands you prefer to use to make corrections. If you can type quickly, without looking at the keys, it is often easier to use **M-DEL** and erase and retype an entire word, than it is to use **DEL** several times to erase two or three characters. However, if you are a good-looking, intelligent, and highly admired person (such as a computer book author) who looks at the keys as he types, you will probably find it easier to erase one character at a time.

One of the most common typing mistakes is to mix up your lower- and uppercase letters. **emacs** has three commands to help you. To change all the letters in the previous word to lowercase, use **M-- M-1**; to change the letters to uppercase, use **M-- M-u**; and to change the letters to lowercase with the first letter capitalized, use **M-- M-c**.

Note: **M--** means "META minus-sign". If you don't have a META key, press ESCAPE and then type the **-** (minus-sign) character.

Although these three commands act on a single word, you can use a prefix argument (explained earlier in the chapter) to change more than one word at a time. For example, say that you have just typed 10 words in lowercase, and you decide to make each word lowercase with an initial capital letter (as in a title). All you have to do is type **ESC 10 M-- M-c**.

The remaining commands transpose (switch around) characters, words or lines. The **C-t** command will transpose two adjacent characters. In general, **C-t** switches the character at the cursor with the character immediately to its left. Thus, if you have typed the word **Halrey** you can correct it by moving to the **r** and pressing **C-t**.

However, there is one special case. If the cursor is at the end of a line (just past the final character in the line), pressing **C-t** will transpose the last two characters. This means that if you are typing on a new line, and you press two keys in the wrong order, you can make an immediate correction by typing **C-t**. (Try it and it will make sense.)

To be more technical, the **C-t** command transposes the two characters on either side of point. At the end of a line, **C-t** switches the two characters before point. (Remember, point is between the character at the cursor, and the character on its left. For example, if the cursor is on the **r** in **Harley**, point is between the **a** and the **r**.)

The **M-t** command is similar except that it transposes two words: the word before point and the word after point. Here is an example. Say that you have just typed the line:

```
I should buy a copy of "The Internet Reference Complete".
```

You decide to switch the last two words. To do so, move the cursor so that point is between the words. (The cursor should be under the space or under the **c**.) Now, press **M-t**. When **emacs** transposes words, it does not change the punctuation, so, in our example, the quotation mark and the period will not be moved, and you will see:

```
I should buy a copy of "The Internet Complete Reference".
```

(Which, of course, is good advice.)

The final command is **C-x C-t**. This command switches two consecutive lines: the current line and the line above it. For example, say that the buffer contains the lines:

```
11111
22222
33333
44444
55555
```

You move the cursor to the fourth line (**44444**) and press **C-x C-t**. The buffer will change as follows:

```
11111
22222
44444
33333
55555
```

The only exception is when you are on the first line of the buffer. In this position, there is no line above the current line, so, as you might expect, **C-t** switches the top two lines. In our example, if you were to move to the top line (**11111**) and press **C-x C-t**, you would see:

```
22222
11111
44444
33333
55555
```

HINT

If you place the cursor below a specific line and then press **C-x C-t** repeatedly, you will move that line down the buffer, one line at a time.

Filling and Formatting Text

As you type regular text (compared to say, typing a computer program), you have two special needs. First, when you reach the end of the line, you will want **emacs** to start a new line for you automatically. Otherwise, you will have to keep track of the cursor position and press RETURN each time you near the right margin.

Second, as you change your text, you will shorten some lines and lengthen others, and you will want to be able to reformat the text to maintain as smooth a right margin as possible.

emacs has commands to perform both of these tasks. These commands are summarized in Figure 21-21.

To tell **emacs** to break long lines automatically as you type, you turn on what is called Auto Fill mode. (We will discuss the idea of modes later in the chapter.) When Auto Fill mode is turned on, **emacs** will break lines for you as you type. When Auto Fill mode is off, **emacs** will not break lines.

How do you know if Auto Fill mode is on or off? When it is on, **emacs** will display the word **Fill** on the mode line. (This is the line at the bottom of your buffer. We discussed the mode line earlier in the chapter.)

When Auto Fill mode is off, you can turn it on by using the command **M-x auto-fill-mode**. When Auto Fill mode is on, you can turn it off by using the same command. Thus, **M-x auto-fill-mode** acts as an on/off toggle switch. Remember, if you are not sure of the current status of Auto Fill mode, just look at the mode line for the word "Fill".

Command	Description
M-x auto-fill-mode	turn on/off Auto Fill mode
M-q	fill a paragraph
ESC 1 M-q	fill+justify a paragraph
M-x fill-region	fill each paragraph in the region
ESC 1 M-x fill-region	fill+justify each paragraph in the region
M-x fill-region-as-paragraph	fill the region as one long paragraph
ESC 1 M-x fill-region-as-paragraph	fill+justify region as one long paragraph
C-x f	set the fill column value
C-h v fill-column	display the current fill column value

FIGURE 21-21. **emacs**: *Commands to fill text*

If you use **emacs** only for typing regular text, you will probably want Auto Fill mode to be on all the time by default. We will explain how to do this later in the chapter, in the section about customizing **emacs**.

HINT

You do not have to type the full command **M-x auto-fill-mode**. As with all such commands, you can use completion (discussed earlier in the chapter) to ask **emacs** to do some of the typing for you. In this case, all you need to type is:

M-x au SPC f RET

One of the limitations of Auto Fill mode is that it will not automatically reformat a paragraph when you make changes. For example, when you delete and insert words, you change the length of the lines and the right margin can become ragged.

To reformat a paragraph, move the cursor to be within that paragraph (or on a blank line before the paragraph), and use the command **M-q**. **emacs** will reformat by removing all the line breaks and inserting new ones as necessary. When this happens, we say that **emacs** FILLS the paragraph.

There are two other fill commands you will find useful. When you want to fill more (or less) than a single paragraph, you can define the region (by setting mark and point) so it contains the text you want to fill. You can then fill the entire region by using the **M-x fill-region** command. (With completion, you only need to type **M-x fil SPC r RET**.)

A variation of this command is **M-x fill-region-as-paragraph**. This command fills an entire region as a single large paragraph. (Again, with completion, you can save keystrokes by typing **M-x fil SPC r SPC SPC RET**.)

The fill commands can also right justify at the same time as they format. That is, they can insert spaces within the text in order to make the right margin line up. To fill and right justify at the same time, just use a prefix argument before a fill command. (We explain prefix arguments earlier in the chapter.) Any numeric value will do, so you might as well use "1".

For example, to fill and right justify a paragraph, use the command **ESC 1 M-q**. You can also use a similar prefix argument with the other fill commands to right justify and fill the region.

When **emacs** fills a paragraph, it ensures that no line is longer than a specific maximum width. By default, this width is 70 characters, but you can change it if necessary.

The value of the fill column width is kept in a variable (storage location) named **fill-column**. You can display the current value of this variable by using the command **C-h v fill-column**. (The **C-h v** command is part of the built-in Help facility. This particular command displays the value of a variable along with a short description.)

There are two ways to change the value of **fill-column**, both of which use the **C-x f** command. First, you can use this command with a prefix argument showing how many characters wide you want your lines to be. For example, to set **fill-column** to a value of 55, you can use **ESC 55 C-x f**. From now on, all lines you fill will be formatted to be no longer than 55 characters long.

The second way to change the value of **fill-column** is to move the cursor to a line that is exactly the width that you want, and then press **C-x f**. **emacs** will use the width of that particular line as the new value for **fill-column**.

The emacs Search Commands

emacs gives you several ways to search for a pattern within the buffer. Figure 21-22 shows a summary of the different search commands. At first, it looks overwhelming, but don't be freaked out—in almost all cases, it boils down to these few simple rules:

To search forward, press **C-s** and type what you want to find. To search backward, press **C-r** and type what you want to find. (Just think of **s** for **search**, and **r** for **reverse**.) Once **emacs** finds what you want, you can search for another occurrence by pressing **C-s** (or **C-r**) as many times as you need. When you get what you want, press **RET** (the RETURN key).

Command	Description
C-s	forward: incremental search
C-s RET	forward: non-incremental search
C-s RET C-w	forward: word search
M-C-s	forward: incremental search for regexp
M-C-s RET	forward: non-incremental search for regexp
C-r	backward: incremental search
C-r RET	backward: non-incremental search
C-r RET C-w	backward: word search
M-C-r	backward: incremental search for regexp
M-C-r RET	backward: non-incremental search for regexp

FIGURE 21-22. **emacs**: *Search commands*

So, most of the time, that's all you need to remember. However, this being **emacs**, there are lots and lots of optional details (which we will get to in a moment). However, before we start, we must deal with a more fundamental problem: The whole thing won't work.

This is because (as we discussed earlier in the chapter), **C-s** is, in reality, the Unix **stop** key. As soon as you press **C-s**, your screen display will freeze and it will look as if your system has hung. To continue, you will need to press **C-q** (the **start** key). So, even if you remember to press **C-q**, it still leaves you back where you started with a big problem: how do you search for a pattern if you can't use the **C-s** key?

For now, we are going to duck the issue. Later in the chapter, we will show you how to customize your **emacs** working environment by putting commands into an initialization file named **.emacs**. At that time, we will show you how to solve the **C-s** problem by telling **emacs** to use the **C-** key instead of **C-s**.

Thus, when you read this section, bear in mind that you will *not* be pressing **C-s** to perform a search. Still, **C-s** is the official **emacs** search key, and that is what you must get used to reading. When it actually comes to using the command, you can press **C-**. The **C-r** key, of course, works just fine. (But then, how often do you want to search backward?)

HINT

The reason that **emacs** makes such heavy use of the **C-s** key is that **emacs** was not developed to run under Unix. Under the operating system for which **emacs** was first written, **C-s** was a perfectly valid and accessible key.

"But," we hear you saying, "isn't it true that most **emacs** users today use Unix, and doesn't that mean they are unable to use the **C-s** key for what is really a fundamental operation (searching for a pattern)?"

Absolutely. But you can rebind any command you want, and you can redefine any key you want, as long as you know how to do it. (We will show you how to do so with the **C-s** command later in the chapter.)

"But," we hear you saying, "that's okay if you already know what you are doing, but what about beginners?"

Ah... who said **emacs** was for beginners?

(By the way, if you've gotten this far, it's too late to go back to **vi**: your brain has already changed permanently. So stick it out and read the rest of the chapter.)

Incremental Searching

The basic type of **emacs** search is called an INCREMENTAL SEARCH. That means **emacs** starts searching as soon as you type a single character. With each character you type, **emacs** refines its search. Here is an example.

Let's say that you want to search for the pattern **harley**. You start by pressing **C-s** (or whatever passes for **C-s** on your system, probably **C-**). **emacs** is now waiting for you to type something. You type an **h** and **emacs** jumps to the first place in the buffer that has the letter **h**. Now you type an **a** and **emacs** jumps to the first place that has the letters **ha**. Now you type an **r** and **emacs** jumps to the first place that has **har**.

In other words, **emacs** starts the search as soon as you begin to type. Each time you type another character, the search becomes more and more specific. The advantage is that, most of the time, you do not have to type the full pattern to find what you want. For instance, it is possible that you would find the pattern **harley** after typing only the first few letters.

The best way to see how this all works is to try it for yourself. Of course, it may be that you have not yet set up your **.emacs** initialization file so that you can use **C-** as a replacement for **C-s**. If this is the case, just use **C-r** to practice. It works the same as **C-s**, only backward.

Here is a good way to set up a practice session. Start **emacs** by entering the command:

```
emacs
```

You will be editing an empty buffer named ***scratch***. Start the Help facility by pressing **C-h b**. This will display a large list of all the key bindings. Press **C-x 0** to delete the window with the ***scratch*** buffer. You will be left in the ***Help*** buffer. Press **M->** (META greater-than sign) to jump to the end of this buffer. You can now use **C-r** to search backward as much as you want. We suggest that you set this up right now, so you can try things out for yourself as you read the following sections.

Keys to Use While Searching

While you are in the middle of a search, there are a number of keys that have special meanings. These are shown in Figure 21-23.

While you are typing the search pattern, you can make a correction by pressing **DEL** (the DELETE key) to erase the last character you typed. When you do, **emacs** will back up to the place that matches those characters that remain.

DEL	erase the previous character
RET	terminate the search
C-s	search forward for same pattern
C-r	search backward for same pattern
C-g	(while search is in progress) stop current search
C-g	(while waiting for input) abort entire command
C-w	use the word after point
C-y	use the rest of the line after point
M-y	use the most recently killed (erased) text

FIGURE 21-23.   **emacs***: Keys to use during a search*

Here is an example. Say that you are searching for the pattern **harley**. After you have typed the first three letters, **har**, **emacs** jumps to the word **share** (because this happens to be the first word that contains these three characters). To continue, you want to type the letter **l**, but, by accident, you press the **p** key. Thus, **emacs** thinks you are searching for **harp** and it jumps to the word **harpoon**. To make the correction, you press **DEL**. This erases the letter **p**, whereupon **emacs** jumps back to the word **share**. You now type **ley** and **emacs** jumps to **harley**.

Don't worry if this is a bit difficult to follow. It will all make perfect sense when you see it.

At any time, you can tell **emacs** to find the next occurrence of the pattern you have specified by pressing **C-s** once again. To go backward, you can press **C-r**. Thus, for example, say that you have typed **harley** and **emacs** has dutifully found the first occurrence of that word. However, that is not the one you want. Simply press **C-s** and **emacs** will find the next one.

If you press **C-s** and **emacs** cannot find any occurrences of the pattern from your current position to the end of the buffer, you will see the message:

Failing I-search

This means the incremental search has failed. That is, you are looking at the last place in the buffer that matches your pattern. However, if you press **C-s** one more time, **emacs** will wrap around and start searching at the beginning of the buffer.

In other words, you can press **C-s** repeatedly to search for a pattern throughout the buffer. When you get to the end (and you see the message), you can press **C-s** and start again from the beginning. Similarly, when you are searching backward with **C-r**, you can press **C-r** twice when you get to the top and wrap around to the bottom.

To terminate your search, you have two options. If **emacs** has found what you want, simply press **RET** (the RETURN key). The search command will stop and you will be left at the current position in the buffer.

If, however, you can't find what you want, and you decide the whole thing was a bad idea, press **C-g**. This will stop the search command, but will leave you back at the exact position at which you started, just as if nothing had happened.

The **C-g** key has another role as well. While you are in the middle of an active search, waiting for **emacs** to find the next occurrence of something or other, pressing **C-g** tells **emacs** to stop searching and come back to where you are. You can now type another character, or press **RET**, or press **C-g** a second time. If you press **C-g** again, you will cancel the whole search process.

In other words, when **emacs** is busy searching for something, **C-g** tells **emacs** to stop without quitting. But when **emacs** is paused, waiting for you to type something, **C-g** cancels and nullifies the search command itself.

There are three other keys that are handy to use during a search. If you press **C-w**, **emacs** copies the word that is immediately after point (the position of the cursor) to the minibuffer. **emacs** then advances point to the end of that word.

What does this mean? It means that you can search for a word in the buffer without having to actually type the word for yourself. Here is an example. You are reading an essay that contains the following quote from Isaac Asimov's final autobiography:

Perhaps writers are so self-absorbed as a necessary part of their profession.

The cursor is under the space before the word **writers**. (That is, point is between the space and the **w**.) You decide to search for further occurrences of the word **writers**.

You press **C-s** (or more probably, its replacement, **C-**). **emacs** is now waiting for you to type something. Instead of typing the actual word, you press **C-w** and **emacs** copies the word **writers** for you into the minibuffer, just as if you had typed the letters yourself. **emacs** then moves the cursor to the next word (to the space before **are**). You can either press **C-w** and pick up the next word, or press **C-s** to begin the search.

You can copy as many words as you want by pressing **C-w**. And you can do so not only when you start the search, but at any point along the way. Thus, whenever **emacs** is paused waiting for you to type something to add to the search pattern, you can press **C-w** to copy the current word. If you make a mistake, you can correct it by pressing **DEL**. When you do, **emacs** will erase an entire word, not just a single character. (In other words, when you are searching and you press **DEL**,

emacs knows whether it should erase a whole word or simply one character. Pretty cool, eh?)

Aside from **C-s**, there are two other commands that will insert text into the minibuffer while you are searching. If you press **C-y** ("yank"), it copies from point to the end of the line. For example, say that you are reading another quote from Asimov's autobiography:

```
I have always thought of myself as a
remarkable fellow, even from childhood,
and I have never wavered in that opinion.
```

(This, of course, is true for all good writers.)

The cursor is at the space before **thought** in the first line, so point is between the space and the **t**. You press **C-s** to start a search. Now you press **C-y**. This will copy the words **thought of myself as a** into the minibuffer.

The final way to automatically copy characters to the minibuffer while searching is to press **M-y**. This copies the most recently erased text.

For example, say that you have just erased the word **heffalump**. (We explained how to erase text earlier in the chapter.) You decide to search for more occurrences of the same word, perhaps to erase some of them as well. Simply press **C-s** and then **M-y**.

Upper- and Lowercase Searching

One issue we have not yet discussed is what **emacs** does about upper- and lowercase letters while it is searching. The general rule is that **emacs** ignores all distinctions between upper- and lowercase as long as you type only lowercase letters in the search pattern. However, once you type even a single uppercase letter, **emacs** will search for an exact match.

Here is an example. If you tell **emacs** to search for **harley** it will find any occurrence of these letters, whether they are upper- or lowercase or mixed. For instance, **emacs** would find **harley**, **Harley**, **HARLEY**, **harLEY** and so on. However, if you tell **emacs** to search for **harley**, it will only find this exact word.

When a program does not distinguish between upper- and lowercase, we say that it is CASE INSENSITIVE. When the distinction is made, we say the program is CASE SENSITIVE.

So let's say that you are searching for the phrase **send money to Harley**. You press **C-s** and then start to type the pattern. As you do, **emacs** begins the search. So far, you have typed **send money to**. Up to this point, you have typed only lowercase letters, so **emacs** is performing a case insensitive search. However, as soon as you type the **H**, **emacs** switches to a case sensitive search.

At this point, you might wonder what would happen if you were to press **DEL** and erase the only uppercase letter? **emacs** would recognize what you did and switch from being case sensitive back to case insensitive.

Non-Incremental Searching and Word Searching

If you look back at Figure 21-22, you will see that there are a number of different types of search commands (and a forward and backward variation for each type). So far, we have discussed the incremental search commands (**C-s** and **C-r**). These commands begin searching as soon as you type a single character. As you type more characters, the search becomes more specific.

It may be that you want **emacs** to wait until you have typed the entire pattern before it starts to search. To do so, you can use one of the non-incremental search commands. This is convenient if you have trouble typing and you make lots of mistakes. If so, it is a bother to have **emacs** jump all over the place like a snipe with a hot foot as you make your corrections.

To request a non-incremental search, simply press **RET** (the RETURN key) before you start typing the search pattern. Thus, to perform a forward non-incremental search, type **C-s RET** and then type the pattern. When you are finished typing, press **RET** once again to start the search. To abort the search, press **C-g**. Similarly, you can request a non-incremental backward search with **C-r RET**.

Another variation is the word search. This tells **emacs** that you want to search only for complete words. To do so, press **C-s**, then **RET**, and then **C-w**. You can now type the words from which you want to search. When you are ready, press **RET** to begin. (The word search is actually a variation of the non-incremental search.)

The great thing about a word search is that it ignores all punctuation, spaces, tabs and ends of lines. Thus, you can look for a series of words that, for example, span more than one line.

For example, say that you are still reading quotes from Isaac Asimov's final autobiography. There is a passage that reads:

```
    My turn will come too, eventually, but I have
had a good life and I have accomplished all I
wanted to, and more than I had a right to expect.
    So I am ready.
    But not too ready.
```

Later, you want to find this passage, but all you can remember are the last two lines. So you press **C-s**, then **RET**, and then **C-w**. You then type **ready but not** and press **RET** again. **emacs** finds the text, even though these particular words are separated by punctuation (a period) and are broken over two lines.

The only commands in Figure 21-22 that we have not yet mentioned are the ones that search for regular expressions. But regular expressions are a topic on their own and deserve their own section.

Searching for Regular Expressions

In Chapter 17, we discussed the idea of a REGULAR EXPRESSION, a compact way of specifying a general pattern of characters. **emacs** has special commands that allow you to search for a regular expression. These commands are shown in Figure 21-24. (Notice that the term "regular expression" is sometimes abbreviated to "regexp".)

Notice that these commands use an **M-C** combination. This means that you must hold down both the META and CTRL keys while you press the other key (either the **s** or **r** key). If you don't have a META key, press **ESC** (the ESCAPE key), and then press either **C-s** or **C-r**.

Regular expressions allow you to expand your search capabilities enormously. For example, using the ordinary search commands, you can tell **emacs** to look for an occurrence of the pattern **Harley**. But with regular expressions, you can have **emacs** search for the pattern **Harley** at the beginning of a line; or a line that consists only of the word **Harley**; or any word that starts with **Har** and ends with **y**.

We discussed regular expressions in detail in Chapter 17. If you need a reminder of how they work, you might want to take a moment to look at that section. In this section, we will confine ourselves to offering a summary of the characters that **emacs** uses for regular expressions, along with a few examples.

Figure 21-25 summarizes the basic characters you can use to create a regular expression with **emacs**. If you understand regular expressions, these characters will make sense to you, although you may see a few new ones.

Command	Description
M-C-s	forward: incremental search for regexp
M-C-s RET	forward: non-incremental search for regexp
M-C-r	backward: incremental search for regexp
M-C-r RET	backward: non-incremental search for regexp

FIGURE 21-24. **emacs**: *Search commands for regular expressions*

char	any regular character matches itself
.	match any single character except **newline**
*	match zero or more of the preceding characters
+	match one or more of the preceding characters
?	match exactly zero or one of the preceding characters
^	match the beginning of a line
$	match the end of a line
\\<	match the beginning of a word
\\>	match the end of a word
\\b	match the beginning or end of a word
\\B	match anywhere not at beginning or end of a word
\\`	match the beginning of the buffer
\\'	match the end of buffer
char	quotes a special character
[ ]	match one of the enclosed characters
[^]	match any character that is not enclosed

FIGURE 21-25. **emacs**: *Characters to use with regular expressions*

Here is an example of a search involving a regular expression. To search for the characters **Harley** at the beginning of a line, press **M-C-s**, then type **^Harley**. If you prefer, you can make the search non-incremental by pressing **RET** (the RETURN key) before you type the regular expression. To search backward, of course, you can use either **M-C-r** or **M-C-r RET**.

Here are a few more examples. To search for a line that consists entirely of the word **Harley**, use:

^Harley$

To search for a word that begins with **Har**, use:

\\<Har

To search for a pattern that starts with **h** or **H**, and is followed by at least one **a**, use:

[hH]a+

As we explained in Chapter 17, you can use a range of characters within square brackets. So, to search for a complete word that consists of a single letter, either upper- or lowercase, possibly followed by a single digit, use:

```
\<[a-zA-Z][0-9]?\>
```

This regular expression will match words like:

```
a0     a     A0     A     B5     z8     Z
```

If you want to search for a character that has a special meaning, you must put a \ (backslash) in front of it. For example, to search for a dollar sign followed by one or more digits, use:

```
\$[0-9]+
```

When you specify all lowercase letters, **emacs** does a case insensitive search. However, if you use at least one uppercase letter, the search becomes case sensitive. Thus, the regular expression **[har]** searches for **h**, **H**, **a**, **A**, **r** or **R**; the regular expression **[Har]** searches only for **H**, **a** or **r**.

Searching and Replacing

There are several commands you can use to search for a particular pattern and then replace it once it is found. For example, say that you have written a long memo to your boss in which you have used the word **jerk** several times. As you read the document for a second time, it occurs to you that an overly sensitive person might take offense, so you decide to change every occurrence of **jerk** to **goofball**.

To do so, you can use one of the search and replace commands. You tell **emacs** what to search for and what to use as a replacement. **emacs** will start from point (the current position within the buffer) and search forward for occurrences of the search pattern. Each time it finds one, **emacs** will make the replacement.

HINT

A search and replacement operation starts from point and continues to the end of the buffer. Thus, if you want to process the entire buffer, you must jump to the beginning before you start.
(Use the **M-<** command.)

With some of the search and replace commands, **emacs** will ask your permission each time it wants to make a change. With other commands, **emacs** makes all the changes automatically.

Figure 21-26 summarizes the **emacs** search and replace commands. Notice that, of the four commands, only one of them is bound to a specific key combination (**M-%**). The other commands must be executed explicitly using **M-x**. However, as you will see, you can use completion (explained earlier in the chapter), so that typing these long names is actually pretty easy.

The basic search and replace command is **M-%**. After you type **M-%**, **emacs** will prompt you to type the search pattern. In the minibuffer, you will see:

Query replace:

Don't be confused, **emacs** is not asking for the replacement characters, it is simply reminding you that you are using the "Query replace" command. Type the search pattern and press **RET** (the RETURN key). In our example, you would type **jerk** and press **RET**. **emacs** will then prompt you for the replacement characters. You will see a message like the following:

Query replace jerk with:

Type the replacement and press **RET**. In our example, you would type **goofball** and press **RET**.

emacs will now jump to the first occurrence of the search pattern and ask you what to do. In our example, you would see the prompt:

Query replacing jerk with goofball: (? for help)

There are several keys that you can use now to control the replacement operation. These keys are described in Figure 21-27. Notice that you can press **?** to display a Help summary.

Command	Description
M-%	query: search and replace
M-x query-replace-regexp	query: regexp search and replace
M-x replace-string	no query: search and replace
M-x replace-regexp	no query: regexp search and replace

FIGURE 21-26. **emacs**: *Search and replace commands*

Command	Description
?	display Help summary
y	(yes) replace
n	(no) do not replace
q	quit immediately
SPC	same as y
DEL	same as n
RET	same as q
!	replace all remaining matches, no questions
. (period)	replace current match and then quit
, (comma)	replace but stay at current position
^ (circumflex)	move back to previous match
C-l	clear screen, re-display, and ask again
C-r	start recursive edit (use M-C-c to return)
C-w	delete matching pattern, start recursive edit

FIGURE 21-27. emacs: *Responses during a search and replace command*

Most of the time, you will need only four of these responses:

- **SPC** (the SPACE bar) to make a replacement and continue

- **DEL** (the DELETE key) to skip a replacement and continue

- **!** (exclamation mark) to make all the rest of the replacements automatically with no more questions

- **RET** (the RETURN key) to quit immediately

The rest of the commands (except for **C-r** and **C-w**) are straightforward and, with a little practice, you should have no trouble. The **C-r** and **C-w** commands are used for "recursive editing", which we will discuss in the next section.

Now take another look at Figure 21-26. You will notice there are three other search and replace commands. The **M-x query-replace-regexp** command is similar to **M-%**, except you can use a regular expression to specify the search pattern. (We explained regular expressions earlier in the chapter.) This command gives you more flexibility than **M-%**. For example, you could search for all the words that begin with **Har** and end with **y**.

The **M-x replace-string** command makes all the replacements automatically without asking you any questions. This is similar to using **M-%** and then pressing the **!** character at the first match. The **M-x replace-string** is handy when you know you want to make all the replacements, and there is no point in stopping at each one to confirm your intentions.

Finally, **M-x replace-regexp** also makes all the replacements automatically, while allowing you to use a regular expression for the search pattern.

You will have noticed that, where the **M-%** command is short and easy to type, the other ones are complicated. However, you do not have to type the entire command name each time. You can use completion (which we discussed earlier in the chapter). If you have not read about completion, take a moment and do so now; it is an especially handy tool. Briefly, you can type part of something and tell **emacs** to complete the rest of the word for you.

Figure 21-28 shows the search and replace commands along with the minimum number of keystrokes you need to use with completion. We have included the **M-x replace-string** command, which is bound to **M-%**. Normally, though, you would just press **M-%**. Notice also that we have described two possible combinations for **M-x query-replace-regexp**; just pick the one you like best.

■ Recursive Editing

In the previous section, we discussed how to perform a search and replace operation. The last concept we want to discuss is RECURSIVE EDITING. This allows you to put a search and replace on hold temporarily, while you perform some editing. When you are finished, you can return to the search and replace operation that is already in progress.

Here is how you might use this facility. Let's say that you are in the middle of a long search and replace operation, and you happen to notice a different change that you want to make. At such times, it is inconvenient to stop what you are doing just to make a single change. And, if you wait until the search and replace operation is finished, you may forget what you wanted to do.

Command	Keystrokes to Use
M-x replace-string	**M-x repl SPC s RET**
M-x replace-regexp	**M-x repl SPC r RET**
M-x query-replace	**M-x que RET**
M-x query-replace-regexp	**M-x que TAB SPC RET**
M-x query-replace-regexp	**M-x que SPC SPC SPC RET**

Note: **M-x replace-string** is the same as **M-%**.

FIGURE 21-28.   **emacs**: *Minimum keystrokes to invoke search and replace commands*

Instead, you can press **C-r**. This pauses the search and replace, and puts you back into the regular editing environment. You can now make any changes you want. When you are finished, press **M-C-c**. (If you don't have a META key, press the ESCAPE key and then press **C-c**.) This will stop recursive editing and return you to the search and replace operation, exactly where you left off.

When you press **C-r**, **emacs** will put square brackets (**[** and **]**) around the name of the mode on your mode line (explained earlier in the chapter). The square brackets are a reminder that you are within a recursive editing environment. For example, say that you are editing a buffer named **document** and your mode line looks like this:

```
--**-Emacs: document              (Fundamental)--33%--------
```

When you press **C-r**, **emacs** will start recursive editing and the mode line will change to:

```
--**-Emacs: document              [(Fundamental)]--33%--------
```

When you press **M-C-c** to quit recursive editing, the square brackets will disappear.

Another way to start recursive editing during a search and replace operation (aside from **C-r**), is by pressing **C-w**. This will delete the current matching pattern and then start recursive editing.

Using **C-w** is handy when you want to replace the matching pattern with something that is not your official replacement. You can delete the match, enter recursive editing, insert the replacement by hand, and then go back to where you were.

For example, say that you are in the middle of changing all the occurrences of **jerk** to **goofball**. You happen upon a particular occurrence of **jerk** that you think should really be **computer book writer**. Press **C-w**. This will erase the word **jerk** and place you in recursive editing. Type the phrase **computer book writer**. Then press **M-C-c** to return to the search and replace operation.

Entering Shell Commands

There are several ways you can use shell commands without having to leave the **emacs** environment. These facilities are summarized in Figure 21-29.

To enter a single shell command, type **M-!** followed by the command. For example, to display a list of all the userids currently logged into your system, you could use either **M-! users** or **M-! who**. (We describe the **users** and **who** commands in Chapter 13.)

Command	Description
M-!	run a shell command
M-|	run a shell command using the region as input
M-x shell	start a separate shell in its own buffer

FIGURE 21-29.   **emacs**: *Running shell commands*

When you run a shell command using **M-!**, **emacs** saves the output in a buffer named ***Shell Command Output***. If this buffer does not already exist, **emacs** will create it. If it does exist, the previous contents will be replaced.

Another way to run a shell command is to use some of the data in the buffer as input for the command. For example, you may have a large number of lines you would like to sort. All you need to do is use these lines as data for the Unix **sort** program.

To perform such an operation, you use the **M-\|** (META vertical-bar) command. This will run whatever shell command you specify, using the contents of the region as input. Earlier in the chapter, in the section called "Operating on a Region", we discussed an example that used the **M-\|** command to create a sorted list of key descriptions. Here is another example.

You want to sort all the lines in the buffer. All you need to do is define the region so as to enclose the entire buffer, and then use **M-\|** to run the **sort** command on the region. Use these commands:

1. **C-x h**: Set the region to be the entire buffer.

2. **M-\| sort**: Sort all the lines in the buffer.

When you use **M-\|**, **emacs** puts the output into a buffer named ***Shell Command Output*** just like when you use the **M-!** command. If the buffer does not exist, **emacs** will create it. If the buffer does exist, its contents will be replaced.

Sometimes, though, you may want to replace the lines in your original buffer with the output of the shell command. All you need to do is use a prefix argument (explained earlier in the chapter); this tells **emacs** not to save the output in a special buffer. Any numeric value will do, so you might as well use "1".

Here is an example. Say that you are working with a buffer that contains names, one name per line. You have just typed in all the names, and now you want to sort them. However, you don't want the output of the **sort** command to be saved in a separate buffer; you want the sorted names to replace the original contents of your buffer. Use these commands:

1. **C-x h**: Set the region to be the entire buffer.

2. **ESC 1 M-| sort**: Sort all the lines in the buffer, replacing the input with the output of the **sort** command.

HINT

When you use the **M-|** command with a prefix argument, the data in your buffer will be replaced by the output of the shell command. If you decide that it was all a mistake, you can undo the effects of the shell command by pressing **C-_** (CTRL-underscore), the regular **emacs** undo command.

Another way to use the shell from within **emacs** is to use the **M-x shell** command. This command will start a separate shell in its own buffer named ***shell***. You can enter as many commands as you want, one after the other. Everything you type, along with all of the output, will be saved in the buffer. Whenever you want, you can switch from this buffer to another one. This means you can have a special buffer just for running shell commands that will be available whenever you want. This allows you to copy the output of a shell command into another buffer.

When you enter the **M-x shell** command, **emacs** will check if a buffer named ***shell*** already exists. If not, **emacs** will create such a buffer; if such a buffer already exists, **emacs** will simply switch you to that buffer (which is already in progress). When you are finished with that particular shell, you can kill it—and stop the shell—by using the **C-x k** command.

HINT

Here is a cool trick. When you tell **emacs** to create a new shell and a buffer named ***shell*** does not already exist, **emacs** will create one. Thus, you can have more than one shell buffer at the same time by changing their names. Here is how it works.

There is a command named **M-x rename-uniquely** that you can use to change the name of a buffer to be unique. So, from within the ***shell*** buffer, you can use this command to change the buffer name to something else. You can then use **M-x shell** to start a brand new shell. Since there is no buffer named ***shell***, **emacs** will create one and you will have two shells.

Here is an example. You start by creating your first "shell in a buffer" by typing **M-x shell**. You now have a buffer named ***shell*** that contains a live shell session. Now type **M-x rename-uniquely**, and **emacs** will change the name of the buffer to ***shell*<2>**. Finally, type **M-x shell** and **emacs** will create a second shell in a new buffer named ***shell***. If you want yet another shell buffer, you can rename the last one and use **M-x shell** again. In this way, you can get as many such shells as you want.

Here are two final hints. First, you do not have to type the full command **M-x rename-uniquely**. Using completion (discussed earlier in the chapter), all you need to type is **M-x ren SPC u RET**. Second, if you are not sure what to get your mother for her birthday, a shell-in-a-buffer is something that just about everybody can use.

Major Modes

As you know, **emacs** was designed to be flexible, especially for advanced users and programmers. The designers of **emacs** realized that your needs will vary depending on what you are doing. For example, if you are working with regular English text, you will be typing and editing in a different manner than if you are, say, writing a computer program. One of the ways in which **emacs** helps you is by acting slightly differently depending on what you are trying to do. For example, when you are typing a computer program, you will want to indent your lines differently than when you are composing an essay.

Thus, **emacs** has what are called MAJOR MODES. The major mode controls a few fundamental aspects of the way **emacs** behaves. At any time, **emacs** is working in one particular major mode. As the need arises, you can tell **emacs** to change to another major mode. If you find yourself using a particular major mode all the time, you can set things up so that, by default, **emacs** starts with this major mode automatically.

The principal difference between the various major modes is that a small number of the keys are redefined in a way that is appropriate for the type of work you are doing. There are various major modes for editing different types of text (such as regular English text, outlines, **nroff** files, TeX, and LaTeX), and for writing different types of programs (such as Lisp, C, and Fortran).

Figure 21-30 shows the major modes. Clearly, you do not have to understand, or even know about, all the major modes. Scan the list and see if there are any major modes that relate to your work. In addition, there are two major modes that are important to just about everybody. The first is Text mode, which is used to edit regular English text. The second is Fundamental mode: a generic editing mode in which each command acts in its most general manner, and each option has its default value.

HINT

If you are not sure which major mode to use, use Fundamental mode.

Major Mode	Type of Data to Edit
asm-mode	assembly language programs
awk-mode	**awk** scripts
bibtex-mode	BibTeX files
c++-mode	C++ programs
c-mode	C programs
change-log-mode	change logs
command-history-mode	command history
completion-list-mode	lists of possible completions
edit-abbrevs-mode	abbreviation definitions
emacs-lisp-mode	**emacs** Lisp programs
forms-mode	field-structured data using a form
fortran-mode	Fortran programs
fundamental-mode	general data, not specialized
hexl-mode	hexadecimal and ASCII data
indented-text-mode	text with indented paragraphs
latex-mode	LaTeX-formatted files
lisp-interaction-mode	typing and evaluating Lisp forms
lisp-mode	non-**emacs** Lisp programs
mail-mode	outgoing mail messages
makefile-mode	makefiles
mh-letter-mode	messages with MH mail system
modula-2-mode	Modula-2 programs
nroff-mode	**nroff**- and **troff**-formatted text files
outline-mode	outlines with selective display
pascal-mode	Pascal programs
perl-mode	Perl scripts
picture-mode	text-based drawings
plain-tex-mode	TeX-formatted files
prolog-mode	Prolog programs
rmail-mode	mail messages with Rmail
scheme-mode	Scheme programs

FIGURE 21-30. emacs: *Major modes* (continued on following page)

Major Mode	Type of Data to Edit
scribe-mode	Scribe-formatted text files
sgml-mode	Standard Generalized Markup Language files
slitex-mode	SliTeX-formatted files
tcl-mode	tcl scripts
tex-mode	TeX- LaTeX- or SliTeX-formatted files
texinfo-mode	TeXinfo files
text-mode	regular human-readable text
vi-mode	makes **emacs** act like **vi** editor
wordstar-mode	makes **emacs** use Wordstar-like key bindings

FIGURE 21-30. **emacs**: *Major modes* (continued from previous page)

We will not go over the particulars of all the major modes. If you are interested in one of them, you can display the details within **emacs** by using the built-in Help and Info facilities (described later in the chapter). The Help facility can show you a brief description of a major mode along with a summary of the key bindings. Type the command **C-h f** followed by the name of the mode. For example, to display all the key bindings for Text mode, use the command **C-h f text-mode**.

Minor Modes

emacs has a large number of optional features you can turn on or off as you work. These features are called MINOR MODES. While you can set only one major mode at a time, you can turn on as many minor modes as make sense within your working environment.

Figure 21-31 contains a summary of all the minor modes. If you want to display a short description of a minor mode from within **emacs**, you can use the **C-h f** command we described in the previous section. For example, to display a description of Auto Fill mode, you can type **C-h f auto-fill-mode**.

We won't go into the details of all the minor modes. However, we will mention three that you will find particularly useful:

■ **auto-fill-mode** Sets automatic filling: as you type, **emacs** will automatically break lines, so you don't have to press the RETURN key at the end of each line.

- **line-number-mode**   Tells **emacs** to display the number of the current line on the mode line.

- **overwrite-mode**   When you type in Overwrite mode, your characters replace the existing text (normally, characters are inserted).

Minor Mode	Description
abbrev-mode	working with abbreviations
auto-fill-mode	automatic filling
auto-save-mode	automatic saving
binary-overwrite-mode	binary overwriting
compilation-minor-mode	compiling programs
delete-selection-mode	typed text replaces selection
double-mode	some keys differ if pressed twice
font-lock-mode	text is fontified as you type
hide-ifdef-mode	hides certain C code within **#ifdef**
indent-according-to-mode	indent appropriately for major mode
iso-accents-mode	display ISO accents
ledit-mode	editing text to be sent to Lisp
line-number-mode	show line numbers on mode line
outline-minor-mode	work with outlines
overwrite-mode	overwrite/insert text
pending-delete-mode	same as **delete-selection-mode**
resize-minibuffer-mode	dynamically resize minibuffer
tpu-edt-mode	TPU/edt emulation
toggle-read-only	buffer contents cannot be changed
transient-mark-mode	highlight region when defined
vip-mode	VIP emulation of **vi**
vt100-wide-mode	132/80 columns for VT-100 terminals

FIGURE 21-31.   **emacs**: *Minor modes*

Setting Major and Minor Modes

To set a major or minor mode, use the **M-x** command, followed by the name of the mode. For example, to set Text mode, use the command **M-x text-mode**. To set Overwrite mode, use **M-x overwrite-mode**. Since mode names can be long, you will find it useful to use completion (discussed earlier in the chapter), so that **emacs** will do some of the typing for you. For example, to set Overwrite mode, you need only type **M-x ov RET**.

Most of the minor modes act as on/off switches (sometimes called "toggles"). Thus, if Overwrite mode is off, you can turn it on by using the command **M-x overwrite-mode**. When you want to turn it off, simply type **M-x overwrite-mode** again.

Each buffer has its own major mode and as many minor modes as you need. Thus, you can work with different types of text at the same time by setting up more than one buffer with different modes.

To help you remember what major mode you are using, **emacs** displays a notation on the mode line (the line at the bottom of the window). **emacs** will also display the name of the major mode and most (but not all) of the minor modes.

At any time, you can use the Help facility to describe the current major and minor modes for the buffer in which you are working. The command is **C-h m**.

To summarize, Figure 21-32 shows the commands you can use to set and describe modes.

HINT

To display a summary of all the modes, you can use the command **C-h a mode**. *The* **C-h a** command displays information about all the **emacs** functions that contain a specific word. (The letter **a** stands for "apropos".) By typing **C-h a mode**, you are asking the Help facility to describe all the functions that contain the word **mode**.

Command	Description
M-x *mode-name*	set the specified mode
C-h m	describe current major and minor modes
C-h f *mode-name*	describe the specified mode
C-h a mode	display summary of all modes

FIGURE 21-32. **emacs**: *Commands to set and describe modes*

Read-Only Mode

On occasion, you may wish to protect a buffer so that you cannot change its contents accidentally. For example, you may want to use **emacs** to read an important file that should not be modified. Or you may have typed some information that, for the time being, must be left untouched.

To help you protect such data, you can set Read-only mode. To do so, use the command **M-x toggle-read-only**. When Read-only mode is on, **emacs** will let you look at the contents of the buffer, but not make any changes. If you try to make a change (say, by typing something), **emacs** will display a warning message:

`Buffer is read-only`

To turn off Read-only mode, just enter the **M-x toggle-read-only** command again.

Earlier in the chapter, we explained how to start **emacs** while specifying that you want to view a file in Read-only mode. When you do this, you can turn off Read-only mode using this same command.

Note: Setting Read-only mode within **emacs** has nothing to do with Unix file permissions (which we explain in Chapter 24).

Customizing Your Working Environment: The `.emacs` File

Whenever **emacs** starts, it looks for a file named `.emacs` in your home directory. If the file exists, **emacs** will read it and execute all the commands it contains as part of the initialization process. By placing certain commands in your `.emacs` file, you can customize just about any facet of your working environment, even to the point of eccentricity. (Files like `.emacs` are called dotfiles. See Chapter 23.)

In the next few sections, we will show you how to use your `.emacs` file to customize your working environment. We are going to get a little technical, so don't worry if you don't understand everything right away. Still, you should at least skim these sections before you move on to the rest of the chapter. In particular, we will show you how to fix the common problems we described earlier in the chapter (such as pressing BACKSPACE and accidentally starting the Help facility, or not being able to use the **C-s** key to start a search).

emacs is written in a computer language called LISP. (The name stands for "List Processing language"). This means that all the commands in your `.emacs` file must be in Lisp, which is unfortunate, because Lisp programs look like nothing on Earth. It is not our intention to explain how to program in Lisp: that would be a book in itself. Rather, we will discuss some of the more important customizations you might make and show you sample commands to place in your `.emacs` file.

Within Lisp, we work with entities called EXPRESSIONS. When Lisp processes an expression, we say that Lisp EVALUATES it. This involves reading the expression, making sense of it, and then performing the appropriate action. So, to be precise, we can say that you can put Lisp expressions in your `.emacs` file, and that Lisp evaluates these expressions as part of the initialization process.

When you create a `.emacs` file, you can put in descriptive comments that are ignored by Lisp. It is a good habit to use such comments to make it easy for you (or someone else) to understand the file. Lisp considers a comment to be any line that begins with a `;` (semicolon) character. You will see such comments in all our examples.

Setting Default Modes

As we explained earlier in the chapter, **emacs** has a minor mode called Auto Fill mode. When Auto Fill mode is turned on, **emacs** will automatically break lines for you as you type. By default, this mode is turned off: if you want to turn it on, you must use the command **M-x auto-fill-mode**.

If you spend most of your time editing regular text, you will probably want to turn on Auto Fill mode (a minor mode) each time you use Text mode (a major mode). To do so, you can place the following lines in your `.emacs` file:

```
; set Auto Fill mode as the default for Text mode
(setq text-mode-hook 'turn-on-auto-fill)
```

Do not leave out the parentheses or the single quote (apostrophe) character. Also, be sure to notice that there is only one single quote.

This particular Lisp expression uses what is called a VARIABLE: a quantity, with a name, that stores a particular value. Lisp and **emacs** make widespread use of variables, and you can modify countless facets of **emacs'** behavior by changing the value of some variable or another.

In this case, the variable is named **text-mode-hook**. The effect of the expression is to give this variable a value of **turn-on-auto-fill**. (The single quote in front of **turn-on-auto-fill** tells Lisp that what follows is an actual value and not an expression that needs to be evaluated.)

The purpose of this expression is to modify what **emacs** does each time it turns on Text mode. We make use of the fact that whenever **emacs** starts Text mode, it looks at the **text-mode-hook** variable and executes its value as a command. In this case, the command will be **turn-on-auto-fill**. Thus, once you put this line of Lisp in your **.emacs** file, Auto Fill mode will be turned on automatically each time you turn on Text mode.

Now let's take another look at the same expression:

```
(setq text-mode-hook 'turn-on-auto-fill)
```

Notice the word **setq**. This is the name of a FUNCTION: something that Lisp can execute. (All Lisp programs consist of one or more functions.)

For our purposes, we don't need to get too technical. All we need to understand is that when Lisp evaluates a function, something happens. In this case, the **setq** function sets the value of a variable (**text-mode-hook**) to a particular value (**turn-on-auto-fill**). (The **q** in **setq** stands for "quote", but we can't explain why without going into esoteric details as to the basic nature of Lisp.)

Here is another example. Each time you create a new buffer, **emacs** will, by default, turn on Fundamental mode. However, it may be that you use **emacs** only for creating regular text documents and that, for you, it would be more convenient to have all your new buffers use Text mode. To do so, use the following lines in your **.emacs** file:

```
; set Text mode as the default major mode
(setq default-major-mode 'text-mode)
```

In this case, we are giving the variable named **default-major-mode** a value of **text-mode**.

Of course, you can change this command and use another major mode as the default, simply by substituting a different mode name. (See Figure 21-30 for a list of major modes.) If you do change the command in this way, be sure not to omit the parentheses or the single quote.

Earlier, we looked at an expression that tells **emacs** to turn on Auto Fill mode each time Text mode is turned on:

```
(setq text-mode-hook 'turn-on-auto-fill)
```

You may decide that you would like Auto Fill mode to be turned on automatically for all major modes, not just for Text mode. To do so, use the following lines instead of the previous command:

```
; set Auto Fill mode as the default for all major modes
(setq-default auto-fill-hook 'do-auto-fill)
```

Here we are using a function named **setq-default**. The purpose of **setq-default** is to set the default value of a particular variable. In this case, we are telling Lisp to set the default value of the variable named **auto-fill-hook** to **do-auto-fill**.

(In **emacs**, a HOOK is a variable whose value is a function that is evaluated automatically whenever a certain condition arises. For example, **emacs** looks at the variable **text-mode-hook** each time Text mode is turned on.)

To summarize, you can customize your **emacs** environment by putting the appropriate expressions in your **.emacs** file. Each time **emacs** starts, it will evaluate the expressions in this file and perform the appropriate actions. The expressions we discussed in this section are as follows:

- Turn on Text mode by default for all new buffers:
  (setq default-major-mode 'text-mode)

- Turn on Auto Fill mode automatically for Text mode only:
  (setq text-mode-hook 'turn-on-auto-fill)

- Turn on Auto Fill mode automatically for all major modes:
  (setq-default auto-fill-hook 'do-auto-fill)

Solving the BACKSPACE and Help Problem

As we explained in Chapter 6, the BACKSPACE key is the same as **C-h**. Thus, when you press BACKSPACE within **emacs**, it is the same as pressing **C-h**. However, **C-h** starts the built-in Help facility.

Unfortunately, many people are used to pressing BACKSPACE to make a correction while they are typing. They expect BACKSPACE to move back one position and erase the previous character. In **emacs**, this function is performed by the **DEL** (DELETE) key.

If you find this inconvenient, you can place the following lines in your **.emacs** file to swap the meanings of BACKSPACE and **DEL**:

```
; swap the meanings of Backspace and DEL
(keyboard-translate ?\C-h ?\C-?)
(keyboard-translate ?\C-? ?\C-h)
```

The first expression tells **emacs** to change every **C-h** keypress into **DEL**. (Notice that the **DEL** key is represented as **C-?**.) The second expression changes **DEL** to **C-h**. Taken together, these two expressions allow you to use BACKSPACE to make corrections, and **DEL** to start the Help facility.

However, you must remember that anywhere you would normally use **DEL**, you must now use BACKSPACE (or **C-h**) instead. For example, the command to erase the previous word is **M-DEL**. If you change the meaning of these two keys, you will have to press **M-**BACKSPACE instead.

If it bothers you to have to mentally translate **DEL** to BACKSPACE all the time, you can solve the problem in a different way. Tell **emacs** to translate BACKSPACE to **DEL**, but do not change the meaning of **DEL**. This means that you can use either key to erase characters, and **DEL** will work in the normal manner. However, you will have to define another key to start the Help facility. The following lines, placed in your **.emacs** file, will do the trick:

```
; make Backspace act like DEL
(keyboard-translate ?\C-h ?\C-?)


; define C-x ? as the Help key
(define-key global-map "\C-x?" 'help)
```

The first expression makes BACKSPACE the same as **DEL**. The second expression tells **emacs** that **C-x ?** should execute the function called **help** (which starts the Help facility). If you set up your **.emacs** file in this way, you can use BACKSPACE and **DEL** interchangeably, and use **C-x ?** to start Help.

HINT

Once you become more experienced with the Help facility, you may want to have **C-x ?** map to a different function named **help-command**. To do so, replace the expression in your **.emacs** file that sets the **C-x ?** key with the following:

```
(define-key global-map "\C-x?" 'help-command)
```

The **help-function** function displays an abbreviated prompt that is faster for an experienced user. Try both mappings and see which one you prefer.

Solving the C-s and C-q Problem

At the beginning of the chapter, we talked a bit about the history of **emacs**. At the time, we explained how **emacs** was written long ago, on a computer system far, far away. The important point is that **emacs** was not developed for Unix. Thus, when **emacs** was first moved to Unix, it was found that some of the choices for key bindings were awkward.

In particular, Unix uses the **C-s** and **C-q** keys for what is called "flow control". **C-s** pauses the screen display, **C-q** restarts it (see Chapter 6). However, **emacs** uses **C-s** and **C-q** for other purposes: **C-s** starts an incremental search, and **C-q** indicates that the next character is to be taken literally. (For example, to type an actual **C-c**, you would press **C-q C-c**.)

Since Unix interprets **C-s** in its own way, you cannot use this key within **emacs**. If you do press **C-s**, all that will happen is that your screen will pause, and it will look as if your system has frozen—to continue, you will have to press **C-q**. Similarly, if you try to use **C-q** to type a special character, nothing at all will happen.

Fortunately, **emacs** provides a simple solution to this problem. By using the **enable-flow-control** function, you can tell **emacs** to assign other keys to take the place of **C-s** and **C-q**. Specifically, **C-** (CTRL-backslash) will replace **C-s**, and **C-^** (CTRL-circumflex) will replace **C-q**. All you have to do is place the following lines in your **.emacs** file:

```
; replace C-s with C-\, and C-q with C-^
(enable-flow-control)
```

Once you make this change, you must substitute these new keys whenever **C-s** and **C-q** would normally be used. For example, the command to save a buffer is **C-x C-s**. After initializing the new key settings, you will have to use **C-x C-**.

Solving the `Esc-Esc` Problem

Certain **emacs** commands can confuse beginners and so **emacs** designates them as DISABLED COMMANDS. When you press the keys that start one of these commands, **emacs** will ask if you really want to use it.

You will not encounter most of the disabled commands unless you press a strange key combination by accident. However, there is one such command that, unfortunately, is all too easy to invoke. This is **eval-expression**. The purpose of the **eval-expression** is to let you type a single Lisp expression and have **emacs** evaluate it immediately. To use this command, you type **ESC** twice in a row (**ESC ESC**).

Most people never need this command (which is why it is disabled). The trouble is that each time you press **ESC ESC**—which is easy to do—**emacs** will display a special set of instructions for disabled commands, and you will have to respond to clear the screen.

To solve this problem, simply place the following lines in your **.emacs** file:

```
; ignore ESC ESC
(global-unset-key "\e\e")
```

This will tell **emacs** to ignore the **ESC ESC** combination. (Notice that the **ESC** key is indicated by **\e**.)

If you ever decide that you want to start using Lisp, you can bring this command back to life by removing the **global-unset-key** command from your **.emacs** file.

The Help Facility

One of the best things about **emacs** is that it has an extensive, built-in Help facility you can use at any time. There is also a complete, online copy of the **emacs** reference manual you can access by using the Info facility (described in the next section).

We suggest you spend a few minutes becoming familiar with the Help facility and its commands. It is always available, and, unless you have a printed manual, there is no other easy way to find out about a particular key or function.

To start the Help facility, press **C-h** followed by a single letter, called an option. The most important Help options are shown in Figure 21-33. If you want to see a list of every possible option, use the **C-h ?** command.

When you press **C-h**, **emacs** will prompt you to select an option. If you change your mind and decide to quit, simply press **q**.

Command	Description
C-h ?	display a summary of all the Help options
C-h q	quit Help
C-h i	start the Info facility (documentation browser)
C-h t	start the **emacs** tutorial
C-h b	display a full list of all the key bindings
C-h c	you specify a key, **emacs** tells you what it does
C-h k	you specify a key, **emacs** describes its function
C-h w	you specify a function, **emacs** shows you its key
C-h a	show all the functions containing a specified word
C-h f	you specify a function, **emacs** describes it
C-h v	you specify a variable, **emacs** describes it
C-h m	describe the current major and minor modes

FIGURE 21-33. emacs: *Help commands*

HINT

It is easy to start the Help facility accidentally by pressing the BACKSPACE key (which is the same as **C-h**). When this happens, all you have to do is press **q** to quit. If that doesn't work, press **C-g**.

emacs comes with two full documentation systems. First, there is a built-in tutorial you can use to teach yourself at your own speed. To start the tutorial, press **C-h t**. We feel that you can get a better introduction to **emacs** by reading this chapter, because the tutorial can be confusing for beginners. However, if you have got this far, you already know the basics, so taking the tutorial now will serve as a nice review.

The Info facility is nothing less than a full-fledged documentation browser. We will discuss the details in the next section. For now, we will just mention that you start the Info facility by using the **C-h i** command.

The next set of commands help you learn about all the different keys. To see a full list of all the key bindings, use the **C-h b** command. This list is more interesting than you might think and is worth checking out from time to time.

The **C-h c** command tells you the name of the function to which a key is mapped. Most of the time, this is enough to tell you what a key does, because the function names are chosen to be descriptive. For example, say that you are wondering what the **C-x C-w** key combination does. Press **C-h c C-x C-w**. You will see:

```
C-x C-w runs the command write-file
```

To display more detailed information about the function, use the **C-h k** command. (This is one of our favorites.) For example, to find out more about the function to which the **C-x C-w** command is mapped, use the command **C-h k C-x C-w**. You will see:

```
write-file:
Write current buffer into file FILENAME.
Makes buffer visit that file, and marks it not modified.
If the buffer is already visiting a file, you can specify
a directory name as FILENAME, to write a file of the same
old name in that directory.
```

Conversely, if you know the name of a function, you can use **C-h w** (the "where is?" command) to tell you what key it uses. For example, if you type **C-h w write-file**, you will see:

```
write-file is on C-x C-w
```

HINT

When you have a spare moment, use the **C-h b** command to display the list of key bindings. Scan the list and find yourself an unfamiliar key that looks interesting. Then use the **C-h k** command to find out about that key.

When you start working with functions and variables, there are three Help options that you will find handy. **C-h a** (the "apropos" command) will show you all the functions whose names contain a specific regular expression. Usually, you specify a word because you are interested in seeing all the functions whose names contain that word. For example, say that you want to see all the functions that have something to do with killing. You can use the command **C-h a kill**. (Try it.)

If you know the name of a function, you can ask **emacs** to describe it for you by using the **C-h f** command. Similarly, you can use **C-h v** to have **emacs** describe a variable.

Finally, the last Help command we will discuss is **C-h m**. This command shows you the current major and minor modes, along with a short description of each one. (We described modes earlier in the chapter.)

The Info Facility

The Info facility is a documentation browser that is built into **emacs**. To start the Info facility, use the **C-h i** command. **emacs** will automatically create a new buffer to hold your Info session.

As you will see, the Info facility has its own special commands. However, you can still use many of the regular **emacs** commands: in particular, you can move away from the Info buffer to another, regular editing buffer.

When the Info facility starts, you will see a menu of selections. All you have to do is move the cursor to the selection you want, and press **RET** (the RETURN key).

Each selection on the main menu represents a full online manual for a particular system. The two most important selections are "Info", the manual for the Info facility itself; and "Emacs", the entire **emacs** reference manual.

The best way to learn how to use the Info facility is to start with the built-in documentation. Type the **C-h i** command, and then press **h** to start the Info tutorial. Follow the instructions and work your way through the various topics. Once you know how to use Info, you will be able to read the **emacs** manual whenever you want.

It is important—very important—that you learn how to use the Info facility. There is so much to learn about **emacs** that you will find yourself using the manual again and again. If you don't learn how to use Info, you will have no way to find out detailed information about **emacs**. The **emacs** Help facility only has summaries. The real information is in Info.

We won't go into all the details of using the Info facility: they are best learned by following the Info tutorial and by practicing. However, we will cover the basic concepts and give you summaries of the important Info commands. The general commands are shown in Figure 21-34.

The first thing you must understand is that, within the Info facility, certain keys work differently than they do within regular **emacs**. For example, as you are reading, you can tell Info to display the next screenful by pressing **SPC** (the SPACE bar), and the previous screenful by pressing **DEL** (the DELETE key). In **emacs**, you would press **C-v** to move forward and **M-v** to move backward.

The next thing to appreciate is the general structure of the menu system. The Info facility organizes information into short sections called NODES. ("Node" is a technical term borrowed from a branch of mathematics called graph theory.) Each node has a name and contains information about one specific topic. As you read, you can move from one node to another.

The nodes themselves are organized into a tree-like arrangement (an upside-down tree, actually). Think of the main menu as being the trunk of the tree. When you choose a selection from a menu, you get either another menu (a sub-branch) or a node.

When you select a node, Info will display it for you to read. As you read, there are commands to move within the node or to jump to another node. These commands are summarized in Figures 21-35 and 21-36.

When you are finished reading, there are three ways to stop. First, you can use an **emacs** command (such as **C-x o** or **C-x b**) to switch to another buffer. This leaves your Info session alive in its own buffer. Second, you can use the **q** (quit) command to stop Info completely. Third, you can use the **emacs C-x k** command to kill the Info window.

When you quit with the **q** command, **emacs** remembers your location within the Info tree. If you later restart the Info facility (with another **C-h i** command), **emacs** will put you back where you were when you quit. When you quit by using **C-x k** to kill the buffer, **emacs** does not remember your location. The next time you start Info, you will be back at the beginning (the main menu).

Command	Description
?	display a summary of Info commands
h	start the Info tutorial
q	quit Info, remember current location
C-x k	quit Info, do not remember current location

FIGURE 21-34.   **emacs**: *General Info commands*

Command	Description
n	jump to next node in the sequence
p	jump to previous node in the sequence
u	jump to the "up" node (the menu you came from)
l	jump to last node you looked at
m *selection*	pick a node from a menu
f	follow a cross-reference
i	look up topic in the index, then jump there
, (comma)	jump to next match from previous i command

FIGURE 21-35. emacs: *Info commands to select a node*

HINT
To learn how to use the Info facility, type **C-h i** and then press **h** to start the tutorial. To quit, press **q**.

Built-In Programs

One of the reasons **emacs** is so robust is that it contains a large number of built-in programs. Before we finish this chapter, we will spend a few minutes describing these programs so you can try them for yourself. In this section, we will discuss the serious programs. In the next section, we will discuss the games.

To execute a program, type **M-x** followed by the name of the program. For example, to run the **doctor** program, type **M-x doctor**. **emacs** will create a new buffer in which to run the program.

Command	Description
SPC	go forward one screenful
DEL	go backward one screenful
b	go to the beginning of the node
.	same as **b**
C-l	re-display the current screen

FIGURE 21-36. emacs: *Info commands to read a node*

There are several ways to stop a program. First, the program itself may have its own quit command, such as **q**. Second, you can use the standard **emacs** quit command, **C-g**. This will stop the program and preserve the buffer. Third, you can use the **C-x k** command to kill the buffer in which the program is running.

Alternatively, you can simply change to a different buffer (by using, for example, the **C-x b** or **C-x o** commands). At any time, you can return to the program and work with it some more.

We don't have the space to explain all of the built-in **emacs** programs in detail. (As you can see, this chapter is almost over.) However, we will give you a quick guided tour to allow you to decide which programs look interesting to you. Figure 21-37 shows the useful programs. Figure 21-38 shows the fun programs.

There are various ways to get information about a program. First, you should try the Info facility. Look for the program within the **emacs** manual and see if you can find some documentation. The larger programs have menus and submenus of their own. The smaller programs may have only a brief mention.

Second, use the Help facility to tell you what it can about the actual function. For example, to find out about **blackbox**, type **C-h f blackbox**.

Third, start the program and see if it has a built-in Help command. For instance, within **dunnet**, you can display a Help document by using the command **help**.

The first useful program is **calendar**. Each time you start the program, it shows you a three-month calendar, which is handy by itself. However, **calendar** is much, much more. One of the basic **calendar** tools is a diary, which you can use to keep daily notes and reminders. Within **calendar**, you will find just about anything you can imagine that has to do with days and calendars. For example, you can display various types of calendars (such as Hebrew, Islamic and astronomical); you can list the dates of the various phases of the moon; and you can display local times for sunrise and sunset.

The **dired** ("directory editor") program provides a complete interface for working with files and directories. You can perform all the common file and

calendar	desk calendar and diary
dired	work with directories and files
gnus	read and respond to Usenet articles
rmail	read and dispose of mail
telnet	open a **telnet** session with a remote host

FIGURE 21-37. **emacs**: *Built-in useful programs*

Program	Description
blackbox	black box puzzle: find objects inside a box
dissociated-press	scrambling text in an amusing way
doctor	the Eliza program: acts like a psychiatrist
dunnet	adventure-style exploration game
gomoku	game of Go Moku
hanoi	visual solution of Towers of Hanoi problem
life	game of Life (auto-reproducing patterns)
mpuz	multiplication puzzle: guess the digits
spook	generates words to get the Fed's attention
yow	displays a quotation from Zippy the Pinhead

FIGURE 21-38. **emacs**: *Games and diversions*

directory operations, such as copy, move, and rename. You can point to a file and tell **emacs** to show it to you. You can print a file, or compress and uncompress it. What we like best about **dired** is that it makes it easy to maintain your directory tree by creating and removing directories, and by moving files from one place to another. (We explain these ideas in Chapters 22, 23 and 24.) Many people keep an active copy of **dired** at all times, so they can switch to it instantly as the need arises.

The **gnus** program runs the GNUS facility, an interface to Usenet. Usenet is a worldwide system of thousands of discussion groups—if your computer is on the Internet, you probably have Usenet access. If so, you can use GNUS to read the discussion groups and to post articles of your own. For more information on Usenet, see *The Internet Complete Reference*, written by Harley Hahn and Rick Stout, and published by Osborne/McGraw-Hill (ISBN 0-07-881980-6).

The **rmail** command starts a system called Rmail, which allows you to read and dispose of electronic mail. Rmail is an alternative to the other mail programs we discussed in Chapter 15 (**mail**, Pine, Elm, and so on). If you use **emacs** as your primary working environment, you will probably want to use Rmail as your mail program.

Finally, there is **telnet**, a program that allows you to establish a connection with a remote computer. If your computer is on the Internet, you can use **telnet** to connect to any other computer on the Internet. For details about such connections and how they work, see the Internet book mentioned above.

Games and Diversions

Now, the fun stuff. First, the **blackbox** program. This is a puzzle game; you must use tomography to find objects that are hidden inside a box. (Tomography involves looking at X-ray images in various planes.)

The **dissociated-press** program is a novelty. It scrambles text in an amusing way, turning selected words into real-looking doubletalk.

The **doctor** program is an old one. Originally it was called "Eliza", after the Eliza Doolittle character in *Pygmalion* and *My Fair Lady*. **doctor** acts like a psychiatrist: the kind that behaves nonjudgmentally, listening with infinite patience, and prompting you to talk about yourself. Just the thing to keep someone busy at the computer, while you are in the next room working on something important.

dunnet is a text-based exploration game in the style of the original **adventure** (which is still included on many Unix systems; see Chapter 7). You play **dunnet** by typing commands consisting of up to several words (for example "eat food"). As you play, you travel around an imaginary place, looking for treasure and trying to stay out of trouble. One of the challenges is to figure out exactly what you are supposed to be doing.

The **gomoku** program plays the game of Go Moku with you. The idea is to try to mark off squares in such a way that you get five in a row. The computer will try to block you and to mark five consecutive squares of its own.

hanoi displays a visual solution to the Towers of Hanoi problem. There are three poles, lined up in a row, as well as a number of different-sized discs with holes. To start, the discs are stacked from largest to smallest on the leftmost pole. The problem is to figure out how to move all the discs from the leftmost pole to the rightmost pole without ever placing a larger disc on top of a smaller disc.

If you were to design a computer program to solve this problem, you would find that it lends itself to what programmers call a "recursive" solution. The Lisp programming language (in which **emacs** is written) is designed to make recursive programming easy, so it makes sense to find such a demonstration program in a Lisp-based system like **emacs**. If you want to see an interesting display, try **ESC 5 M-x hanoi**.

The Game of Life (the **life** program) is based on a simple two-dimensional grid-like universe. A number of "lifeforms", called cells, exist. Each cell fills exactly one position in the grid, which is surrounded by 8 other positions. The cells reproduce according to a few well-defined rules. If a cell is surrounded by 4 or more cells, it dies of overcrowding. If a cell is all alone or has only one neighbor, the cell dies of loneliness. An empty location will be filled with a brand new cell if that location has exactly 3 neighbors. As the game progresses, you can watch the patterns change from one "generation" to the next. (The Game of Life was invented by John Horton Conway and introduced publicly by Martin Gardner in the October 1970 issue of *Scientific American*.)

mpuz is a multiplication puzzle. The program creates a multiplication calculation of medium complexity. However, each different digit is represented by a letter and not a number. You must guess which letters stand for which numbers.

The **spook** program was designed to insert special words—with no meaningful context—into your buffer. These words are of the type that the American FBI (Federal Bureau of Investigation), or CIA (Central Intelligence Agency), or NSA (National Security Agency) would be looking for within electronic messages in order to identify subversive people.

The intention is that, after composing a mail message, you execute the **spook** program to add a collection of these words to the buffer. Then, if the FBI or CIA or NSA has a program that checks for subversive messages traveling around the Internet, your message will be snagged and archived. Later, some government flunky will have to waste time reading your mail, just to make sure you are not a bad guy. Here is some sample output from **spook**:

```
Delta Force Panama Croatian Noriega FBI radar
strategic Legion of Doom AK-47 class struggle
SEAL Team 6 NORAD Rule Psix Kennedy cryptographic
```

Of course, no one knows for sure if the FBI or CIA or NSA really scan mail in this way. However, the idea is that if everyone uses the **spook** program regularly, it would overwhelm such agencies if they did indeed try to spy on us.

Finally, the **yow** program displays a quotation from Zippy the Pinhead. Zippy is a freakish, counterculture comic character whose life is punctuated by a repeated series of non sequiturs. Here are three such examples:

```
Equip me with MISSILES!!
*Help*I'm RELIGIOUS!!
I love a man with a HAIRPIECE!!

I don't know why but, suddenly, I want to
discuss declining I.Q. LEVELS with a blue
ribbon SENATE SUBCOMMITTEE!

My pants just went on a wild rampage through a
Long Island Bowling Alley!!
```

(By the way, "pinhead" is the pejorative term for a cretin: a person with deformity and mental retardation that was caused by a thyroid deficiency.)

HINT

After reading this section, you might wonder what would happen if Zippy the Pinhead were to have a conversation with the **emacs** psychiatrist. If you want to find out, try the command:

M-x psychoanalyze-pinhead

When you try this command, you will find the conversation moves quickly. Let it go for a while, and then stop it by pressing **C-g**. You can now move back to the beginning of the buffer (by using **M-<**) and read what happened.

To end this chapter, Figure 21-39 (on the following page) shows excerpts from a sample conversation between Zippy and the doctor. In order to make the excerpts easy to follow, we have indented Zippy's comments and put them in italics.

I am the psychotherapist.
Please, describe your problems.
Each time you are finished talking, type RET twice.

   If I am elected no one will ever have to do their
   laundry again!

Why do you say that?

   Yow! I want my nose in lights!

What makes you believe you want your nose in lights?

   I selected E5... but I didn't hear "Sam the Sham
   and the Pharaohs"!

Is it because you didn't hear sam the sham and the
pharaohs that you came to me?

   Spreading peanut butter reminds me of opera!!
   I wonder why?

Can you elaborate on that?

   Civilization is fun! Anyway, it keeps me busy!!

Earlier you said you didn't hear sam the sham and
the pharaohs"?

   I'm EMOTIONAL now because I have
   MERCHANDISING CLOUT!!

When did you first know that you have
merchandising clout?

   I have seen these EGG EXTENDERS in my Supermarket...
   ...I have read the INSTRUCTIONS...

You mentioned that it keeps you busy?

   All right, you degenerates!
   I want this place evacuated in 20 seconds!

FIGURE 21-39.   emacs: *Zippy the Pinhead talks to the Psychiatrist*

CHAPTER 22

The Unix File System

The most important part of any computer system is its data: the information that is stored and manipulated by the programs. Unix has a FILE SYSTEM whose job it is to maintain all the data that is stored in the computer. This includes programs, documents, databases, text files and so on.

Most of the time, the Unix file system runs automatically. The file system does need some care and feeding occasionally, but this is the responsibility of your system manager. All you need to understand are the basic concepts and how to use a few of the commands.

In this chapter, we will orient you to the Unix file system. In Chapters 23 and 24, you will learn how to use the file system commands that will help you in your day-to-day work.

What Is a File?

In everyday life, the idea of a file is straightforward: a collection of papers, such as you might keep in a folder in your desk. If you have used a computer, you may know a more specific meaning for the word "file". On most computer systems, a file is a collection of data, stored on a disk, compact disc (CD) or tape. A computer file might contain a document, program, spreadsheet, picture, message or whatever. Each file has a name by which you can reference it.

Within Unix, the definition of a file is much broader. A FILE is any source from which data can be read, or any target to which data can be written. Thus, the term "file" refers not only to a repository of data like a disk file, but to any physical device. In particular, the keyboard (a source of input) is a file, the display (an output target) is a file, and each printer (also an output target) is a file.

In this chapter, you will learn that all files are named in a standard way. In fact, it is just as easy to send input to one of your disk files as to, say, the screen of the terminal that your friend is using in the next room.

To put this in perspective, remember that the disk is inside the host computer which may be, say, in the office of the system administrator on the other side of the building. (See Chapter 3.)

This generality is of enormous importance: It means that Unix programs are much more flexible than programs that run on other computer systems. Any program that reads and writes using standard input/output (see Chapters 16 and 17) can use any input source and any output target. Moreover, you will find that the Unix file system has a compelling beauty: everything makes sense.

HINT

In Unix, the term "file" refers to any source of input or target of output, not only to a repository of data.

The Three Types of Unix Files

Unix has three types of files: ordinary files, directories and special files.

An ORDINARY FILE is what most people think of when they use the word "file". Ordinary files contain data and are stored on disk or, less often, on compact disc (CD) or tape. These are the files that you will work with most of the time. For example, when you use a text editor program to modify a document, both the document and the editor program itself are stored in ordinary files. Sometimes, these types of files are called REGULAR FILES.

The next type of file is a DIRECTORY. A directory is stored on disk and contains information that is used to organize and access other files. Conceptually, a directory "contains" other files. For example, you might have a directory named

vacation within which you keep all the files having to do with your upcoming trip to Syldavia.

You yourself do not create the directory, nor do you put files in it or maintain it. You use commands to tell Unix to do the work for you. For example, if you want to see what is in a directory, you don't actually look inside. You use a command to tell Unix to look inside, figure out what it means, and display a summary for you. (This is the **ls** [list] command.)

If you did look inside a directory, all you would see is gibberish. A directory does not really contain files, it contains the information Unix needs to access the files. The best way to understand a directory is to think of it as pointing to a number of files.

A directory can also point to other directories. This allows you to organize your files into a hierarchical system using whatever design suits your needs. As we will see later, the whole Unix file system is organized as one large hierarchy with directories inside of directories inside of directories. Whenever you want, you can tell Unix to make or remove directories. Thus, you can change your organization as your needs change.

The last type of file, a SPECIAL FILE or DEVICE FILE, is an internal representation of a physical device. For example, your keyboard, your display screen, a printer, the disk drive—all the devices on your system can be accessed as files. To send data to the screen on someone else's terminal, all you have to do is write the data to the file that represents that device.

What's in a Name?   File

There are three types of Unix files: ordinary files, directories and special files. However, the word "file" is often used, informally, to refer to just ordinary files.

When you see or hear the word "file", you must decide, by context, what it means. Sometimes it means any type of file, sometimes it means just ordinary files.

For example, say that you read the following sentence: "The **ls** command lists the names of all the files in a directory." In this case, the word "file" refers to any type of file: an ordinary file, special file or directory. All three types of files can be stored in a directory and, hence, listed with the **ls** command.

But what if you read, "You can use the **vi** editor to modify your text files." In this sentence, the word "file" refers only to ordinary files—files that contain data—because they are the only type of files it makes sense to edit.

Thus, the word "file" is used in two ways: to mean any type of Unix file, and to mean the plain vanilla ordinary files we work with from minute to minute. Most of the time, the difference is clear by context.

Text Files and Binary Files, Bits and Bytes

Special files represent physical devices; directories organize other files. It is the ordinary files that contain actual data (including programs).

There are as many types of ordinary files as there are types of data. However, broadly speaking, we can categorize ordinary files into two groups: text files and binary files.

TEXT FILES are ordinary files that contain only ASCII characters: the type of data that you can generate by typing at a keyboard. In fact, the term ASCII FILE is often used as a synonym for text file.

(The ASCII character set is explained in Chapter 17. Briefly, it is a set of 128 different codes that represent the different characters we use for textual data: upper- and lowercase letters, numerals, the space, the tab, punctuation, as well as the control characters.)

Text files are used to hold documents, memos, shell scripts and so on. You can edit a text file with a text editor, such as **vi** or **emacs** (see Chapters 20 and 21). When you display a text file on your screen, it is composed of normal, everyday characters, and it makes sense when you look at it.

BINARY FILES are ordinary files that contain non-textual data, such as pictures. If you try to display or edit a binary file, the output will look like gibberish (although you may see some recognizable characters). Binary files contain data that only makes sense when processed by a program. For example, say that you use a program that maintains a database. Chances are that the data will be stored in a binary file, using a format that makes sense only to the database program.

Here is a more common example involving binary files. You are writing a computer program, say, in the C programming language. You create the program by editing a text file that contains instructions in the C language. However, the computer cannot execute instructions in the C language. They must first be translated into so-called machine instructions that the computer can understand.

To do so, there are two special programs you use—a compiler and a linker—to make the translation. We won't go into the details here. The main idea is that the C program you write is stored in a text file that you can edit and understand. The compiler and linker use this text file and generate a binary file that contains the equivalent machine language program.

The original C program—the one you create with a text editor—is called the SOURCE PROGRAM or, more simply, the SOURCE. The machine language program, the binary file you can execute, is called the EXECUTABLE PROGRAM. Thus, when you program, you create a text file, but the computer executes a binary file.

The distinction between text files and binary files becomes important when you transfer data from one computer to another. In many cases, you have to use different commands to transfer the two types of data. Thus, you need to be aware of what type of file you are using.

HINT

If an ordinary file contains data you can display or edit in a meaningful way, it is a text file. Otherwise, it is a binary file.

Technical Differences Between Text Files and Binary Files

If you have followed the discussion carefully, you may have felt dissatisfied. So far, we have not really defined the difference between text files and binary files, we have only given examples and appealed to your intuition.

The difference between these two types of files is highly technical. We will explain it briefly, but if you don't understand it at first, don't worry.

Within a computer, data is stored as a long series of BITS. A bit consists of a single binary digit: that is, a single element that is either a 0 or a 1. In other words, computers store data as long strings of 0s and 1s.

A string of bits is divided into groups of 8, each group being known as a BYTE. Thus, we can consider computer data as being stored in bytes, each of which contains 8 bits, each bit consisting of a 0 or a 1.

Data is represented using codes of 0s and 1s. The ASCII code contains the rules for representing textual data. You can look at the ASCII code (see Appendix E) and see the bit pattern for each character. For example, the uppercase letter "A" is represented by the bits 01000000. The lowercase letter "a"—a completely different character—is represented by the bits 01100001.

Using the ASCII code, a text file stores one character per byte. Thus, a file that contains 1000 characters will be 1000 bytes long.

Strictly speaking, the ASCII code uses only 7 bits per character. The 8th bit—the leftmost one—is always set to 0. Thus, when a text file (which contains ASCII data) is transferred to another computer, the transferring programs need only pay attention to the rightmost 7 bits in each character. The 8th bit is ignored, or is used for other purposes (which we won't go into).

Binary files also store data in bytes. However, the data in binary files does not necessarily use the ASCII code. Each binary file contains data that was stored in the way that makes sense to the program that created the file.

The important idea is that, where text files only use 7 bits out of each byte, binary files use all 8 bits. That means that when you transfer a binary file, the transferring programs need to make sure that all 8 bits are accounted for. This is why you must tell the transferring program whether you are using text files or binary files.

To summarize: A text file contains ASCII characters that use 7 bits per byte. A binary file contains data that uses the full 8 bits per byte.

Directories and Subdirectories

We use directories to organize files into a hierarchical system. To do so, we collect files together into groups and keep each group in its own directory. Since directories are themselves files, a directory can contain other directories. This is what creates the hierarchy.

Here is an example. Say that you are a student and you are taking three classes for which you have to write essays: History, Literature and Surfing. You use the **vi** editor (Chapter 20) to write the essays, of which there are several for each class.

To organize all this work, you make a directory called **essays** (don't worry about the details for now). Within this directory, you make three more directories: **history**, **literature** and **surfing**. Within each of these directories, you keep your essays. Each essay is stored in a text file that has a descriptive name. Figure 22-1 shows a diagram of what it all looks like.

A PARENT DIRECTORY is one that contains other directories. A SUBDIRECTORY is a directory that lies within another directory. In Figure 22-1, **essays** is a parent directory that contains three subdirectories: **history**, **literature** and **surfing**. Sometimes a subdirectory is called a CHILD DIRECTORY.

It is common to talk about directories as if they contain other files. For example, we might say that **essays** contains three subdirectories. Or we might say that **literature** contains four text files.

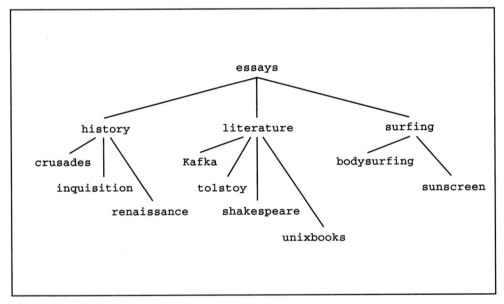

FIGURE 22-1. *An example of organizing with directories*

Thus, you might imagine that if we looked inside the **literature** directory we would actually see the four files. Actually, Unix stores all files as distinct items. If we were to look inside **literature** (and we can't really) we would see, not four text files, but the information that Unix needs to access these files.

However, there is no reason to care about the technical details. Unix maintains the whole file system for us automatically. All we need to do is use the appropriate command, and Unix will do whatever we want: make a directory, remove a directory, move a file from one directory to another and so on. From our point of view, everything just works, and we can, indeed, think of directories as containing other files.

The Tree-Structured File System

Unix systems contain many, many files that are organized using directories and subdirectories. The Unix file system is based upon a single main directory called the ROOT DIRECTORY. (The name will make sense in a moment.) The root directory is the parent or ancestor of every directory in the system.

Figure 22-2 shows the outline of the Unix file system. You can see the root directory at the top. This figure shows the directories that are used with systems based on Berkeley Unix. If your system is based on System V (see Chapter 2) or another variation of Unix, your file system may be somewhat different, but the idea will be the same.

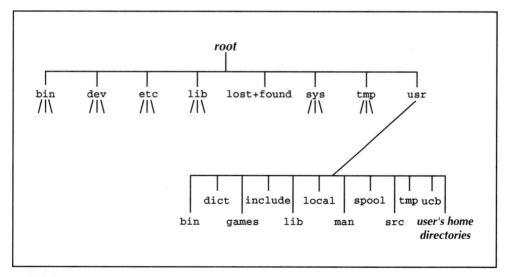

FIGURE 22-2. *The Unix file system*

What you see in Figure 22-2 is the bare skeleton. All Unix systems will have other directories created by the system manager. It is not really important to memorize the name of each directory. All you need is a general idea of how the file system is organized. (We will take a quick look at these directories in a moment.)

As you can see, the outline of the Unix file system is like an upside-down tree. The name "root" was chosen to indicate the main trunk of the tree. (Only a weenie would have called it the "trunk" directory.)

Since the root directory is so important, its name must often be specified as part of a command. It would be tiresome to always have to type the letters "root". Instead, the root directory is indicated by a single **/** (slash).

For example, the **ls** command will list the names of all the files in a specific directory. To list all the files in the root directory, you use:

```
ls /
```

What's in a Name?   Root

If you are old enough (or if you have studied English history), you may remember a song that had the line: "Her name was McGill and she called herself Lil, but everyone knew her as Nancy."

With the Unix file system, we might say: "It acts as the trunk and we call it the root, but everyone knows it as **/** (slash)."

When you specify the name of a directory or a file that lies within the root directory, you type a **/** followed by the name. For example, the formal name of the **etc** directory is **/etc**. To list all the files in this directory, use:

```
ls /etc
```

Formally, this means "the directory named **etc** that lies within the **/** (root) directory".

To indicate a directory or file within another directory, separate the names with a **/**. For example, within the **/etc** directory is a file named **passwd**. The formal name of this file is **/etc/passwd**. Similarly, within the **/usr** directory is another directory named **dict**. Within this directory is a file named **words**. The formal name of this file is **/usr/dict/words**.

HINT

The **/** character has two different meanings. At the beginning of a file name, **/** stands for the root directory. Within a file name, **/** acts as a delimiter.

Once you understand the tree in Figure 22-2, you can see that all directories, except the root directory, lie within another directory. Thus, all directories, except the root directory, are actually subdirectories. In day-to-day speech, we use the term "subdirectory" only when we want to emphasize that a particular directory lies within another directory. Mostly, we just say "directory".

What's in a Name?   etc, tmp, usr

Within the root directory are three subdirectories named **etc**, **tmp** and **usr**. These names were chosen because they are short and easy to type. However, when we talk, these names are hard to pronounce.

The convention is to call **etc** the "etcetera" directory; **tmp** is the "temp" directory; and **usr** is the "user" directory. Notice that we pronounce **usr** and **tmp** as if the "e" were there, even though we don't spell them that way.

As a general rule, if you are talking about Unix and you come across a missing letter or two, put it in when you pronounce the word. For example, the name of the **/etc/passwd** file is pronounced "slash etcetera slash password".

A Tour of the Root Directory

The root directory is the base of the entire file system. Mostly, it contains only other directories. However, the root directory does contain at least one important file: the program that is the heart of Unix (called the "kernel"). On Berkeley Unix systems, this program is in a file named **vmunix**. (The name stands for "virtual memory Unix". Virtual memory is a technique for using disk space to simulate large amounts of memory.) On other systems, the kernel may have a different name. To find the kernel on your system, look for a very large file in the root directory.

What's in a Name? root

In Chapter 4, we explained that the system manager logs in with a userid of **root** when he or she needs to become the superuser. Now you can see where the name comes from: this userid is named after the root directory, the most important directory in the file system.

The **/bin** directory contains basic programs that are part of Unix. This is where many of the Unix commands are stored. The name "bin" refers to the fact that many of these programs are binary files. However, we like to think of this directory as a storage bin for programs.

The **/dev** directory contains the special files that represent the physical devices. You usually won't need to use these files, but if you do, here they are.

The **/etc** directory is mostly for the system administrator. Here lie the programs and files that are used for managing the system. Perhaps the most well-known file is **passwd**, the system password file (see Chapter 13). Another well-known file is **termcap**, a database that contains technical descriptions of all the terminals Unix can use. (Some Unix systems use a different database called **terminfo**.)

The **/lib** directory contains libraries of programs used by programmers.

The **/lost+found** directory is used by a special program that checks the Unix file system. Whenever this program finds a file that does not seem to belong anywhere (accidents do happen), it will put it in the **/lost+found** directory. The system manager can then look at the file and dispose of it appropriately.

The **/sys** directory contains what are called system source files. These are of interest only to the system manager and to programmers.

The **/tmp** directory is used for temporary storage. Anybody is allowed to store files in this directory, and, from time to time, all the files in this directory are removed automatically. Typically, a program will use the **/tmp** directory to store files that are needed for only a short time.

For example, when you use **vi** editor (Chapter 20), it makes a copy of the file you want to edit. This copy is stored in the **/tmp** directory. Thus, you are always working with a temporary copy and not with the original file.

The **/usr** directory contains a number of important subdirectories of its own, which we will discuss later in the chapter.

Using the Special Files in the /dev Directory: tty

We have already explained how special files are used to represent physical devices. All the special files are kept in the **/dev** directory. To display the names of the special files on your system, use the command:

```
ls /dev
```

You will see many names. You will rarely have a need to use most of these special files. For the most part, they are for system programs. However, there are a few special files that are interesting to know about.

All the files that begin with the letters "tty" represent terminals. For example, terminal **tty01** is represented by the special file **/dev/tty01**. If you send output to this file, it is just like sending output to the screen of that terminal.

For example, say that you have a file named **scary** that displays a short, scary message. You use the **who** command (Chapter 13) and find out that one of your friends is logged in to terminal **tty01**. You can use the **cp** (copy) command (see Chapter 24) to copy the contents of the **scary** file directly to your friend's terminal screen:

```
cp scary /dev/tty01
```

The message will appear from nowhere, thus scaring him into an early decline. On some systems, this command will work even if your friend has set **mesg** to **n** (see Chapter 13).

(Disclaimer: The above command is given only as an example. Only a bored, immature person would actually play such a trick.)

If you want to display the name of the special file that represents your terminal, use the command:

```
tty
```

For example, you might see the output:

```
/dev/tty02
```

This means that you are logged in to terminal **tty02**.

As a convenience, you can always use the file **/dev/tty** as a synonym to represent your terminal. Thus, you could display data on your screen by copying it to **/dev/tty**. If you ever use a program that must write its output to a file, you can display the output by telling the program to write to **/dev/tty**.

The most useful file in the **/dev** directory is named **null**. This file represents an non-existent, empty device. When you read from **/dev/null** you get nothing; when you write to **/dev/null** the output disappears.

The **null** file is handy when you have a program that writes spurious output you want to ignore. If you send the output to **/dev/null**, it will disappear forever.

For example, say that you have a program that updates data in certain files. The program is named **updatefiles**. The usual way to run the program would be to enter its name as a command:

```
updatefiles
```

However, as the program runs, it generates lines of output that are displayed on your terminal: output you would just as soon not have to look at. Using the symbol, you can redirect the output to the **/dev/null** file:

```
updatefiles > /dev/null
```

Essentially, this runs the program, but throws away the output. (Redirection is explained in Chapter 16.)

When you read the Usenet discussion groups (Chapter 26), you will sometimes see a remark like: "If you don't like my comments, send your criticisms to **/dev/null**." This is a not-so-subtle way of telling people who disagree with you to go pound sand.

A Tour of the **/usr** Directory

The **/usr** directory is one of the most important subdirectories in the root directory. The **/usr** directory holds a number of subdirectories of its own. (As you will see, the name "usr" indicates that some of these subdirectories are given to users to hold their personal files.)

The **/usr/bin** directory, like its namesake in the root directory, is used to hold executable programs.

The **/usr/dict** directory contains files used by the Unix dictionary (actually a word list). For more details, see the discussion of the **look** command in Chapter 17.

The **/usr/games** directory contains the Unix games and diversions (see Chapter 7).

The **/usr/include** directory contains the so-called "include" files that are used by programmers. These hold predefined instructions that are included in many different programs.

The **/usr/lib** directory, like its counterpart **/lib**, contains libraries of programs and data used by programmers.

The **/usr/local** directory is used for the convenience of the system manager. He or she can use this directory to store local programs and documentation.

The **/usr/man** directory contains the directories and files used by the online Unix manual (explained in Chapter 8).

The **/usr/spool** directory acts as a way station. It is used to hold data that is waiting to be sent somewhere. For example, when you print a file (see Chapter 19), a copy of the file, along with some system information, is kept in this directory. The file waits here until it can be printed. Similarly, when you send mail (see Chapters 14 and 15), it is kept in this directory until it can be delivered. As we explained in Chapter 19, the word "spool" is an old acronym, originally meaning "simultaneous peripheral operations offline".

The **/usr/src** directory holds source programs. If your site has the right type of Unix license (software is licensed, not sold), this directory may contain the actual programs that make up Unix itself. If so, you can look at them to your heart's content. If you can read the C programming language, reading the Unix programs can be a fascinating (and time-consuming) venture into the unknown.

The **/usr/tmp** directory, like the **/tmp** directory, is used for temporary storage.

The **/usr/ucb** directory contains programs that were developed at the Computer Science department of the University of California at Berkeley. If you want to see the principal commands that were added to standard System V Unix by the developers of Berkeley Unix, you can list the files in this directory. Use the command:

```
ls /usr/ucb
```

This directory is found in all modern systems, since, these days, virtually all Unix systems contain the Berkeley programs. (For a discussion of the different types of Unix, see Chapter 2.)

Why Do We Have Both /bin and /usr/bin for Holding Programs?

We mentioned that many programs and other executable files are kept in the **/bin** and **/usr/bin** directories. The name "bin" stands for binary, as many of these programs are binary files. However, we can also think of these directories as bins in which we store programs.

You might be wondering, why does Unix have two such directories? Why not simply store all the programs in **/bin** (or, for that matter, in **/usr/bin**)?

The answer is that the two "bin" directories are a historical legacy. In the olden days (the early 1970s), the Unix developers used a computer called a PDP 11/45. (The PDP 11/45 was sold by the Digital Equipment Corporation and was the type of machine that used to be referred to as a "mini-computer".)

This computer had more than one device for data storage. The primary device was a "fixed-head disk". That is, the read/write head did not move in and out. There was also a regular disk (in which the read/write head did move) called an RP03. The fixed-head disk, sometimes referred to as a "drum", could store only a small amount of data (less than 2 megabytes), but could do so relatively quickly, because the head did not need to move. The RP03 could store 40 megabytes (which was large in those days), but was slower, as the head needed to move back and forth as the various "tracks" of the disk were accessed.

In order to accommodate multiple storage devices on the same computer, the Unix programmers used a design in which each device had its own "file system". The main device (the drum) held the root file system; the other device (the RP03 disk) held the **/usr** file system.

The idea was that when Unix started, it had immediate access to the root file system and everything it contained. Once Unix was up and running, it would "mount" the **/usr** file system, at which time Unix could access all the files on both systems. However, during the startup procedure, before the **/usr** system was mounted, Unix only had access to the relatively small storage area of the root file system.

It would have been nice to keep the entire Unix system (including extra space for temporary files) on the drum, as it was a lot faster to access than the RP03 disk. However, there just wasn't enough room. So the Unix designers divided all the programs and files into two categories. Those that were absolutely crucial to the startup process and to running the bare-bones operating system were stored in the root file system, in the **/bin** directory. The rest of the programs were stored in the **/usr** file system, in the **/usr/bin** directory.

Similarly, the library of programmers' files were divided into two directories, **/lib** and **/usr/lib**. And temporary files were kept in **/tmp** and **/usr/tmp**.

Of course, these days, storage devices are much less expensive and a lot faster. Thus, there is no practical reason why the system programs need to be divided into two directories. Indeed, modern versions of System V Unix (starting with V.4) have moved the contents of the **/bin** directory to **/usr/bin**, and the contents of **/lib** to **/usr/lib**. However, there is a "symbolic link" from **/bin** to **/usr/bin** (and from **/lib** to **/usr/lib**) so that you can still access the files in their old locations if necessary.

(Briefly, a symbolic link lets you access a file as if it were in a particular directory, even though it is in another. We will describe links in Chapter 24, at which time we will be more precise.)

On Unix systems that still use pairs of directories, you will usually see that the directories on the root file system hold the basic system files, while the directories in the **/usr** file system hold most everything else.

Home Directories

With so many system directories chock-full of important files, it is clear that we need an orderly system for users to store their personal files. Of course, people like you and me wouldn't make a mess of things if we were allowed to, say, store our own personal programs in the **/bin** directory. But, for the most part, we can't have people putting their files, willy-nilly, wherever they want.

The solution is to give each user a HOME DIRECTORY. This is a directory, associated with a particular userid, that is completely under the auspices of that userid. When your system manager registers you with the system, he or she assigns you a home directory. The name of your home directory is kept in the system password file (see Chapter 13). When you log in, the system automatically places you in this directory. (The idea of being "in" a directory will make more sense after you have read Chapter 23.)

Within this home directory, you can do whatever you want. You can store files and create other subdirectories as you see fit. Many people have large elaborate tree structures of their own, all under their personal home directory.

The traditional place for the system manager to create home directories is under the **/usr** directory. The name of the home directory is the name of the userid. For example, if your userid is **harley**, your home directory would be **/usr/harley**. Many system managers place home directories elsewhere. On some systems, home directories are within a directory named **u**; on other systems, they are within a directory named **users**. Still others use parent directories that categorize users into groups. For example, a systems manager at a university might divide the home directories into **undergrad**, **grad**, **prof** and **staff**; at a real estate company you might see **agents**, **managers** and **admin**. You get the idea.

When you log in, the global variable **$HOME** is set to the name of your home directory. (Global variables are discussed in Chapter 11 for the C-Shell and in Chapter 12 for the Korn shell.) Thus, one way to display the name of your home directory is to enter:

```
echo $HOME
```

(The **echo** command simply displays the values of its arguments.)

As a shortcut, the symbol ~ (tilde) can be used as an abbreviation for your home directory. For example, you can display the name of this directory by using:

```
echo ~
```

Whatever its name, the important thing about your home directory is that it is yours to use as you see fit. (However, there will probably be a quota that limits the total amount of disk space you can use.) One thing many people do is create a **bin** subdirectory to store their own programs. You can put the name of this directory—for example, **/usr/harley/bin**—in your search path.

(The search path is explained in Chapters 11 and 12. Basically, your search path is a list of directories. This list is stored in the global variable named **PATH**. Whenever you enter the name of a command that is not built into the shell, Unix looks in the directories specified in your search path to find the appropriate program to execute.)

Figure 22-3 shows a typical directory structure based on the home directory of **/usr/harley**. This home directory has three subdirectories: **bin**, **essays** and **jokes**. The **essays** directory has three subdirectories of its own: **history**, **literature** and **surfing**. All of these directories contain files (which are not shown in the diagram). As you will see in Chapter 23, making and removing subdirectories is easy. Thus, it is a simple matter to enlarge or prune your directory tree as you see fit.

Variations in the Unix Directory Structure

What we have discussed so far describes the standard organization of the Berkeley Unix file system (the one shown in Figure 22-2). You will probably find variations

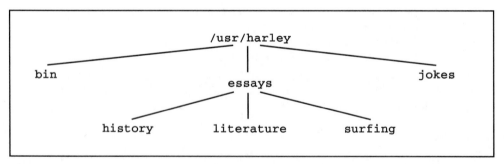

FIGURE 22-3. *A typical home directory-based tree structure*

on your system, especially if you are using a version of Unix that leans more toward System V. (See Chapter 2 for a discussion of the different types of Unix.)

Actually, it is not all that important to know exactly how your system is organized; let the system manager worry about that. Most of the time, all you need to care about are your own personal files, the ones under your home directory. However, in case you are interested, here are a few common variations that you can look for.

We have already mentioned that System V (starting with version V.4) has moved all the programs from **/bin** to **/usr/bin**, and all the library files from **/lib** to **/usr/lib**. Another major change is that the spool files under **/usr/spool** have been moved to a new directory called **/var**. (The name stands for "variable", as these files tend to change.)

Aside from **/bin** and **/usr/bin**, your system may have other directories to hold programs. The most important of these are **/usr/ucb**, which contains programs that are specific to Berkeley Unix, and **/usr/5bin**, which contains programs for System V compatibility. (Remember, the "V" is a Roman numeral 5.) These directories are important because, if they exist on your system, they should be in your search path. (The search path tells Unix what directories to look in when it needs to find a program. See Chapter 11 for the C-Shell and Chapter 12 for the Korn shell.)

Another pair of "bin" directories you might see is **/sbin** and **/usr/sbin**. If your system has such directories, they will contain the system management programs that were previously stored under **/etc**. (Hence the name **sbin**: "system bin".)

HINT

If your system has both the **/usr/ucb** and **/usr/5bin** directories, you can customize your working environment by changing the order of these directories in your search path. If you want your system to act like Berkeley Unix, put **/usr/ucb** first. If you want your system to act like System V Unix, put **/usr/5bin** first.

This will ensure that when Unix looks for a program that is contained in both directories, it will find the appropriate version. (Remember, Unix looks in the directories in the order in which they appear in the search path.)

The only other variation that is at all interesting to non-nerds has to do with where the system stores the users' files. In the classical setup, all the home directories are contained in the **/usr** directory. For example, the home directory for userid **harley** would be **/usr/harley**.

Some systems place the home directories in a different directory. Common locations are **/u**, **/user** (with an "e"), **/home**, and **/var/home**. Thus, following are some typical home directories (from different systems):

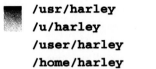

/usr/harley
/u/harley
/user/harley
/home/harley
/var/home/harley

On large systems, especially those where files are stored on a network, the exact
location of the home directories may be more involved; much depends on how the
system manager has decided to organize the file system. In any case, you can
always find out the exact name of your home directory by entering the command:

echo $HOME

HOME is a global variable that contains the name of your home directory.
(Global variables are explained in Chapter 11 for the C-Shell and Chapter 12 for
the Korn shell.)

CHAPTER 23

Working with Directories

In Chapter 22, we described how the Unix file system is organized as a hierarchy of directories and subdirectories. We explained how each user is assigned a home directory to organize as he or she sees fit.

In this chapter, you will learn the commands and techniques you need to organize your directories. You will also learn how to move from one directory to another as you work. Finally, you will learn how to use **ls**, one of the most important Unix commands, to display the contents of a directory.

Pathnames and Your Working Directory

In Chapter 22, we saw how to write the full name for a file. Start with a **/** (slash), which stands for the root directory. Then write the names of all the directories you have to pass through to get to the file. Separate each name with a **/**. Finally, write the name of the file. Here is an example:

/usr/dict/words

In this case, the file **words** lies in the **dict** directory, which lies in the **usr** directory, which lies in the root directory.

When we write the name of a file in this manner, we call it a PATHNAME, because it shows the path through the directory tree from the root directory to the file in question.

Let's say that your userid is **harley** and your home directory (see Chapter 22) is **/usr/harley**. You have a file named **memo** that you want to edit using the **vi** editor (Chapter 20). You enter:

vi /usr/harley/memo

Later, you want to edit another file, named **document**. You enter:

vi /usr/harley/document

As you can see, it is a lot of bother to have to specify the full pathname every time you want to use a file. To make life easier, Unix allows you to designate one directory at a time as your WORKING DIRECTORY (also known as your CURRENT DIRECTORY). When you want to use a file that is in your working directory, you do not need to specify the whole path: you only need to type the file name.

For example, if you tell Unix that you will be working in the directory **/usr/harley**, you can enter the commands:

vi memo
vi document

Another way of expressing this idea is that if a file name does not start with a **/**, Unix will assume the file is in your working directory.

The best way to understand how all this works is to remember that the Unix file system can be understood as a large tree. The trunk of the tree is the root directory. Think of the various directories as being branches of the tree. For example, if a directory has three subdirectories, you can think of that branch as having three sub-branches. (If you want a more visual picture, look at the figures in Chapter 22.)

Now, imagine you are sitting on some branch of the tree. The branch you are sitting on is your working directory. If you want to change your working directory, you must move to a different branch of the tree.

When you log in, Unix automatically sets your working directory to be your home directory. In other words, as soon as you log in, you instantly find yourself sitting on the branch of the tree that represents your home directory.

Absolute and Relative Pathnames

There are two main ways to specify file names. You can choose whichever method is most convenient at the time.

In order to show you how it all works, we will use the sample directory tree in Figure 23-1. This tree shows several subdirectories based on a home directory of **/usr/harley**.

Under the home directory, we have two subdirectories, **bin** and **essays**. In keeping with the Unix tradition, the files in the **bin** directory contain our personal programs. There are two such programs, **funky** and **spacewar**. The **essays** subdirectory contains two subdirectories of its own, **history** and **literature**. Each of these directories contains two files.

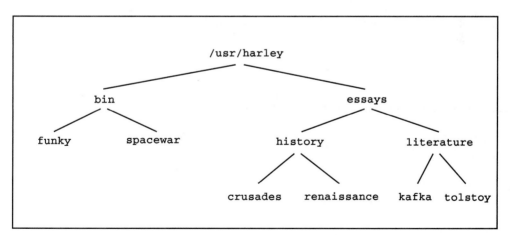

FIGURE 23-1. *A sample directory tree*

(To recall the terminology of Chapter 22, we have eleven files: five directories and six ordinary files. Of the ordinary files, the two programs are binary files and the four **essays** are text files.)

Let us say that we have just logged in. Our working directory is automatically set to be the home directory, **/usr/harley**. Now let's take a look at how we might specify the names of the various files.

Say that we want to use a command in which we need to refer to the **bin** directory. Of course, we can call it **/usr/harley/bin**, which is the pathname. However, an easier way is to take advantage of the current setting of our working directory.

Unix assumes that any file name that begins with a **/** shows the full path to the file, starting from the root directory. However, if a file name does not begin with a **/**, Unix assumes that it describes a path starting from the working directory.

In this case, the working directory is **/usr/harley**. Thus, you do not have to type the long name **/usr/harley/bin**. All you need to type is **bin**.

Here is another example using the same working directory. You want to enter a command for which you need to specify the name of the **tolstoy** file in the **literature** directory. The full name—the pathname—of this file is:

```
/usr/harley/essays/literature/tolstoy
```

However, since the working directory is **/usr/harley**, you can refer to the file as:

```
essays/literature/tolstoy
```

Here is one final example. Say that you want to do a lot of work with the files **kafka** and **tolstoy**. It is inconvenient to refer to these files using the full pathnames:

```
/usr/harley/essays/literature/kafka
/usr/harley/essays/literature/tolstoy
```

Moreover, it is only slightly more convenient to use names relative to the working directory:

```
essays/literature/kafka
essays/literature/tolstoy
```

The best thing to do is to change the working directory to be:

```
/usr/harley/essays/literature
```

(We will show you how to do this in a moment.) Having changed the working directory, you can refer to the files more simply as:

```
kafka
tolstoy
```

The idea is to choose your working directory so as to make file names easy to type. Think of the working directory as a base of operations you can change whenever you want. When you log in, you start out in your home directory, but you can change to any directory you want, whenever you want.

To distinguish between the two ways of specifying file names, we sometimes call a pathname—a name that starts with a **/**—an ABSOLUTE PATHNAME. When we use a name that does not start with a **/**, we call it a RELATIVE PATHNAME.

In other words, an absolute pathname starts from the root directory. A relative pathname starts from the working directory. The idea is to set your working directory so you can use short, relative pathnames whenever possible.

When we show sample commands in this book, such as:

```
vi document
```

we are actually using relative pathnames. In this case, the command will start the **vi** editor using the file named **document**. We assume that **document** resides in the working directory.

Three Handy Pathname Abbreviations: .. . ~

Unix provides three handy pathname abbreviations. The first is two periods in a row:

```
..
```

which is often called "dot-dot". When you use **..** in a pathname, it refers to the parent directory.

To illustrate how this works, let us use the sample directory tree from Figure 23-1. Within our home directory **/usr/harley**, we have two subdirectories, **bin** and **essays**. The **bin** directory contains two files. The **essays** subdirectory contains two subdirectories of its own, **history** and **literature**. Each of these directories contains two files.

Say that we set the working directory to be:

```
/usr/harley/essays/literature
```

We can now refer to the two files in this directory as **kafka** and **tolstoy** (using relative pathnames). From this working directory, the specification .. refers to the parent directory. From within our current working directory, .. means the same as:

```
/usr/harley/essays
```

So, let's say we wanted to use the file **crusades** within the **history** directory. One way is to use the absolute pathname:

```
/usr/harley/essays/history/crusades
```

An easier way is to use .. to stand for the parent directory:

```
../history/crusades
```

Unix will replace the .. with the name of the parent directory. Now, say that we want to refer to the **bin** directory. We could use the absolute pathname:

```
/usr/harley/bin
```

Alternatively, we can use the .. abbreviation twice:

```
../../bin
```

The first parent directory is:

```
/usr/harley/essays
```

The second parent directory is:

```
/usr/harley
```

Here is another example. Let's say we want to refer to the **funky** file within the **bin** directory. The absolute pathname is:

```
/usr/harley/bin/funky
```

But, starting from our working directory, we can use:

```
../../bin/funky
```

Finally, here is one last extreme example. From our working directory:

/usr/harley/essays/literature

we can refer to the root directory as:

../../../..

And we can refer to the **/etc** directory as:

../../../../etc

Of course, you would probably never use these examples, as it is a lot easier to type **/** and **/etc**. The **..** abbreviation is most useful when you want to refer to directories near your working directory, without having to actually change your working directory.

The second pathname abbreviation is a single period:

.

This is usually called "dot".

A single **.** refers to the working directory itself. For example, if the working directory is:

/usr/harley/essays/literature

the following three specifications all refer to the same file:

/usr/harley/essays/literature/kafka
./kafka
kafka

Certainly, it is a lot easier to type **.** than the full name of the working directory. But, as you can see, you don't really need to specify any directory name. As long as a file name does not begin with a **/**, Unix will assume that the name is relative to your working directory.

You might ask, why would you ever need to use a single **.** abbreviation? The answer is, you rarely do. However, there are certain situations in which you must specify an absolute pathname. In such cases, you can use the **.** abbreviation and Unix will replace it with the name of your working directory.

The idea is to avoid typing a long pathname, but not only out of laziness (although that is a good idea). Using the **.** makes it much less likely that you will make a spelling mistake. And, as you probably know by now, it is far too easy to make spelling mistakes when you are typing Unix commands.

Here is a quick example. Let's say you have written a program called **plugh**. (We leave it to your imagination as to what this program might do.) The program is in the directory **/usr/harley/adventure**, which is your working directory.

Normally, you run a program by entering its name:

```
plugh
```

However, Unix can only run a program when it lies in one of the directories in your search path (see Chapter 11 for the C-Shell and Chapter 12 for the Korn shell). In this case, it happens that the directory containing the program is not in your search path.

As an alternative, Unix will find any program if you specify the absolute pathname of the file. In this case, you can run the program by typing:

```
/usr/harley/adventure/plugh
```

An easier way is to use **.** to stand for your working directory:

```
./plugh
```

As this example illustrates, when you start a file name with **..** or **.** you are really specifying an absolute pathname. The **..** and **.** are abbreviations that Unix replaces appropriately.

The third pathname abbreviation is the tilde:

```
~
```

You can use this symbol at the beginning of a file name to stand for your home directory. For example, to use the **ls** command to list the names of all the files in your home directory, you can use:

```
ls~
```

To refer to the subdirectory **bin** that lies within your home directory, you can use:

```
~/bin
```

Note: You cannot use the **~** abbreviation with the Bourne shell, although you can use it with the C-Shell, the Korn shell, Bash, the Tcsh and the Zsh. (The various shells are discussed in Chapter 10.)

Moving Around the Directory Tree: cd, pwd

To change your working directory, use the **cd** (change directory) command. The syntax is:

cd [*directory*]

where *directory* is the name of the directory to which you want to change. If you enter the command without a directory name, **cd** will, by default, change to your home directory.

To display the name of your working directory, use the **pwd** (print working directory) command. The syntax is easy:

pwd

pwd is one of the most useful Unix commands. You will find yourself using it a lot.

What's in a Name?   pwd

In Chapter 6, we explained how the early Unix developers used teletype terminals that printed output on paper. Over the years, Unix has retained the convention of using the word "print" to mean "to display information".

Thus, the name **pwd** stands for "print working directory", even though it has been a long time since anyone actually printed the name of their working directory.

If you are using the C-Shell, it is a simple matter to create an alias for the **pwd** command (say, **dwd**, for "display working directory"):

```
alias dwd pwd
```

With the Korn shell, you would use:

```
alias dwd=pwd
```

However, nobody really bothers. **pwd** is kind of a cute name, even if it is anachronistic. (Using aliases is explained in Chapter 11 for the C-Shell and in Chapter 12 for the Korn shell.)

HINT

When we talk about **cd**, it is common to talk as if the user were really the one changing directories. For example, we might say, "You can use the **cd** command to change to the **/usr/harley/essays** directory," as if you yourself were doing the changing.

Sometimes, we use the name of the command as a verb: "You can **cd** to **/usr/harley/essays** and check for the file you want."

This convention recalls our earlier metaphor in which you imagine yourself sitting on a branch of the directory tree. Wherever you are sitting is your working directory. Using the **cd** command moves you from branch to branch.

Here are some examples of how to use the **cd** command. When you practice using your own examples, remember that you can use the **pwd** command from time to time to check where you are.

To change your working directory to **/usr/harley/essays**, use:

```
cd /usr/harley/essays
```

To change to **/bin**, use:

```
cd /bin
```

To change to **/** (the root directory) use:

```
cd /
```

The **cd** command is convenient when you use relative pathnames or abbreviations. For example, say that your working directory is **/usr/harley**. Within this directory, you have two subdirectories, **bin** and **essays**. To change to **bin** (which is really **/usr/harley/bin**), enter:

```
cd bin
```

Because the directory name (**bin**) does not start with a **/**, Unix assumes it is a relative pathname, based on the current value of the working directory.

Here is another example. Again, your working directory is **/usr/harley**. This time you want to change to:

```
/usr/harley/essays/history
```

Using a relative pathname, you can enter:

cd essays/history

As we mentioned above, entering the **cd** command without a directory name:

cd

will change to your home directory, no matter where you are in the tree. Thus, you never really need to know the full pathname of your home directory.

> **HINT**
> Whenever you get lost in the directory tree, just enter:
>
> **cd**
>
> to return to your home directory. (Using the **cd** command in this way is equivalent to clicking your heels together and repeating "There's no place like home...")

Using the **cd** command in this way is convenient when you are exploring in some distant branch of the file system and you want to work with your own files. For example, say that your working directory happens to be **/etc/local/programs**. You want to move to the **bin** directory within your home directory. Just enter:

cd
cd bin

To make it more convenient, recall that you can enter more than one command on the same line as long as you separate the commands with a semicolon (see Chapter 9). Thus, no matter where you are in the tree, you can move to your own personal **bin** directory by entering:

cd; cd bin

The first command changes to your home directory. The second command changes to the **bin** directory within your home directory.

You can also use the standard pathname abbreviations we discussed earlier. As you remember, **..** stands for the parent directory. For example, say that your working directory is:

```
/usr/harley/essays/history
```

To change to **/usr/harley/essays** directory, you can use:

```
cd ..
```

From the same working directory, you could change to **/usr/harley/essays/literature** by using:

```
cd ../literature
```

As with other commands, you can use the **..** abbreviation more than once. For example, from the same working directory, you can change to **/usr/harley/bin** by using:

```
cd ../../bin
```

Question: What happens if you are in the root directory and you enter:

```
cd ..
```

Answer: The root directory does not have a parent directory. Nothing happens.

The other useful abbreviation is **~** (tilde), which stands for the name of your home directory. (Remember, you cannot use this abbreviation with the Bourne shell.) Thus, the following two command lines are equivalent:

```
cd ~/bin
cd; cd bin
```

Both will change to the **bin** directory within your home directory.

HINT

To make it easy to remember where you are in the directory tree, here is an alias you can use with the C-Shell to display the name of your working directory every time you use a **cd** command:

```
alias 'cd 'cd \!*; echo $cwd'
```

This alias replaces the **cd** command with two commands: a **cd** command followed by an **echo** command. The **echo** command displays the value of the built-in variable **cwd** which contains the name of your current working directory. For example, if your home directory is **/usr/harley** and you enter:

```
cd ~/bin
```

you will see:

```
/usr/harley/bin
```

If you like what this alias does, place it in your **.cshrc** file to make it a permanent part of your personal toolbox. (The details of this alias are discussed in Chapter 11, as is the **.cshrc** file.)

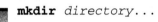

Making a New Directory: `mkdir`

To make a directory, use the **mkdir** command. The syntax is:

```
mkdir directory...
```

where *directory* is the name of a directory you want to make.

Using this command is straightforward. You can name a new directory anything you want as long as you follow a few simple rules. We will go over the rules in Chapter 24 when we talk about naming files. (Remember, as we explained in Chapter 22, directories are really files.) Basically, you can use letters, numbers, and those punctuation symbols that do not have a special meaning.

HINT

When you name directories, life will be easier if you stick to lowercase letters only.

For example, to make a directory named **extra**, within your working directory, use:

```
mkdir extra
```

When you specify a directory name, you can use either an absolute or relative pathname, as well as the standard abbreviations.

As an example, let's say that you want to create the directory tree in Figure 23-2. (These are the directories we used as examples earlier in the chapter.) Within your home directory, you want to make two subdirectories, **bin** and **essays**. Within the **essays** directory, you want to make two more subdirectories, **history** and **literature**.

To start, make sure you are in your home directory:

```
cd
```

Now, make the first two subdirectories:

```
mkdir bin essays
```

Next, change to the **essays** directory:

```
cd essays
```

and make the final two subdirectories:

```
mkdir history literature
```

To illustrate the various ways to specify pathnames, let's take a look at two more ways to create the same directories. First, you could have done the whole thing without leaving the home directory:

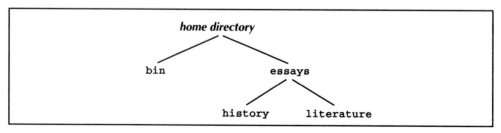

FIGURE 23-2.   *Making a sample directory tree*

```
cd
mkdir bin essays essays/history essays/literature
```

The first command changes to the home directory. The second command specifies all four names, relative to the new working directory.

In the following example, we don't even bother changing to the home directory:

```
mkdir ~/bin ~/essays ~/essays/history ~/essays/literature
```

Remember, the **~** (tilde) character is an abbreviation for your home directory.

There are times when it is handy to use the **..** abbreviation to indicate a parent directory. For example, say that you have changed to the **essays** directory:

```
cd ~/essays
```

You now decide to create a subdirectory named **extra** within the **bin** directory. The **bin** directory and the **essays** directory have the same parent (the home directory). You can use:

```
mkdir ../bin/extra
```

When you create a directory, Unix makes you follow two sensible rules. First, within a single parent directory, you cannot make two directories with the same pathname. For example, you cannot have two directories that are named **~/essays/history**. (How would you tell them apart?)

However, you can have two directories with the same name if they are in different parent directories. For example:

```
~/essays/history
~/homework/history
```

The second rule is that you cannot make a subdirectory if its parent directory does not exist. For example, you cannot make **~/homework/history** unless you have already made **~/homework**.

When you specify more than one directory within a single **mkdir** command, Unix will make the directories in the order you specify. Thus, the command:

```
mkdir ~/homework ~/homework/history
```

will work, because the **homework** directory is made before Unix tries to make the **history** directory. However, the command:

```
mkdir ~/homework/history ~/homework
```

will not work.

Recall for a moment our analogy comparing the file system to a tree. The main trunk is the root directory, and each branch is a subdirectory. The two rules merely say that (1) you cannot make two identical branches, and (2) you cannot make a new branch that has nowhere to attach to the tree.

Removing a Directory: `rmdir`

To remove a directory, use the **rmdir** command. The syntax is straightforward:

```
rmdir directory...
```

where `directory` is the directory you want to remove.

For example, to remove the directory **extra** from within the working directory, use:

```
rmdir extra
```

When you use **rmdir**, you can specify one or more directory names using absolute or relative pathnames. You can also use the standard abbreviations: `..` for the parent directory, and `~` (tilde) for the home directory.

Let's take a look at some examples using the sample directory tree that we built in the previous section. Within the home directory, we have two subdirectories, **bin** and **essays**. Within the **essays** directory, we have two more subdirectories, **history** and **literature**. Figure 23-2 shows this tree.

Say that you want to delete all of these directories. There are several ways to do the job. First, move to the **essays** directory:

```
cd ~/essays
```

From here, you can delete the two subdirectories:

```
rmdir history literature
```

Next, move to the parent directory (the home directory):

```
cd ..
```

Remove the two main subdirectories:

```
rmdir bin essays
```

An alternate method would be to move to the home directory and remove all four subdirectories in one command:

```
cd
rmdir essays/history essays/literature essays bin
```

As a final example, you could do all the work without moving to the home directory:

```
rmdir ~/essays/history ~/essays/literature ~/essays ~/bin
```

When you remove a directory, Unix makes you follow two sensible rules. First, you cannot remove a directory unless it is empty. This is a safeguard. (A directory is not empty if it contains a subdirectory or a file.)

For example, say that you have two directories, **data** and **olddata**. The **data** directory contains 100 important files. The **olddata** directory is empty.

You decide to remove the **olddata** directory. However, just as you enter the command, a meteorite smashes through the window hitting the nerd sitting at the next terminal. In the confusion, you accidentally type:

```
rmdir data
```

Fortunately, Unix is prepared for just such an eventuality. You see the message:

```
rmdir: data: Directory not empty
```

Your **data** directory is left untouched.

There may be occasions when you really do want to remove a directory that is not empty. For this operation, you can use the **rm** command with the **-r** option. Using **rm -r** will also remove all subdirectories and their contents. This command is explained in Chapter 24. Obviously, this is a command to use carefully.

The second rule for removing directories is that you cannot remove any directory that lies between your working directory and the root directory. For example, say that your working directory is:

```
/usr/harley/essays/literature
```

You cannot remove the **essays** directory, because it lies between you and the root directory. However, you can remove the directory:

```
/usr/harley/essays/history
```

by using:

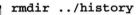

```
rmdir ../history
```

After all, the **history** directory does not lie between you and the root directory. If you want to remove **essays**, you must first move closer to the root directory, say to **/usr/harley**. Now you can remove the directory:

```
cd /usr/harley
rmdir essays/history essays/literature essays
```

(This example assumes that you have already removed all the files from the three directories. To remove files, use the **rm** command which we discuss in Chapter 24.)

Question: Your working directory is **/etc**. Can you remove a subdirectory that lies within your home directory? The answer is yes, because your working directory (**/etc**) does not lie between the root directory and the directory you want to remove.

To remember this rule, just recall our analogy to a real tree. The trunk is the root directory. Each branch is a subdirectory. At any time, you are sitting on some branch that is your working directory. You can think of removing a directory as sawing off a branch of the tree.

The restriction on removing directories simply states that you cannot saw off a branch that is holding up the one you are sitting on.

HINT
It is possible to remove your working directory. This is like cutting off the branch of the tree that you are sitting on. Probably Unix shouldn't let you do this, but it does.

Removing your working directory will only cause you problems. Don't do it.

Moving or Renaming a Directory: mv

To move or rename a directory, use the **mv** command. The syntax is:

```
mv directory target
```

where *directory* is the name of the directory you want to move or rename, and *target* is the name of the target.

The **mv** command will perform either a move or rename operation, whichever is appropriate. (Note: The **mv** command can be used to move or rename any type of file, not just a directory. In Chapter 24, we will use **mv** with ordinary files.)

Here is an example. Say that you have a directory named **data** in your working directory. You want to change the name of this directory to **extra**. Assuming that a directory named **extra** does not already exist (in your working directory), you can use the command:

```
mv data extra
```

As you can see, renaming a directory is essentially the same as "moving" it to a different name. Thus, the **mv** command performs both these operations.

If the target directory already exists, **mv** will move the original directory into the target. For example, say that the following two directories already exist:

```
/usr/harley/data
/usr/harley/storage
```

You want to move the **data** directory to lie within the **storage** directory. Use:

```
mv /usr/harley/data /usr/harley/storage
```

The pathname of the **data** directory is now:

```
/usr/harley/storage/data
```

Of course, if your working directory is **/usr/harley**, you can simplify the command:

```
mv data storage
```

When **mv** moves a directory, it also moves all the files and subdirectories that lie within that directory. For example, say that, before the move, you had a file named **document** within the **data** directory. Its absolute pathname was:

```
/usr/harley/data/document
```

After the move, the absolute pathname becomes:

```
/usr/harley/storage/data/document
```

If you had subdirectories—perhaps even a whole subtree—under **data**, they are moved as well.

Thus, you can use the **mv** command for three purposes:

1. Rename a directory.

2. Move a directory.

3. Move an entire subtree.

Listing the Contents of a Directory: `ls -rCFR1`

To display information about the contents of a directory, use the **ls** (list) command. You will find that **ls** is one of the most frequently used Unix commands. As such, it has many options to control its output: the Berkeley Unix **ls** command has 18 options; the System V version has 22 options. (We discussed the different types of Unix in Chapter 2.)

In our discussion of **ls**, we will show you the most important options used with the Berkeley Unix version of the **ls** command; the System V command varies only slightly. If you would like the exact details for your particular system, you can display the **ls** manual page by using the command **man ls**. (The online Unix manual is explained in Chapter 8.)

In this section, we will introduce the **ls** command and discuss the simple options. In the following sections, we will talk about the advanced features of **ls** and discuss the more complex options.

The syntax for the **ls** command is:

```
ls [-adglrsCFR1] [name...]
```

where *name* is the name of a directory or an ordinary file.

Notice that **ls** has a **-l** (the lowercase letter "*L*") option and a **-1** (the number "1") option. Do not confuse them. (Actually, the **-l** [letter] option is used a lot. The **-1** [number] option is used rarely.)

The basic function of **ls** is to display an alphabetical list of names of files in a directory. For example, to list the files in the **/bin** directory, use:

```
ls /bin
```

To list the files in both the **/bin** and **/etc** directories, use:

```
ls /bin /etc
```

It is useful to use the **..** abbreviation with the **ls**. For example, to list the files in the directory that contains your working directory, use:

```
ls ..
```

To list the files in the directory that contains the parent directory, use:

```
ls ../..
```

The most common way to use **ls** is without parameters:

```
ls
```

By default, **ls** will display the names of all the files in your working directory.

HINT

To list the names of the files in your working directory, use the **ls** command with no parameters:

```
ls
```

This is possibly the single most frequently used Unix command (after **mail harley**).

When **ls** sends its output to your terminal (which is usually the case), the output will be organized into columns. For example, here are the first five lines of output of a directory listing of the **/bin** directory. (On this particular system, the actual output was 23 lines.)

[	e	li	nice	sh5
ar	echo	line	nm	shutdown
as	ed	ll	od	size
awk	expr	ln	pagesize	strip
cat	false	login	passwd	stty
.	.	.	.	.
.	.	.	.	.
.	.	.	.	.

Notice that the file names are arranged alphabetically by column. That is, you read down, not across. As we explained in Chapter 22, the **/bin** directory contains many of the Unix commands, so some of the names in this directory will look familiar.

(Yes, in answer to your question, there really is a command with the odd name of **[**. It is used in writing Bourne shell scripts.)

When you redirect the output of **ls** to a file or to a pipeline, **ls** will write only one file name per line. This makes it easy to process the output of **ls** with another program. (Redirection and pipelines are explained in Chapter 16. Filters—programs that are used in pipelines—are explained in Chapter 17.)

A common example is:

```
ls | wc -l
```

The **wc -l** command counts the number of lines of input it receives. Thus, this combination of **ls** and **wc** tells you how many files you have in your working directory.

If you want to force **ls** to write columns to a file or pipeline, use the **-C** option (uppercase "C"):

```
ls -C
```

If you want to force **ls** to write one line per file name to your terminal, use the **-1** option (the number "1"):

```
ls -1
```

By default, **ls** displays file names in alphabetical order. (More precisely, **ls** uses the order of the characters in the ASCII code. See Chapter 17.) If you want to display the names in reverse order, use the **-r** (lowercase "r") option:

```
ls -r
```

You will often find yourself in the position of wanting to find out what types of files a directory contains. In such cases, you can use the **-F** (flag) option. This option flags certain file names with an identification character. Names of directories are followed by a **/** (slash). Names of ordinary files that contain executable programs are followed by an ***** (asterisk). Other types of ordinary files are not marked.

For example, say that your working directory contains a directory named **documents**, a text file named **memo**, and a binary file named **spacewar** that contains a program. The command:

```
ls -F
```

will display:

```
documents/     memo     spacewar*
```

The last **ls** option that we will discuss in this section is **-R**, which stands for "recursive". This option can be used when you specify a directory name. The option tells **ls** to list information about all the subdirectories and files that lie within the directory you name. In other words, **ls -R** displays information about an entire subtree.

For example, to list all the files and subdirectories that are descendants of your home directory, use:

```
ls -R ~
```

(Remember, ~ is an abbreviation for your home directory.) Be careful not to confuse the **-r** and **-R** options when you enter a command.

What's in a Name?   Recursive

There are several file and directory commands that have either a **-R** or **-r** option to process an entire subtree. When you use such an option, it tells the command to process all the subdirectories and files that are descendants of the directory you specify.

The letters "R" or "r" stand for the word "recursive", which is actually a technical term with several meanings. In computer science, a recursive program is one that can put itself on hold and start a new copy of itself. (Yes, this makes sense as long as the programmer ensures that everything works properly.)

It is hard to see how this has anything to do with processing a directory tree. The only real connection is that it is possible to write recursive programs to work with tree structures. However, this really doesn't apply to Unix commands.

So don't worry if the name makes no sense to you. Just remember that, with Unix file commands, "recursive" (**-R** or **-r**) means "process the entire subtree".

Keeping Track of Your Disk Space Usage: `ls-s`, `du`, `quota`

One use for the **ls** command is to see how much storage space your files use on the disk. It is possible that your userid has some type of quota restricting you to a maximum amount of disk space. So, from time to time, it is a good idea to see how much storage you are using.

Disk storage is measured in kilobytes, megabytes and gigabytes. One KILOBYTE is 1,024 (2^{10}) bytes; one MEGABYTE is 1,048,576 (2^{20}) bytes; one GIGABYTE is 1,073,741,824 (2^{30}) bytes. Within a text file, one byte holds one character. For example, 100 characters requires 100 bytes of disk storage. Most of your files will be measured in kilobytes.

If you want to find out how much disk space a directory or file uses, you can use the **ls** command with the **-s** (size) option. **ls** will preface each file name with its size in kilobytes. If you specify a directory name, **ls** will also show a total for the entire directory.

For example, here are the first six lines of output of a directory listing of the **/bin** directory using the **-s** option. (On this particular system, the actual output was 38 lines.)

```
total 4055
  12 [            40 init           1 pr
   1 ar           96 init.old     168 ps
   1 as           24 kill          24 pwd
   1 awk           1 ksh           24 radisk
  28 cat          128 l           168 rdump
   .              .               .
   .              .               .
   .              .               .
```

On the top line, you can see that the total space used by all the files in the directory is 4,055 kilobytes. The other lines show how much space the various files require. The **cat** file, for example, uses 28 kilobytes.

Another command you can use is **du** (disk usage). The syntax is:

```
du [-as] [name...]
```

where *name* is the name of a directory or file.

When you specify the name of one or more directories, **du** will show you the number of kilobytes used by those directories and all the subdirectories that come under them. If you do not specify a name, **du** will assume you mean your working directory.

If you use the **-s** (sum) option, **du** will display only the grand total. If you use the **-a** (all) option, **du** will break down the total and show the size of each directory and file it counted. To see a nice display of all your file usage:

```
du -a ~
```

(Remember, ~ is an abbreviation for your home directory.) This command will show you each of your files and directories and how much space they use. The last line of the output will show your home directory and the grand total.

When you specify the name of one or more files, you must use the **-a** option. For example:

```
du -a /bin/cat /bin/echo
```

When you use **du** in this way, you will see how much space is used by each of the files you specify.

Many systems impose a quota on how much disk space each userid is allowed to use. If your system has such a quota, you can use the **quota** command to check on your usage and limits:

```
quota
```

To display extra information, use the **-v** (verbose) option:

```
quota -v
```

Note: The three commands **ls -s**, **du** and **quota** estimate storage usage in different ways, so don't be surprised if the numbers vary somewhat.

HINT
It is important to remember that you are sharing your file system, usually with many other people. Disk space is often at a premium, and you should make sure you don't use more than you really need.

From time to time, check how much space you are using. If you have files that you do not need, especially large files, be considerate and remove them.

Don't think of it as being forced to live within your quota. Think of it as being a good neighbor.

Wildcards, Filename Substitution, Globbing

When you use directory and file commands, you can employ special characters called WILDCARDS to specify a pattern of file names.

For example, say that you want to list the names of all the files in your working directory that start with "h". You can use:

```
ls h*
```

Using wildcards is a lot like using the regular expressions we described in Chapter 17 (filters) and Chapter 20 (the **vi** editor). In fact, you can think of wildcards as being a limited type of regular expression. However, there are important differences. Figure 23-3 shows the basic wildcards and how they are used to specify file names. You might find it interesting to compare this table with the ones that describe the standard regular expressions. (Figures 17-2 and 20-2.)

When you use a wildcard, the shell interprets the pattern and replaces it with the appropriate file names. For example, when you enter:

```
ls h*
```

the shell replaces the **h*** with all the file names that begin with the letter **h**. For instance, if your working directory contains six files: **a**, **b**, **h**, **h1**, **h2** and **z**, the previous command is changed to:

```
ls h h1 h2
```

What's in a Name?   Wildcard

The term "wildcard" comes from poker and other card games in which certain cards are designated as being "wild". Such cards can take on any value the player assigns them. For example, say that you are playing poker and 2s are wild. Your hand consists of 2, 3, ace, ace, ace. Since a 2 can be anything, you would use your 2 to stand for either a 3, which would give you a full house (3, 3, ace, ace, ace) or an ace, which would give you four of a kind (four aces). In this case, you would choose four of a kind because it is the higher hand.

Wildcards within Unix are similar, but not exactly the same. The ***** and **?** characters do not really stand for anything you want. Rather, they stand for everything that can possibly be matched.

For example, the pattern **h*** stands for all the files whose names begin with the letter "h".

The idea of using wildcards to specify files is known formally by different names, depending on what shell you are using. With the C-Shell and Tcsh, it is called FILE NAME SUBSTITUTION. With the Bourne shell, the Korn shell and the Zsh, it is called FILE NAME GENERATION. With Bash, it is called PATHNAME EXPANSION. You get the idea.

SYMBOL	MEANING
*	match any sequence of zero or more characters
?	match any single character
[ ]	match one of the enclosed characters

Note: You must specify a **/** (slash) character explicitly. You cannot match it with a wildcard.

FIGURE 23-3. *Summary of wildcards used to specify file names*

The actual operation of substituting file names for a wildcard pattern is called GLOBBING. Sometimes, the word GLOB is used as a verb, as in, "Unless you set the **noglob** variable, the C-Shell globs automatically."

What happens if you specify a wildcard pattern that does not match any files? The shell will display an appropriate message and abort the command. The message you see depends on what shell you are using. Shells in the C-Shell family (C-Shell, Tcsh) display a message like:

```
No match
```

Shells in the Bourne shell family (Bourne shell, Korn shell, Bash, Zsh) display your pattern followed by:

```
not found
```

(The various shells are discussed in Chapter 10.)

Here are some examples so you can see how it all works. The first character with a special meaning is **∗** (the asterisk). This stands for zero or more of any character except a **/** (which, as you know, has a special meaning within a pathname). For example, the following wildcard specifications match patterns as indicated:

Ha∗	names that begin with **Ha**
Ha∗y	names that begin with **Ha** and end with **y**
Ha∗l∗y	names that begin with **Ha**, contain an **l**, and end with **y**

The **?** (question mark) stands for any single character. For example, to match file names that start with **d**, followed by a single character, use **d?**. To match file names that start with any character and end with **y**, use **?*y**. To find all the 2-character file names, use **??**.

To specify characters from a set, use **[** and **]** (square brackets) to enclose the set. This represents a single instance of any of the specified characters. For example, to match file names that begin with either **H** or **h**, use **[Hh]***. To match the file names **spacewar.c** or **spacewar.o**, use **spacewar.[co]**.

To specify a range of characters within square brackets, you can use a **-** (hyphen). For example, the wildcard pattern **[a-z]** represents all the lowercase letters. The pattern **[a-zA-Z]** represents all the lowercase and uppercase letters.

Thus, to match all the file names that begin with a lowercase letter, use **[a-z]***. To match all the file names that begin with a lowercase or uppercase letter and end with a numeral, use **[a-zA-Z]*[0-9]**.

Here is an example. You want to display the name and size of the files that hold the oldest Unix commands. Most of these command names consist of two lowercase letters, like **ls**. The best place to look for old commands is in the **/bin** and **/usr/bin** directories (see Chapter 22). Thus, we can use the **ls** command with the **-s** (size) option to examine these directories:

```
ls -s /bin/[a-z][a-z] /usr/bin/[a-z][a-z]
```

Try it on your system and see what you find.

If you use the C-Shell, Tsch or Bash, there are two types of abbreviations you can use in addition to the wildcard symbols. These are shown in Figure 23-4.

First, as we explained earlier, you can use a **~** (tilde) at the beginning of a file name to stand for the name of your home directory.

Second, you can use **{** and **}** (the brace brackets) to enclose a list of patterns, separated by commas. For example:

```
{harley,addie}
```

SYMBOL	MEANING
~	the name of your home directory
{ }	use separate instances of specified patterns

FIGURE 23-4. *Abbreviations used to specify file names (C-Shell only)*

The shell will form a separate file name using each pattern in turn. Note: Do not put spaces before or after the commas.

For example, say that you want to list the names of all the files in the directories **/usr/harley**, **/usr/addie** and **/usr/tln**. You could specify all the names:

```
ls /usr/harley /usr/addie /usr/tln
```

Or you can use brace brackets to abbreviate:

```
ls /usr/{harley,addie,tln}
```

Here is another example. You want to combine the contents of the files **olddata1**, **olddata2**, **olddata3**, **newdata1**, **newdata2** and **newdata3**. You want to store the result in a new file named **master**. Use the command:

```
cat {old,new}data{1,2,3} > master
```

(The **cat** command, which combines files, is discussed in Chapter 17. The **>** character, which redirects the standard output, is discussed in Chapter 16.)

Dotfiles (Hidden Files): `ls -a`

Any file whose name begins with a **.** (period) is called a DOTFILE or a HIDDEN FILE. The names of hidden files, such as **.login**, are not listed when you use the **ls** command unless you use the **-a** (all) option.

You would probably not use a dotfile to hold your own personal data. However, there are standard dotfiles that are normally found in each user's home directory. By convention, these files are used by programs to hold startup or configuration information.

If you want to see all your dotfiles, change to your home directory and enter:

```
ls -a
```

Figure 23-5 lists the names of the standard dotfiles you may one day want to modify. There may be other dotfiles in your home directory, but unless you really know what you are doing, you should leave them alone.

FILE NAME	USED BY	TO CONTAIN
`.bash_logout`	Bash	logout commands
`.bash_profile`	Bash	login initialization commands
`.bashrc`	Bash	initialization commands
`.cshrc`	C-Shell	initialization commands
`.elm`	Elm	directory of configuration files
`.emacs`	**emacs** editor	initialization commands
`.exrc`	**vi** editor	initialization commands
`.forward`	mail delivery	address for forwarding mail
`.gopherrc`	**gopher**	initialization file
`.inputrc`	Bash	changes to default key bindings
`.login`	C-Shell	login initialization commands
`.logout`	C-Shell	logout commands
`.netrc`	**ftp**	auto-login information
`.newsrc`	newsreaders	info about Usenet newsgroups you read
`.nn`	**nn**	directory of configuration files
`.mailrc`	**mail**	initialization commands
`.pinerc`	Pine	configuration file
`.plan`	**finger**	info displayed when fingered
`.project`	**finger**	more info displayed when fingered
`.profile`	Bourne shell	initialization commands
`.profile`	Korn shell	initialization commands
`.rcrc`	rc shell	initialization commands
`.signature`	newsreaders	signature for when you post articles
`.tcshrc`	Tcsh shell	initialization commands
`.tin`	**tin**	directory of configuration files
`.xsession`	X Window	auto-startup initialization commands
`.xinitrc`	X Window	other startup initialization commands
`.zshenv`	Zsh	initialization commands
`.zshrc`	Zsh	initialization commands
`.zlogin`	Zsh	login initialization commands
`.zlogout`	Zsh	logout commands
`.zprofile`	Zsh	login initialization commands

FIGURE 23-5. *Dotfiles (hidden files) you might want to change*

HINT

Many of the dotfiles are crucial. Before you edit a dotfile, make a backup copy. For example:

```
cp .login .login.bak
```

(The **cp** command is explained in Chapter 24.) If you accidentally ruin the file, you will be able to restore it.

On occasion, you will see directory names that start with a dot. Such directories are also hidden, and you will not see them with **ls** unless you use the **-a** option. Three common examples are the **.elm** directory (used by the Elm mail program), the **.nn** directory (used by the **nn** newsreader), and the **.tin** directory (used by the **tin** newsreader). (A newsreader is a program used to read articles from Usenet discussion groups.)

Long Directory Listings: `ls -dgl`

To display the most information about a directory or file, use the **ls** command with the **-l** (long) option. The output consists of a disk storage summary followed by one line per file. Here is an example. You enter:

```
ls -l
```

and you see:

```
total 7
-rw-rw-r--  1 harley        2255 Oct  3 21:52 article
drwxrwxr-x  2 harley         512 Oct  1 11:40 bin
drwxrwxr-x  2 harley         512 Oct  1 11:41 essays
-rw-rw-r--  1 harley        1825 Sep 26 20:03 memo
```

The first line tells us that the files in this directory use approximately 7 kilobytes of disk storage. The rest of the lines show us information about the files.

At the far left, the first character of each line shows you the type of file. There are several possibilities, but the only ones you need care about are **d**, which means a directory, and **-**, which means an ordinary file. In this listing, we have two directories and two ordinary files. (You may also see the letter **l**, which indicates a symbolic link. This is explained in Chapter 24.)

Let's look at the rest of the information from right to left. At the far right are the file names. Next, we see the time and date the file was last modified. For example, the file named **article** was last modified on October 3 at 9:52 PM. (Remember, Unix uses a 24-hour clock.)

To the left of the date is the size of the file in bytes. With a text file, one byte holds one character of data.

To the left of the size is the userid of the owner of the file. All of these files are owned by **harley**. To the left of the owner's userid is a number that shows how many links there are to this file. Finally, the string of nine characters at the far left (just to the right of the initial character) shows the file permissions.

We will discuss file ownership, links and permissions in Chapter 24, at which time we will look at the output of the **ls -l** command in more detail.

System V Unix displays the name of the group just to the right of the owner's userid. (Groups are also discussed in Chapter 24.) Berkeley Unix does not display this information unless you use the **-g** (group) option.

The information displayed by the **-l** option can be used in many imaginative ways by piping the output to a filter (see Chapters 16 and 17). For example, to list the names of all the files that were last modified in September, you can use:

```
ls -l | grep Sep
```

To count how many files were last modified in September, use:

```
ls -l | grep Sep | wc -l
```

When you specify the name of a directory, **ls** lists information about the files in that directory. For example, to display a long listing about all the files in the **/bin** directory, you would use:

```
ls -l /bin
```

If you want information about the directory itself, use the **-d** (directory) option. Thus, to display information about the **/bin** directory as a file in its own right, use:

```
ls -dl /bin
```

Useful Aliases for Using ls

The **ls** command is used a lot. For this reason, it is common to define certain aliases to make it easy to use **ls** with the most useful options. (Defining aliases with the C-Shell is explained in Chapter 11; defining aliases with the Korn shell is explained in Chapter 12.)

Here are the most common aliases as you would define them with the C-Shell:

```
alias ll  'ls -l'
alias la  'ls -a'
alias lla 'ls -la'
```

With the Korn shell, you would use:

```
alias ll='ls -l'
alias la='ls -a'
alias lla='ls -la'
```

These aliases make it easy to display a long listing (**ll**), a listing of all files (**la**), and a long listing of all files (**lla**). For example, once you have defined the **ll** alias, you can display a long listing of the **/bin** directory by using:

```
ll /bin
```

To display a long listing of your working directory, use:

```
ll
```

Two other common aliases use the **-F** option. With the C-Shell:

```
alias ls  'ls -F'
alias ls  'ls -lF'
```

and with the Korn shell:

```
alias ls='ls -F'
alias ls='ls -lF'
```

These aliases make **ls**, by default, always display the flag that marks the file type (**/** for directories, ***** for executable files). The second alias makes **ls**, by default, display a long listing as well. (Of course, you would define only one of these aliases.)

It may be that your system manager has already set up some of these aliases in your initialization file (**.cshrc** for the C-Shell) or your environment file (for the Korn shell). To check what aliases you have, enter the command:

```
alias
```

If you don't like your aliases, you can change or remove them by editing your
`.cshrc` file or your environment file. Note: If you decide to edit this file, be sure
to make a copy first.

HINT

With the C-Shell, it is best to place alias definitions in your `.cshrc`
file (see Chapter 11). With the Korn shell, you should place them in
your environment file (see Chapter 12).

When you first start using a Unix system, it is a good idea to
check your initialization file (`.login` for the C-shell, `.profile`
for the Korn shell). Sometimes system managers—with the best of
intentions—put alias definitions in these files. If so, you should delete
the aliases you don't want and move the others to the appropriate file.

CHAPTER 24

Working with Files

In Chapter 22, we discussed the Unix file system. We explained that there are three types of files: directories, special files and ordinary files. In Chapter 23, we discussed directories and covered the commands you use to work with directories.

With this chapter, we finish our discussion of the file system by showing the commands you use with ordinary files. You will learn how to create and manipulate files. You will also learn how to control the permissions that let Unix users share files with one another. Finally, we will explain what goes on behind the scenes and how manipulating files really means working with links.

Note: The commands we discuss in this chapter work with ordinary files. Thus, in this chapter, when we say "file" we are referring to an ordinary file. When we need to refer to directories we do so explicitly.

Creating a File: touch

How do you create a file? Strangely enough, you don't. Unix will create files for you as the need arises. You never really need to create a new file for yourself.

There are three common situations in which a file will be created for you automatically. First, many programs will create a file on your behalf. For example, let's say you start the **vi** editor (Chapter 20) by using the command:

```
vi memo
```

This command specifies that you want to edit a file named **memo**. If **memo** does not exist, **vi** will create it for you.

Second, when you redirect output to a file (Chapter 16), Unix will create the file if it does not already exist. For example, say that you want to save the output of the **ls** command to a file named **listing**. You enter:

```
ls > listing
```

If **listing** does not exist, Unix will create it for you.

Third, when you make a copy of a file, Unix will create the new file automatically. For example, say that you want to copy the file **data** to a file named **extra**. You enter the following command:

```
cp data extra
```

Unix will create the file **extra** for you. (The **cp** command is explained later in the chapter.)

In Chapter 23, we explained that you use the **mkdir** command to make a new directory. Is there an analogous command that will make an ordinary file? The answer is no, but there is a command that has the side effect of creating an empty file. This command is **touch**. Here is how it works.

When we discussed the **ls** command in Chapter 23, we explained that the **-1** (long listing) option displays the time and date that a file was last modified. The job of the **touch** command is to change this modification time to the current time and date.

For example, let's say that a file named **memo** was last modified on July 8 at 2:30 PM. You enter:

```
ls -1 memo
```

and you see:

```
-rw-------  1 harley      4883 Jul  8 14:30 memo
```

It is now 10:30 AM, December 21. You enter:

```
touch memo
```

Now when you enter the same **ls** command you see:

```
-rw-------  1 harley      4883 Dec 21 10:30 memo
```

(By the way, **touch** works by reading a character from the file and writing it back. On some systems, **touch** will let you specify the exact time and date you want. For information on how **touch** works on your system, see the online manual (Chapter 8). Use the command **man touch**.)

For most people, the **touch** command is of limited usefulness. (Although it does come in handy when you want to make people think you have updated a memo.) However, **touch** has one important side effect: if the file you specify does not exist, **touch** will create it. Thus, you can use **touch** to create a brand new, empty file.

For example, to create a file named **newfile**, use:

```
touch newfile
```

The modification time will be the current time and date.

Normally, though, there is no need to use **touch**. As we explained above, new files are usually created for you automatically as the need arises.

HINT
The **touch** command is handy for creating a group of temporary files in order to experiment with the Unix file commands.

Choosing a File Name

Unix is liberal with respect to naming files. There are only two basic rules:

1. File names can be up to 255 characters long. (Some older System V Unix systems allow only 14 characters.)

2. A file name can contain any character except **/** (which, as we explained in Chapter 23, has a special meaning within a pathname).

HINT
Create file names that are meaningful to you. When you have not used a file for a while, it is helpful if the name reminds you of what the file contains.

The rules allow you to create a file name that contains all sorts of weird characters: control characters, backspaces, punctuation, even space characters. Obviously, such file names will cause trouble.

For example, what if you use the **ls -l** command to list information about a file named **info;date**:

```
ls -l info;date
```

Unix would interpret the semicolon as separating two commands:

```
ls -l info
date
```

Here is another example. Say that you have a file named **-info**. It would be a lot of trouble using the name in a command, for example:

```
ls -info
```

Unix would interpret the **-** (hyphen) character as indicating an option.

Generally speaking, you will run into trouble with any name that contains a character with a special meaning (**<,>**, **|**, **!** and so on). The best idea is to confine yourself to characters that cannot be misinterpreted. These are shown in Figure 24-1.

---

a, b, c...	(lowercase letters)
A, B, C...	(uppercase letters)
0, 1, 2...	(numbers)
.	(period)
=	(equals sign)
_	(underscore)

FIGURE 24-1. *Characters that are safe to use in file names*

As we explained in Chapter 23, files whose names begin with a **.** (period) are called dotfiles or hidden files. When you use **ls**, such files are listed only if you specify the **-a** (all) option. By convention, such names are used to indicate files that initialize or support a particular program. Figure 23-5 contains a list of the common dotfiles.

Remember that Unix distinguishes between upper- and lowercase. Thus, the names **info**, **Info** and **INFO** are considered to be completely different.

There is a convention that names that begin with uppercase letters are reserved for files that are important in some special way. For example, you might see a file named README.

Because uppercase comes before lowercase in the ASCII code (Chapter 17), such names will come first in the directory listing and will stand out.

HINT

When you name files or directories, it is a good idea to stick to lowercase letters.

Some programs expect to use files whose names end in a period followed by one or more specific letters. For example, the C compiler expects C programs to be stored in files that end in **.c**, such as **myprog.c**. The **uncompress** command expects input files that end in **.Z** (uppercase "Z"), such as **data.Z**.

In such cases, the suffix is sometimes referred to as an EXTENSION. For example, we might say files that hold C programs should have an extension of **.c**.

Such extensions are convenient as they allow you to use wildcard specifications to refer to a group of files. For example, you can list the names of all the C programs in a directory by using:

```
ls *.c
```

(Wildcards are explained in Chapter 23.)

Copying a File: cp

To make a copy of a file, use the **cp** command. The syntax is:

```
cp [-ip] file1 file2
```

where *file1* is the name of an existing file, and *file2* is the name of the destination.

Using this command is straightforward. For example, if you have a file named **data** and you want to make a copy named **extra**, use:

```
cp data extra
```

Here is another example. You want to make a copy of the system password file (see Chapter 13). The copy should be called **pword** and should be in your home directory. Use:

```
cp /etc/passwd ~/pword
```

(As we explained in Chapter 23, the ~ character is an abbreviation for the pathname of your home directory.)

If the destination file does not exist, **cp** will create it. If the destination file already exists, **cp** will replace it. Consider the first example, shown in the following:

```
cp data extra
```

If the file **extra** does not exist, it will be created. But if the file **extra** does exist, it will be replaced. All the data in the original **extra** file will be lost, and there is no way to get it back.

> ### *HINT*
> If you want to append data to the end of a file, use the **cat** command and redirect the output. (See Chapter 17.) For example, the command:
>
> ```
> cat data >> extra
> ```
>
> appends the contents of **data** to the end of **extra**. The original contents of **extra** are preserved.

If you want to be cautious about replacing data, use the **-i** (interactive) option. For example:

```
cp -i data extra
```

This tells **cp** to ask your permission before replacing a file that already exists. If you type an answer that begins with the letter **y** or **Y** (for "yes"), **cp** will replace the file, If you type any other answer, **cp** will not make the replacement.

The second option is **-p** (preserve). This option makes the destination file have the same modification time and permissions as the source file. (Permissions are explained later in the chapter.)

Copying Files to a Different Directory: cp

The **cp** command will also copy one or more files to a different directory. The syntax is:

cp [-ip] *file... directory*

where *file* is the name of an existing file, and *directory* is the name of an existing directory. The **-i** and **-p** options work as described above.

Here is an example. To copy the file **data** to a directory named **backups**, use:

cp data backups

To copy the three files **data1**, **data2** and **data3** to the **backups** directory, use:

cp data1 data2 data3 backups

HINT
You may be able to use wildcards to specify more than one file name (see Chapter 23). For example, to copy the three files **data1**, **data2** and **data3** to the backups directory, you can use:

cp data[123] backups

If there are no other files whose names begin with data, you can use:

cp data* backups

If there are no other files whose names begin with "d", you can use:

cp d* backups

Copying a Directory to Another Directory: cp -r

You can use **cp** to copy a directory and all of its files to another directory by using the **-r** option. The syntax is:

cp -r [-ip] *directory1... directory2*

The **−i** and **−p** options work as described above. The **−r** (recursive) option tells **cp** to copy an entire subtree.

Here is an example. Say that within your working directory you have two subdirectories: **essays** and **backups**. Within the **essays** directory, you have many files and subdirectories. You enter:

```
cp -r essays backups
```

A copy of **essays**, including all its files and subdirectories, is now in **backups**. The **cp** command will create the new directories automatically.

For instance, say that **essays** contains a subdirectory named **literature** that contains a file named **kafka**:

```
essays/literature/kafka
```

The copy of this file is:

```
backups/essays/literature/kafka
```

HINT

To copy all the files in a directory, and only the files, use **cp** with a ***** wildcard (see Chapter 23). To copy the directory itself (as well as its contents), use **cp** with the **−r** option.

For example, to copy the files in a directory named **documents** to another directory named **backups**, use:

```
cp documents/* backups
```

To copy the directory **documents** itself to the directory **backups**, use:

```
cp -r documents backups
```

Moving a File: mv

To move a file to a different directory, use the **mv** (move) command. The syntax is:

```
mv [-if] file... directory
```

where `file` is the name of an existing file, and `directory` is the name of the target directory.

The **mv** command will move one or more files to an existing directory. (You can make a directory using the **mkdir** command, explained in Chapter 23.)

Here are two examples. The first moves a file named **data** to a directory named **archive**:

```
mv data archive
```

(If a directory named **archive** does not exist, **mv** will think you want to rename the file. See below.)

The next example moves three files—**data1 data2** and **data3**—to the **archive** directory:

```
mv data1 data2 data3 archive
```

As with most file commands, you can use a wildcard specification. For example, the last command can be abbreviated to:

```
mv data[123] archive
```

If the target to which you move a file already exists, **mv** will replace the file. All the data in the original file will be lost, and there is no way to get it back (so be careful). If you want to be cautious about losing data, use the **-i** (interactive) option. For example:

```
mv -i data archive
```

This tells **mv** to ask your permission before replacing a file that already exists. If you type an answer that begins with the letter **y** or **Y** (for "yes"), **mv** will replace the file. If you type any other answer, **mv** will not make the replacement.

In this case, **mv** would ask your permission before replacing a file named **archive/data**.

The second option is **-f** (force). This forces **mv** to replace a file. The **-f** option will override the **-i** option as well as restrictions imposed by file permissions (explained later in the chapter). Use **-f** with care and only when you know exactly what you are doing.

Renaming a File or Directory: mv

To rename a file or directory, use the **mv** (move) command. The syntax is:

```
mv [-if] oldname newname
```

where *oldname* is the name of an existing file or directory, and *newname* is the new name. The **-i** and **-f** options work as described above.

Renaming a file or directory is straightforward. For example, to rename a file from **memo** to **important**, use the following:

```
mv memo important
```

If the target (in this case, **important**) already exists, it will be replaced. All the data in the original target will be lost, and there is no way to get it back (so be careful). You can use the **-i** and **-f** options, described above, to control the replacement.

As you might expect, you can use **mv** to rename and move at the same time. For example, say that **memo** is a file and **archive** is a directory. Consider the command:

```
mv memo archive/important
```

This command moves a file named **memo** to the directory named **archive** (which must already exist). As part of the move, the file will be renamed **important**.

Removing a File: rm

To remove (delete) a file, use the **rm** command. The syntax is:

```
rm [-fir] file...
```

where *file* is the name of a file you want to remove.

To remove a file, just specify its name. Here are some examples:

```
rm data
rm ~/memo
rm bin/spacewar
```

The first command removes a file named **data** in the working directory. The second command removes a file named **memo** in your home directory. The next command removes a file named **spacewar** in the directory named **bin**, which lies in the working directory.

What's in a Name?   Remove

(Note: The following explanation will be easy to understand after you have learned about links, which are discussed later in this chapter.)

In Unix, we do not talk about deleting or erasing a file. We talk about "removing" the file.

When Unix creates a file, it establishes a link between the file name and the actual file the name represents. When we use the **rm** or **rmdir** commands, Unix removes this link.

Removing a link is not really the same as deleting. There may be more than one link to the file, and Unix will not delete the actual file until the last link is removed.

In almost all cases, there is only one link to a file, so removing this link deletes the file. This is why, most of the time, **rm** and **rmdir** act as delete commands.

As with all file commands, you can use wildcard specifications (see Chapter 23). Here are two examples:

```
rm data[123]
rm *
```

The first command removes the files **data1**, **data2** and **data3** in the working directory. The second command is a powerful one: it removes all the files in your working directory.

Once you remove a file, it is gone for good. There is no way to get back an erased file, so be careful.

HINT

If you are using **rm** with a wildcard specification, it is a good idea to test it first with an **ls** command (Chapter 23) to see what files are matched.

Say that you want to delete the files named **data.backup**, **data.old** and **data.extra**. You are thinking about using the wildcard specification **data***, which would match all files whose names begin with **data**. However, to be prudent, you check this specification by entering:

```
ls data*
```

The output is:

```
data.backup    data.extra    data.important    data.old
```

You see that you had forgotten about the file **data.important**. If you had used **rm** with **data*** you would have lost this file. Instead, you can use:

```
rm data.[beo]*
```

This will match only those files you really want to remove.

How to Keep from Removing the Wrong Files: **rm -if**

As we mentioned in the previous section, it is a good idea to check a file specification with **ls** before you use it with an **rm** command. However, even if you check the specification with **ls**, you might still type it incorrectly when you enter the **rm** command.

If you use are a C-Shell user, you can put the following alias in your **.cshrc** file to prevent such an occurrence.

```
alias del 'rm \!ls:*'
```

If you use the Korn shell, you can put the following in your environment file:

```
alias del='fc -e - ls=rm'
```

We discuss these aliases in detail in Chapter 11 (C-Shell) and Chapter 12 (Korn shell).

Here is how to use the alias, which is named **del**. First, enter an **ls** command with the wildcard specification that describes the files you want to remove. For example:

```
ls data.[beo]*
```

Take a look at the list of files. If they are really the ones you want to remove, enter:

```
del
```

This will execute the **rm** command using the file names from the previous **ls** command.

A handy alternative is to use the **-i** (interactive) option. This tells **rm** to ask your permission before removing each file. For example, you can enter:

```
rm -i data*
```

rm will display a message for each file, asking your permission to proceed. For example:

```
rm: remove data.backup?
```

If you type a response that begins with **y** or **Y** (for "yes"), **rm** will remove the file. If you type anything else (including simply pressing RETURN), **rm** will leave the file alone.

It is common for people to create an alias that automatically inserts the **-i** option every time they use the **rm** command. With the C-Shell, you would use:

```
alias rm 'rm -i'
```

With the Korn Shell, you would use:

```
alias rm='rm -i'
```

Some system managers even put this alias in everybody's **.cshrc** file or Korn shell environment file, thinking they are doing their users a favor.

This practice is to be deplored for two reasons. First, Unix was designed to be terse and exact. Having to type **y** each time you want to remove a file slows down your thought processes. Using an automatic **-i** option makes for sloppy thinking because users come to depend on it.

(If you feel like arguing the point, think about this: It is true that, during the first week, a new user may accidentally remove one or two files. However, it won't be long before he or she will learn to use the commands well. In the long run, developing your skills is always the better alternative to being coddled.)

The second reason for not automatically using the **-i** option is that, eventually, everyone uses more than one Unix system. When people become used to a slow, clunky, ask-me-before-you-remove-each-file **rm** command, they forget that most Unix systems do not work in this way. Because they never learn how to use **ls** and **rm** properly, it is easy to make a catastrophic mistake when they move to a new system.

For this reason, if you really must create an alias for **rm -i**, give it a different name, for example:

```
alias erase 'rm -i'
```

Later in the chapter, we will discuss file permissions. At that time, you will see that there are three types of permissions: read, write and execute. We won't go into the details now. All we want to say is that, without write permission, you are not allowed to remove a file.

If you try to remove a file for which you do not have write permission, **rm** will ask your permission to override the protection mechanism.

For example, say that the file **data.important** has file permissions of **400**. (The "400" will make sense later. Basically, it means that you have read permission, but not write or execute permission.) You enter the following:

```
rm data.important
```

You will see the question:

```
rm: override protection 400 for data.important?
```

To remove the file, type a response that starts with **y** or **Y**. If you type anything else, **rm** will leave the file alone.

The **-f** (force) option tells **rm** to remove all the files you specify regardless of file permissions. For example:

```
rm -f data.important
```

This option will also override the **-i** option. Use **-f** only when you are one hundred percent sure of what you are doing.

Removing an Entire Subtree: rm -r

To remove an entire subtree, use the **rm** command with the **-r** (recursive) option and specify the name of a directory. **rm** will remove not only the directory, but all the files and subdirectories that lie within the directory. This, in effect, removes an entire subtree.

For example, say that you have a directory named **extra**. Within this directory are a number of files and subdirectories. Within each subdirectory are still more files and subdirectories. To remove everything, enter:

```
rm -r extra
```

Here is another example: deceptively simple, yet powerful. To remove everything under your working directory, use:

```
rm -r *
```

Obviously, **rm** **-r** can be a dangerous command. If you are not sure what you are doing, **-r** is a good option to forget about. At the very least, use the **-i** option if you have the least doubt as to what files you want to remove. For example, you might enter:

```
rm -ir extra
```

rm will now ask permission before removing each file and directory.

If you want to remove an entire subtree quickly and quietly, you can use the **-f** option. For example:

```
rm -fr extra
```

rm will not ask your permission for anything. (Remember, **-f** will override the **-i** option, so there is no point in using them together.)

HINT

Before using **rm** **-r** to delete files, use the **pwd** command to display your working directory. If you are in the wrong directory, you will remove the wrong files.

To conclude the discussion of the **rm** command, let's take a quick look at how easy it is to wipe out all your files. Say that your home directory contains many subdirectories, the result of months of hard work. You want to remove all the files and directories under the **extra** directory.

As it happens, you are not in your home directory. What you should do is change to your home directory and then enter the **rm** command:

```
cd
rm -fr extra
```

However, you think to yourself, "There is no point in typing two commands. I can do the whole thing in a single command." You intend to enter:

```
rm -fr ~/extra
```

(Remember, as we explained in Chapter 23, the~ (tilde) character is an abbreviation for the pathname of your home directory.)

But, being in a hurry, you accidentally type a space before the slash:

```
rm -fr ~ /extra
```

In effect, you have entered a command to remove all the files in two subtrees: ~ (your home directory) and **/extra**.

Once you press RETURN, don't even bother trying to hit **^C** or DELETE (whichever is your **intr** key) to abort the command. The computer is a lot faster than you, and there is no way to catch a runaway **rm** command. All your files are gone, including your dotfiles. (Note: We tested this command so you don't have to. Just believe us.)

In Chapter 4, we explained that there is a special userid named **root** that offers superuser privileges. When your system manager logs in as **root**, he or she can do just about anything, including remove any file or directory in the system.

What would happen if someone logged in as superuser and entered the command:

```
rm -fr /
```

(Kids, don't try this at home unless you have your parents' permission.)

Is It Possible to Restore a File That Has Been Removed?

No.

File Permissions

In order to control access within the file system, Unix maintains a set of FILE PERMISSIONS (often called PERMISSIONS) for each file. These permissions control who can access the file and in what way.

There are three types of permissions, each independent of one another. They are READ PERMISSION, WRITE PERMISSION and EXECUTE PERMISSION. With respect to a particular file, you either have a permission or you don't. For example, you might have read and write permission, but not execute permission.

When applied to an ordinary file, the meaning of a permission is straightforward: Read permission means that you are allowed to read the file. Write permission means that you are allowed to write to the file. Execute permission means that you are allowed to execute the file.

Of course, it makes no sense to try to execute a file unless it is executable. In practice, a file is executable if it is a program or a script of some type. (A shell script, for example, contains commands to be executed by the shell.)

The three types of permissions are distinct, but they do work together. For example, in order to change a file, you need both read and write permission. In order to execute a shell script, you need both read and execute permission.

As you will see later in the chapter, you are able to set and change the permissions for your own files. You do so for two reasons:

■ To restrict access by other users

■ To guard against your own errors

If you want to protect a file from being deleted accidentally, you can make sure that there is no write permission for the file. Many commands that replace or delete data will ask for confirmation before changing a file that does not have write permission.

With directories, the permissions are analogous, but have somewhat different meanings. Read permission means you can read the names in the directory. Write permission means you can make changes to the directory (create, move, copy, remove). Execute permission means you can search the directory.

If you have read permission only, you can list the names in a directory, but that is all. Unless you have execute permission, you cannot, for example, check the size of a file, look in a subdirectory, or use the **cd** command to change to the directory.

Although it is an unlikely combination, what would it mean if you had write and execute permission for a directory, but not read permission? You would be able to access and modify the directory without being able to read it. Thus, you could not list the contents, but, if you knew the name of a file, you could remove it.

HINT

When you first learn about the directory permissions, they may seem a bit confusing. Later in this chapter, you will learn that a directory entry contains only a file name and a pointer to the file, not the actual file itself.

Once you understand this, the directory permissions make sense. Read permission means you can read directory entries. Write permissions means you can change directory entries. Execute permission means you can use directory entries.

For reference, Figure 24-2 contains a summary of file permissions as they apply to ordinary files and directories.

How Unix Maintains File Permissions: **id**

The programmers at Bell Labs who created the first Unix system (see Chapter 1) organized file permissions in a way that is still in use today. At the time Unix was developed, people at Bell Labs worked in small groups that needed to share

Ordinary File
Read: you can read from the file
Write: you can write to the file
Execute: you can execute the file

Directory
Read: you can read the directory
Write: you can create, move, copy or remove entries
Execute: you can search the directory

FIGURE 24-2. *Summary of file permissions*

programs and documents. From the point of view of a single user, the programmers divided the entire world into three parts: the user, the user's group, and everybody on the system.

Thus, for each file, Unix keeps three sets of permissions: one for the userid, one for the userids in the group, and one for all the userids on the system. This means that, for each file and directory, you can assign separate read, write and execute permissions for yourself, for the people in your group, and for everybody else. Figure 24-3 shows the possibilities.

Here is an example. The people in your group maintain a particular program. The file that contains this program resides in one of your personal directories. You can set up the file so that you and your group have read, write and execute permission, while all the other users on the system have only read and execute permission. This means that, while anyone can execute the program, only you or members of your group can change it.

Here is another example. You have a document you don't want anyone else to see. Give yourself read and write permission. Give no permissions to your group or to everybody else.

You: read, write, execute
Your group: read, write, execute
Everybody: read, write, execute

FIGURE 24-3. *The possible file permissions*

Note: The permissions for "everybody" also apply to you and to the members of your group. Thus, you can imagine a strange example in which you give read permission for a file to everybody but no permissions to your group. Members of your group will still be able to read the file because "everybody" means anyone at all.

When your system manager created an account for you, he or she also assigned you to a group. Just as each user has a name called a userid, each group has a name called a GROUPID (pronounced "group-eye-dee"). The list of all the groupids in your system is kept in the file **/etc/group**, which you are free to examine.

If you want to see the name of your group, use the command:

```
id
```

This will show you your userid and your groupid.

Although groups sound like a good idea, in practice they are ignored most of the time. System managers generally don't find it worthwhile to maintain groups that are small enough to be useful. For example, if you are an undergraduate student at a university, your userid is probably part of a large group (such as all social science students) with whom sharing would be a meaningless experience.

HINT

Ignore your group by giving it the same permissions that you give to everybody.

■ Displaying File Permissions: `ls -l`

To display the file permissions for a file, use the **ls** command with the **-l** (long listing) option. The permissions are shown on the left-hand side of the output. If you want to display permissions for a specific directory itself, you can use the **-d** option along with **-l**. (The **ls** command, along with these options, is explained in Chapter 23.)

Here is an example. You enter the following command to look at the files in your working directory:

```
ls -l
```

The output is:

```
total 109
-rwxrwxrwx   1 harley    28672 Oct 11 16:37 program.everybody
-rwxrwx---   1 harley    36864 Oct 11 16:38 program.group
-rwx------   1 harley    24576 Oct 11 16:32 program.user
-rw-rw-rw-   1 harley     7376 Oct 11 16:34 text.everybody
-rw-rw----   1 harley     5532 Oct 11 16:34 text.group
-rw-------   1 harley     6454 Oct 11 16:34 text.user
```

We discussed most of this output in Chapter 23. Briefly, the file name is on the far right. Moving to the left, we see the time and date of last modification, the size (in bytes), and the userid of the owner. To the left of the owner is the number of links (which we will discuss later in this chapter).

At the far left, the first character of each line shows us the type of file. An ordinary file is marked by **-**, a hyphen; a directory (there are none in this example) is marked by a **d**.

If you want to display the name of the group as well as the owner, you can use **ls** with the **-g** (group) option. (Note: With some System V types of Unix — see Chapter 2 — this is the default; that is, the **ls** command will display the group name without your having to ask for it. On such systems, you may find that the **-g** option will cause **ls** to *not* show the group. A little experimenting will quickly show you how the **ls** command works on your system.)

What we want to focus on here are the 9 characters to the right of the file type character. Their meaning is as follows:

    r ← read permission

    w ← write permission

    x ← execute permission

    - ← permission not granted

To analyze the permissions for a file, divide the 9 characters into three sets of 3. From left to right, these sets show the permissions for the owner of the file, the owner's group, and for everybody else. (The owner is the userid that created the file.)

owner	group	everybody
rwx	rwx	rwx

Let's do this for all the files in the example:

<u>owner</u>	<u>group</u>	<u>everybody</u>		
`rwx`	`rwx`	`rwx`	←	`program.everybody`
`rwx`	`rwx`	`---`	←	`program.group`
`rwx`	`---`	`---`	←	`program.user`
`rw-`	`rw-`	`rw-`	←	`text.everybody`
`rw-`	`rw-`	`---`	←	`text.group`
`rw-`	`---`	`---`	←	`text.user`

We can now see exactly how each permission is assigned. For instance, the file **text.user** has read and write permissions for the owner, and no permissions for the group or for everybody else.

File Modes

Unix uses a compact, three-number code to represent the full set of file permissions. This code is called a FILE MODE or, more simply, a MODE. For example, we will see that the mode for the **text.user** file in the last example is **600**.

Within a mode, each number stands for one set of permissions. The first number represents the owner's permissions. The second number represents the group's permissions. The third number represents everybody else's permissions. Using the example we just mentioned, we get:

6	←	permissions for owner
0	←	permissions for group
0	←	permissions for everybody

Here's how the code works. We start with the following numeric values for the various permissions:

read permission = **4**
write permission = **2**
execute permission = **1**
no permission = **0**

read	write	execute	VALUE	read		write		execute
-	-	-	**0**	0	+	0	+	0
-	-	yes	**1**	0	+	0	+	1
-	yes	-	**2**	0	+	2	+	0
-	yes	yes	**3**	0	+	2	+	1
yes	-	-	**4**	4	+	0	+	0
yes	-	yes	**5**	4	+	0	+	1
yes	yes	-	**6**	4	+	2	+	0
yes	yes	yes	**7**	4	+	2	+	1

FIGURE 24-4. *Numeric values for file permission combinations*

Now, for each set of permissions, we add the appropriate numbers. For example, to indicate read and write permission, we add **4** and **2**. Figure 24-4 shows each possible combination along with its numeric value.

Let's do an example. What is the mode for a file in which:

—the owner has read, write and execute permissions?

—the group has read and write permissions?

—everyone else has read permission only?

Owner: read + write + execute = **4+2+1 = 7**
Group: read + write = **4+2+0 = 6**
Everyone: read = **4+0+0 = 4**

Thus, the mode is **764**.

Let's look at the examples from the previous section:

owner	group	everybody		mode
rwx 7	rwx 7	rwx 7	← program.everybody	777
rwx 7	rwx 7	--- 0	← program.group	770
rwx 7	--- 0	--- 0	← program.user	700
rw- 6	rw- 6	rw- 6	← text.everybody	666
rw- 6	rw- 6	--- 0	← text.group	660
rw- 6	--- 0	--- 0	← text.user	600

Now, let's do an example going backwards. What does a file mode of **540** mean? Using Figure 24-4, we see:

Owner:	**5**	→	read, execute
Group:	**4**	→	read
Everyone:	**0**	→	nothing

Thus, the owner can read and execute the file. The group can only read the file. Everybody else has no permissions.

Changing File Permissions: chmod

To change the permissions for a file, use the **chmod** (change mode) command. The syntax is:

chmod *mode file*...

where *mode* is the new file mode, and *file* is the name of a file or directory. Only the owner or the superuser can change the file mode for a file. Unix automatically makes you the owner of each file you create.

Here are some examples. The first command changes the mode for the specified files to give read and write permission to the owner, and read permission to the group and to everyone else. These permissions are suitable for a file you want to let anyone read, but not modify.

chmod 644 memo1 memo2 document

The next command gives the owner read, write and execute permissions, with read and execute permissions for the group and for everyone else. These permissions are suitable for a file that contains a program you want to let other people execute, but not modify.

chmod 755 spacewar

In most cases, it is best to restrict permissions unless you have a reason to do otherwise. The following commands set permissions only for the owner. First, read and write permissions:

chmod 600 homework.text

Next, read, write and execute permissions:

`chmod 700 homework.program`

When you create a script using a text editor (see Chapters 20 and 21), it will have only read and write permissions by default. In order to execute the script, you will have to add execute permission. Use **chmod 700** (or **chmod 755** if you want to share).

HINT

To avoid problems, do not give execute permission to a file that is not executable.

How Unix Assigns Permissions to a New File: umask

When Unix creates a new file, it starts with a file mode of:

666: for non-executable ordinary files

777: for executable ordinary files

777: for directories

From this initial mode, Unix subtracts the value of the USER MASK. The user mask is a mode, set by you, showing which permissions you want to restrict.

To set the user mask, use the **umask** command. The syntax is:

`umask [`*mode*`]`

where *mode* specifies which permissions you want to restrict. It is a good idea to put a **umask** command in your initialization file so that your user mask will be set automatically each time you log in. For the C-Shell (see Chapter 11), this file is `.login`; for the Korn shell (Chapter 12) the file is `.profile`.

Here is an example. You want write permission to be withheld from your group and from everybody else. Use a mode of **022**:

`umask 022`

This user mask shares your files without letting anyone change them.

To be as private as possible, you can withhold all permissions — read, write and execute — from your group and from everybody else. Use a mode of **077**:

`umask 077`

HINT

Unless you have reason to do otherwise, make your files completely private by using **umask 077** in your **.login** file. If you want to share, you can do so on a file-by-file basis by using the **chmod** command.

To check the current value of your user mask, enter the **umask** command without a parameter:

```
umask
```

Note: With some shells, the **umask** command will not display leading zeros. Thus, if your user mask is **022**, you may see:

```
22
```

If your user mask is **002**, you may see:

```
2
```

If this is the case with your shell, just pretend the zeros are there.

The Idea of a Link

The rest of the material in this chapter is supplementary. It is useful and interesting, but not as important as what we have covered so far. If you have the time, do take a few minutes to read through the next few sections. They will help you understand a lot more about the Unix file system, and show you how everything actually makes sense.

When Unix creates a file, it does two things. First, it sets aside space on a disk to store whatever data is in the file. Second, it creates a structure called an INODE or INDEX NODE to hold the basic information about the file. (The word "inode" is pronounced "eye-node".)

The inode contains all the information Unix needs to make use of the file. As a user, you don't really need to know what is in an inode, but, in case you are interested, Figure 24-5 will show you.

Unix keeps all the inodes in a large table. Within this table, each inode is known by a number called the INUMBER or INDEX NUMBER. For example, say that a particular file is described by inode #24. We say that the file has an inumber of 24.

When we work with directories, we talk as if they actually contain files. For example, you might hear someone say that his **bin** directory contains a file named **spacewar**.

- the name of the userid that owns the file
- the type of the file (ordinary, directory, special...)
- the size of the file
- where the data is stored
- file permissions
- the last time the file was modified
- the last time the file was accessed
- the last time the inode was modified
- the number of links to the file

FIGURE 24-5. *The contents of an inode (index node)*

However, the directory does not really contain the file. All the directory contains is the name of the file and its inumber. Thus, the contents of a directory are actually quite small. They consist of a list of names and, for each name, an inumber.

Let's look at an example. What happens when you create a file named **spacewar** in your **bin** directory? First, Unix sets aside storage space on the disk to hold the file. Next, Unix looks in the inode table and finds a free inode. Let's say that it is inode #24. Unix fills in the information in the inode that pertains to the new file. Finally, Unix places an entry in the **bin** directory. This entry contains the name **spacewar** along with an inumber of 24.

When Unix needs to use the file, it is a simple matter to look up the name in the directory, use the corresponding inumber to find the inode, and then use the information in the inode to access the file.

The connection between a file name and its inode is called a LINK. Conceptually, a link connects a file name with the file itself.

Multiple Links to the Same File

One of the most elegant features of the Unix file system is that it allows multiple links to the same file. In other words, the same file can be known by more than one name.

Remember, the unique identifier of a file is its inumber, not its name. There is no reason why more than one name cannot reference the same inumber.

Here is an example. Let's say that your home directory is **/usr/harley**. Within your home directory, you have a subdirectory called **bin**. You have created a file in the **bin** directory by the name of **spacewar**. It happens that this file has an inumber of 24.

Using the **ln** command (described later in the chapter), you create another file, in the same directory, named **funky**, so that it has the same inumber as **spacewar**. Since both **spacewar** and **funky** have the same inumber, they are, essentially, different names for the same file.

Now you move to your home directory and create another file named **extra**, also with the same inumber. Then you move to the home directory of a friend, **/usr/addie**, and create a fourth file named **myfile**, also with the same inumber.

At this point, you still have only one file, the one identified by inumber 24, but it has four different names:

```
/usr/harley/bin/spacewar
/usr/harley/bin/funky
/usr/harley/extra
/usr/addie/myfile
```

Would you ever want to do this? Probably not. (Although it can be handy to have various people access the same file by different names.)

But it is important to understand how links work, because they underlie the operation of the basic file commands: **cp** (copy), **mv** (move), **rm** (remove) and **ln** (link). If you just memorize how to use the commands, you will never really understand what is happening, and the rules for using the file system will not make sense.

You might ask, which of these names is the most important one? Does the original name have any special significance?

The answer is that Unix treats all links as equal. It doesn't matter what the original name of the file was. A new link is considered to be just as important as the old one. Files are not controlled by their names or locations. Files are controlled by ownership and permissions.

Creating a New Link: ln

To create a new link to an ordinary file, use the **ln** command. There are two forms of this command. To make a new link to a single file, use the syntax:

```
ln file newname
```

where *file* is the name of an existing ordinary file, and *newname* is the name you want to give the link.

For example, say that you have a file named **spacewar**. To make a new link with the name **funky**, use:

```
ln spacewar funky
```

You will end up with two file names, each of which refers to the same file (that is, to the same inumber). Once a new link is created, it is indistinguishable from the original directory entry.

You can also use **ln** to make new links for one or more ordinary files and place them in a specified directory. The syntax is:

```
ln file... directory
```

where *file* is the name of an existing ordinary file, and *directory* is the name of the directory in which you want to place the new links.

Here is an example. Your home directory is **/usr/harley**. In this directory, you have two files, **data1** and **data2**. Your friend has a home directory of **/usr/addie**. In this directory, she has a subdirectory named **work**. You want to create new links to the two files and place them in your friend's **work** directory. Use the command:

```
ln /usr/harley/data1 /usr/harley/data2 /usr/addie/work
```

Of course, you can use a wildcard specification (see Chapter 23):

```
ln /usr/harley/data[12] /usr/addie/work
```

Another way to simplify this command is to change to your home directory before entering the **ln** command:

```
cd
ln data[12] /usr/addie/work
```

Once you have created these links, the two files reside simultaneously in both directories: **/usr/harley** and **/usr/addie/work**.

How the Basic File Commands Work

All of the basic file commands can be understood in terms of changing file names and links. There are four basic operations:

1. COPY [the **cp** command]   When you copy a file, Unix creates a brand new file with its own inumber. (Remember, the inumber — inode number — is what really identifies a file.) You end up with two files. The old file name points to the old inumber; the new file name points to the new inumber.

2. RENAME or MOVE [the **mv** command]   When you rename or move a file, Unix changes the file name, but keeps the same inumber. You end up with one file. The new file name points to the old inumber.

3. CREATE A LINK [the **ln** command]   When you create a new link, Unix makes a new directory entry using the file name you specify. You end up with one file and two file names. Both file names point to the same inumber.

4. REMOVE [the **rm** and **rmdir** commands]   When you remove a file, Unix deletes the link between the file name and the inumber by removing the directory entry. If this happens to be the only link to the file, Unix also deletes the file. This means that the actual file is not deleted until the last link is removed.

Here is an example. You have a file named **spacewar**. You decide to make a new link to this file and call it **funky**:

```
ln spacewar funky
```

Now you remove **spacewar**:

```
rm spacewar
```

Even though the original file name is gone, the file still exists. The file itself will not be deleted until the last link (**funky**) is removed.

This is why Unix has a remove command and not a "delete" or "erase" command.

HINT
If you want to see how many links a file has, use the **ls -l** command. The number of links is displayed between the permissions and the name of the owner. For example, say that you enter:

```
ls -l data spacewar
```

The output is:

```
-rw----- 1 harley        4070 Oct 14 09:50 data
-rw----- 2 harley       81920 Oct 14 09:50 spacewar
```

You can see **data** has only one link, while **spacewar** has two links.

Symbolic Links: `ln  -s`

The links that we described in the previous two sections allow you to have more than one name refer to the same file. However, such links have two limitations.

First, you cannot create a link to a directory. Second, you cannot create a link to a file in a different file system.

(On many systems, parts of the directory tree are stored separately, perhaps on different devices, perhaps in different "partitions" on the same disk. Each of these parts is called a FILE SYSTEM. Unix combines all the file systems into a single integrated tree structure. To you, it looks like one big file system. To Unix, it is really several file systems joined together.)

To create a link to a directory or to a file in a different file system, you need to use `ln` with the `-s` option. Such a link does not contain the inumber of the original file. Rather, it contains the pathname of the original file. Thus, it is called a SYMBOLIC LINK. When you access a symbolic link, Unix uses the pathname to find and access the original file.

It is unlikely that you would ever need to create a symbolic link (or, for that matter, a regular link). We only mention such links because you may encounter them if you explore your system.

When you use `ls  -l` to display the long listing for a file that is a symbolic link, you will notice two things. First, the leftmost character of the output line will be the letter `l`. Second, the actual symbolic link is shown at the right side of the line.

Here is an example from a system where there is a symbolic link from **/bin/csh** to **/usr/bin/csh**. You enter:

```
ls -l /bin/csh
```

The output is:

```
lrwxr-xr-x 1 root    14 Sep 25 14:17 /bin/csh -> ../usr/bin/csh
```

As you can see, this "file" is only 14 bytes long: just long enough to hold the pathname of the real file. To see the long listing for the real file, you enter:

```
ls -l /usr/bin/csh
```

The output is:

```
-rwxr-xr-x 1 root  249856 Mar 19  1991 /usr/bin/csh
```

This file has 249,586 bytes. As you might have guessed from the name, this file holds the C-Shell program.

(Note: Some Unix systems show you the size of the actual file when you display information about the symbolic link.)

To distinguish between the two types of links, a regular link is called a HARD LINK, while a symbolic link is called a SOFT LINK. When we use the word "link" by itself, we mean a hard link.

HINT

When you use the `ls -l` command, you see the number of hard links. There is no easy way to see how many soft links there are to a file.

CHAPTER 25

Processes and Job Control

There are times when you want to be able to put some task on hold and work on something else for awhile. For example, you may be editing a document when, all of a sudden, you think of a message that you want to mail to someone right away. You *could* stop the editor, start the mail program, compose and send your message, restart the editor program, find the place where you stopped editing and then go back to what you were doing.

However, Unix makes it a lot easier. At any time, you can temporarily pause a program, do something else, and then return to the original program, picking up exactly where you left off. Indeed, you can pause more than one program and jump back and forth from one to another.

There are also other ways you can manage your programs: You can start programs and have them run on their own without your direct intervention. You can display a list of all the programs that are currently executing. If a program is giving you trouble, you can stop it—even if it won't respond properly.

All this, and more, is what we will cover in this chapter.

Foreground and Background Processes

A PROCESS is a program that is executing. Every time you enter a command that executes a program, Unix creates a new process. Even if you are doing nothing in particular, you will always have at least one process: the one for the shell that Unix started for you when you logged in.

For most processes, all the input and output is associated with your terminal. That is, the input comes from your keyboard (and possibly a mouse), and the output goes to your screen.

Some programs, though, can run by themselves without tying up your terminal. For example, say that you want to run a program that reads a large amount of data from a file, sorts that data, and then writes the output to another file. There is no reason why such a program can't work on its own without your intervention.

When you enter a command to run a program, the shell normally waits for the program to finish before asking you to enter another command. However, if you were using the sorting program that we described, there would be no need to wait for it to finish. You could enter the command to start the program, wait for the program to begin, and then move right along to the next command.

To do this, all you have to do is type an **&** character at the end of the command. For example, say the command to run the sorting program is as follows:

sort <bigfile >results

If you enter this command, the shell will run the program, wait until it finishes, and then display a shell prompt (to tell you that it is waiting for a new command). However, if you enter the command with an **&** at the end:

sort <bigfile >results &

the shell will not wait for the program to finish. As soon as the program has started, the shell will display a prompt, and you can enter another command.

When the shell waits for a program to finish before asking you to enter a new command, we say the process is running in the FOREGROUND. When the shell starts a program, but then leaves it to run on its own, we say the process is running in the BACKGROUND. In the first example, we ran the **sort** program in the foreground. In the second example, we ran the **sort** program in the background by typing the **&** character.

Each time you run a program in the background, the shell displays a unique number, called the PROCESSID (pronounced "process-eye-dee"). The processid acts as an identification number for that particular process. You can use this number with certain commands (which we will discuss later) to control the activity of the process. For example, if the program doesn't seem to be working properly, you can abort it.

A program is a candidate to run as a background process if it does not need to run interactively; that is, if it does not need to read from your keyboard or write to your screen. In our example, we could run the program in the background because it gets its input from one file (**bigfile**) and writes its output to another file (**results**).

Sometimes, the term JOB is used as a synonym for "process". For example, you might say, "Since the sorting program takes so long and runs by itself, I think I will run it as a background job." Each time you run a program in the background, the shell assigns a JOB NUMBER as well as a processid. Later, you can refer to the process by using either number. Job numbers always start from **1** and count up.

Here is an example that you can try for yourself. Enter the command:

```
ls >temp &
```

This will run the **ls** command in the background, with its standard output redirected to a file named **temp**. As the shell processes the command, it will display a job number and a processid. The actual number will be assigned by the shell at the time the command is run. Here is a typical example:

```
[1] 6167
```

This means that job number **1** has been started with a processid of **6167**.

When a background process finishes its job, the shell will send you a short message telling you that the process is done. For example:

```
[1]   Done      ls > temp
```

In this case, job number **1** (the **ls temp** command) has finished. (If you want to erase the **temp** file, you can use the command **rm temp**.)

TECHNICAL HINT

Compiling a program is a great activity to run in the background. For example, let's say that you are using the **cc** command to compile a C program named **myprog**. You might use one of the following commands:

```
cc -O myprog.c >&errors &
cc -O myprog.c 2>errors &
```

(The **-O** option tells the C compiler to use optimization. The first command is for the C-Shell; the second command is for the Korn shell. In each command, the error messages are redirected to a file named **errors**.)

Another common situation occurs when you have to build a program that uses a makefile. For example, say that you have downloaded a program named **game** using Anonymous FTP over the Internet. After unpacking all the files, you need to build the program using **make**. You might enter the command:

```
make game &
```

This allows you to continue with other work while **make** is executing. When **make** is finished, the shell will display a message showing you that the process is over.

When You Should Not Run a Job in the Background

The best programs to run in the background are those which are not interactive. Such programs do not need you to type input, nor do they write output to your screen. For example, it would not be a good idea to try to run a text editor, like **vi** or **emacs**, in the background. Such programs are built around the keyboard and screen.

However, Unix *will* allow you run any program in the background: all you have to do is put an **&** character at the end of the command that starts the program.

So what happens when you do run such a program in the background? To answer this question, we have to ask two other questions: What happens when a background process tries to read from the keyboard? And what happens when a background process tries to write to the screen?

When a background process tries to read from the keyboard, the process stops, and it stays stopped until you do something to bring it into the foreground. (Later in the chapter, we will show you how to do this.) The way to think about it is that the program wants to read, and it is going to wait and wait and wait until you give it something to read.

And what happens when a background process tries to write to the terminal? The output will appear on your screen and, as far the program is concerned, there is no problem. However, you will probably be in the middle of something else, and when a bunch of output suddenly appears out of nowhere your screen is going to be cluttered.

If you would like to see this for yourself, try this experiment. Enter the following two commands quickly, one right after the other:

```
w &
vi
```

The first program is the **w** command (which tells you who is logged in and what they are doing); the second program is the **vi** editor.

Because you typed an **&** character after the **w**, the first program will be started as a background process. This means that the shell will not wait for **w** to finish before it starts **vi**, and **w** will be writing its output to the screen after **vi** has started. The result will be a mixed-up screen that will give you a graphic illustration of what happens when two processes write to the screen at the same time.

(If you would like to clear the **vi** screen, press **^L**. To quit **vi**, type **:q** and then press RETURN.)

The moral of all this is: Don't run programs in the background if they read or write from the terminal.

HINT

If a program writes to the terminal, but takes a long time to execute, you can run it in the background by redirecting the standard output to a file. Later, you can look at the output of the program by displaying the file.

For example, the following commands run the **w** command in the background—saving its output to a file named **w-data**—and then start the **vi** editor:

```
w w-data &
vi
```

By the time you finish with **vi**, the output of **w** will be waiting for you.

Suspending a Process: Job Control

If you are working with a program and you want to pause it temporarily, you can do so by pressing **^Z**, a special key that sends the **susp** code. When you do this, we say that you SUSPEND the process. The **susp** key is almost always **^Z**.

However, if you suspect that this is not the case on your system, you can check it by using the **stty** command (described in Chapter 6).

When you suspend a process, the shell tells you that the job has been stopped. For example, say that you are using the **vi** editor, and you decide to suspend it so you can check your mail. You press **^Z** and you see:

```
Stopped
```

You can now enter any commands that you want (such as the command to start your mail program).

At any time, you can return to the suspended program (in this case **vi**) by using the **fg** (foreground) command. Simply enter:

```
fg
```

The shell will reactivate your program and you will be back where you left off.

When a process is suspended, it waits indefinitely. To restart it, you use either the **fg** or **bg** commands (explained later). This capability—being able to suspend and restart processes—is called JOB CONTROL.

You can only use job control if (1) your shell offers it and (2) it is supported by the version of Unix that is running on your system. All modern shells (including the C-Shell and the Korn shell) offer job control. However, the Bourne shell does not. With respect to Unix, Berkeley Unix supports job control, while System V supports it starting with version V.4.

Thus, unless you are using the Bourne shell or an older version of System V, you should be able to use job control and suspend processes.

(For a discussion of the various types of Unix, see Chapter 2. For a discussion of the various shells, see Chapter 10.)

HINT FOR KORN SHELL USERS

Within the Korn shell, you cannot use job control unless the **monitor** option is turned on. This may already be the case for your system. If not, you will have to turn this option on for yourself. The command to use is:

```
set -o monitor
```

Normally, you would place this command in your environment file so that the **monitor** option will be turned on automatically each time a new Korn shell is started. For information about the Korn shell and the environment file, see Chapter 12.

Displaying a List of Suspended Jobs: jobs

To keep track of your suspended jobs you can use the **jobs** command. The syntax is:

jobs [-1]

To display a list of all your suspended jobs, simply enter the command name by itself:

jobs

Here is some sample output:

```
[1]     Stopped     vi document
[2]   - Stopped     make game
[3]   + Stopped     elm
```

In this case, we have three suspended jobs; job number **1** is the **vi** editor. Job number **2** is the **make** program; and job number **3** is the **elm** mail program.

If you would like to see the processid as well as the job number and command name, use **jobs** along with the **-1** (long listing) option:

jobs -1

Here is some sample output:

```
[1]       6727 Stopped     vi
[2]   -   3662 Stopped     make game
[3]   +   3709 Stopped     elm
```

Moving a Suspended Job to the Foreground: fg

When you want to resume working with a job that is suspended, you can move it to the foreground. To do so, use the **fg** command. The syntax is:

fg [%*job*]

where *job* is the name or number of a suspended job.

If you enter the command by itself:

fg

the shell will restart what is called the CURRENT JOB. This is the job you see marked with a **+** (plus sign) character when you use the **jobs** command. In the example in the previous section, the current job is number **3**, the **elm** program.

The current job is the most recently suspended job. If you do not have any suspended jobs, the current job is the most recent background job.

If you want to move a different program to the foreground, you can specify the one you want. There are several ways to do this, and they are summarized in Figure 25-1.

Most of the time, it is easiest to use a **%** (percent) character, followed by a job number. For example, to move job number **1** into the foreground, you can use:

fg %1

You can also specify a job by referring to the name of the command. For example, if you want to restart the job that was running the command **make game**, you can use:

fg %make

Actually, you only need to specify enough of the command to distinguish it from all the other jobs. If there are no other commands that begin with the letter "m", you could use:

fg %m

SPECIFICATION	MEANING
%*nn*	job number *nn*
%*name*	command that begins with **name**
%?*name*	command that contains **name**
%	the current job
%+	same as **%**
%−	the previous job

FIGURE 25-1. *Specifying a job for the* **fg** *or* **bg** *commands*

An alternative is to use **%?** followed by part of the command. For example, another way to move the **make game** command to the foreground is to use:

```
fg %?game
```

Note: If your shell interprets the **?** character as a wildcard (see Chapter 23), you may have to put a **** (backslash) character in front of the **?** to tell the shell to take the **?** literally:

```
fg %\?game
```

When you do this, we say you are "quoting" the **?** character.

As we mentioned, it you use the **fg** command without specifying a particular job, **fg** will move the current job into the foreground. (This is the job that is marked with a **+** character when you use the **jobs** command.) Alternatively, you can use either **%** or **%+** to refer to the current job. Thus, the following three commands are equivalent:

```
fg
fg %
fg %+
```

Similarly, you can use **%-** to refer to the previous job:

```
fg %-
```

This is the job that is marked with a **-** (minus sign) character when you use the **jobs** command.

As a convenience, some shells will assume that you are using the **fg** command if you simply enter a job specification that begins with a **%** character. For example, if job number **2** is the command **make game**, then all of the following commands will have the same effect:

```
%2
fg %2
fg %?game
fg %make
```

In each case, the shell will move job number **2** into the foreground.

There is one final abbreviation that you can use: a command consisting of nothing but the single character **%** will tell the shell to move the current job to the foreground. Thus the following four commands are equivalent:

```
%
fg
fg %
fg %+
```

HINT

Although our examples showed more than one suspended job, most of the time you will suspend only a single job, do something else, and then restart the original. In this case, job control becomes simple: all you need to do is press **^Z** to suspend the original job, and enter **%** or **fg** to restart it.

Moving a Suspended Job to the Background: bg

To move a suspended job to the background, you use the **bg** command. The syntax is:

bg [%*job*]

where *job* is the name or number of a suspended job.

To specify a job, you follow the same rules as with the **fg** command. In particular, you can use the variations in Figure 25-1. For instance, to move job number **2** into the background, you can use:

bg %2

If you use the command by itself, without a job specification:

bg

the shell will move the current job into the background.

As you might imagine, you will use the **fg** command more often than the **bg** command. But there is one important situation when **bg** comes in handy. Say that you enter a command (in the regular manner) that seems to be taking a long time. If the program is not interactive, you can suspend it and move it to the background.

For example, let's say that you want to use **make** to build a program named **game**, so you enter the command:

```
make game
```

After waiting a while, you realize that this could take a long time. Since **make** does not need anything from you, there is no point in tying up your terminal. Simply press **^Z** to suspend the job, and enter **bg** to move the job to the background. Your terminal is now free, and you can enter another command.

HINT
If you meant to run a program in the background, but you forgot to type the **&** character when you entered the command, you can suspend the job by pressing **^Z**, and then use the **bg** command to move the job into the background.

Displaying the Status of Your Processes: ps

To display information about all the processes that are currently running under the auspices of your userid, you can use the **ps** (process status) command.

The **ps** command has a large number of options which vary from system to system. In particular, the options for Berkeley Unix are different than the options for System V Unix. (We discuss the various types of Unix in Chapter 2.) By using these options, you can display a great deal of technical information about each process. You can also display information about processes that belong to other userids.

However, most of the time you will only care about your own processes and you will only want to display the basic information. To do so, simply enter the name of the command by itself:

```
ps
```

Here is some typical output:

```
  PID TT STAT   TIME COMMAND
 3662 r2 TW     0:05 make game
 3709 r2 TW     0:00 elm
 6087 r2 S      0:00 -csh (csh)
 6727 r2 TW     0:00 vi document
23895 r2 R      0:00 ps
```

In this case, we have five processes associated with our userid. As you can see, the first column shows us the processid.

The second column shows the name of the terminal from which the process was started. The **ps** command only shows you the last two characters of the terminal name, in this case **r2**. The full name of the terminal would be **ttyr2**. (We discuss terminal names in Chapter 22. Most of the time you can ignore them.)

The next column shows the status of each process. Again, this is something that you can ignore.

The fourth column shows how much processor time the process has used so far. Processor time is measured in minutes and seconds, and a little goes a long way. In our example, the **make** program has used about 5 seconds of processor time, but the other processes have used so little time that each shows 0 seconds.

The last column tells you which command started the process. Even if you are doing nothing else, you will always see at least one line for your basic shell, and at least one line for the **ps** command itself. Here is a typical example:

```
PID TT STAT   TIME COMMAND
25015 q6 S     0:00 -csh (csh)
25034 q6 R     0:00 ps
```

In this case, we see our shell **csh** (the C-Shell) and the **ps** command. Of course, as soon as **ps** finishes, it will vanish, so we really only have one process: the shell which is waiting for us to enter a command.

HINT
You can find out a lot of details about your processes by using various options with **ps**. You can even snoop on other people and check out what processes they are running. (The w also comes in handy here.)

To find out about these options and how they work on your particular system, check the entry for **ps** in the online manual by using the command **man ps**. The manual page will also explain what all the different status codes mean. (We discuss the online Unix manual in Chapter 8.)

Killing a Process: `kill`

When you are using a regular program running in the foreground, you can terminate it by pressing the **intr** key. On most systems, this is the **^C** key; on some systems, it is the DELETE key. (We discuss this in Chapter 6.)

However, how can you stop a program that is running in the background? You do this by using the **kill** command. The syntax is:

kill [-*signal*] *process*

where *signal* is the type of signal you want to send (explained in a moment), and *process* identifies the process you want to terminate. When you terminate a process in this way, we say you KILL the process.

Most of the time, you will use the **kill** command with a single processid. Before you use the **kill** command, you can use **jobs** or **ps** to display the processid. Here is an example.

You have entered the command **make game &** to run the **make** program in the background. Some time later, you decide to kill the job. First, you use the **ps** command to find out the processid. You enter:

ps

The output is:

```
  PID TT STAT   TIME COMMAND
 3662 r2 TW     0:05 make game
 3709 r2 TW     0:00 elm
 6087 r2 S      0:00 -csh (csh)
 6727 r2 TW     0:00 vi document
23895 r2 R      0:00 ps
```

The processid you want is **3662**. To kill this process, enter:

kill 3662

The shell will kill the process and display a message. In this case, the message is:

[2]   Terminated   make game

This means that the process that was running the program **make game** has been killed. The number at the beginning of the line means that the process was job number **2**.

An alternative way to list the various processes is to use the **jobs -l** command. Let's say you had used this command instead of **ps**:

jobs -l

Here is what you would have seen:

```
[1]       6727 Stopped      vi
[2]    -  3662 Stopped      make game
[3]    +  3709 Stopped      elm
```

Again, you could use the command **kill 3662** to kill the **make** program. However, you can also use the same type of job description as with the **fg** and **bg** commands (see Figure 25-1), so you can use the command:

```
kill %2
```

HINT

If you are running a program in the foreground and you encounter trouble, you would normally try to kill it by pressing **^C**. However, in some circumstances this will not work, and the offending program will be beyond your reach.

In this case, you can press **^Z** to suspend the job, enter the **jobs** command to find out the job number, and then use **kill** to kill the process.

Remember this hint. It is often the only way to kill an otherwise inaccessible program that is off in the Twilight Zone.

Technically speaking, the purpose of the **kill** command is not to kill a process: the **kill** command is actually designed to send a SIGNAL to a process. In Chapter 6, we mentioned signals when we discussed the special keys (**intr**, **stop**, **start**, **susp**, and so on). Whenever you press one of these keys (**^C**, **^S**, **^Q**, **^Z**, and so on), it sends a signal to the current foreground process. It is up to the process to recognize this signal and either do something or pass the signal on to Unix to do something.

Each signal has its own name and identification number. Most Unix systems have at least thirty or so different signals, but only two are of interest to regular users. Signal number **15** is called **TERM**. This is the signal the **kill** command uses to kill a process. (The name stands for "terminate".) Signal number **9** is called **KILL**. This is a stronger form of **TERM** that we will discuss in a moment.

When you use the **kill** command, you can specify a specific signal as an option. If you do not specify a signal, **kill** will, by default, send signal **15**. Thus, the following three commands (all acting upon process **3662**) are equivalent:

```
kill 3662
kill -15 3662
kill -TERM 3662
```

As we mentioned, there are many different signals and the purpose of the **kill** command is to send whichever signal you specify to the process you specify. In this sense, it might have been better to name the command **signal**. However, by default, **kill** sends signal **15**, which has the effect of killing the process—this is why the command is called **kill**. Indeed, most people use **kill** only for killing a process and not for sending other signals.

Most of the time, a program will recognize the **TERM** signal and gracefully shut itself down. Sometimes, though, a program will be designed to ignore this signal (or something may go wrong). In such cases, you may not be able to kill the program by using a simple **kill** command.

Instead, you can use the **KILL** command which, by definition, cannot be ignored. In other words, using **KILL** ensures a sure **kill**. For example, if you are having trouble killing process **3662**, you could use either of the following commands:

```
kill -9 3662
kill -KILL 3662
```

Most people use the **-9** option rather than **-KILL**, because it is easier to type.

HINT

When you want to kill a process, always try the regular **kill** command first. Use **kill -9** only as a last resort.

When you use **kill** without an option (that is, **kill -15**), it allows the process a chance to close all the files that it may have had open. When you use **kill -9**, it kills the process instantly. If there were files open that were not closed properly, it may cause you a problem later on.

HINT FOR NERDS

If you want to see the full list of signals, there are certain system files that you can check. Try either of the following commands:

```
more /usr/include/signal.h
more /usr/include/sys/signal.h
```

Alternatively, you can display the page in the online manual that describes a programming interface named **signal**. Here you will see a full list of signals. Use the command:

```
man signal
```

(We explain the online Unix manual in Chapter 8.)

The End of the Last Chapter

I would like to thank you for spending so much time with me talking about Unix. I wrote this book in order to make Unix accessible to intelligent people and, to the extent that I have helped you, I am grateful for the opportunity.

Unix has traditionally attracted the most talented computer users and programmers, for whom working on Unix is a labor of love. One reason Unix is so wonderful is that most of it was designed before the men in suits sat up and took notice. Perhaps you have wondered why Unix works so well and why it is so elegant: It is because the basic Unix philosophy was developed long before the business and marketing people started trying to make money from it.

You may remember me saying, several times, that Unix is not easy to learn, but it is easy to use. By now, you will realize what this means: it is more important for a tool to be designed well for a smart person, than it is for a tool to be easy enough to be used on the first day by someone whose biggest intellectual challenge in life is working the remote control on their VCR.

You have my word that every moment you spend learning and using Unix will repay you generously. I can't be by your side as you work, but you do have this book, and I have put in a great deal of effort to provide you with the very best Unix companion that I could.

Although I may be irreverent at times—indeed, whenever I am able to make a joke that the editors can't catch—I would like to take a moment to wish you the very best. As you read and re-read this book, please remember: I am on *your* side.

—Harley Hahn

HINT
Unix is fun.

APPENDIX A

Summary of Unix Commands Covered in this Book

Chapter references are indicated by the numbers in parentheses.

colrm (17)	remove specified columns from each line of data
cp (24)	copy files
craps (7)	craps dice game
cribbage (7)	cribbage card game
crypt (17)	encode or decode text using a specified key
csh (10,12)	the C-Shell
cut (17)	extract selected portions (columns) of each line
date (7)	display the time and date
du (23)	display disk storage usage statistics
echo (11,12)	write arguments to standard output
ed (20)	old standard Unix line-oriented text editor
egrep (17)	like **grep**, searches for full regular expressions
emacs (21)	the **emacs** text editor
ex (20)	standard Unix line-oriented text editor
exit (4)	exit a shell
export (12)	Korn shell: place shell variable in the environment
factor (7)	decompose a number into its prime factors
fg (25)	move a job into the foreground
fgrep (17)	like **grep**, searches for fixed character string
finger (13)	display information about a specified userid
fish (7)	the Go Fish card game
fmt (15)	format text to fit a 72-character line
fortune (7)	display an interesting message
from (15)	show if mail is waiting
gmacs (21)	the **emacs** text editor
gnuemacs (21)	the **emacs** text editor
gnumacs (21)	the **emacs** text editor
grep (17)	extract lines that contain a specified pattern

Chapter references are indicated by the numbers in parentheses.

hack (7)	fantasy game (a replacement for **rogue**)
hangman (7)	hangman word game
head (18)	display the first part of a file
history (11)	C-Shell: display commands from history event list
history (12)	Korn shell: display commands from history file
hostname (7)	display the name of your system
hunt (7)	multiplayer shooting game
id (24)	display userid and groupid
jobs (25)	show suspended jobs
kill (25)	terminate a job; send a signal to a job
kpasswd (4)	change your login password (Kerberos)
ksh (10,12)	the Korn shell
last (4)	check the last time that a userid has logged in
leave (7)	display reminder at specified time
less (18)	display data, one screenful at a time
ln (24)	make a link between two directory entries
lock (7)	temporarily lock your terminal
login (4)	terminate a login shell and initiate a new login
logout (4)	terminate a login shell
look (17)	extract lines beginning with a specified pattern
lp (19)	System V: send a file to be printed
lpq (19)	Berkeley Unix: show what print jobs are waiting
lpr (19)	Berkeley Unix: send a file to be printed
lprm (19)	Berkeley Unix: remove a job from the print queue
lpstat (19)	System V: show what print jobs are waiting
ls (23)	display information about files
mail (15)	send or read mail
Mail (15)	Berkeley Unix version of **mail**

Chapter references are indicated by the numbers in parentheses.

mailx (15)	System V version of **mail**
man (8)	display entries from online Unix reference manual
mesg (13)	allow or deny receiving messages at your terminal
mille (7)	Mille Bournes board game
mkdir (23)	make (create) a directory
monop (7)	Monopoly board game
moo (7)	guessing game
more (18)	display data, one screenful at a time
msgs (7)	display local system messages
mv (23, 24)	move or rename files
mwm (5)	the Motif window manager
news (7)	display the local system news
nl (19)	add line numbers to text
number (7)	convert a number to English words
olwm (5)	the Open Look window manager
passwd (4)	change your login password
paste (17)	combine columns of data
pg (18)	display data, one screenful at a time
ping (13)	check if an Internet computer is responding
ppt (7)	convert text to paper tape format
pr (19)	format text, suitable for printing
primes (7)	generate prime numbers larger than specific value
print (12)	Korn shell: write arguments to standard output
printenv (11)	C-Shell: display values of environment variables
ps (25)	display information about processes
pwd (23)	display pathname of current (working) directory
quiz (7)	question and answer game
quota (23)	display your system resource quotas

Chapter references are indicated by the numbers in parentheses.

r (21)	Korn shell: reuse a command from the history file
rain (7)	display animated raindrops
rev (17)	reverse order of characters in each line of data
rm (24)	remove (delete) files or directories
rmdir (23)	remove empty directories
robots (7)	shooting-at-robots game
rogue (7)	fantasy game, exploring the Dungeons of Doom
ruptime (7)	display how long local systems have been up
rwho (13)	display info about userids on local network
sail (7)	multiplayer sailing game
set (11)	C-Shell: set/display the value of shell variables
set (12)	Korn shell: set/display shell options and variables
setenv (11)	C-Shell: set or display value of environment variables
sh (10)	the Bourne shell
snake (7)	chase game
sort (17)	sort or merge data
spell (17)	check text for words that may be spelled wrong
stty (6)	set/display operating options for your terminal
tail (18)	display the last part of a file
talk (13)	send messages back and forth to another user
tcsh (10)	the Tcsh shell
tee (16)	copy standard input to a file and standard output
touch (24)	update access and modification times of a file
tr (17)	translate or delete selected characters
traceroute (14)	display Internet route to another computer
trek (7)	Star Trek-inspired game
tset (4, 17)	initialize your terminal
tty (22)	show special file that represents your terminal
type (12)	Korn shell: show what type of command
twm (5)	the Tab window manager

Chapter references are indicated by the numbers in parentheses.

umask (24)	set user (file mode) mask for file creation
unalias (11)	C-Shell: remove a name previously defined by **alias**
unalias (12)	Korn shell: remove a name previously defined by **alias**
uniq (17)	remove adjacent repeated lines in a text file
unset (11)	C-shell: remove a shell variable
uptime (7)	display how long your system has been up
users (13)	display userids that are currently logged in
vi (20)	the **vi** text editor
view (20)	same as **vi**, in read-only mode
w (13)	display info about userids and active processes
wc (17)	count number of lines, words or characters
whatis (8)	display one-line summary of specified command
whence (12)	Korn shell: display pathname of specified command
who (13)	display info about currently logged in userids
whoami (7)	display the userid that is currently logged in
worm (7)	worm-growing game
worms (7)	display worms on your terminal
write (13)	send messages back and forth to another local user
wump (7)	the game of Hunt-the-Wumpus
xbiff (15)	X Window version of **biff** (show if mail waiting)
xcalc (5)	X Window calculator
xclock (5)	X Window clock
xhost (5)	tell X server that you will use a remote computer
xinit (5)	start X Window
xterm (5)	start an X Window terminal session
yppasswd (4)	change your login password (Sun NIS)
zsh (10)	the Zsh shell

Chapter references are indicated by the numbers in parentheses.

APPENDIX B

Summary of Unix Commands By Category

This appendix contains a summary of all the Unix commands covered in this book, organized by category. The categories are:

Directories
Displaying Data
Diversions
Editing
Entering a Command: C-Shell
Entering a Command: Korn Shell
Files
Filters
Games
Information
Job Control

Logging In and Out
(Online) Manual
Mail
Numbers
Printing
Shells
Terminals
Time and Dates
Users
Variables
X Window

Directories

cd (23)	change the current (working) directory
chmod (24)	change permissions (mode) of a file or directory
ln (24)	make a link between two directory entries
ls (23)	display information about files
mkdir (23)	make (create) a directory
pwd (23)	display pathname of current (working) directory
rm (24)	remove (delete) files or directories
rmdir (23)	remove empty directories
umask (24)	set user (file mode) mask for file creation

Displaying Data

head (18)	display the first part of a file
less (18)	display data, one screenful at a time
more (18)	display data, one screenful at a time
pg (18)	display data, one screenful at a time
tail (18)	display the last part of a file

Diversions

arithmetic (7)	help you practice simple computation
banner (7)	write large characters, suitable for printing
bcd (7)	convert text to BCD cardpunch format
ching (7)	display advice from the Book of Changes
fortune (7)	display an interesting message
number (7)	convert a number to English words
ppt (7)	convert text to paper tape format
rain (7)	display animated raindrops
worms (7)	display worms on your terminal

Chapter references are indicated by the numbers in parentheses.

Editing

ed (20)	old standard Unix line-oriented text editor
emacs (21)	the **emacs** text editor
ex (20)	standard Unix line-oriented text editor
fmt (15)	format text to fit a 72-character line
gmacs (21)	the **emacs** text editor
gnuemacs (21)	the **emacs** text editor
gnumacs (21)	the **emacs** text editor
vi (20)	the **vi** text editor
view (20)	same as **vi**, in read-only mode

Entering a Command: C-Shell

! (11)	repeat specified command
!! (11)	repeat previous command
^^ (11)	repeat previous command with substitution
alias (11)	assign a name to specified command list
history (11)	display the history event list
unalias (11)	remove a name previously defined by **alias**

Entering a Command: Korn Shell

alias (12)	assign a name to specified command list
r (21)	resuse a command from history file
history (12)	display commands from history file
type (12)	Korn shell: show what type of command
unalias (12)	remove a name previously defined by **alias**
whence (12)	Korn shell: display pathname of specified command

Chapter references are indicated by the numbers in parentheses.

Files

chmod (24)	change permissions (mode) of a file or directory
cp (24)	copy files
ln (24)	make a link between two directory entries
ls (23)	display information about files
mv (23,24)	move or rename files
rm (24)	remove (delete) files or directories
touch (24)	update access and modification times of a file
umask (24)	set user (file mode) mask for file creation

Filters

fmt (15)	format text to fit a 72-character line
head (18)	display the first part of a file
less (18)	display data, one screenful at a time
cat (17)	combine, copy standard input to standard output
colrm (17)	remove specified columns from each line of data
crypt (17)	encode or decode text using a specified key
cut (17)	extract selected portions (columns) of each line
egrep (17)	like **grep**, searches for full regular expressions
fgrep (17)	like **grep**, searches for fixed character string
grep (17)	extract lines that contain a specified pattern
look (17)	extract lines beginning with a specified pattern
nl (19)	add line numbers to text
more (18)	display data, one screenful at a time
paste (17)	combine columns of data
pg (18)	display data, one screenful at a time
pr (19)	format text, suitable for printing
rev (17)	reverse order of characters in each line of data
sort (17)	sort or merge data
spell (17)	check text for words that may be spelled wrong
tail (18)	display the last part of a file
tee (16)	copy standard input to a file and standard output
tr (17)	translate or delete selected characters
uniq (17)	remove adjacent repeated lines in a text file
wc (17)	count number of lines, words or characters

Chapter references are indicated by the numbers in parentheses.

Games

adventure (7)	the original text-based adventure game
backgammon (7)	backgammon dice/board game
battlestar (7)	an adventure game
bj (7)	blackjack card game
boggle (7)	Boggle word game
btlgammon (7)	backgammon dice/board game
canfield (7)	solitaire card game
chess (7)	chess game
craps (7)	craps dice game
cribbage (7)	cribbage card game
fish (7)	Go Fish card game
hack (7)	fantasy game (a replacement for **rogue**)
hangman (7)	hangman word game
hostname (7)	display the name of your system
hunt (7)	multiplayer shooting game
mille (7)	Mille Bournes board game
monop (7)	Monopoly board game
moo (7)	guessing game
quiz (7)	question and answer game
robots (7)	shooting-at-robots game
rogue (7)	fantasy game, exploring the Dungeons of Doom
sail (7)	multiplayer sailing game
snake (7)	chase game
trek (7)	Star Trek-inspired game
worm (7)	worm-growing game
wump (7)	the game of Hunt-the-Wumpus

Chapter references are indicated by the numbers in parentheses.

Information

du (23)	display disk storage usage statistics
msgs (7)	display local system messages
news (7)	display the local system news
quota (23)	display your system resource quotas
ruptime (7)	display how long local systems have been up
uptime (7)	display how long your system has been up

Job Control

bg (25)	move a job into the background
fg (25)	move a job into the foreground
jobs (25)	show suspended jobs
kill (25)	terminate a job; send a signal to a job
ps (25)	display information about processes

Logging In and Out

kpasswd (4)	change your login password (Kerberos)
last (4)	check the last time that a userid has logged in
login (4)	terminate a login shell and initiate a new login
logout (4)	terminate a login shell
passwd (4)	change your login password
yppasswd (4)	change your login password (Sun NIS)

(Online) Manual

apropos (8)	display command names based on keyword search
man (8)	display entries from online Unix reference manual
whatis (8)	display one-line summary of specified command

Mail

biff (15)	notify when mail arrives
fmt (15)	format text to fit a 72-character line
from (15)	show if mail is waiting
mail (15)	send or read mail
Mail (15)	Berkeley Unix version of **mail**
mailx (15)	System V version of **mail**

Chapter references are indicated by the numbers in parentheses.

Numbers

bc (7)	an arbitrary-precision, easy to use calculator
factor (7)	decompose a number into its prime factors
primes (7)	generate prime numbers larger than specific value
xcalc (5)	X Window calculator

Printing

cancel (19)	System V: remove a job from the print queue
lp (19)	System V: send a file to be printed
lpq (19)	Berkeley Unix: show what print jobs are waiting
lpr (19)	Berkeley Unix: send a file to be printed
lprm (19)	Berkeley Unix: remove a job from the print queue
lpstat (19)	System V: show what print jobs are waiting
nl (19)	add line numbers to text
pr (19)	format text, suitable for printing

Shells

bash (10)	the Bash shell
chsh (10)	change your default shell
csh (10)	the C-Shell
exit (4)	exit a shell
ksh (10)	the Korn shell
sh (10)	the Bourne shell
tcsh (10)	the Tcsh shell
zsh (10)	the Zsh shell

Terminal

lock (7)	temporarily lock your terminal
mesg (13)	allow or deny receiving messages at your terminal
stty (6)	set/display operating options for your terminal
tset (4,17)	initialize your terminal
tty (22)	show special file that represents your terminal

Chapter references are indicated by the numbers in parentheses.

Time and Dates

cal (7)	display a calendar
date (7)	display the time and date
calendar (7)	display current reminders from **calendar** file
leave (7)	display reminder at specified time
xclock (5)	X Window clock

Users

chfn (13)	change your **finger** information
finger (13)	display information about a specified userid
id (24)	display userid and groupid
rwho (13)	display info about userids on local network
talk (13)	send messages back and forth to another user
users (13)	display userids that are currently logged in
w (13)	display info about userids and active processes
who (13)	display info about currently logged in userids
whoami (7)	display the userid that is currently logged in
write (13)	send messages back and forth to another local user

Variables

echo (11,12)	write arguments to standard output
export (12)	Korn shell: place shell variable in the environment
print (12)	Korn shell: write arguments to standard output
printenv (11)	C-shell: display values of environment variables
set (11)	C-Shell: set/display the value of shell variables
set (12)	Korn shell: set/display shell options and variables
setenv (11)	C-Shell: set or display value of environment variables
unset (11)	C-Shell: remove a shell variable

Chapter references are indicated by the numbers in parentheses.

X Window

mwm (5)	the Motif window manager
olwm (5)	the Open Look window manager
twm (5)	the Tab window manager
xbiff (15)	X Window version of **biff** (show if mail waiting)
xcalc (5)	X Window calculator
xclock (5)	X Window clock
xhost (5)	tell X server that you will use a remote computer
xinit (5)	start X Window
xterm (5)	start an X Window terminal session

Chapter references are indicated by the numbers in parentheses.

APPENDIX C

Summary of vi Commands

This appendix contains a summary of all the **vi** commands covered in this book. For more information, see Chapter 20 in which we discuss **vi** in detail.

Starting

vi *file*	start **vi**, edit specified file
vi -R *file*	start **vi** read-only, edit specified file
view *file*	start **vi** read-only, edit specified file

Stopping

:q!	stop without saving data
ZZ	save data and stop
:wq	save data and stop
:x	save data and stop

Recovering After System Failure

vi -r	display names of files that can be recovered
vi -r *file*	start **vi**, recover specified file

Controlling the Display

^L	redisplay the current screen
:set number	display internal line numbers
:set nonumber	do not display internal line numbers

Moving the Cursor

h	move cursor one position left
j	move cursor one position down
k	move cursor one position up
l	move cursor one position right
LEFT	move cursor one position left
DOWN	move cursor one position down
UP	move cursor one position up
RIGHT	move cursor one position right
BACKSPACE	move cursor one position left
SPACE	move cursor one position right
-	move cursor to beginning of previous line
+	move cursor to beginning of next line
RETURN	move cursor to beginning of next line
0	move cursor to beginning of current line
$	move cursor to end of current line
^	move cursor to first non-space/tab in current line
w	move cursor forward to first character of next word
e	move cursor forward to last character of next word
b	move cursor backward to first character of previous word
W	same as **w**; ignore punctuation
E	same as **e**; ignore punctuation
B	same as **b**; ignore punctuation
)	move forward to next sentence beginning
(	move backward to previous sentence beginning
}	move forward to next paragraph beginning
{	move backward to previous paragraph beginning
H	move cursor to top line
M	move cursor to middle line
L	move cursor to last line

Moving Through the Editing Buffer

^F	move down (forwards) one screenful
^B	move up (backwards) one screenful
*n***^F**	move down *n* screenfuls
*n***^B**	move up *n* screenfuls
^D	move down a half screenful
^U	move up a half screenful
*n***^D**	move down *n* lines
*n***^U**	move up *n* lines

Searching for a Pattern

/*rexp*	search forward for specified regular expression
/	repeat forward search for previous pattern
?*rexp*	search backward for specified regular expression
?	repeat backward search for previous pattern
n	repeat last **/** or **?** command, same direction
N	repeat last **/** or **?** command, opposite direction

Special Characters to Use in Regular Expressions

.	match any single character except **newline**
*****	match zero or more of the preceding characters
^	match the beginning of a line
$	match the end of a line
\<	match the beginning of a word
\>	match the end of a word
[ ]	match one of the enclosed characters
[^]	match any character that is not enclosed
****	interpret the following symbol literally

Line Numbers

*n***G**	jump to line number *n*
1G	jump to first line in editing buffer
G	jump to last line in editing buffer
:map g 1G	define macro so **g** will be the same as **1G**

Inserting

i	change to insert mode: insert before cursor position
a	change to insert mode: insert after cursor position
I	change to insert mode: insert at start of current line
A	change to insert mode: insert at end of current line
o	change to insert mode: open below current line
O	change to insert mode: open above current line
ESCAPE	leave insert mode, change to command mode

Making Changes

r	replace exactly 1 character (do not enter input mode)
R	replace by typing over
s	replace 1 character by insertion
C	replace from cursor to end of line by insertion
cc	replace entire current line by insertion
S	replace entire current line by insertion
c*move*	replace from cursor to *move* by insertion
~	change the case of a letter

Replacing a Pattern

`:s/pattern/replace/`	substitute, current line
`:lines/pattern/replace/`	substitute, specified line
`:line,lines/pattern/replace/`	substitute, specified range
`:%s/pattern/replace/`	substitute, all lines

Undoing or Repeating a Change

u	undo last command that modified the editing buffer
U	restore current line
.	repeat last command that modified the editing buffer

Controlling the Length of Lines

rRETURN	replace a character with a **newline**
J	join lines
`:set wm=`n	auto line break within n positions of right margin

Deleting

x	delete character at cursor
X	delete character to left of cursor
D	delete from cursor to end of line
dd	delete the entire current line
d_move_	delete from cursor to _move_
dG	delete from current line to end of editing buffer
d1G	delete from current line to start of editing buffer
:_line_**d**	delete specified line
:_line,line_**d**	delete specified range

Copying the Last Deletion

p	copy buffer; insert after/below cursor
P	copy buffer; insert before/above cursor
xp	transpose two characters
deep	transpose two words (start to the left of first word)
ddp	transpose two lines

Copying and Moving Lines

:_line_**co**_target_	copy specified line; insert below target
:_line,line_**co**_target_	copy specified range; insert below target
:_line_**m**_target_	move specified line; insert below target
:_line,line_**m**_target_	move specified range; insert below target

Executing Shell Commands

:!_command_	pause **vi**, execute specified shell command
:!!	pause **vi**, execute previous shell command
:sh	pause **vi**, start a shell
:!csh	pause **vi**, start a new C-Shell

Reading Data

:*liner file*	insert contents of *file* after specified line
:**r** *file*	insert contents of *file* after current line
:*liner* !*command*	insert output of *command* after specified line
:**r** !*command*	insert output of *command* after current line
:**r** !**look** *pattern*	insert words that begin with specified pattern

Using Shell Commands to Process Data

n!!*command*	execute *command* on *n* lines
!*move command*	execute *command* from cursor to *move*
!*move* **fmt**	format lines from cursor to *move*

Writing Data

:**w**	write data to original file
:**w** *file*	write data to specified file
:**w>** *file*	append data to specified file

Changing the File While Editing

:**e** *file*	edit the specified file
:**e**! *file*	edit the specified file, omit automatic check

Abbreviations

:**ab** *short long*	set *short* as an abbreviation for *long*
:**ab**	display current abbreviations
:**una** *short*	cancel abbreviation *short*

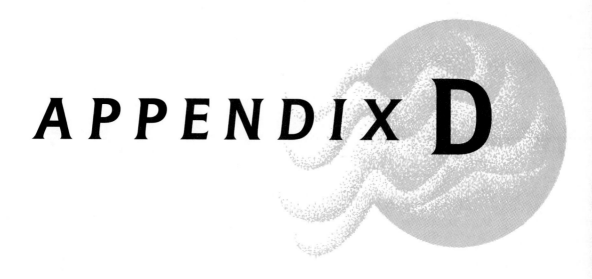

APPENDIX D

Summary of emacs Commands

This appendix contains a summary of all the **emacs** commands covered in this book. For more information, see Chapter 21 in which we discuss **emacs** in detail.

Names for Special Keys

C-	CTRL
M-	META
DEL	DELETE
ESC	ESCAPE
LFD	LINEFEED (CTRL-J)
RET	RETURN
SPC	SPACE
TAB	TAB

Status Characters Within the Mode Line

--	the buffer has not yet been modified
**	the buffer has been modified
%%	the buffer cannot be modified (Read-only mode)

Completion Keys

TAB	complete text in minibuffer as much as possible
SPC	complete text in minibuffer up to end of word
RET	same as **TAB**, then enter the command
?	create new window, display list of possible completions

Keys to Use While Typing

DEL	delete one character to the left of cursor
C-d	delete one character at the position of cursor
C-o	open a new line
C-_	undo the last change to the buffer
C-x u	same as **C-_**
C-q	insert the next character literally

Note: **C-_** is "CTRL underscore".

Commands for Controlling Windows

C-x 0	delete the selected window
C-x 1	delete all windows except selected window
C-x 2	split selected window vertically
C-x 3	split selected window horizontally
C-x o	move cursor to the next (other) window
C-x }	make selected window wider
C-x {	make selected window narrower
C-x ^	make selected window larger
M-x shrink-window	make selected window smaller

Note: In older versions of **emacs**, the command to split a window horizontally was C-x 5, not C-x 3.

Commands for Controlling Buffers

C-x C-b	display a list of all your buffers
C-x b	display a different buffer in selected window
C-x k	kill (delete) a buffer
C-x 4 b	display a different buffer in next window
C-x 4 C-o	same as C-x 4 b, but don't change selected window

Commands for Working With Files

C-x C-f	switch to buffer containing specified file
C-x C-v	replace buffer contents with specified file
C-x C-s	save a buffer to file
C-x C-w	save a buffer to specified file
C-x i	insert contents of a file into buffer
C-x 4 C-f	read contents of file into next window
C-x 4 f	same as C-x 4 C-f
C-x 4 r	same as C-x 4 C-f, read-only

Commands for Moving the Cursor

Backward	Forward	
C-b	C-f	a single character
LEFT	RIGHT	a single character
M-b	M-f	a word
C-p	C-n	a line
UP	DOWN	a line
M-a	M-e	a sentence
M-{	M-}	a paragraph

Beginning	End	
C-a	C-e	the current line
M-<	M->	the entire buffer

Prefix Argument Combinations

M-*number*	repeat command specified number of times
ESC *number*	repeat command specified number of times
C-u *number*	repeat command specified number of times
C-u	repeat command 4 times
C-u C-u	repeat command 16 times
C-u C-u C-u	repeat command 64 times
C-u C-u C-u C-u	repeat command 256 times

Commands to Move Throughout the Buffer

C-v	scroll down one screenful
M-v	scroll up one screenful
C-x >	scroll to the right
C-x <	scroll to the left
M-C-v	scroll down in the next window
M-<	jump to the beginning of buffer
M-<	jump to the end of buffer
C-l	re-display the screen, current line in middle

Commands to Use Line Numbers

M-x line-number-mode	display current line number
M-x goto-line	jump to line with specified number

Commands to Set Mark and Define a Region

C-SPC	set mark to current location of point
C-@	same as **C-SPC**
M-x set-mark-command	same as **C-SPC**
C-x C-x	interchange mark and point
M-@	set mark after next word (do not move point)
M-h	put region around paragraph
C-x h	put region around entire buffer

Commands that Act Upon the Region

C-w	kill (erase) all the characters
C-x C-l	convert the characters to lowercase
C-x C-u	convert the characters to uppercase
M-=	count the lines and characters
M-|	run a shell command, use characters as data

Commands to Delete Text

DEL	delete one character to the left of cursor
C-d	delete one character at the position of cursor
M-	delete spaces & tabs around point
M-SPC	delete spaces & tabs around point; leave one space
C-x C-o	delete blank lines around current line
M-^	join two lines (delete **newline** + surrounding spaces)

Commands to Kill Text

C-k	kill from cursor to end of line
M-d	kill a word
M-DEL	kill a word backwards
M-k	kill from cursor to end of sentence
C-x DEL	kill backwards to beginning of sentence
C-w	kill the region
M-z *char*	kill through next occurrence of *char*

Commands to Move and Kill by Word or Sentence

	Words			*Sentences*	
	Backward	**Forward**		**Backward**	**Forward**
Move:	**M-b**	**M-f**	Move:	**M-a**	**M-e**
Kill:	**M-DEL**	**M-D**	Kill:	**c-x DEL**	**M-k**

Commands to Yank Text

C-y	yank most recently-killed text
C-u C-y	same as **C-y**, cursor at beginning of new text
M-y	replace yanked text with earlier killed text
M-w	copy region to kill ring, without erasing
M-C-w	append next kill to newest kill ring entry
C-h v kill-ring	display the actual values in the kill ring

Commands for Correcting Common Typing Mistakes

DEL	delete one character to the left of cursor
M-DEL	kill the previous word
C-x DEL	kill to the beginning of sentence
M-- M-l	change the previous word to lowercase
M-- M-u	change the previous word to uppercase
M-- M-c	change previous word to lowercase, initial cap
C-t	transpose two adjacent characters
M-t	transpose two adjacent words
C-x C-t	transpose two consecutive lines

Note: **M--** is "Meta minus-sign".

Commands to Fill Text

`M-x auto-fill-mode`	turn on/off Auto Fill mode
`M-q`	fill a paragraph
`ESC 1 M-q`	fill+justify a paragraph
`M-x fill-region`	fill each paragraph in the region
`ESC 1 M-x fill-region`	fill+justify each paragraph in the region
`M-x fill-region-as-paragraph`	fill the region as one long paragraph
`ESC 1 M-x fill-region-as-paragraph`	fill+justify region as one long paragraph
`C-x f`	set the fill column value
`C-h v fill-column`	display the current fill column value

Search Commands

`C-s`	forward: incremental search
`C-s RET`	forward: non-incremental search
`C-s RET C-w`	forward: word search
`M-C-s`	forward: incremental search for regexp
`M-C-s RET`	forward: non-incremental search for regexp
`C-r`	backward: incremental search
`C-r RET`	backward: non-incremental search
`C-r RET C-w`	backward: word search
`M-C-r`	backward: incremental search for regexp
`M-C-r RET`	backward: non-incremental search for regexp

Keys to Use During a Search

`DEL`	erase the previous character
`RET`	terminate the search
`C-s`	search forwards for same pattern
`C-r`	search backwards for same pattern
`C-g`	(while search is in progress) stop current search
`C-g`	(while waiting for input) abort entire command
`C-w`	use the word after point
`C-y`	use the rest of the line after point
`M-y`	use the most recently killed (erased) text

Search Commands for Regular Expressions

M-C-s	forward: incremental search for regexp
M-C-s RET	forward: non-incremental search for regexp
M-C-r	backward: incremental search for regexp
M-C-r RET	backward: non-incremental search for regexp

Characters to Use With Regular Expressions

char	any regular character matches itself
.	match any single character except **newline**
*	match zero or more of the preceding characters
+	match one or more of the preceding characters
?	match exactly zero or one of the preceding characters
^	match the beginning of a line
$	match the end of a line
\<	match the beginning of a word
\>	match the end of a word
\b	match the beginning or end of a word
\B	match anywhere not at beginning or end of a word
\'	match the beginning of the buffer
\'{	match the end of buffer
char	quotes a special character
[ ]	match one of the enclosed characters
[^]	match any character that is not enclosed

Search and Replace Commands

M-%	query: search and replace
M-x query-replace-regexp	query: regexp search and replace
M-x replace-string	no query: search and replace
M-x replace-regexp	no query: regexp search and replace

Responses During a Search and Replace Command

?	display help summary
y	(yes) replace
n	(no) do not replace
q	quit immediately
SPC	same as **y**
DEL	same as **n**
RET	same as **q**
!	replace all remaining matches, no questions
. (period)	replace current match and then quit
, (comma)	replace but stay at current position
^ (circumflex)	move back to previous match
C-l	clear screen, re-display, and ask again
C-r	start recursive edit (use **M-C-c** to return)
C-w	delete matching pattern, start recursive edit

Minimum Keystrokes to Invoke Search and Replace Commands

M-x replace-string	M-x repl SPC s RET
M-x replace-regexp	**M-x repl SPC r RET**
M-x query-replace	M-x que RET
M-x query-replace-regexp	M-x que TAB SPC RET
M-x query-replace-regexp	M-x que SPC SPC SPC RET

Note: **M-x replace-string** is the same as **M-%**.

Running Shell Commands

M-!	run a shell command
M-|	run a shell command using the region as input
M-x shell	start a separate shell in its own buffer

Major Modes

asm-mode	assembly language programs
awk-mode	**awk** scripts
bibtex-mode	BibTeX files
c++-mode	C++ programs
c-mode	C programs
change-log-mode	change logs
command-history-mode	the command history
completion-list-mode	lists of possible completions
edit-abbrevs-mode	abbreviation definitions
emacs-lisp-mode	**emacs** Lisp programs
forms-mode	field-structured data using a form
fortran-mode	Fortran programs
fundamental-mode	general data, not specialized
hexl-mode	hexadecimal and ASCII data
indented-text-mode	text with indented paragraphs.
latex-mode	LaTeX-formatted files
lisp-interaction-mode	typing and evaluating Lisp forms
lisp-mode	non-**emacs** Lisp programs
mail-mode	outgoing mail messages
makefile-mode	makefiles
mh-letter-mode	messages with MH mail system
modula-2-mode	Modula-2 programs
nroff-mode	**nroff**- and **troff**-formatted text files
outline-mode	outlines with selective display
pascal-mode	Pascal programs
perl-mode	Perl scripts
picture-mode	text-based drawings
plain-tex-mode	TeX-formatted files
prolog-mode	Prolog programs
rmail-mode	mail messages with Rmail
scheme-mode	Scheme programs
scribe-mode	Scribe-formatted text files
sgml-mode	Standard Generalized Markup Language files
slitex-mode	SliTeX-formatted files
tcl-mode	tcl scripts
tex-mode	TeX- LaTeX- or SliTeX-formatted files
texinfo-mode	TeXinfo files
text-mode	regular human-readable text
vi-mode	makes **emacs** act like **vi** editor
wordstar-mode	makes **emacs** use Wordstar-like key bindings

Minor Modes

abbrev-mode	working with abbreviations
auto-fill-mode	automatic filling
auto-save-mode	automatic saving
binary-overwrite-mode	binary overwriting
compilation-minor-mode	compiling programs
delete-selection-mode	typed text replaces selection
double-mode	some keys differ if pressed twice
font-lock-mode	text is fontified as you type
hide-ifdef-mode	hides certain C code within **#ifdef**
indent-according-to-mode	indent appropriately for major mode
iso-accents-mode	display ISO accents
ledit-mode	editing text to be sent to Lisp
line-number-mode	show line numbers on mode line
outline-minor-mode	work with outlines
overwrite-mode	overwrite/insert text
pending-delete-mode	same as **delete-selection-mode**
resize-minibuffer-mode	dynamically resize minibuffer
tpu-edt-mode	TPU/edt emulation
toggle-read-only	buffer contents cannot be changed
transient-mark-mode	highlight region when defined
vip-mode	VIP emulation of **vi**
vt100-wide-mode	132/80 columns for VT-100 terminals

Commands to Set and Describe Modes

M-x *mode-name*	set the specified mode
C-h m	describe current major and minor modes
C-h f *mode-name*	describe the specified mode
C-h a mode	display summary of all modes

Help Commands

C-h ?	display a summary of all the Help options
C-h q	quit Help
C-h i	start the Info facility (documentation browser)
C-h t	start the **emacs** tutorial
C-h b	display a full list of all the key bindings
C-h c	you specify a key, **emacs** tells you what it does
C-h k	you specify a key, **emacs** describes its function
C-h w	you specify a function, **emacs** shows you its key
C-h a	show all the functions containing a specified word
C-h f	you specify a function, **emacs** describes it
C-h v	you specify a variable, **emacs** describes it
C-h m	describe the current major and minor modes

General Info Commands

?	display a summary of Info commands
h	start the Info tutorial
q	quit Info, remember current location
C-x k	quit Info, do not remember current location

Info Commands to Select a Node

n	jump to next node in the sequence
p	jump to previous node in the sequence
u	jump to the "up" node (the menu you came from)
l	jump to last node you looked at
m *selection*	pick a node from a menu
f	follow a cross-reference
i	look up topic in the index, then jump there
,	jump to next match from previous **i** command

Info Commands to Read a Node

SPC	go forwards one screenful
DEL	go backwards one screenful
b	go to the beginning of the node
.	same as **b**
C-l	re-display the current screen

Built-In Useful Programs

calendar	desk calendar and diary
dired	working with directories and files
gnus	reading and responding to Usenet articles
rmail	reading and disposing of mail
telnet	open a **telnet** session with a remote host

Games and Diversions

blackbox	black box puzzle: find objects inside a box
dissociated-press	scrambling text in an amusing way
doctor	the Eliza program: acts like a psychiatrist
dunnet	an adventure-style exploration game
gomoku	plays the game of Go Moku with you
hanoi	visual solution of Towers of Hanoi problem
life	game of Life (auto-reproducing patterns)
mpuz	multiplication puzzle: guess the digits
spook	generates words to get the Fed's attention
yow	display a quotation from Zippy the Pinhead

APPENDIX E

The ASCII Code

Character	Decimal	Hex	Octal	Binary	
`.`	0	00	000	0000 0000	(null)
Ctrl-A	1	01	001	0000 0001	
Ctrl-B	2	02	002	0000 0010	
Ctrl-C	3	03	003	0000 0011	
Ctrl-D	4	04	004	0000 0100	
Ctrl-E	5	05	005	0000 0101	
Ctrl-F	6	06	006	0000 0110	
Ctrl-G	7	07	007	0000 0111	(beep)
Ctrl-H	8	08	010	0000 1000	**backspace**
Ctrl-I	9	09	011	0000 1001	**tab**
Ctrl-J	10	0A	012	0000 1010	**newline**
Ctrl-K	11	0B	013	0000 1011	
Ctrl-L	12	0C	014	0000 1100	
Ctrl-M	13	0D	015	0000 1101	**return**
Ctrl-N	14	0E	016	0000 1110	
Ctrl-O	15	0F	017	0000 1111	
Ctrl-P	16	10	020	0001 0000	
Ctrl-Q	17	11	021	0001 0001	
Ctrl-R	18	12	022	0001 0010	
Ctrl-S	19	13	023	0001 0011	
Ctrl-T	20	14	024	0001 0100	
Ctrl-U	21	15	025	0001 0101	
Ctrl-V	22	16	026	0001 0110	
Ctrl-W	23	17	027	0001 0111	
Ctrl-X	24	18	030	0001 1000	
Ctrl-Y	25	19	031	0001 1001	
Ctrl-Z	26	1A	032	0001 1010	
Ctrl-[	27	1B	033	0001 1011	**escape**
Ctrl-	28	1C	034	0001 1100	
Ctrl-]	29	1D	035	0001 1101	
Ctrl-^	30	1E	036	0001 1110	
Ctrl-_	31	1F	037	0001 1111	

Character	Decimal	Hex	Octal	Binary	
(space)	32	20	040	0010 0000	**space**
!	33	21	041	0010 0001	(exclamation mark)
"	34	22	042	0010 0010	(double quote)
#	35	23	043	0010 0011	(number sign)
$	36	24	044	0010 0100	(dollar sign)
%	37	25	045	0010 0101	(percent)
&	38	26	046	0010 0110	(ampersand)
'	39	27	047	0010 0111	(single quote)
(	40	28	050	0010 1000	(left parenthesis)
)	41	29	051	0010 1001	(right parenthesis)
*	42	2A	052	0010 1010	(asterisk)
+	43	2B	053	0010 1011	(plus)
,	44	2C	054	0010 1100	(comma)
–	45	2D	055	0010 1101	(minus/hyphen)
.	46	2E	056	0010 1110	(period)
/	47	2F	057	0010 1111	(slash)
0	48	30	060	0011 0000	
1	49	31	061	0011 0001	
2	50	32	062	0011 0010	
3	51	33	063	0011 0011	
4	52	34	064	0011 0100	
5	53	35	065	0011 0101	
6	54	36	066	0011 0110	
7	55	37	067	0011 0111	
8	56	38	070	0011 1000	
9	57	39	071	0011 1001	
:	58	3A	072	0011 1010	(colon)
;	59	3B	073	0011 1011	(semicolon)
<	60	3C	074	0011 1100	(less than)
=	61	3D	075	0011 1101	(equals)
>	62	3E	076	0011 1110	(greater than)
?	63	3F	077	0011 1111	(question mark)

Character	Decimal	Hex	Octal	Binary	
@	64	40	100	0100 0000	(at sign)
A	65	41	101	0100 0001	
B	66	42	102	0100 0010	
C	67	43	103	0100 0011	
D	68	44	104	0100 0100	
E	69	45	105	0100 0101	
F	70	46	106	0100 0110	
G	71	47	107	0100 0111	
H	72	48	110	0100 1000	
I	73	49	111	0100 1001	
J	74	4A	112	0100 1010	
K	75	4B	113	0100 1011	
L	76	4C	114	0100 1100	
M	77	4D	115	0100 1101	
N	78	4E	116	0100 1110	
O	79	4F	117	0100 1111	
P	80	50	120	0101 0000	
Q	81	51	121	0101 0001	
R	82	52	122	0101 0010	
S	83	53	123	0101 0011	
T	84	54	124	0101 0100	
U	85	55	125	0101 0101	
V	86	56	126	0101 0110	
W	87	57	127	0101 0111	
X	88	58	130	0101 1000	
Y	89	59	131	0101 1001	
Z	90	5A	132	0101 1010	
[	91	5B	133	0101 1011	(left square bracket)
\	92	5C	134	0101 1100	(backslash)
]	93	5D	135	0101 1101	(right square bracket)
^	94	5E	136	0101 1110	(circumflex)
_	95	5F	137	0101 1111	(underscore)

Character	Decimal	Hex	Octal	Binary	
`	96	60	140	0110 0000	(backquote)
a	97	61	141	0110 0001	
b	98	62	142	0110 0010	
c	99	63	143	0110 0011	
d	100	64	144	0110 0100	
e	101	65	145	0110 0101	
f	102	66	146	0110 0110	
g	103	67	147	0110 0111	
h	104	68	150	0110 1000	
i	105	69	151	0110 1001	
j	106	6A	152	0110 1010	
k	107	6B	153	0110 1011	
l	108	6C	154	0110 1100	
m	109	6D	155	0110 1101	
n	110	6E	156	0110 1110	
o	111	6F	157	0110 1111	
p	112	70	160	0111 0000	
q	113	71	161	0111 0001	
r	114	72	162	0111 0010	
s	115	73	163	0111 0011	
t	116	74	164	0111 0100	
u	117	75	165	0111 0101	
v	118	76	166	0111 0110	
w	119	77	167	0111 0111	
x	120	78	170	0111 1000	
y	121	79	171	0111 1001	
z	122	7A	172	0111 1010	
{	123	7B	173	0111 1011	(left brace bracket)
|	124	7C	174	0111 1100	(vertical bar)
}	125	7D	175	0111 1101	(right brace bracket)
~	126	7E	176	0111 1110	(tilde)
	127	7F	177	0111 1111	**del**

APPENDIX F

List of Internet Top-Level Domains

This appendix shows the top-level domains that were current at the time we wrote the book. As new countries connect to the Internet, new domains will be created using the standard international country codes.

The only country that uses more than one international domain is Great Britain. They use **uk** (United Kingdom) as well as **gb**. (Of course, they also speak English with an accent.)

Old-Style Top-Level Domains

com	commercial organization
edu	educational institution
gov	government
int	international organization
mil	military
net	networking organization
org	non-commercial organization

International Top-Level Domains

aq	Antarctica
ar	Argentina
at	Austria
au	Australia
az	Azerbaijan
be	Belgium
bg	Bulgaria
br	Brazil
ca	Canada
ch	Switzerland ("Confoederatio Helvetica")
cl	Chile
cm	Cameroon
cn	China
co	Colombia
cr	Costa Rica
cs	Czechoslovakia
cy	Cyprus
cz	Czech Republic
de	Germany ("Deutschland")
dk	Denmark
dz	Algeria
ec	Ecuador
ee	Estonia
eg	Egypt

es	Spain ("España")
fi	Finland
fj	Fiji
fr	France
gb	Great Britain
gr	Greece
gu	Guam (US)
hk	Hong Kong
hr	Croatia
hu	Hungary
id	Indonesia
ie	Ireland
il	Israel
in	India
ir	Iran
is	Iceland
it	Italy
jp	Japan
kr	Korea (South)
kw	Kuwait
lb	Lebanon
li	Liechtenstein
lk	Sri Lanka
lt	Lithuania
lu	Luxembourg
lv	Latvia
ma	Morocco
md	Moldavia
mo	Macao
mx	Mexico
my	Malaysia
ni	Nicaragua
nl	Netherlands

no	Norway
nz	New Zealand
pa	Panama
pe	Peru
ph	Philippines
pl	Poland
pr	Puerto Rico
pt	Portugal
re	Reunion (France)
ro	Romania
ru	Russian Federation
se	Sweden
sg	Singapore
si	Slovenia
sj	Svalbard & Jan Mayen Islands
sk	Slovakia (Slovak Republic)
su	Soviet Union
th	Thailand
tn	Tunisia
tr	Turkey
tw	Taiwan
ua	Ukraine
uk	United Kingdom (England, Scotland, Wales, Northern Ireland)
us	United States
uy	Uruguay
ve	Venezuela
yu	Yugoslavia
za	South Africa

Glossary

absolute pathname: A pathname in which the full name of every directory is specified, from the root directory to the actual file. (23)

account: An arrangement that allows someone to use a Unix system. An account keeps track of resources, such as disk space. Before you can use a Unix system, your system manager must set up an account for you and give you a userid. (4)

address: A formal description of the destination of a mail message. (14)

alias: 1. In the C-Shell or Korn shell, an alternate name given to a command or a list of commands. (11, 12) 2. In the **mail** program, a name given to a list of addresses. (15)

arguments: When you type a command, the items that follow the name of the command. The arguments for a commands are the options and the parameters. (9)

ASCII code: A standardized system in which character data is represented as bits. Each character is stored in one byte (8 bits). Within a byte, the leftmost bit is ignored. The other 7 bits form a pattern of 0s and 1s that represents the particular character. The ASCII code contains 128 distinct bit patterns. The full ASCII code is shown in Appendix E. (17)

ASCII file: A file that contains data in the form of characters. Same as **text file. (22)**

auto save file: Within **emacs**, a backup file that is maintained automatically. (21)

backbone: A high-speed link connecting together parts of a network. (3)

background: Describes a process for which the shell does not wait to complete before displaying the next shell prompt. We refer to such processes as being "in the background". (25)

bang path: An address used with UUCP consisting of a list of computer names and a userid, the names being separated by an ! character. For example, **tinker!evers!chance**. (The term "bang" is slang for the ! character.)

banner page: When printing with System V Unix commands, an extra page at the beginning of the printout that contains identification information. (19)

Bash: An upwards-compatible replacement for the Bourne shell developed by Free Software Foundation as part of the GNU project. (10)

binary file: A file that contains data that makes sense only when read by a program. Binary files use a full 8 bits per byte to store data. Text files contain characters that use only 7 bits per byte. Compare to **text file**. (22)

bind: Within **emacs**, to associate a particular key combination with a command. (21)

bit: The basic element of data storage. A bit can hold a single element which is either in one state or another. The custom is to speak of a bit as containing either a **0** or a **1**. A bit that contains a **0** is said to be "off". A bit that contains a **1** is said to be "on". The term **bit** is a contraction of "binary digit". (22)

body: The main part of a mail message, the text. (15)

Bourne shell: The original Unix shell, named after its creator Steven Bourne. The Bourne shell has since been updated although it lacks the advanced features of other shells. Many people consider the Bourne shell to be the best shell for executing scripts. However, as a primary interface, most users choose a shell that provides a more modern command processor. (10)

Bourne shell family: Collective name for the Bourne shell, Korn shell, Bash and the Zsh. (10)

BSD: A multitasking, multiuser operating system developed at the University of California at Berkeley, originally based on UNIX. The name stands for "Berkeley Software Distribution". (2)

buffer: Within **emacs**, a work area, separate from other work areas, in which **emacs** stores the output associated with a specific task. (21)

built-in editor: In the Korn shell, a facility that lets you recall, edit, and re-execute commands from the history file. (12)

byte: A unit of data storage, a collection of 8 consecutive bits. One byte can hold a single character. (22)

Chapter references are indicated by the numbers in parentheses.

C: A programming language, originally developed by Ken Thompson and Dennis Ritchie. C has since been extended and standardized and is used throughout the world. (10)

C++: A programming language, developed by Bjarne Stroustrup. C++ is upwards-compatible with C and incorporates facilities for object-oriented programming. The name C++ is pronounced "see-plus-plus". (10)

case insensitive: Describes a program, system, or operation that does not distinguish between upper- and lowercase letters. (21)

case sensitive: Describes a program, system, or operation that distinguishes between upper- and lowercase letters. (4, 21)

child directory: A directory that lies within another directory. All directories, except the root directory, can be considered to be child directories. The directory that contains the child directory is called the parent directory. Same as subdirectory. (22)

character terminal: A terminal that displays only characters: letters, numbers, punctuation and so on. (3)

click: To press a button on a pointing device (usually a mouse). (5)

client: A program that requests a resource from a server. (3)

client/server relationship: Describes the connection between a client (resource requester) and a server (resource provider). (3)

command line: 1. When you enter a Unix command, the entire line that you type before you press the RETURN key. (9) 2. When using the `vi` editor, the bottom line of the screen, upon which certain commands are echoed as they are typed. (20)

command mode: Within the `vi` editor, when the characters you type are interpreted as commands. Compare to **input mode**. (20)

command processor: A program that reads and interprets commands that you enter at your terminal. The shell is a command processor. (10)

command substitution: A feature of the shell in which the output of one command is inserted into another command which is then executed. (17)

command syntax: The formal description of how a command must be entered. (9)

completion: Within **emacs**, a service in which you can ask **emacs** to guess what you are about to type and then complete the typing for you. (21)

console: The terminal (screen, keyboard, possibly a mouse) that is built into a host computer. (3)

current window: Within **emacs**, the window in which you are currently working; the window that contains the cursor. Synonym for **selected window**. (21)

CPU: A synonym for processor, the main component of a computer. Originally, this term was an acronym standing for "Central Processing Unit". In Unix, the term simply refers to the processor. For example, the amount of processor time used by a program is called CPU time. (13)

cracker: A person who tries to break into computer systems for fun. (4)

C-Shell: A shell, developed by Bill Joy as the Berkeley Unix alternative to the Bourne shell. The programming language offered by this shell resembles the C language, hence the name C-Shell. The C-Shell is the default shell on many Unix systems, especially those derived from Berkeley Unix. The name C-Shell is pronounced "see-shell". (10)

C-Shell Family: Collective name for the C-Shell and the Tcsh. (10)

current directory: The designation for the directory that will be used, by default, when entering Unix commands. The current directory is set by using the **cd** (change directory) command and displayed by using the **pwd** (print working directory) command. Synonym for **working directory**. (23)

current message: Within the **mail** program, the default message upon which a command will act. Usually the last message that was read. (15)

Chapter references are indicated by the numbers in parentheses.

cursor: A special character—often an underscore that blinks—that marks your current position on the screen of your terminal. (3)

daemon: A program that executes in the background, usually to provide a service of general interest. (19)

default: An assumed value that will be used when a particular item is not specified. (9)

delete: Within **emacs**, to erase characters which are not saved. When you **kill** characters, **emacs** does save them. (21)

delete command: Within **emacs**, a command that erases characters that are not saved. (21)

demodulation: The conversion of telephone signals to computer signals. (3)

device file: Synonym for special file. (22)

directory: A type of file that, conceptually, contains other files, some of which might be other directories. Actually, a directory does not contain actual files, it contains the information that Unix needs to access the files. One of the three types of Unix files. Compare to **ordinary file**, **special file**. (22, 23)

disabled command: Within **emacs**, a command that might confuse a beginner and, as such, cannot be executed until you explicitly confirm your intention. (21)

display manager: An X Window program that handles the login procedure, automatically starting X Window and a window manager. (5)

display server: A program that takes care of the details of interfacing with a graphical user interface on behalf of other programs. (5)

display: In the X Window system, the screen, keyboard and pointing device (usually a mouse) associated with a particular terminal. (5)

domain: The part of a standard Internet address that indicates the name of the complete computer. For example, in the address **harley@nipper.ucsb.edu**, the domain is **nipper.ucsb.edu** (14)

dotfile: A file whose name begins with a **.** (period) character. When listing file names with the **ls** command, dotfiles are not listed unless requested specifically. Same as **hidden file**. (23)

doubleclick: To press a button on a pointing device (usually a mouse) twice in rapid succession. (5)

drag: To use a pointing device (usually a mouse) to move a graphical object on the screen of your terminal. You point to the object, hold down a button, move the pointing device to indicate the new location, and then release the button. (5)

dragon: A type of daemon that is not invoked explicitly, but is always there, waiting in the background to perform some task. (19)

echo: To display a character on the screen that corresponds to a key pressed by a user. For example, when you press the A key, Unix echoes the letter "A". (3)

echo area: Within **emacs**, the bottom line of the screen, used by **emacs** to echo the commands that you type and to display error messages. The echo area shares this line of the screen with the **minibuffer**. (21)

editing buffer: A working area, used by the **vi** editor, to hold the data you are editing. (20)

editor: A program used to create and modify text files. (20, 21)

emacs: An editor, originally developed by Richard Stallman, that offers a full working environment that is highly customable. (21)

email: Same as **mail**. The term **email** is a contraction of "electronic mail". (14)

emulate: To run a program that causes a computer to act like a different device. For example, when you use a PC to connect to a Unix host computer, you run a program on the PC that emulates a terminal. (3)

entry: The documentation for a single topic within the online manual. Same as **page**. (8)

Chapter references are indicated by the numbers in parentheses.

environment: A collection of information that is passed to a program when it is started by the shell. (12)

environment file: Within the Korn shell, a file that contains initialization commands that are executed each time a new copy of the shell is started. (12)

environment variable: 1. Within the C-Shell, a variable that is accessible to any program. Same as global variable. (12) 2. Within the Korn shell, such a variable is called a shell variable. (12)

escape character: A character, that when read by a program, tells the program that the data that follows is to be treated in a special way. (15)

evaluate: Within **emacs**, the processing of a Lisp expression. (21)

event: Within the shell, a command that has been entered. (11)

event number: Within the shell, a number that identifies an event (a command that has been entered). (11)

executable program: A program that, having been translated into machine language and linked, is ready to be executed. (22)

execute: To follow the instructions contained in a program. Same as **run**. (2)

execute permission: A type of file permission that allows the execution of an ordinary file or the searching of a directory. (24)

export (a variable): To make a variable and its value available to a program that is started by the shell. (12)

expression: Within **emacs**, a Lisp entity that can be processed. (21)

extension: The last part of a file name that follows a **.** (period) character. For example, the file name **foobar.c** has an extension of **.c**. (24)

file: Any source of input or target of output. There are three types of files: ordinary files, directories and special files. (22, 24)

file mode: A three-number value, for example **755**, that describes three sets of file permissions, read, write and execute permissions. The first number describes the permissions for the userid that owns the file. The second number describes the permissions for the userid's group. The third number describes the permissions for everybody else. (24)

file permission: One of three types of authorizations (read, write and execute) that specifies how a file may be accessed. (24)

filename generation: The term used with the Bourne shell, Korn shell and Zsh as a synonym for filename substitution. (23)

filename substitution: Within the C-Shell, replacing a pattern that is part of a command by all the file names that match the pattern. Within the pattern, certain characters named wildcards have special meanings. See also **globbing**, **wildcard**. (23)

file server: A program, sometimes a computer, that provides access to files over a network. (3)

fill: Within **emacs**, to reformat text so as to make line widths as uniform as possible. (21)

filters: Any program that reads data from the standard input and writes data to the standard output. (17)

finger: To display information about a userid by entering the **finger** command. (13)

focus: When using a graphical user interface, describes which window is active by being logically connected to the keyboard of your terminal. Once you focus on a window, whatever you type on the keyboard is used as input for the program running in that window. (5)

foreground: Describes a process for which the shell is waiting to complete before displaying the next shell prompt. We refer to such processes as being "in the foreground". (25)

function: Within **emacs**, a Lisp entity that can be executed and that returns a result. (21)

Chapter references are indicated by the numbers in parentheses.

gateway: A computer that acts as a link between programs running on two different networks. (3)

GECOS field: Part of each entry in the password file. For each userid, the GECOS field contains the name and other information relating to the person using that userid. (13)

gigabyte: A unit of storage measurement, 2^{30} bytes. One gigabyte is 1,073,741,824 bytes. See also **kilobyte**, **megabyte**. (23)

global variable: 1. A variable whose value is available to the shell and any programs that you may run. (6) 2. Within the C-Shell, a global variable is called an **environment variable** (11) 3. Within the Korn shell, a global variable is called a **shell variable**. (12)

globbing: Within a shell, the act of performing filename substitution. We say that a shell globs when it replaces a pattern in a command by all the file names that match the pattern. See also **filename substitution**, **wildcard**. (23)

GNU: A project of the Free Software Foundation dedicated to developing an entire Unix system independent of commercial software. The name GNU is a recursive acronym standing for "GNU's not Unix". (10, 21)

graphical user interface: A system in which the user interacts with the host computer by using a pointing device (usually a mouse) to manipulate windows, icons, menus and other graphical elements. (5)

graphics terminal: A terminal that displays, not only characters, but anything that can be drawn on the screen using small dots. (3)

groupid: The name of a group of userids. The groupid is used to allocate file permissions. (24)

GUI: Abbreviation for graphical user interface. (5)

hack: To put forth a massive amount of nerd-like effort, usually by programming. (4)

hacker: A person who hacks. (4)

hard link: Synonym for **link**. (24)

hardware: The physical components of a computer: keyboard, display, mouse, disk, processor, memory, and so on. (2)

header: A number of lines at the beginning of a mail message that contain descriptive information. (15)

hidden file: A file whose name begins with a **.** (period) character. When listing file names with the **ls** command, dotfiles are not listed unless requested specifically. Same as **dotfile**. (23)

history file: Within the Korn shell, a list of commands that have been entered. (12)

history list: Within the C-Shell, a list of commands that have been entered. (11)

history substitution: Within the shell, a facility that lets you edit and re-enter a previous command without having to retype it. (11)

home directory: The directory that is designated to hold the files for a particular userid. Whenever you log in, your current directory is automatically set to be your home directory. (22)

hook: Within **emacs**, a variable whose value is a function that is evaluated automatically whenever a certain condition arises. (21)

hop: A single link in a chain of computers through which data must pass in order to reach a final destination. For example, say that a mail message must pass through three computers, **tinker** to **evers** to **chance**. We say that the mail took two hops to reach its destination. Similarly, we might say that **chance** is two hops away from **tinker**. (14)

host: The computer that runs Unix. Users log in to the host to initiate a Unix work session. (3)

icon: When using a graphical user interface, a small picture that represents a window. (5)

iconize: To change an open window into an icon. (5)

Chapter references are indicated by the numbers in parentheses.

incremental search: Within `emacs`, a search operation that starts as soon as you type the first character of the search pattern, and that is modified as you type each subsequent character. (21)

index node: In the Unix file system, a structure that holds the basic information about a file. Same as **inode** (24)

index number: In the Unix file system, a number that identifies a particular index node (inode) within the table of index nodes. Same as **inumber**.

inode: In the Unix file system, a structure that holds the basic information about a file. Same as **index node.** (24)

input mode: Within the `vi` editor, when the characters you type are inserted into the editing buffer. Compare to command mode. (20)

Internet: The global wide area network that uses the IP protocol to communicate. The Internet connects countless computers around the world and provides many important services such as mail, file transfer and remote login. (3,14)

Internet address: See **standard Internet address**. (14)

interpret: The action of an interpreter as it reads and executes a command. (11, 12)

interpreter: A program that reads and executes a list of commands called a script. (11, 12)

inumber: In the Unix file system, a number that identifies a particular index node (inode) within the table of index nodes. Same as **index number**.

IP: One of the TCP/IP protocols. IP is used to move packets of raw data from one computer to another. IP is the basic protocol of the Internet. The name IP stands for "Internet Protocol". (14)

job: A synonym for **process**: a program that is executing. (25)

job control: A facility, supported by Unix and implemented by the shell, that allows you to suspend and restart processes. (25)

job number: 1. When printing a file, the number designated to identify the print job. (19) 2. When entering a background command or suspending a foreground command, a number that is created to identify the job. Job numbers start from **1** and count up. (25)

key: A password, used by the **crypt** program to encode data. (17)

key binding: Within **emacs**, the connection between a particular key combination and the command that it invokes. (21)

kill: 1. Within **emacs**, to erase characters which are automatically saved. When you **delete** characters, **emacs** does not save them. (21) 2. To terminate a process. (25)

kill command: Within **emacs**, a command that erases characters that are automatically saved. (21)

kill ring: Within **emacs**, a series of storage areas in which **emacs** saves characters that have been killed. (21)

kill ring entry: Within **emacs**, a specific storage area within a kill ring. A kill ring entry stores the characters that were erased by a kill command. (21)

kilobyte: A unit of storage measurement, 2^{10} bytes. One kilobyte is 1,024 bytes. See also **gigabyte**, **megabyte**. (23)

Korn shell: An upwards-compatible replacement for the Bourne shell, developed by David Korn. The Korn shell is the default shell on many Unix systems, especially those derived from System V. (10)

LAN: Abbreviation for local area network. (3)

line editor: An editor which numbers lines of text and which uses commands based on these numbers. Same as **line-oriented editor**. Compare to **screen editor**. (20)

line-oriented editor: Same as line editor. (20)

link: Within the Unix file system, the connection between a file name and its inode. Same as **hard link**. See **inode**, **symbolic link**. (24)

Chapter references are indicated by the numbers in parentheses.

Lisp: The computer language in which **emacs** is written, and which you can use to customize the **emacs** environment. (21)

local area network: A network in which the computers are connected directly by some type of cable. (3)

log in: To initiate a Unix work session. (4)

log out: To terminate a Unix work session. (4)

login: Describes the process of logging in. (4)

login shell: The shell that Unix starts automatically when you log in. (10)

logout: Describes the process of logging out. (4)

lowercase: Describes small letters, "a" to "z". (4)

macro: Within **vi**, a one-character abbreviation for a command. (20)

major mode: Within **emacs**, an environment in which a number of aspects of **emacs'** operation are customized to facilitate a particular type of work. (21)

mail: 1. A system in which messages, usually stored as files of text, are sent and received. For example, "You can use mail to send a message to someone else." 2. To send or receive such a message. For example, "Mail me the document that you want me to read." 3. The message itself. For example, "When I logged in there was mail waiting for me." (14, 15)

mail server: A computer that acts as a way station for electronic mail. (3)

main menu: When using X Window, the menu that appears when you move to an empty area of the screen and press a particular button on your pointing device. The main menu is used to start certain programs and to control your X Window session. (5)

manual: Same as the online manual. When Unix people refer to "the manual", they always mean the online manual. (8)

mark: Within **emacs**, a location that you can set, that forms one boundary of the region (the other boundary being point). (21)

mask: Within the Unix file system, a three-number value that indicates which files' permissions should be assigned by default to newly created files. (24)

maximize: To expand a window to its largest possible size. (5)

megabyte: A unit of storage measurement, 2^{20} bytes. One megabyte is 1,048,576 bytes. See also **kilobyte**, **gigabyte**. (23)

menu: A list of items from which you can make a selection. (5)

message of the day: A message, created by the system manager, that is displayed whenever someone logs in. (4)

message list: Within the **mail** program, the specification of one or more message numbers. (15)

minibuffer: Within **emacs**, the bottom line of the screen, used by **emacs** to ask you for information and to read your reply. The minibuffer shares this line of the screen with the **echo area**. (21)

minimize: Same as **iconize**. (5)

minor mode: Within **emacs**, an optional feature that can be turned on or off. (21)

mode: 1. Within **emacs**, either a **major mode** or **minor mode**. 2. Synonym for **file mode**. (24)

mode line: Within **emacs**, the line at the bottom of each window in which **emacs** displays information about the buffer that is being displayed in that window. (21)

modem: A device—modulator/demodulator—that provides an interface between a computer and a telephone line. (3)

modulation: The conversion of computer signals to telephone signals. (3)

Chapter references are indicated by the numbers in parentheses.

multitasking: Describes an operating system that can execute more than one program at the same time. (2)

multiuser: Describes an operating system that can support more than one user at the same time. (2)

numeric argument: Synonym for **prefix argument**.

network: Two or more computers connected together in order to facilitate communication and to share resources. (3)

newline   The character, used in textual data, to indicate the end of a line. The **newline** character is **^J**.

news: Announcements of local interest, displayed by using the **news** or **msgs** commands. (7)

news server: A computer that provides users on a network with access to the Usenet news. (3)

next window: Within **emacs**, the window to which **emacs** moves as you cycle from the current window to another. (21)

node: Within the **emacs** Info facility, a section that contains information about one specific topic.

one or more: Indicates that you must use at least one of something. For example, the syntax for a command might allow you to specify one or more file names. This means that you can specify more than one name, but you must use at least one name. Compare to **zero or more**. (9)

online manual: Information, available to all users at all times, that contains documentation about Unix commands and important system facilities. The online manual is divided into sections. Each section contains many entries (also called pages), each of which documents a single topic. To access the online manual, use the **man** command. With X Window, use the **xman** command. Users are encouraged to check the online manual before asking for help. (See **RTFM**.) (8)

operating system: A complex master control program whose principal function is to make efficient use of the hardware. The operating system acts as the primary interface to the hardware for both users and programs. (2)

options: An argument for a command, almost always prefaced with a – character, that specifies how you want the command to execute. For example, you might enter the command `ls -l`. This is the `ls` command with the `-l` option. In conversation, the – character is pronounced "minus" even though it has nothing to do with arithmetic. If you were to talk about the last example, you would say that you used the `ls` command with the "minus L" option. (9)

ordinary file: A file that contains data to be accessed by a person or a program. An ordinary file is what most people mean when they use the word "file". One of the three types of Unix files. Compare to **directory, special file**. (22)

page: The documentation for a single topic within the online manual. By tradition, the documentation for each topic is called a page even though it might be large enough to fill many printed pages. Same as **entry**. (8)

pager: A program that displays a text file or data, one screenful at a time. (18)

paragraph: Within **vi**, a section of text that starts and ends in a blank line. (20)

parameter: An argument for a command that is used to pass information to the program that will be executed. For example, a parameter might specify the name of a file. (9)

parent directory: A directory that contains another directory. The contained directory is called a subdirectory or child directory. (22)

parse: The action of the shell as it analyzes the components of a command. (11, 12)

password: A secret pattern of characters that must be typed as part of the login process to ensure that the user has proper authorization to use a particular userid. (4)

Chapter references are indicated by the numbers in parentheses.

password file: A file, maintained by Unix, that contains information about all the userids in the system. Each entry in this file contains information about one userid. On some systems, the password file also contains the passwords (encoded, of course). On other systems, the passwords are kept separately in a shadow file. (13)

pathname: A description of a sequence of subdirectories. (23)

pathname expansion: The term used with Bash as a synonym for filename substitution. (23)

permission: Same as file permission. (24)

ping: To display information about the status of an Internet computer by entering the `ping` command. (13)

pipe: To pass data from one program to another so as to form a pipeline. (16)

pipeline: An arrangement in which two or more programs process data in sequence, the output of one program becoming the input to the next program. (16)

point: Within `emacs`, the location between the position of the cursor and the character to its left. The place within the buffer at which most `emacs` commands take effect. Point forms one boundary of the region (the other boundary being **mark**). (21)

point and click: To use a pointing device (usually a mouse) to select a graphical object by moving to it and then clicking a button. (5)

pointing device: An instrument (usually a mouse) used to manipulate the elements of a graphical user interface. (5)

pop-up: Describes a menu that appears from no apparent location as a result of some action you have taken. (5)

port: The part of the host computer to which a terminal is connected. (6)

prefix argument: Within **emacs**, a key combination typed before a command, usually meaning that **emacs** should execute the command a specified numbers of times. Same as **numeric argument**. (21)

print: 1. To display information on the terminal. For example, the command to display the name of your working (current) directory is named **pwd**, "print working directory". (6) 2. To print data on paper. (19)

print job: Refers to a file that is printing or is waiting to be printed. (19)

print server: A program that coordinates the printing of data using various printers. (3)

process: A program that is executing. Same as **job**. (25)

processid: A unique number that identifies a process. (25)

program: A list of instructions that, when carried out by a computer, performs a task. (2)

protocol: A set of rules that allow different computers and programs to communicate with one another. (14)

pull-down: Describes a menu which appears below a word once you use a pointing device (usually a mouse) to click on the word. (5)

queue: When printing, describes the list of files waiting to print. (19)

read permission: A type of file permission that allows the reading of an ordinary file or directory. (24)

real time: Describes a program or system that reacts instantly. (3)

recursive: For Unix file commands, describes options that process an entire subtree of directories. (23)

recursive editing: Within **emacs**, a facility that allows you to stop a search and replace operation temporarily in order to do some editing. (21)

Chapter references are indicated by the numbers in parentheses.

redirect: To send the output of a program to a designated destination. (16)

region: Within **emacs**, an area enclosed by the locations of mark and point, on which you can perform an operation. (21)

regular expression: A compact way of specifying a general pattern of characters. (17, 21)

regular file: Synonym for **ordinary file**. (22)

relative pathname: A pathname that is interpreted as starting from the current directory. (23)

remove: To erase a file by deleting its link. (24)

request id: When printing with System V Unix commands, a job number that identifies the print request. (19)

root: The userid used by the system manager to become superuser. (4)

root directory: The main directory of the Unix file system. The root directory is, directly or indirectly, the parent directory of all the other directories. (22)

root menu: Same as main menu. (5)

routers: A special-purpose computer that directs data from one network to another. (14)

run: To follow the instructions contained in a program. Same as **execute**. (2)

screen editor: An editor that allows you to enter and display data anywhere on the screen. Commands are not oriented toward line numbers. Compare to **line editor**. (20)

script: A list of commands to be executed by an interpreter. (11, 12)

scroll: To move lines on the screen of a terminal, usually up or down, to make room for new lines. (6, 21)

search path: Names of the directories in which the shell looks to find a program. (11, 12)

selected window: Within **emacs**, the window in which you are currently working; the window that contains the cursor. Same as **current window**. (21)

sentence: Within **vi**, a string of characters—ending in a period, comma, question mark or exclamation mark—and followed by at least two **space** characters or a **newline** character. (20)

server: A program, sometimes a computer, that offers a resource, often over a network. A program that requests such a service is called a client. (3)

set: Within the Korn shell, to turn on a **shell option**.

shadow file: A file that contains passwords (encoded of course) as well as data relating to passwords, such as an expiration date. (13)

shell: A program that provides the primary interface to Unix by acting as a command processor and by interpreting scripts of commands. (10)

shell escape character: Within a program, the **!** character when used to indicate that the following command should be sent to the shell to be executed. (16)

shell option: 1. Within the Korn shell, a variable that acts as an off/on switch. (12) 2. Within the C-Shell, such a variable is called a **shell variable**. (11)

shell prompt: One or more characters displayed by the shell to indicate that it is ready to accept a new command. (4, 11, 12)

shell script: A list of commands that can be executed by a shell. (11, 12)

shell variable: 1. Within the C-Shell, a variable that represents a value of some type within the shell. There are two types of shell variables: those that act as off/on switches and those that store a string of characters. (11) 2. Within the Korn Shell, the same as a **global variable**. (12)

signal: To send a control code to a program by pressing a special key. (6)

Chapter references are indicated by the numbers in parentheses.

smiley: Several consecutive characters that, when viewed sideways, look like a small face. The basic smiley is **:-)** (Turn your head sideways to the left to see the face). A smiley is used in electronic communication to indicate a sense of irony or frivolity. The smiley replaces the charming smile that you would use in person to avoid the wrath of someone to whom you have just said something obnoxious or argumentative. (13)

smiley face: Same as **smiley**. (13)

snail mail: Slang for regular postal office mail. In Unix, the unqualified term "mail" always refers to electronic mail. (14)

soft link: Synonym for **symbolic link**. (24)

software: Computer programs of all types. (2)

source: A program that has been written in a computer language. A synonym for **source program**. Before a source program can be executed it must be translated into machine language. (22)

source program: A program that has been written in a computer language. Before a source program can be executed it must be translated into machine language. Informally, a source program is referred to simply as "source". (22)

special file: A file that represents a physical device. One of the three types of Unix files. Compare to **directory**, **ordinary file**. (22)

spool file: A file that holds data for further processing, often for printing. (19)

spool: To hold a file for further processing, such as printing, and to perform such processing at a convenient time. The name "spool" comes from an old acronym meaning "simultaneous peripheral operations offline". (19)

spool file: A temporary file that holds data for further processing at a convenient time, usually for printing. (19)

standard input: The technical designation for the default source of input for Unix programs. (16)

standard output: The technical designation for the default target of output for Unix programs. (16)

standard Internet address: An address in the form *userid@domain*. For example, `harley@nipper.ucsb.edu`. In this address, the userid is `harley`, the domain is `nipper.ucsb.edu` (14)

subdirectory: A directory that lies within another directory. All directories, except the root directory, can be considered to be child directories. The directory that contains the child directory is called the parent directory. Same as **child directory**. (22)

sub-domain: In a standard Internet address, one part of the domain. For example, in the address `harley@nipper.ucsb.edu` there are three sub-domains, `nipper`, `ucsb` and `edu` (14)

superuser: A user, usually the system manager, who has logged in using the `root` userid (which affords special privileges). (4)

suspend: To pause a program by pressing the `susp` key (usually `^Z`). (25)

symbolic link: Within the Unix file system, a special type of link that is actually the pathname of another file. A symbolic link is sometimes called a **soft link** to distinguish it from a regular link. See **link**. (24)

syntax: Informally, a synonym for **command syntax**: the formal description of how a command must be entered. (9)

system administrator: Same as system manager. (4)

system mailbox: The file in which your mail is stored until you read it. (15)

system manager: The person who administers and manages a Unix system. Same as **system administrator**. (4)

TCP: One of the TCP/IP protocols. TCP is used to coordinate the moving of data from one computer to another by breaking the data into packets. TCP stands for "transmission control protocol". (14)

Chapter references are indicated by the numbers in parentheses.

TCP/IP: A collection of more than 100 different protocols used to connect computers within a network and to transmit data. TCP/IP is widely used, especially within the Internet. (14)

Tcsh: An upwards-compatible replacement for the C-Shell. The name Tcsh is pronounced "tee-see-shell". (10)

tee: A program, used within a pipeline, to save data in a specified file while, at the same time, sending the data to another program. (16)

teletype: An electro-mechanical communications device that printed its output on paper. Teletypes are the (spiritual) ancestors of modern Unix terminals. (6)

termcap database: A collection of technical descriptions of all the different types of terminals. (6)

terminal: The hardware used by the someone to access a Unix system. A terminal has a keyboard, screen and, possibly, a mouse. (3)

terminal server: A special computer that acts as a switch, connecting terminals to host computers. (3)

text: Data that consists of ASCII characters: letters, numbers, punctuation, and so on. (22, 21)

text editor: Synonym for **editor**. (20,21)

text file: A file that contains characters and can be displayed or printed. Text files use only 7 bits per byte because each character, as defined by the ASCII code, uses only 7 of the 8 bits. Same as **ASCII file**. Compare to **binary file**. (22)

tilde escape: Within the **mail** program, a command, prefaced by a ~ (tilde) character, that can be issued while you are typing a message. (15)

top-level domain: In a standard Internet address, the most general sub-domain. The top-level domain is the last sub-domain in the address. For example, in the address **harley@nipper.ucsb.edu** the top-level domain is **edu**. (14)

trap: For a program that is executing, to notice and react to a specific signal that otherwise might abort or affect the program. (6)

TTY: A terminal. (6)

Unix: 1. Any operating system that meets generally accepted "Unix-like" standards with respect to providing user and programming services. Modern Unix operating systems are both multitasking and multiuser and are usually derived, at least in spirit, from UNIX, BSD or both. 2. Describes a worldwide culture, based on the Unix operating systems, involving interfaces, shells, programs, languages, conventions and standards. (2)

UNIX: The specific family of operating system products and associated software originally developed by AT&T. (2)

unset: Within the Korn shell, to turn off a **shell option**.

uppercase: describes capital letters, "A" to "Z". (4)

user: A person who uses a Unix system in some way. (4)

userid: The name, registered with a Unix system, that identifies an account. A userid usually represents a particular user. The word userid is pronounced "user-eye-dee". (4)

UUCP: A Unix-based networking system that allows any Unix computer to exchange files with any other Unix computer. (14)

UUCP address: An address, in the form of a bang path, used to send mail over the UUCP network. (14)

UUCP network: Same as **UUCP**. (14)

UUCP MAPPING PROJECT: A group that regularly publishes updated connection maps for the UUCP network. (14)

variable: A quantity, known by a name, that represents a value. (6, 11, 12, 21).

vi: A screen-oriented editor, part of every Unix system. (20)

Chapter references are indicated by the numbers in parentheses.

view mode: In **emacs**, a situation in which you can read but not change a file. (21)

visit: Within **emacs**, to copy the contents of a file into a buffer. (21)

WAN: Abbreviation for Wide Area Network. (3)

whitespace: Consecutive space and tab characters that separate two items. (9)

wide area network: A network connecting local area networks. (3)

wildcard: A character that has a special meaning when interpreted as part of a filename substitution pattern. See also **filename substitution, globbing**. (23)

window: 1. A bounded region of the screen, manipulated by a graphical user interface. (5) 2. Within **emacs**, an area of the screen that is used to display the contents of a buffer. (21)

window manager: A program that, under the auspices of a graphical user interface, controls the appearance and characteristics of windows and other graphical elements. (5)

working directory: The designation for the directory that will be used, by default, when entering Unix commands. The working directory is set by using the **cd** (change directory) command and displayed by using the **pwd** (print working directory) command. Synonym for **current directory**. (23)

workstation: A Unix computer that is used by one person at a time. (3)

write permission: A type of file permission that allows writing to an ordinary file or modifying the entries in a directory. (24)

X client: An X Window program that calls upon an X server to act as its interface with the terminal. (5)

X server: An X Window display server. (5)

X terminal: A graphics terminal designed to run X Window. (5)

xterm: An X client that provides a virtual terminal within a window. (5)

X   Same as **X Window**. (5)

X Window: A widely used system designed to support graphical user interfaces. The correct usage of this term is singular, "X Window", not plural, "X Windows". The X Window system is often referred to simply as "X". (5)

zero or more: Indicates that you can use one or more of something or that you can omit the item entirely. For example, the syntax for a command might allow you to specify zero or more file names. This means that you can specify one or more names, or to omit the name entirely. Compare to **one or more**. (9)

Zsh: A replacement for the Bourne shell and C-Shell developed by Paul Falstad. The name Zsh is pronounced "zee-shell". (10)

Chapter references are indicated by the numbers in parentheses.

Quick Index
for the **vi** Editor

Topics

vi Commands

ex Commands

Special Characters

Keys

Quick Index for the
emacs Editor

Topics

Commands

Functions

Special Characters

Keys

Index

B

C

Q

R

T

V

W

X

Z

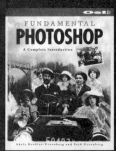

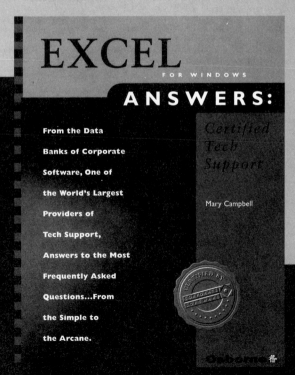

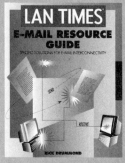
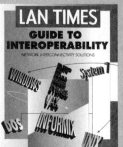

BC640SL

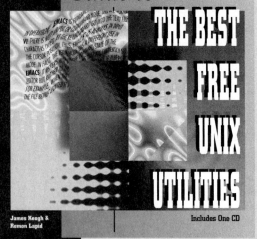

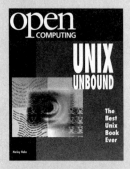

Ship to:

Name _____

Company _____

Address _____

City / State / Zip _____

Daytime Telephone: _____
(We'll contact you if there's a question about your order.)

ISBN #	BOOK TITLE	Quantity	Price	Total
0-07-88				
0-07-88				
0-07-88				
0-07-88				
0-07-88				
0-07088				
0-07-88				
0-07-88				
0-07-88				
0-07-88				
0-07-88				
0-07-88				
0-07-88				

Shipping & Handling Charge from Chart Below

Subtotal

Please Add Applicable State & Local Sales Tax

TOTAL

Shipping & Handling Charges

Order Amount	U.S.	Outside U.S.
Less than $15	$3.45	$5.25
$15.00 - $24.99	$3.95	$5.95
$25.00 - $49.99	$4.95	$6.95
$50.00 - and up	$5.95	$7.95

Occasionally we allow other selected companies to use our mailing list. If you would prefer that we not include you in these extra mailings, please check here: ☐

METHOD OF PAYMENT

☐ Check or money order enclosed (payable to Osborne/McGraw-Hill)

☐ AMERICAN EXPRESS   ☐ DISCOVER   ☐ MasterCard   ☐ VISA

Account No. [ ][ ][ ][ ][ ][ ][ ][ ][ ][ ][ ][ ][ ][ ][ ]

Expiration Date _____

Signature _____

In a hurry? Call 1-800-822-8158 anytime, day or night, or visit your local bookstore.

Thank you for your order   Code BC640SL

Take Hold of Your Future

The future of computing is wide open, and if you're working in an open-computing environment – or are making the change soon – your choices are more complicated than ever. You need the right mix of technical and business information to make the right decisions. You should be reading *Open Computing*.

Written for professionals who integrate, manage, and program interoperable systems, *Open Computing* gives you the up-to-the-minute information that you need to reduce information costs, create strategic computing solutions, select the right hardware and software, and improve productivity.

Yes, I want to receive Open Computing at Great Savings off the newsstand price!*

Please enter my subscription as shown:

☐ 1 year (12 issues) $18 *Save 50%
☐ 2 years (24 issues) $32 *Save over 55%
☐ 3 years (36 issues) $42 *Save over 60%

CANADIAN RESIDENTS: 1 yr. $24, 2 yrs. $44, 3 yrs. $60. OTHER FOREIGN: 1 yr. $51, 2 yrs. $98, 3 yrs. $142. air delivery. All Canadian and other foreign orders must be prepaid in U.S. funds.

Name: (please print) _____ Title: _____

Company Name: _____

Address: _____ ☐ Home ☐ Office

City: _____ State: _____ Zip: _____

☐ Payment Enclosed   Please Charge My: ☐ Visa ☐ Mastercard ☐ Am/Exp   ☐ Bill Me

Card #:_____ Exp. Date:_____ Signature:_____

Please complete all questions to qualify for the rates shown above. Subscriptions at the above rates are limited to persons with active professional, functional, and managerial responsibilities in open computing. Other subscriptions: U.S., $36; Canada, $48; Other Foreign, $102 air delivery.

CIRCLE ONE
My Company's Primary Business
a. Mfg. of Comp./Comp. Equip.
b. Other Manufacturing
c. Systems Integrator/House
d. Software Developer
e. VAR, Dealer, or Distributor
f. Communications/Telephone
g. Transportation/Utilities
h. Mining or Construction
i. Financial/Insurance/
   Real Estate
j. Wholesale or Retail Trade
k. Consulting
l. Government or Military
m. School or University
n. Other_____
o. Medical/Dental/Legal
p. Research/Development

CIRCLE ONE
My Primary Job Function
a. Corp. or Fin. Mgmt.
b. IS/IT/MIS Mgmt.
c. Office Mgmt./Admin.
d. Network Mgmt./Telecomm.
e. Systems Integration
f. Design or Dev. Eng.
g. Prog./Software Dev.
h. Research/Analysis
i. Marketing or Sales
j. Purchasing
k. Mfg./Production
l. Distribution
m. Education
n. Consulting
o. Government/Public Admin.
p. Other_____
q. Technical Staff/Eng. Support

CIRCLE ONE
The Number of Employees
at All Locations of My
Company
a. Fewer than 10
b. 10—49
c. 50—249
d. 250—999
e. 1,000—4,999
f. 5,000 or more

CIRCLE ALL THAT APPLY
I Purchase/Influence the
Purchase of the Following:
a. Mainframe Computers
b. Midrange/Minis/Superminis
c. PCs/Micros
d. Workstations
e. Board-Level Products

f. Terminals (X/Character)
g. Printers
h. Storage Products
j. Modems
k. LAN Equipment/
   Bridges/Routers/Hubs
m. Operating Syst. Software
n. Network/Systems Mgmt.
   Software
o. Applications Software
p. Communications Software
q. Databases
r. Development Tools
s. E-Mail
t. Consulting/ Systems
   Integration
u. Maintenance/Support
v. Training/Education

EX40C26

YOUR NO-RISK GUARANTEE: I may cancel at any time and receive a refund for the balance of my subscription.
Please add appropriate state and local sales tax.

Please allow 6 - 8 weeks for processing.

Save 60%

Realize the Promise of Open Computing

The open computing era will reward both the individuals and the organizations that can put their knowledge to use and harness the potential of interoperable systems. Build your knowledge through the in-depth features, industry news, comprehensive product reviews, and technical insights in every issue of *Open Computing*. Subscribe Today!